Security and Development

A project of the International Peace Institute

SECURITY AND DEVELOPMENT

Searching for Critical Connections

edited by
Neclâ Tschirgi
Michael S. Lund
Francesco Mancini

Viva Books

New Delhi | Mumbai | Chennai | Kolkata | Bangalore | Hyderabad | Kochi | Guwahati

First Indian Edition 2011

VIVA BOOKS PRIVATE LIMITED

- 4737/23 Ansari Road, Daryaganj, New Delhi 110 002
  E-mail: vivadelhi@vivagroupindia.net, Tel. 42242200
- 76, Service Industries, Shirvane, Sector 1, Nerul, Navi Mumbai 400 706
  E-mail: vivamumbai@vivagroupindia.net, Tel. 27721273, 27721274
- Jamals Fazal Chambers, 26 Greams Road, Chennai 600 006
  E-mail: vivachennai@vivagroupindia.net, Tel. 28290304, 28294241
- B-103, Jindal Towers, 21/1A/3 Darga Road, Kolkata 700 017
  E-mail: vivakolkata@vivagroupindia.net, Tel. 22836381, 22816713
- 7, Sovereign Park Apartments, 56-58, K. R. Road, Basavanagudi, Bengaluru 560 004
  E-mail: vivabangalore@vivagroupindia.net, Tel. 26607409, 26607410
- 101-102 Mughal Marc Apartments, 3-4-637 to 641, Narayanguda, Hyderabad 500 029
  E-mail: vivahyderabad@vivagroupindia.net, Tel. 27564481, 27564482
- Beevi Towers, First Floor, SRM Road, Kaloor, Kochi 682 018, Kerala
  E-mail: vivakochi@vivagroupindia.net, Tel: 0484-2403055, 2403056
- 232, GNB Road, Beside UCO Bank, Silpukhuri, Guwahati 781 003
  E-mail: vivaguwahati@vivagroupindia.net, Tel: 0361-2666386

www.vivagroupindia.com

Published by arrangement with

Lynne Rienner Publishers, Inc.
1800 30th Street, Suite 314
Boulder, Colorado 80301
USA

ISBN : 978-81-309-1534-0

Published by Vinod Vasishtha for Viva Books Private Limited, 4737/23, Ansari Road, Daryaganj, New Delhi - 110 002. Printed and bound by Raj Press, R-3, Inderpuri, New Delhi - 110 012.

S0000 / S0810

Contents

Foreword

Terje Rød-Larsen
President, International Peace Institute

The International Peace Institute (IPI) is proud to present *Security and Development: Searching for Critical Connections*, edited by Neclâ Tschirgi, Michael Lund, and Francesco Mancini. This volume makes an important contribution to the broad debate on the links between security and development as both interconnected challenges and coordinated policies.

A growing awareness during the 1990s of both the developmental costs of armed conflict and the impact of economic and social development on security conditions has generated a vast field of research and policy focused on the intersection between security and development. From the former Yugoslavia to Somalia and Afghanistan, the international involvement in these countries brought out the inherent problems and risks of compartmentalizing issues of security and development. As a result, it is now widely recognized that a better understanding of the intersection between the two is critical for responding effectively to potential threats to international and human security.

The overlapping nature of security and development challenges has increasingly led to a new international agenda that calls for integrated security and development policies, culminating in the 2005 World Summit's Outcome Document at the UN, which declared that "without security there is no development, and without development there is no security." Numerous donor governments have employed whole-of-government approaches, integrating defense, diplomacy, and development efforts. International organizations from the World Bank to the United Nations are promoting greater integration between and among donors to advance reform and promote peace, security, and development in postconflict states. In short, stovepiped policy responses are out, integrated approaches are in.

The security-development nexus has generated both new intellectual discourse and policy activity; however, the implications for policy intervention still require further investigation. This lack of clarity is reflected in the fundamental dilemmas and difficulties of the donors' quest for policy integration. The connection between security and development is often generalized for differing stages of conflict, differing timeframes, differing country contexts, and multiple levels of policy activity—local, national, regional, and international. Another crucial distinction that gets muddied in the current discourse is that between security and development as societal goals and as policies to achieve goals. These ambiguities often lead to the broad assumptions that (1) development and security pose no trade-offs and (2) policy interventions in one area will have concurrent benefits in the other.

This book aims to shed some light on this discussion through the contributions of policy experts, field practitioners, and social science scholars who take a multifaceted approach. It aims to identify critical connections between security and development through a combination of thematic and country case studies. Thus, the first three chapters examine the body of existing research on the interactions between armed conflict and three key factors in development: poverty, the environment, and demography. The case studies, by comparison, take a country-specific approach, investigating how a common set of variables has affected respective levels of security and development. The result is a set of policy ideas grounded in hard realities that, we trust, will advance our understanding of the ways that security and development interplay on the ground, as well as how international interventions can be more effective in promoting human and international security.

The book represents the culmination of a multiyear research and policy development program at IPI titled the Security-Development Nexus. The program explored the linkages between security and development and produced policy ideas on how coherent and mutually supportive security and development policies can be designed and implemented.

The project would not have been possible without the generous support provided by the Rockefeller Foundation and the governments of Australia, Belgium, Canada, Germany, Luxembourg, Norway, and the UK through the Department for International Development. Additionally, IPI thanks the Rockefeller Brothers Fund's Pocantico Conference Center and the Mission of Switzerland to the United Nations in New York for hosting the authors' meetings.

IPI is also extremely grateful to the governments of Denmark, Sweden, and Switzerland, as well as the Ford Foundation and the William and Flora Hewlett Foundation, all of which have provided core support to IPI during the lifetime of this project. Finally, we at IPI are deeply grateful to the book's editors and authors. The volume in your hands is the fruit of their long-term commitment and intellectual contributions.

Acknowledgments

This volume is the product of a multiyear research program at the International Peace Institute (IPI) known as the Security-Development Nexus. The program was launched in response to a growing discomfort with the assertion of a necessary interdependence between security and development in policy circles and consisted of three parallel research tracks to investigate that assertion critically and empirically. The first two tracks focused on the rule of law and security sector reform as new areas of policy and programming for both security and development actors. Research under those two tracks led to the publication of *Security and Development in the Pacific Islands,* edited by M. Anne Brown, in 2007; *Managing Insecurity: Field Experiences of Security Sector Reform,* edited by Gordon Peake, Eric Scheye, and Alice Hills, in 2007; and *Civil War and the Rule of Law: Security, Development, Human Rights,* edited by Agnès Hurwitz with Reyko Huang, in 2008. The third track adopted a broader approach to test the notion of the security-development nexus in both selected thematic areas and concrete country contexts. The present volume brings together the combined insights from the extensive research undertaken under the third track.

The chapters included here were researched and written over a several-year period against a fast-changing backdrop and were updated periodically by their authors in light of new research and shifting country realities. The authors' efforts were continually overtaken by new developments, as well as by the editors' search for greater analytical and policy consistency between the thematic and empirical dimensions of the study. We owe a tremendous debt of gratitude to the chapter authors for their hard work, patience, and sustained commitment to this project. They not only contributed their own chapters, but also provided critical insights and comments that helped to shape the volume overall. We have been extremely fortunate to work with such a dedicated and knowledgeable group of scholars and practitioners.

Similarly, we are grateful to former colleagues at IPI who provided early and consistent intellectual guidance to the project. In particular, we acknowledge our appreciation to former IPI president David M. Malone and our colleagues in the Security-Development Nexus program: Agnès Hurwitz, Gordon Peake, Kaysie Studdard Brown, and Reyko Huang. We are equally grateful for the continuing support of the current leadership at IPI, namely IPI's president, Terje Rød-Larsen, and its senior vice president and director of studies, Edward C. Luck.

Throughout the course of the Security-Development Nexus program, which included two major conferences and several authors' meetings, we received invaluable input from many colleagues. We would especially like to thank David Carment, Caty Clément, Devon Curtis, Ann Fitz-Gerald, David J. Francis, Michele Griffin, Francisco Gutiérrez Sanín, Macartan Humphreys, Chetan Kumar, Haile Menkerios, Madalene O'Donnell, 'Funmi Olonisakin, Robert Picciotto, Balakrishnan Rajagopal, John Rapley, Gay Rosenblum-Kumar, Luis Benjamin Serapiao, Jose da Silva Campino, Gulden Turkoz-Cosslet, and Dan Varisco. We also extend our appreciation to the peer reviewers of the individual chapters, as well as to the anonymous reviewers of the entire manuscript, for their constructive suggestions. At IPI, our thanks go to Monica Bernardo, Eddie Bearnot, Amanda Gunton, Alison Gurin, and Njambi Ouattara for their contributions in seeing the volume through to completion; Adam Lupel and Eleanor Hearne for reliably leading the publication process; and Sara Abbasey for her research assistance. We would also like to thank the staff at Lynne Rienner Publishers for their expert work on the manuscript, as well as Lynne Rienner herself for her early and sustained support for the project.

Finally, this project would not have been possible without the generous support of our donors, who are identified in the Foreword. We also want to thank the Rockefeller Brothers Fund's Pocantico Conference Center and the Mission of Switzerland to the United Nations in New York for hosting the authors' meetings. In addition to their financial support, our donors participated actively in many aspects of the Security-Development Nexus program, from its inception to its final products. For this, we are truly grateful.

—the Editors

Security and Development

1

The Security-Development Nexus

Neclâ Tschirgi, Michael S. Lund, and Francesco Mancini

Academic research bears some good news: the number of wars and the lethality of warfare have been declining since 1992.[1] This includes civil wars, which decreased from a high of forty-six in 1992 to twenty-one in 2006.[2] In the same stretch of time, the most severe conflicts declined by 80 percent.[3] Yet deeper analysis of these trends provides disturbing findings. The University of Maryland's report *Peace and Conflict 2008* notes that the downward trend in conflict is not the result of effective prevention of new conflicts but rather the termination of ongoing wars. The report confirms that the number of ongoing active conflicts dropped significantly over the post–Cold War period. Meanwhile, there has been no discernible change in the number of newly initiated conflicts. In fact, in the report's words, "for the past sixty years, the rate at which new armed conflicts emerge each year has been essentially unchanged."[4] This suggests that, despite almost two decades of research, advocacy, and action, international efforts to prevent violent conflicts have seriously lagged behind efforts to resolve existing conflicts. If the steady outbreak of new wars is to be arrested and reversed, the conflict prevention agenda that gained prominence in the immediate post–Cold War years needs to be revitalized. This requires deeper investigation of the sources of violent intrastate conflicts that threaten both human and international security.

Not all countries face an equal risk of conflict. Some are more vulnerable than others. Various institutions have developed indexes or criteria to classify and rank the countries at greatest risk of conflict and insecurity, referring to them as either "fragile states," "failed states," "weak states," or "countries at risk of instability."[5] Many of these countries are also home to the world's poorest, comprising the *bottom billion* of the globe's population, living in some fifty-eight countries. Of these, seventy percent are in Africa, but various lists also include countries from other regions like Haiti, Bolivia, Yemen, Tajikistan, Laos, Cambodia, Burma, and North Korea.[6] The combined gross domestic product (GDP) of these countries is estimated at about US$350 billion per year, less than the GDP of metropolitan Chicago.[7]

Many of these countries are chronic development laggards: their economic conditions have remained weak or shown little improvement year after year. In addition to suffering from underdevelopment, these countries also tend to be in constant turmoil—experiencing widespread human insecurity, political instability, political and criminal violence, and various forms of ethnic or religious conflict. Paul Collier, who popularized the concept of the bottom billion, asserts that "seventy-three percent of people in the societies of the bottom billion have recently been through a civil war or are still in one."[8] They are increasingly seen as being caught in a so-called conflict trap, created by a vicious circle of insecurity and underdevelopment.[9]

The overlapping development and security challenges facing these countries have increasingly led to a new international agenda that calls for integrated security and development policies. Initially motivated by the activist internationalism of the immediate post–Cold War years, the new agenda gained greater urgency after September 11, 2001, due to heightened awareness of the impact of insecurity in distant countries on the vital interests of the world's major powers. From the United Nations to the African Union, from bilateral donors to international nongovernmental organizations (INGOs), policymakers and practitioners have enthusiastically embraced the refrain that security and development are interdependent and require integrated policies. The final outcome of the September 2005 World Summit at the United Nations was a document that boldly declared, "Without security there is no development, and without development there is no security."[10] Contributing to the impetus behind this agenda was growing acceptance of the idea of *human security.* Its proponents sought to broaden the definition of security outside its traditional association with interstate relations and apply it to the wider dimensions of human welfare, thus incorporating both security and development in a single overarching concept.[11]

Despite the new policy discourse, the nature of the interplay between security and development and its policy implications are far from clear. The interdependence between security and development is often assumed to apply indiscriminately to greatly differing phases of conflict, different time frames, and far-reaching policy activity at the local, national, regional, and international levels. Another crucial distinction that gets muddied in the current discourse is that between security and development as societal goals and as policies to achieve goals. These ambiguities in the discourse often lead to broad assumptions that development and security conditions change in tandem, and that policy interventions in one area will have concurrent impacts in the other. Such assumptions have led to the mantra that there is no development without security and no security without development.

Given the breadth and vagueness of the security-development nexus proposition, this study approaches their presumed interdependence as an open question. Its central aim is to examine the nature of their actual interactions as evidenced within both the existing general research and the particular developing countries that have already experienced various forms of violent conflict. The study's focus is particularly relevant for the UN, as Secretary-General Ban Ki-moon has strongly affirmed his intention to make conflict prevention, along with a commitment to the bottom billion, high priorities during his tenure, which began on January 1, 2007.[12] This is a welcome development, provided that international strategies for conflict prevention and sustainable development are firmly grounded in reality rather than in high-minded, generalized rhetoric. While recognizing the impressive body of literature on conflict prevention that has been produced since the mid-1990s, we as the authors of this study have been motivated by the continued shortcomings of international efforts in preventing deadly conflict.[13] Thus, we hope to contribute to a better understanding of the utility as well as the limitations of the call for integrated security-development policies that reflect a renewed commitment to the international conflict-prevention agenda.

Searching for Critical Connections

At a general level, there is considerable evidence of a correlation between levels of underdevelopment and levels of insecurity. The higher the level of development, the lower is the likelihood of internal violent conflict and insecurity.[14] Indeed, since the end of World War II, developed countries have overwhelmingly been spared the ravages of war and violent conflict.[15] Meanwhile, since the early 1990s, 80 percent of the world's poorest countries have suffered violent conflict.[16] These facts clearly suggest a link between low levels of development and high risks of violent conflict.

However, when it comes to unpacking the relationship, the

results are far from clear. It is not easy to determine how developmental factors contribute to conflict. Conversely, it is not obvious to what extent conflict is the source of a country's development problems rather than the consequence.[17] The generality of the concept of a security-development nexus obscures the difficulties in determining the causal connections between the two phenomena and, even more important, in extracting appropriate policy guidelines as to what combination and sequence of policies are relevant in different contexts. Since the concerted call for integrated policies remains highly abstracted, it does not adequately reflect the causal lags, disconnects, blowbacks, tensions, and trade-offs involved in addressing multifaceted security and development challenges in diverse circumstances. Indeed, advocating in vague terms for policy integration between security and development not only fails to provide any practical guidance, it also potentially leads to ineffective and possibly counterproductive actions, widening the gap between rhetoric and reality. While it is important to affirm a concept of security that extends beyond the absence of war, the concrete challenge for policymakers is to understand the impact of such an extension and how to work toward its achievement while avoiding the contradictions that may arise.

To cut through the confusion left by the current discourse, this volume searches for the most critical connections between security and development as reflected both in societal outcomes and the various policies that might achieve those outcomes. One thing that is clear is that those who assert the security-development nexus want to see the achievement of both in the given countries of concern. Yet much academic and policy literature focuses separately on one or the other. By contrast, this volume seeks to understand how both security and development can be pursued complementarily and how developing societies can escape the conflict trap. Several international bodies have coined terms that seek to capture this dualism, among them *structural stability, secure development,* and *structural prevention.* Similarly, NGOs have used the term *preventive peacebuilding* to describe programs that alloy conflict prevention and development aims and components.[18] However, few studies have looked at how the amalgamation of security and development captured by these hybrid terms actually comes into being on the ground. Going beyond the postulated vicious circle of conflict and poverty, this volume seeks to identify the critical factors and dynamics that can lead to a virtuous circle of security and development.

In particular, the volume is designed to address three interrelated questions, each of which probes for critical connections:

1. What are the critical causal interactions between conditions of security and development in societies?
2. What are the basic ingredients of environments of mutually-compatible security and development?
3. What kinds of policies are more likely to achieve these outcomes?

The answers to these questions go to the heart of international efforts to assist countries that face concurrent development and security challenges. Although there is no presumption that greater knowledge will necessarily prevent all forms of violent conflict or hold the key to lasting development, what it can do is contribute to averting counterproductive or harmful interventions based on simplistic formulas and faulty analysis. Gaining a better understanding of trends and pressures that can lead to conflict and thwart development and addressing them through appropriate policy responses is the best route toward achieving the twin goals of security and development in challenging environments. Yet the task is far from easy, as is evidenced by the shortcomings of numerous efforts to date.

The call for greater convergence between security and development policies emerged in response to the complex and interlocking humanitarian, human rights, security, and development crises that confronted international policymakers in the immediate aftermath of the Cold War. Throughout the 1990s, a steady stream of policy documents by international institutions and bilateral and multilateral donors called for concerted international action to address these complex and multidimensional challenges.[19] By the early 2000s, many UN documents and policy reports asserted the connections between security and development "to the point of monotony."[20] The UN High-level Panel on Threats, Challenges, and Change noted that "development and security are inextricably linked. A more secure world is only possible if poor countries are given a real chance to develop."[21] While focusing on *Investing in Development,* Jeffrey Sachs, director of the UN Millennium Project, noted that "many world leaders in recent years have rightly stressed the powerful relationship between poverty reduction and global security."[22] In his report *In Larger Freedom,* former UN Secretary-General Kofi Annan reiterated that "development, security and human rights go hand in hand."[23]

Interestingly, academic researchers initially had little to offer to the international policy debates and were slow in removing the blinders of their particular disciplines so as to better examine the linkages between security and development—two realms of study and practice that had developed in separate tracks for much of the twentieth century.[24] Indeed, much of the early post–Cold War academic literature was firmly grounded in conventional disciplinary perspectives. Security scholars had traditionally focused on interstate conflicts and approached their subject primarily from a statecentric perspective; development scholars, meanwhile, had been concerned primarily with the sources of economic growth and socioeconomic development to the neglect of societal conflicts. Researchers in both fields had to undergo significant retooling to address the intrastate conflicts that came to the forefront of international affairs in the immediate post–Cold War years. From Rwanda and Somalia to Haiti and East Timor, violent conflicts around the world were instrumental in expanding disciplinary boundaries and stimulating cross-disciplinary fertilization. However, despite a great deal of innovative research, the dominant approaches toward poor and unstable countries are still greatly informed by divergent disciplinary perspectives, which are, in turn, employed selectively to generate widely varying policy prescriptions. Indeed, policymakers frequently become frustrated while trying to make sense of competing interpretations of the complex and pressing problems in such societies. This may explain their frequent resort to ready-made policy formulas such as the security-development nexus, which has come to mean many things to many people.

In This Volume

This volume is our effort to advance beyond the legacy of fragmented disciplines dealing with security and development even as we challenge some of the current orthodoxy on the need for integrated security-development policies. It approaches the possible links between security and development empirically, namely by gathering evidence-based insights and applying them to societies that face concurrent security and development problems in the search for coherent approaches. Eschewing the equally unhelpful blanket claims that security and development are mutually dependent and that each is so unique as to defy generalization, it further aims to reveal critical connections between security and development through thematic and country case studies.

Thus, the next three chapters examine the body of existing general research on the interactions among conflict and three key factors in development: poverty, the environment, and demography. Unpacking the postulated nexus between development and security, these thematic chapters seek to identify the principal causal paths at work within and across key issue areas and their policy implications. The subsequent seven chapters are detailed case studies that both examine a wide spectrum of countries that have contended with security and development challenges and explore how a common set of variables might have determined respective levels of security and development.

The three thematic chapters disentangle the intertwined phenomena of security and development by pulling together the leading findings in the extant empirical research on the various effects violent conflict has on development and, reciprocally, the effects of low development and the structural vulnerability it causes societies with respect to conflict. In Chapter 2, Sakiko Fukuda-Parr investigates the strong mutual influences between poverty and insecurity and the various factors commonly advanced to explain the so-called poverty-conflict trap. Despite the analytical richness of this body of research, Fukuda-Parr argues against monocausal and unidirectional explanations. Indeed, the evidence points to multilayered and two-way relationships in that poor countries show a greater disposition to conflict and that poverty increases as an outcome of violent conflict. She makes a strong plea for the greater use of several theories and tools in explaining the divergent paths that societies often take in the quest for economic development, and she calls for increased emphasis on economic and other structural sources of conflict. Further, she turns a critical eye to the largely unexamined tendency of many current aid policies to neglect or even increase conflict risks—for instance, those that apply Millennium Development Goals (MDGs) in all contexts regardless of their varied security environments. The author stresses that the policy challenge is not simply to accelerate development and reduce poverty but to realign the priorities and instruments of development cooperation to deliberately address the security risks created by the development process. Thus, she concludes that current aid policies entail serious contradictions that can only be redressed by reconceptualizing development.

Chapters 3 and 4 focus on two major forces that affect all societies—environmental and demographic change—and show how they are especially threatening to the security and development of poor societies, thus requiring that we pay specific attention to how conservation and other policies are applied thereto. In Chapter 3, Richard Matthew surveys the links between the environment and security that have come under scrutiny since the Earth Summit in Rio de Janeiro, Brazil, in 1992. He traces various causal pathways that link specific environmental, social, and demographic factors and thus help shape societies' security and development. Environmental degradation can trigger or exacerbate violent conflict, contribute to vulnerability and inequity, and bolster infectious disease. Moreover, environmental policies can involve complex feedback loops that lead to unanticipated outcomes, such as worsening conflicts. Matthew adds, however, that societal adaptability and resilience fortunately defy any deterministic outcomes. Instead, environmental factors come into play in various indirect ways. Thus, the influence of environmental change and the responses thereto that generate violence and conflict are difficult to specify; further, conflicts often have histories that go beyond these structural determinants.

In Chapter 4, Richard Cincotta examines the mounting quantitative and qualitative evidence that certain demographic forces such as population growth and movement increase the risk of civil strife as well as reduce material welfare. Drawing upon strong statistical data, he shows that countries with very youthful age structures are most at risk of conflict, and that there is a tight correlation between youthful age structure and very rapid growth rates of urban population. Yet he also shows that demographic risk factors are not the direct causes of civil war or the so-called triggers that ignite political violence. For countries in the early phases of demographic transition, there are policy options that can have positive short-term implications for development. These can help to alter the age structure and slow urban growth and rates of other demographic risks, thereby reducing the likelihood of instability and civil strife in the medium and long term.

Chapters 5 through 11 concern the interplay between security and development at the level of particular countries. The country case studies on Yemen, Somalia, Guinea-Bissau, Namibia, Guyana, Kyrgyzstan, and Tajikistan first examine the respective security and development levels each country has attained. They then address the factors that have contributed to each country's particular trajectory and performance. The seven countries were selected from a larger group of relatively small, low- to medium-income developing countries that have experienced various forms and degrees of violence or armed conflict since 1989 and/or still face some risk of conflict or insecurity. Five of them have had civil wars, although only Somalia is still engaged in open warfare. The other four (Yemen, Guinea-Bissau, Namibia, and Tajikistan) have already outlived what is often considered the high-risk period, namely the first five years since the end of their violent conflicts, without relapsing into war. However, they continue to face development challenges that can have security consequences.

Despite their differences, all seven countries have witnessed considerable turbulence over the last twenty years. Yemen was unified, had a short civil war, and then reunited; Somalia had a vicious civil war and collapsed as a state; Guinea-Bissau's civil war and recurrent intra-elite clashes have brought it to the brink of state failure; Namibia gained its independence through a long armed struggle but has enjoyed relative security and development ever since; Guyana has had no war but has seen a steady rise in political and criminal violence in the midst of an ongoing political stalemate; and neighboring Kyrgyzstan and Tajikistan have both been grappling with instability and violence following their independence from the Soviet Union. The seven countries represent a wide spectrum in terms of their conflict histories and levels of insecurity and socioeconomic development. For the purposes of this study, the diversity of experiences among them is particularly instructive, since it allows a greater understanding of how security and development vary in different contexts and thus of how to identify appropriate strategies to affect change.

In view of the differences among the seven countries, the case-study authors have employed a common framework in order to foster a systematic analysis of the levels and sources of development and security conditions in each case. This framework has allowed the authors to first trace the evolution of postindependence security and development, then explore the extent to which a set of common variables helps to explain each country's current status and future prospects. Yet they have also adapted the framework to fit the realities of each case so as to provide a country-specific analysis of the significance of said variables. Accordingly, each chapter provides a grounded characterization of the specific security and development conditions and their sources in each country. By employing this common framework, the case studies allow for a comparative analysis from which broader conclusions may be extracted.[25]

The sets of variables considered are drawn from the existing cross-country research and literature to cover the historical, geographic, sociocultural, economic, environmental, political, and international factors that are most likely to determine security and development outcomes.[26] Although the conflict literature has provided the leading factors for examination, these often overlap with what the development literature presents as the factors most likely to be important. The following pages provide a brief review of the main sets of variables the authors examined in their cases. Their findings are summarized in the concluding chapter.

The authors initially consider the historical legacies that have shaped recent security and development prospects in their countries of study. Regarding the eruption of new conflicts after the imposed stability of the Cold War era, they explore the dominant view among academics that some war-torn countries have tended to experience repeated cycles of violent conflict following short periods of respite. They also draw attention to the structures and dynamics of intergroup relations in developing countries as well as to how imperial or colonial-era policies may have helped shape ethnic, racial, religious, and social divides.[27]

Socioeconomic structural factors create widely felt problems that may become the bases for grievances and increase the chances that violent conflict will occur, even if they do not directly trigger its outbreak. Among more recent structural risk factors, poverty and inequality are consistently cited as root causes of conflict. As discussed extensively in Chapter 2, there is a strong statistical correlation between the incidence of poverty and conflict, although the causal mechanisms are still being understood. Among the socioeconomic causes of conflict, it is less the incidence of poverty per se than its distribution across ethnic, religious, and social groups that requires special attention.[28]

Since the mid-1990s, the literature on civil wars and intrastate conflict has also been greatly enriched by economic analysis. Economists have not only studied factors such as poverty, inequality, and lack of economic growth as sources of conflict but also examined the political-economic drivers of conflict.[29] The greed thesis emerged from econometric research by Paul Collier and Anke Hoeffler, who found a correlation between dependence on natural resources (or primary commodity exports as a proportion of GDP) and higher risk of conflict.[30] As a result, resource predation has been seen as providing rebels with the motivation and/or opportunity to wage war. Thus, private greed rather than social or political grievance has been posited as an important explanation for conflict.

Another promising area of recent research has focused on new or nontraditional security threats in relation to demographics, the environment, and health. As discussed in Chapter 3 and 4, this body of research has been instrumental in expanding the scope and parameters of the conventional security discourse by demonstrating the security implications in each of these areas, as well as in the intersections among them. Indeed, the country case studies demonstrate the cumulative impacts of changing health, population, and environmental trends on both human and national security.

In addition to such long-term trends, several variables more intimately associated with the outward expression of conflict are also examined in the chapters. These have to do with group ideologies, religious and cultural value systems, organizations, institutions, politics, and government policies that enable the structural conditions for violent action or, alternatively, peaceful forms of conflict or even cooperation. These factors are also deeply rooted but can be amenable more to change. In the immediate post–Cold War era, psychosocial factors gained considerable attention as multiethnic societies broke into conflict that led to the rapid dissolution of states in the Balkans, central Asia, and Africa. State failure and state weakness were catapulted onto the center stage of academic and policy interest with the events of September 11, 2001.[31] Many analysts came to view state failure and state weakness as the sources of contemporary conflict and thus to focus primarily on the dynamics of state collapse. Others, by contrast, consider state fragility as a consequence of prolonged conflict—including the Cold War, which interrupted the process of state formation in many postcolonial countries.[32]

Beyond state failure, researchers have cited the absence of democratic processes, specifying the lack of rule of law, violations of human rights, the repression of basic freedoms, and authoritarian rule as crucial sources of conflict and arguing that democracy is an important instrument for nonviolent conflict resolution. However, it is also recognized that although democracy can serve as an instrument for peaceful conflict management, the process of democratization itself can be conflict inducing.[33] There is an ever-expanding body of literature on the roles played by elections, political parties, civil societies, the media, human and minority rights, constitution making, local administrations, interest groups, transparency and accountability mechanisms, and political mobilization in restraining or fueling conflict.[34]

Another set of variables examined in the chapters concerns external influences on security and development. Geostrategic factors have always been recognized as key explanatory factors for war.[35] However, researchers are now going beyond geographic variables to explore the role of regional political dynamics in increasing risk of conflict. After 9/11 and the changes it caused in the international security environment, and despite the marked decline in interstate wars since the end of the Cold War, international relations experts and security specialists continue to view violent domestic conflicts in the context of global systemic factors, including the fluid regional and international balance of power at the end of the Cold War.[36] More recently, the growing reach of globalization has brought about new transnational threats such as terrorism and criminal networks, which can cause violence and undermine socioeconomic development.[37] Finally, given the changing roles of donors and external actors in the post–Cold War era, the nature and extent of deliberate international diplomatic, development, and security interventions have attracted growing attention as important factors in influencing security and conflict outcomes. The postindependence time frame of the case studies precludes identifying the impact of more recent policy changes. Yet the chapters all consider the dynamic interplay between domestic and international forces and the likely impact of new policy directions.

As this quick survey highlights, the range of factors that can influence the interplay between security and development is not only very broad but also contextually shaped. This volume is designed to provide a more nuanced and context-specific understanding of those factors in order to contribute to the dual goal of promoting security and advancing development. The findings from the thematic chapters and country case studies are summarized and analyzed in the volume's conclusion along with the policy implications they suggest. Meanwhile, three broad conclusions help to link the insights from the thematic and country case studies. First, structural development factors pose conflict risks in each of the seven countries—although there is no consistent pattern that can easily lend itself to uniform policy changes across different contexts. Second, at the country level, political uncertainty and instability emerge as causes rather than consequences of development failures and insecurity and so provide a key to their remedy. Therefore, countries actually need to find a *development-politics-security* nexus that is highly context specific. Finally, despite the current tendency to search for causes of conflict mainly at the country level, external factors—both regional and international—have far-reaching influence on a country's development and security prospects and require solutions at the global as well as domestic level. These findings imply that the next generation of research, policy, and action to prevent conflict and redress chronic development problems need to be better grounded in hard realities. It is hoped that the chapters that follow are important steps in that direction.

Notes

1. Human Security Centre, "Human Security Report 2005," (New York: Oxford University Press, 2005), www.humansecurityreport.info/.

2. Uppsala Conflict Data Program, Non-State Conflict Dataset v.2 2002–2006, www.ucdp.uu.se/database.

3. Human Security Report Project, *Human Security Brief 2007*, May 2008, p.6, http://www.humansecuritybrief.info/.

4. Peace and Conflict 2008, http://www.cidcm.umd.edu/pc.

5. See, for example, *Foreign Policy,* "The Failed States Index 2008," http://www.foreignpolicy.com/story/cms.php?story_id=4350 (July/August 2008); the Brookings Institution, "Index of State Weakness in the Developing World," July 16, 2009, http://www.brookings.edu/reports/2008/02_weak_states_index.aspx; Monty G. Marshall and Benjamin R. Cole, "Global Report on Conflict, Governance and State Fragility," http://www.systemicpeace.org/Global%20Report%202008.pdf; and World Bank, "2007 IDA Country Performance Ratings and Components, Ranked by CPR," http://siteresources.worldbank.org/IDA/Resources/73153-1181752621336/3878278-1213817150625/ICPR2007Rank.pdf.

6. Paul Collier, *The Bottom Billion, Why the Poorest Countries Are Failing and What Can Be Done About It* (New York: Oxford University Press, 2007), 7; see also, "Springing the Traps," *The Economist,* August 2, 2007, http://www.economist.com/books/displaystory.cfm?story_id=E1_JVRTVSG.

7. Michael Clemens, "Smart Samaritans," *Foreign Affairs* 86, no. 5 (September/October 2007): 132.

8. Collier, *The Bottom Billion,* 1.

9. Paul Collier, V. L. Elliott, Håvard Hegre, Anke Hoeffler, Marta Reynal-Querol, and Nicholas Sambanis, *Breaking the Conflict Trap: Civil War and Development Policy* (Washington, DC: World Bank, 2003).

10. UN, *2005 World Summit Outcome*, UN Doc. A/RES/60/1, October 24, 2005.

11. Indeed, the Commission on Human Security, launched at the 2000 UN Millennium Summit, defines human security to include "protecting fundamental freedoms—freedoms that are the essence of life," and called in its 2003 *Human Security Now* report for a strong and integrated response to the challenges this new, broader type of security represents. See Commission on Human Security, *Human Security Now* (Commission on Human Security: New York 2003), 2, 4, http://www.humansecurity-chs.org/finalreport/index.html. For a critique of the "human security" concept see Roland Paris, "Human Security: Paradigm Shift or Hot Air?," *International Security* 26, no. 2 (2001), 102.

12. See the Secretary-General's address to the forty-third executive session of UNCTAD's Trade and Development Board in Geneva on March 3, 2008, in which he said that 2008 would be the year of the "bottom billion." http://www.un.org/News/Press/docs/2008/sgsm11449.doc.htm.

13. Following the major contribution of the Carnegie Commission on Preventing Deadly Conflict, the conflict prevention literature has continued to grow, although there remain large gaps between research, policy rhetoric, and policy implementation. For a recent review of the status of that subject, see Michael S. Lund, "Conflict Prevention: Theory in Pursuit of Policy and Practice," in Jacob Bercovitch, Viktor Kremenyk, and William Zartman, eds. The SAGE Handbook of Conflict Resolution (Thousand Oaks, CA: SAGE Publications, 2008).

14. For an analysis of the conflict-poverty traps, see Macartan Humphreys and Ashutosh Varshney, "Violent Conflict and the Millennium Development Goals: Diagnosis and Recommendations," Working Paper Series, Center on Globalization and Sustainable Development, New York: The Earth Institute at Columbia University, August 2004.

15. Human Security Centre, *Human Security Report*, 2005.

16. World Bank, "Global Challenges: Fragile States," October 10, 2008, http://web.worldbank.org/WBSITE/EXTERNAL/EXTABOUTUS/0,,contentMDK:21708932~pagePK:51123644~piPK:329829~theSitePK:29708,00.html.

17. Frances Stewart posits three types of connections between security and development: (1) security (or lack of conflict) as a necessary component within development and well being (security and development as synonymous); (2) the impact of insecurity (or conflict) on nonsecurity elements of development and economic growth (i.e., security as a cause of development); (3) the impact of development on security (i.e., development as a cause of security). For the full report, see Frances Stewart, "Development and Security," CRISE Working Paper No. 3 (Oxford: University of Oxford, 2004).

18. See e.g., http://www.wanep.org/programs/cbp.html.

19. UN, *An Agenda for Peace: Preventive Diplomacy, Peacemaking and Peace-keeping*, report of the Secretary-General pursuant to the statement adopted at the Summit Meeting of the Security Council on 31 January 1992, UN Doc A/47/277-S/2411; UN, *An Agenda for Development, report of the Secretary-General,* 1994, UN Doc A/48/935, January 31, 1992; OECD, *OECD-DAC Guidelines on Conflict, Peace, and Development Co-operation*, (Paris: OECD 1997); OECD, *DAC Guidelines: Helping Prevent Violent Conflict*, (Paris: OECD 2001), http://www.oecd.org/dataoecd/15/54/1886146.pdf; UN, *Prevention of Armed Conflict*: report of the Secretary-General, UN Doc A/55/985-S/2001/574, June 7, 2001.

20. Mark Duffield, "Getting Savages to Fight Barbarians: Development, Security, and the Colonial Present," *Conflict, Security and Development* 5, no. 2 (2005): 1.

21. UN, *A More Secure World: Our Shared Responsibility*, UN Doc. A/59/565, December 2, 2004, viii, http://www.un.org/secureworld/report2.pdf.

22. UN Millennium Project, *Investing in Development. A Practical Plan to Achieve the Millennium Development Goals,* report to the UN Secretary-General, (London: Earthscan 2005), 6, www.unmillenniumproject.org/documents/MainReportComplete-lowres.pdf.

23. UN Secretary-General, *In Larger Freedom: Towards Development, Security and Human Rights for All*, UN Doc. A/59/2005, March 21, 2005, 5, http://www.un.org/largerfreedom/contents.htm.

24. Exceptions to this trend were, for example, Mark Duffield, *Global Governance and the New Wars: The Merging of Development and Security* (London: Zed Books, 2001) and Frances Stewart, "Development and Security," *Conflict, Security & Development* 4, no. 3 (December 2004), 261–288.

25. This procedure seeks to follow the method of "structured, focused comparison" that is widely used in international relations and comparative politics for deriving grounded generalization from a small number of cases.

See Alexander George and Andrew Bennett, 2005, *Case Studies and Theory Development in the Social Sciences* (Cambridge, MA; MIT Press).

26. For example, an earlier review of the conflict literature is found in Michael E. Brown, "The Causes of Internal Conflict: An Overview," in *Nationalism and Ethnic Conflict*, eds. Michael E. Brown, Owen R. Coté Jr., S. M. Lynn-Jones, and S. E. Miller (Cambridge, MA: MIT Press, 2001), 3–25; See also A. M. Gardner, "Diagnosing Conflict: What Do We Know?" in *From Reaction to Conflict Prevention: Opportunities for the UN System*, eds. F. O. Hampson and D. M. Malone (Boulder, CO: Lynne Rienner Publishers, 2002), 15–40. For another synthesis, see Jonathan Goodhand, *Aiding Peace? The Role of NGOs in Armed Conflict* (Boulder, CO: Lynne Rienner Publishers, 2006) especially Chapters 2 and 3.

27. See, for example, Ted Robert Gurr and Barbara Harff, *Ethnic Conflict and World Politics.* (Boulder, CO: Westview, 1994), Chapter 5; Hakan Wiberg and Christian P. Scherrer, eds., *Ethnicity and Intra-State Conflict: Types, Causes, and Peace Strategies* (Brookfield, VT: Ashgate, 1999); James D. Fearon and David Laitin, "Ethnicity, Insurgency and Civil War," *American Political Science Review* 97, no. 1 (2003): 75–90.

28. Ravi Kanbur, "Poverty and Conflict: The Inequality Link," Coping with Crisis working paper series (New York: International Peace Academy, June 2007).

29. For a review of research on the relationships between economics and violent conflict see Macartan Humphreys, "Economics and Violent Conflict," Harvard University, February 2003, http://www.preventconflict.org/portal/economics/Essay.PDF.

30. Paul Collier and Anke Hoeffler, "On Economic Causes of Civil War," Oxford Economic Papers, no. 50. Oxford Center for International Studies, October 1998.

31. Susan Strange, *The Retreat of the State: The Diffusion of Power in the World Economy* (New York: Cambridge University Press, 1989); Georg Sorenson, *The Transformation of the State: Beyond the Myth of Retreat* (New York: Palgrave Macmillan, 2004).

32. For a useful review of why states fail and policy responses to state failure, see Sebastian von Einsiedel, "Policy Responses to State Failure," in *Making States Work: State Failure and the Crisis of Governance*, eds. Simon Chesterman, Michael Ignatieff, and Ramesh Thakur (Tokyo: United Nations University, 2005).

33. Jeroen de Zeeuw and Krishna Kumar, eds., *Promoting Democracy in Postconflict Societies* (Boulder, CO: Lynne Rienner Publishers, 2006).

34. See, for example, Jack Snyder, *From Voting to Violence* (New York: W.W. Norton, 2000); Benjamin Reilly and Per Nordlund, eds., *Political Parties in Conflict-Prone Societies* (Tokyo: United Nations University, 2008); Terrence Lyons, *Demilitarizing Politics: Elections on the Uncertain Road to Peace* (Boulder, CO: Lynne Rienner Publishers, 2005).

35. See, for example, Kristian S. Gleditsch, "Transnational Dimensions of Civil War," *Journal of Peace Research* 44, no. 3 (2007): pp. 293–309; Michael Pugh and Neil Cooper, *War Economies in a Regional Context* (Boulder, CO: Lynne Rienner Publishers, 2004).

36. For an early discussion of this point, see Michael E. Brown, *The International Dimensions of Internal Conflict* (Cambridge, MA: MIT Press, 1996).

37. On global terrorism see, for example, Eric Rosand, "Global Terrorism: Multilateral Responses to an Extraordinary Threat," Coping with Crisis working paper series (New York: International Peace Academy, April 2007). On transnational organized crime see, for example, James Cockayne, "Transnational Organized Crime: Multilateral Responses to a Rising Threat," Coping with Crisis working paper series (New York: International Peace Academy, April 2007).

2

Poverty and Violent Conflict: Rethinking Development

Sakiko Fukuda-Parr

Ending poverty and achieving peace are central objectives of the twenty-first century as envisioned by the world leaders who adopted the Millennium Declaration at the historic UN General Assembly in September 2000, and their importance has been reaffirmed in subsequent policy documents.[1] Ending poverty and achieving peace are not new objectives for the international community: the vision of the UN was founded on guarantees of freedom from fear and freedom from want for all people. Together with the freedom to live in dignity, they formed the three pillars of the Secretary-General's 2005 agenda *In Larger Freedom.* What is new is the idea that these two objectives are interrelated—that global security threats are inextricably intertwined with the challenges of global poverty and that eradicating one is not only an important end in itself but a means to resolving the other.

Today's wars are increasingly concentrated in the poorest countries of the world. More than half of the countries that have been affected by conflict since 1990 are low-income countries, up from just over a third in previous decades.[2] In the 1990s, nine out of the ten countries ranked lowest in the Human Development Index (HDI) were affected by violent conflict, as were seven out of the ten countries with the lowest per capita gross domestic product (GDP), five out of the ten countries with the lowest life expectancy, nine out of the ten countries with the highest infant mortality and child mortality rates, and nine of the eighteen countries whose HDI was on the decline.[3] As the 2005 *Human Security Report* shows, even though the number of conflicts in the world declined in the 1990s, it remained and remains high in sub-Saharan Africa.[4] A third of all violent conflicts from 1990 to 2003 occurred in Africa, the world's poorest region.[5]

Though freedom from fear and freedom from want for all people were the founding objectives of the United Nations, they have been pursued as separate and unrelated ends, with political and security institutions rarely interacting with economic and social institutions.[6] Indeed, reporting on the San Francisco Conference in 1945, Secretary of State Edward R. Stettinius of the United States noted, "The battle of peace has to be fought on two fronts. The first front is the security front, where victory spells freedom from fear. The second is the economic and social front, where victory means freedom from want. Only victory on both fronts can assure the world of an enduring peace."[7]

Thus, world leaders created the Bretton Woods Institutions alongside the United Nations to assist with the reconstruction of war-torn countries and the socioeconomic development of newly emerging nations. The Cold War drastically shifted international priorities, and the early commitment to addressing poverty became subordinate to the dynamics of political and military rivalry between two superpowers and their respective blocs. As a result, the security and development institutions that were put into place at the end of World War II evolved on parallel tracks, as did the related academic research. It was only with the end of the Cold War that the development and security agendas became linked. In the new millennium, there is renewed recognition that peace and development are interrelated and should be pursued together; that global security threats are inextricably intertwined with the challenge of global poverty; and that the two objectives of security and development are not only important ends in themselves but that each can be used as a means to achieve the other.

If the problems of poverty and violent conflict are interrelated, they need to be addressed through a coherent agenda with mutually reinforcing priorities, instruments, and approaches. It is not enough to assert that "there will be no development without security and no security without development."[8] A concerted effort is required to merge the two agendas and achieve a major departure from the last half of the twentieth century, when the two were deliberately kept apart. Despite some progress since the end of the Cold War, these two agendas are still far from aligned. In fact, there are serious contradictions in priorities and instruments. Aid for development can and does—wittingly or unwittingly on the part of those who provide it—empower repressive regimes and increase tensions.[9] The international community uses sanctions and other punitive measures to pressure regimes that are either repressing their own people or threaten world peace, but such measures also undermine and can even have devastating effects on development.

The purpose of this chapter is to explore the gaps and inconsistencies between current international policies and evolving development and security agendas. A wide range of international policies influences global development and security. These include trade, foreign investment, the environment, migration, technology transfer, and the arms trade. This chapter focuses primarily on development aid, examining debates about its priorities and ongoing efforts to coordinate its approaches. Although aid policies are formulated by individual donor countries and specific programs are negotiated on a bilateral basis, enormous efforts are expended on achieving consensus and coordination through mechanisms such as the Organization for Economic Cooperation and Development–Development Assistance Committee (OECD-DAC).[10] Since the late 1990s, the OECD-DAC and other development actors have increasingly become aware of the role of conflict in development. However, the overall thrust and organization of international development are still not tailored to addressing conflict. As a result, the stated objective of bringing security and development policies together falls seriously short of delivering on its promise.

Building on the literature review in Chapter 1, this chapter begins by examining recent research on the causal links between development and poverty on the one hand and conflict and security on the other. It then explores the implications of these findings for international development policy and argues that there is a major gap between what we know about these links and the international cooperation agenda, including contradictions between the conflict prevention objectives and the international cooperation instruments and paradigms. It concludes by offering a number of ideas about aligning international priorities, policies, and instruments.

Development-Conflict Links

In response to the growing number of civil wars in developing countries, in the early 1990s economists began to study the causal relationship between development and conflict. This was not only of academic interest. It became clear that understanding the linkage—identifying both the mechanisms by which war's destructive impact undermined development in both the short and long term and the roles of economic and social factors in conflict—was imperative for policymaking. Development agencies sponsored policy-oriented studies, including two large-scale projects that built on cross-country econometric analyses and case studies. The first was a project of the World Institute for Development Economics Research of the UN University (UNU-WIDER) and Queen Elizabeth House at Oxford University, which led to the 2000 publication *War, Hunger, and Displacement: The Origins of Humanitarian Emergencies*.[11] The second project, at the World Bank, led to a series of publications culminating with the 2003 volume *Breaking the Conflict Trap: Civil War and Development Policy*.[12]

These studies represented a new direction in the fields of both development and conflict research, bringing an economic perspective to the understanding of the origins, evolution, and impact of conflict. Until then, economists rarely examined war as an obstacle to development and the eradication of poverty.[13] Similarly, explanations of civil wars had generally focused on geostrategic, political, or social factors such as colonialism, the construction of ethnic identities and their associated political and economic advantages, long-standing enmity between groups on cultural and identity grounds, and the political motives of key actors. Economists offered new analyses of the economic motives and dynamics that were key among the root causes of violent conflict. These analysts not only offered important economic perspectives to development and conflict studies but also took on broader multidisciplinary perspectives, incorporating political science, history, and anthropology.

By now, a rich literature has been established on the links between development and conflict, including data sets, cross-country statistical studies, and country case studies and covering a large range of questions.[14] The diversity of studies has also generated considerable disagreement to become known as a field of controversies. This is unfortunate, since the disagreements have often taken attention away from the many findings on which there is agreement—studies that offer a great deal of insight that could help formulate better policies. Above all, the studies find strong evidence that economic and political-economy factors can be underlying causes or exacerbaters of conflict. They dispel the commonly accepted theory that so-called ancient hatreds explain the conflicts that have emerged since the end of the Cold War among, primarily, ethnic groups in developing countries, arguing instead that economic and political interests play an important role in mobilizing individuals for war. They also identify and document the direct and indirect developmental costs of war. Most important, they agree that economic and development policies make a difference. They conclude firmly that the international community has often been blind to these causal linkages and that as a result its actions have exacerbated human suffering or fueled violence.[15]

The following discussion provides a brief overview of the current debates with a view to highlighting those findings for which there is strong support among researchers and that have important policy implications. The links fall into two areas: the consequences of conflict for development and economic and structural factors as causes of conflict.

The Consequences of Conflict for Development

Much has been learned about the human and development consequences of modern civil wars. Today's civil wars are particularly devastating to populations because civilians, not soldiers, are the main victims. Wars in developing countries have been particularly destructive. About 1 million people died in Rwanda in 1994; the war in the Democratic Republic of Congo is estimated to have killed 7 percent of its population; and 2 million people have died in Sudan over a period of twenty years.[16] A detailed empirical review of eighteen countries in the UNU-WIDER/Queen Elizabeth House study found that over the course of war, per capita income fell in fifteen of them, food production in thirteen, and export growth in twelve, whereas debt increased in all eighteen.[17] These consequences have immediate impacts on human lives. Incomes fall as employment opportunities shrink and shift to the informal sector. Nutrition deteriorates with the disruption of food supplies. Diseases spread with population movements. These consequences are reflected in such indicators as infant and child mortality rates, nutritional status, school enrollment, and others. These costs are not always spread evenly across the population; generally, some suffer much more than others. Children and women tend to be particularly vulnerable in most situations.

But it is not direct destruction that is necessarily the most devastating consequence of war for development. Civil wars have many indirect consequences that compromise longer-term development in diverse and complex ways. They undermine the economy, reducing economic growth, capital flows, exports, investments, and savings.[18] As GDP shrinks, government revenues also decline—and as resources are diverted to war efforts, expenditures shrink further for the productive and social sectors. Paul Collier estimates that the cumulative effect of a seven-year war would be around 60 percent of annual GDP.[19] Wars also weaken government administration, social institutions, social networks, and trust among people. Thus they weaken state capacity and erode social capital along with the human potential of entire generations.

The aforementioned eighteen-country review shows that over the course of war, thirteen of the countries studied experienced rising infant mortality and declining per capita caloric intake.[20] Wars weaken a country's foundation by affecting the stock of human and physical capital as well as social capital and institutional capacity in public, private, and community sectors. The distributional impacts are important to analyze. Wars can worsen both individual and horizontal inequalities in the immediate future, with longer-term consequences.[21]

While these destructive consequences of war may be inevitable, economists such as Frances Stewart argue that government policies and the actions of the international community can either exacerbate or mitigate the impact of conflict on the economy and on human well-being. Some countries do better at keeping economic activities going, sustaining government revenues, and protecting social expenditures during wartime and thus mitigating the negative consequences on both the economy and human survival. For example, Indonesia, Nicaragua, Uganda, and Sri Lanka have all experienced significant conflict, yet have continued to make progress on key social and economic indicators. Granted, in the cases of Uganda and Indonesia, the impact of violence was geographically contained, so national averages masked the declines in regions affected by conflict. However, in the cases of Nicaragua and Sri Lanka, governments that continued to provide services for their populations made a huge difference.[22]

In short, when the national government does not abandon its developmental role, the nation as a whole is less negatively impacted by war. An important policy implication for international donors is that it is better that they not withdraw support to the economy or resort exclusively to humanitarian relief efforts. Indeed, actions such as economic sanctions and withdrawal of aid or trade often have adverse consequences.[23]

Structural Factors as Underlying Causes of Conflict

As noted in Chapter 1, the academic literature on conflict and development offers a number of important theories about the root causes of conflict, the nature of war economies, and the political-economy processes at work during conflicts. This literature also identifies factors that increase a country's risk of violent internal conflict. The main factors include (1) low incomes and stagnant growth, (2) horizontal inequalities and the exclusion of cultural-identity groups, (3) environmental pressure, (4) demographic structures and the youth bulge, (5) dependence on mineral resources, and (6) failure to manage spillovers from conflicts in neighboring states. However, as the following discussion demonstrates, it is not any single factor but the mutual influence of various factors that increases a country's vulnerability to conflict. Thus, what is required is a holistic understanding of the complex and interlocking dynamics of poverty, inequality, exclusion, environmental degradation, and demographic pressures, which create the conditions for the outbreak or recurrence of conflict.

One of the most striking findings of several recent studies is the strong statistical correlation between low levels of GDP per capita and the risk of conflict. [24] It is estimated that the risk of war is three times greater for a country with a per capita income of US$1,000 than for a country with a per capita income of US$4,000.[25] Besides the level of GDP, a country's rate of growth is also inversely correlated with the risk of conflict: the risk is twice as high for a country with a GDP growth rate of negative 6 percent as it is for a country whose growth rate is positive 6 percent.[26] In a study on the causes of slow growth between 1980 and 2002, Branko Milanovic identifies war and civil strife together as the most important factor, accounting for an income loss of about 40 percent, while poor policies and slow reforms have played minimal roles and democratization, education, and health attainments had zero or negligible effect.[27] Another strong statistical correlation found by Collier, Stewart, and others is the high risk of conflict recurring after a society has experienced internal war.[28] These studies conclude that once a country experiences conflict, it can get trapped in a vicious circle whereby poverty undermines prospects for peace and conflict undermines prospects for development.[29] Building on the aforementioned World Bank study, *Breaking the Conflict Trap*, Paul Collier, in his book *The Bottom Billion,* makes a strong case for viewing conflict as an integral part of the international development agenda.[30]

Why do low incomes and stagnant growth rates increase the risk of war? One explanation is low opportunity cost: people have little to lose in waging war. In particular, in periods of stagnation, there are larger numbers of disaffected people, especially young men, who are more easily mobilized to join armed rebel groups.[31] As covered in Chapter 4, research on demographic factors by Richard Cincotta and others has found that, in the 1990s, populations showing rapid growth and a high proportion of young adults (fifteen to twenty-nine years of age) were more likely to suffer an outbreak of civil conflict. Outbreak of civil conflict was more than twice as likely in countries where the youth comprised more than 40 percent of the adult population than in countries with lower proportions of young people. War was also twice as likely in countries with urban population growth rates above

4 percent than in countries with lower rates.[32] Countries experiencing the early stages of high population growth, especially among young people and in urban areas, are characterized by low incomes, low levels of female education, and high levels of unemployment and poverty, as well as surges in the adolescent population that outpace job growth. As a result, young men become frustrated and easily subject to mobilization calls by armed groups.

Another important explanation for conflict is horizontal inequality between identity groups (such as ethnic groups) that gives rise to grievances that lead to political tension and, ultimately, violence.[33] Such inequalities involve denying ethnic or religious groups access to economic, political, and social opportunities. This theory builds on the idea that people mobilize for group rather than individual interests. While many recognize the significant empirical evidence for this from both cross-country analyses and qualitative case studies, skeptics question the quality of data and point out measurement challenges.[34] Critics also point out that many excluded groups do not take up arms in the absence of aggravating factors—whether at the individual or group level. Nonetheless, the horizontal inequalities thesis offers a relevant explanatory factor for investigation in concrete contexts.

Collier and Hoeffler argue that dependence on primary commodities increases the risk of conflict. They found that countries with more than 25 percent dependence on primary commodity exports are more than five times as likely to experience conflict as countries with lower dependence on these resources.[35] This is especially true for countries rich in mineral resources, which can be misused by rebel groups and governments alike. Resources that are easily transportable, such as diamonds, are particularly susceptible to capture by rebel groups, since their capture does not require control over large territory.[36] When rebel groups get access to such natural resources, they are able to raise funds to finance their activities, and the control of these resources in itself fuels conflict. Moreover, rebel groups can mobilize popular support by galvanizing public resentment over the expropriation of these benefits by the ruling elite. Corporate corruption becomes another facilitating factor. Poor countries with weak financial and institutional capacities are less able to manage these negative dynamics or to deter rebellion. Although some studies have challenged the empirical basis for the Collier/Hoeffler hypothesis of the "resource curse,"[37] many researchers continue to explore the weak governance of natural resources as a conflict risk.

Thomas Homer-Dixon and the so-called Toronto Group argue that struggles over resources in the context of environmental deterioration can escalate into civil war, thereby espousing what is known as the theory of *green wars.* As population growth puts pressure on the environment, people migrate. Local communities compete with migrant groups for increasingly scarce resources while refugee flows create cross-border problems.[38]

Several authors argue that spillover from neighboring countries can significantly affect both conflict and development. Taylor Seybolt found that in 2002, eleven of fifteen conflict cases were in fact spillover cases.[39] Three mechanisms can explain these spillovers: economic disruptions that lead to slower growth; *demonstration effects,* such as ethnic grievances, that develop into armed rebellion; and transborder population movements and illicit activities.[40] Poor countries with weak state capacity are particularly vulnerable to these spillovers because they are less able to manage the consequences; specifically, they are less able to absorb refugee populations and/or resist getting involved in illicit trade in arms and minerals. It is estimated that a country bordering a conflict zone can expect about half a percent decline in its growth rate.[41]

There is energetic debate over the merits of these different theories, and recent reviews of the literature have provided useful assessments of what we know, what we do not know, and where further research is needed.[42] Differences of view are not surprising given the methodological and measurement constraints in this field of study.[43] Several sources of cross-country data exist, each of which uses a different set of definitions and measures. Country case studies collectively offer another source of data and qualitative findings, but the latter are not as consistent as the cross-country data. Furthermore, explaining conflict requires an understanding of the complex motivations that lead people to take up arms.[44]

Implications for the International Development Agenda

The controversies have diverted attention away from the policy implications of the points of consensus that do exist. Indeed, there is widespread consensus on several important issues that challenge the mainstream intellectual framework underpinning international development agendas, starting with the need to take conflict as an important factor in a more systematic way. It is also important to view the various factors as not competing but complementary theories. Although the demographic conditions of the youth bulge may lead to high unemployment and a low opportunity cost for joining rebel groups in general, horizontal inequalities may leave particular groups of youth significantly more disadvantaged. These factors may combine with control by rebels over mineral resources, as in Liberia and Angola. They may also lead to migration and competition over land and other environmental resources in land-scarce contexts. Many country studies show multiple factors operating and interacting at the same time. The capture of blood diamonds, the youth bulge, and the horizontal inequality that results from political domination by a given ethnic group coexist in many countries in conflict.

The literature on conflict-development links demonstrates several important points. First, conflict is a source of poverty and undermines long-term development. The policy implication is that conflict prevention should be a major objective of domestic development policy in a given country as well as of the international development agenda. Second, structural factors are among the underlying causes of conflict and need to be addressed to reduce vulnerability to conflict. An analysis of the underlying causes of conflict should be carried out in conflict-affected and low-income countries as part of poverty-reduction strategy analysis. Special attention should be paid to the relevance of the critical factors identified in the literature. Third, to mitigate the poverty impact of conflict and because economic and social policies during conflict affect both human well-being and longer-term development, attempts must be made to continue development policies, sustain the economy, maintain macroeconomic stability, provide social services, and ensure that people do not lose their basic entitlements to food, health care, and income-earning activity must be made to help mitigate the poverty impact of conflict.

Aligning International Development Priorities: More Aid for Peace

These research findings have significant implications for global development priorities. Given the long-term correlation between security and development, the importance of economic growth is evident. Those who formulate development strategies have traditionally not paid sufficient attention to the growing divergence among developing countries and the special needs of the development laggards. Indeed, within the current globalization paradigm, neoliberal policies that promote international trade and investment as the engine of growth are not geared to addressing the persistent development problems of low-income countries that are also at high risk of insecurity.[45] Unless mainstream economics takes long-term insecurity seriously, it is likely that the rhetorical commitment to structural prevention will continue to ring hollow. These range from new patterns of trade, investment, and technology development to international charters. This chapter focuses primarily on development cooperation and its corollary, economic sanctions, because of their special relevance for conflict-affected countries.

Since the end of the Cold War, it has become increasingly clear that development actors can no longer afford to work *in* or *around* conflict; they also need to work *on* conflict.[46] The donor community has a major role to play by providing greater support to low-income countries and weak states that are most vulnerable to conflict, continuing development activities in times of conflict, and tailoring development aid to address the structural factors at the root of a given conflict. More concretely, development failures that are identified as sources of vulnerability—such as horizontal inequalities and exclusion, youth unemployment, environmental deterioration, certain population dynamics, and weak governance—need to be addressed from a development as well as a conflict perspective. Although these principles are no longer contested, the dominant development-aid paradigm has yet to undergo a radical change. Instead, the primary approach has been to incorporate conflict into the current development cooperation framework, with predictable tensions.

One of the earliest policy initiatives to bring a conflict perspective to development cooperation was presented in a 1997 publication by the OECD-DAC, *The DAC Guidelines: Helping Prevent Violent Conflicts*. The guidelines were groundbreaking in legitimating the notion that development agencies can and should address the sources of violent conflicts in developing countries. From El Salvador to Rwanda to Afghanistan, international aid agencies have increasingly begun to work on the challenges of peacebuilding and postconflict reconstruction on multiple levels. New types of programs have been developed, such as postconflict reconciliation, security sector reform (SSR), and disarmament, demobilization, and reintegration (DDR) of ex-combatants. Resource allocation to these programs has increased sizably. Many development agencies, such as the UN Development Programme (UNDP), have developed specialized capacities in these areas. However, such approaches have not yet become an integral part of the dominant development paradigm or of ongoing efforts to rethink the aid architecture and improve aid effectiveness. The primary focus of development aid has so far been on responding to conflict and postconflict contexts rather than on incorporating conflict prevention objectives more generally into the development agenda.

The Dominant Development Paradigm

The two main features of the international development framework that began to take shape around 2000 are the focus on poverty reduction as a central policy objective—as codified by the Millennium Development Goals (MDGs)—and a new interest in ex post conditionality to ensure aid effectiveness. With the end of the Cold War, during which development aid was greatly influenced by political considerations, the international donor community increasingly came to focus on questions of aid effectiveness and gave priority to countries that were considered good performers based on the quality of their policies and institutions. In the aid effectiveness model, donors promise additional resources to countries that demonstrate a commitment to implementing reforms and policies for maintaining a well-functioning market economy, fighting corruption to strengthen governance, and eradicating poverty. This shift has been a result of a desire within the donor community to show results and demonstrate effectiveness in aid spending in the context of a decline in political support for aid in donor countries. It also represents a departure from the tendency in the 1990s to use conditionality as a tool of policy change. Influential research on aid policy showed that ex ante conditionality did not work and that aid was only effective in contributing to economic growth among countries that had sound policies.[47]

The new emphasis on performance is not surprising, since donor countries faced increasing difficulty in mobilizing political support for aid as a budget priority during the 1990s. Flows of official development assistance (ODA) experienced a secular decline from 1994 to 2000.[48] There was increasing pressure to prove that aid was being used effectively and delivering tangible results. The problem with the current aid model, however, is that it marginalizes the neediest countries and those most at risk—even though there is a growing understanding of the special needs of these countries.[49] From 1996 to 2001, for instance, the percentage allocation of aid flows to the least well-performing states declined, while it increased for the well-performing countries.[50] In other words, development aid favors middle-income countries; low-income countries facing serious entrenched problems are left behind.

New Attention to Fragile States

Perhaps due to new concern for global security after September 11, increasing attention is gradually being paid to *fragile states,* or countries that are not good performers.[51] The concept of fragile states is ambiguous. It combines the categories of diverse organizations, notably the Low Income Countries under Stress of the World Bank and the Countries of Difficult Partnership of the OECD-DAC. Although there is no formal definition, the term covers countries that are unwilling and/or unable to improve governance. The standard most commonly used in a growing number of studies and debates involves the two bottom quintiles of the World Bank's Country Policy and Institutional Assessments (CPIA). The CPIA incorporates in its measurements policies for economic management, structural policies, social inclusion and poverty reduction, and the management and institutions of the public sector. According to data for the period 1999–2003, the group of fragile states identified by the CPIA would include forty-six states containing 870 million people, or 14 percent of the world population.[52]

Donors are now paying closer attention to both total levels of aid and aid allocation to those states that do not meet the aid effectiveness criteria. In *Monitoring Aid to Fragile States,* the OECD confirmed that, in general, aid to fragile states was not keeping up with the recent growth in aid to other low-income countries; this remains the case. Some fragile states are receiving less aid than they should given their extreme poverty, combined with governance indicators that are no worse than other low-income countries receiving more aid. Rather, these countries tend to be less strategically important to other countries and thus attract relatively little international attention.[53] In 2004, for example, thirty-eight fragile states received about 28 percent of total aid compared to 72 percent received by forty-three nonfragile states. Factoring in differences in their populations, the net ODA per capita in 2004 also showed significant differences, with fragile states receiving US$19 per capita while nonfragile states received US$39 per capita. Yet as a group, nonfragile states experienced a significant increase in income levels from 1992 to 2004 (when the average gross national income, or GNI, increased from US$250 to US$490) compared to the fragile states (in which the average GNI increased from US$298 in 1992 to US$348 in 2004).[54] The OECD-DAC data also indicates that the average aid volatility for the fragile states was significantly higher than it was for the nonfragile states from 1992 to 2004.[55]

Aligning International Cooperation Instruments: Aid for Peace

While aid volumes and volatility matter greatly for fragile states, both the positive and the negative impacts of aid are much broader.

Although its policy objective has been conceptualized as economic growth, development aid inevitably has a significant impact on the internal political dynamics of a country by virtue of the fact that it brings sizable resources and international endorsement to one or another political actor. One of the most important lessons of the turn of the millennium—first argued by Peter Uvin in his study of Rwanda prior to the genocide—has been that aid can never be neutral.[56] Aid has significant consequences on political dynamics in the recipient country, especially in low-income countries that are highly dependent on aid. Development aid can contribute to the dynamics of violence or the dynamics of peace in several different ways—before, during, and after violence.[57] Many of these consequences are unintended, as donors act without foreseeing them. At the same time, sanctions—the international instruments for global security, conceptualized to change political dynamics—have huge social and economic consequences. Development aid and conflict are intertwined in multiple ways. Aid can (1) unintentionally perpetuate conflict, (2) be a powerful tool for peacebuilding, (3) provide incentives for conflict prevention; (4) promote development even during war, and (5) have a devastating impact on development once it is withdrawn and sanctions are implemented.

The Impact of Aid on Peace and Conflict

Many well-documented studies of conflicts, from Rwanda to Afghanistan to Sierra Leone, have argued persuasively that both development and humanitarian relief aid—before, during, and after violent conflict—represent financial resources and influence that can reinforce tensions and repressive behavior.[58] In preconflict situations of high social and political tension, these resources, particularly significant in poor countries that are aid dependent, can help parties in conflict. During periods of violence, their effect is starker; humanitarian assistance to provide food, shelter, and health services in conflict zones can worsen tensions among groups and even strengthen the leadership of warring factions.

Aid can also be used intentionally for peace. In situations of rising tension, aid can be applied deliberately to shift the dynamics in favor of reducing tension. It can act as an incentive to influence the behavior of repressive regimes, help strengthen pro-peace actors' capacities, change relations between conflicting actors, and/or influence the socioeconomic environment in which conflict and peace dynamics take place. It can strengthen the capacity of national actors, for example, through human rights training for the military and police.

In the long term, aid can help address some of the strongest dynamics linking poverty and conflict we have discussed: horizontal inequalities and exclusions among ethnic and other identity groups, weaknesses in governance and civil society, and poor management of natural resources. All of these increase a country's vulnerability to armed conflict. Aid can promote the socioeconomic and political inclusion of marginalized groups and help reduce the horizontal inequalities that feed grievance. It can also help build state capacity by providing critical support to the judiciary, the media, and civil society organizations that promote equity and justice. This approach acknowledges that lack of state capacity in delivering basic social services is a critical weakness that undermines the legitimacy of the state.[59]

Donors can use disincentives to violence by threatening to cut off recipient states' funds. Donors have resorted to withdrawing aid as a diplomatic statement of protest against government policies or actions that are repressive or corrupt and willfully neglect peoples' needs. The effectiveness of these measures is uncertain. One study commissioned by the OECD concluded that conditionality rarely works.[60] For these incentives for peace and disincentives for violence to take effect, donor coordination is clearly important, yet it is often lacking. Much more systematic analysis is needed on the impact of aid conditionality and aid withdrawal. At the time of this writing, there is no comprehensive study that looks not only at the impact of aid withdrawal on its intended purpose but also at the broader impact on the population and longer-term development of the country. All too often, donors withdraw in situations of rising political tension or when governments are engaging in increasingly unacceptable behavior. Donors can feel pressure to be accountable to their own publics, who may object to supporting human rights violations, corruption, and repression; in addition, withdrawing aid sends a strong message to the recipient regime. But withdrawing aid also incurs an opportunity cost for building a longer-term safeguard for peace. While the socioeconomic consequences are not as heavy as comprehensive sanctions, there is nonetheless a large opportunity cost to development.

Economic Sanctions as a Lever

Besides withdrawal of aid, sanctions can also influence conflict dynamics. Until the 1990s, there had been only two cases of UN sanctions—which were imposed against South Africa and Southern Rhodesia (now Zimbabwe)—but they became more common in the 1990s, mostly involving developing countries with internal conflicts. The experience of the 1990s has shown economic sanctions to be highly problematic for three reasons. The first is humanitarian and developmental; they have devastating consequences for ordinary citizens and destroy institutions that are necessary for long-term development.[61] Second, sanctions have spillover effects on neighboring countries that depend on trade routes through the countries in question. Third, sanctions are a weak instrument for changing the behavior of a regime. In fact, they can even have the perverse effect of strengthening rather than weakening the ruling elite.

Extensive analyses of the 1990s sanctions in Iraq, Haiti, and elsewhere conclude that the most adverse impacts of sanctions on ordinary people result from comprehensive sanctions, which have deep and far-reaching macroeconomic consequences that destabilize and weaken the economy.[62] These economic disruptions lead not only to failures in health care and food supplies that directly compromise survival but also to business closures, layoffs, roads that do not get repaired, buses that do not run, electricity blackouts, and so on. They lead to social dislocation as families become desperate to survive. The most ironic consequence of sanctions is the perverse political impact they can have on the behavior of the ruling elites. Sanctions provide ruling elites with an excuse to blame the international community for deteriorating conditions in their country even as they engage in sanctions-busting through smuggling and other methods. Sanctions then create incentives rather than disincentives for the ruling elite to continue their hold on power through repressive means. Comprehensive and trade sanctions effectively penalize the population of the country rather than the targeted political elite.

These conclusions are now widely accepted, and have led to efforts to reform sanctions and put in place targeted sanctions aimed at specific actors, such as travel bans, and their most vulnerable activities, freezing bank accounts and transfers to undermine the resources and activities of political leaders and their key supporters. The key drawback of targeted sanctions is that they are difficult to design and implement. Requirements include careful preparation and design based on analysis of the vulnerabilities of the ruling elite; the monitoring of implementation by tracking flows of goods, capital, and travel; and the introduction of measures to penalize sanctions busting. Such challenges are huge, requiring significant reforms and additional capacity within the UN.

Despite these drawbacks, sanctions will no doubt continue to be an important instrument, since they represent the main nonmilitary tool the international community can use against regimes that patently breach human rights and international law. As the 2004 *Report of the High-level Panel on Threats, Challenges, and Change* notes,

> In dealing preventively with threats to international peace and security, sanctions are a vital though imperfect tool. They constitute a necessary middle ground between war and words when nations, individuals, and rebel groups violate international norms and where a failure to respond would weaken those norms, embolden other transgressors, or be interpreted as consent.[63]

However, making sanctions work requires major new initiatives that would equip the secretariats of the UN and other bodies to design, monitor, and implement targeted sanctions that would effectively change behavior.

Reconceptualizing Aid: New Priorities, New Approaches

While we now know more about poverty not only as a consequence but also as a source of war and civil strife, current frameworks for development cooperation have not caught up with the implications, leaving many contradictions. Notwithstanding incremental changes, the development cooperation agenda is not designed to deal effectively with the dynamics of poverty and conflict; its logic even leads to policies that are perverse, often achieving the opposite of what is needed in terms of priorities for aid allocation among countries, criteria for evaluating aid effectiveness, and approaches for engaging with fragile states about aid.

Reconceptualizing Aid Effectiveness

Concern with aid effectiveness continues to drive many of the policy debates surrounding aid. The researchers and policymakers concerned with aid effectiveness have defined aid goals primarily in terms of development, without factoring in conflict prevention. This perversely leads then to consider ineffective aid that could be helpful for peace. If conflict prevention is an end in itself as well as a means to development, aid can be as much an investment in conflict prevention as in development and economic growth. Its effectiveness should be judged not only against an economic benchmark but also against its level of contribution to building democratic governance.

Aid to Tanzania in the 1980s was declared an unmitigated disaster by the 1998 World Bank study *Assessing Aid: What Works, What Doesn't, and Why?*[64] The World Bank concluded that millions spent on building roads was washed away, along with the roads themselves, by poor government policies that did not provide for maintenance. However, that aid may well have been important for the lead that Tanzania has in educational attainment among low-income countries as well as in its progress toward democratization. By standard efficiency criteria, aid for Tanzanian roads may have had low returns in the context of weak macroeconomic policy and administrative capacity. But even badly maintained roads may have been better than none, particularly if they helped keep communications open to the hinterland and represented a response to the needs of otherwise neglected populations. Tanzania has been less successful than its neighbors by measures of GDP growth—but more successful by measures of social indicators.[65] It is a poor country that enjoys more social peace and stronger democratic governance than its neighbors.

If conflict prevention were accepted as a goal for aid, several important principles and practices would be challenged. The principle of political neutrality would need to be redefined. Policies of political neutrality, when interpreted as being politically blind, can unwittingly fuel conflict. The common practice of limiting development aid prior to conflict and withdrawing during conflict may make sense when the objective is to use aid effectively for development, but it does not help conflict prevention. Intuitively, aid during violent conflict would appear to be a total waste. But evidence shows that economic and social investment in health, education, and social infrastructure can mitigate the human costs of conflict and protect longer-term development.

In light of this analysis, we see that it is particularly important that socioeconomic policies prioritize and target specific vulnerabilities that can exacerbate insecurity and conflict. This requires national governments and international actors to undertake rigorous conflict analyses and conflict-impact assessments of development policies in high-risk contexts. Indeed, the introduction of planning and policy tools such as the UN Development Assistance Framework/Common Country Assessment (UNDAF/CCA) and the World Bank's Country Assessment Framework, as well as of efforts to view national Poverty Reduction Strategy Papers (PRSPs) through a conflict-oriented lens, are significant innovations. Such tools allow national governments and international agencies to identify the differential impacts of development policies across geographic, rural/urban, sociocultural, and gender divides. They can thus be used to address inequities that heighten vulnerabilities while providing protection for particularly disadvantaged groups.

Integrating conflict considerations into development thinking, however, needs to be done at multiple levels and by all relevant development actors rather than by international donors, who are currently leading the agenda. For example, the 2008 report issued by the UN Conference on Trade and Development (UNCTAD) on the least developed countries (many of which are also the most at risk of conflict for the reasons we have already discussed) is totally silent on conflict issues—even as a constraint to development.[66] If conflict were an integral part of the development paradigm, it would be inconceivable to prepare a report on the least developed countries without factoring conflict into the equation.

In this context, it should be recalled that the Millennium Declaration identified peace, security, and disarmament as the key international objectives alongside development and poverty eradication. Yet, when the MDGs were adopted, no attention was paid to their implementation in conflict-affected countries. If, as the research amply demonstrates, conflict retards development, then the MDGs also need to be monitored from a conflict perspective to redress this original oversight. The World Bank's *Global Monitoring Report 2006: Strengthening Mutual Accountability, Aid, Trade, and Governance* called for key actions to strengthen mutual accountability to accelerate progress toward the MDGs. These include improving the domestic environment for growth in order to reduce poverty and facilitate better aid, fair trade, greater debt relief, and more effective and accountable governance both at the state and the global levels.[67] The *Global Monitoring Report 2007* went further in recognizing that fragile states face special risks in meeting the MDGs and called for targeted attention to these countries to assist them in meeting their MDG commitments.[68]

Revising Allocation Priorities and Approaches: The Fragile-States Agenda

As we have noted, there is growing recognition among international donors that fragile countries constitute a special category that requires new approaches, as evidenced by the establishment of the OECD-DAC Fragile States Group and the adoption of new policies by the World Bank and other bilateral and multilateral donors. They agreed to develop a set of principles on good international engagement in fragile states to complement the partnership commitments set out in the earlier *Paris Declaration on Aid Effectiveness.*[69] The adoption by the OECD-DAC of the *Principles for Good International*

Engagement in Fragile States and Situations in April 2007 represents an important policy development. The ten principles are intended to maximize the positive impact of international engagement in fragile states while minimizing unintentional harm.[70] These principles do not only prioritize conflict prevention but also explicitly recognize the links between political, security, and development objectives as well as focus on state building as an objective.

Meanwhile, there are ongoing efforts to incorporate the fragile-states agenda within existing aid effectiveness platforms. In September 2008, a high-level meeting on aid effectiveness was held in Accra by the ministers of developing and donor countries and the heads of bilateral and multilateral development institutions. The Accra meeting predictably focused on three main challenges to accelerate progress on aid effectiveness: (1) recognizing country ownership, (2) building more effective and inclusive partnerships, and (3) achieving development results and openly accounting for them.[71] However, the meeting also occasioned a special session on aid policies in fragile situations. As a background document prepared for the meeting noted, "The restoration of security, peace, and stability; the establishment of functioning institutions and basic administrative capacity; the rebuilding of the trust and confidence of society in the state; and the protection and participation of women are preconditions for development and aid effectiveness."[72]

In fact, participants at an earlier, preparatory meeting held in Kinshasa in July 2008 had already adopted the *Kinshasa Statement,* which declared the following:

> We agree on the fundamental importance of peacebuilding and state building in situations of fragility and conflict. . . . We agree on the need to launch an international dialogue on objectives for peacebuilding and state building. Such objectives can serve as an international reference point to generate support at [the] country level to address causes of fragility and conflict, including, for example, natural resource management. We will use this process to bring together different policy communities in order to strengthen coherent responses beyond aid. . . . At [the] country level, peacebuilding and state-building objectives are currently not sufficiently integrated into national development plans. We resolve to strengthen joint partner country–donor strategic frameworks or compacts to integrate peace building and state building with development objectives and to set up appropriate mechanisms to jointly monitor progress. We will support the UN to effectively facilitate this process.[73]

These ideas were carried over to the Accra meeting. The Accra Agenda for Action (AAA) is designed to reform development aid in order to improve its effectiveness. While its primary focus is on conventional development contexts, it also calls on donors and developing countries to conduct assessments of governance and capacity and examine the causes of conflict, fragility, and insecurity; to agree on a set of realistic peace- and state-building objectives that address the root causes of conflict and fragility; to support capacity development for core state functions and for early and sustained recovery; and to identify appropriate funding modalities. In light of the shortcomings of the conventional aid effectiveness model, this is a belated but encouraging development.

These are positive developments, but many of their policy implications have yet to be explored. Apart from the focus on conflict-security links and conflict prevention, the rest of the OECD-DAC principles, such as the need to promote inclusive development and coordination among donors, could as well apply to nonfragile states.

Aiming for Policy Coherence

The growing interest in state-building and peacebuilding offers an opportunity to push for greater policy coherence and corresponding institutional and operational reforms across the international system at the intersection of security and development. In recent years, both at the UN and in donor capitals, there has been a steady push for greater coherence, collaboration, and coordination among departments and agencies working on development, diplomacy, and security.[74] *Whole-of-government approaches* or WGAs launched by various countries aim at policy coherence.[75] Whether defined as the 3-Ds (development, diplomacy, and defense) or the 4-Ds (with the addition of democracy), the WGAs are still mainly rhetorical and limited to only a few governments; but they are potentially important for monitoring and assessing the cumulative impacts of discrete policy interventions—analytically as well as empirically. A whole-of-government strategy can point to gaps, contradictions, and dilemmas across policy sectors—possibly helping to avoid conflicting and counterproductive strategies.

Equally important, WGAs provide the basis for collaboration across governments and international organizations by identifying common transnational solutions and alliances. For example, environmental problems (such as global warming and the depletion of oceanic resources) or demographic problems (such as migration) are still handled by experts and policymakers with the primary mandate for the environment or migration. However, given that these problems can affect economic growth as well as human security in both industrial and developing countries, they require cross-cutting policy platforms nationally, regionally, and globally. Such multiagency and multinational platforms are better able to remove the institutional/national blinders that prevent actors from identifying common priorities and mobilizing the resources necessary to address them.

Yet WGAs are intertwined with national interests and may involve competing priorities that can have serious adverse effects in conflict-prone and fragile states. As the premier organ of multilateral and bilateral donor cooperation, OECD-DAC has noted,

> Development actors have come to realize that successful long-term development in impoverished nations is impossible when incapacitated states cannot deliver the collective goods of basic security and effective governance. Both development and military actors are also aware of the fact that short-term, ad hoc responses in which national and international policies lack coherence and coordination will not be successful. As a result, the focus has now shifted to improving state-building capacities through better joined-up working.[76]

In the same document, the OECD also notes:

> The challenge for governments involved in fragile states is to establish clarity on and coherence in objectives. These objectives are likely to differ among the departments involved. For instance, the promotion of sustainable development is not the primary mandate of all government departments. Therefore, ministries may promote national interests rather than the interests of a partner country, which, from the perspective of development cooperation, is problematic. When dealing with the problems of precarious statehood—and in particular the wide range of potential threats emanating from them—the issue therefore is how governments determine their priorities for engagement in fragile states. From the perspective of the OECD-DAC, the question more specifically is where development outcomes should rank vis-à-vis trade, counterterrorism, national defense, and other political objectives of donor countries.[77]

The Search for a New Paradigm: Human Security and Human Development

Efforts to bring the fragile-states agenda within the framework of the *Paris Declaration on Aid Effectiveness* provide a useful reality check in terms of monitoring development and security objectives simultaneously. This chapter has sought to demonstrate that in order to develop aid policies appropriate for conflict prevention, more empirical research is needed. These would supplement the useful evidence and debates that have been generated on aid, growth, and the achievement of the MDGs. Similarly, in devising normative criteria for aid allocation, aid effectiveness must be assessed against a broader set of factors that are important for conflict prevention, including state building and democratic governance.

The 2008 midterm progress report on the MDGs provides a compelling demonstration of the merits of setting universally agreed and realistic goals for development that are people centered and can be closely monitored to gauge progress. Unfortunately, the MDGs do not include a key dimension of human well-being: security. As a result, the 2008 MDG progress report makes only a passing reference to conflict. Creating a parallel set of Millennium Security Goals (MSGs) in tandem with the MDGs would serve to bring the development and security agendas into greater harmony and could lead to a comprehensive reconceptualization of international development cooperation. Many elements of such a paradigmatic shift are suggested in an important study commissioned by the Swedish government, authored by Robert Picciotto and others. They propose a more comprehensive approach to international cooperation for human security, encompassing existing approaches that developmentalize security and securitize development.[78] Their proposals are captured in the idea of eight additional MSGs that would make for a more balanced agenda for the twenty-first century:

1. Reduce the number, length, and intensity of conflicts between and within states.
2. Reduce the number and severity of terrorist attacks.
3. Reduce the number of refugees and displaced persons.
4. Regulate the arms trade.
5. Reduce the extent and severity of core human rights violations.
6. Protect civilians and reduce women's and children's participation and victimization in war.
7. Reverse weapons proliferation and achieve progress toward nuclear, radiological, chemical, and biological disarmament.
8. Combat transnational crime and illegal trafficking.

While the proposed MSGs are not yet on the international agenda, they provide a possible way of overcoming many of the shortcomings of the current approaches to security and development. There are many gaps in knowledge about the dynamics of the development/conflict nexus, and much more research is needed. However, the larger gap is between what we already know about failed development as a cause and consequence of conflict and our efforts to implement those policy lessons.

Notes

An earlier version of this chapter was published in the *Kokuren Kenkyu Journal*, Japan. I am grateful for useful comments from Arunabha Ghosh, Francesco Mancini, and Neclâ Tschirgi.

1. UN, *United Nations Millennium Declaration,* UN Doc. A/RES/55/2, September 18, 2000; UN Secretary-General, *In Larger Freedom: Towards Development, Security and Human Rights for All,* UN Doc. A/59/2005, March 21, 2005; UN, *2005 World Summit Outcome,* UN Doc. A/RES/60/1, October 24, 2005.
2. UNDP, *Human Development Report 2005* (New York: Oxford University Press, 2005).
3. UNDP, *Human Development Report 2005.*
4. Human Security Centre, *Human Security Report 2005: War and Peace in the 21st Century* (New York: Oxford University Press, 2005).
5. UNDP, *Human Development Report 2005;* see also the UK Department for International Development's (DFID) April 2008 briefing update on conflict in Africa, "Africa: Conflict," http://www.dfid.gov.uk/Documents/publications/factsheet-africa-reg-conflict.pdf, which notes that the level and intensity of conflict in Africa is easing after peaking in the 1990s
6. Peter Uvin, "The Development/Peacebuilding Nexus: A Typology and History of Changing Paradigms," *Journal of Peacebuilding and Development* 1, no. 1 (2002): 5–22.
7. Stettinius, of course, was drawing from Franklin D. Roosevelt's wartime speech on the four freedoms: "In the future days [that] we seek to make secure, we look forward to a world founded upon four essential human freedoms. The first is freedom of speech and expression—everywhere in the world. The second is freedom of every person to worship God in his own way—everywhere in the world. The third is freedom from want, which, translated into world terms, means economic understandings [that] will secure to every nation a healthy peacetime life for its inhabitants—everywhere in the world. The fourth is freedom from fear, which, translated into world terms, means a worldwide reduction of armaments to such a point and in such a thorough fashion that no nation will be in a position to commit an act of physical aggression against any neighbor—anywhere in the world. That is no vision of a distant millennium. It is a definite basis for a kind of world attainable in our own time and generation." Franklin D. Roosevelt, Address to US Congress, January 6, 1941, chapter 36.
8. UN, *In Larger Freedom.*
9. Peter Uvin, "The Influence of Aid in Situations of Violent Conflict," *DAC Journal* 2, no. 3, (2001).
10. OECD, *The DAC Guidelines: Helping Prevent Violent Conflict* (Paris: OECD, 2001).

11. Wayne Nafziger, Frances Stewart, and Raimo Vayrynen, eds., *War, Hunger, and Displacement: The Origins of Humanitarian Emergencies,* Vols. 1 and 2 (New York: Oxford University Press, 2000).

12. Paul Collier, V. L. Elliott, Havard Hegre, Anke Hoeffler, Marta Reynal-Querol, and Nicholas Sambanis, "Breaking the Conflict Trap: Civil War and Development Policy," policy research report (Washington, DC: World Bank, 2003).

13. Macartan Humphreys, *Economics and Violent Conflict* (Cambridge, MA: Harvard University Press, 2003), http://www.preventconflict.org/portal/economics/Essay.pdf.

14. Excellent reviews of the literature have been published as well. See, for example, on poverty, Jonathan Goodhand, "Enduring Disorder and Persistent Poverty: A Review of the Linkages Between War and Chronic Poverty," *World Development* 31, no. 3 (2003): 629–646; on the range of economic analyses, Humphreys, *Economics and Violent Conflict*; on policy implications, Macartan Humphreys and Ashutosh Varshney, "Violent Conflict and the Millennium Development Goals: Diagnosis and Recommendations," Working Papers Series, Center on Globalization and Sustainable Development (New York: The Earth Institute at Columbia University, August 2004); on motivations, Frances Stewart, "Conflict and the Millennium Development Goals," *Journal of Human Development* 4, no. 3 (2003): 325–351; and on diverse schools of thought, Human Security Centre, "Mapping and Explaining Civil War: What to Do About Contested Datasets and Findings?" Workshop Report, Oslo, August 18–19, 2003, www.hsrgroup.org/workshops/oslo/osloreport.pdf.

15. Both the World Bank and UNU-WIDER/QEH studies come to these conclusions. See, for example, Collier et al., "Breaking the Conflict Trap," 121–188, and Frances Stewart and Valpy FitzGerald, "The Costs of War in Poor Countries: Conclusions and Policy Recommendations," in *War and Underdevelopment, Volume I: Economic and Social Consequences of Conflict,* eds. Frances Stewart and Valpy FitzGerald (New York: Oxford University Press, 2001), 225–245.

16. UNDP, *Human Development Report 2005.*

17. Frances Stewart, Cindy Huang, and Michael Wang, "Internal Wars: An Empirical Overview of the Economic and Social Consequences," *War and Underdevelopment, Volume I: Economic and Social Consequences of Conflict,* eds. Frances Stewart and Valpy FitzGerald, (New York: Oxford University Press, 2001), 67–103.

18. Stewart and FitzGerald, *War and Underdevelopment, Volume I;* Collier et al., "Breaking the Conflict Trap."

19. Paul Collier, "On the Economic Consequences of Civil War," *Oxford Economic Papers* 51 (1999): 168–183.

20. Collier, "On the Economic Consequences of Civil War."

21. Stewart and FitzGerald, *War and Underdevelopment, Volume I.*

22. Stewart and FitzGerald, *War and Underdevelopment, Volume I.*

23. Stewart and FitzGerald, *War and Underdevelopment, Volume I.*

24. Wayne Nafziger, Frances Stewart, and Raimo Vayrynen, *War, Hunger, and Displacement* (New York: Oxford University Press, 2000); Collier and Hoeffler, 2004, "Greed and Grievance in Civil Wars," *Oxford Economic Papers*; Collier et al., "Breaking the Conflict Trap"; James D.

Fearon and David D. Laitin, "Ethnicity, Insurgency, and Civil War," *American Political Science Review* 97, no. 1 (February 2003): 75–90.

25. Humphreys, *Economics and Violent Conflict.*

26. Fearon and Laitin, "Ethnicity, Insurgency, and Civil War."

27. Branko Milanovic, "Why Did the Poorest Countries Fail to Catch Up?" Carnegie Paper no. 62 (Washington, DC, Carnegie Endowment for International Peace, November 2005).

28. Collier et al., "Breaking the Conflict Trap"; Stewart, "Conflict and the Millennium Development Goals."

29. Estimates regarding the frequency of the recurrence of civil war have become quite controversial. Drawing upon the estimate of Paul Collier and Anke Hoeffler in the *Journal of Conflict Resolution* in 2002, policymakers often refer to a 50 percent risk that a postconflict country will slide back into war within five years (although Collier and Hoeffler have now revised their estimate to 20 percent). An article by Astri Suhrke and Ingrid Samset, "What's in a Figure? Estimating Recurrence of Civil War," *International Peacekeeping* 14, no. 2 (April 2007): 195–203, analyzes how academic research gets adopted into policy discourse.

30. Paul Collier, *The Bottom Billion: Why the Poorest Countries Are Failing and What Can Be Done About It* (Oxford: Oxford University Press, 2007).

31. Paul Collier, "Economic Causes of Civil Conflict and Their Implications for Policy," *Turbulent Peace: The Challenges of Managing International Conflict,* eds. Chester A. Crocker, Fen Osler Hampson, and Pamela Aall (Washington, DC: United States Institute of Peace Press, 2001), 143–161.

32. Richard P. Cincotta, Robert Engelman, and Daniele Anastasia, *The Security Demographic: Population and Civil Conflict After the Cold War* (Washington, DC: Population Action International, 2003).

33. Stewart, Huang, and Wang, "Internal Wars."

34. Human Security Centre, *Human Security Report 2005.*

35. Paul Collier and Anke Hoeffler, "Aid, Policy, and Peace," Working Paper no. 28125 (Washington, DC, World Bank, 2002); Collier and Hoeffler, "Greed and Grievance in Civil War."

36. Mick Moore, "Political Underdevelopment: What Causes 'Bad Governance,'" *Public Management Review* 1, no. 3 (2001): 385–418; Philippe Le Billon, "The Political Ecology of War: Natural Resources and Armed Conflicts," *Political Geography* 20 (2001): 561–584.

37. See, for example, Syed Mansoob Murshed, "The Conflict-Growth Nexus and the Poverty of Nations," UN DESA, DESA Working Paper no. 43, UN Doc. ST/ESA/2007/DWP/43, June 2007, available at www.un.org/esa/desa/papers/2007/wp43_2007.pdf. This paper refers to work by Michael L. Ross, "What Do We Know About Natural Resources and Civil Wars?" *Journal of Peace Research* 41, no. 3 (2004): 337–356, and by James Fearon, "Primary Commodity Exports and Civil War," *Journal of Conflict Resolution* 49, no. 4 (2005): 483–507.

38. Aristide R. Zolberg, Astri Suhrke, and Sergio Aguayo, *Escape from Violence: Conflict and the Refugee Crisis in the Developing World* (New York: Oxford University Press, 1989).

39. Taylor Seybolt, "Major Armed Conflicts," in *SIPRI Yearbook 2002:*

Armaments, Disarmament, and International Security (Oxford: Oxford University Press, 2002), 21–62, and Taylor Seybolt, "Measuring Violence: An Introduction to Conflict Data Sets," in *SIPRI Yearbook 2002,* 81–96.

40. Collier et al., "Breaking the Conflict Trap"; James Murdoch and Todd Sandler, "Economic Growth, Civil Wars and Spatial Spillovers," *Journal of Conflict Resolution* 46, no. 1 (2002): 91–110.

41. UNDP, *Human Development Report 2005.*

42. For an excellent review of the literature, see David M. Malone and Heiko Nitzschke, "Economic Agendas in Civil Wars," Discussion Paper no. 2005/07, New York: UNU-WIDER, April 2005, and Murshed, "The Conflict-Growth Nexus and the Poverty of Nations."

43. See Human Security Centre, "Mapping and Explaining Civil War," for an excellent summary of issues.

44. Stewart classifies explanations of causal links as based on group motivation, whereby individuals act out of loyalty to a group, or on private motivation, whereby individuals act out of personal interest such as material gain. See Frances Stewart, "Crisis Prevention: Tackling Horizontal Inequalities," *Oxford Development Studies* 28 (3): 245–262.

45. See Collier, *The Bottom Billion.*

46. See Goodhand, "Enduring Disorder and Persistent Poverty."

47. Craig Burnside and David Dollar, "Aid, Policies, and Growth," *American Economic Review* 90, no. 4 (2000): 847–868; Paul Collier and David Dollar, "Development Effectiveness: What Have We Learnt?" *The Economic Journal* 114 (2004): F244–F261; Paul Mosely, John Hudson, and Arjan Verschool, "Aid, Poverty Reduction, and the New Conditionality," *The Economic Journal* 114 (2004): F217–F243.

48. See OECD, "Monitoring Resource Flows to Fragile States: 2005 Report" (Paris: OECD, 2006), http://www.oecd.org/dataoecd/61/9/37035045.pdf. After 2001, there was a significant increase in total ODA flows.

49. There is no formally agreed definition of *fragile states,* but most studies use the bottom two quintiles of the World Bank's Country Performance Index rankings.

50. UK DFID, "Why We Need to Work More Effectively in Fragile States" (London: DFID, January 2005).

51. OECD-DAC, "The Security and Development Nexus: Challenges for Aid," DAC High-Level Meeting, Paris, April 15–16, 2004; Oxford Policy Management, "Aid Allocation Criteria: Managing for Development Results in Difficult Partnerships," prepared for the OECD-DAC Learning and Advisory Process on Difficult Partnerships for the Senior Level Forum on Development Effectiveness in Fragile States, London, January 13–14, 2005.

52. This would include, for 1999–2003, Afghanistan, Angola, Azerbaijan, Burma, Burundi, Cambodia, Cameroon, Central African Republic, Chad, Comoros, Côte d'Ivoire, Democratic Republic of Congo, Djibouti, Dominica, Eritrea, Ethiopia, The Gambia, Georgia, Guinea, Guinea-Bissau, Guyana, Haiti, Indonesia, Kenya, Kiribati, Lao People's Democratic Republic, Liberia, Mali, Nepal, Niger, Nigeria, Papua New Guinea, São Tomé and Príncipe, Sierra Leone, Solomon Islands, Somalia, Sudan, Tajikistan, Timor Leste, Tonga, Togo, Uzbekistan, Vanuatu, Yemen, and Zimbabwe.

53. However, there are also important exceptions. Aid volumes tend to rise in the early stages of postconflict recovery because the fragile state in question often represents a strategic interest to the international community.

54. OECD, *Monitoring Aid to Fragile States* (Paris: OECD, 2006).

55. OECD, *Monitoring Aid to Fragile States.*

56. Peter Uvin, *Aiding Violence: The Development Enterprise in Rwanda* (West Hartford, CT: Kumarian Press, 1998).

57. Peter Uvin, "The Influence of Aid in Situations of Violent Conflict," paper prepared for the OECD-DAC Informal Task Force on Conflict, Peace, and Development Cooperation (Paris: OECD-DAC, 1999).

58. Mary B. Anderson, *Do No Harm: How Aid Can Support Peace—or War* (Boulder, CO: Lynne Rienner Publishers, 1999); Uvin, *Aiding Violence.*

59. OECD-DAC, "The Security and Development Nexus: Challenges for Aid."

60. Uvin, "The Influence of Aid in Situations of Violent Conflict."

61. See, for example, the case of Haiti in Elizabeth D. Gibbons, *Sanctions in Haiti: Human Rights and Democracy Under Assault* (Washington, DC: Praeger, 1999).

62. David Cortright and G. A. Lopez, *The Sanctions Decade: Assessing UN Strategies in the 1990s* (Boulder, CO: Lynne Rienner Publishers, 2000); Gibbons, *Sanctions in Haiti.*

63. UN, *A More Secure World: Our Shared Responsibility*, UN Doc. A/59/565, December 2, 2004.

64. World Bank, *Assessing Aid: What Works, What Doesn't, and Why* (New York: Oxford University Press, 1998).

65. See, for example, data in the annual *Human Development Reports* published by UNDP that shows Tanzania ranks higher by HDI than by GDP per capita, such as UNDP, *Human Development Report 2008* (New York, Macmillan, 2007).

66. See UNCTAD, *The Least Developed Countries Report 2008* (New York: UN Publications, 2008).

67. World Bank, *Global Monitoring Report 2006: Strengthening Mutual Accountability—Aid, Trade, and Governance* (Washington, DC: World Bank, 2006).

68. World Bank, *Global Monitoring Report 2007* (Washington DC: World Bank, 2007).

69. OECD-DAC, *The Paris Declaration on Aid Effectiveness,* 2005.

70. See OECD, "Principles for Good International Engagement in Fragile States and Situations," April 2007, http://www.oecd.org/fragilestates.

71. See OECD-DAC, "Accra Agenda for Action," September 2–4, 2008, http://www.oecd.org/department/0,3355,en_2649_33721_1_1_1_1_1,00.html.

72. OECD-DAC, "Discussion Paper for Roundtable 7 on Situations of Fragility and Conflict," *Third High Level Forum on Aid Effectiveness,* Accra, Ghana, September 2–8, 2008, http://siteresources.worldbank.org/ACCRAEXT/Resources/4700790-1225142330310/RT7-Fragility-Conflict.pdf.

73. OECD-DAC, "Discussion Paper for Roundtable 7 on Situations of Fragility and Conflict."

74. For a quick review of efforts at the UN, see Michele Griffin, "The

Helmet and the Hoe: Linkages Between United Nations Development Assistance and Conflict Management," *Global Governance* 9, no. 2 (2003): 295–361.

75. For a review of various governments' efforts in this regard, see OECD-DAC, "Whole-of-Government Approaches in Fragile States" (Paris: OECD, 2006), http://www.oecd.org/department/0,2688,en_2649_33721_1_1_1_1_1,00.html.

76. OECD, "Whole of Government Approaches in Fragile States," DAC Guidelines and Reference Series (Paris: OECD, 2006), http://www.oecd.org/document/4/0,3343,en_2649_33693550_35237252_1_1_1_1,00.html.

77. OECD, "Whole of Government Approaches to Fragile States."

78. OECD, "Whole of Government Approaches to Fragile States."

3

Environment, Conflict, and Sustainable Development

Richard A. Matthew

The purpose of this chapter is to present the research-based arguments that, since the Earth Summit in Rio de Janeiro, Brazil, in 1992, have systematically explored the complex linkages among environmental change, human and national security issues (including violent conflict), and sustainable development.[1] While perspectives and emphases vary, the chapter argues that there is broad agreement on several key issues: (1) environmental problems can cause or amplify security problems such as violent conflict, population displacement, poverty, and the spread of infectious disease; (2) conservation strategies that are not attentive to the social causes of conflict and security may exacerbate them; and (3) pro-poor and conflict-sensitive conservation and sustainable development hold great promise for improving human and national security as well as alleviating poverty and protecting living systems. In short, this growing body of literature supports the argument, made by the so-called Brundtland Report in 1987 and since reiterated in successive international documents, that we live at a time of global and interlocking crises, and only a holistic approach that accommodates ecological, moral, developmental, and security needs is likely to succeed in managing these.[2]

The chapter is divided into several sections. After this introduction, the next section briefly presents highlights of the pre-Rio concern for the aforementioned linkages. It is followed by a short discussion of the dramatic increase in interest after Rio, which sets up more extensive treatment of four general themes that have been investigated and discussed throughout the world: (1) the relationship between environmental change and conflict; (2) the relationship between environmental change and human security; (3) the relationships among conservation, conflict, and peace; and (4) the impact of climate change. Each of these thematic sections is divided into two or more subsections. The chapter concludes with several recommendations for the UN community.

Pre-Rio Concerns About Environment, Conflict, and Security

More than 200 years ago, in 1798, Thomas Malthus wrote *An Essay on the Principle of Population,* in which he argued "that the power of population is indefinitely greater than the power of the earth to produce subsistence for man."[3] The imbalance between human needs and food availability, Malthus predicted, would lead to famine, disease, and war. As the scale of global change increased, the link between environment and security gained more attention. In 1948, Fairfield Osborn asked, "When will it be openly recognized that one of the principal causes of the aggressive attitudes of individual nations and of much of the present discord among groups of nations is traceable to diminishing productive lands and to increasing population pressures?"[4]

This notion surfaced regularly throughout the latter half of the twentieth century. For example, Paul Ehrlich's *The Population Bomb* (1968) and the limits-to-growth thesis propounded by Donella Meadows and others in 1972 combined with the first Organization of Petroleum Exporting Countries (OPEC) oil crisis in 1973 to stimulate fear about how resource scarcity might endanger economic growth in the North and create competitive conditions ripe for armed conflict.[5] The Carter Doctrine, affirming the strategic value of the oil-rich Middle East, was in part a response to these arguments.

While some worried that resource scarcity might trigger war, others voiced concern about war's impact on the environment. In particular, evidence of the harmful effects of using defoliants in southeast Asia during the Vietnam War led to two important international agreements: the *Additional Protocol I to the 1949 Geneva Convention on the Protection of Victims of International Armed Conflicts* (1977) and the *Convention on the Prohibition of Military or Any Other Hostile Use of Environmental Modification Techniques* (1977).

Still other analysts began to frame a more ambitious approach to thinking about the linkages between the environment and security. The environmentalist Lester Brown wrote a widely read exploratory piece titled *Redefining National Security* in 1977.[6] In 1982, the

Independent Commission on Disarmament and Security Issues, chaired by the Swedish socialist Olaf Palme, released a report titled "Common Security." The authors of this report distinguished between collective security (the sort of security against armed force provided to its members by the NATO alliance) and common security, which focused on nonmilitary threats such as those posed by environmental degradation and poverty. This conceptual trajectory was pushed further in the 1983 article "Redefining Security," in which author Richard Ullman sought to broaden the concept of national security to include nonmilitary threats to a state's range of policy options or to the quality of life of its citizens.[7] In the mid-1980s, President Mikhail Gorbachev of the then Soviet Union expressed a similar perspective through his notion of comprehensive security.

In 1986 the Chernobyl nuclear facility experienced a meltdown that caused widespread harm and even wider anxiety. Arguments about environmental threats to human welfare and security seemed suddenly very persuasive. The following year, 1987, the World Commission on Environment and Development—mandated by the UN and chaired by Gro Harlem Brundtland, then Norway's prime minister—issued its report *Our Common Future* (commonly known as the Brundtland Report).[8] Focusing on the interlocking processes of population growth, food production, ecosystem protection, energy use, industrialization, and urbanization, the authors argued for a global commitment to sustainable development. To fail to make this commitment, they contended, would place the future of much, perhaps all, of humankind in jeopardy.

By the late 1980s, as the Cold War approached its endpoint, environmental awareness rose to unprecedented levels, and some of the more threatening implications of rapid technological change were being worked out by researchers, and more articles began to appear making explicit linkages among environmental change, security, and sustainable development. Influential writings by Charles Barber, Lothar Brock, Simon Dalby, Odelia Funke, Peter Gleick, Jessica Mathews, Patricia Mische, Norman Myers, Nico Schrijver, Arthur Westing, and others began to be widely circulated in academic and policy circles in Europe and North America.[9] Perhaps in response to these arguments, then President George H. W. Bush added threats posed by environmental change to the National Security Strategy of the United States in 1991. The idea that environmental change was serious enough to be considered a security issue was making sense to a growing community of analysts, activists, and practitioners.

Post-Rio Efforts to Link Environment, Conflict, Security, and Development

In the early 1990s, conditions were ripe for an especially vigorous foray into exploring the linkages among environmental change, sustainable development, and security. A flood of reliable scientific information about global climate change and biodiversity loss was channeled into the 1992 Earth Summit. At the same time, as we have noted, the end of the Cold War had triggered a wide-ranging process of rethinking security. Flush with new resources and interest, the subfield of environmental security expanded rapidly.

A considerable amount of this growth was in response to the work of Canadian scholar Thomas Homer-Dixon, which focused on the relationship between natural-resource scarcity and violent conflict.[10] Homer-Dixon's position was popularized in the United States via a 1994 magazine article by Robert Kaplan titled "The Coming Anarchy."[11] Kaplan's own bleak vision of a violent future—resulting from a combination of weak political systems, burgeoning urban populations, grinding poverty, and a flood of cheap weapons—was widely distributed in the American foreign-policy community. In Kaplan's easily digested account of a post–Cold War world, the root of these interlocking forces of social collapse was environmental degradation—a problem the entire world was experiencing and failing to resolve. The state of the environment, Kaplan concluded, had become a matter of national security.

If Homer-Dixon's acceptance into US policy circles stimulated considerable interest in the linkages among environment, conflict, and security, his work was only a part of a much larger global effort to "bring nature back in" to the study of world politics. According to Daniel Deudney, bringing nature back in meant recalling and investigating the complex and ongoing interplay among climate, natural geography, and human history.[12] Through this larger effort, many scholars writing during the two decades after the end of the Cold War years have been able to draw attention to the environmental underpinnings of historical patterns of conflict and insecurity that, during much of the twentieth century, were linked primarily to processes of economic development, colonialism, state building, and ideological rivalry.[13] They have also identified many areas of concern and trends that do not bode well for the future.

Deudney argued persuasively that insights from what he described as the tradition of geopolitics could be an invaluable supplement to much contemporary work, yielding richer understandings of complex issues such as the potential for economic development and the likelihood of conflict in the southern hemisphere.[14] Deudney also noted the existence since antiquity of "a diverse array of claims about the natural environment as a cause of political, economic, and social outcomes" that he described as *naturalist theories.*[15] Today, insights from the naturalist and geopolitical theories discussed by Deudney are evident in the work of prominent environmental historians such as Jared Diamond, Brian Fagan, and John McNeill.[16]

These insights are frequently ignored by policymakers, especially in the United States, where familiarity with the environment and with security literature depends heavily on Kaplan's account; this ignorance has meant a lack of research and focus on how the historical distribution of natural resources (as well as attempts to control and exploit these resources) have predisposed certain regions of the world to the precise forms of violence and conflict studied by Homer-Dixon and others.[17] For example, although much has been written about unconstrained population growth, political corruption, institutional failure, and lack of ingenuity in the South, rather less has been said about the highly destructive patterns of colonialism that preceded and contributed to these phenomena. The world's so-called hot zones, from South and Southeast Asia through East and West Africa and the Middle East to Central and South America, are inadequately described and explained by theories that are generally ahistorical. Many of the countries in these regions are also products of a particularly violent colonial experience that was, in large measure, shaped by four centuries of Western competition to control the planet's natural resources.

Included in the important work of this period are the critical studies of Canadian scholar Simon Dalby.[18] So is Jon Barnett's research in Australia.[19] Typological work on conflict and the environment by Gunther Baechler in Switzerland and the quantitative work of numerous Scandinavian scholars, including Nils Petter Gleditsch, continue to make an enormous, empirically driven contribution to the literature as well.[20] Research on the linkages between environment and security has also been undertaken by local scholars throughout South and Southeast Asia, in Russia, in different parts of Africa and the Middle East, and through much of Central and South America, as well as in a number of small island states. In short, through the work of scholars around the world, a vibrant literature connecting environment, development, and security has emerged since the 1992 Earth Summit, although only a portion of this literature has made a significant impression on security policy. This vast literature reveals a number of environmental security challenges and opportunities that might be of interest to both the academic and practitioner communities. In the following pages, I discuss several topics prominent in the literature, loosely inspired by the evolving categorization of the field found in the bibliographic section of the *Environmental Change and Security Project Report*.[21]

The next section begins with an overview of arguments linking environmental change to conflict, followed by a discussion of efforts, primarily in the United States, to institutionalize this perspective after the Cold War and also to use it in attempts to describe new roles for the military. The United States is emphasized here because, given the vast size of its military, had a reorientation around environmental concerns succeeded, the impact would have been of global significance. Moreover, with the end of the Cold War, the image of a green military, managing enormous tracts of land in a sustainable manner and poised to respond to environmental disasters and support humanitarian efforts, appeared to many in the United States to be within reach. During the George W. Bush administration, their security concerns, especially global terrorism, shifted attention away from a green agenda and diminished the optimism that characterized the 1990s. This shift, however, appears to be reversing. The publication of a series of reports by the Intergovernmental Panel on Climate Change (IPCC) in 2007 stimulated a new wave of research and policy debate around the security implications of climate change, and the Barack Obama administration has not only engaged in these debates but seems far more receptive in general than its predecessor to insights and warnings from environment and security research. The chapter then turns to linkages between the environment and human security, focusing especially on questions of vulnerability, demography, equity, and health. Here it also considers the recently articulated notion of pro-poor conservation. It concludes with a discussion of how conservation efforts can adversely affect human security and how they might be used to instead promote peace.

Environmental Change, Violence, and Conflict

The weight of environmental change in generating violence and conflict is difficult to specify. Clearly, the conflicts to which environmental stress contributes often have long histories and many contributing variables. They are, in analytical terms, overdetermined. In places such as Indonesia, Nepal, Pakistan, Liberia, Sierra Leone, and

Rwanda, for example, conflict is grounded in patterns of insecurity based on long-standing political and economic practices of exclusion and exploitation that have distorted and degraded the natural environment, creating a variable that can trigger new conflicts or amplify old ones. In spite of the complexity of the issue, a number of scholars have sought to clarify the contribution of environmental factors to conflict. Such understanding could be of enormous benefit to conflict prevention, conflict resolution, peacekeeping, postconflict reconstruction, and transition strategies. In particular, it would facilitate the integration of environmental concerns into the system-wide humanitarian and peacebuilding efforts of the UN. Further, it might identify elements of postconflict reconstruction that affect the likelihood of a country's return to violent conflict.

In his 1999 study, Homer-Dixon focuses on the adverse social effects of the scarcity of resources such as water, cropland, and pasture. In his model, which receives some confirmation from the work of Wenche Hauge and Tanja Ellingsen but not from the *1999 State Failure Task Force Report: Phase II Findings,* scarcity may be the result of changes in access, demand, or supply.[22] According to Homer-Dixon, scarcity can cause a host of negative social effects, including social segmentation, resource capture, economic stress, and population movement. These in turn can trigger, amplify, or otherwise contribute to conflict—especially diffuse, violent civil conflict. Other writers such as Paul Collier and Indra de Soysa examine the so-called resource curse.[23] Collier regards as especially serious the plight of societies whose economies are dependent on a plentiful and lucrative natural resource to which access can be controlled (for instance, gold or oil rather than water or biodiversity); a fractious ethnic cleavage that the dominant group has been unable to resolve; low education and high infant mortality rates; inadequate dispute-resolution mechanisms and corrupt governance institutions; a history of violent conflict; and a diaspora community of angry emigrants and refugees forced to leave and willing to back one side in a civil war.

Of course, as extensive research on conflict makes clear, the outcome of any cluster of variables is never assured. Why this is the case is explained, at least partially, by those environmental security researchers who study the capacity of communities at all scales to adjust and adapt to many forms of stress, including those related to environmental change. Both the simplified, Malthus-inspired, scarcity conflict story and the resource curse story tend to downplay and, in some cases, explicitly deny this capacity.[24] But recent human history identifies few Easter Islands—or states that, confronted with severe environmental stress, collapsed into violence and subsequently disappeared—and many Rwandas, or states confronted with severe environmental stress that have experienced great violence and then begun to recover. In fact, many of the cases used to demonstrate the validity of the scarcity conflict thesis are not nearly as straightforward as has been suggested.[25]

For example, Northern Darfur State is one of three states in western Sudan. It has a population of about 1.5 million people, who subsist primarily through farming and herding. Population growth has dramatically increased population density in the region, placing enormous pressure on its arid lands. In recent years, declining rainfall, possibly a manifestation of global warming, has added considerably to the region's woes. Historically, the region was neglected by the more populous and oil-rich South, a neglect due partly to ethnic prejudice and partly to the civil war that has plagued Sudan for much of its existence. Ironically, as the civil war has diminished in recent years, culminating in the December 2004 peace agreement, years of drought have intensified long-standing conflicts over access to land and water between the farmers, who are also predominantly black and Muslim, and the herders, who tend to identify themselves as Arab Muslims. As the conflict has matured, survival strategies have included selling land, produce, and livestock cheaply so that they will not be stolen and working the land unsustainably to extract nutritional value—the region suffers from a severe food shortage—as quickly as possible. As the market serving the region has collapsed, poverty and malnutrition have intensified and local residents have become highly vulnerable to a range of health threats including malaria, yellow fever, cholera, and diarrhea. Since 2003, hundreds of thousands of people have died or been displaced.

In *Hegemony or Survival,* Noam Chomsky writes, "Humans have demonstrated that [destructive] capacity throughout their history, dramatically in the past few hundred years, with an assault on the environment that sustains life, on the diversity of more complex organisms, and, with cold and calculated savagery, on each other as well."[26] Sudan is a particularly harsh and unsettling case in point. As in many parts of the world, conflict in Sudan is linked strongly to economic and ethnic factors operating at the local level. But corrupt government, ethnic rivalry, intransigent poverty, and an arid environment also create great vulnerability to the transnational problem of climate change, which enters into Sudan as drought and very quickly amplifies both the vulnerability of the people and the multiple forms of violent conflict and abject misery to which they are more or less permanently exposed.

An interesting feature of the activity in the field of environmental security in the 1990s was the extent to which it was seized upon by some in the United States to reorient security policy after the Cold War. The US security community gravitated toward the argument that resource scarcity caused or contributed to acute violence and especially civil conflict. Vice President Al Gore and others took seriously the claim that the health of the environment was a matter of utmost importance to the long-term interests of the United States and the world. Often working behind the scenes and in a context of stiff resistance from other senior White House officials, Gore used a variety of strategies to introduce environmental concerns into key agencies and policy areas.[27] Bolstered by excitement about the opportunity afforded by the end of the Cold War to tackle global problems through multilateral institutions and programs, Gore's initiatives were widely applauded.

These efforts have largely been halted, partly because of new priorities such as the global war on terrorism enunciated by the second Bush administration following the September 11 attacks and partly because they were based on an incomplete understanding of the connections between environment and security. Although the environmental concerns of the 1990s have largely disappeared from the US defense agenda, some of the achievements of the period are noteworthy, especially those that involved cooperation with other countries, and others seem poised to resurface. For example, Sweden and the United States developed guidelines for environmental standards for military training and operations—standards of the sort that the new Africa Command would like to help spread throughout Africa as part of its goal of assisting with the professionalization of militaries in the region. The United States also worked with Russia and other Arctic nations to reduce radioactive contamination in the Arctic region. Under the aegis of Vice President Gore, civilian scientists were given access to archived intelligence material that might be useful in assessing environmental degradation worldwide.

Since the Clinton administration, the US military has been engaged primarily in the conventional activities of war. It has, however, contributed to multilateral efforts to respond to environmentally amplified humanitarian disasters. But if the suitability of multilateral military forces for such roles was demonstrated during responses to the 2004 South Asian tsunami, Hurricane Katrina and Hurricane Rita in 2005, the October 2005 earthquake in northern Pakistan, the 2008 earthquake in Sichuan Province in China, and the 2009 bushfires in Australia, the political will to help has been more difficult to find.

Environmental Change and Human Security

Since the publication of *Our Common Future,* sustainable development has been presented and widely endorsed as a reasonable solution to a complex of social and environmental problems. But for all too many people in the world, the step toward sustainable development seems implausible or even dangerous.[28] The Global Environmental Change and Human Security Project (GECHS) was established in 1996 to examine linkages between environmental change and human security in order to clarify the conditions prerequisite to the success of sustainable development programs.[29]

The concept of human security received its most familiar early definition in the UNDP's 1994 *Human Development Report:* "Security has far too long been interpreted narrowly: as security of territory . . . or as protection of national interests . . . or as global security from the threat of nuclear holocaust. . . . Forgotten were the legitimate concerns of ordinary people who sought security in their daily lives."[30] The authors of the UNDP report suggested that introducing the concept of human security could help to recover the earlier on-the-ground focus of the state's security practices.

Human security can be said to have two main aspects. It means, first, safety from such chronic threats as hunger, disease, and repression. And second, it means protection from sudden and hurtful disruptions in the patterns of daily life.[31] Over time, the idea has been given at least two very simple formulations: freedom from fear and want on the one hand, protection and empowerment on the other. Although the concept of human security has been criticized as too broad to be analytically useful, its development has been steady and it has held considerable attraction for scholars, policymakers, and activists in the developing world and Europe.[32] Tariq Banuri, for example, offers a concise argument in defense of human security:

> Security denotes conditions [that] make people feel secure against want, deprivation, and violence or the absence of conditions that produce insecurity, namely the threat of deprivation or violence. This brings two additional elements to the conventional connotation (referred to here as political security), namely human security and environmental security.[33]

The fact that the term *human security* embodies a great deal may make it less analytically interesting to some scholars, but it would be wrong to suggest that there is not much analytical value in broad inclusive concepts that tell a compelling general story.[34] In his analysis of the concept, Roland Paris notes that such a high level of inclusiveness can "hobble the concept of human security as a useful tool of analysis," but he ultimately concludes that "definitional expansiveness and ambiguity are powerful attributes of human security . . . human security could provide a handy label for a broad category of research . . . that may also help to establish this brand of research as a central component of the security studies field."[35] Much of the effort to focus the concept of human security and use it as a basis for analysis has been undertaken by scholars in the field of environmental security. This strand of inquiry has tended to emphasize issues of vulnerability and equity as opposed to conflict and violence.

Environmental Security, Vulnerability, and Demography Issues

Researchers have studied the vulnerabilities associated with environmental stress for at least seventy years.[36] Most of this work was sparked by attempts to reduce the social and economic costs of natural hazards like floods, earthquakes, and severe weather. The majority of the research focused on determining such characteristics of environmental stress as magnitude, frequency, and location relative to human population. Many landmark examples of environmental stress have led to cooperation at all levels, ranging from the collaboration of local authorities on, for example, watershed management and flood-control systems to major international engineering and science efforts (such as dam building on rivers traversing international boundaries). This early work almost exclusively focused on environmental stress itself; so-called natural disasters were often attributed solely to the environmental stress in question with little or no consideration of intervening factors.

Since the Rio Conference, vulnerability researchers have expanded their focus to consider how social, economic, and political conditions converge to heighten and differentiate people's vulnerability to the same environmental stress. Such maturation of the research has led to a growing recognition that social vulnerability is latent in human systems prior to the onset of an environmental stress; disaster occurs when stress exceeds the coping capacity of the human system.

One promising line of research concerns rethinking the relationships between demographic and environmental change from a vulnerability perspective.[37] The concepts of population explosion and the youth bulge have been the traditional entry points for understanding demographic and environmental conflict issues. The first concept suggests that the demands of a rapidly increasing population for basic, life-sustaining commodities such as food, water, and shelter have increasingly pressured environmental systems and finite stores of natural resources. The second contends that large numbers of young men—a feature of developing rather than developed countries—facilitate volatile environments, especially when there is competition for a dwindling resource base. These concepts are the backbone of the Malthusian perspective, which has been refined over a 200-year period. In the 1990s, the demography and environmental security debate expanded to include discussions of demographic inequities and of globalization's tendency to alter the ways in which communities interact with their local environments.

Global population is now projected to level off at about 9 billion people around the end of this century—although this middle-scenario prediction could prove quite inaccurate. Population growth rates have declined in much of the world due to factors such as continued urbanization, decreasing reliance upon child labor, the prevalence of social safety nets, and increases in female education and employment outside the home. Two key topics, demographic inequities and gender, have emerged within the debate on demographics and environmental security; it is now widely accepted that inequities have a greater social and environmental effect than population growth. It is well known that the consumption rate of the wealthiest 20 percent of the population in the developed world is many times that of the poorest fifth.[38] Economic globalization may have widened this gap, and contemporary overexploitation of environmental resources by the rural poor may be driven by Northern tastes and demands rather than by population growth. Gender inequalities such as the undervaluation of women's contributions to household income, less access to education, and violence against women, especially during armed conflict, have also emerged as important issues within demographic and environmental security research. In this light, researchers should cast demography and environmental security in a context that transcends population trends and focuses on demographic inequities.

In the context of demographic change, considerable attention has been given to the idea that environmental scarcity is a key factor in motivating people to move. Environmental refugees move from depleted rural areas to more abundant rural areas and to cities. They are sometimes compelled to cross cultural and national boundaries, whereby their sudden presence can deepen or trigger group violence. Assessing the plight of displaced peoples is difficult, however, because of the absence of reliable data for establishing baselines or trends, let alone causal sequences and impacts. This is another relationship that needs to be studied for humanitarian reasons as well as ecological, political, and intellectual ones.

Environmental Security, Vulnerability, and Equity Issues

Despite frequent references to intergenerational equity in discussions of global environmental change and human security, the concept is only beginning to be framed as an issue of equity.[39, 40] In these equity-based analyses, the focus is typically limited to questions of equity in the mitigation of greenhouse gas emissions. Relatively less attention is paid to equity in the impacts climate change will have on people and the tools and strategies available for adaptation to these impacts, and there is virtually no mention of the connections among global environmental change, equity, and issues of human security.[41]

Yet despite such limited attention, there is widespread recognition that the effects of global environmental change are likely to be highly uneven, with some individuals, households, communities, or regions experiencing significant negative effects such as the loss of life and property due to climate extremes, a rise in skin cancer due to stratospheric ozone depletion, the loss of agricultural productivity, increased water stress, and so on.[42] Others may experience only minor negative effects or may be able to successfully adapt to changing environmental conditions. Still others may experience net benefits, such as lower winter heating costs due to warmer temperatures, a longer agricultural growing season, increased forest productivity, or an expansion of tourism due to land use changes. These inequities in impacts and adaptive capacities suggest that global environmental change is likely to create both winners and losers.[43]

If all humans were contributing equally to global environmental change, the emergence of winners and losers might be considered an inevitable outcome of human development. However, all humans are *not* contributing equally to the environmental transformations that are occurring today and that are likely to occur in the future. The drivers of global environmental change—such as fossil fuel consumption, urban and coastal development, industrialization, deforestation, and other land use changes—are also inequitable and can be disproportionately attributed to some nations, regions, and social groups. In general, those who consume more energy, raw materials, and land are making a more substantial contribution to global environmental change than those who consume less. Moreover, all humans do not have an equal voice in key decisions about energy usage patterns, land use changes, industrial emissions, and so forth, even though these decisions affect the integrity of the ecological systems on which all humans and all other species depend.[44]

Equity concerns are thus central to global environmental change, and they are clearly linked to human security for some regions and groups as well. The implications of inequities related to global environmental change for human security have not, however, been systematically considered. To date, equity concerns have been largely framed as a North-South issue, relevant to debates about development and sustainability.[45] Human security issues, in contrast, have largely been framed in terms of conflict or cooperation. Framing global environmental change as an equity issue involves, first and foremost, a recognition of the differential consequences for human security, particularly for regions or social groups that are more vulnerable to environmental changes. Furthermore, it involves acknowledging that equity-based responses to global environmental change may require different approaches than responses that address the science alone. When framed in terms of equity, global environmental change is transformed from a unifying discourse for responding to environmental problems that threaten the security of all humans into an issue of differential vulnerability that draws attention to some key questions: For instance, whose security is at stake? Why? And how can equity issues be resolved when addressing global environmental changes?[46]

Pro-Poor Conservation

One further promising new opportunity has emerged since 2003 that is beginning to gain substantial momentum in the conservation community:

> Pro-poor conservation may be defined as an approach that optimizes conservation and livelihood benefits with an explicit emphasis on poverty reduction and social justice. It aims to ensure that environmental resources are sustainably managed and positively employed to empower the poor and help them secure a desirable livelihood, increase their assets, and reduce vulnerability to shocks. This approach is based on the concept of sustainable livelihoods and is related to other approaches such as integrated conservation and development.[47]

The concept of sustainable livelihoods concerns both an approach to and a goal for sustainable development—namely, creating livelihoods that are appropriate to the particular cultures, ecologies, and needs of real communities and that are able to adapt to change and withstand stress.[48] Pro-poor conservation is a concept designed to encourage the conservation community to recognize that its activities have sometimes succeeded at the expense of the poor, for example by restricting or denying access to resources needed for survival and development. Proponents of the concept also encourage conservationists to correct this deficiency by mainstreaming poverty-alleviation practices and values into their programs. This is regarded as an ethical stance that the International Union for the Conservation of Nature (IUCN) likens to the Hippocratic Oath—first, do no harm to the poor—but it is also regarded as a pragmatic position that will bolster conservation programs challenged by conflict and make conservation relevant—and hence desirable—to a broader constituency.

Having accepted that conservation practices can impose penalties on vulnerable social groups, the IUCN has acted quickly to conceive an alternative approach and operationalize it through a series of implementation principles that it is sharing with its vast NGO membership.[49] These include working closely with local communities to preserve and create livelihoods while also acting at various levels of governance to reduce the likelihood that local needs and programs will be derailed by measures adopted at a different scale of social organization. IUCN members are now active in refining their understanding of poverty and of how the needs and aspirations of the poor can, on a case by case basis, be reconciled with ecological imperatives, even in harshly degraded environments.[50]

Pro-poor conservation is a direct response to years of studying the linkages between environmental change and security as impacted by conflict; it could provide the conservation community with the motivation and tools it needs to become more fully part of the global effort to achieve sustainable development.

Environmental Change and Infectious Disease

A growing amount of public, media, and policy attention has focused on potential threats to human and national security from biological organisms. Throughout much of the twentieth century, it appeared that the dangers posed to human societies by infectious diseases would be minimized and perhaps even eradicated due to improvements in water and sanitation systems, systematic vaccination efforts, and the development and widespread use of antibiotics. However, events during the later half of the twentieth century—including the Hong Kong flu pandemic of 1968–1969, the concern about a possible swine flu outbreak in 1976, and the emergence of previously unknown diseases such as HIV/AIDS and hemorrhagic fevers like Marburg and Ebola—demonstrated that infectious diseases remained a threat to the lives and well-being of the world's peoples. Despite advances in medical and public health efforts, billions of people continue to be afflicted by disease, and each year millions succumb. As well as causing death and illness, "The ability of infectious agents to destabilize populations, economies, and governments is fast becoming a sad fact of life. The prevention and control of infectious diseases are fundamental to individual, national, and global health and security."[51]

Naturally occurring infectious diseases emerge and spread primarily through interactions among people and animals in their shared environments. Throughout history, natural infectious diseases have had a significant impact on human societies. An outbreak of bubonic plague that struck Europe between 1346 and 1350 is estimated to have killed one-third of the continent's population.[52] The Spanish influenza pandemic of 1918 sickened 20 to 40 percent of the global population and is estimated to have killed more than 500,000 people in the United States alone and another 20 million globally.[53] Two additional influenza pandemics occurred in the twentieth century: Asian flu in 1957, which caused more than 2 million fatalities worldwide, and Hong Kong flu in 1968, which resulted in over 1 million deaths.[54] The eradication of smallpox as a naturally occurring disease is often cited as one of the great triumphs of medicine in the twentieth century—for good reason. Smallpox had ravaged hundreds of millions of lives and by some estimates killed half a billion people in the century prior to its eradication.[55]

During the latter part of the twentieth century, numerous voices cautioned against complacency in the face of threats from infectious diseases, warning that diseases thought to be eradicated could reemerge to affect human populations, while new diseases could emerge to pose additional challenges to medical and public health systems. In 1992, *Emerging Infections,* a report from the Institute of Medicine, observed the following:

> Infectious diseases remain the major cause of death worldwide and will not be conquered during our lifetimes. With the application of new scientific knowledge, well-planned intervention strategies, adequate resources, and political will, many of these diseases may be prevented by immunization, contained by the use of drugs or vector-control methods, and, in a very few cases, even eradicated—but the majority are likely to persevere. We can also be confident that new diseases will emerge.[56]

The emergence and reemergence of infectious diseases have been linked to a number of environmental and social factors.[57] Additionally, an outbreak of hantavirus in the United States in 1993 has been linked to that year's El Niño event, which caused increased rainfall and warmer temperatures that enabled in turn the rapid growth of the deer mouse population that carries the virus.[58]

Human settlement and land use patterns also play an important role. For example, the conversion of grassland to farmland in Asia has encouraged the growth of disease-carrying rodent populations.[59] Today there is widespread concern about the erosion of historical boundaries between wild and domestic animals—evident, for example, in the wet markets throughout Asia—which creates conditions conducive to the transfer of zoonotic diseases from wild animal to domestic animal to human. This, for example, is how avian flu, H5N1, has invaded the human population in China, Vietnam, and elsewhere. Of course, the misuse of antibiotics and the rapid pace of microbial adaptation to changing environmental conditions are also important factors. According to David Gordon and others, "[80] percent of *Staphylococcus aureus* isolates in the United States . . . are penicillin resistant"—that is, they have adapted to the hospital environments in which they now thrive.[60] Finally, processes of globalization that create pathways for the rapid movement of microbes and poor-quality health care further encourage human vulnerability to infectious disease.[61]

The toll taken by infectious disease involves more than human lives. Direct economic costs include lost productivity, decreases in tourism and travel, and reduced markets for goods. A report by Bio Economic Research Associates found SARS (severe accute respiratory syndrome) to be "the costliest in a series of infectious disease outbreaks in human and animal populations . . . that have cost over [US]$100 billion (not including HIV/AIDS) to economies around the world" from 1996 to 2005.[62] Compounding these direct costs are long-term costs resulting from the link between poverty and illness. According to the World Health Organization (WHO), HIV/AIDS has killed more than 20 million people worldwide and is the leading global cause of death for adults aged between fifteen and fifty-nine years. An estimated 34 to 46 million people are currently living with the disease.[63] People with HIV/AIDS tend to die during their most productive years, leaving social networks and economies in shambles throughout areas such as sub-Saharan Africa, where the HIV incidence rate in 2007 ranged from 2 percent to as high as 25 percent, with some 22 million people—or two-thirds of the world's total—infected.

It is important to emphasize that, by any standard measure, public health gains over the past century have been dramatic in most of the world. But observers such as Laurie Garrett argue that we should not be complacent in the face of these indicators. As we modify our environments and become increasingly urbanized, we also become vulnerable to the periodic epidemics that have afflicted humankind over the millennia.[64] At the time of finalizing this chapter (June 2009), the WHO is declaring that swine flu, or influenza A virus subtype H1N1, has become a global pandemic, and some observers worry that this could impose enormous human and economic costs on the world over the next few years. To this, we might add that environmental degradation, poor sanitation, malnutrition, and poverty—which constitute the day-to-day living conditions of some 2.6 billion people living on less than US$2 per day—dramatically increase the sensitivity of these people to emerging and reemerging diseases. Zoonotic infectious diseases like SARS and HIV/AIDS flourish in these conditions. Hence, in the case of HIV/AIDS, the attention given by the world health community to sexual practices, condom use, and drug therapies has not stemmed the spread of the disease, which will continue until the underlying conditions favorable to infection are addressed.[65]

Conservation, Conflict, and Peace

The Security Effects of Conservation Efforts

In the mid-1990s, the IUCN undertook a state-of-the-art review of the literature on environmental security and determined that there were good reasons for conservationists to take heed of this research. In 1999, a case study was carried out by the IUCN in Pakistan's Northwest Frontier Province.[66] It was presented at both the Earth Forum and the World Conservation Congress, each held in Amman, Jordan, in 2000. This led to the formation of an IUCN task force that undertook a dozen further studies, several of which were gathered in the volume *Conserving the Peace: Resources, Livelihoods, and Security*, which was released at the 2002 World Summit in Johannesburg.

The task force agreed with the claim that different forms of environmental degradation and change were linked to violent conflict and other types of human insecurity, especially in areas where livelihoods relied heavily on direct access to natural resources. It underscored the difficulties faced by conservationists working in high-conflict areas and concluded that the value of their efforts could extend beyond conservation to include conflict mitigation and hence help create conditions for peace and social reconstruction. However, the task force also noted that additional benefits were not assured: conservation efforts undertaken without adequate attention to their social impacts could themselves generate social conflict and insecurity. In 2002, the task force called for further research in this area, especially to explore possible linkages among conservation efforts, resource rights, and livelihood security.[67]

The conclusions of *Conserving the Peace* informed an eighteen-month study completed in 2004 by the IUCN's Regional Environmental Law Programme, Asia, in cooperation with several country offices. Directed by Patti Moore, the research team incorporated local experts associated with the IUCN or other nongovernmental organizations in Bangladesh, India, Nepal, and Pakistan. The study sites included two wetlands (Tanguar Haor in Bangladesh and Koshi Tappu Area, or KTA, in Nepal) and two forest areas (Dir-Kohistan in northern Pakistan and a group of villages in Orissa, India). Following an inception workshop held in Kathmandu in July 2003, teams of two or three researchers spent several weeks in each study site gathering data on environmental conditions; the structure of livelihoods, with an emphasis on those that were resource based; systems of local resource rights and the extent to which they were respected and adequate from a livelihood perspective; and expressions of insecurity and violence, especially those that appeared to be linked to disagreements over access to natural resources or related issues.[68]

Although sporadic violence and severe flooding occasionally disrupted data collection, the efforts were, overall, very successful and provided a solid information base for analysis. The teams met again in Nepal in August 2004 to discuss their findings. During the workshop, distinct patterns emerged within and across the four cases that have had clear lessons for the conservation community as well as important policy implications; they also set the stage for research in other areas where the particular set of conditions they studied is evident (that is, where poor, resource-dependent people are living in a situation that is precarious from environmental, legal, and human security perspectives).

For our purposes, the case of Nepal is of particular interest. In the 1950s, people were encouraged to migrate to the KTA to reduce population pressure on Kathmandu Valley. Once settled, they were displaced again to accommodate conservation imperatives as the KTA evolved into a new, hybrid entity, with part of it leased to India to support irrigation and part of it protected as a Ramsar site. From 1996 to 2006, the Maoists aligned themselves with the people pushed out of the KTA. Theirs is a powerful hillside insurgency, perhaps supported by a majority of people outside Kathmandu Valley. Regardless of the justice or injustice of their cause, it is awkward for conservationists to be identified as the enemy in Maoist recruitment discourse. Further adding to this untenable situation, the wardens of the KTA have introduced corruption into the local economy, allowing some people into the wetland at their discretion and for a fee.

This and many other cases demonstrate that, from a conservation perspective, it is extremely difficult to work alongside a community that is being forced to survive in an economy in which, increasingly, only short-term gains appear reliable.[69] Well-respected resource rights that can be enforced and adjudicated in ways that poor communities trust and can afford may be a prerequisite to successful conservation efforts. Conservationists must make some effort to understand what is happening in this regard to ensure that their efforts are truly pro-poor.

Peace Parks in Theory and Practice

In 1932, Canada's Waterton Lakes National Park and the Glacier National Park in the United States were formally combined into the world's first international peace park. Waterton-Glacier International Peace Park was at once a symbol of the commitment to peaceful relations between the two countries and an attempt to facilitate management of a shared ecosystem. Over the years, attempts to build on this example and expand the concept of the peace park into a proactive force that protects living systems, facilitates the lives of transboundary indigenous peoples, and promotes peace in regions of conflict and tension have received considerable support from world leaders, environmental organizations, and academics. The IUCN, which has acted to coordinate the global effort, defines a transboundary area as "an area of land and/or sea that straddles one or more borders between states, subnational units such as provinces and regions, autonomous areas and/or areas beyond the limit of national sovereignty or jurisdiction whose constituent parts are especially dedicated to the protection and maintenance of biological diversity and of natural and associated cultural resources and managed cooperatively through legal or other effective means." It continues to define peace parks as "transboundary protected areas that are formally dedicated to the protection and maintenance of biological diversity and of natural and associated cultural resources and to the promotion of peace and cooperation."[70]

Although this idea has received considerable attention, little research has been done on its demonstrated or potential value. The IUCN's World Commission on Protected Areas has created the Global Transboundary Protected Areas Network, hosted a variety of workshops, and supported several initiatives to create peace parks. Considerable progress has been made in South Africa under the leadership of the late Anton Rupert as well as Nelson Mandela. An extensive effort is also underway to turn the Siachen Glacier, the world's highest warzone, into an international peace park as a step toward ending Pakistani-Indian hostilities in the areas of Kashmir and Jammu.[71] Although the peace park movement is at an early stage of its development, and a variety of economic, administrative, and political obstacles may prove insurmountable, it is easy to appreciate the appeal of the concept. Areas such as Kashmir are physically beautiful and could sustain a valuable industry or serve as potent symbols of peace for the fractious Indian subcontinent. Transboundary management could build trust on both sides, create economic opportunities, preserve shared ecosystems, reassure the global community, and resolve a violent conflict that has lasted almost sixty years. At the same time, it is naive to suggest that transforming conflict zones into peace parks and developing a structure for comanagement that is acceptable to all parties will be easy.

The Impact of Climate Change

The 2007 reports of the Intergovernmental Panel on Climate Change (IPCC), Al Gore's documentary *An Inconvenient Truth,* and the awarding of the Nobel Peace Prize to Gore and the IPCC in 2007 have dramatically raised the profile of climate change, notably in the environmental security community. For example, in the same year, a CNA Corporation report prepared by a group of retired generals and admirals known as the Military Advisory Board, concluded that "climate change acts as a threat multiplier for instability in some of the most volatile regions of the world" and would "add to tensions even in stable regions of the world."[72]

Also in 2007, the German Advisory Council on Global Change argued that "climate change [would] overstretch many societies' adaptive capacities within the coming decades" and identified a set of what it called *conflict constellations* related to climate change–

induced scarcities of water and food; increases in droughts, floods, and severe weather events; and population movements, especially in large swathes of Africa, Asia, and Latin America.[73]

It seems reasonable to conclude that the increase in droughts, floods, heat waves, and hurricanes—together with the impacts of microbial invaders, ecosystem failures, and water, food, and energy shortages predicted by the IPCC—will place an enormous burden on fragile communities in the developing world and hence contribute to human insecurity and intergroup conflict. These communities are vulnerable to climate change in the same way they are vulnerable to other threats like infectious disease—they are poor and lack both the capacity to mitigate stresses and the resilience to adapt.

In this context, the thrust of multilateral negotiations may be somewhat inimical to the needs of the developing world. First, much attention has been given to validating the science (an eighteen-year process to date, and one that inevitably creates a lag time between what is known and what is agreed upon), as well as to exploring the appropriate mix of regulation, market mechanisms, and education for attaining what are to date very modest goals. Second, while it is too early to be certain, there may be a shift in emphasis taking place from mitigation to adaptation as the developed world reconciles itself to the fact that climate change will occur for decades no matter what actions are taken in the near future. Third, there are clearly reasonable grounds for expressing the concern that climate change is displacing other issues from the global agenda—including other forms of environmental change that are most pronounced in the developing world.

All of this raises an important question: how in fact will post-Kyoto targets be established? It is certainly plausible that oil-producing states like Saudi Arabia and wealthy states, like Canada, Japan, and the United States, that consume a lot of energy will be comfortable accepting much higher concentrations of carbon in the atmosphere than might be acceptable from the perspective of countries like Pakistan, Sudan, or Tuvalu. After all, none of the wealthier countries mentioned will come close to meeting the Kyoto targets by 2012, and they may conclude both that (1) the impacts on them will be mixed and (2) they have the capacity to adapt to the negative ones.

The moral and prudent course of action would be to develop climate change policy around the pressing needs of the developing world, recognizing that its higher level of vulnerability calls for aggressive targets for emissions reduction along with broad support for poverty alleviation and appropriate adaptation technologies. But given the decades-old resistance to meeting the goal of doubling development assistance, one must be concerned that the continuation of this trend could result in a bifurcated climate change response. For the North, the goal would be to stabilize the climate at a level that can be managed through adaptation. For the South, the goal could be to find ways to contain population movements. From this perspective, securitizing climate change—even though it clearly does have positive security implications at the local, national, subregional, and regional levels—poses a grave risk: that climate change policy will become a Security Council issue for the South and more of a World Trade Organization (WTO) issue for the North.

Conclusion

This chapter has sought to demonstrate that an increasingly compelling body of literature is supporting the intuition that environmental change is often linked to insecurity at both human and national levels. In particular, it can trigger or exacerbate violent conflict, contribute to vulnerability and inequity, and bolster infectious disease. These are not linear relationships, and they involve complex feedback loops. Further complicating matters, conservation efforts designed to protect living systems have at times themselves exacerbated conflict and insecurity, especially for the poor.

Fortunately, progress is being made on a number of fronts. Militaries are accepting some environmental constraints on their activities; pro-poor conservationists are demonstrating the commitment of the conservation community to sustainable development; and the concept of peace parks is being taken seriously and pursued aggressively in some of the most troubled regions of the world. Unifying these efforts is the widely held intuition that as the world moves toward sustainability, it will reduce and move away from certain forms of violence and insecurity. Much remains to be done, but there are grounds for optimism. Whether these forces will be able to gain the upper hand in the struggle in and over the world's environment remains to be seen.

It is essential to continue to extend the research on the complex linkages described in this chapter, especially through fine-grained field work. Researchers must improve their understanding of other work on conflict and cooperation that focuses on nonenvironmental variables such as identity and material issues. It is also clear that in order to reduce environmental stress as a source of insecurity and integrate conservation and sustainable development into conflict prevention, peacemaking, and postconflict reconstruction, it is essential to focus on institutional and/or governance constraints and opportunities.

Finally, it is worth recalling that the field of security has traditionally had three elements. Security studies, or big-picture analyses, aim to identify trends and relationships at the macro level; tactics studies have as their objective the construction of tools that can be used in the field; and strategic studies help connect the tools that are available or that can be developed to the challenges we face in best understanding the world we inhabit. In the environmental arena, there is a vast literature that looks persuasively at the big picture. There are also thousands of laws, adages, projects, and NGOs that operate at the tactical level. But there is surprisingly little work at the strategic level, especially in the subliterature of environmental security. Through conservation and sustainability, the environment might well have the potential to unite security and development goals. But to realize this potential will require a concerted and inclusive effort to think strategically about how to bring environmental tools to bear on global challenges.

Notes

1. This chapter adapts, updates, and synthesizes arguments from a series of writings about different aspects of environmental security that I have published, alone or with coauthors, over the course of a decade. These are listed in the bibliography. The author would like to thank the Woodrow Wilson Center's Environmental Change and Security Program for permission to reprint material from its *Environmental Change and Security Project Reports* of 2001 and 2002, http://www.wilsoncenter.org. Discussions of the impact of environmental security on US policy are adapted from Richard Matthew, "The Environment as a National Security Issue," *Journal of Policy History* 12, no. 1 (2000): 101–122. The author would like to acknowledge Mike Brklacich, Karen O'Brien, and Bryan McDonald for contributing to the sections on vulnerability, equity, and infectious disease respectively. With regard to the latter, the ideas included here were developed and presented in a different format in Richard Matthew and Bryan McDonald, "Cities under Siege: Urban Planning and the Threat of Infectious Disease," *Journal of the American Planning Association* 72, no. 1 (2006): 109–117.

2. World Commission on Environment and Development, *Our Common Future* (New York: Oxford University Press, 1987), commonly known as the Brundtland Report.

3. Thomas Malthus, *An Essay on the Principle of Population,* 1798, http://www.econlib.org/library/Malthus/malPop.html.

4. Fairfield Osborn, *Our Plundered Planet* (New York: Grosset and Dunlap, 1948), 200–201.

5. Paul Ehrlich, *The Population Bomb* (New York: Ballantine, 1968);

Donella Meadows, Dennis L. Meadows, Jørgen Randers, and William W. Behrens III, *Limits to Growth* (New York: Universe, 1972). See also William Ophuls, *Ecology and the Politics of Scarcity* (San Francisco: W. H. Freeman, 1976).

6. Lester Brown, *Redefining National Security,* Worldwatch Paper no. 14 (Washington, DC: Worldwatch Institute, 1977).

7. Richard Ullman, "Redefining Security," *International Security* 8, no. 1 (1983): 129–153.

8. World Commission on Environment and Development, *Our Common Future.*

9. See Charles Barber, "Global Environmental Security and International Cooperation: Conceptual, Organizational, and Legal Frameworks," working paper (Washington, DC: World Resources Institute, 1989); Lothar Brock, "Peace Through Parks: The Environment on the Peace Research Agenda," *Journal of Peace Research* 28, no. 4 (1991): 407–423; Lothar Brock, "Security Through Defending the Environment: An Illusion?" in *New Agendas for Peace Research: Conflict and Security Reexamined,* ed. Elise Boulding (Boulder, CO: Lynne Rienner Publishers, 1992), 79–102; Simon Dalby, "Ecopolitical Discourse: 'Environmental Security' and Political Geography," *Progress in Human Geography* 16, no. 4 (1992): 503–522; Odelia Funke, "Environmental Dimensions of National Security: The End of the Cold War," in *Green Security or Militarized Environment,* ed. Jyrki Kakonen (Brookfield, VT: Dartmouth, 1994), 55–82; Peter H. Gleick, "The Implications of Global Climate Changes for International Security," *Climate Change* 15 (1989): 303–325; Jessica Matthews, "Redefining Security," *Foreign Affairs* 68, no. 2 (1989): 162–177; Jessica Matthews, "Power Shift," *Foreign Affairs* 76, no. 1 (1997): 50–66; Patricia Mische, "Ecological Security and the Need to Reconceptualize Sovereignty," *Alternatives* 14, no. 4 (1992): 389–427; Norman Myers, *Ultimate Security: The Environmental Basis of Political Stability* (New York: W. W. Norton, 1993); Nico Schrijver, "International Organization for Environmental Security," *Bulletin of Peace Proposals* 20, no. 2 (1989): 115–122; and Arthur Westing, "Comprehensive Human Security and Ecological Realities," *Environmental Conservation* 16, no. 4 (1989): 295–298.

10. See Thomas Homer-Dixon, "On the Threshold: Environmental Changes as Causes of Acute Conflict," *International Security* 16, no. 2 (1991): 76–116; Thomas Homer-Dixon, "Environmental Scarcities and Violent Conflict: Evidence from Cases," *International Security* 19, no. 1 (1994): 5–40; and Thomas Homer-Dixon, *Environment, Scarcity, and Violence* (Princeton, NJ: Princeton University Press, 1999).

11. Robert Kaplan, "The Coming Anarchy," *The Atlantic,* February 1994, 61.

12. See Daniel Deudney, "Bringing Nature Back In: Geopolitical Theory from the Greeks to the Global Era," in *Contested Grounds: Security and Conflict in the New Environment Politics*, eds. Daniel Deudney and Richard A. Matthew (Albany, NY: SUNY Press, 1999), 25–57.

13. See, for example, Jared Diamond, *Guns, Germs, and Steel: The Fates of Human Societies* (New York: W. W. Norton, 1997).

14. Deudney, "Bringing Nature Back In."

15. Deudney, "Bringing Nature Back In," 27.

16. Diamond, *Guns, Germs, and Steel*; Brian Fagan, *Floods, Famines, and Emperors: El Niño and the Fate of Nations* (New York: Basic, 1999); John McNeill, *Something New Under the Sun: An Environmental History of the Twentieth Century World* (New York: W. W. Norton, 2002).

17. For a discussion, see Nancy Peluso and Michael Watts, eds., *Violent Environments* (Ithaca, NY: Cornell University Press, 2001), and Richard Matthew, "In Defense of Environment and Security Research," *Environmental Change and Security Project Report* 8 (2002): 109–124, http://www.wilsoncenter.org.

18. Simon Dalby, "Ecopolitical Discourse: 'Environmental Security' and Political Geography," *Progress in Human Geography* 16, no. 4 (1992): 503–522; Simon Dalby, "The Environment as Geopolitical Threat: Reading Robert Kaplan's 'Coming Anarchy,'" *Ecumene* 3, no. 4 (1996): 472–496; Simon Dalby, "Threats from the South? Geopolitics, Equity, and Environmental Security," in *Contested Grounds: Security and Conflict in the New Environment Politics*, eds. Daniel Deudney and Richard A. Matthew (Albany, NY: SUNY Press, 1999), 155–185.

19. Jon Barnett, "Reclaiming Security," *Peace Review* 9, no. 3 (1997): 405–410; Jon Barnett, "In Defense of the Nation-State: Securing the Environment," *Sustainable Development* 6, no. 1 (1998): 8–17; Jon Barnett, *The Meaning of Environmental Security: Ecological Politics and Policy in the New Security Era* (London: Zed Books, 2001).

20. Nils Petter Gleditsch, "Armed Conflict and the Environment: A Critique of the Literature," *Journal of Peace Research* 35, no. 3 (1998): 381–400.

21. See Matthew, "In Defense of Environment and Security Research."

22. Wenche Hauge and Tanya Ellingsen, "The Causal Pathway to Conflict: Beyond Environmental Security," *Journal of Peace Research* 35 (1998): 299–317.

23. Paul Collier, "Economic Causes of Civil Conflict and Their Implications for Policy," *Turbulent Peace: The Challenges of Managing International Conflict,* eds. Chester A. Crocker, Fen Osler Hampson, and Pamela Aall (Washington, DC: United States Institute of Peace Press, 2001), 143–161.

24. Homer-Dixon, *Environment, Scarcity, and Violence.*

25. Richard Matthew, Ted Gaulin, and Bryan McDonald, "The Elusive Quest: Linking Environmental Change and Conflict," *Canadian Journal of Political Science* 36, no. 4 (2003): 111–137.

26. Noam Chomsky, *Hegemony or Survival: America's Quest for Global Dominance* (New York: Metropolitan, 2003), 2.

27. Gore proved especially adept at restructuring in situ policies and institutions and at using environmental initiatives as a basis for advancing diplomatic goals. The so-called Gore bilaterals, forged with his counterparts in Russia, South Africa, and elsewhere, are a series of high-level agreements to cooperate on shared environmental problems that are typical of Gore's resourcefulness. For a sense of his perspective on environmental issues, see Al Gore, *Earth in the Balance: Forging a New Common Purpose* (Boston, MA: Houghton Mifflin, 1992).

28. This argument receives considerable treatment in Mark Halle, Richard Matthew, and Jason Switzer, eds., *Conserving the Peace: Resources,*

Livelihoods, and Security (Geneva: International Institute for Sustainable Development, 2002).

29. Steve Lonergan, "Global Environmental Change and Human Security: Science Plan," Global Environmental Change Report no. 11 (Bonn: International Human Dimensions Programme, 1999).

30. UNDP, *Human Development Report 1994* (Oxford: Oxford University Press, 1994), 22.

31. UNDP, *Human Development Report 1994,* 23.

32. See, for example, Caroline Thomas and Peter Wilkins, eds., *Globalization, Human Security, and the African Experience* (Boulder, CO: Lynne Rienner, 1999), and Majid Tehranian, ed., *Worlds Apart: Human Security and Global Governance* (London: I. B. Tauris, 1999). A more explicit union of environmental security and human security is evident in Naqvi Nauman, ed., *Rethinking Security, Rethinking Development: An Anthology of Papers from the Third Annual South Asian NGO Summit* (Islamabad: Sustainable Development Policy Institute, 1996).

33. Tariq Banuri, "Human Security," in *Rethinking Security, Rethinking Development: An Anthology of Papers from the Third Annual South Asian NGO Summit,* ed. Naqvi Nauman (Islamabad: Sustainable Development Policy Institute, 1996), 163–164.

34. Concepts such as class relations, human rights, and democracy are broad and inclusive and do an enormous amount of work in contemporary political analysis.

35. Ronald Paris, "Human Security: Paradigm Shift or Hot Air?" *International Security* 26, no. 2 (2001): 87–102, 102.

36. This section draws on short texts prepared by Mike Brklacich (vulnerability) and Karen O'Brien (equity) in the development of an edited volume titled *Global Environmental Change and Human Security,* scheduled for publication by MIT Press in late 2009

37. For more on demographic challenges, see Chapter 4.

38. See, for example, the United Nations University's World Institute for Development Research Report, "Estimating the Level and Distribution of Global Household Wealth," 2006, http://www.wider.unu.edu/publications/working-papers/research-papers/2007/en_GB/rp2007-77/. In the UK, the richest 20 percent of the population enjoys 43 percent of the state's wealth, while the poorest 20 percent command only 6.6 percent of the wealth. See World Bank, "DepWeb: GNP Per Capita," 2001, http://www.worldbank.org/depweb/english/modules/economic/gnp/chart3a.html.

39. This section also draws on short texts prepared by Mike Brklacich and Karen O'Brien in the development of an edited volume titled *Global Environmental Change and Human Security,* to be published by MIT Press in late 2009.

40. Claudia Kemfert and Richard Tol, "Equity, International Trade, and Climate Policy," *International Environmental Agreements: Politics, Law and Economics* 2 (2002): 23–48; Bruce Tonn, "An Equity-First, Risk-Based Framework for Managing Global Climate Change," *Global Environmental Change* 13, no. 4 (2003): 295–306; and Donald Brown, "The Importance of Expressly Examining Global Warming Policy Issues Through an Ethical Prism," *Global Environmental Change* 13, no. 4 (2003): 229–234.

41. Benito Müller, "Equity in Climate Change: The Great Divide,"

working paper (Oxford: Oxford Institute for Energy Studies, 2002); and Neil Adger, "Commentary: The Right to Keep Cold," *Environment and Planning A* 36 (2004): 1711–1715.

42. Adger, "Commentary."

43. Karen O'Brien and Robin Leichenko, "Winners and Losers in the Context of Global Change," *Annals of the Association of American Geographers* 93, no. 1 (2003): 99–113; Robin Leichenko and Karen O'Brien, *Double Exposure: Global Environmental Change in an Era of Globalization* (New York: Oxford University Press, 2005).

44. For further discussion, see the articles in David A. Crocker and Toby Linden, eds., *Ethics of Consumption: The Good Life, Justice, and Global Stewardship* (Lanham, MD: Rowman and Littlefield, 1998).

45. J. Agyeman, R. D. Bullard, and B. Evans, eds., *Just Sustainabilities: Development in an Unequal World* (Cambridge, MA: MIT Press, 2003).

46. Lonergan, "Global Environmental Change and Human Security: Science Plan," and Leichenko and O'Brien, *Double Exposure*.

47. International Union for the Conservation of Nature, "Pro-Poor Conservation: Elements of IUCN's Conceptual Framework," 2003, draft document.

48. For a more elaborate discussion, visit the website supported by the International Institute for Sustainable Development (IISD), http://sdgateway.net/livelihoods/introduction.htm.

49. International Union for the Conservation of Nature, "Pro-Poor Conservation," 2.

50. See, for example, Livestock and Wildlife Advisory Group, UK Department for International Development (DFID), *Wildlife and Poverty Study,* December 2002, http://www.bushmeat.org/pdf/DFIDWildlifePoverty Study.pdf.

51. Mark S. Smolinski, Margaret A. Hamburg, and Joshua Lederberg, eds., *Microbial Threats to Health: Emergence, Detection, and Response* (Washington, DC: National Academies, 2003), xi.

52. William H. McNeil, *Plagues and Peoples* (New York: Anchor, 1998), 179.

53. Alfred Crosby, *America's Forgotten Pandemic: The Influenza of 1918* (Cambridge, UK: Cambridge University Press, 1990).

54. WHO, *The World Heath Report 2005: Changing History* (Geneva: World Health Organization, 2005), http://www.who.int/whr/2005/en/index.html.

55. Jonathan Tucker, *Scourge: The Once and Future Threat of Smallpox* (New York: Grove Press, 2002).

56. Joshua Lederberg, Robert E. Shope, and Stanley C. Oakes, eds., *Emerging Infections: Microbial Threats to Health in the United States* (Washington: National Academy Press, 1992), 2, http://www.nap.edu/openbook.php?isbn=0309047412.

57. Laurie Garrett, *The Coming Plague: Newly Emerging Diseases in a World Out of Balance* (New York: Farrar, Straus, and Giroux, 1994); Jennifer Brower and Peter Chalk, *The Global Threat of New and Reemerging Infectious Disease: Reconciling US National Security and Public Health Policy* (Arlington, VA: RAND, 2003); Smolinski et. al., *Microbial Threats to Health.*

58. Smolinski et al., *Microbial Threats to Health;* Terry Yates, James Mills, Cheryl Parmenter, Thomas Ksiazek, John Castle, Charles Calisher, Stuart Nichol, Kenneth Abbott, Joni Young, Michael Morrison, Barry Beaty, Jonathan Dunnum, Robert Baker, Jorge Salazar-Bravo, and Clarence Peters, "The Ecology and Evolutionary History of an Emergent Disease: Hantavirus Pulmonary Syndrome," *Bioscience* 52, no. 11 (2002): 989–998.

59. David F. Gordon, Don Noah, and George Fidas, *The Global Infectious Disease Threat and Its Implications for the United States*, NIE 99-17D (January 2000), http://www.cia.gov/cia/reports/nie/report/nie99-17d.html.

60. Gordon et al., *Global Infectious Disease.*

61. Gordon et al., *Global Infectious Disease.*

62. James Newcomb, *Biology and Borders: SARS and the New Economics of Biosecurity* (Cambridge, MA: Bio-Era Research Associates, 2003).

63. WHO, *The World Health Report 2004: Make Every Mother and Child Count* (Geneva: World Health Organization, 2004).

64. Laurie Garrett, *The Coming Plague.*

65. Eileen Stillwaggon, *AIDS and the Ecology of Poverty* (Oxford: Oxford University Press, 2006). See especially Chapter 1.

66. See Richard Matthew, "Environment and Conflict in Northern Pakistan," *Environmental Change and Security Project Report* 7 (2001): 21–35.

67. This idea has been explored by the IISD, which supported the IUCN studies noted in the text. Further information is available at http://www.iisd.org/natres/security/cac.asp.

68. Information about this project is available at http://www.iucn.org/places/asia/livelihood/index.html.

69. See, for example, Andrew Balmford, Joslin L. Moore, Thomas Brooks, Neil Burgess, Louis A. Hansen, Paul Williams, and Carsten Rahbek, "Conservation Conflicts Across Africa," *Science* 291, no. 5513 (2001): 2616–2619.

70. Both definitions are taken from the IUCN's Global Transboundary Protected Areas website, available at http://www.tbpa.net.

71. Information available at T. V. Padham, "A Greener Peace in the Himalaya Peaks," SciDev, September 22, 2003, http://www.scidev.net/Features/index.cfm?fuseaction=readfeatures&itemid=199&language=1.

72. CNA Corporation, *National Security and the Threat of Climate Change,* April 2007, 6–7, http://cna.org/nationalsecurity/climate/report/National%20Security%20and%20the%20Threat%20of%20Climate%20Change.pdf.

73. German Advisory Council on Global Change, *World in Transition: Climate Change as a Security Risk* (London: Earthscan, 2007), 1, http://www.wbgu.de/wbgu_jg2007_kurz_engl.pdf.

4

Demographic Challenges to the State

Richard P. Cincotta

Demographic conditions and the course of population trends have only recently begun to work their way into the consciences and priorities of security analysts. While this recent awakening is encouraging, its limited scope is not surprising. With the exception of mass migrations of refugees and the impacts of catastrophic illness and death, most demographic trends move more slowly and more deliberately than political reversals, economic perturbations, and fast-paced careers in foreign service. Why, then, should national security policymakers take a good look at their national demographic statistics? Why should foreign assistance donors take seriously claims of a nexus between global security and the progress of high-fertility countries toward lower fertility, a more mature age structure, and slower population growth? And does the eventual completion of the demographic transition secure a "demographic peace," or should policymakers be wary of other concerns about political stability at the end of this transition?[1]

Answers to these questions are being sought through analyses of *demographic transition*—the transformation of populations with large families and short lives into those containing smaller families with longer lifespans (Figure 4.1). Recent research indicates that this transformation initiates far-reaching secondary and even tertiary economic and social impacts that have proved consequential to the political stability of countries and the welfare and security of their citizens.

The following chapter reviews research efforts to determine the security impacts of conditions and trends that have a substantial demographic component: a youthful age structure; the declining availability of natural resources; the rapid growth of and deteriorating human conditions in urban slums; high rates of death in the working-

Figure 4.1 Birth-rate and Death-rate Transitions

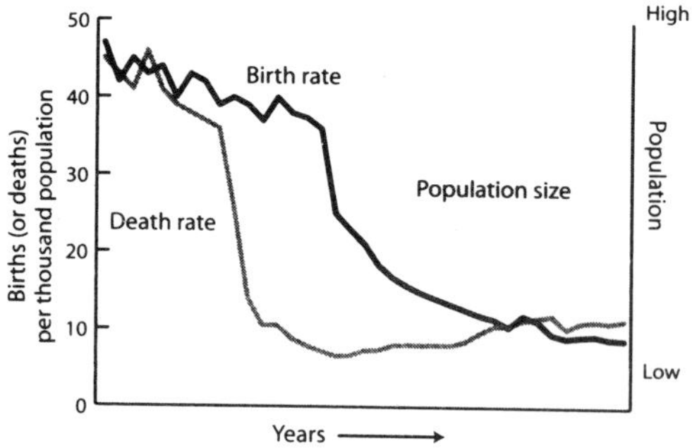

The demographic transition (an idealized version of which is pictured) is comprised of two components, birth-rate and death-rate transitions. Historically, death rates have dropped first. Population growth occurs when a gap opens between birth and death rates. Individually, birth-rate and death-rate transitions have taken from less than fifty to more than 150 years to complete. Some developing countries are passing through these transitions rapidly, much faster than European or North American populations did during the nineteenth and twentieth centuries.

age population (largely from HIV/AIDS); demographic aging and declines in population size; differential population growth rates among ethnic populations; cross-border and domestic migration; and an unusually high marriage-age sex ratio (showing the demographic dominance of males). In reviewing these topics, the chapter is organized to present (1) what is known with a reasonable degree of statistical certainty (the state of current knowledge); (2) what is only partially understood, difficult to prove, and often contentiously debated (the lacunae of current knowledge); and (3) what remains highly speculative or virtually unexplored yet is of acute or growing interest to the security community (the future of knowledge).

This review finds that, among the factors presented, a youthful age structure has, so far, been shown to offer the most serious challenges to the political stability of states. The other demographic factors, however, are not unimportant; they can and often do produce stresses that seriously impede social and economic development, widen rifts between regional and ethnic groups, confine communities and families to poverty, and erode the legitimacy of governments. Yet such sources of grievance, by themselves, have not generally been associated with a level of violence that has unduly threatened states. In addition, ongoing trends in the industrial world—unprecedented demographic aging, population decline, and sustained immigration into low-fertility countries—have yet to reach their most challenging stages. Most analysts agree that, if sustained long enough, these trends will produce conditions that could prove to be politically and economically disruptive—an end stage to the demographic transition that is not at all conducive to a future demographic peace.

What lessons can policymakers take from this field of research? For countries at the end of their transition, lessons are still being learned. For high-fertility developing countries, however, the long-term policy response recommended to governments in this chapter is straightforward: advance demographic transition by giving higher priority in national development strategies to women-focused development. Moreover, in each ethnoreligious community, increase the level of girls' educational attainment, improve access to modern contraception, provide adequate and informed maternal and child health care, and improve women's basic rights and establish their legal status in secular terms rather than through religious family courts. As fertility declines, policies should help make workplaces and job markets more inviting and rewarding for women, and allow working women to bear and raise children in accord with their ambitions.

The World in Demographic Flux

The twenty-first century is unfolding in a world of extraordinary demographic diversity. In 2008, about one-half of all countries had populations more than 60 percent of which were aged under thirty years. Among this group, the countries with the youngest age structures had a population more than half of which was under eighteen years of age. The vast majority of the so-called youngest of the young are in sub-Saharan Africa; the others are Yemen, the Palestinian territories, Afghanistan, and East Timor.[2] At the same time, almost 15 percent of the world's countries now have age structures whereby the percentage of the population over age sixty is greater than twenty. Among the "grayest" of these are Japan, Germany, and Italy, where people over sixty years of age comprise more than 25 percent of the population and the median age has increased to values above forty years. Declining fertility has been the controlling factor in this unprecedented age-structural divergence, setting in motion a gradual transformation of the population's age distribution that ultimately shifted the majority of the population into the working ages (fifteen to sixty-four years of age) and reduced the proportion of the youngest age groups (Figure 4.2).[3]

Despite this widening age gap between the youngest and the most mature age structures, the stark juxtaposition of the high-fertility South against the low-fertility North is breaking down. According to

Figure 4.2 The Direction and Sequence of Age Structural Change, 2005

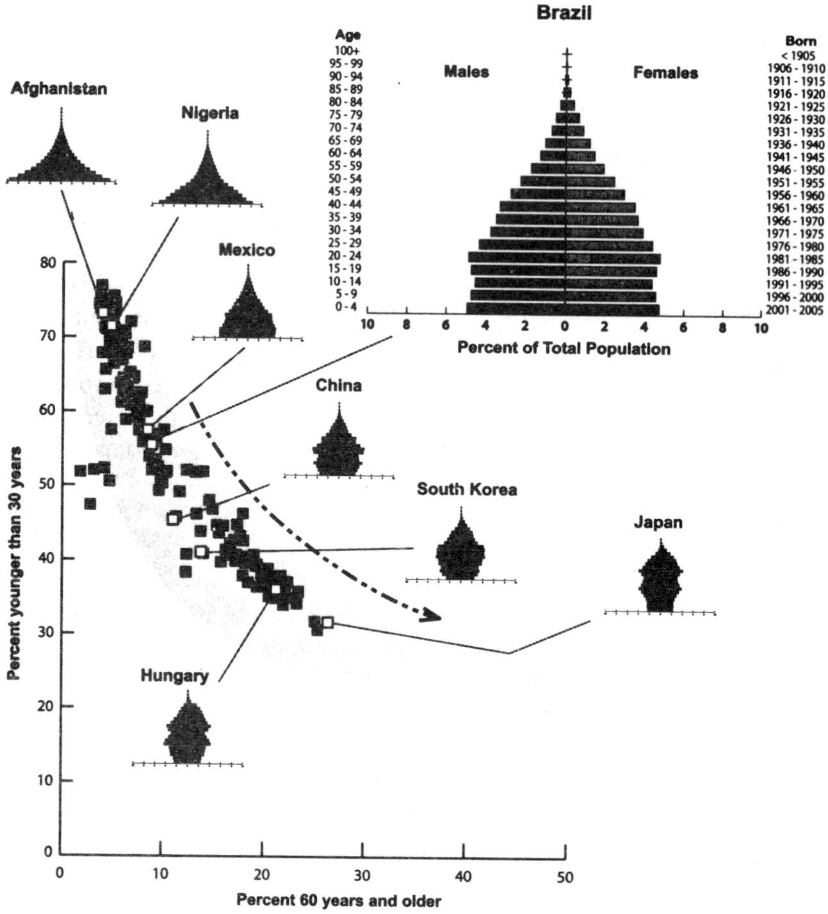

As fertility and infant mortality rates decline, the age structure of a population passes through a fairly predictable sequence of patterns. Because of the wide variation in their progress through the demographic transition, the world's countries can be used to illustrate this sequence and its path. Outliers, mostly to the left of the path, are countries where labor migrants comprise a substantial proportion of the population. Data are from the UN Population Division, 2007.

the UN Population Division, slightly more than half of the world's countries have undergone transitions to a fertility level below 2.5 children per woman. Of all the UN's standard geographic regions, in only three regions of sub-Saharan Africa, plus the Micronesian region of the South Pacific, has no single country dropped below a total fertility rate of 2.5 children per woman. Since 2005 the varied collection of countries with near-replacement-level fertility (that is, with total fertility rates between 1.6 and 2.5 children per woman) has grown to include Algeria (2.4), Brazil (2.3), Costa Rica (2.1), Indonesia (2.2), Iran (2.0), Lebanon (2.2), Mexico (2.2), Morocco (2.4), Turkey (2.1), and Vietnam (2.1).[4]

Reviews of past trends show that income growth was not essential for substantial fertility declines to have occurred in high-fertility, low-income countries.[5] For example, most East and Southeast Asian countries saw their total fertility rate decline to nearly three children per woman before their economies emerged from the World Bank's low-income category. The current situation of stalled fertility declines, principally among sub-Saharan African countries, indicates to some analysts that economic development, women's status, or both may play significant roles in fertility decline in the middle and later phases of this transition.[6]

Since the 1960s, national programs that made modern contraceptives and associated information available and affordable to low-income individuals have been instrumental facilitators of fertility change.[7] These programs typically operate under the assumption that, among low-income households, preferences for wider spacing between childbirths and for smaller families than were seen in previous generations are initial responses to the high risks of maternal and infant mortality. Later declines in desired family size and increases in the demand for modern contraception are assumed to be driven by the increasing costs of investments made in children and the higher returns realized from those investments; by higher female educational attainment; and—where women are entering labor markets—by high opportunity costs for child rearing. In nearly every country, rural populations tend to lag behind urban populations in their advancement to this second stage.

These once high-fertility, now low-fertility countries are soon due to experience a so-called demographic bonus: a set of opportunities associated with age structures that have many workers and few dependents.[8] While some states have clearly outperformed others in this demographic window of favorability, it has in general been associated with social and economic gains—increasing rates of household and government savings, greater investments in school-aged children, slowing workforce growth, and upward pressure on wages—in countries as diverse as China, Chile, South Korea, Ireland, and Trinidad. These reversals have also signaled the approach of demographic aging and thus the need both to establish sustainable pension systems and to prepare, in some fashion, for an eventual falloff in the size of the working-age population.

In much of Europe and in several countries in East Asia, fertility has declined to very low levels—below 1.6 children per woman. In these chiefly urban societies, where maternal and infant mortality risks are almost negligible, the costs of raising children appear to be driven upward by parental competition for educationally and culturally endowed children, while the benefits are depressed by opportunity costs that increase as societies recognize women's claims to status in terms of professional and economic accomplishments and discount claims based solely on childbearing. Meanwhile, another demographic trend—increasing life expectancy among those older than fifty—is promoting an unprecedented accumulation of population in older age groups.

The State of Current Knowledge

The Youth Bulge and Political Instability

Several studies analyzing contemporary and historical data show that countries with very youthful age structures—those with a large proportion of young adults relative to the total population of adults—have an elevated risk of experiencing the emergence of a new civil conflict.[9] Richard Cincotta and Elizabeth Leahy have shown that, in each decade since 1970, 80 to 85 percent of all civil conflicts involving the state (more than twenty-five battle-related deaths per year) have emerged in countries with youthful age structures.[10] A recent, more comprehensive study by Henrik Urdal extends this relationship to other forms of political violence and to domestic terrorism.[11]

Measures used to assess this age-structural condition vary, but show similar results in analyses of conflict risk. Several studies use the UN definition of young adults—aged fifteen to twenty-four years—to calculate the proportion in the entire adult population (aged fifteen years and older).[12] Others measure the proportion aged fifteen to twenty-nine in the adult population, or among working-age adults (fifteen to sixty-four).[13] Still others calculate ratios of non-overlapping cohorts, such as the population of fifteen- to twenty-nine-year-olds divided by the population of thirty- to fifty-four-year-olds, or age thirty and older.[14] A 2007 study used the proportion aged under thirty as a guide to differentiating young age structures from more mature configurations.[15] Despite variations in their indicators, both controlled and comparative studies suggest that the conflict-risk levels associated with a large youth bulge are of roughly similar magnitude to risks associated with low levels of economic development or with high levels of infant mortality—around 2.3 times that of background risks.[16] These studies maintain that a youthful age structure is a significant risk factor but neither a necessary nor a sufficient condition for the initiation of political violence.

Do declines in the youth bulge reduce civil conflict? So far, the answer has been no; civil violence tends to persist long after age structure has matured. However, there are hopeful indications that increasing age-structural maturity, along with economic development, makes recruitment more difficult and qualitatively affects the conflict environment. For example, as the youth bulge declined and the economy began to recover during Northern Ireland's Troubles and Sri Lanka's Tamil-separatist civil war, insurgents shifted from troop-intensive confrontations to bombing and, in the case of the Tamil separatists, to aerial bombardment from small propeller-driven airplanes. In Colombia, this aging effect, coupled with job growth, appears to be diminishing rebel recruitment and could alter the parameters of that insurgency as well. The aging of Lebanon's Shiite population ultimately could undercut recruitment to Hezbollah's militia and speed its integration into state forces.

The results of my own research suggest that the political volatility associated with a large youth bulge can impede a country's capacity to attain liberal democracy or destabilize a liberal regime already in place.[17] Regimes faced with this demographic condition typically concentrate their resources on preserving their position by limiting dissent and maintaining order, a focus that engenders the support of commercial elites and other propertied segments of society. The dissipation of a large youth bulge tends to yield relative political calm, ease unemployment, and relieve pressure on social and economic institutions. With much of a society's political volatility depleted, authoritarian executives often lose the support of commercial elites who find the regime's grip on communication and commerce economically stifling and the extractive privileges of family members and cronies of the political elite financially debilitating. As several studies of democratic transition have noted, political calm and improved economic and social conditions—which tend to advance hand-in-hand with the maturing of age structures—provide authoritarians with opportunities to make a deal for a safe and peaceful exit.[18]

Rapid Urbanization and Dwindling Rural Resources

For the other demographic stresses, however, the conclusions of the research are less straightforward. For example, while countries with a high rate of urban population growth were about twice as likely as other states to experience civil conflict in the 1990s, statistically these outbreaks have been inseparable from the risks associated with low per capita income.[19] The relationship between natural resource scarcities and the risk of civil conflict is also somewhat complex and debatable. Researchers using case-study methodologies have convincingly identified sets of pathways by which scarcities of basic natural resources and attempts to relieve and overcome these scarcities can exacerbate political and ethnic tensions at the subnational level.[20] In addition, population growth, by diminishing per capita levels of cropland and fresh water, has increased the vulnerability of low-income countries to price spikes in international grain markets—a condition that, in 2008, contributed to high food prices in urban areas, triggering in turn protests and riots in at least thirty countries.[21] Despite evidence of sporadic local violence, cross-country statistical studies have not been able to demonstrate that these resource scarcities are on their own sufficient to increase the risk of a full-fledged, state-involved civil conflict.

The Lacunae of Knowledge

While there now may be sufficient statistical knowledge and conclusions from case studies to alert policymakers to the security relevance of population age structures, valid questions remain as to what social processes these demographic indicators reflect, how severe these stresses are in terms of state stability, and how amenable they are to state mediation and adaptation. Thus, the debates surrounding group behaviors and the role of the state are contentious and will likely remain so.

The Behavioral Sources of Youth-Bulge Volatility

Several loosely related mechanisms have been proposed to explain the political volatility of the youth bulge. Studies have convincingly documented the risks of criminal and coalitional violence associated with concentrations of adolescent and young adult males (aged from the mid-teens to the late twenties) and the tendency of this group to reward aggression within its hierarchy.[22] Others have argued that the coincidence of youth bulges with urban growth and economic downturns promotes conditions in which young males are easily organized into volatile and potentially violent political movements.[23] And

Christian G. Mesquida and Neil I. Weiner have speculated that the high intensity of conflicts that often occur in countries with large youth bulges reflects the latter's ability to amplify the inherent tensions between young males setting out to claim economic and social status and adult males who hold society's reins.[24] Jack Goldstone has also called attention to a recurring link between large family sizes among elites and the involvement of their young sons in the leadership of religious movements, political revolutions, and colonial adventures in states in early modern Europe and Asia.[25] According to this theory (from which ominous parallels can be drawn with contemporary conditions in parts of the oil-rich Middle East), young men arrived at adulthood to discover that the system of patronage under which they lived could no longer provide them with the land, military commissions, or bureaucratic jobs commensurate with their family titles and education. Political and religious movements provided alternative paths of social mobility.

Societies in which large families, and thus large proportions of young people, are the norm are exposed to two processes that can make them vulnerable to civil and political violence. The first of these is a vibrant and experimental youth culture. In populations with extremely youthful age structures, boys grow up in youth-packed neighborhoods where authority in the home competes with male hierarchies on the street. Youthful populations tend to produce local, self-organizing adolescent subcultures where intimidation, violence, risk-taking, and demonstrations of loyalty are exercised to sort out and maintain hierarchies.[26]

The second critical process is synergistic with the first. In youth-bulge societies, the surge of adolescents virtually guarantees that the number of dropouts will outpace job growth, leaving even educated young men underemployed, frustrated, and resentful of those who enjoy the opportunities they lack. Without the structure, competition, and mobility afforded by jobs, young men in this transitionary stage of life—when they are most eager to achieve identities, assert their independence from parental authority, and gain respect from their male and female peers—become increasingly vulnerable to mobilization by and recruitment into criminal and political organizations. According to this explanation, both large proportions of young adults and the rate of their growth as groups are likely to aggravate political and social tensions in the context of economic factors that inhibit job opportunities for youth, including inflation, disincentives to investment, and lack of access to land or credit. Where insurgents and criminal networks have been successful at taxing elites and the private sector through kidnapping, extortion, control of exports of drugs and other contraband (as in Colombia) or by capturing or threatening to destroy natural resources (also in Colombia, as well as in Sierra Leone, Liberia, and Angola), these nonstate actors have become major employers of and avenues for social and political mobility.

For youth-bulge theorists, the nature of grievances and fears in a society are of relatively minor importance. They merely represent opportunities for leadership to circumscribe, mobilize, and recruit young adult supporters. The critical factors are, first and foremost, the presence of a large proportion of young adults in a population with limited or restricted opportunities and, second, a political or military organization's capacity to manage and financially support its recruits' activities, not least by supplying weaponry.

Coupled Demographic Factors

If a large youth bulge imparts a substantial amount of risk to state stability, what might the convergence of several challenging demographic factors mean? For example, could youth-bulge countries experiencing very low levels of per capita availability of cropland and/or fresh water bear higher risks than youth-bulge countries without such environmental constraints? So far, evidence for such compound relationships is weak. The results of my analysis suggest that even when there is an increased risk of conflict, it is not, statistically speaking, significantly greater than that of the youth-bulge effect alone (Table 4.1).[27]

Yet there are reasons to be concerned for the future security of poorly developed, agriculture-based economies with youthful age structures. In countries where farm plot size is already marginal and nearly all arable land is occupied or restricted from settlement, young adults—particularly second and third sons who lack an inheritance and access to other rural employment—typically migrate to cities in search of education, employment, social mobility, and opportunities for international migration. More often than not, however, they find themselves among millions of other job seekers, trapped in the squalor of slums with few assets besides their own unskilled labor.[28]

Other aspects of urban growth could also help explain the association between youth bulges and elevated risks of civil conflict. Urban populations tend to be diverse, bringing disparate ethnic, religious, and regional groups into close social contact. Such interactions can have positive social implications where local governments and community leaders have the political convictions, incentives, and finan-

Table 4.1 Demographic Stress Factors and Associated Risks of the Emergence of Civil Conflict

Demographic Stress Factor	Factor Name	Factor Set (Key Criteria)	Likelihood of New Civil Conflict (%)[a]		
			1970–1980	1980–1990	1990–2000[b]
YB	Youth bulge	The proportion of young adults (aged fifteen to twenty-nine) is greater than 40 percent of all adults (aged fifteen and up). Rapid rates of urban population growth (3.5 percent per year or more) tend to be coupled with this factor.[c]	28*	30**	30**
CFSS	Cropland and/or freshwater scarcity	There is per capita cropland and/or per capita freshwater scarcity, which likely constrains rural employment opportunities.[d]	14	15	17
YB and CFSS	Youth bulge coupled with cropland and/or freshwater scarcity	There is both a large proportion of young adults and per capita cropland and/or freshwater stress.	19	19	33
Not YB	No youth bulge	The proportion of young adults is less than 40 percent of all adults.	12	5	11

Source: Conflict data from Uppsala/PRIO Conflict Database, 2008; demographic data from UN Population Division, 2007; cropland data from FAOSTAT, 2008; freshwater data from World Resources Institute, 2008.

Notes: a. *Armed conflict* is defined as a violently contested incompatibility including the use of armed force. In this research, an armed conflict is regarded as a civil conflict when it involves principally parties originating from the same country, at least one of which is associated with the state, and results in at least twenty-five battle-related deaths. Values of demographic factors are measured during the first year of a given decade. Likelihood of a conflict is calculated by determining the proportion of countries in the set that experienced a conflict over the course of said decade. Countries with persistent conflicts (continuing from the last five years of the prior decade) are omitted from the analysis.

b. These results differ slightly from those published by Cincotta et al. in *The Security Demographic,* which uses demographic data from 1995 rather than 1990 to predict civil conflict during the 1990–2000 period.

c. While a rapid rate of urban population growth has been shown to be associated with elevated risk of civil conflict, the high correlation of this demographic stress factor to the youth bulge suggests that these factors should be statistically handled as one. This chapter discusses the synergies between these two stress factors.

d. In this research, countries with less than 0.07 hectare per person are assumed to experience conditions of per capita cropland scarcity. Countries with less than 1,000 cubic meters per person are assumed to experience conditions of per capita freshwater scarcity.

* Statistically significant in comparison with expectations of null hypothesis, $p < 0.10$

** Statistically significant in comparison with expectations of null hypothesis, $p < 0.05$

cial resources to overcome differences. Very often, however, cities are where these communities engage most intensely in economic and political competition and where historic grievances and cultural misunderstandings are most likely to surface. Urban housing and job markets tend to illuminate disparities in access to education, capital, and political power. For centuries the sites of organized criminal activity, social protest, and labor unrest, urban areas—particularly those in Asia—are increasingly the principal locus of ethnic and religious conflict as well.

A 1992 incident in India reflects the urban influence on conflict. Outside the normally sleepy, rural northern town of Ayodhya, a crowd of some 150,000 Hindu militants descended upon a virtually abandoned sixteenth-century mosque, believing it to be situated on the birthplace of Ram, an important Hindu deity. The militants attacked security forces and onlookers and destroyed the mosque. The violence, however, did not spread through the nearby rural countryside, where Muslim and Hindu communities coexisted peaceably. Instead, the hatred returned hundreds of kilometers by bus and by rail to its origins in the growing Indian cities of Mumbai, Calcutta, Ahmedabad, and Delhi. Nearly 95 percent of the 1,500 lives lost in communal riots triggered by this incident were those of urban dwellers. In March 2002, more than 850 people died and thousands lost their homes in three days of rioting in Ahmedabad and nearby Vadodara.[29] These incidents, some of which were reported to have been condoned by local government leaders, unraveled efforts by moderates to broker cooperation between Indian Muslim and Hindu politicians and aggravated already delicate relations between India and neighboring Pakistan.[30]

Yet with adequate investments, even the most salient demographic risk factors—a large youth bulge and closely linked rapid urban growth—can yield net benefits. During the 1980s and early 1990s, Southeast Asia's industrializing urban areas accounted for about 80 percent of the region's economic growth.[31] In this development success story, early investments in education and family planning were key: workers delayed marriage, had smaller families than their parents, and were able to put more money in the bank—which ultimately financed the lion's share of the region's growth. And in the late 1980s when workforce growth slowed, wages rose, attracting large numbers of women to jobs in the manufacturing sector and further encouraging saving and investments in schooling.[32] By the early 1990s, the region had become a net exporter of capital to the West.[33]

Nonetheless, Southeast Asia's successes did not come without an ample share of political turbulence and violence. And some of these states still experience large proportions of young adults in their adult populations—upwards of 35 percent in both Thailand and Indonesia—as well as youthful populations in minority-populated subnational regions, including Thailand's southern isthmus and Indonesia's eastern islands. In these regions, employment lags and centralized state power, historic grievances, and ongoing discrimination remain the bases for political organization.

The State as a Mediator of Demographic Stress

Some states with unusually high levels of demographic stress manage to remain free of civil conflict. What explains this resilience? Several researchers have argued that the state itself—by exercising innovative policies, funding relevant programs, and relying on responsive state-sanctioned institutions—can reduce the risks associated with demography-related stresses.[34] There are numerous ways to do this. States with large natural resource endowments (for example, Saudi Arabia, and Nigeria) or military budgets subsidized from abroad (for example, both Israel and the Palestinian Authority) have tended to draw large numbers of young men into their militaries and internal security forces, using them to extend state control to suppress political opposition and violence. Other states, particularly small island states in the Caribbean and the South Pacific, have encouraged a creative variety of strategies to relieve demographic stresses, including temporary and permanent labor out-migration, contracts with merchant marine services and foreign navies (as are found in Samoa), UN peacekeeping (as occurs in Fiji), facilitated remittances (that is, savings sent home by foreign workers), and so-called diaspora tourism.[35]

What Should Be Known and Why

Ethnic Demographic Shifts and Migration

Although subnational ethnic population data are politically sensitive and difficult to obtain, there is widespread consensus that large differences in ethnic growth rates as made clear through censuses or electoral returns, or even perceptions thereof, can add to the risk of political violence.[36] Even as countries progress through the demographic transition, ethnic groups within them tend to progress at differing rates, and experience emigration and immigration at varying rates. In Asia, some ethnic groups began their demographic transition early and their fertility fell fast; Lebanese Christians, Indonesian Chinese, and India's Malayalis are examples of this. In the same countries, other groups have lagged far behind, among them Lebanese Shiites, Timoreans in Indonesia, Israeli Arabs and Israeli ultra-Orthodox Jews, and Indians of the north-central Hindi-speaking states. Researchers have generally attributed these gaps to a set of interrelated factors, including differences in levels of urbanization, in household income, in women's level of education and their participation in the job market (perhaps the most tangible indicators of their status), and in knowledge of and ease of their access to contraceptives.[37]

Ethnoreligious shifts (that is, shifts in their proportions within the population) tend to become politically salient to the group with whom the nation-state has been identified when changes in ethnic or religious composition are perceived as threats to the political character, traditions, or cultural practices of the group and therefore the state. Tensions can also arise when growing ethnoreligious groups are denied political access and economic rewards commensurate with their perceived share of the population. According to some researchers, political protest and violence seem more likely to occur when contesting groups not only gain a sizable proportion of the population[38] but also have a significantly higher proportion of youths than the more politically powerful group.[39] Such tensions are especially likely to rise in the twenty-first century as ethnic populations progress at varied paces through the demographic transition, particularly in sub-Saharan African and Latin American states where ethnic political organizations already hotly compete for political power. Differences in group fertility rates are already shifting Russia's ethnic and religious composition and influencing party politics in Israel.[40]

Al-Qaida's activities in the United States in 2001, Madrid in 2004, and London in 2005 motivated intelligence organizations to closely review the security implications of current trends in international migration. While subsequent reviews of immigration and border-control policies led to a tightening of efforts to filter out potential terrorists during the visa application process, identify suspects at borders, and redouble efforts to monitor and infiltrate those terrorists operating within immigrant communities, the dynamics of migration to industrial countries remains fundamentally unchanged. Continued population growth and political instability in developing regions, demand for labor within industrial countries, and wide gaps between rich and poor countries almost assure that migration will remain a powerful force, reshaping the ethnic and religious makeup of many industrial countries.[41]

The root of European concern may lie in the ethnic makeup of fast-growing minority populations, the low fertility of the continent's native majority, and the history of its ethnoreligious strife and persecution.[42] Many of western Europe's immigrants were born in North Africa, Turkey, the Middle East, Eastern Europe, Latin America, or sub-Saharan Africa. As many as 15 to 18 million foreign-born migrants are Muslims. Today they work in countries in which national histories and myths emerged over some 900 years of frequent military confrontations with Berber, Arab, and Ottoman forces on land and sea. Moreover, European states and their institutions have facilitated the forging of national identities among disparate ethnic, linguistic, and Christian religious traditions. Thus, as native European populations level off and decline, issues of language, religion, and culture—which have been integral in forging European national identities—tend to color discussions of population decline and aging.

An influx of refugees and other cross-border migrants often evokes fears and provokes anti-immigrant tensions in host countries. While the vast majority of migrants seek only to eke out a living or assimilate, a small fraction unduly influences host-country politics, aids insurgents, and/or actively participates in insurgencies.[43] And some members of wealthy diaspora populations—for example, Sri Lankan Tamils, Irish Catholics, and Sikhs in the United States—have helped underwrite political instability in their countries of origin from afar.[44] Yet immigrants also legitimately remit sizable portions of their wages to improve their relatives' educational status and economic welfare, and they often account for a substantial portion of foreign direct investment in their country of origin. For these and numerous other reasons, trends and policies that influence migration, ethnic relations, separatism, and assimilation warrant closer study and more accurate data.

Skewed Sex-Distribution

Political scientists Valerie Hudson and Andrea den Boer focus their research on regions of contemporary China and India, where sons are strongly preferred to daughters and a large number of expectant parents have recently gained access to ultrasound technology and amniocentesis, facilitating sex-selective abortion. Hudson and den Boer show that this selection will ultimately produce a high sex ratio (the number of males in the population divided by the number of females) among marriageable young adults, and it could leave many Chinese and Indian men unmarried. They draw upon contemporary studies and historical accounts that suggest that, in general, unmarried men are more likely to be involved in violent crime than those in their cohort who are married, and they warn that this effect could spawn political instability in parts of Asia.[45]

However, the changing social and economic contexts of marriage in Asia make some political demographers skeptical of Hudson and den Boer's concerns. For example, Asian men are marrying later, improving their economic security and social status while a larger pool of younger women reaches maturity.[46] Perhaps more importantly, women need not marry only once; today, in some countries of the developing world, divorce rates rival or surpass those in some industrial countries.[47] Moreover, the youth bulge is gradually dissipating in Asia and capitalism is extending its reach, promising more opportunities for employment, particularly in India and China. In addition, there is counterevidence: in 2007, researchers at the Berlin Demographic Institute found that eastern German twenty-year-olds—a population with a high sex ratio—did not experience higher rates of criminal or political violence.[48] Thus, it remains to be seen what social adjustments will be made as young generations with skewed sex ratios advance into the adult years.

Policy Recommendations

While the plethora of unresolved controversies and unanswered questions will no doubt drive researchers to further unravel the relationships between demography and security, the state of research should not delay policymakers from implementing policies and programs that have proved successful in addressing risks. The price for policy inaction and disengagement in the world after September 11 is extraordinarily high—to be measured in future security crises, failed states, and lost human lives. How can development practitioners and policymakers act in a timely fashion?

If the research conclusions of this chapter are correct, then the responses that states and international development donors should make to counter the most addressable demography-related insecurities are fairly intuitive. Diplomats and development policymakers should turn their focus and resources toward countries in the early and middle phases of their demographic transition and should be mindful of both a short- and a long-term strategy.

In the short term, many of the risks associated with demography could be addressed by policies and programs in youth-bulge countries that would do the following:

1. Reduce the financial risk to domestic and foreign investors who could introduce and expand labor-intensive industries and technologies capable of improving urban job markets for young adults, diversifying rural job markets, and stimulating a demand for schooling and job training.[49]
2. Promote opportunities for labor emigration in places where the growth of the young working-age population has far outstripped the national job market.
3. Integrate minorities into secular schools and increase their participation in government while promoting minority access to public services, urban job markets, and professional careers.

To promote the demographic transition in the medium and long terms, international development donors should scale up efforts to help countries

1. improve girls' school enrollment and lengthen their educational attainment;
2. improve women's access to family planning, maternal health care, and income-generating opportunities;
3. encourage states to enhance minority women's opportunities to access services, improve their educational status, and succeed in the job market;
4. encourage, where applicable, a shift of women's rights and family issues into state judicial systems and out of religious courts, which tend to impede women's social and economic mobility;
5. encourage policies that promote workplace conditions allowing women to achieve and compete even as they meet their childbearing intentions.

Conclusion

While advancing the demographic transition in high-fertility countries is not a panacea for political violence, the evidence that has accumulated suggests that its contribution to reducing conflict risks is underappreciated. Globally, this transition is incomplete. About one-fifth of all countries today experience total fertility rates of four children per woman or more—and 85 percent of these are in sub-Saharan Africa. When two high-fertility north-central states of India (Uttar Pradesh and Bihar) are added to these countries, their total population—the most conflict-affected population in the world—is more than 1.1 billion.[50] The significant risks of delaying progress through the demographic transition—which in turn can only be reduced over time—underscore the need for the governments of developing countries and aid donors alike to increase financial and political support for policies and programs that, by focusing on women's development, could lead to further fertility declines among high-fertility countries.

Where fertility has reached very low levels—namely in parts of Europe and East Asia—the coming decades will bear witness to concerted efforts by policymakers to reverse demographic aging, halt population declines, and, in some cases, minimize the impact of immigration and ethnic shifts. For these demographic challenges there are, as yet, no easy solutions. Coming, as they have in the wake of political stability and development facilitated by a country's advance through the demographic transition, such challenges may, in hindsight, prove to have been a small price to pay—and then again, they may not.

Notes

1. Neil Howe and Richard Jackson, "Battle of the (Youth) Bulge," *The National Interest* 96, no. 4 (2008): 33–41.

2. UN Population Division, *World Population Prospects: The 2006 Revision* (New York: United Nations, 2007).

3. Fertility is expressed by the total fertility rate for any given time, which estimates the number of children, on average, that women are bearing during the span of a normal reproductive lifetime.

4. UN Population Division, *World Population Prospects.*

5. John Bongaarts and Susan Cotts Watkins, "Social Interactions and Contemporary Fertility Transitions," *Population and Development Review* 22, no. 4 (1996): 639–682; John Bongaarts, "Population Policy Options in the Developing World," *Science* 263, no. 5148 (1994): 771–776.

6. John Bongaarts, "Fertility Transitions in Developing Countries: Progress or Stagnation?" Poverty, Gender, and Youth Working Paper Series no. 7 (New York: Population Council, 2008).

7. Rudolfo A. Bulatao, "The Value of Family Planning Programs in Developing Countries," RAND Monograph Report Series (Santa Monica, CA: RAND, 1998).

8. David E. Bloom, David Canning, and Jaypee Sevilla, "The Demographic Dividend: A New Perspective on the Economic Consequences of Population Change," RAND Monograph Report Series (Santa Monica,

CA: RAND, 2002); Ronald Lee and Andrew Mason, "What Is the Demographic Dividend?" *Finance and Development* 43, no. 3 (2006): 16–17.

9. Jack A. Goldstone, "Demography, Environment, and Security: An Overview," in *Demography and National Security,* eds. Myron Weiner and Sharon Staunton Russell (New York: Berghahn, 2001), 38–61; Gary Fuller, "The Demographic Backdrop to Ethnic Conflict: A Geographic Overview," paper presented at the conference The Challenge of Ethnic Conflict to National and International Order in the 1990s: Geographic Perspectives, Washington, DC, September 30, 1993; Gary Fuller and Forrest R. Pitts, "Youth Cohorts and Political Unrest in South Korea," *Political Geography Quarterly* 9, no. 1 (1990): 9–22; Jack A. Goldstone, *Revolution and Rebellion in the Early Modern World* (Berkeley, CA: University of California Press, 1991); Herbert Moller, "Youth as a Force in the Modern World," *Comparative Studies in Society and History* 10, no. 3 (1968): 237–260.

10. Richard P. Cincotta and Elizabeth Leahy, "Population Age Structure and Its Relation to Civil Conflict: A Metric," *Environmental Change and Security Project Report* 12 (Washington, DC: Woodrow Wilson Center for International Scholars, 2006–2007).

11. Henrik Urdal, "A Clash of Generations? Youth Bulges and Political Violence," *International Studies Quarterly* 50, no. 3 (2006): 607–630.

12. Urdal, "A Clash of Generations?"; see also Sarah Staveteig, "The Young and the Restless: Population Age Structure and Civil War," *Environmental Change and Security Project Report* 11 (Washington, DC: Woodrow Wilson Center for International Scholars, 2005).

13. Richard P. Cincotta, "How Democracies Grow Up," *Foreign Policy* March–April 2008, 80–82; Richard P. Cincotta, Robert Engelman, and Daniele Anastasion, *The Security Demographic: Population and Civil Conflict After the Cold War* (Washington, DC: Population Action International, 2003).

14. Richard A. Easterlin, *Birth and Fortune: The Impact of Numbers on Personal Welfare* (Chicago: University of Chicago, 1987); Christian G. Mesquida and Neil I. Wiener, "Human Collective Aggression: A Behavioral Ecology Perspective," *Ethology and Sociobiology* 17, no. 4 (1996): 247–262; Christian G. Mesquida and Neil I. Wiener, "Male Age Composition and the Severity of Conflicts," *Politics in the Life Sciences* 18, no. 2 (1999): 181–189.

15. Elizabeth Leahy, Robert Engelman, Carolyn G. Vogel, Sarah Haddock, and Tod Preston, *The Shape of Things to Come: Why Age Structure Matters to a Safer, More Equitable World* (Washington, DC: Population Action International, 2007).

16. Leahy et al., *The Shape of Things to Come.*

17. Cincotta, "How Democracies Grow Up"; Richard P. Cincotta, "Half a Chance: Youth Bulges and Transitions to Liberal Democracy," *Environmental Change and Security Project Report* 13 (Washington, DC: Woodrow Wilson Center for International Scholars, 2008–2009).

18. Samuel P. Huntington, *The Third Wave: Democratization in the Late Twentieth Century* (Norman, OK: University of Oklahoma, 1991), 115–116; Philippe C. Schmitter, *Speculations About the Prospective Demise*

of Authoritarian Regimes and Its Possible Consequences (Washington, DC: Woodrow Wilson Center, 1980).

19. Urdal, "A Clash of Generations?"

20. Thomas Homer-Dixon, *The Environment, Scarcity, and Violence* (Princeton, NJ: Princeton University Press, 1999); Colin H. Kahl, "Population Growth, Environmental Degradation, and State-sponsored Violence: The Case of Kenya, 1991–1993," *International Security* 23, no. 2 (1998): 80–119; Richard A. Matthew, "Environmental Stress and Human Security in Northern Pakistan," *Environmental Change and Security Project Report* 7 (2001): 17–31, http://www.wilsoncenter.org.

21. IRIN News, "NGOs Call for More Funds, Investment in Agriculture," July 2, 2008, http://www.irinnews.org/PrintReport.aspx?ReportId=79047.

22. Martin Daly and Margot Wilson, *Homicide* (New York: Aldine de Gruyter, 1988); Glen Weisfeld, "Aggression and Dominance in the Social World of Boys," in *Male Violence,* ed. John Archer (New York: Routledge, 1994), 42–69.

23. Moller, "Youth as a Force"; Nazli Choucri, *Population Dynamics and International Violence: Propositions, Insights, and Evidence* (Cambridge, MA: MIT Press, 1973).

24. Mesquida and Wiener, "Human Collective Aggression."

25. Goldstone, *Revolution and Rebellion.*

26. John Archer, "Gender Roles as Developmental Pathways," *British Journal of Social Psychology* 23 (1984): 245–256. Conflict data are from the Uppsala Conflict Data Program and International Peace Research Institute Oslo, *UCDP/PRIO Armed Conflict Dataset Codebook: Version 4-2008.* (Oslo: UCDP/PRIO, 2008); demographic data are from the UN Population Division, *Population Prospects, the 2006 Revision* (New York: United Nations, 2007); cropland data are from the Food and Agriculture Organization of the United Nations, *FAOSTAT,* http://faostat.fao.org; freshwater data are from the World Resources Institute, *World Resources 2008: Roots of Resilience—Growing the Wealth of the Poor Share Delicious* (Washington, DC: WRI, 2008). Also see Cincotta et al., *The Security Demographic.*

27. Conflict data are from the Uppsala Conflict Data Program and International Peace Research Institute Oslo, UCDP/PRIO *Armed Conflict Dataset Codebook: Version 4-2008* (Oslo: UCDP/PRIO, 2008); demographic data are from the UN Population Division, *Population Prospects, the 2006 Revision* (New York: United Nations, 2007); cropland data are from the Food and Agriculture Organization of the United Nations, *FAOSTAT,* http://faostat.fao.org; freshwater data are from the World Resources Institute, *World Resources 2008.* Also see Cincotta et al., *The Security Demographic.*

28. Leif Ohlsson, "Livelihood Conflicts: Linking Poverty and Environment as Causes of Conflict," Policy Paper (Stockholm: SIDA Environmental Policy Unit, 2000); Peter Xenos, "Demographic Forces Shaping Youth Populations in Asian Cities," in *Youth, Poverty, and Conflict in Southeast Asian Cities,* eds. Lisa M. Hanley, Blair A. Ruble, and Joseph S. Tulchin (Washington, DC: Woodrow Wilson International Center for Scholars, 2004); Fuller and Pitts, "Demographic Backdrop."

29. Raj Chengappa and Ramesh Menon, "The New Battlefields," *India*

Today, January 31, 1993, 28; Peter Gizewski and Thomas Homer-Dixon, "Urban Growth and Violence: Will the Future Resemble the Past?" *Project on Environment, Population and Security* (Washington, DC: American Association for the Advancement of Sciences, 1995), 3.

30. Human Rights Watch, "We Have No Orders to Save You: State Participation and Complicity in Communal Violence in Gujarat," *Human Rights Watch* 4, no. 3C (2002): 2–68.

31. Asian Development Bank, *Emerging Asia: Changes and Challenges* (Manila: ADB, 1997).

32. John G. Bauer, "How Japan and the Newly Industrialized Economies of Asia Are Responding to Labor Scarcity," *Asia-Pacific Research Report* 3 (Honolulu: East-West Center, 1995), 5–12.

33. World Bank, *The East Asian Miracle: Economic Growth and Public Policy* (Oxford: Oxford University Press, 1993), 40–43.

34. Thomas Homer-Dixon, "The Ingenuity Gap," *Population and Development Review* 21, no. 3, (1995): 587–612.

35. Helen Ware, "Demography, Migration, and Conflict in the Pacific," *Journal of Peace Research* 42, no. 4 (2005): 435–434.

36. Bhagat, "Religious Identity, Demography, and Social Tension in India."

37. Cross et al., "Completing the Demographic Transition in Developing Countries."

38. Elia Zureik, "Demography and Transfer: Israel's Road to Nowhere," *Third World Quarterly* 24, no. 4 (2003): 619–630.

39. Christian Leuprecht, "Migration as the Demographic Wild Card in Civil Conflict: Mauritius and Fiji," *Environmental Change and Security Project Report* 13 (2008/2009): 34–39.

40. Richard P. Cincotta and Eric Kaufmann, "The Changing Face of Israel," *Foreign Policy Online,* June 1, 2009, http://www.foreignpolicy.com/story/cms.php?story_id=4956.

41. National Intelligence Council, *Growing Global Migration and Its Implications for the United States* (Washington, DC: NIC, 2001).

42. Timothy M. Savage, "Europe and Islam: Crescent Waxing, Cultures Clashing," *Washington Quarterly* 27, no. 3 (2004): 25–50; Jonathan Grant, Stijn Hoorens, Suja Sivadasan, Mirjam van het Loo, Julie DaVanzo, Lauren Hale, Shawna Gibson, and William Butz, "Low Fertility and Population Aging: Causes, Consequences, and Policy Options," working paper (Berlin: RAND Europe, 2004); Michael S. Teitelbaum and Jay Winter, *A Question of Numbers: High Migration, Low Fertility, and the Politics of National Identity* (New York: Hill and Wang, 1998).

43. Myron Weiner, *The Global Migration Crisis* (New York: Longman, 1995).

44. Yossi Shain, "Democrats and Secessionists: US Diasporas as Regime Destabilizers," in *International Migration and Security*, ed. Myron Weiner (Boulder, CO: Westview Press, 1993).

45. Valerie Hudson and Andrea den Boer, *Bare Branches: The Security Implications of Asia's Surplus Male Population* (Cambridge, MA: MIT Press, 2004).

46. Richard P. Cincotta, "From Ultrasound to Insurgency," *Environmental Change and Security Project Report* 11 (2005): 70–109.

47. Karen O. Mason, Noriko O. Tsuya, and Minja Kim Choe, *The Changing Family in Comparative Perspective: Asia and the United States* (Honolulu: East-West Center, 1998).

48. Steffen Kröhnert and Reiner Klingholz, *Not am Mann* (Berlin: Berlin Institute for Population and Development, 2007).

49. UN Office for West Africa (UNOWA), Youth Unemployment and Regional Insecurity in West Africa (New York: United Nations, 2005).

50. Data from UN Population Division, *World Population Prospects: The 2006 Revision;* A. R. Nandra and Carl Haub, The Future Population of India: A Long-range Demographic View (Washington, DC: Population Reference Bureau, 2007).

5

The Security Paradox in Unified Yemen

Laurent Bonnefoy and Renaud Detalle

Located in the southwestern corner of the Arabian Peninsula, with a territory about the size of France, Yemen is the poorest yet most populated country of the Arabian Peninsula, with around 25 million people. It is one of the rare Arab countries to have experienced relatively free elections in which multiple candidates competed, such as during the parliamentary elections of 1993 or even, despite a clear trend towards the monopolization of power by the ruling party, the presidential election of 2006. Few remember that former South Yemen was the only Arab state with a Marxist government or that under British rule in the 1940s, Aden was one of the most active ports in the world. Yet since its unification in 1990, Yemen has acquired a negative reputation for backwardness, tribalism, violence, instability, and fundamentalism.

Although Yemen has been caught in the midst of geostrategic struggles between global and regional powers for many centuries, its desert and mountainous hinterland were largely immune to modernization and foreign influence until the 1960s. British colonization in the south, which ended in November 1967, basically limited itself to Aden. The north remained independent, although an Ottoman military presence remained until the end of World War I under the rule of the Zaydi imamate, which dominated much of the Yemeni highlands for over a thousand years. Following the 1962 Nasserist military takeover in the north, a civil war between republicans and royalists lasted until 1970. With the emergence of two republics—the Yemen Arab Republic (YAR) in Sanaa and the People's Democratic Republic of Yemen (PDRY) in Aden—Cold War politics ensured the continued partition of the country. The Yemeni leaders proved quite adept at embracing foreign ideologies (especially in the southern PDRY), leaving the country highly susceptible to foreign influence, whether from the Soviets, Egyptians, Americans, Chinese, or Saudis.

The role of external actors in the historical development of the two Yemens should not lead to an underestimation of domestic dynamics such as internal competition for power, deep-rooted tribal and social structures, and economic challenges. For instance, the January 1986 purge and civil war in the PDRY (which left thousands dead and the city of Aden severely damaged) was an intense power struggle among socialist elites over ideological and regional loyalties. Meanwhile, North Yemen's affiliation with the West remained loose and uncertain throughout the 1970s and early 1980s, as the government steadily sought to maintain its independence.

Although the country had rarely been unified throughout its long history, Yemenis shared a strong sense of common identity. Nonetheless, the unification of North and South Yemen into the Republic of Yemen on May 22, 1990, was far from a smooth transition and lacked proper preparation. It was preceded by the wars of 1972 and 1979 as well as by continuous cross-border guerrilla activities, plots, and assassinations. Although official rhetoric claimed equality between the two former Yemeni states, northerners exerted some dominance over their ex-socialist counterparts, who had remained unaware of the south's oil reserves. The euphoria of unity, accompanied by political reforms and democratization, soon vanished due to this perceived sociopolitical inequality as well as to economic difficulties compounded by Yemen's international isolation after its government opposed military intervention in Iraq during the 1990–1991 Gulf War. In short, unified Yemen's early years were rocked by severe economic, political, and security crises. After months of skirmishes and unsuccessful mediation attempts, from April to July of 1994, a civil war broke out between the so-called secessionists (an odd alliance of southern socialists, Adeni liberals, and supporters of the preindependence Sultans) and proponents of national unity under the dominance of northerners. The secessionists lost and unity prevailed. By the mid-1990s, the government, aided by international donors, managed to stabilize the economy and devalue the Yemeni riyal as well as confront some of the country's serious problems.

Although national unity has been strengthened since 1994, there is a continued risk of instability and insecurity, albeit in new and changing forms. In the South, antinorthern sentiment is still widespread and, in 2007, new tensions appeared with still unknown consequences. The post–September 11 international environment has plainly revealed the fragility of Yemen's situation. Under strong external pressure—and despite widespread anti-Americanism among the population—the Yemeni government decided to cooperate in the so-called global war on terror, hosting US Army Special Forces to train Yemeni troops in and advise them on counterterrorism. This was a sharp departure from its lack of cooperation during the US investigation into the bombing of the USS *Cole* on October 12, 2000. Since 2001, the stability provided by President Ali Abdallah Salih and the relatively low intensity of terrorist violence has created an impression that Yemen has handled this trying period rather well.[1] However, this assessment is seriously challenged by the fact of the state's continued fragility, which has become more and more apparent since 2007 with the conjunction of multiple crises, including the government's brutal repression of the anti-US Zaydi movement in northern Yemen since June 2004. Various ceasefires have been proclaimed but all have proved fragile and most grievances have remained unaddressed.[2] These factors give rise to the security paradox—whereby Yemen's internal insecurity is exacerbated by attempts to obtain international security—that is the subject of this chapter.

Caught between regional and international security pressures on the one hand and domestic priorities on the other, Yemen has treaded a very difficult course since 1990. This chapter analyzes the country's security and development challenges with a view to assessing whether both can be consistently addressed. It also focuses on the impact and consequences of national and international responses to Yemen's pressing problems—especially in the changed international environment since 9/11. The chapter ends with remarks about Yemen's security paradox and policy recommendations for reconciling the country's security and development needs.

Security and Development Trends Since Unification

Security: From Terrorist Haven to Ally in the War on Terror?

Since its unification in 1990, Yemen has experienced different forms of conflict and insecurity, all of which have contributed to its domestic problems and generated a negative international reputation. Yemen's first serious crisis after unification was the Iraqi invasion of Kuwait and the following Gulf War in 1991. Still struggling with internal political issues yet finding itself on the UN Security Council, the Yemeni government objected to military intervention in Iraq, although it had good relations with Kuwait. The Yemeni position was considered pro-Iraq and seriously affected its relationships with its embittered Arab neighbors as well as with Western donors. Yemeni migrant workers were deported from Kuwait and Saudi Arabia in massive numbers while foreign aid from the United States decreased significantly.[3]

Additionally, at the time of unification, Yemen had no delineated borders with its immediate neighbors (Saudi Arabia and Oman) or with those across the sea (Djibouti, Ethiopia, and, after 1993, Eritrea). Violent clashes with neighbors occurred regularly and threatened to escalate rapidly. In 1999, an international arbitration board ruled in favor of Yemen's sovereignty over the Hunaysh islands, which had been contested by Eritrea. The signature of border treaties with Oman in 1992 and Saudi Arabia in 2000 settled remaining territorial disputes.[4] Since then, Yemen has not faced external threats likely to fuel a territorial conflict, although sea and land border control remains a serious concern.

Domestically, Yemen's tribal social system has contributed to routine violence in which hundreds of Yemenis are injured or die each year.[5] With large proportions of the population affiliated with tribes, a coherent system of customary law has sometimes been instrumental in mitigating potential conflict, especially given its perceived legitimacy in contrast to Yemen's largely corrupt and ineffectual judicial system.[6] Despite the strengthening of the state following unification, the retribalization of some southern governorates is a possible contributor to rising insecurity.[7] Yet it is important to note that this tribal violence is not the expression of a national political agenda, nor should it be associated with international forms of terrorism.

Yemen's political conflicts are also largely the by-product of a unification for which it was ill prepared. The new political system was unable to merge two very different political and bureaucratic cultures. Moreover, at first, the status of the armies of the two former Yemeni entities was left unresolved. The assassination of about 150 socialist militants over the four-year transitional period exacerbated existing tensions, leading to the May 1994 civil war.[8] Fortunately, the war was short lived, as unification enjoyed popular support and southern secessionists lacked military resources (despite financial support from rich emigrants). Assisted by Islamist militias, the central government achieved a rapid victory on July 7, 1994, in Aden, which is referred to as the "secessionists' capital." The speed of this achievement allowed for the near-total eradication of political socialism and allowed the victors to control the narrative of the conflict. As a result, numerous aspects of the war—such as the number of casualties, the role of Saudi Arabia, and the roles played by Yemeni fighters or *mujahidin* (some of whom are now associated with Al-Qaida) returning from the Afghan-Soviet conflict—remain unclear.[9]

More than fifteen years after the civil war, the destabilizing competition between elites has largely disappeared. The defeated socialists have lost legitimacy among the population; not only do they no longer represent a political alternative, but they lack sufficient material resources to oppose the government, even at a local level. According to official statistics, the Yemeni Socialist Party (YSP) only gathered 4.69 percent of the votes in the April 2003 parliamentary elections. The party's boycott of the 1997 elections might have contributed to its decline. Nevertheless, the feeling that unification was achieved at the expense of the southern populations is increasingly popular, while the contestation of domination by the north has been rising and taking different, largely noninstitutional forms since 2007.

Another security issue that has plagued Yemen since the 1980s is the kidnapping of tourists and foreign residents by tribal groups. Initially, kidnappings were viewed as a curious manifestation of North Yemen's tribal fabric. Since 1994, the international media and many analysts have begun to erroneously link these kidnappings to violent Islamist groups. In fact, most of these incidents have had nothing to do with an anti-Western political agenda and were resolved peacefully through tribal mediation. Only in 1998 did a kidnapping end tragically, when four tourists kidnapped by the Aden-Abyan Islamic Army (a violent Islamist group) were killed during a botched rescue attempt by the Yemeni Army.[10] Notably, no kidnappings occurred between the end of 2001 and late 2005, as the Yemeni government declared the kidnappings of foreigners as acts of terrorism punishable by death. In late 2005 and early 2006, three kidnappings of foreigners occurred, but all ended well. However, this practice appears to be on the rise again, indicating a deteriorating political situation.

The post–Cold War preoccupation with radical Islam contributed to this perception of Yemen as a safe haven for terrorists. Indeed, Yemen's geography, social conservatism, and remoteness made it look like the so-called Afghanistan of the Near East. Remote mountainous and desert areas made Yemen an ideal place for violent groups to install training camps and plot attacks against Western interests. Not only did Yemen welcome individuals who had fought in the 1980s in Afghanistan, but throughout the 1990s, Yemenis also participated in various jihadist fronts in Bosnia, Sudan, and

Chechnya. As a result, Yemen became host to assorted groups which had connections with international jihadist movements and to which the government turned a blind eye.

Yet Yemeni leadership was able to achieve a political and power-sharing equilibrium that served to preserve peace among domestic factions. Local Islamist parties remained closely associated with people in power. An Islamist party, al-Islah, was part of the coalition government that imposed several conservative reforms between 1993 and 1997.[11] Although al-Islah represents various religious clerics, it also includes conservative business people, tribal segments of the population, and members of the Muslim Brotherhood.[12] Despite the participation of radical Islamist groups in government, during the 1990s little internal political violence occurred and Western interests were rarely targeted. This changed with the October 2000 bombing of the USS *Cole* in Aden, which killed seventeen US Navy personnel and wounded thirty-eight; Yemen thereby became associated with terrorism and was placed on Washington's security agenda.[13] Yemeni reluctance to fully support the subsequent investigation contributed to the perception of the nation's long-standing leniency toward terrorism. Although prominent figures in the army and the administration were suspected of having supported the attack, none have been tried as of the time of this writing.

The 9/11 terrorist attacks were a harsh reality check. The fact that Yemeni citizens had participated in the planning of the New York and Washington attacks seemed to confirm the country's links with terrorism, especially once Yemeni native Ramzi bin al-Shaybah, the alleged coordinator of the attacks, was arrested in Pakistan in September 2002. Many Yemenis were caught in Afghanistan and imprisoned in the US-run Guantanamo Bay detention center (as of June 2009, following the return of many Saudis and Pakistanis to their home countries, Yemenis constituted the largest contingent, and the Obama administration's plan to close the camp was hampered in part by the alleged incapacity of the Yemeni government to manage and control these militants upon their return to their country). As an inevitable consequence, Yemen came under intense international pressure—which, in turn, has significantly affected the government's policies on many fronts. Despite the attack on the French oil carrier *Limburg* in October 2002, the murder of Jarallah Umar—a prominent leader of the YSP—and the murders of three Baptist missionaries from the United States in December 2002, the country has not faced large-scale terrorist attacks for some time.[14] Vague plans of attacks against different Western embassies and officials, including US ambassador Edmund Hull, have been foiled.[15] Yet the deaths of eight Spanish tourists and their two Yemeni guides in a suicide attack in Ma'rib in July 2007, the murders of two Belgian tourists in January 2008, and most of all the attack on the American embassy in Sanaa in September 2008, as well as various targeted attacks against oil facilities, point to a new kind of instability that has further affected the country's reputation and that questions the efficiency of both national and global antiterror policies. The Yemeni government has often blamed the terrorist attacks on isolated individuals rather than on a transnational terrorist network, the existence of which it only started to acknowledge in 2006 and was forced to fully acknowledge with the announced merger of the Saudi and Yemeni branches of Al-Qaida in 2009. Nevertheless, it is recognized that in particular tribal areas, Yemen offers ample training ground for secretive groups who could plan terrorist attacks.

Remarkably, since 9/11, Yemen has been able to transform itself from a potential target as a supposed safe haven for terrorists to a perceived US ally in the war on terror. Through the exchange of intelligence, the arrests and trials of militants, and its security cooperation with the United States, the government has been walking a thin line, trying to satisfy the competing demands of the international community and of a population that favored Iraq in 1991 and opposed the US invasion in 2003. Nonetheless, Yemen's transformation into a US ally was accompanied in 2004 by an invitation to President Salih to join the US-hosted G8 summit in Florida and the official lifting of US sanctions on arms sales to Yemen, which had been in force since the 1994–1995 Foreign Relations Authorization Act. Though there have also been tensions and accusations that it is still too soft on terror groups, Yemen has reacted to its new status in ways that have had far-reaching impact on its domestic policies, as we will discuss.

Development: Poor Indicators, Great Challenges

Tracking development trends in Yemen is difficult due to missing, incomplete, or contradictory data. Despite international assistance, the country has still not been able to carry out a reliable population census.[16] Such an absence of data is symptomatic of the state's incapacities. International organizations such as the World Bank have acknowledged the absence of reliable and comparable indicators, on poverty for example, prior to 1998.[17] Given the limitations of quantitative data, this chapter relies greatly on qualitative analysis based on extensive field experience to supplement available statistical data.

Yemen is poorly developed and faces many development challenges with security implications. After unification, the country suffered from high inflation, budget deficits, and growing poverty. According to the UN's 2001 "Yemen Common Country Assessment," real gross domestic product (GDP) per capita fell from US$701 in 1990 to US$328 in 1995.[18] The debt inherited by the newly unified Republic of Yemen in 1990 amounted to twice the country's gross national product (GNP).[19]

In September 1990, very early in the unification process, Yemen's pro-Iraq stance regarding the invasion of Kuwait prompted Saudi Arabia to make residence and work conditions harsher, which led an estimated 800,000 Yemeni immigrants to leave the country. It deprived the country of valuable remittances, an essential source of revenue. Most returnees were from North Yemen, as southerners enjoyed a more secure status in Saudi Arabia. As a result of the return of migrants, the Yemeni labor population expanded by almost 30 percent, increasing unemployment and drastically reducing remittances, which were estimated in 1989 at around US$1 billion.[20] Meanwhile, in February 1991, the United States dropped its aid from US$20.5 million to less than US$3 million because of Yemen's lack of support for the Gulf War. In December 1992, demonstrations against high living costs, unemployment, and inflation turned riotous.[21] However, decreasing regional tensions after the mid-1990s allowed the migration of Yemenis abroad to reach pre–Gulf War levels. Nevertheless, remittances have declined from their high point at the end of the 1980s. Yemeni immigrants no longer enjoy a privileged status, and they face competition from other immigrants, primarily from Asia.[22]

Due to a costly military campaign and the subsequent destruction of Aden, the 1994 civil war only exacerbated these difficulties. That year, the budget deficit reached 18 percent of the GDP.[23] At the end of the civil war, there was an increase in international attention, aid, and investment, which led to a modest improvement in Yemen's development prospects. Furthermore, in 1995, structural reforms launched by the government in cooperation with international financial institutions strengthened the service and oil sectors and lessened the contribution of the agricultural sector to GDP. In the late 1990s, through donor-backed policies, the Yemeni government managed to decrease inflation and budget deficits. In 1997, the Paris Club, which covered about one-third of Yemen's US$9 billion debt, agreed to restructure the government's foreign debt.[24] According to the 2002 World Bank "Poverty Update" on Yemen:

> During the second half of the [1990s], the stabilization program stimulated growth [that] may have positively affected living standards, especially in rural areas. However, the evidence available does not allow assessing the extent to which the economic trend during the first half of the 1990s was offset by the positive performance of the economy during the second half of the 1990s. Based on actual economic growth rates between 1998 and 2001, it is estimated that poverty incidence has stagnated at around 41 percent.[25]

The *Human Development Report 2004* ranked Yemen 149th out of 177 countries and 153rd three years later.[26] The World Bank's 2006 "Country Assistance Strategy" report indicated that Yemen's development was negatively affected by its low GDP (US$550 per capita in 2004), low literacy rates (52 percent overall but only 28.5 percent for women), extremely high gender gaps in all sectors, high population growth (3.5 percent according to the Yemeni government), and fragile state, characterized by an inadequate infrastructure and a poorly performing industrial production center (in 2001, for example, industries employed only 16.8 percent of the workforce).[27]

Underdevelopment is also evident in the state's heavy dependency on oil. In 2001, oil revenues accounted for 15 percent of the GDP, 71 percent of the state budget, and 83 percent of goods and services exports.[28] As a result of the oil boom of the 1990s and mid-2000s, manufacturing's share in the economy decreased. While manufacturing accounted for 12.7 percent of the GDP in 1993, ten years later it was only 4.9 percent.[29] The long-awaited contract for liquefied natural gas (LNG) exports is expected to further increase dependence and to discourage economic diversification, yet it will not be able to compensate for the depletion of oil reserves. Gross annual value of exports, starting in 2009 when facilities and infrastructures were due to be completed, will be around US$1.5 billion (in 2005 prices)—that is, around one-fourth of the level of crude oil exports.[30]

Despite these acute challenges, over the last eighteen years there have been positive changes in various areas. The country's Human Development Index shows an upward trend, from 0.392 in 1990 to 0.508 in 2007. Access to education and health care has improved. According to the *Human Development Report 2007/2008*, access to basic education increased from 51 percent in 1991 to 75 percent in 2005.[31] Improvements in health care might be attributed to growing urbanization (around 35 percent of the population is urbanized), since healthcare facilities are absent in rural areas. Consequently, life expectancy has risen from forty years in 1975 to sixty-two in 2007, while infant mortality was down to 76 per thousand in 2007. The World Bank's 2003 paper "Yemen and the Millennium Development Goals" notes:

> Yemen has made significant progress on the MDG [Millennium Development Goals] targets, especially when one considers that Yemen started relatively late, largely due to historical reasons. It seems likely that by 2015, Yemen may achieve the primary education target, the elimination of [the] gender gap within [the] primary education target, and the absolute poverty reduction target, provided that the policy and institutional reforms recommended are implemented and donor support is forthcoming. However, the reforms required are difficult and may be opposed by many.[32]

Despite a 2.5 percent annual growth rate in GDP per capita between 1990 and 2002 and a 4.6 percent growth in 2006 due to extra oil-related revenues, most Yemenis have been affected by decade-long price hikes (18.4 percent in 2006) and rising unemployment rates, estimated at 12.5 percent by the government in 2005 but probably much higher. The Ministry of Planning and Development's second Five Year plan, for 2001–2005, estimated that in 2000 "37 percent of the labor force is unemployed in the general sense, of which 11.9 percent is explicit and 25.1 percent is underemployed." Furthermore, the UN's 2001 "Yemen Common Country Assessment" states that "wages have been falling in real terms since the early 1990s."[33] In 2005, in a new "Yemen Common Country Assessment," the UN asserted that "reducing poverty and unemployment substantially over the coming years is contingent upon the adoption of a radically different and human-centered approach to development."[34] Although inequalities are not high compared to other countries (in 1998, which was the most recent figure available at the time of this writing, the UN Development Programme (UNDP) measured a Gini index of 33.4), fast growth is contributing to a sense of increasing inequality. Divergences between nationally and internationally aggregated figures and the rising grievances of Yemenis are a normal feature of growing social and economic tensions.[35] The informal sector, community loans, and self-help mechanisms explain why negative trends have not led to large-scale crime and insecurity in the face of accelerating urbanization.[36] Nonetheless, following years of drought since 2001, a growing sense of poverty has pervaded Yemen's rural areas.

According to international organizations, development prospects remain poor and the situation is deteriorating. Despite "steady progress" during the end of the 1990s, the World Bank notes that "Yemen's macroeconomic outcomes show increasing fragility," with long-term growth stifled by insufficient reforms and policies to tackle socioeconomic challenges, including economic diversification and the deleterious influence of *qat*, a mildly narcotic plant chewed daily by most Yemenis.[37] The fragility of the state and its citizens' livelihoods has become more evident, despite growing international aid.

Meanwhile, the country's youth bulge, matched with an inadequate education system, darkens development prospects. According to the UN, in 2005, around 50 percent of Yemenis were under fifteen years old.[38] Primary school children in Yemen are taught in shifts and secondary schools rarely have fewer than eighty pupils per class.[39] Professional school education has been overlooked by the government and by international organizations. Vocational training is underdeveloped, accounting for only 0.4 percent of total enrollment.[40]

The inadequacy of the public education system has led to an increase in the number of private, mostly religious, schools. In the 1990s, the so-called scientific institutes *(al-ma'had al-'ilmiyya)* constituted a parallel religious education system. These institutes were closely associated with the aforementioned al-Islah party and were accused of spreading religious fundamentalism.[41] In 2002, the government was finally able to assume control of some 1,000 schools funded by Saudi Arabia, which taught around 600,000 pupils. The growing number of religious educational institutes actually had more to do with poor job prospects for students and underutilization of human potential than with terrorism, religious fanaticism, or the preaching of hatred. Nonetheless, as part of the global war on terror, the government announced in late 2004 that hundreds of private religious institutes would be closed or put under state control. Yet, the state's assumption of control over curricula is not likely to solve the problems of the education sector—much less combat terrorism.

A Difficult Juggling Act: Reconciling Security and Development

Since unification, Yemen has experienced serious structural difficulties and instability resulting from the 1990–1991 Gulf War, the 1994 civil war, terrorist attacks, and intermittent violence. These have adversely affected its development prospects. Unable to prevent or reverse these momentous events, the country's political system seems to be caught in a particularly difficult predicament as it faces internal political struggles, rising domestic discontent, and strong international pressures. The principles underlying unification were initially built on equal power sharing between the rulers of the two former sovereign states. The 1994 war caused a power shift and favored an alliance between the president's General People's Congress and different and competing Islamist parties, whether Zaydi or the Muslim Brotherhood. Over the years, the political system has been characterized by the growing role of the president, whose power was strengthened by constitutional amendments adopted by referendum in 2001. Yet the opposition remains active through its press and in Parliament. Since unification, opposition activity has mainly revolved around two competing groups: the YSP, which lost most of its leading figures in the war of 1994, and al-Islah, which brings together Islamists and tribal elements. Since 2002, opposition parties have tried to unite their forces by formulating a common platform and by presenting a unique candidate—namely Faysal bin Shamlan, a former Socialist Party oil minister—during the September 2006 presidential election; he garnered 22 percent of the vote and even managed to win a majority in certain southern regions.

Until now, the various levels of power sharing offered to opposition movements by the ruling party have allowed the legitimate representation of all political forces, and thus have reduced many political tensions. Shaikh Abdallah al-Ahmar, for example, chief of the Hashid tribal confederation, was speaker of Parliament and chairman of the al-Islah opposition party until his death in late December 2007.

Since the late 1990s, developments have suggested autocratic tendencies on the part of President Salih, who has been in power since 1978. Discussion of his succession is taboo; nonetheless, his son Ahmad, head of the Special Forces and first elected to Parliament in 1997, is slowly being put forward. However, the consequences of the death of Shaikh al-Ahmar could in the medium term be critical for the country's stability, as he was considered to be the link among the multiple and contradictory identities of Yemen's ruling groups.[42]

Since the 1994 civil war, grievances have been less focused on the effectiveness of power sharing and more on internal inequalities and the interregional development gap. Although economic divisions do not fall along a north-south divide, southerners claim discrimination and from 2007 onward were more vocal than they had been in denouncing their situation, organizing demonstrations that were repressed by the army in Aden, and by the Abyan and Lahej governorates. Overall, the most unstable areas include al-Jawf, Ma'rib, Shabwa, Abyan, and Sa'ada, all of which have strong tribal structures and poor infrastructure, although Ma'rib and Shabwa have oil resources. In these parts of the country, communities feel they are benefiting neither from oil revenues nor from state policies. State investment in health, education, and transportation infrastructure is absent. These areas also suffer from high levels of car thefts and tribal confrontations. Government negligence intensifies demonstrations of resentment by tribes who have used tourist kidnappings as a source of income and a means to gain attention from the capital. Similarly, drug and arms smuggling into Saudi Arabia offers good income opportunities while challenging the control of the state.[43]

Economic hardship in urban areas has also caused violent demonstrations. Demands for reform formulated by the international monetary institutions led in July 2005 to a cut in government subsidies and a doubling of diesel and gasoline prices. Spontaneous demonstrations then occurred in all the main cities. The intervention by state security forces caused forty casualties and destroyed public property. According to the government daily newspaper *al-Thawra*, "Price reforms aim at fighting corruption, ending smuggling and accelerating development."[44] Indeed, the government seems critically aware that the population will not accept austerity measures if corruption, which is becoming increasingly visible in the cities, is not tackled.[45] The fight against corruption was one of the main themes of the presidential campaign of September 2006. Trying to show his commitment, President Salih named Ali Muhammad Mujawar, a former minister of electricity with strong anticorruption credentials, as prime minister in April 2007.

At the regional level, economic difficulties increase pressures for migration, especially to Saudi Arabia. However, since 2002, the so-called Saudization of certain economic sectors in which foreigners are no longer allowed to work has reduced opportunities and increased illegal migration to the main Saudi cities. Tensions are exacerbated because the Yemeni government is unable to efficiently patrol its northern border with Saudi Arabia, finally delimited by the Jeddah Treaty of 2000. Besides arms and drug smuggling across the northern border, in the mid-2000s trafficking of women and children was estimated at 200 cases per week.[46] Border tensions between the two countries escalated during the May and November 2003 terrorist attacks in Saudi Arabia. Saudi Arabia asserted that terrorists had imported explosives from Yemen. In violation of the 2000 border treaty, Saudi Arabia has threatened to build a security fence along its southern border with Yemen.[47] Strict border control would negatively affect tribal communities living along the border who benefit from commerce, smuggling, and migration.

The growing contradiction between the Yemeni government's original disagreement with the 2003 war in Iraq and its close cooperation with the United States in the ensuing war on terror is a likely source of instability. There is evidence that violent groups capitalize on this gap by seeking support in isolated communities in regions where the state is weak. In November 2002, the assassination of Ali Qa'id Sunyan al-Harithi, accused of being a prominent Al-Qaida member, along with five other car passengers by an American drone left the Yemeni government in the difficult position of contending with internal anti-Western pressures on the one hand and external pressures to defend Western action on the other. Over the years, widespread anti-Western sentiments, whether legitimate or not, have increased communities' economic and ideological shows of support of Islamist groups, from financing Hamas to agreeing with Osama Bin Laden's political discourse. Small groups such as the Aden-Abyan Islamic Army have planned attacks targeting the state, civilians, and/or foreigners, but few have succeeded. In this context, few in Yemen saw the attack on the USS *Cole* as terrorism, because the act was directed at a military target on its way to enforce the Iraq embargo.[48]

Notably, the upheaval around the Zaydi leader Husayn Badr al-Din al-Huthi and his kin marks the convergence of internal inequalities and resentment toward international policies, highlighting the links between security and development. The Sa'ada region, a Zaydi and royalist stronghold in the 1960s with a strong Saudi influence, had been long neglected by the government.[49] Husayn al-Huthi—scion of a learned Zaydi family, former member of Parliament, and virulent preacher—gathered supporters based on tribal and sectarian loyalties. A brutal but localized war erupted in mid-June 2004 when the government decided to arrest al-Huthi. The operation was justified on the grounds that al-Huthi preached hatred against Israel and the United States and was supported by an unnamed foreign power (most likely Iran, so as to raise the specter of a pan-Shia plot). Al-Huthi and his group, The Believing Youth *(al-Shabab al-Mumin),* represented no immediate security threat and shared little with Al-Qaida. In an open letter to the president published in the summer of 2004, al-Huthi even declared his allegiance to the government and said his grievances only concerned foreign policy.[50] Nevertheless, the army launched violent operations in the region of Sa'ada, underestimating the resistance. According to unofficial opposition sources, despite religious and tribal attempts at reconciliation, weeks of intense fighting resulted in thousands of casualties; the brutal killing of al-Huthi on September 10, 2004; and the displacement of over 11,000 families who were left homeless. The fighting flared up sporadically afterward, including in early 2008, with al-Huthi's father, a respected scholar, and brothers leading the rebels.[51] The conflict threatened to take on an international dimension. Ayatollah Ali al-Sistani in Iraq and scholars of Qum in Iran pleaded in favor of their Zaydi Shia brethren. The government managed to limit the visibility of this supposed upheaval by denying journalists, nongovernmental organizations (NGOs), and international organizations access to the area. Hence, these events did not make international headlines—a fact that demonstrated not only the limited visibility of Yemen but also the government's successful manipulation of the media in communicating its policy against religious extremism in the war on terror. In early 2007, the renewed violence forced the government to accept international mediation, mainly from Qatar, which despite promised financial aid and the signature of an agreement between the rebels and the government in February 2008 did not prevent another brutal round of fighting between April and July 2008. Since 2007, the International Committee of the Red Cross, as well as international NGOs like Médecins Sans Frontières, have been given access to the battleground, but information on the war remains scarce and grievances go unaddressed. At the time of this writing in May 2009, low-level fighting has led analysts and actors alike to anticipate a new round of more severe fighting.

Intellectuals, the press, and many Yemeni citizens believe that Ali Abdallah Salih's campaign sought to display his government's commitment to fighting terrorism.[52] Although the causes and consequences of this conflict are still debated, many argue that the incident actually demonstrated the weakness of the army and the state.

The fact that the military officer in charge of the repression was accused of protecting radical Islamists and having close connections to Osama bin Laden gave the al-Huthi insurgency additional fodder. Ever since, the fighting has continued, albeit sporadically, and there continue to be reports of heavy-handed government measures against opponents and journalists, including occasional reports of torture.[53] The government's inability to confront the opposition peacefully has only increased grievances; meanwhile, the military campaign, the arrests and persecution of Zaydi intellectuals and magistrates, and growing governmental repression have increased support for the rebellion. These violent confrontations demonstrate how political, religious, social, historical, and tribal issues can overlap and escalate into conflict.

Capacities for Peace and Risk Factors

In addition to the events described above, there are also unique internal factors that influence Yemen's security and development trends, either by amplifying or mitigating challenges and risks. Yemen has significant assets, including a large youthful population, great natural resources (minerals, oil, gas, fish, and agricultural wealth), a temperate climate with highlands-reaching monsoons, and an ideal geographic position with great potential for tourism. Compared to other countries with limited levels of development, Yemen has relatively low social inequality, and urbanization is not so extensive as to destabilize rural communities. As a consequence, the country's main cities, including Sanaa, Aden, Taiz, Hudeidah, and Mukalla have very low crime rates. Although it is one of the poorest countries in the world, Yemen faces no serious food insecurity and its population has not suffered from famine in forty years, although the recent replacement of traditional wholesome cereals such as sorghum with imported flour has increased nutrition problems in remote areas.

The ethnic and religious homogeneity of Yemen should also be considered a source of stability. Zaydi and Shafi'i (the latter being one of the four major branches of Sunni Islam) identities tend to converge and become secondary in defining most communities, though this assertion could be challenged after the recent war against al-Huthi, which contributed to the stigmatization of the Zaydi identity.[54] However, Yemen's president, like a significant proportion of the ruling elite, is of Zaydi origin, which is likely to prevent universal stigmatization.

Yemen's relatively homogenous nature could be challenged by the growing flow of refugees from the Horn of Africa. Many of the migrants have entered illegally, taking great risks to reach Yemen by sea, then ending up in camps or moving to Saudi Arabia in search of a better future.[55] Those who stay in Yemen often end up being integrated into the *akhdam* (servant class), a social group that suffers significant discrimination, especially as its members' employment prospects are systematically limited to unskilled work such as sweeping streets and collecting garbage.

Meanwhile, emigration has played an important role in Yemen's modern history. Over the years, many people have left the country searching for job opportunities abroad. Yemeni expatriates do not form an institutionalized diaspora, although many have kept ties with the homeland. Until 1990, Yemenis were able to migrate to Saudi Arabia with a privileged status and their remittances positively affected the country's economy and stability. Despite decreases in the 1990s, migration to the Gulf States, the United States, and Asia is rising again, although opportunities in all of these places have become scarcer. The Yemeni origin of many Saudi families important in the private business sector (including bin Laden, bin Mahfuz, al-'Isa'i, and Buqshan families) has been an important source of development projects often launched in coordination with the Yemeni state. These initiatives, in the form of hospitals, schools, roads, and private industrial investments, have often been aimed at developing the regions of origin of these rich individuals, thus indirectly contributing to regional inequalities.

Qat, the stimulant flowering plant, plays a complex role in Yemen.[56] A large part of the household budget is devoted to qat. On a daily basis, hours are spent on its consumption and cultivation. While it requires large quantities of water to grow and has negative health implications, qat is also a strong source of social and national cohesion. It reduces internal migration by employing many in the rural sector as farmers and traders; it not only allows money to flow between social groups but prevents the destabilizing results of rapid urbanization. Qat is also an important source of revenue through taxation. Incidentally, qat revenues are currently being decentralized and directly accrued to newly established local authorities in order to reduce tax evasion through closer local monitoring. Yet, in addition to its health risks, qat may also become a future source of instability, as water resources become depleted and the price of diesel used to pump water rises.

For Yemen, water is a serious security concern and could result in important and destabilizing internal migrations. Rapidly declining water resources are exacerbated by intensive qat farming, wasted water because of a poor pipe network, and inefficient irrigation. Frequent droughts have increased rural poverty and encouraged urban migration. In the past, water scarcity has contributed to intertribal conflict that could potentially escalate in the future. According to the World Bank 2006 "Country Assistance Strategy," "Water scarcity...is serious and getting worse; per capita availability of water in Yemen is at 2 percent of [the] world and 10 percent of [the] regional average."[57]

Natural endowment of oil reserves has been a double-edged sword. While oil has become a source of easy government revenue, oil has also been extracted from some of the most impoverished and excluded tribal territories, thereby fueling grievances. Yemen has significantly fewer oil reserves than its rich neighbors. With 160 million barrels extracted annually, the country's reserves represent less than 1 percent of Saudi Arabia's. If no others are found, Yemen's reserves will be depleted by 2012.[58] The heavy reliance on oil reserves for revenue, an increasing youth population, and unemployment all make a compelling case for the need to diversify the economy.

The widespread existence of small arms, which is considered a part of Yemen's "tribal culture," is a potential risk. According to the Small Arms Survey, in 2002, 6 to 9 million small arms were in circulation.[59] Interpersonal conflicts can escalate into deadly intertribal war, however localized. For example, in December 2004, a long-lasting financial quarrel between two tribes in the al-Jawf region led to the deaths of twenty-eight people after conciliation efforts failed.[60]

Even though the spread of small arms and distrust of the state can be attributed to the low levels of infrastructure development in some regions, they have also been effective guarantees against autocratic rule. As such, Yemen's tribal system appears to be a mixed blessing. The state is formed by complex and sometimes competing networks in which power sharing remains effective. In contrast to many other countries in the Middle East, nationalist and even socialist governments in Yemen have proved incapable of destroying traditional structures and therefore have been forced to work constructively with them. Active tribal structures have functioned as participation structures that facilitate certain processes of democratization. The existence of diverse political parties and media should be considered an indirect result of an armed civil society that is able to balance the state and the military.

Policy Responses in a Changing Environment

This section examines the evolution of security and development policies since unification at both the domestic and international levels. Special focus is devoted to the post-9/11 environment.

An Unfinished State

Yemen is a state in construction, one that has found itself in the midst of momentous events. Its policies reflect changing priorities as well as contradictory impulses. In the first decade following unification, the government showed strong commitment to structural reforms and its progress was acknowledged by international actors. The Economic, Financial, and Administrative Reform Program (EFARP), implemented during the first Five Year Plan (1996–2000) and negotiated with the International Monetary Fund (IMF), managed to reduce the budget deficit, curb inflation, and stabilize the exchange rate. The 2001–2005 Economic and Social Development Plan was equally promising in its commitment to tackle poverty, to develop a responsible fiscal policy, and to promote decentralization. Government documents such as the 2003 Poverty Reduction Strategy Paper (PRSP), assert a commitment to reaching the MDGs. Similarly, the 2006–2010 plan announced by the Yemeni government outlines a comprehensive development strategy.[61]

However, security considerations have repeatedly affected the government's development plans. For example, in 1996, following the destruction of Aden during the civil war, the government, advised by international financial institutions, decided to create a free zone in the Aden port. The national company Yeminvest received the concession to manage the project. Despite a good geographic position and high levels of internal investment, the project did not fare well. Poor management, unsettled land property regulation, corruption, and stiff competition from other ports in the region (including Dubai, Salalah, and Djibouti) did little to attract investors. The October 2000 attack on the USS *Cole* and the 2003 attack on the *Limburg* made ship owners and their insurance companies reluctant to station boats and merchandise in Yemeni ports. According to Aden Free Zone sources, traffic volume fell by 67 percent between 2002 and 2003. In 2003, the government attempted to revitalize the Aden Free Zone by transferring management from Yeminvest to an international private company.

After unification, the government also undertook efforts to integrate its territory through infrastructure rather than through military consolidation. A number of private-public projects successfully built roads, schools, cellular phone networks, and hospitals; they also improved water supply and electricity provision. These projects simultaneously increased state capacity and empowered isolated communities. As a result, in areas where the state is absent, communities and tribes are increasingly demanding a greater state presence. Indeed, both infrastructure and reconstruction programs in Sa‘ada after the 2004 killing of al-Huthi and the creation of a special Sa‘ada reconstruction fund in 2007 (and another in 2008) demonstrate the government's awareness of security-development linkages. Road construction not only gives local communities access to the outside world, but also enables military access to isolated areas. As a result, after years of neglect, development projects are focusing on rebellious regions but remain hampered by the instability of the situation in the field.

Under donor pressure, the Yemeni government also launched an ambitious decentralization program to empower local communities, including the 2000 Local Authorities Law and the 2001 elections of local councils. The program was an attempt to revive the successful cooperative movement in North Yemen of the 1970s and 1980s. However, decentralization is a double-edged sword. Given the limited institutional capacities and resources at the local level, the overlapping of tribal and political networks has created multiple opportunities for corruption as well as conflict. The socialist-era legacy of southern governorates has complicated decentralization of resources and salaries. For example, in 1999, while only 2.38 percent of the population were employed as civil servants, 12.41 percent were employed as such in the governorate of Aden.[62] The government's postponement of local council elections from 2003 to 2006 reflected a reassessment of the decentralization strategy in light of its limitations, from the lack of institutional capacity to the need to redistribute resources among regions.

Notwithstanding its reformist development record after unification, it is important to remember the government's political roots. While President Salih cultivates an international image of himself as a civilian Arab reformer, he is a former member of the military and occupies its highest grade as field marshal. The army is the most powerful institution in Yemen's recent history, although it remains deeply influenced by tribal affiliations. It is used as a conduit of redistribution to many different populations, particularly in zones where other institutions and infrastructures are deficient. The lack of any strong small-arms-control initiative except in the capital city is the result of its prominence, as is the pervasive culture of impunity for well-connected tribal shaikhs doubling as army officers. Military expenditures account for a very high proportion of GDP (7 percent in 2005) according to the UNDP's *World Development Report 2007*, although the national army continues to be poorly trained, ill-disciplined, and ineffective.[63] This ineffectiveness has led to brutal military tactics, as evidenced by the high rate of casualties and the duration of the al-Huthi campaign as well as by allegations by converging Zaydi sources of the indiscriminate bombing of villages.[64]

Given the army's important role, political and security considerations were a key part of Yemen's unification process. Starting in the mid-1990s, however, when Western interests were seen to be threatened, security concerns gained even more importance under the increasing external pressure. After 9/11, the government's priorities shifted radically—with immediate and far-reaching domestic repercussions. For example, international criticism of Yemen's education system and of the Zaydi insurgency spurred a government public campaign to close hundreds of religious teaching centers and gain control over another 4,000 institutions training 300,000 students.[65] Indeed, the government has tried to exert more control over religious elements in general. Many Muslim clerics have been dismissed by the Ministry of Religious Affairs for being too openly anti-Western. The al-Iman University, headed by prominent Islamist figure 'Abd al-Majid al-Zindani, a former member of the president-appointed consultative council, was temporarily closed down in September 2001. It reopened after many foreign students were expelled from the country. Many individuals were arrested, some of whom were tried, and new student visa regulations were implemented.

On the other hand, since the 1990s, and especially after 9/11, the government has pursued a parallel strategy, allowing a number of jihadis to return. These people, supported by prominent figures, have been successfully reintegrated into the economic system and even the state and are said to have abandoned violence. Such a strategy has probably proved more effective than repression in keeping Yemen free of large-scale terrorist attacks.

Yemeni collaboration in the global war on terror has coincided with considerable regression in the area of human rights. A 2003 Amnesty International report on Yemen highlights the use of security concerns to sideline the rule of law: "The government's security policies adopted in the wake of the events of [9/11] represent a serious setback to its previous progressive undertakings and a further drift away from its obligations under international human rights treaties."[66]

In 2005, Yemen dropped thirty-three places in just two years in Reporters Without Borders' annual ranking of country press freedom. In September 2004, opposition journalist 'Abd al-Karim al-Khaywani, editor of the weekly *al-Shura,* was arrested and imprisoned for criticizing the government's overreaction in the war against al-Huthi. *Al-Shura* was shut down for six months. Individuals close to the ruling party continued to publish a progovernment paper called *Minbar al-Shura* with the same layout as that of the banned paper in order to fool the readers and spread government propaganda. In early 2008, al-Khaywani, accused of betrayal, faced another trial and was sentenced to six years in prison, only to receive a presidential pardon a few months later. After the al-Huthi war, Zaydi identity has been increasingly marginalized—a number of Zaydi books were withdrawn from bookshops, and the commemoration of Ghadir Khum, a yearly Shia holiday and a popular festival among some Zaydis, was declared illegal in January 2005. Those caught breaking the ban were arrested.

Yet the government has also undertaken various initiatives on human rights. For example, signaling its commitment to women's rights, the government successively appointed four women (Wahiba Fara', Amat al-'Alim al-Suswa, Khadija al-Haysami, and Huda al-Ban) to head the Ministry of Human Rights. In January 2004, it organized an international conference on human rights to discuss liberty restrictions associated with the global war on terror. President Salih used this conference as an opportunity to announce Yemen's intention to ratify the US-opposed International Criminal Court (ICC). Parliament ratified the treaty in March 2007, only to nullify the vote a few weeks later as it was claimed the quorum had not been reached. As of June 2009, the issue was still on standby.

Expanding External Engagement and Deepening Dilemmas

Yemen was an important arena for East-West power struggles throughout the Cold War, as was reflected in the deep division between the two Yemens. The end of the Cold War coincided with Yemen's unification. Because of changing geostrategic considerations, external powers were only marginally concerned with the security and development challenges Yemen faced following its unification and the 1994 civil war. After 9/11, however, Yemen's potential instability and reputation as a terrorist safe haven led to a sharp increase in international attention and an immediate surge of assistance. For example, regional aid for infrastructure projects (mainly from Saudi Arabia, Kuwait, and the United Arab Emirates), which had dropped since the 1990s, increased again after 9/11. In 2002, Yemen received a total of US$583.7 million in development assistance (around US$30.2 per capita or 5.8 percent of the GDP). This figure was reduced to US$234 million and US$252 million in 2003 and 2004, respectively. Key bilateral donors include Germany, the United States, Japan, the Netherlands, and the European Commission, with Arab agencies and Arab countries providing relatively limited aid.

Operating in Yemen since 1969, the World Bank has been a major donor, financing and implementing some 131 projects. In 1997, the Bank backed the establishment of the Yemeni Social Fund for Development (YSFD). Its 2006 "Country Assistance Strategy" makes recommendations to improve governance and to create an attractive investment environment.[67] It also includes programs focused on primary education access and rural development. In 2003, the ambitious US$23.4 million Port Cities Development Program was launched.

Although Yemen has great needs, the state has not been able to manage the massive cash flow provided by international donors effectively. Private and public actors (including different ministries) and NGOs compete fiercely for external aid and seem to have developed more expertise in attracting donor funds than in delivering effective projects on the ground. The most immediate effect of the rise in aid has been an increase in high-level corruption. Yemen's rank in Transparency International's corruption perception index fell from eighty-eight in 2003 to 111 in 2006.[68] In retaliation against growing corruption and the slow rate of progress in carrying out reforms, the World Bank reduced the budget of its Yemeni programs by a third in 2006, only to increase them once again as the government began to tackle the issue of corruption more seriously.

Donors have been keen to assist Yemen in meeting the MDGs. In 2001, the government initiated the Basic Education Development Project based on MDG education goals, including the universal completion of primary education and gender parity by 2015. According to the World Bank, there is some progress on meeting the education goals—the ratio of female school enrollment has improved from 36 percent in 2000–2001 to 39 percent in 2003–2004.

The government's May 2002 PRSP identified several priorities, including economic growth, human resources development, infrastructure building, and enhancement of social protection. In October 2002, a conference of donors in Paris pledged US$2.3 billion to finance PRSP projects; in November 2006, another conference organized in London managed to gather US$4.7 billion for various development projects.

Although development donors remain committed to poverty eradication, the nature of development assistance has changed in important ways since 9/11, with growing donor interest in weak states and conflict prevention. Although the Parliament has been commended by the National Democratic Institute for its capacity building, it still faces opposition by the ruling elite and certain tribes, especially to a program aimed at mitigating conflict with tribal shaikhs.[69]

Yemen's identification as a fragile state, with the potential to become a terrorist safe haven, has in some ways been a blessing for Yemen's development. The trajectory of US aid to Yemen is particularly revealing. During the 1990s, American assistance to Yemen consisted almost entirely of food aid. USAID closed its Yemeni offices in 1996 after working in North Yemen for twenty-five years as a Cold War front against socialist South Yemen. In June 2003, USAID reopened its operations and, in cooperation with international NGOs (such as the Adventist Development and Relief Agency), implemented a three-year strategic plan focused on 'Amran, al-Jawf, Ma'rib, Sa'ada, and Shabwa—all of which are considered high-risk areas due to the preservation of strong tribal customs and the heavy weaponry available. For the 2004 fiscal year, the budget of USAID in Yemen reached US$15 million. For example, in the Ma'rib region, in response to high poverty indicators, the absence of the state, and rising anti-Americanism, USAID announced plans to build a hospital.[70] It was in this region that a US Army drone had killed suspected Al-Qaida members in November 2002.

USAID is explicit about its combined security and development concerns in Yemen:

> USAID's overall goal in Yemen is to support [the] USG [United States government] foreign policy objectives in the war on terrorism by helping to develop a healthy and educated population with access to diverse economic opportunities. . . . The USG's foreign policy interests in Yemen are to expand the USG and ROYG [Republic of Yemen government] partnership against terrorism, to neutralize Al-Qaida's ability to threaten US interests both inside and from Yemen, and to enhance regional security by building a close partnership between the [United States] and [the] Yemeni military.[71]

September 11 should not be considered a complete turning point in international policies toward Yemen. The post-9/11 emphasis on security has merely deepened a trend that first emerged in the mid-1990s, as violence began to affect Western interests. Nevertheless, the attacks on New York and Washington led to greatly increased military and security cooperation with the governments of the United States and other nations, as demonstrated in the cases above. Additionally, increasing security collaboration with Saudi Arabia through intelligence sharing and prisoner exchanges has transformed the region. In April 2005, military maneuvers were organized for the first time between the two countries in the desert north of Hadhramawt.

Since the attack on the USS *Cole,* security cooperation with the United States has increased but has been deliberately discreet. In 2003, a permanent US Federal Bureau of Investigation (FBI) office was opened in Sanaa. The Yemeni army, navy, and a newly established coast guard now receive training by and equipment from the

United States. In March 2002, Vice President Dick Cheney made the first high-ranking trip to Yemen since George H. W. Bush's 1984 visit to inaugurate an oil refinery. Despite close collaboration, however, in light of the destabilizing effect of US bases in Saudi Arabia, the Yemeni government has persistently refused to allow the United States to establish military bases on its territory.

Increasing the security of Yemen's borders has been a main concern for the United States. Immediately after 9/11, computers were delivered to entry points and custom officers were trained. In 2004, the first batch of US-funded coast patrol boats was delivered. Furthermore, French and German forces stationed in neighboring Djibouti conducted joint maneuvers with the Yemeni national army. Although no relevant figures are available, the military budget is noticeably on the rise, as important arms and missile contracts have been signed.

Assessing the Policy Mix

As we have now demonstrated, both national and international actors recognize the interplay between Yemen's security and development challenges and the need for an adequate policy mix. However, their priorities do not necessarily converge. While the exact impact a given policy will have is difficult to assess in the short term, the evidence demonstrates that security-oriented policies pursued by foreign actors can weaken state control over certain populations and territories. These policies also seem to have contributed to reversing the democratization processes that were initiated in Yemen after unification and diverted state attention from much-needed domestic reforms. The country's stability remains uncertain and its image abroad is still negative. Future events could jeopardize aforementioned developments such as Yemen's evolution into a US ally, since the national interests of these two countries sometimes conflict. For example, in December 2002, a commercial ship carrying fifteen North Korean Scud missiles that were hidden under a cargo of cement was apprehended in the international seas by the Spanish military. After having first denied it, the Yemeni government admitted that it was the intended recipient. Under US Navy escort, the missiles were transported to Aden. Furthermore, the Yemeni authorities' refusal in 2006 to freeze the assets of 'Abd al-Majid al-Zindani—the aforementioned prominent figure in the al-Islah party and the head of the Islamic al-Iman University accused of financing terrorism—has troubled relations with the United States.

In their focus on security, Yemeni government initiatives have served at times to restrain violent groups and their activities. For example, private investment projects in poor Red Sea–coastal areas have been announced and a new Sanaa international airport, partly funded by Saudi Arabia, has been planned. The 2001 decision to consider kidnappings of foreigners as terrorist acts and the subsequent military campaigns against certain tribes have for some time lowered the frequency of these activities. Through its actions, the government undertook significant risk by suggesting a link between tribal activities and terrorism. For a time, the absence of kidnappings allowed the much-needed tourist industry to develop, but since 2007 terrorist attacks directly targeting tourists have once again hampered its growth.

These developments could be construed as improvements in Yemen's security situation since 9/11. Yet if security seemed to increase between 2001 and 2007 for Western interests despite brief periods of crisis, it came at a high price for Yemenis. Political repression and the ongoing war in northern Yemen have increased insecurity among citizens. According to French researcher François Burgat, Yemen has progressively been moving towards the "Arab Political Formula."[72] Indeed, most of the characteristics that made the Yemeni political system unique are increasingly under threat. From the 1962 Republican Revolution to the end of the 1990s, the legitimacy of Yemen's political regime was based on a tacit power-sharing agreement among various social groups, including Islamists and tribes, which was not the case in other Arab states such as Iraq, Algeria, and Egypt. In the 1990s, the participation of Islamist figures and parties in the government revealed a level of freedom no other country in the region experienced. Free elections were organized; opposition parties were established, ranging from a traditional Zaydi party *(Hizb al-haqq)* to a Green party *(Hizb al-khadhr al-ijtma'i al-yamani);* independent publications and newspapers were founded; and a dynamic and independent civil society emerged.[73] Yet the 1999 presidential elections brought with them an increase in authoritarianism. No candidate from any opposition party was given the right to compete, and President Salih was challenged only by a member of his own party who nonetheless admitted that he himself was not the right man for the job either.

In February 2001, constitutional amendments strengthened the power of the president and extended his stay in power. Ever since, the space provided for opposition appears to have been shrinking, and the presidential elections in September 2006, in spite of substantive debate, ended up maintaining the status quo. Despite attempts to unify opposition parties through an informal Joint Meeting of Parties

(Ahzab al-Liqa al-Mushtarak) and the agreement of the Socialist, Nasserist, and Islamist Parties around a common platform of government, Ali Abdallah Salih could not be seriously challenged. In early 2009, President Salih (with the agreement of the opposition that had expressed dissatisfaction over the electoral law and threatened to boycott the ballot) decided to postpone for two years the parliamentary elections that had been planned for that April.

In December 2004, following the launch of the war against al-Huthi, reappointments in the judicial sector included the transfer of experienced Zaydi judges away from politically sensitive areas. These steps by the government indirectly weakened the state, as citizens are now more likely to rely on traditional forms of conflict resolution than trust in the neutrality of the state courts. Consequently, the role and legitimacy of tribal and religious actors have been reinforced at the expense of the state.

Despite developments that have affected power sharing among political groups, the government must balance many elements, including a well-armed tribal population. The government is acutely aware of the limits of its legitimacy. Media and public statements have been forceful in stating that despite foreign pressures, Yemen is still sovereign. In 2002, the Parliament voted for a resolution calling on Arab countries to stop all cooperation with the United States until it put an end to its pro-Israel policy. Indeed, there are numerous instances of serious tensions in the government's alliance with the United States. For example, at the time of the US-led war in Afghanistan (which was formally condemned by the government), allied warplanes were banned from entering Yemeni airspace. A year later, the government was highly critical of the war against Iraq, organizing supposedly spontaneous demonstrations against US policy in the Middle East. When prominent Islamist figures (including 'Abd al-Majid al-Zindani) were accused by foreign governments of supporting terrorism, the government came to their defense. Tensions increased in January 2003 with the arrest in Germany of Muhammad 'Ali Hasan al-Muayyad and his subsequent rendition to the United States. Al-Muayyad, a member of al-Islah, was tried for funding Al-Qaida and Hamas and sentenced to seventy-five years in prison by a New York court in July 2005.

The Security Paradox and Its Policy Implications

Since unification in 1990, Yemen has changed dramatically, as have its sources of grievance and societal tensions. The sense of national unity has evolved and there have been improvements in its development indicators. Moreover, in the new millennium thus far, the vast majority of the population has not experienced physical violence, and terrorism is not a direct threat faced by Yemenis.

Yet Yemen's security has been negatively affected by national and international policies strongly focused on security issues. The deaths of thousands of civilians and soldiers since the summer of 2004 after al-Huthi's insurgency illustrate this situation. Although it claims loyalty to Arab nationalism and strongly opposes the US intervention in Iraq, President Salih's government is losing credibility and legitimacy. There is a widespread impression that the government is following an agenda formulated in Washington and that its autonomy in decisionmaking is limited. In other words, the pressure put on the government—mainly by the United States—for enhanced security cooperation risks weakening the state vis-à-vis its own population.[74]

The military campaign against al-Huthi illustrated an acute paradox that regional and international actors should take into account if they aim to effectively link security and development policies. Considering the potential for instability on Yemen's domestic front, the prioritization of Western security interests in the post-9/11 context threatens to exacerbate the insecurities of the local population. This security paradox that privileges international security at the expense of local security is counterproductive in an increasingly globalized world.

The current link between security and development initiatives by national and international actors has largely missed the point. The increases in donor funding and development projects in Yemen, with their focus on inequalities and poverty, cannot sufficiently undo the security paradox. Alongside efforts to build a political economy geared toward a fair distribution of wealth, political solutions are needed to accommodate and empower marginalized groups, provide alternative conflict resolution mechanisms, and develop respect for rules-based interaction among individuals, communities, and the government. So far, the increased focus on security has failed to address many of the development risks and challenges identified in this chapter.

The Yemeni case demonstrates that if terrorism and insecurity cannot be addressed solely in military terms, focusing on underdevelopment is not adequate either. Fundamental political questions—most notably the extent of the state's authority, insufficient political participation, recurrent violations of human rights, spreading corruption, and the weak rule of law—need to be addressed in order to bolster domestic security and stability.

Contrary to its international reputation, Yemen faces no massive conflict even though security in some of its regions is tenuous and the potential for conflict among some tribal groups is ever present. It is unlikely that Yemen will plunge into large-scale internal conflict, although localized tribal conflicts, sometimes brutal and deadly (with or without state participation), will probably continue and may target foreigners. It is these sorts of civil conflicts rather than terrorism that pose the greatest threat to Yemen's security. The al-Huthi conflict, an example of the Yemeni security paradox, should be considered more than just a minor and isolated event. The absence of state infrastructure and services in certain regions has been an important source of inequality and resentment. In such contexts, rebellion would probably prove to be popular, even if it is limited in nature. However, such resistance would likely invite fierce military intervention and repression—creating a vicious circle of violence. These cases of violence would probably have less to do with terrorism and the activity of foreigners; they are more likely to be internal and similar in nature to the al-Huthi crisis. Such localized conflict could occur in the near future in the former southern governorates.

Given Yemen's vulnerability to external developments, it is difficult to propose long-term policy options. Yemen—like North Yemen before unification—has been open to new ideas and initiatives. Yemen's development and politics have been largely shaped by the external context. Thus it is to be expected that international and regional actors will continue to play an important role in Yemen. However, that role has to be in tune with Yemen's particular developmental challenges and security dilemmas.

The diagnoses by international development actors—including UN agencies, the World Bank, the European Commission, and bilateral donors—of Yemen's challenges are increasingly positive. However, the effectiveness of these initiatives suffers from insufficient coordination and the absence of strong and clear-cut long-term priorities. International actors should make a special effort to understand and respect the specificities of the Yemeni political regime and its fragile balances and should shape their initiatives accordingly. The Yemeni political system and its attendant power sharing with, among others, tribes and Islamists, are vital to Yemen's security and development. Thus, instead of promoting their own models of political or judicial development, international actors need to recognize and support the potentially beneficial roles of traditional and religious actors at all levels. However, the particular emphasis put on education since 2002 should not merely be maintained but increased in the coming years.

Even though local discourses and practices often cause international concern, the inclusion of Islamist opposition parties as well as traditional and religious actors serves to strengthen the Yemeni political system by creating some parameters around their activities. They are legitimate actors and have shown themselves to be ready to cooperate and able to change. Pressuring the government (directly or indirectly) to repress opposition groups or to close religious centers is counterproductive in terms of enhancing domestic security and democratizing Yemen. The goal of reducing the military and symbolic violence associated with Western domination, both in the Middle East and globally, require reevaluation.

The heightened focus on security in Yemen, especially since 9/11, has contributed to increasing militarization that undermines development, contradicts the democratization process, and threatens the social equilibrium. Given that the Yemeni armed forces have been a conduit for the distribution of resources and political power to social and tribal groups, alternative channels of redistribution—including nationwide income taxes—need to be identified. International actors should not encourage the government to relegate its development priorities through their development assistance. Instead, they should support the Yemeni government by investing in education, health, and infrastructure projects that are essential for strengthening the state and addressing socioeconomic grievances. Similarly, to address the impending water shortage and its potential for causing conflict, technical solutions such as the desalinization of sea water, the building of dams, and more effective water re-treatment, are vital. These require investments the Yemeni government is incapable of making without external support. Stronger government programming in these sectors can effectively link security and development and potentially counter anti-Western rhetoric.

Another neglected area is the Yemeni judicial sector.[75] Given Yemen's relatively poor human rights record, it could also be an instrument for strengthening the state. Effective rule of law institutions serving marginalized rural communities could enhance allegiance to the central government and limit the function of tribal leaders as arbitrators and mediators in disputes. Judicial actors, including traditional ones, could be trained and given the capacity to conduct independent investigations or, through professional syndicates, cooperate with human rights NGOs. Donors could further support democratic processes and institutions by requiring that they play a central role in monitoring and auditing development assistance programs. Such programs, along with a sustained dialogue with the press, would help develop important mechanisms of internal and external accountability with respect to the use of public and donor funds.

Yemen's large—however poorly educated—workforce is an asset that has yet to be fully utilized. The government lacks an appropriate employment policy and does too little for the unemployed, despite heavy investment in vocational training. Better incentives, such as contractual guarantees and tax incentives, could encourage investment from successful Yemenis abroad. Responsible development partners should not let the government entertain the fantasy of finding new oil reserves, which the conclusion of the 2000 border treaty with Saudi Arabia and the signatures of LNG export contracts in 2005 reactivated. International actors can also use their influence to support Yemen's integration into the Gulf Cooperation Council (GCC), a natural partnership that would open GCC markets to Yemen's workers and products (agricultural and fishery-related) and facilitate remittances, transfers, and investments. In 2006, for the first time, Saudi Arabia did not object to Yemen's candidacy for the GCC, thus increasing the likelihood of its membership by 2016. Technical support by the European Commission for Yemen's application to join the World Trade Organization should be used to maintain the pressure on the government to expand democratization.

These broad policy guidelines are suggested primarily to tackle the Yemeni security paradox. The case of Yemen illustrates how much common perceptions of security and development have been eclipsed by a purely security-based approach to development. Consequently, many have forgotten that inequality, poverty, malaria, AIDS, and human rights abuses remain more deadly than actual terrorist attacks, however brutal and unjustifiable. The work of development partners should not end up sustaining and perpetuating authoritarian systems in countries that express sympathy for Western security concerns. Development cooperation in Yemen and elsewhere should not be about keeping the political status quo along with incremental economic change; it should be about addressing the bottlenecks and rigidities in the economic, social, and political structures that obstruct Yemen's growth and the empowerment of its people.

Notes

1. President Ali Abdallah Salih has been head of state since July 1978, first of North Yemen and then of the Republic of Yemen. He is, after Muammar Qaddafi of Libya and Sultan Qabus of Oman, the third-longest-standing Arab leader.

2. Specific to Yemen, Zaydism is a sect of Shia Islam representing probably around 40 percent of the population and concentrated in the northern highlands. On the Sa'ada conflict, see the International Crisis Group

(ICG), "Yemen: Defusing the Sa'ada Time Bomb," *Middle East Report* no. 86 (Brussels: ICG, 2009).

3. For an overview of the social and economic effects of the involuntary return of migrants to Yemen in 1990, see Nicholas Van Hear, "The Socio-economic Impact of the Involuntary Mass Return to Yemen in 1990," *Journal of Refugee Studies* 7, no. 1 (1994): 18–38.

4. For details and analysis of the border issue with Saudi Arabia, see Renaud Detalle, ed., *Tensions in Arabia: The Saudi-Yemeni Fault Line* (Baden Baden: Nomos Verlagsgesellschaft, 2000), or Askar Halwan Al-Enazy, "The International Boundary Treaty (Treaty of Jeddah) Concluded Between the Kingdom of Saudi Arabia and the Yemeni Republic on June 12, 2000," *The American Journal of International Law* 96, no. 1 (2002): 161–173.

5. ICG, "Yemen: Coping with Terrorism and Violence in a Fragile State," *Middle East Report* no. 8 (Brussels: ICG, January 2003), 13.

6. For an anthropological analysis of the tribal system in the Yemeni northern highlands, see Paul Dresch, *Tribes, Governments, and History in Yemen* (Oxford: Clarendon, 1993); see also Najwa Adra, "Qabyala: The Tribal Concept in the Central Highlands, the Yemen Arab Republic" (PhD diss., Temple University, 1982). For a monographic study of the judicial system in a court in Sanaa, see Anna Würth, *Ash-sharî'a fî Bâb al-Yaman: Recht, Richter, und Rechtpraxis an det familienrechtlichen Kammer des Gerichts Süd-Sanaa, Republik Jemen (1983–1995)* (Berlin: Duncker and Humblot, 2000).

7. See Würth, *Ash-sharî'a fî Bâb al-Yaman*.

8. Fred Halliday, "The Third Inter-Yemeni War and Its Consequences," *Asian Affairs* 26, no. 2 (June 1995): 131–140, 132.

9. Analysis of the 1994 civil war is scarce and incomplete, with the notable exception of Jamal S. Al-Suwaidi, ed., *The Yemeni War of 1994: Causes and Consequences* (London: Saqi Books, 1995) and Halliday, "The Third Inter-Yemeni War."

10. For a study of the Aden-Abyan Islamic Army, see Sheila Carapico, "Yemen and the Aden-Abyan Islamic Army," *Middle East Report Online*, October 18, 2000, http://www.merip.org/mero/mero101800.html.

11. For an account of the relations between the Islamists and the state, see Renaud Detalle, "Les islamistes yéménites et l'Etat: vers l'émancipation?" in *Les Etats arabes face à la contestation islamiste*, eds. Basma Kodmani-Darwish and May Chartouni-Dubarry (Paris: Ifri-Armand Colin, 1997), 271–298.

12. For analysis of the al-Islah opposition party, see Paul Dresch and Bernard Haykel, "Stereotypes and Political Styles: Islamists and Tribesfolk in Yemen," *International Journal of Middle East Studies* 27, no. 4 (1995): 405–431.

13. Charles Schmitz, "Investigating the *Cole* Bombing," *Middle East Report Online*, September 6, 2001, http://www.merip.org/mero/mero090601.html.

14. The assassination of Jarallah 'Umar, vice secretary-general of the YSP, occurred as he was attending the congress of the other main opposition party, al-Islah, on December 28, 2002. An extremist former member of al-Islah, AliAhmad Jarallah opened fire on Jarallah 'Umar and killed him. The

reasons for the murder remain controversial; see, for example, Muhammad Muhammad Maqaleh, *Min qatal Jarallah 'Umar: al-jarima bayn al din wa al-siyassa* (Sanaa: Markaz 'Ubadi, 2005).

15. James Morrison, "Embassy Row," *Washington Times*, March 7, 2006, 2, http://www.washtimes.com/world/20060306-105313-1811r_page2.htm.

16. A nationwide population census was carried out by the government and funded by donors in 2004; however, the official population figure of 21,422,000 can only be considered an estimate, as many individuals, particularly in rural areas, refused to give the exact number of members of their households because of lack of trust in the government. Indeed, many feared this data would be used to implement new taxes.

17. World Bank, "Republic of Yemen Poverty Update: Volume I," World Bank Report no. 24422-YEM (Washington, DC, December 11, 2002), 18, http://www-wds.worldbank.org/servlet/WDS_IBank_Servlet?pcont=details&eid=000094946_03011404014323.

18. UN, "Yemen Common Country Assessment," (Sanaa: UN, 2001), 2, http://www.undg.org/archive_docs/1706-Yemen_CCA_-_Yemen_2001.pdf.

19. Paul Dresch, *A History of Modern Yemen* (Cambridge, UK: Cambridge University Press, 2000), 198.

20. For an account of the impact of the deportations from Saudi Arabia in 1990, see Van Hear, "The Socio-economic Impact."

21. Thomas Stevenson, "Yemeni Workers Come Home: Reabsorbing One Million Migrants," *Middle East Report* 181 (March 1993): 15–20, 18.

22. Zainy Abbas, "Illegal Yemeni Migrants Talk of Their Journeys North," *Arab News*, April 9, 2006, http://www.arabnews.com/?page=1&section=0&article=80460&d=9&m=4&y=2006.

23. Renaud Detalle, "Ajuster sans douleur? La méthode yéménite," *Maghreb-Machrek* no.155 (1997): 20–36.

24. "Paris Club Conditions Are Being Implemented: Yemen's 2nd Round of Debt Rescheduling," *Yemen Times*, October 20–26, 1997, http://www.yementimes.com/97/iss42/front.htm.

25. World Bank, "Republic of Yemen Poverty Update," iii.

26. UNDP, *Human Development Report 2004: Cultural Liberty in Today's Diverse World* (New York: UNDP, 2004), 141; UNDP, *Human Development Report 2007/2008: Fighting Climate Change—Human Solidarity in a Divided World* (New York: Palgrave Macmillan, 2007), 231.

27. World Bank, "Country Assistance Strategy for the Republic of Yemen for the Period of FY2006–FY2009," http://www-wds.worldbank.org/external/default/WDSContentServer/WDSP/IB/2006/08/08/000090341_20060808101759/Rendered/PDF/36014.pdf.

28. World Bank, *World Development Indicators* 2002 (Washington, DC: World Bank, 2002).

29. For more information on the structure of the Yemeni economy, see World Bank, "Yemen Republic at a Glance," September 2004, http://www.worldbank.org/data/countrydata/aag/yem_aag.pdf.

30. World Bank, "Country Assistance Strategy for the Period 2006–2009," (Washington, DC: May 17, 2006), 11, http://www-wds.worldbank.org/external/default/WDSContentServer/WDSP/IB/2006/08/08/000090341_20060808101759/Rendered/PDF/36014.pdf.

31. UNDP, *Human Development Report 2007/2008*, 271.

32. Qayser Khan and Susan Chance, "Yemen and the Millennium Development Goals," World Bank Discussion Paper, Middle East and North Africa Working Paper Series no. 31 (Washington, DC: World Bank, March 2003), 23, http://www-wds.worldbank.org/external/default/WDSContentServer/WDSP/IB/2003/10/20/000090341_20031020140717/Rendered/PDF/270220PAPER0MNA031.pdf.

33. UN, "Yemen Common Country Assessment," 2001, xi.

34. UN, "Yemen Common Country Assessment," (Sanaa: UN, 2005), 38, http://www.undg.org/docs/8078/Yemen%20CCA%20English.pdf.

35. Sarah Philipps, "Foreboding About the Future in Yemen," *Middle East Report Online*, April 3, 2006, http://merip.org/mero/mero040306.html.

36. For details on poverty in Yemen, see Blandine Destremau, "Pauvreté et droits au Yémen," *Chroniques Yéménites*, no. 8 (2001): 117–132; Government of the Republic of Yemen, "Poverty Reduction Strategy Paper: 2003–2005," policy paper, May 31, 2002, http://povlibrary.worldbank.org/files/Yemen_PRSP.pdf (accessed December 15, 2006).

37. World Bank, *Yemen Economic Update* (Sanaa: World Bank Sanaa Office, Spring 2005), http://siteresources.worldbank.org/INTYEMEN/Resources/310077-1098870168865/YemenUpdate-Spring05.pdf.

38. UN, "Yemen Common Country Assessment," 2005, 2.

39. As a result of the shortage of teachers and of low education levels, the Yemeni government had to bring in teachers from other Arab countries, mainly Egypt and Sudan, until the beginning of the 1990s.

40. World Bank, "Project Performance Assessment Report: Yemen Vocational Training Project," World Bank Report no. 32593 (Washington, DC: World Bank, 2005), http://www-wds.worldbank.org/external/default/WDSContentServer/IW3P/IB/2005/06/21/000160016_20050621174604/Rendered/INDEX/32593.txt.

41. For information on and a history of the scientific institutes, see Fâris Al-Saqqaf, *Ilghâ' al-ma'had al-'ilmiyya wa tawhîd al-ta'alîm* (Sanaa: Markaz dirasât al-mustaqbal, 2004).

42. Dresch, *A History of Modern Yemen*.

43. ICG, "Yemen: Coping with Terrorism and Violence in a Fragile State."

44. *Al-Thawra*, July 20, 2005.

45. Sarah Phillips, "Cracks in the Yemen System," *Middle East Report Online*, July 28, 2005, http://www.merip.org/mero/mero072805.html.

46. Peter Willems, "Rude Awakening," *Yemen Times*, May 17, 2004, http://www.yementimes.com/article.shtml?i=738&p=culture&a=1.

47. John Bradley, "Saudi Arabia Enrages Yemen with Fence," *Independent*, February 11, 2004, 28.

48. François Burgat, "The Sanaa Chronicles," ISIM Newsletter, no. 9 (2002): 17.

49. The revolution of September 26, 1962, after putting an end to the 1,000-year-old Zaydi imamate that ruled the Yemeni highlands, started an eight-year-long war in which Egypt and Saudi Arabia intervened, respectively supporting the republicans and the royalists.

50. Mohammed bin Sallam, "Al-Hothy Appeals," *Yemen Times*, June 28, 2004, http://www.yementimes.com/article.shtml?i=750&p=front&a=1.

51. François Burgat, "Le Yémen après le 11 septembre 2001: entre construction de l'Etat et rétrécissement du champ politique," *Critique internationale* 3, no. 32 (2006): 11–21.

52. See, for example, D. Sa'udi 'Ali 'Ubayd, "Al-Huthi, azma al-sulta fi al-fikr wa al-mumarisa," *Sawt al-Shura* no. 50, October 4, 2004.

53. Amnesty International, "Yemen," *Amnesty International Report 2005*, http://web.amnesty.org/report2005/yem-summary-eng (accessed December 15, 2006).

54. For an analysis of the origins of this historical convergence movement, see Bernard Haykel, *Revival and Reform in Islam: The Legacy of Muhammad al-Shawkânî* (Cambridge, UK: Cambridge University Press, 2003).

55. In January 2003, eighty people, mostly Somalis, drowned when their boat caught fire on its way to Yemen. Tragedies like this one regularly hit the news; indeed, since 2003, the number of such accidents has significantly increased. It is estimated that 20,000 refugees, mostly Somalis but also Ethiopians, annually try to reach the coast of Yemen illegally. See IRIN News, "SOMALIA-YEMEN: Over 80 African Migrants Die as Boat Capsizes Off Coast," December 4, 2007, http://www.irinnews.org/Report.aspx?ReportId=75670.

56. Daniel Varisco, "The Elixir of Life or the Devil's Cud: The Debate over *Qat* (*Catha edulis*) in Yemeni Culture," in *Drug Use and Cultural Context: Tradition, Change, and Intoxicants Beyond "The West,"* eds. Ross Coomber and Nigel South (London: Free Association Books, 2004), 101–118.

57. World Bank, "Country Assistance Strategy for the Republic of Yemen," 13.

58. World Bank, "Country Assistance Strategy for the Republic of Yemen," 4.

59. Derek B. Miller, "Demand, Stockpiles, and Social Controls: Small Arms in Yemen," Small Arms Survey Occasional Paper no. 9 (Geneva: Small Arms Survey, May 2003), vii, http://www.smallarmssurvey.org/files/sas/publications/o_papers_pdf/2003-op09-yemen.pdf.

60. Hassan Al-Zaidi, "Bloody Tribal Warfare," *Yemen Times,* December 6, 2004, http://yementimes.com/article.shtml?i=796&p=front&a=1.

61. All three national development plans are available on the Yemeni Ministry of Planning and International Cooperation's website, http://www.mpic-yemen.org.

62. World Bank, "Assessment of Administrative Decentralization in Yemen," (Washington, DC, 2002).

63. In comparison, according to the World Bank, *World Development Report 2007: Development and the Next Generation* (Washington, DC: World Bank, 2006), military expenditures were 3.4 percent in the United States, 4.1 percent in France, and 8.2 percent in Saudi Arabia.

64. Amnesty International, "Yemen: Killing of Civilians Must Be Investigated," AI Index no. MDE 31/008/2004, July 9, 2004, http://web.amnesty.org/library/Index/ENGMDE310082004?open&of=ENG-YEM.

65. For official discourse on the issue of religious education, see "Al-shatat al-ta'limi," *al-Thawra*, April 7, 2005.

66. Amnesty International, "Yemen: The Rule of Law Sidelined in the Name of Security," AI Index no. MDE 31/006/2003, September 24, 2003, http://web.amnesty.org/library/Index/ENGMDE310062003?open&of=ENG-YEM.

67. World Bank, "Country Assistance Strategy for the Republic of Yemen."

68. Transparency International, "Corruption Perceptions Index," August 11, 2006, http://www.transparency.org/policy_research/surveys_indices/cpi.

69. For an account of the failure of a National Democratic Institute program financed by USAID, see David Finkel, "U.S. Ideals Meet Reality in Yemen," *Washington Post,* December 18, 2005, 1-A.

70. Kareem Fahim, "First the Guns, Now the Butter," *Village Voice*, October 12, 2004, http://www.villagevoice.com/2004-10-12/news/first-the-guns-now-the-butter/.

71. For information on USAID initiatives in Yemen, see USAID, "Budget: Yemen," January 14, 2005, http://www.usaid.gov/policy/budget/cbj2005/ane/ye.html.

72. François Burgat, "Les élections présidentielles de 1999 au Yémen: du 'pluralisme armé' au retour à la norme arabe," *Maghreb Machrek* no. 174 (2000): 67–75.

73. For an account and analysis of this period of Yemen's history, see Sheila Carapico, *Civil Society in Yemen: The Political Economy of Activism in Modern Arabia* (Cambridge, UK: Cambridge University Press, 1998).

74. For an analysis of the link between state construction in Yemen and US foreign policy, see Ludmila du Bouchet, "La politique étrangère américaine au Yémen," *Chroniques Yéménites*, no. 11 (2004): 101–121, http://cy.revues.org/document154.html (accessed December 15, 2006).

75. The UNDP has an insufficiently funded project to modernize the judicial sector at a time when the government's main commitment is to bring supposed terrorists to trial. For details of the Integrative Justice Sector Development Program of the UNDP, see http://www.undp.org.ye/reports/d_12ProjectDocument.pdf. Within the framework of this program, the UNDP launched a help desk and telephone hotline for free legal assistance in March 2005.

6

Beyond the Conflict Trap in Somalia

Kenneth Menkhaus

By almost every yardstick, Somalia is one of the least developed countries in the world. Since the collapse of the central government in January 1991, Somalia has been plagued by endemic criminal violence, intermittent armed conflict, and an Ethiopian military occupation that has provoked widespread armed resistance. The horrific levels of violence associated with the insurgency and counterinsurgency have plunged Somalia into the country's worst humanitarian crises since 1991. The protracted nature of Somalia's collapse has resulted in unexpected patterns of not only the aforementioned armed conflict and criminality but also informal governance and economic activity, making Somalia a compelling subject for those studying security and development linkages in failed states.[1]

At first glance, it is tempting to conclude that Somalia's crises of underdevelopment, insecurity, and state collapse constitute a vicious circle as well as an acute and pathological example of the *conflict trap*.[2] To an extent, this explanation of the Somalia security-development nexus makes sense. But a closer look at trends in Somalia since 1991 reveals a more complex relationship between development and security. Fueled by remittances, interstate commerce, and private-sector investment, significant if limited economic development has occurred despite daunting security conditions and the lack of a central government. Likewise, despite extremely high levels of poverty and unemployment, coalitions of businesspeople, traditional elders, Islamists, and community leaders have at times successfully built a patchwork quilt of local, informal polities and systems of conflict management in an effort to reduce criminal violence and armed conflict. As a result, Somalia has periodically enjoyed a measure of governance without government, as common parlance would have it, and is somewhat less anarchic than is often believed. Somali communities have demonstrated that the conflict trap is indeed a powerful short-term dynamic but that in the longer run, evolving local interests in basic public order and the revival of commerce have the potential to slow, if not reverse, the vicious circle of insecurity and underdevelopment—even in the absence of a central government. What remains unclear is whether these local adaptations and small successes in improving security and livelihoods constitute the genesis of sustained development and a new political order or whether they are merely coping mechanisms of limited long-term significance. Equally uncertain is whether those involved in external state building and governance initiatives can learn to work with rather than against these local, organic processes. International development sponsors' and peacebuilders' efforts have to date rarely demonstrated this capacity, viewing existing local systems of governance either as irrelevant to state revival or as active hindrances.

This chapter uses the Somali case to explore how and to what extent the conditions of state collapse do not always lead simply to high levels of insecurity and low levels of development. It documents how local adaptations to state failure produce a wide array of coping mechanisms that reduce at least some insecurity and can generate hot spots of economic activity and recovery. Evidence is drawn from the period before the December 2006 Ethiopian military occupation of southern Somalia and the subsequent insurgency and counterinsurgency that has done so much to destroy the local economy and reduce the country to 1991–1992 levels of criminal violence. It is impossible, at the time of this writing in mid-2008, to ascertain whether the massive dislocations and violence since 2007, as well as the rise of extremist Islamist movements, will permanently disrupt the types of governance and economic recovery documented in this chapter or whether the post-2006 violence will constitute a brutal but temporary disruption of a more enduring trend toward innovative local adaptation to state collapse in Somalia. I make no attempt to assess security-development dynamics in the country since 2007.

Historical Background

Although Somalia's poverty is a chronic condition, its descent into protracted civil war and state collapse is the result of a more recent period of political decay and repression, which began in the 1970s. Somalia's first ten years of independence (1960–1969) were marked by a vibrant but eventually dysfunctional and corrupt multiparty democracy. When the military came to power in a coup in 1969, it was initially greeted with broad popular support. The regime of President Mohamed Siad Barre degenerated into a police state by the mid-1970s and eventually possessed one of the worst human rights records in Africa. Somalia's disastrous defeat in the Ogaden War with Ethiopia in 1977–1978 prompted the rise of several liberation movements intent on overthrowing the regime.

In its first decades of independence, Somalia exploited its strategic location on the Horn of Africa to attract very high levels of foreign aid, both from the Eastern Bloc (in the 1970s) and the West (in the 1980s). Unfortunately, very little of this aid produced tangible improvements in economic development in Somalia. Instead, the aid subsidized a bloated, unsustainable Somali state and fueled a corrupt patronage system that, in combination with ruthless repression, enabled the regime to stay in power for twenty-two years. Not coincidentally, the Somali state withered and collapsed when foreign aid was frozen on human rights grounds in the late 1980s, as the Cold War ended and Somalia's strategic importance to the superpowers evaporated.[3]

The period of open civil war against the state from 1988 to 1990 and the subsequent period of state collapse and warfare in 1991–1992 produced horrific security conditions for most Somali communities. The government's war against the Somali National Movement in northern Somalia in 1988–1990 resulted in tens of thousands of casualties and hundreds of thousands of refugees.[4] In the south, the government militia engaged in scorched-earth tactics and looted towns as it retreated. When the last government forces fled the capital of Mogadishu in January 1991, the city was beset by looting and violence. For two years, the entire zone of south-central Somalia was wracked by armed conflict, criminal violence, and a complete breakdown in law and order. Persistent looting and atrocities committed by uncontrolled militias produced widespread famine, refugee flows, and massive internal displacement. Every aspect of the economic infrastructure—telephone lines, factories, bridges, seaports, electricity grids, canal systems—was either dismantled for scrap metal, damaged by war, or left in serious disrepair. International relief efforts were frustrated by the diversion of food aid by militias, and aid agencies were troubled by the growing realization that their relief efforts had become part of a broader war economy in which merchants, warlords, and gunmen were profiteering from the conditions of famine, looting, and lawlessness they had created.[5]

In December 1992, President George H. W. Bush of the United States approved a major US-led, UN-sanctioned peace operation in Somalia. That 45,000-troop humanitarian intervention quickly ended the famine and stabilized the country but left the much more difficult tasks of reconciliation, state building, and disarmament to a successor UN peace operation, the UN Operation in Somalia (UNOSOM). UNOSOM's political initiatives to build a transitional government quickly led to tensions with some powerful warlords and their constituencies, and in June 1993 UNOSOM and US forces became embroiled in armed conflict with the militia of General Mohamed Farah Aideed. The conflict culminated in the disastrous Black Hawk Down firefight in Mogadishu in which seventeen US soldiers and hundreds of Somalis died, prompting a US-phased withdrawal. The derailed UN mission departed Somalia in March 1995, having failed to achieve national reconciliation or revive the central government. Somalia became synonymous with failed UN peacekeeping and served as fodder for critics of nation building.

Despite a marked reluctance on the part of much of the international community—especially the United States—to remain engaged in Somalia following the UNOSOM debacle, postintervention Somalia has continued to attract sporadic external efforts to promote national peace and a revived state. Those initiatives have yet to bear fruit, however. A national dialogue convened in Arte, Djibouti, in 2000 produced the Transitional National Government (TNG), but the TNG was never able to extend its authority beyond portions of the capital city and gradually faded into irrelevance. A successor body, the Transitional Federal Government (TFG), was established in January 2005 after two years of negotiations sponsored by a regional organization, the Inter-Governmental Authority on Development (IGAD). Like the TNG, the TFG immediately faced major difficulties in establishing itself as a functional administration. At the time of this writing, the TFG remains deeply divided internally, faces heavily armed resistance in Mogadishu, and is barely functional in the fourth year of its existence. It has made almost no progress in the five-year transition period that is supposed to culminate in elections in 2009. Moreover, even if efforts to broker power sharing succeeded in rendering it more inclusive and external support for building its capacity were sustained, the TFG would only gradually be able to extend its authority over Somalia; for the coming years, then, most if not all of Somalia is likely to remain a de facto zone of state collapse.

Security and Development Trends in Somalia, 1991–2007

Conflict Trends

Somalia has been a zone of intermittent, low-intensity armed conflict since 1988. Despite several spikes in armed conflict since 1995—most notably the post-2006 clashes—the overall trend in the past seventeen years has been a diminution in the scale and intensity of fighting. Until 2006, the armed clashes of 1988–1992 had been most destructive and widespread, as Somalia was then in a genuine state of civil war. In that period, an estimated 90,000 Somalis died directly due to combat and another 220,000 died of famine-related causes.[6] Since the 1993–1994 UNOSOM intervention, Somalia's armed clashes have generally been more localized and brief, hence much less costly in terms of both loss of life and damage to property. Somalia's situation was categorized as a war in 1990–1992 and again in 2002.[7] By comparison, from 1995 through 2001, the Stockholm International Peace Research Institute (SIPRI) catalogued it as an intermediate armed conflict, in which fewer than 1,000 battle-related deaths per year were recorded.[8] Some regions of the country—most notably Puntland—have been almost entirely spared from war, while other locations have been enjoying relatively long stretches without armed conflict since 1995.

A breakdown of conflict trends reveals more subtle shifts from year to year. From 1988 through 1990, armed conflict pitted the government against a growing number of clan-based liberation movements. The warfare was concentrated first in the northwest of the country; then it moved southward through the central regions of the country toward Mogadishu. Some heavy weaponry was used, including tanks and occasional government warplanes, but the fighting mainly involved small arms. Liberation fronts developed *technicals*—modified pick-up trucks with mounted guns on the back—that could strike quickly and handle rough track-roads. Government forces indiscriminately targeted civilians, using a combination of scorched-earth tactics, looting, executions, and other atrocities, including, in northern Somalia, aerial attacks targeted at civilians fleeing toward the Ethiopian border.[9]

The nature of warfare and armed violence shifted following the collapse of the government in January 1991. From January to November 1991, two large clan-based coalitions fought each other in sweeping, fast-moving campaigns across southern Somalia. Direct and sustained armed conflict between the militias was infrequent;

most of the armed violence instead targeted civilians caught in the so-called shatter zone between the Jubba Valley and Mogadishu. The militias, who were unpaid, fought primarily for the opportunity to loot. Because they killed anyone identified as a member of a rival clan, this period saw an extraordinary level of internal displacement in Somalia, as families fled to the relative safety of their respective clan's home territory.[10]

By late 1991, the forces driving Somalia's fragmentation led to a new and highly destructive phase of internal quarrels in both the Hawiye and Darood clans. In Mogadishu, the Hawiye clan split erupted into heavy warfare. Extensive and indiscriminate use of mortars and rocket-propelled grenades leveled the Mogadishu city center and incurred thousands of casualties. To the south, tensions within the Darood clan culminated in an explosion of clashes in and around Kismayo. Unlike the first phase of warfare, which was fueled by a mixture of grievances and opportunistic looting, the fighting in 1992 was driven more by clannish attempts to control key real estate—cities, seaports, and airports through which famine relief flowed. Disputes over control of pivotal real estate remain unresolved and a constant source of tensions.[11]

One of the most significant trends of armed conflict between 1995 and 2006 was the continuing devolution of warfare to lower and lower levels of clan lineages. With few exceptions, most armed conflicts up to 2006 consisted of extended family feuds fueled by political rivalries, communal disputes over resource access, or unresolved criminal acts that had degenerated into a spiral of revenge attacks and armed clashes. This devolution of warfare to lower levels of lineage identity and the subsequent fragmentation of power had many implications. Warfare was more localized; clashes were contained within a subclan's territory or neighborhood. Conflicts were of shorter duration and less deadly because there was limited support for such internal squabbles: clan elders were in a better position to intervene, and money and ammunition were scarcer.[12] Conflicts were somewhat less predictable, often precipitated by a series of incidents involving theft or other misdemeanors. Atrocities against civilians were almost unheard of, as combatants were much more likely to be held accountable in the event of clan reconciliation. Pillaging and looting were no longer as common. Little territory was either gained or lost in localized clashes; commodities worth stealing were generally in the hands of businessmen with paid security forces protecting them.[13] Somalia was still rocked by flare-ups of deadly violence but was better understood (at least through 2006) as a zone of "not peace not war."[14]

No single explanation accounts for the gradual deceleration of armed conflict in Somalia into something less than war between 1991 and 2006, but a number of partial explanations help us understand it. The single most important explanation is the apparent shift in interests of some of the political and economic elite in Mogadishu. In the early 1990s, many of these elites had taken part in the wartime economy of plunder; upon acquiring significant wealth and shifting to more legitimate business activities, some developed a keener appreciation for basic public order and the rule of law and began to play a role in the funding of local governance and security arrangements.[15]

The Somali business community has been a critical driver of conflict and governance trends in Somalia and yet has been reluctant to assume a visible role in the political arena. As a group, it is diverse in its interests and activities and hence difficult to generalize about. While there are thousands of petty traders and mid-size entrepreneurs in Somalia, a relatively small group—estimated to number no more than several dozen—forms the powerful core of the community. Almost all of these businessmen run their businesses throughout Somalia, keeping main offices in Mogadishu, but they themselves reside outside Somalia—in Dubai, Nairobi, Djibouti, and elsewhere, where they can enjoy better security, access to amenities, and contact with banks and trading partners. Many of their business activities focus on interstate commerce—for instance, the importation of basic consumer goods into Somalia for local consumption or for transit trade into East Africa. Others have made fortunes in telecommunication services, remittances companies, construction, the transport sector, and the operation of private seaports and airports. They are careful to diversify their investments and activities, and they cultivate cross-clan partnerships in order to ensure that their businesses can operate nationally. Some are former warlords clever enough to have created sustainable sources of income; others are businessmen who have had to acquire large private security forces to protect their investments. Some members of the business elite engage in activities that would be considered illegal in the context of a functioning state, such as charcoal exports, while others engage in legitimate commerce and service sectors. Wide-ranging interests exist within the business community: some profit from lawlessness and conflict; others benefit from public order but are reluctant to embrace the return of a central state, mainly out of fear the state will lay claim to their investments in seaports, air strips, control of currency, and so on. Most, however, would directly benefit from a revived central government—provided it engaged in good governance rather than predatory behavior. Some businesspeople have plunged into Somali politics, but for the most part the business group shows reluctance to get too directly engaged politically—and that reluctance has grown exponentially since post–September 11 sanctions were imposed by the US government on some Somali companies accused of having unspecified links to Al-Qaida.[16]

The most important and visible contribution of the Somali business community to peace and development occurred in 1999, when, after years of providing financial support to warlords in their respective clans, the businessmen refused to pay any more so-called taxes on the grounds that they were not receiving security in return. Businessmen bought militiamen away from the Mogadishu warlords and cooperated with a short-lived Benadir regional authority to demobilize and provide vocational training to some while routing others to serve as paid security guards or members of the *sharia* court police.[17] This weakened the capacity of the warlords to fight and paved the way for the rise of local sharia courts in Mogadishu. For gunmen, it meant modest but steady income as private security guards—a coveted and respectable job among unskilled young men in Mogadishu. Serving in a warlord's militia was a less attractive option: it is dangerous, pays infrequently, and is viewed with scorn by most of the Mogadishu population. Many young gunmen remained unaffiliated with either private security or militias through 2005, instead making a living operating roadblocks in Mogadishu.[18]

In addition to shifting economic interests, other factors played a role in the decline in armed conflict up to 2006. By the mid-1990s, warlords were increasingly unable to rally the Somali diaspora to contribute funds to their war coffers; local communities were war weary and reluctant to support wars; traditional elders had reasserted some of their authority and were better able to manage conflict; and a general stalemate between rival clans had led to establishment of new, de facto spheres of influence and militia occupation difficult to overturn by force.

The growing capacity of civic groups to mobilize against militia violence and lawlessness was most visible in the spring and summer of 2005 in Mogadishu. At that time, Mogadishu-based opposition political leaders announced the Mogadishu Stabilization and Security Plan (MSSP). Many political figures sought to use the MSSP to undermine President Abdullahi Yusuf Ahmed's claim that Mogadishu was too unsafe to serve as the capital. But civic groups took the MSSP seriously and pressed hard for the removal of militia roadblocks and the encampment of 1,400 militiamen outside Mogadishu. Women's groups fed and managed the camps. Public demonstrations around roadblocks shamed some of the militia into abandoning the roadblocks, at least temporarily. The public mobilization referred to by Mogadishu residents as *kadoon* (political mobilization) took both political and militia leaders by surprise. Although the MSSP enjoyed only temporary success, it was an indication of the potential for civic groups to mobilize in support of peacebuilding efforts.

The trend toward diminished armed conflict in Somalia was not without reversals, even before the so-called great reversal of 2006. In 2002, multiple and fairly serious outbreaks of armed conflict from Gedo to Puntland produced casualty levels that briefly qualified Somalia as a zone of civil war.[19] These outbreaks were triggered by a number of factors, but some can be attributed to political maneuvering linked to the IGAD-sponsored October 2002 peace talks.

The creation of the TFG in January 2005 also became a driver of renewed armed conflict. The first sign that the TFG might produce new levels of armed conflict came with its split into rival wings, the Mogadishu wing (led by Sharif Hassan, then Speaker of Parliament) and the Yusuf wing (led by then president Abdullahi Yusuf and Ali Mohamed Ghedi, then prime minister). The Mogadishu wing included many of the most powerful Hawiye militia leaders, enjoyed core support from some Mogadishu-based Hawiye clans, showed hostility toward Ethiopia, insisted on the establishment of government in Mogadishu, and rejected proposals for peacekeeping forces, including frontline troops. The Yusuf wing, dominated by the Majerteen and Abgal clans, was a client of Ethiopia, fiercely opposed Islamists, had a weak foothold in Mogadishu, insisted that Mogadishu was too insecure to serve as the capital, and set up a provisional capital in Baidoa. This split mirrored the broad division of Somali politicians into two camps that had been occurring since the late 1990s; it can be traced in part to Ethiopia and its regional rivals, notably Egypt and Eritrea, which increasingly served as drivers of conflict in Somalia.

In 2006, conflict dynamics grew even more complex in Somalia, as the Mogadishu wing itself split and engaged in increasingly fierce battles in the capital. The 2005 alliance between the Union of Islamic Courts (UIC)—an umbrella group of the eleven clan-based sharia courts operating in Mogadishu—and the many clan-based militia leaders in the city had been a marriage of convenience, a temporary pact created solely in opposition to President Yusuf and his wing of the TFG. Disputes over control of a proposed Mogadishu administration had fractured the Mogadishu alliance by October 2005. When, in February 2006, a group of Mogadishu-based militia leaders announced the formation of the Alliance for Restoration of Peace and

Counterterrorism (ARPCT), the Islamists quickly mobilized in response. The US-backed ARPCT was taken by surprise by the strength and superior commitment of the Islamist militias, and over the four-month course of the heaviest fighting Mogadishu had experienced since 1992, the UIC earned a decisive victory. By June, the Islamists had consolidated control over not only Mogadishu but the strategic surrounding regions. The unexpected victory temporarily brought much greater security to the streets of Mogadishu and was greeted enthusiastically by most residents.

In the first days of the UIC's victory, there was widespread hope among Somalis and external observers that the Islamists' consolidation of power in Mogadishu might also produce a new opportunity for nationwide peace and political dialogue toward the establishment of a government of national unity. Both TFG and Islamist leaders made promising public statements about the need for dialogue and ceasefire. But events quickly conspired to dampen those hopes. Hard-liners in all camps—the Islamist leadership, the TFG, and the Ethiopian government—made provocative statements and took actions designed to sabotage dialogue and put Somalia on a path of very serious and dangerous confrontation. In December 2006, Ethiopia launched a major offensive against the UIC, routing its militias and forcing it to retreat to Mogadishu, where angry clan elders, UIC moderates, and business leaders forced disbandment. This allowed Ethiopian forces to advance into the capital without a shot—a shocking turn of events none had foreseen. Unfortunately, Ethiopia opted to occupy Mogadishu, which opened the door for new levels of violence in 2007 and 2008.

Internal Security Trends

Like armed conflict, lawlessness in Somalia changed considerably over the course of the 1990s. The early years of civil war—from 1988 to 1992—featured a level of impunity and gratuitous violence that was largely brought under control for the remainder of the decade. Looting, rape, and murder associated with armed clashes rarely occurred between 1995 and 2006. In instances where such atrocities did take place, as in intra-Rahanweyn conflicts in 2003, they provoked local and international condemnation.[20] Violent crimes and thefts were much more likely to be addressed via customary law and blood payments. These both deterred would-be criminals and reassured communities. Some neighborhoods and towns (often of mixed clan composition) organized the equivalent of neighborhood watch systems, sometimes absorbing young former gunmen into paid protection forces. Kinsmen carried out vigilante justice against individual criminals and gangs.[21] Militia gangs that had terrorized villages in the early 1990s increasingly settled down, making arrangements to tax a portion of village harvests in return for protection. Although these protection rackets and Mafioso behaviors were hardly ideal and sometimes engendered local resistance, they did provide a more predictable security environment for local communities. In some cases, these arrangements moved into a gray area between extortion and taxation, protection racket and nascent security force. This tendency for criminals and bandits to gravitate toward more routine, safe, and "respectable" forms of predation, whereby they established relationships with and provided a service to their erstwhile victims, gave hope that armed anarchy was not sustainable.[22] Instead, there appeared to be a natural tendency for gunmen to seek to legitimate their appropriation of resources, protect their human sources of wealth, and engage in reciprocal behavior (protection for money). Under the right circumstances, this might have constituted a basis for state building.

Yet lawless behavior in Somalia remained a serious problem in the 1995–2006 period, especially in the troubled south. The most egregious crimes (if measured in property and goods stolen or lives lost) were committed by some of the top political and business leaders, whom the international community still convenes for peace conferences. These included the public incitement of deadly violence for narrow political purposes, the embezzlement of foreign aid funds, the introduction of counterfeit currency into circulation (which, by creating hyperinflation, robbed average Somalis of most of their savings), huge landgrabs by force of arms, the export of charcoal (previously illegal and highly environmentally destructive), and involvement in piracy, which has since grown to epidemic proportions on the Somali coast and which has been very lucrative for the Somali elites behind it. The prevalence of this type of criminality supports the worrisome claim that some Somali elites either have a vested interest in blocking the revival of a central government or will accept it only if it is too weak and compromised to enforce the rule of law.

One of the most troubling and prevalent types of crime affecting both international agencies and locals during the 1995–2006 period was kidnapping. Though most common in Mogadishu, it was not unheard of elsewhere. Kidnapping for profit exploded as a major criminal activity because it was one of the few profitable ventures for Mogadishu street criminals. Somali nationals linked to sources of funds, whether via jobs with international agencies or family members in the diaspora, were likely targets. Unemployment and decreased opportunities for looting made kidnapping an obvious alternative income-generating activity for armed gangs.[23] Kidnapping also involved debtors who defaulted on repayments; in still other instances, it was a political tool designed to frighten off international agencies or humiliate political opponents.

The ascendance of the sharia courts in Mogadishu and the attempt by the UIC to expand their presence into the Somali hinterland were important sources of improved security in south-central Somalia. Because the sharia courts were based on subclans and thus had jurisdiction only over members of a single lineage, it was never clear how a broader Islamic administration based on the sharia courts would function to provide all Somalis protection and equal rights before the law. This was one of several dilemmas the UIC leaders faced but were never able to resolve before the Ethiopian invasion ousted them from power.

Collectively, these various sources of governance and local security arrangements not only served to provide households with at least some protection from lawlessness and anarchy, but they also at times provided adequate security to permit the rise of a vibrant commercial economy and modest development opportunities up until 2006.

Development Trends

Accurate economic data on Somalia, an extremely poor country based largely on a subsistence economy, has always been difficult to secure. Economic data has been especially unreliable for Somalia since the 1990 state collapse, so generalizations about economic trends must be made with caution. Still, a number of useful studies and surveys help provide us with a basic portrait of the Somali economy between 1990 and 2006.[24]

Absent a central government, virtually all economic growth in Somalia in that period was produced by the private sector—that is, the collection of tens of thousands of petty traders, small farmers, nomads, middle men, contractors, for-profit service providers, and multimillion-dollar partnerships (parties to which would seek to make profits in Somalia). Economic growth in this period was concentrated in a few urban hotspots such as Mogadishu, Bosasso, and Galkayo.[25] Mogadishu's city center remained in ruins, but the outer rings of the city hosted an impressive economic revival. According to the World Bank, Mogadishu's region, Benadir, enjoyed the highest per capita income of any region in south-central Somalia.[26] Towns such as Bosasso, Galkayo, and to a lesser extent Beled Weyn and Bardhere enjoyed more robust economies than they had prior to the civil war—in part because they are located along strategic commercial routes where thousands of middle-class Mogadishans who were internally displaced during the war settled. Towns and cities that failed to thrive in the 1995–2006 period were in almost all cases contested cities, where chronic insecurity and periodic armed clashes discouraged investment: Kismayo, a southern port city that has been occupied and disputed for seventeen years, is a classic case in point.

Several factors explain the economic boom in urban areas up to 2007. First and foremost is the rise of a remittance economy in Somalia. Remittances from Somalia's large diaspora have long played a role in the economy. Since 1995, however, remittances have rapidly come to dominate it, due in part to the sharp growth of the Somali diaspora during the civil war and in part to the revolution in telecommunications and global finances that occurred in the mid-1990s, allowing Somalis abroad to send funds back to Somalia instantly and at very low cost. By 2001, total remittances coming into Somalia annually were estimated at between US$500 million and US$1 billion, dwarfing all other sources of hard currency.[27] Nearly all remittances flow to urban households, so this infusion of capital from abroad sustained urban economic growth but did little for rural populations.[28] The remittances provided urban households with purchasing power, fueling robust economic growth in commerce (mainly imports of basic consumer goods), local trade, housing construction, and services. The service sector—comprising telecommunications, remittance companies, schools and health services, airlines, water and electricity companies, hotels and restaurants, and so on—was the fastest growing part of the economy. By the late 1990s, remittances were increasingly used to finance small- and medium-sized businesses and housing construction. Towns like Bosasso enjoyed a construction boom, attracting migrant labor from not only southern Somalia but Ethiopia as well. Even so, unemployment in Somali urban areas remained over 60 percent.[29]

A second explanation for Somalia's urban growth was the boom in interstate commerce since 1995. Before 1990, Somalia's borders with its neighbors Ethiopia and Kenya were closed to commercial traffic. With the collapse of the state, Somalia's borders were open, especially to Kenya. Transit trade through Somalia became a lucrative business, fueling a dramatic growth in the importation of basic consumer goods through the Bosasso and Mogadishu ports. Although they did pay for protection to ensure that their goods passed safely through southern Somalia, merchants did not pay custom duties. As a result, they were able to sell imported goods in Kenya at a lower price than the goods that passed through Kenyan seaports.[30] Somalia's status as the world's largest duty-free shop generated a considerable number of jobs and commercial business opportunities in port cities.

By contrast, the rural economy was, with few exceptions, in a prolonged downward spiral. This is of major significance, since 66 percent of the Somali population is rural.[31] Livestock terms of trade continued to decline against the value of dry foodstuffs, impoverishing pastoral families. The periodic Saudi embargo on Somali livestock exports badly damaged the pastoral economy as well. Agricultural production was also down from the prewar era, especially in zones of irrigated cash-cropping, but also among subsistence farmers in rain-fed areas. Chronic insecurity and the lack of agricultural extension services were mainly to blame. The rural sector did have a few areas of niche growth—the commercial production of sesame, vegetables, and dried limes for export expanded, and cattle production in the Transjubba area enjoyed profitable access to the Kenyan market—but generally the rural sector was in a state of serious recession.[32]

By the late 1990s, standards of living were increasingly varied within Somali society, more so than perhaps any other time in recent history. Historically, kinship assistance worked as an informal system of income redistribution. Though that system remained in place, it was being eroded by the ability to bank savings abroad and by the rise of a remittance economy. In general, households enjoying access to monthly remittances from family members working abroad (half of all urban households at most and only a small fraction of rural households) enjoyed improved standards of living and arguably better than most enjoyed during the prewar era.[33] This is in part because the average amount of remittances sent to households—between US$50 to US$200 per month—vastly exceeded the salaries civil servants were earning in the 1980s (typically about US$15–$20 per month). In addition, postwar Somalia was very inexpensive; US$100 to US$200 per month allowed for a relatively comfortable standard of living. Households that owned or co-owned medium- to large-scale business enterprises—trucking companies, hotels, import-export businesses—tended to enjoy a better standard of living than had been possible in the prewar era. For the rest of the population—urban households without access to remittances, the internally displaced, and almost the entire rural population—standards of living were very low and did not improve in the period prior to 2007.

By 2005, the total number of internally displaced persons (IDPs) in Somalia was estimated at roughly 350,000, or about 5 percent of the population, down from the 1992 wartime high of as many as 1.6 million.[34] The enormous wave of IDPs in the early 1990s was driven by fear, as Somalis all fled to their clans' home areas for security. The result was a spontaneous, nationwide episode of ethnic cleansing. Until the disastrous levels of displacement occurred in 2007, gradual reintegration was the trend, as Somalis began to negotiate access to the homes they fled in 1991.

In some locations, IDPs in the 1995–2006 period were increasingly difficult to distinguish from economic migrants. Some moved seasonally between their rural farms and their urban settlements in an effort to maximize economic opportunities. Though no major wave of new IDPs occurred until 2007, chronic insecurity, predation, and depressed economic conditions in rural areas produced a significant rural-urban drift throughout the 1990s.[35]

Economic growth and development went through several distinct phases between 1991 and 2006. The years of open civil war from 1990–1992 marked a period of profound negative development in which an already poor economy collapsed, producing famine conditions for the worst-affected regions of the country and a mere survival economy for the rest. Only a small percentage of war entrepreneurs—arms dealers, warlords and their militiamen, and merchants engaged in the export of scrap metal and theft of food relief—profited during this period.

The Somali economy took a dramatic turn with the arrival of the UN peace operation in December 1992. The arrival of 45,000 peacekeepers, joined by several thousand civilians working in diplomatic, humanitarian, and logistical support positions in the UNOSOM mission, transformed the Mogadishan economy. The years of 1993 and 1994 saw a major increase in employment, business opportunities, and property rental in Mogadishu. For the rest of the country, the cessation of hostilities that generally accompanied the UN mission allowed for gradual improvements in economic growth and production, though they were still far below prewar levels.

The postintervention period (from 1995 to 2007) constituted a third phase in economic growth in Somalia. UNOSOM's departure shocked the Mogadishan economy, initially producing a severe recession. Yet a simultaneous rapid rise of remittance money and rise of the nascent Somali business class increased investment in the service economy and commerce. Almost entirely generated by private sector activity, economic growth in several urban centers was instrumental in sustaining the overall Somali economy. It also produced business dynamics of immediate relevance to broader political trends, including cross-clan business partnerships, private business security forces, and, most important, the rise of a powerful commercial interest in basic law and order.

Analyzing the Trends from 1991 to 2007

Overall, phases in Somalia's security and development from 1991 to 2007 roughly coincided. The 1990–1992 civil war period—marked by horrific levels of armed conflict, unchecked violent crime, and economic collapse—constituted a classic example of a conflict trap. The vicious circle in which warfare, plunder, and gratuitous violence led to an almost total cessation of economic activity and the collapse of the economy meant young men had no other source of livelihood than looting and extortion. The UNOSOM mission from 1993–1994 constituted a temporary, dramatic, and abrupt intervention by deus ex machina—imposing an immediate cease-fire, providing at least marginally improved public security, and jump-starting the local economy with a massive infusion of cash for property rental, procurement, contracting, and local employment. Notably, the financial impact of UNOSOM's contracting and employment activities far outweighed the impact of the fairly modest reconstruction and development aid the international community funded. Although the economic impact followed gradually, months after the cease-fire, UNOSOM's two-year mission provided ample opportunities for merchants previously engaged in wartime economic activities to shift into more so-called legitimate businesses. That shift proved to be a crucial factor in creating a powerful new elite with vested interests in basic law and order, open roads, and peacetime economies. By the mid- to late 1990s, war was generally bad for business in Mogadishu. Ironically, although UNOSOM had failed in its principal mission, it inadvertently contributed to the transformation of economic interests in Mogadishu.

The postintervention period was by far the most complex and nuanced in terms of the security-development nexus. In the mid-1990s, business ventures grew impressively but tended to be risk averse, involving short-term imports of commercial goods as well as investments that had wheels (that is, the transportation sector) and could quickly move out of harm's way. But those investments produced jobs, including coveted positions as security guards by militiamen seeking less dangerous and more socially acceptable employment. By the late 1990s, urban economic growth had increased rapidly and tended to involve more expensive, fixed investments—small factories, telecommunications centers, warehouses, private seaports and airstrips, and hotels. This trend coincided with the growing capacity of large business partnerships to protect their investments with substantial private security forces, which in turn improved public security in adjacent neighborhoods and businesses in the area.[36]

Violent crime and armed conflict still plagued Somalia, and certain areas of the country were still prone to spikes in severe armed clashes. But in general, both violent crime and armed conflict were somewhat easier to contain than they had been in the 1991–1992 period. In one especially noteworthy instance in 2004, a warlord in north Mogadishu attempted to extort money from a large business consortium running the El Ma'an seaport. His militia was soundly defeated by the private, cross-clan security forces of the seaport. The ascendance of the business elite as a new, powerful actor with an interest in basic public order contributed directly to a reduction in street crime and warlordism and to modest levels of economic growth.

The short-lived ascendance of the UIC in 2006 was even more important in reducing criminal violence in much of south-central Somalia. The UIC's ability to bring comprehensive public order across such a large area in so short a period of time challenged the conventional wisdom that Somalia was ungovernable. Whether the UIC could have institutionalized its success in governance as part of a revived central state is a question that will haunt Somalia for years to come; the Islamist experiment was cut short by a combination of the rash posturing of its own hard-liners and a violent response by neighboring Ethiopia.

Explaining the Risk Factors

Explanations of war and peace in Somalia up to 2007 encounter an intriguing paradox—namely, many of the factors that drove armed conflict also played a role in managing, ending, or preventing war. Clanism and clan cleavages were sources of conflict; they divided Somalis, fueled endemic clashes over resources and power, were used to mobilize militia, and made broad-based reconciliation very difficult to achieve. Most of Somalia's armed clashes since 1991 have been fought in the name of clans, often resulting from political manipulation. Yet traditional clan elders were also the primary source of conflict mediation, clan-based customary law served as the basis for negotiated settlements, and clan-based blood-payment groups served as a deterrent to armed violence.

Likewise, the central state was conventionally viewed as a potential source of rule of law and the peaceful allocation of resources, though it was also at times a source of violence and predation. Economic interests, too, intersected ambiguously with conflict in Somalia. As we have noted, in some places, war economies emerged, perpetuating violence and lawlessness, while in other instances business interests were a driving force for peace, stability, and the rule of law. A more nuanced understanding of Somalia's patterns of war and peace in the period leading up to the Ethiopian intervention requires a focus on the particular circumstances that enable these and other variables to serve as escalators or de-escalators of violence.

Geography, Environment, and Land

Geography is unquestionably a vital piece of the Somali puzzle. Somalia's crisis has played out in a harsh, semi-arid environment in the eastern coastal zone of the Horn of Africa. Rainfall is seasonal and prone to severe periodic failure. Rain-fed farming is only possible in the interriparian region of southern Somalia. Until recent decades, the vast majority of the population of 7 to 8 million Somalis subsisted as pastoralists or agropastoralists, moving seasonally with herds of camels, goats, sheep, and cattle in search of pasture and water. Despite decades of urbanization, 65 percent of the population remains rural.[37]

An environment of chronic scarcity and the subsistence orientation of the rural sector are major underlying factors in the very high levels of poverty and underdevelopment in Somalia. Even in the decades before its civil war, Somalia consistently ranked among the least developed countries in the world.

In pastoral zones, competition for scarce resources—pasture and water—results in chronic conflict in rural zones. In recent years, a combination of environmental degradation, the overuse of fragile pasture, deforestation for charcoal production, the commercialization of livestock exports, and easy access to semiautomatic weaponry has rendered once-manageable pastoral disputes into higher-casualty confrontations.[38]

In recent decades, a rapid increase in the value of irrigable riparian farmland along the Shabelle and Jubba river valleys has also produced endemic conflict. Large-scale landgrabs in the 1980s, facilitated by corrupt land tenure and registration procedures, dispossessed tens of thousands of small landholders. In the 1990s, powerful clans used their militias to occupy and claim valuable riparian areas, engendering local resistance.[39] The fact that much of southern Somalia is in some manner occupied by "newcomer" clans using their superior firepower to lay claim to towns and farmland is a major, unresolved source of conflict. This same problem of occupation and hegemony exists in the capital city, Mogadishu, transformed from a cosmopolitan, multiclan city to one dominated by the Hawiye clan.

Land conflicts are not only about ownership and access; they are also at the heart of debates over political rights and representation. Somalis continue to debate whether and under what conditions a Somali can enjoy full citizenship—the right to representation, the right to own property, equality of opportunity, and equality before the law—based on one's clan and its home territory. One (nationalist) strand of thought argues for the right of any Somali to enjoy full rights in any region of the country, irrespective of birthplace or clan affiliation. A second school of thought contends that clan membership is the basis for full rights in a clan homeland; others may live there as so-called guests but cannot claim the same rights as the indigenous clan. A third school of thought argues that birthright is the determining factor for full rights—anyone born in a region may claim full citizenship rights there, including the right to own property, even if they are not members of the dominant clan in that area.[40] Since issues of rights and representation in contemporary Somalia center directly on land and clan claims on that land, discussion of a revived state and system of representation of governance—especially federalism—may increase the risk of conflict.

Demography and Clans

Clans have been the main but by no means sole source of social identity and organization in Somalia. In the context of a collapsed state, they assume a central role in Somali affairs. Lineage affiliation is a key source of protection and social obligation—a form of group insurance against calamity and physical threat. It has also played a very destructive and divisive role in Somalia's long-running crisis and is easily manipulated by political elites to advance narrow agendas, including the derailing of peace accords and the rebuilding of government institutions. The key feature of lineage affiliation in Somalia is its essentially fluid and situational nature. Somalis mobilize around a range of clan and subclan identities according to circumstances. So clans are at once key political and social actors and yet fracture prone.

Among the more reliable predictors of instability is the youth bulge phenomenon.[41] Somalia has been experiencing a youth bulge since about 2005, fueling problems of unemployment, recruitment into militias and criminal gangs, and social violence.[42] Likewise, projections for successful economic development tend to be linked closely to levels of education and literacy. On this score, Somalia faces major challenges, as only 17 to 19 percent of the adult population is literate and the gross enrollment rate for primary school in 2001 stood at only 17 percent.[43] The mid-1980s collapse of the education sector means an entire generation of young adults and teenagers have had no formal schooling.[44] Yet the rapid growth of private Islamic schools, mainly in Mogadishu, is increasing primary-school enrollment among those who can afford tuition.

The Legacy of the State

The legacy of the state in Somalia—in its colonial and postcolonial forms—has been negative for peace and development. Somalis' experience with a central government has been as an instrument of domination and expropriation. Some observers argue that the British colonial policy of indirect rule and general neglect in what was once known as British Somaliland (northern Somalia) partially protected indigenous, traditional structures, allowing them to fill the void left by the collapse of the state. Some contend that these allowed Somaliland to maintain greater levels of peace and security than those found in south-central Somalia, where repressive Italian colonial rule displaced or corrupted traditional authority and customary law.[45] The legacy of authoritarianism has rendered much of the Somali population suspicious of attempts to revive a central government, and makes state-building exercises inherently conducive to conflict. Of growing importance in terms of governance legacies is the fact that a whole generation or more of Somalis—as of 2005, the entire population under the age of twenty-five—has only a distant memory, if that, of a functioning central state. How that generation will react to state authority if and when it is reestablished is an open question.

The Role of Diaspora

The Somali diaspora, estimated to comprise as many as 1 million people, is a central pillar of the Somali economy as the source of nearly US$1 billion of remittance annually.[46] The political impact of the diaspora has changed over the past decade. In the early 1990s, the diaspora was a major source of funding for warring militias. In recent years, it has been reluctant to support armed conflict and has instead channeled money into private investments. Occasionally the diaspora funds community projects: scholarships, hospital wings, libraries. Diaspora members have also been important sources of political leadership. Many have returned to Somaliland, Puntland, and Mogadishu to assume positions in local or national governments. The size and central role of the diaspora alone make Somalia a globalized nation.

Political Mobilization and the Elite

Since 1991, political mobilizers, factions, and leaders in Somalia have tended to work against rather than for peace. At the national level, political elites have used ethnic and factional mobilization to advance narrow political agendas—including attempts to sabotage peace accords and power-sharing agreements. With the notable exception of recent Islamic movements, almost all factional solidarity and political mobilization in Somalia has been based on clan memberships. Cross-clan alliances have proved relatively weak and transient. No major nationalist movement has emerged in the past fifteen years, even though Somalia is one of the few African nation-states with a common language, religion, and national/ethnic identity.[47] Only political Islam has cross-clan appeal and enjoys a significant presence in urban Somali politics. Political Islam in Somalia is divided into a number of competing schools of thought: the progressive al-Islah movement (mainly based in Mogadishu and comprised principally of intellectuals and businessmen); the very conservative Salafist movements such as Takfir; the hard-liners in the now dormant al-Itihad al-Islamiyya (AIAI); and the jihadists of the Al-Shabaab. Although the various Islamist schools argue for unity among Somalis based on a common Islamic identity, none—including the UIC—has successfully served as an umbrella movement under which to keep the diverse strands of Islamist thinking together in Somalia. Indeed, by 2007, divisions between rival Islamist movements in Somalia were open and acrimonious, with Al-Shabaab publicly disavowing the exiled Islamist leadership of the UIC.

Constructive political leadership promoting reconciliation and development has emerged mainly at the local level. Some municipalities have secured mayors with a strong sense of commitment to maintaining peace and rebuilding basic public services. In some locations, clan elders have devoted enormous energy to managing conflict and enforcing customary law. Loose coalitions of businessmen have emerged in some cities and towns as major promoters of commerce and the rule of law. Finally, a small but increasingly influential group of civil leaders—organized in nonprofit groups, professional associations, and the al-Islah movement—provide needed leadership to maintain peace and promote development at the local level. Although these leaders were not able to prevent serious setbacks in their own communities in the pre-2007 period—almost every town and region of Somalia saw at least one major crisis between 1995 and 2007—there was still a notable difference between communities that enjoyed better leadership (including some in Bosasso, Jowhar, Beled Weyn, Luuq, and certain neighborhoods in Mogadishu) and those that did not (such as those in Kismayo and Bulo Hawa).

The Rule of Law

An impressive array of traditional mechanisms—clan-based customary law *(xeer),* blood compensation *(diya)* groups, and clan elders—help manage conflict in Somalia. Historically, these have been the primary source of law and order in Somalia's relatively ungoverned pastoral zones. Clan customary law, enforcement of blood payments for wrongs committed, and Islamic law applied by local sharia courts have assured high levels of lawful behavior and personal security in communities.[48] The latter complements rather than replaces traditional sources of law. For customary law to successfully maintain order, it must at least restore the authority and responsibility of clan elders who negotiate disputes and establish a rough balance of power within local clan groupings. The capacity of a lineage to seek revenge for a wrong committed induces other clans to seek dispute settlements through customary law. Weak and powerless clans (including the minority or low-caste clans) rarely enjoy the protection of enforced customary law; the best they can do is seek client status with a more powerful clan and hope that it fulfills its obligations. Clans constantly seek a rough balance of power both to avoid being overrun and to enhance routinized patterns of cooperation reinforced by repeated adherence to customary law. Although such understandings broke down during the early 1990s, clan elders gradually reestablished their ability to enforce customary law.

Notably, historically speaking, rule of law in Somalia was rarely associated with a formal judiciary or police force. Most aspects of law and order before the late 1980s—when Somalia was unquestionably one of the safest places in Africa—reflected adherence to a social contract more than police capacity. Most Somalis took their legal disputes to a local shaikh or elder rather than a court of law for mediation or adjudication.

During the UIC's brief period of rule in 2006, the Islamists did not supplant traditional mechanisms of conflict management. Instead, the sharia courts generally integrated customary practices into their operations, allowing families of the victims of crime to opt between blood-payment compensation (the traditional mechanism) or sharia justice. The fact that the jurisdiction of the courts was explicitly defined by subclan was the most obvious indication that the courts were still required to work within, not against, the reality of clan. There was evidence that the Islamist leadership hoped to move the sharia court system from clan-based to neighborhood-based jurisdiction, but those plans were derailed with the ouster of the UIC by Ethiopia.

Capacities for Peace, 1995–2006

Local Coping Mechanisms

In the context of protracted state collapse, country-level institutions and policies do not exist. Instead, local, often informal systems of governance gradually replace the vacuum left by the collapsed central state. These in turn provide a modest level of key public goods for local communities—including basic rule of law and public security in both traditional and contemporary forms.

From 1995 to 2007, sharia courts managed conflict and reduced crime. Most sharia courts were formed locally—at the town or neighborhood level—by a coalition of clan elders who oversaw them, businessmen who financed them, and Muslim clerics who administered them. They included sharia militias to apprehend criminals and patrol streets. As we have noted, sharia courts operated in tandem with customary law. They provided some towns and neighborhoods with much improved security.

In addition, neighborhood watch groups hired local gunmen to patrol their streets to prevent crime. Municipalities and regional administrations also emerged in some parts of the country. Although this loose collection of polities and service providers did not replace the state, it did give Somalia greater levels of security and governance. This reassertion of rules-based transactions and public security came at the expense of warlords and local militia—who, although weaker, were still dangerously troublesome.

Though these substate polities and conflict management mechanisms varied from place to place, they tended to share a common set of features. First, they were *organic*—they sprang up as a result of the actions of local communities to provide basic rule of law and more predictable environments; few were imposed by political authorities or occupying militia. Second, in every case, security and governance regimes in south-central Somalia were *fragile* and prone to spoilers. Third, governance and public security regimes remained *local;* their reach was limited geographically and by clan. Fourth, governance and public security regimes in south-central Somalia were *patchy* in coverage—many areas lay outside the effective reach of local administrations and authorities. Fifth, security was increasingly *privatized;* absent a state, it was a commodity that businesses and wealthier Somalis privately obtained.

In the absence of a state, the private sector provided most social services and employment. It provided major urban centers with electricity, piped water, telecommunications, veterinary and health services, seaports, international airports, and quasi-banking services. Businesses often formed complex partnerships with local political authorities. For example, some businesses operated municipal water systems with regulatory oversight provided by town councils or local electrical grid fees regulated by clan elders. Local and regional governments rarely attempted to provide competing services with the private sector and only occasionally exercised modest regulatory control. They often lacked the capacity to enforce regulations.

Local nonprofit groups, usually Islamic charities, expanded social services for education and health care in Mogadishu. These were generally cost-recovery, fee-based services affordable only to those with access to employment or remittances, though some scholarships were available for poor families. The network of Islamic schools in the Mogadishu area, the Formal Private Education Network in Somalia (FPENS), enrolled over 100,000 students, while the University of Mogadishu had over 1,400 students enrolled in one of five faculties.[49]

The two instances in which serious attempts were made to reestablish national government—the aforementioned TNG in 2000–2001 and TFG in 2005–2008—revealed a number of problems with formal government policies. First, the TNG immediately laid claim to a number of governmental functions that had been provided to some degree by nongovernmental actors. Businessmen sponsoring sharia courts handed over their judicial and policing roles to the TNG. When the latter failed to become operational, public security deteriorated. The TNG also attracted a modest amount of foreign aid—up to US$55 million from some Gulf states—but instead of using it for governance and development, it went to corrupt officials or was used to provide lucrative contracts to TNG-supporting businessmen. The TNG not only failed to promote development but also left Mogadishu less secure. The TFG has a distressingly similar story. In 2006, it immediately began restricting the activities of the private and nonprofit sectors, in some cases seeking to nationalize them and in every instance seeking to extort money from them. The inclination on the part of aspiring state authorities to view nonstate actors as dangerous rivals rather than partners in the delivery of key public services has tended to reinforce public distrust of the state and thus dampen enthusiasm for externally funded state-building efforts.[50]

The Role of Regional Actors

Even before the armed occupation of southern Somalia by neighboring Ethiopia in December 2006, regional actors were extensively involved in the Somali crisis. Some of their interventions were positive (or at least were intended to be positive), but more often they constituted obstacles to peace. Regional rivals such as Ethiopia and Eritrea fought proxy wars inside Somalia and, in the process, contributed to chronic insecurity and undermined the establishment of national unity governments.

The region's role has changed considerably over the past fifteen years. In the late 1980s and early 1990s, neighboring states—Kenya, Ethiopia, and to a lesser extent Djibouti and Yemen—were safe havens for over 1 million refugees fleeing war-torn Somalia. Overwhelmed by their own internal political problems, Kenya and Ethiopia were in no position to mediate the conflict in Somalia. They were preoccupied with containing the dangerous spillover of refugees and arms from Somalia.

In the mid-1990s, after the UN peacekeeping mission, Somalia was benignly neglected by the world's major powers. Second-tier and regional powers were thus able to pursue their interests there. The rivalry between Ethiopia and Egypt, driven by hydropolitics and aspirations for regional dominance, was particularly problematic. Each country sponsored a competing peace process and rival Somali coalitions in an effort to undercut the other's diplomatic initiatives. Egypt fiercely promoted a unitary Somali state, backed the TNG, and strongly rejected Somaliland's secessionist bid. It also used its leverage in the Arab League to convince various Persian Gulf States to fund its Somali clients, enabling the latter to purchase weapons on the international market despite a UN arms embargo against their nation. Ethiopia, meanwhile, supported a federalist, decentralized Somalia; opposed the TNG; and established informal working relationships with Somaliland. On more than one occasion, Ethiopia sent troops into Somalia and provided arms and training to its Somali clients.[51] Briefly after 2003, these regional rivalries appeared to subside due to sustained external pressure placed on Ethiopia, Egypt, and Djibouti to work together for a durable solution in Somalia. The 2002–2004 Kenyan peace process, sponsored by the IGAD, provided a structured context for regional coordination and cooperation on Somalia policy. But such cooperation proved elusive. Ethiopia directly interfered in the political process in a way that led to the selection of Abdullahi Yusuf as president of the TFG, while rival Eritrea backed the emerging opposition to the TFG. This proxy war became a major factor when the UIC took power in Mogadishu in 2006; it received significant assistance from Eritrea, which used it in an attempt to weaken Ethiopia. Since 1999, the Ethiopian-Eritrean rivalry has become a major impediment to peace in Somalia.

The growing influence on Somalia of the Persian Gulf States as both a base of Somali business and a source of assistance (governmental and private) is also significant. For example, in 2000, Saudi Arabia gave an estimated US$55 million to the TNG and was a major donor to the Barre regime. Islamic charities in the Gulf are also a major source of assistance in Somalia, especially in the education and health sectors. Gulf State governments (and the Middle East in general) remain strongly committed to the unity of Somalia. Wahhabist missionaries from the Gulf have been aggressive in promoting their brand of Islam in Somalia. Al-Shabaab is believed to receive funds from private sources in the Gulf. Somalia is increasingly being drawn into the economic and social orbit of the Islamic world and South Asia as more and more of its young people study in Malaysia, Pakistan, and Sudan, and more of its commercial activities are linked to Asia.

Regional states have played an essential part in the broader regional economy. Kenya is a major market for transit trade through Somalia, and it is also the site of a large Somali business hub (namely Eastleigh in Nairobi). Ethiopia generates a modest demand for transit goods and is also a source of livestock. Dubai has served as Somalia's de facto financial and commercial capital; and Djibouti is emerging as an important base for Somali business as well. Yemen, Kenya, and Ethiopia are gateways for the flow of Somali refugees and economic migrants. Despite its radically fragmented and localized political authority, Somalia has seen its economy steadily globalize.

International Intervention, 1991–2006

International involvement in Somalia can be broken down into four distinct periods: the 1991–1992 period of humanitarian response, the 1993–1994 UN intervention, the 1995–2001 period of benign neglect, and the post-9/11 era up to 2007. Each has had a dramatically different—and often unintended—impact on Somalia's security and development. Indeed, the law of unintended consequences defines features of post-1991 external intervention and mediation in Somalia.

In 1991 and 1992, the external response to the war and famine in Somalia was humanitarian in nature. The international community provided little diplomatic mediation to end the civil war from 1989 to 1992. The global preoccupation with the end of the Cold War and the Gulf War as well as an abiding diplomatic frustration all contributed to a period of missed opportunities.[52] As for humanitarian engagement, international relief agencies found that their food aid, contracts, and security needs became the principal items over which militias fought—thus bearing witness to the first in a series of unintended consequences in stateless Somalia.

The 1993–1994 UNOSOM intervention was the largest and most ambitious peace enforcement mission in UN history to date. Although many consider UNOSOM a complete failure, the mission's enormous impact on the Mogadishu economy sowed the seeds for the rise of a business class engaged in legitimate or at least quasi-legitimate commerce. Businessmen have not only been the source of economic growth but also a major force for improving security. However unintended, the economic impact of the UN peace operation constitutes an important and positive legacy.

Postintervention international development policies were modest in scope and impact. Aid levels shrank dramatically in this period, staying under US$100 million annually—a tenth of the value of remittance flows into the country. Much of that money was devoted to salaries, overhead, and travel expenses for international staff based in Nairobi.[53] Absent a functional government, Somalia was not eligible for World Bank or IMF loans—although, in 2002, the World Bank began a modest reengagement in Somalia. The European Union, the chief donor since 1995, provided technical assistance primarily to the peaceful northern regions of Somaliland and Puntland. Foreign aid programs focused on capacity-building in local governments, municipalities, and nonprofits; security sector reform, including police training, demobilization, and de-mining; repatriation of refugees; rehabilitation and upgrading of key economic infrastructure, including seaports, roads, and urban water supplies; provision of food aid; and assistance to the health and education sectors. The modest funds provided were often channeled through local nongovernmental organizations (NGOs).

Southern Somalia received mainly humanitarian aid during this period. Due to the increasing insecurity of foreign aid workers and diplomats, who were often faced with threats over contract disputes and the possibility of being kidnapped, internationals in southern Somalia reduced their presence, thereby putting more pressure and responsibility on national staff. All UN agencies, international NGOs, and diplomatic missions tasked with work in Somalia continued to be based in Nairobi.

Although aid flows were low, the impact of aid projects at the local level was considerable. Consistently, the principal impact of foreign aid projects was not so much their intended project objectives (improved access to health care, stronger local governance capacity, and so on) but rather the broader economic opportunities they offered as sources of employment, contracts, and rent. International NGOs and UN agencies constituted major sources of salaried employment and at times became central pillars of the local economy. Local competition for coveted jobs, contracts, compound and vehicle rentals, and money exchange services was fierce and could produce lethal disputes. For instance, having managed to escape from the ravages of the 1990–1992 civil war, the town of Saakow in the Middle Jubba region was largely destroyed in 1999 by communal fighting sparked by clan disputes over who controlled the lucrative money exchange for the sole international NGO in town.[54] In another case, a borehole dug by an aid agency led to armed conflict between two clans over control of the well; clan elders resolved the issue by ordering their men to fill the well with dirt. Clan elders in the city of Beled Weyn, at times a major hub of international relief and development activity, grew so concerned by the conflicts over aid resources that they created a board that allocates all aid agency contracts and hiring by clan.[55]

At its worst, postintervention foreign aid in Somalia up to 2006 was actively if inadvertently harmful, either triggering armed conflict or serving as a source of income for warlords.[56] More often, it had little, if any, impact. Projects were either unsustainable or seen by local communities as their responsibility. UNOSOM devoted considerable energy to forming, training, and providing technical assistance to dozens of district councils. Virtually none survived after UNOSOM departed. The countryside is littered with empty schoolhouses constructed by aid agencies because communities lack teachers and funds for salaries.

Some carefully conceived aid projects have, however, had a positive and lasting impact. The most successful have worked for rather than against the interests of key political and economic actors and have integrated existing practices and structures. For instance, the UN Children's Fund (UNICEF), in sponsoring the rehabilitation and expansion of municipal water systems, has successfully partnered with local business consortiums that run the systems at a profit, while municipal authorities and local elders serve as regulatory bodies.

From 2001 to 2006, Somalia's status as a potential safe haven for terrorists brought the nation to the attention of the West once again.[57] Its reengagement was primarily in the form of aerial surveillance, naval patrols, and stepped-up border patrols with US-Ethiopian and US-Kenyan military forces. US military and intelligence agencies sought to build networks of local informants and counterterrorism partners to better track terrorist activity inside Somalia and engaged local proxies in snatch-and-grab missions. Partnerships with local militia leaders were not effective, however. Furthermore, counterterrorism policies in Somalia tended to work against international efforts to revive a functional central state. Some warlords working with the US had no interest in the revival of a central government and were deeply unpopular inside Somalia, a fact that became painfully evident when the ARPCT was defeated by the Islamists in Mogadishu in 2006. Their defeat prompted widespread celebrations among a war-weary Somali public. Of course, the tension between short-term security arrangements and long-term state-building agendas is hardly unique to Somalia. The United States has faced similar trade-offs in Afghanistan, where its military has relied heavily on regional warlords as counterterrorism partners. Somalia's long-term security is partly dependent on how the United States reconciles its state-building and counterterrorist policies.

Finally, China's petrol-driven foreign policy may become a major driver for political developments in Somalia. China has been aggressively pursuing oil concessions in Africa and moved quickly to forge ties to President Yusuf during his tenure. It is important to note that China's petro-diplomacy does not depend on good governance or democratization. This could work against most international donor agendas in the region.

Conclusion

Between 1995 and 2006, Somalia's vicious circle of economic collapse and insecurity was gradually and partially transformed. Local communities were not passive in the face of the conflict trap: due to their own shifting interests, key local actors (businesspeople, professionals, neighborhood leaders, Islamists, and even militias) were able to break this vicious circle. Local communities actively sought to build and maintain systems of risk management, law and order, and predictability. And although merchants and warlords often profit politically and economically from lawlessness, warfare, and plunder in the short term, the Somali case suggests that as they accumulate riches and valuable real estate, they become increasingly interested in the benefits of law and legitimate commerce.

Likewise, although spoilers remain an enduring problem, most Somali businessmen and political leaders are interested in pursuing real reconciliation and state building. But all are risk averse, fearful of the revival of a predatory state. In such a context, the rule of law, security sector reform, law enforcement, and antiterrorism projects will encounter either active resistance and sabotage by powerful political actors or quiet subversion by local partners.[58]

The Somalian experience up to 2007 demonstrates that organic processes can create livelihoods and provide basic security, at least at the local level. And these organic processes are sustainable in the long run. Postconflict strategies and external interventions that build on and mesh rather than clash with organic efforts to improve security are more likely to succeed. This requires tailoring postconflict assistance to local conditions and institutions rather than relying on off-the-shelf governance and demobilization packages. A strategy of building on success rather than displacing local systems requires that actors recognize organic, informal systems of conflict management based on long-standing cultural practices and attempt to harmonize more formal, statecentric mechanisms of conflict management with existing local practices.[59]

Peacebuilders and development strategists wishing to align external aid with local initiatives must embrace the "do no harm" principle. Positive political and economic developments are providing livelihoods and basic security in Somalia. These developments must be safeguarded from ill-conceived interventions undermining local coping mechanisms. Food relief should not undermine local producers by driving market prices to unprofitable levels; development aid should not displace promising private sector approaches to the delivery of key services; state-building efforts should not trigger armed conflict; and counterterrorism policies should not empower destructive elements that impede reconciliation and the rule of law. More knowledge of local conditions requires increased diplomatic engagement in the country itself, which is the only viable way to avoid unintended negative consequences.

Yet the harmonization of external initiatives and local processes requires more than avoiding harm. Effective harmonization efforts must also create a *multiplier effect.* Local, regional, and informal systems of governance remain the primary source of rule of law in the country and collectively constitute an organic state-building mechanism in Somalia. The TFG, by contrast, was a top-down, inorganic state-building initiative, and the policies initially pursued by top TFG officials appeared to be actively hostile to any nonstate source of political authority and service delivery, despite their own weaknesses in those areas.

One possibility involves the TFG or a successor government ceding de facto authority to nonstate, local, and informal actors on some matters of public security and governance, at least in the interim. This mediated form of government may in fact be the only viable option during a political transition, when the central government lacks the capacity to provide security and services.

This harmonization may not always be simple or appropriate. Local patterns of governance can fail to meet international human rights standards. For example, sharia courts and customary clan law are often effective sources of public order and are generally supported by local communities. Yet they both deny international standards of due process and occasionally impose penalties that violate human rights. For aid agencies, the choice of incorporating sharia and customary law into governance programs poses considerable problems. To provide technical support for these alternative sources of law is to legitimize practices considered unacceptable by the international community.

The complete and sustained collapse of the central government in Somalia has created or contributed to numerous problems not inherently linked to criminality and armed conflict. Indeed, Somalia has repeatedly shown that, in some places and at some times, communities, towns, and regions enjoy relatively high levels of peace, reconciliation, security, lawfulness, and economic recovery despite an absent central authority. Somalia's state collapse has extracted high costs and state building is important, but not all of Somalia's problems can be attributed to the collapse of the central government.

In fact, attempts to revive a central state structure have actually exacerbated armed conflicts in the short term. State building and peacebuilding are two separate and, in the short term, mutually antagonistic enterprises in Somalia. Reviving state structures is viewed in some Somali quarters as a zero-sum game: winners and losers have high stakes at play.[60]

Notes

1. In May 1991, the northwestern portion of Somalia unilaterally seceded from the rest of the country and declared itself the Republic of Somaliland. While south-central Somalia has been beset by years of state collapse, armed conflict, and warlordism, Somaliland's political trajectory has been quite different. Somaliland enjoys much greater adherence to rule of law, a minimally functional (though unrecognized) central government, high levels of security, and a relatively robust local economy. Because the situations in Somaliland and south-central Somalia are so different, it is unhelpful and confusing to generalize about both in a single case study. For that reason, this chapter does not include discussion of Somaliland. For recent scholarship and analysis of Somaliland, see Mark Bradbury, Adan Yusuf Abokar, and Haroon Ahmed Yusuf, "Somaliland: Choosing Politics over Violence," *Review of African Political Economy* 30, no. 97 (September 2003): 455–478; WSP-International, *Rebuilding Somaliland: Issues and Possibilities* (Lawrenceville, NJ: Red Sea, 2005); and International Crisis Group (ICG), "Somaliland: Democratisation and Its Discontents," *ICG Africa Report* series no. 66 (Brussels: ICG, July 28, 2003).

2. Paul Collier, V. L. Elliott, Havard Hegre, Anke Hoeffler, Marta Reynal-Querol, and Nicholas Sambanis, "Breaking the Conflict Trap: Civil War and Development Policy," policy research report (Washington, DC: World Bank, 2003).

3. David Rawson, *The Somali State and Foreign Aid* (Washington, DC: US Department of State Foreign Service Institute, 1993).

4. Africa Watch, *Somalia: A Government at War with Its Own People* (Washington, DC: Africa Watch, January 1990).

5. Among the many analyses of the Somali civil war in 1991 and 1992, see Terrence Lyons and Ahmed I. Samatar, *Somalia: State Collapse, Multilateral Intervention, and Strategies for Political Reconstruction* (Washington, DC: Brookings Institution Occasional Papers, 1995), and Ahmed I. Samatar, ed., *The Somali Challenge: From Catastrophe to Renewal* (Boulder, CO: Lynne Rienner Publishers, 1994).

6. These figures are from the most careful and authoritative study of deaths in the Somali crisis. See Refugee Policy Group (RPG), *Lives Lost, Lives Saved: Excess Mortality and the Impact of Health Interventions in the Somalia Emergency* (Washington, DC: RPG, 2004), 24.

7. It should be noted that many reports estimate that over 1,000 Somalis died during the four-month urban battle pitting General Aideed's militia against UNOSOM peacekeepers in 1993. The SIPRI (Stockholm

International Peace Research Institute) database may not have coded this conflict as a war since it involved UN peacekeepers. A war is considered to be 1,000 battle deaths or more.

8. See Stockholm International Peace Research Institute (SIPRI) yearbooks 1990–2004 (Oxford: Oxford University Press); SIPRI relies on coded data on armed conflict from the Uppsala Conflict Database, a project of the Department of Peace and Conflict Research, University of Uppsala, Sweden, http://www.pcr.uu.se/database/index.php.

9. Africa Watch, *Somalia: A Government at War with Its Own People.*

10. Ken Menkhaus, *Somalia: State Collapse and the Threat of Terrorism*, Adelphi Paper no. 364 (Oxford: Oxford University Press, 2004).

11. Menkhaus, *Somalia: State Collapse.*

12. One close observer to the fighting in Mogadishu reports that the average cost of a full-scale armed clash by a militia costs about US$4,000 an hour in ammunition, a steep price that few warlords are capable of sustaining; hence it is unusual for armed clashes to last more than a few hours.

13. Menkhaus, *Somalia: State Collapse*, 28–31.

14. Among recent studies that have explored this liminal state, see P. Richards, ed., *No Peace, No War: An Anthropology of Contemporary Armed Conflicts* (Oxford: James Currey, 2005).

15. This explanation is pursued in more detail later in the chapter.

16. Menkhaus, *Somalia: State Collapse.*

17. Personal interview with former Benadir regional governor, July 2008.

18. Menkhaus, *Somalia: State Collapse.*

19. Matt Bryden, "No Quick Fixes: Coming to Terms with Terrorism, Islam, and Statelessness in Somalia," *Journal of Conflict Studies* 23, no. 2 (Fall 2003): 24–56.

20. UN Office for the Coordination of Humanitarian Affairs, *Somalia Humanitarian Situation Report,* (Nairobi: UN-OCHA, July 30, 2003), 5–6.

21. In some instances, kinsmen lose patience with the costs of criminality by a member of their *diya* (blood compensation) group and have the individual arrested or executed. Vigilante justice is also associated with neighborhood security groups and with the militia of private businessmen, who occasionally hunt down criminal gangs. One such posse killed six professional criminals in an attack outside of Mogadishu in November 2002 (personal correspondence, November 2002).

22. The seminal work on this topic is Charles Tilly, "War Making and State Making as Organized Crime," in *Bringing the State Back In,* eds. Peter Evans, Dietrich Rueschemeyer, and Theda Skocpol (New York: Cambridge University Press, 1985), 169–191. Similar patterns of shifts in interest on the part of warlords have recently been documented in eastern Congo. See Koen Vlassenroot and Tim Raeymaekers, "The Politics of Rebellion and Intervention in Ituri: The Emergence of a New Political Complex?" *African Affairs* 103 (July 2004): 385–412.

23. An excellent journalistic piece on the interests entangled in kidnapping in Somalia is Alexis Masciarelli, "Somalia's Kidnapping Industry," BBC News, May 24, 2002, http://news.bbc.co.uk/2/hi/africa/2005567.stm.

24. Among the most comprehensive surveys of the Somali economy are UNDP, *Somalia Human Development Report 2001* (Nairobi: UNDP, 2001);

World Bank, *Somalia: Socio-Economic Survey 2002*, Somalia Watching Brief Report No. 1 (Nairobi: World Bank, September 2003); Jamil Mubarak, "The Hidden Hand Behind the Resilience of the Stateless Economy in Somalia," *World Development* 25, no. 12 (December 1997): 2027–2041; and Peter Little, *Somalia: Economy Without State* (Bloomington, IN: Indiana University Press, 2003).

25. The most impressive economic growth in Somalia is actually concentrated in the secessionist state of Somaliland, especially Hargeisa, but that region is outside the purview of this study.

26. World Bank, *Somalia: Socio-Economic Survey 2002*, 23.

27. UNDP, *Somalia Human Development Report 2001*, 104–105. By contrast, estimates of income earned by livestock exports is around US$100 million per year, and foreign aid infusions are generally under US$100 million annually.

28. One study in Somaliland found that only 5 percent of rural households received remittances, while over half of urban households did. See Ismail Ahmed, "Remittances and Their Economic Impact in Post-War Somaliland," *Disasters* 24, no. 4 (2000): 380–389.

29. World Bank, *Somalia: Socio-Economic Survey 2002*, xii.

30. Ken Menkhaus, "Gedo Region," *UN Development Office for Somalia, Studies on Governance Series*, no. 5 (Nairobi: UNDOS, December 1999).

31. World Bank, *Somalia: Socio-Economic Survey 2002*, xii.

32. Author's fieldwork.

33. The term *household* in the Somali context is broader than is common, as extended family members and several generations of a family frequently live together in a single compound.

34. UN Coordination Unit (UNCU), *A Report on Internally Displaced Persons in Somalia* (Nairobi: UNCU, 2002), i; UNDP, *Somalia Human Development Report 2001*, 60–61.

35. The World Bank estimates that the percentage of Somalia's urban population has increased from 23.5 percent in the prewar era to 34 percent today. See World Bank, *Somalia: Socio-Economic Survey 2002*, xii.

36. Menkhaus, *Somalia: State Collapse.*

37. UNDP, *Somalia Human Development Report 2001.*

38. In arid central Somalia, for instance, two subclans of the Haber Gedir clan have engaged in a war over pasture and wells, which has produced several hundred deaths. This new and highly lethal pastoral warfare is increasingly common throughout the Horn of Africa, in areas such as Mandera (in Kenya) and the Karamoja cluster (at the Kenya-Uganda border).

39. Catherine Besteman and Lee V. Cassanelli, eds., *The Struggle for Land in Southern Somalia: The War Behind the War* (Boulder, CO: Westview, 1995).

40. ICG, "Somalia: Continuation of War by Other Means?" *ICG Africa Report* series no. 88, (Brussels: ICG, December 21, 2004), 14–15.

41. Technically, a youth bulge is said to exist when the ratio of the population aged fifteen to twenty-nine to the population aged thirty to fifty-four exceeds 1.27. See US Government, National Intelligence Council, *Global Trends 2015* (Washington DC: NIC, 2000), 25.

42. World Bank, *Somalia: Socio-Economic Survey 2002*, 11.

43. UNDP, *Somalia Human Development Report 2001*, 83.

44. UNDP, *Somalia Human Development Report 1998* (Nairobi: UNDP, 1998), 16.

45. The extent to which traditional practices actually survived colonial and postcolonial state manipulation, as well as the extent to which the strength or weakness of customary law and clan elders accounts for the very different trajectories experienced by Somaliland and south-central Somalia, remains a matter of fierce debate in Somali circles.

46. UNDP, *Somalia Human Development Report 2001*, 61.

47. The collapse of Somali nationalism and the dominance of subnational clan identity has been the subject of considerable discussion and debate in Somalia; some bemoan this state of affairs, others challenge the premise that Somalia was ever as homogeneous as nationalists claimed. Tragically, some of the ethnic communities that predated ethnic Somalis in Somalia and that served as the best evidence of ethnic diversity in the country have been partially displaced by the civil war; some, like the Benadiri, Bajuni, and Barawan coastal people, have suffered heavy population losses to permanent relocation to Kenya and other countries.

48. Andre Le Sage, "Stateless Justice in Somalia: Formal and Informal Rule of Law Initiatives," working paper (Nairobi: UNDP, Rule of Law and Security Programme, January 2005).

49. Andre Le Sage and Ken Menkhaus, "The Rise of Islamic Charities in Somalia: An Assessment of Impact and Agenda," paper presented at the International Studies Association Conference, Montreal, March 2004, 17.

50. Appointed prime minister to the TFG in 2008, Hassan Hussein Nuur "Adde" has taken a new approach, seeking partnerships with nonstate actors.

51. For details on violations of the UN Arms Embargo on Somalia, see various reports by the UN Panel of Experts on Somalia, including Ernst Jan Hagendoorn, "Report of the Panel of Experts on Somalia pursuant to Security Council Resolution 1425 (2002)," UN Doc. S/2003/223, March 25, 2003.

52. Mohamed Sahnoun, *Somalia: The Missed Opportunities* (Washington, DC: US Institute of Peace, 1994), and Ken Menkhaus and Lou Ortmayer, "Somalia: Misread Crises and Missed Opportunities," in *Preventive Diplomacy in the Post–Cold War World: Opportunities Missed, Opportunities Seized, and Lessons to be Learned,* ed. Bruce Jentleson (New York: Carnegie Commission on Preventing Deadly Conflict, 1999), 211–237.

53. UNDP, *Somalia Human Development Report 2001*, 119–120.

54. Ken Menkhaus, "Middle Jubba Region," UN Development Office for Somalia, Studies on Governance Series No. 6 (Nairobi: UNDOS, December 1999).

55. Ken Menkhaus, "Hiran Region," UN Development Office for Somalia, Studies on Governance Series No. 8 (Nairobi: UNDOS, December 1999).

56. For years, a major international NGO presence in the town of Buale was completely captured by one militia, which monopolized the renting of vehicles to the NGO, cornered all employment and security for the NGO, and diverted most of the aid intended for the community. For devastating critiques of the harmful effects of aid in Somalia, see Michael Maren, *The Road*

to Hell: The Ravaging Effects of Foreign Aid and International Charity (New York: Free Press, 1997).

57. Matt Bryden, "No Quick Fixes"; ICG, "Somalia: Combating Terrorism in a Failed State," *ICG Africa Report* series no. 45 (Brussels: ICG, May 2002).

58. Ken Menkhaus, "Quasi-States, Nation-Building, and Terrorist Safe Havens," *Journal of Conflict Studies* 23, no. 2 (Fall 2003): 7–23.

59. Le Sage, "Stateless Justice in Somalia," 3.

60. Ken Menkhaus, "International Peacebuilding and the Dynamics of Local and National Peacebuilding in Somalia," in *Learning from Somalia: The Lessons of Armed Humanitarian Intervention,* eds. Walter Clarke and Jeffrey Herbst (Boulder, CO: Westview, 1997), pp. 42–63.

7

Anatomy of State Fragility: The Case of Guinea-Bissau

Joshua B. Forrest

Guinea-Bissau was a colony of Portugal until 1974. National independence was won through full-scale guerrilla war (1962–1974) pursued by the African Party for the Independence of Guinea-Bissau and Cape Verde (PAIGC), which succeeded in politically unifying the country's diverse ethnic groups. Despite national unity during the twelve-year anticolonial war, Guinea-Bissau's postliberation history is characterized by a tendency toward an authoritarian centralization of executive power punctuated by multiple coup attempts and a short civil war in 1998 and 1999. Moreover, despite a relatively robust base of natural resources, Guinea-Bissau has made scant progress toward development and remains mired in economic difficulties, urban food shortages, and infrastructural inefficiencies. In the 2000s, Guinea-Bissau's political fragility has been accentuated by the rise of new security threats, as drug traffickers and criminal networks have begun using the country as a transit route from South America to Europe.

In this chapter, I examine security and development in Guinea-Bissau from its civil war to 2006, and seek to address three main questions. First, in a small country whose various ethnic groups were politically united for more than a decade to pursue the anticolonial struggle, why has there been so much political conflict since independence? Why has multiparty democratization failed to provide adequate institutional mechanisms of conflict resolution? What can be done now to encourage greater political stability? Second, given the relative ecological advantages enjoyed by Guinea-Bissau, why have successive strategies of socialism, capitalism/privatization, and intensive international assistance all failed to generate economic development? Third, what are the connections among political instability, persistent development failures, and security threats that have characterized the past quarter century in Guinea-Bissau? How can policy responses become better tailored to address the country's political, security, and development concerns?

The answers to these questions are important if we are to understand Guinea-Bissau's precarious situation in the early twenty-first century. Based on this analysis, guidelines can be suggested for the establishment of more effective security and economic policies. Thus, after reviewing the security and development conditions and policies in Guinea-Bissau since the early 1990s, I conclude with several policy recommendations.

It is important to add that research for this chapter was undertaken prior to the discovery of mounting evidence that Guinea-Bissau is being used as a transit route for South American drugs destined for Europe, which has rendered the country's policy dilemmas more complex. However, this development should not be surprising. With approximately four hundred kilometers of coastline dotted by more than ninety largely uninhabited islands and with a government that is increasingly unable to govern, Guinea-Bissau is highly vulnerable to both internal and external security threats. Although I do not attempt to assess the implications of these new and evolving threats, the overall analysis makes possible a better understanding of the consequences of chronic and cumulative problems in a fragile state.

Tracking the Problem

A History of Military Coups

In 1974, a twelve-year full-scale guerrilla war led by the PAIGC ended Portugal's colonial rule over Guinea-Bissau and unified most of the country's various ethnic groups. Since then, Guinea-Bissau has suffered continual political instability. Just prior to independence, agents allied with the Portuguese assassinated Amílcar Cabral, an immensely popular leader of the country's anticolonial war effort. Cabral was succeeded as head of the PAIGC by his half-brother Luiz Cabral, who was then elected as the country's first president; he went on to establish a single-party political system led by the PAIGC.[1] Early political stability, reflecting the postwar national euphoria over the departure of the Portuguese and accompanying expectations of rapid economic development, ended with a 1980 coup d'état carried out by General João Bernardo "Nino" Vieira, a key military commander during the liberation struggle.[2]

Throughout his first presidency (1980–1998), Vieira centralized his political power and became politically isolated, particularly after purported coup attempts in 1983 and 1986.[3] Beginning in 1991, political pressure from the World Bank and the International Monetary Fund (IMF), among others, involving structural policy adjustments and advances toward democratization led Guinea-Bissau to achieve modest political liberalization and hold its first multiparty elections in 1994.[4] Despite the elections, however, the Vieira regime's continued political repression fueled increasing resentment in most parts of the countryside. Moreover, Vieira's centralization of power and his growing distrust of military officers produced political tensions between the army and the executive office.

In 1998 and 1999, most of the soldiery, supported by the vast majority of the populace, rose up in a mass popular rebellion.[5] Although anger over their low wages contributed to the soldiers' rebellion, Vieira's political strain with army leaders and the government's general repression were the main triggers. For more than a year, the majority of the armed forces, aided by citizens throughout the countryside, fought against a small number of troops loyal to the president. Vieira was only able to hold onto power thanks to external military support from neighboring Senegal. But the Guinea-Bissauan rebel soldiers proved better fighters than the Senegalese, as they demonstrated during the highly destructive street battles that took place in the capital city of Bissau in the spring of 1999.[6] Agreements between the two sides mediated by the Economic Community of West African States Monitoring Group (ECOMOG) were repeatedly broken by the Vieira regime.[7] Vieira was finally defeated by mid-1999, when he fled to Portugal. In economic terms, the war disrupted farming practices for two years, and the destruction wrought on the country's infrastructure is still felt today. In political terms, the war helped to consolidate a culture wherein violence was seen as a legitimate mechanism for obtaining power.

The end of the civil war of 1998 and 1999 was followed by a short period of relative calm, due in part to internal diplomacy among Guinean politicians and in part to international aid, which included the provision of large quantities of food and other necessities. From December 1999 to January 2000, the country's military leaders allowed national elections to proceed; handed political power to the newly elected president, Kumba Yala; and refrained from taking direct responsibility for policymaking. The military seemed interested in being seen as upholding the political will of the people by assuring the installation of a newly elected president and enabling the transition to a civilian regime. At the same time, its success in the 1998–1999 uprising served as a de facto warning to the incoming president to take into account its demands for political stability, the cessation of governmental repression, legitimate popular rule, and both adequate compensation for officers and regular pay for soldiers.

Nonetheless, the period of 2000–2003 was marked by a return to a combination of electoral processes and presidential repression. A democratic political culture did not take root under President Yala.[8] By mid-2000, to the disappointment of many voters, Yala was beginning to circumvent the reelected Parliament and the Supreme Court. Moreover, he and his immediate military advisers considered Army Chief Ansumane Mané, a popular hero of the 1998–1999 uprising, a threat to Yala's full control over the army high command. In November 2000, Mané was shot dead during his attempted arrest.[9]

During 2001 and 2002, Yala concentrated political power into the office of the president and intimidated or repressed political opponents.[10] He sought to hold onto power by repeatedly postponing elections for a new People's National Assembly and by appointing military commanders whom he personally preferred. In November 2002, he dissolved Parliament.[11] The extent of repression under Yala's presidency, the growing sense of the illegitimacy of his regime, and the exclusion of key military commanders from his circle of power led to a September 2003 coup d'état led by General Verissimo Correia Seabra.[12]

The period of 2003–2005 was characterized by alternating coups d'état, military rule, and parliamentary elections. Although Henrique Rosa was appointed as interim president, General Seabra and the military council retained the key decisionmaking powers until March 2004, when they allowed parliamentary elections, resulting in a new National Assembly.[13] However, General Seabra was killed and his regime ended by yet another army coup d'état in October 2004. This time, the provocation was the lack of salary payments to Guinea-Bissauan army units that had been deployed with the United Nations Mission in Liberia (UNMIL), but continuing disregard for the conditions of soldiers' barracks and the perception of corruption among some of Seabra's staff were also contributing factors.[14]

Shortly after the October 2004 coup, General Tagme Na Wai was appointed chief of staff of the armed forces and sixty-five military officers who had been purged under previous administrations were reinstated, easing intra-army factional tension.[15] President Rosa retained his office until the next presidential election, and Prime Minister Carlos Gomes Junior headed Parliament. However, it was clear that neither the president nor the prime minister held real political power, as General Na Wai and his fellow military officers ruled through a council consisting of army officers and civilians.[16]

General Na Wai directed the country on a steady path toward presidential elections in 2005 despite the emergence of serious political tensions. For example, immediately prior to the 2005 poll, Yala and his supporters briefly seized the presidential palace. Yala declared that he deserved to be reinstated as president, since he had been illegally ousted in the 2003 coup, and that elections had to be postponed. Though General Na Wai ordered the army to oust Yala from the palace (a mission that was accomplished without bloodshed), he decided not to prosecute—and in fact allowed Yala to participate in the presidential campaign as a bona fide candidate.[17] This was intended to assure a return to a peaceful political climate and to encourage Yala's supporters to commit themselves to the electoral process.

The first round of the 2005 presidential election proved peaceful yet competitive; of thirteen candidates, none obtained the 50 percent of the vote necessary to avoid a second round. In the weeks between the first and second presidential ballots, the country was wracked by political tension when Yala rejected the first-round results as fraudulent (he had finished in third place, making him ineligible for the second-round runoff).[18] Eventually, Yala announced his acquiescence to the official electoral results, and a relatively smooth second-round run-off between former President João Bernardo Vieira and PAIGC leader Malam Sanha resulted in Vieira's return to the presidency. Citizens held their breath during this interim period—a sign of how fundamentally unstable and insecure the political system remained. After President Vieira's installation, the competition between the main political parties and the country's entrenched political and military elite proceeded with little relief. International mediation efforts (organized by the UN) during Vieira's second presidency failed to quell the fierce competition among key power brokers in the government and the armed forces. This was made more dramatic by the assassination of President Vieira in March 2009 by a group of disgruntled army men (the coup leaders and motives are not known as of this writing), with the army leaders immediately announcing their determination to hold multiparty presidential elections later that same year.[19]

It should be noted that the decision of Guinea-Bissau's military coup-makers of the 2000s to restore a civilian regime did not reflect their abiding commitment to formal democratic institutions so much as their view that elections constituted a convenient way of selecting a president, reestablishing political stability, and generating a sense of political legitimacy. Moreover, they realized, elections tended to produce increased international aid, which directly benefited the military. Even after elections, however, army leaders have generally played a decisive role in political decisionmaking, especially regarding security matters and any policy issues that affect the army, such as officer appointments and salaries. The armed forces of Guinea-Bissau are well respected at home and abroad, but the government's periodic inability to disburse military salaries or reliably provide food does contribute to disquiet within their ranks.

There are multiple reasons for the military coups in Guinea-Bissau. Most have sought to protect the political and fiscal interests of the armed forces, end the reign of a repressive president, and reduce the general insecurity produced by repression. In many cases, coup leaders were applauded for their actions by the peasantry for ending elected regimes that had proved unaccountable to the public. Most coup efforts also reflected factional power struggles and competition both among military officers and within the government. Since the beginning of Yala's presidency, most military officers have been of Balanta origin—the country's largest ethnic group—such that ethnic factionalism was not a major factor in coups during the 2000s. (Previously, however, Balanta officers had often been overlooked for promotion—which may indeed have contributed to coup attempts prior to Yala's reign). Once in power, military generals have tended to move relatively quickly toward reinstalling civilian bureaucrats and politicians, whether by appointment or election. Thus, despite its history of coups, Guinea-Bissau has been spared extended direct army rule.

Politics and Persistent Poverty

Guinea-Bissau consistently ranks as one of the world's ten poorest nations. The UNDP (UN Development Programme) *Human Development Report 2005* ranked Guinea-Bissau 172nd out of 177 nations, with a gross domestic product (GDP) per capita of US$160.[20] The country has an overwhelmingly agrarian subsistence economy characterized by the growth and consumption of rice and cassava, modest levels of export-oriented cashews, and lesser amounts of exported peanuts and timber. Various development approaches have not made a major difference in the country's overall low economic performance. After an initial effort at socialist development (1974–1984) proved disastrous, privatization reforms led the government to promote the cultivation of marketable cash crops, especially cashews. The effect, however, has been mixed at best. Only a tiny group of farmers and traders benefited, while many peasants found themselves short of food and income, provoking rising levels of out-migration.[21]

From 1984 to 1998, when privatization was gradually being implemented, the economy was marked by sectoral disarticulation. It lacked any economic integration of peasant farming with urban industries and marketing institutions. High levels of international assistance did not resolve this rural-urban split. Apart from a single beverage factory and several dozen very small handicrafts shops, the lack of an industrial sector meant that economic growth came mainly from cash-crop sales. Since most economic activity took place in the rural informal sector, it did not contribute to the integration of rural-urban economic sectors or to national economic growth.[22]

From 1984 to 1998, economic liberalization reforms helped to encourage the spread of cashew farming, which had only been recently introduced to Guinea-Bissau. Some rice farmers switched to the increasingly more lucrative cashews, selling the harvested cashews to urban purchasers who exported them, which yielded the government a portion of the profits through the export tax.[23] Gradually rising export sales of cashews provided the country with a fiscal base sufficient to begin repaying international loans. Yet the country remains mired in debt, which increased from US$126 million in 1980 to US$284 million in 1990 and US$435 million in 2000.[24]

The 1998–1999 civil war destroyed private property and basic infrastructure on a massive scale—particularly in the capital city of Bissau—with estimated losses of US$90 million.[25] Sales of cashews (the main export) and rice (the main food crop) were severely reduced. The country's GDP declined an estimated 28 percent and the out-migration of peasant labor intensified.[26]

The decline in crop sales persisted through subsequent agricultural seasons. Guinea-Bissau had zero or negative economic growth rates from 1999 to 2003, during which time electric power was shut down for extended periods and many civil service salaries went unpaid.[27] In 2004, despite a slight rise in economic growth due to a temporary cashew-harvest expansion, GDP remained 25 percent below its prewar level.[28] In 2005, Guinea-Bissau's budget deficit was US$84 million.[29]

From 1999 to 2004, extensive population dislocations caused by privatization and the impact of war led to a reduction in wet-rice cultivation, increasing the pressure on subsistence peasant farmers to obtain foodstuffs. However, problems in securing monetary income made it increasingly difficult for families to maintain a year-round food supply. For example, the Tombali region has traditionally served as Guinea-Bissau's central source of domestically produced rice, but it is less capable of performing that role today.[30] Many cashew growers in 2004 sold their harvests for cash instead of exchanging them for rice from Senegalese traders (as they had done in the 1990s), further exacerbating food supply deficits.[31] Thus, the country had to rely even more dramatically on rice imports to satisfy national food demands.

Nonetheless, in the countryside, where 82 percent of the populace lives, peasants have survived by growing their own foods and selling cash crops. Out-migration—sending family members away from the farm to work—may be used as a coping strategy to keep household incomes at secure levels. After the 1998–1999 civil war, most rural families have had at least one household member working for cash wages in a town in Guinea-Bissau or abroad.[32] A long history of temporary cross-border migration by those in search of employment (directed both north to Senegal and south to Guinea and Sierra Leone) has enabled Guinea-Bissauans to make ends meet in the wake of the economic stagnation that characterizes their country.[33]

Most Guinea-Bissauans rely heavily on the production and purchase of food, clothing, bicycles, radios, batteries, fishing nets and hooks, utensils, cooking pots, kola nuts, and other items through so-called informal markets.[34] This informal trade is largely unrecorded, making it difficult to accurately assess the per capita income earnings of Guinea-Bissauans or to know with certainty the extent of changes in the nation's standard of living. Thus, while the 1998–1999 civil war caused infrastructural decay and marketing blockages, the basic standard of living for most Guinea-Bissauans may not have declined appreciably from its already relatively low prewar level—and it may even be higher than that suggested by GDP indicators or UNDP ratings.

It is nonetheless the case that increased reliance on cash-based income sources, especially cashew crops, has contributed to the attenuation of traditional social links. Anthropological studies suggest a partial breakdown of community institutions, particularly in light of the decline in the social influence exerted by traditional councils, elders, and chiefs.[35] In the countryside, particularly in rice-farming villages, the weakening of social safety nets and the accompanying economic dislocations have strained the fabric of rural society and, in some areas, weakened a sense of community altogether. Food production has been inconsistent, reflecting in part the inadequate integration of the country's economic sectors, and it has been exacerbated by the country's political insecurity. As a result of unreliable domestic grains, the nation has increasingly depended on global largesse for food aid.

There is, however, no clear-cut evidence that endemic poverty is a cause of political conflict in Guinea-Bissau. The coup attempts in 1983 and 1985–1986 took place when rice production and rice-related social support systems were relatively intact in the countryside. Rice may have played a minor role in the generation of some coup attempts—in 1980, for example—due to the army's discontent regarding poor rice distribution mechanisms; however, this was not an economic so much as a political problem, reflecting internal factional and personal power struggles. It was only during the 1990s, when cashews came to be regarded as a more desirable export crop than rice and social changes disrupted traditional social support systems, that the civil war erupted. In other words, although the economic and social changes caused by privatization and structural adjustment reforms caused some discontent among the populace, there is no evidence of a direct causal connection between those reforms and the war. The military interventions and coups of 2003 and 2004 did not reflect any noteworthy change in economic conditions. That said, the country's political instability between coups has had far-reaching economic consequences. The political leadership tends to be preoccupied with intra-army factionalism, detracting attention from the country's underdevelopment and relative lack of economic integration. Economic development has been repeatedly disrupted by political factionalism and military coups. Consistent political crises have made it very difficult both to engage in coherent economic planning and to implement macroeconomic policy.

Ongoing political instability in Guinea-Bissau has contributed to the fact that the majority of the people are bereft of adequate social support from government-based agencies. As the central state's infrastructural capacity has proven nearly paralyzed and the government has relied largely on a handful of internationally funded programs, economic development plans have not been effectively implemented. Food security in the capital city, Bissau, is consequently often imperiled, while population dislocations have left many rural communities without essential labor forces.[36] Meanwhile, adding to the country's political and economic malaise has been the rise of a new security threat.

Rising Insecurity

Based largely on intelligence assessments gathered by international agencies, there is growing evidence of a steady influx of narcotrafficking (involving cocaine and other illegal narcotics) through Guinea-Bissau from South America to Europe.[37] It is estimated that drug flows through Guinea-Bissau represent a larger dollar amount than the country's GDP and that the national budget is roughly equal to the wholesale value of 2.5 tons of cocaine.[38] The transnational character of this operation as well as the continuing fragility of the state in Guinea-Bissau have become issues of grave international concern. Specifically, it is feared that narcotraffickers (who seem to operate with considerable impunity) might be linked to other illicit activities, such as the trafficking of people or small arms. In addition, some believe that the flow of drug money has already penetrated various levels of government and society, seriously challenging the rule of law, fostering corruption, and financing other illegal activities.[39] Concern over the potential consequences of narcotrafficking has resulted in a revival of international interest in and support for Guinea-Bissau. Following a formal request by the government of Guinea-Bissau in July 2007, the UN Security Council referred the country to the newly established Peacebuilding Commission with a special request that the Commission provide the Council with advice on (1) the government's capacity to effectively oversee and manage national finances as well as to undertake comprehensive public sector reform, including effective anticorruption measures; (2) action by the national government and the international community to develop effective, accountable, and sustainable security systems as well as to strengthen the independence of the judiciary and the rule of law, taking into account in particular the dangers posed by drug trafficking and organized crime; and (3) continuing improvements in democratic accountability.[40] However, by mid-2009, little visible progress in curtailing the spread of narcotics-related corruption had been made; in fact, some observers theorize that the March 2009 assassination of President Vieira may have reflected a reaction by narcotraffickers within the government itself against the late president's anti-drug-trade and anti-corruption efforts.[41]

Understanding Interlocking Legacies

Guinea-Bissau's low level of economic development, high level of political instability, and rising insecurity are in large part a product of its cultural and colonial legacies, which set in motion certain ethnic tensions and minimized the extent to which the country's extensive natural resources would be effectively exploited. These policy legacies have been exacerbated by a series of postcolonial institutional and policy choices that are addressed in the next section.

Natural Resources

As previously noted, Guinea-Bissau is an agrarian society. Peasant farming remains the principal economic activity and the main source of food for some four-fifths of the population.[42] Rice is the principal food crop as well as a key cash crop, produced mostly through wet-rice farming on riparian fields in the marshy south of the country. Since the early 1990s, more profitable cashew nuts have gradually replaced rice cultivation in parts of the countryside, including the rice-producing south. By the end of the 1990s, cashews had become the country's principal cash crop, and Guinea-Bissau was ranked sixth in the world in cashew production.[43]

Peasants grow a variety of additional agronomic crops for both sale and subsistence, including groundnuts, maize, cassava, beans, corn, and vegetables. Cashew nuts account for 90 percent of exports, with shrimp, groundnuts, and palm kernels making up most of the rest.[44] Peasant farmers are adept at operating between the capitalist market in cash crops and the bartering-oriented world of informal trade and self-reliant production processes. The country receives adequate, if declining, levels of rainfall for crop and livestock production. Palm tree products such as palm oil and palm kernels are cultivated and used for subsistence, local market sales, and exports.[45] The country's many rivers and coasts provide ample supplies of fish and shellfish. Tropical fruits found wild in the forest, such as bananas, plantains, papayas, and mangoes, grow in large numbers seasonally and are harvested for subsistence use, but are generally not grown or harvested for sale or export.

Guinea-Bissau also has substantial deposits of phosphate and bauxite, but these minerals are buried deeply inland and are therefore considered too expensive to profitably export. The discovery of small offshore oil deposits led the government to sign exploration pacts with several oil companies; however, it is not yet clear how much is actually retrievable and, in any case, it will take several years before this resource can be exploited. Overall, Guinea-Bissau's natural resources remain as yet underexploited and could potentially contribute significantly to the country's economic development. Guinea-Bissau's social, colonial, and political history, on the other hand, has created long-lasting development challenges.

Cultural and Colonial Legacies

Portugal's principal colonial legacies included a poorly staffed state government, bureaucratic fragility and a tendency toward corruption at the lower levels, inadequate policy implementation, and exploitation of peasants—especially those who lived in decentralized societies and practiced animism. In Guinea-Bissau as in their other African colonies, the Portuguese tended to favor those who lived in hierarchical societies, because they had easily identifiable chiefs to collaborate with; many of those societies were Muslim (as is 37 percent of the population in Guinea-Bissau today). Guinea-Bissau's animist (especially Balanta) majority and some of the poorer Muslim peasants were engaged in forced labor. The animists' frequent rebellions were suppressed, although peasant rebels were often able to elude colonial soldiers.

Many of these peasants, particularly the Balanta, joined the fighters in the national liberation struggle (1962–1974), during which an anticolonial stance increasingly united all of Guinea-Bissau's ethnic and religious groups and helped provide the social glue required for nation-state formation.[46] Moreover, intermarriage and interethnic trade helped assure that social conflicts at the interpersonal and community levels did not take the form of ethnic violence. Guinea-Bissauans—especially in rural areas—are highly conscious of the fact that their violent struggle was a key factor in the departure of the Portuguese colonialists. This has contributed to the belief that there is no need to defer to any centralized political authority that lacks popular legitimacy.

Political Mobilization and Ethnic Politics

With a population of 1.4 million, Guinea-Bissau is ethnically quite diverse, consisting of the following main groups: Balanta (30 percent), Fulbe (20 percent), Manjaco (14 percent), Mandinga (13 percent), and Pepel (7 percent), as well as Beafada, Brames, Bijago, Nalu, Djola, and several other small groups.[47] However, ethnic antagonisms are not deeply rooted in the social history of Guinea-Bissau. Thus, ethnic imbalances do not play a decisive role in the country's security problems. Coups d'état tend to reflect constantly shifting factional and political cleavages rather than ethnic antagonisms. However, in the 1980s–1990s, ethnic tensions occasionally served as contributing factors toward intra-army mobilization for coups. Under Luiz Cabral's rule as the first president, Cape Verdeans tended to predominate among the educated elite and to hold key positions in the ruling party and the state, a fact that was resented by many Guinea-Bissauans.[48]

During his 1980–1998 reign, President Vieira brought his own ethnic group, the Pepel, representing about 5 percent of the population, to bureaucratic and ministerial high posts, along with several allied small groups such as the Banhun.[49] He also appointed Pepel members to commanding posts in the armed forces and filled his newly created special security force largely with Pepel soldiers. In contrast, as previously noted, leading members of the Balanta—the country's largest ethnic group, with about 30 percent of the populace—often did not receive high-level government appointments. This created army unrest and political instability, possibly contributing to coup attempts in the 1980s.

Following the 1994 elections, rising levels of oppression under Vieira seriously hurt his regime's popularity. In response, the president proceeded to cobble together a coalition of Islamic groups—the Fulbe, Mandinka, and Biaffada—although he did rely on his own Pepel group to shore up his rule. This coalition kept his regime afloat until the 1998–1999 multiethnic rebellion removed him from power.[50]

The next president, Kumba Yala, a Balanta intellectual, had woven together an interethnic coalition to win the 2000 elections, although he subsequently ruled in a way that marginalized many of his initial supporters. His 2003 ouster was orchestrated by military men who belonged to the same Balanta ethnic group, including the coup leader, chief of staff Verissimo Seabra. The next coup d'état, in 2004, was also led by a Balanta general, Na Wai.[51] Thus, interethnic tensions have not been a primary cause of military violence.[52] Most of the intra-army tensions and coup efforts have reflected political and fiscal demands or factional disputes rather than ethnic ones, and interethnic ties continue to be forged among officers and among politicians in the political arena.

Shifting Development Strategies

In the postcolonial period, Guinea-Bissau has been marked by a series of diverse development strategies. The country started out in 1974 with a socialist economic policy framework. In the late 1970s through the mid-1980s, expectations for economic growth were dashed, as the government's state-based policies proved unworkable in the context of the highly fragile state bureaucracy bequeathed by the Portuguese. Both efforts to promote industrial enterprises in the capital city of Bissau and plans to create a profitable rural agronomic economy went awry. Purchase prices offered to rice producers were inadequate. Government-run stores, intended to provide peasants with a fair exchange of finished goods for cash crops, did not offer products that were sufficiently valuable to make it worthwhile for peasants to sell their crops.[53] The road and transport system made large-scale crop delivery unrealistic, and the political elite did not sufficiently focus on the actual implementation of rural-urban infrastructural and economic development plans.[54]

In the face of economic decay, President Vieira began to work with the IMF and the World Bank in the mid-1980s on economic reforms. Structural adjustment, combined with privatization, had several effects. First, the new policy provoked a gradual shift in many peasants' choice of cash crop—from rice to cashew nuts.[55] Out-migration and the growing preference for cashew production led to a decline in the availability of rice for Guinea-Bissauan consumers. The government's inability to deal with this growing deficit eventually resulted in the country's increased dependency on external rice aid.[56] Second, privatization generated higher profits for a small number of traders and agricultural producers (successful cashew growers) and boosted the fledgling private sector. Third, the switch from rice to cashew nuts in some parts of the countryside provoked the individualization of land tenure patterns and presented new challenges. Whereas wet-rice cultivation reinforced communal labor practices and encouraged cooperative social institutions, cashew growing led to single-household management of land-tenure systems. Cashew cultivation required only individualized production, exacerbating radical declines in the efficiency and social cooperation of the production process. This, in turn, strained the ability of rural communities to care for their less fortunate members and led to out-migration.[57]

Fourth, structural adjustment facilitated the debureaucratization of the national government. In eliminating 5,000 of about 26,000 government posts, the government enjoyed a better overall expenditure account. However, the country remained mired in debt due to overspending in other sectors.[58] Fiscal unaccountability and outright corruption remained major problems despite repeated efforts by the international community at oversight reforms.[59] One final unintended impact of the structural adjustment reforms was that they deepened and intensified the culture of dependency on subcontracted ministerial assignments to international development agencies in areas such as health, agriculture, rural development, and education.[60]

By early 2000, the government had come to rely heavily on international assistance to address the country's most severe social problems. In September 2000, the post–civil war government, in collaboration with the armed forces, Parliament, and civil society representatives, produced a national poverty reduction strategy paper (PRSP) with the assistance of the World Bank and the IMF.[61] The Ministry of Social Solidarity, Reinsertion of Combatants, and Fight Against Poverty was created to support the mission of poverty reduction.

The goals established in the PRSP included reducing poverty by one-third by 2015 and by 100 percent by 2050, based on an uninterrupted national GDP annual growth rate of 5 percent. The government aimed to implement fiscal transparency, reduce the budget deficit, improve bank oversight, liquidate additional public enterprises, increase the retention rate of schoolchildren, and expand water provision services.[62] While these development goals may have been worthy, it was by no means clear how the government would develop the bureaucratic and financial capacity to implement them, as production levels in fact declined in 2002 and 2003 and electric power was unreliable.[63] At the time of this writing, there is no evidence of appreciable progress on the ground toward carrying out the poverty reduction measures due to the incapacity of governmental institutions to implement them. Indeed, in applying to be placed on the agenda of the UN Peacebuilding Commission, the government acknowledged its inability to meet its targets without significant additional external support.

Institutional Developments

State Institutions

Guinea-Bissau has a presidential-parliamentary system in which the separately elected president has the responsibility to manage the government and establish the country's overall political direction, while the National Popular Assembly makes most policy-related decisions—although in practice, the president tends to predominate in macropolicy domains. Parliamentary elections were held in November 1994 and December 1999. The Assembly was dissolved by President Yala in 2003 and restored through a third set of parliamentary elections held in March 2004. Those election results gave a plurality to the erstwhile ruling PAIGC.[64] However, following Vieira's 2005 reelection to the presidency, fourteen members of Parliament bolted from the PAIGC to help form a new coalition of parties, the Forum of Convergence for Development (FCD). The FCD, whose largest party is the PRS, claimed a new ruling coalition of fifty-three seats that ensured the president's policymaking capacity and threatened to undercut the capacity of opposition parties such as the PAIGC to hinder presidential initiatives.[65] Subsequent interparty squabbling was temporarily eased by a national stability pact intended to last ten years as well as by a government stability agreement signed in 2007. However, these pacts ultimately failed to overcome the enduring distrust and competition among the country's political elites.

From 1994 to 2004, instead of leading to a deeper phase of democratization, each election actually resulted in greater presidential efforts toward a monopolization of political power and the repression of opponents. Open destructive conflict took place after each of three national elections: the 1998–1999 war following the 1994 election, the increase in presidential repression subsequent to the 1999 election, and the September 2004 coup that followed the March 2004 elections. These events do not necessarily suggest a causal relationship between elections and conflict. Rather, the destructive conflicts that emerge during elections reflect antagonisms generated by autocratic rule or by unrelated factional disputes that would probably have occurred regardless of the incidence of elections.

The National Assembly includes a number of opposition political parties. They do not hesitate to speak out against government policy during parliamentary debate and many (though not all) of these civilian political elites appear prepared to work together to iron out policy differences.[66] After Vieira's 2005 reelection, the PRS, led by former President Yala, decided to join Vieira's government, with six PRS officials being assigned ministerial portfolios.[67] This was the closest any Guinea-Bissau government has come to power sharing. The parliamentary opposition led by the PAIGC remains persistently critical of the government, but its ability to thwart the president proved limited, as Vieira held a loyalist majority, however slim, in the National Assembly after November 2005.[68] This could lead to the marginalization of the National Assembly, as was the case during the earlier presidencies of Vieira (1980–1998) and Yala (2000–2003).

The national Supreme Court has not been able to establish itself as an effective counterweight to the Office of the President. In 2001, President Yala removed half its members, including its president. More recently, the court appeared to gain momentum. In 2004, a new Supreme Court president, Maria do Céu Silva Monteiro, was elected by seven prominent justices.[69] In August 2005, the Monteiro-led Supreme Court played a key role in validating the results of the second round of the presidential election.[70] Yet before that, in May 2005, it had approved the presidential candidacies of Vieira and Yala—despite the fact that both had signed political charters making them ineligible to run for political office until 2008. One analyst interpreted the court's decision as a combination of a genuine interest in political stability and the *fear factor*, whereby judges have traditionally toed the presidential line so as to avoid possible career termination.[71] The court may also have been concerned about instability in the event of a ban on either candidate.[72] The Supreme Court's willingness to subordinate the rule of law to political considerations again seemed apparent in January 2006, when it upheld Vieira's appointment of a loyalist as prime minister, even though the largest party in Parliament, the opposition PAIGC, insisted that it had the right to nominate the prime minister. The Constitution confusingly establishes that Parliament can nominate the prime minister but also that the president can overrule the nomination. The court's decision to uphold President Vieira's appointment may have been inspired by the practical need to avoid political stalemate, but PAIGC supporters concluded that the Supreme Court was simply unwilling to defy the president.[73]

Public Service and Corruption

Although Guinea-Bissau has well-trained policymakers, public services suffer from poor implementation due to the country's inadequate infrastructure and communications and transport systems as well as to insufficient funds for the purchase of fuel for government vehicles. These problems are further exacerbated by intragovernmental political rivalries and factionalism.[74]

The UN and other international actors put into place programs to facilitate administrative management, accountability, and probity during the 1990s and early 2000s. Most of these oversight efforts were abandoned during the 2000–2003 reign of President Yala. A nearly empty government treasury from 1999 to 2004 left state ministries unable to pay the salaries of key service workers. From 2001 to 2004, primary and secondary schoolteachers and health care staffs repeatedly went on strike to protest the nonpayment of their salaries over the course of several months.[75] As previously noted, Guinea-Bissau, which for much of the twentieth century was a rice exporter, has been dependent on external aid to feed its urban populace since the 1990s—a dramatic sign of the extent to which government institutions have proved unable to effectively grapple with the country's basic needs.[76] The country's chronic budget deficit has not only contributed to the weakening of state capacities but also established a context of fiscal instability that has been favorable to the influx of drug money.

Adding to the problems of public service efficiency has been the growth of corruption at the highest levels of government. In November 2001, a review of national accounts overseen by the Supreme Court found US$16 million to be missing and unaccounted for.[77] Expectations of bribes for job placements in government units and the disappearance of portions of ministerial budgets appear to be increasingly common.

In 2004, the national government began to make noteworthy improvements in fiscal management and oversight.[78] With support from the IMF and UNDP, government ministries demonstrated marked increases in the degree of fiscal rigor and accountability.[79] As a result, during the first half of 2005, there was a 41 percent increase in revenues, while government expenditures were kept to manageable levels.[80] To combat corruption, it was decided that public employees would be required to collect their wages in person at the national bank.[81] These were impressive accomplishments, but the government still had considerable difficulty in meeting its payroll in the second half of 2005 due to lower-than-expected revenues from the annual cashew harvest. It remains to be seen whether corruption can be reduced at the middle and lower levels of the bureaucracy.[82]

The Role of Civil Society

Guinea-Bissau's civil society started to mobilize politically during the first stages of multiparty democratization in the early 1990s, but it often faced governmental repression. Yet the government has also tolerated a surprisingly wide range of political behavior. Excepting criticisms of the president, political grievances are often aired without resulting in political persecution. However, governmental tolerance is arbitrary and can change quickly, depending on the extent of the opposition to the regime in power. Since April 2004, concurrent with activities related to the parliamentary elections, civil society groups have gradually become more active. In December 2004, for example, as previously noted, teachers and health care employees held a week-long strike to protest wage arrears.[83]

Citizens have been increasingly involved in supporting electoral processes. In recent years, the National Electoral Commission, staffed predominantly by civil society representatives, has been generally successful in assuring free and fair voting procedures. In 2005, the Citizens' Goodwill Task Force, consisting of small community-level groups, played a noteworthy role in fostering a peaceful electoral campaign. The task force mobilized so-called peace brigades to encourage people at voting places to focus on campaign issues rather than on the personalities of the candidates, with a view toward reducing potential political tensions.[84]

Civil society is mostly represented by trade unions, teachers, the media, local nongovernmental organizations (NGOs), opposition political parties, and hundreds of grassroots mini-groups. Private media began to operate in the mid-1990s but are constrained by political pressure and lack of funding.[85] That said, the urban intellectual elite has consistently given voice to alternative views.

In some rural areas, Islamic mosques represent civil society.[86] In others, multiethnic spiritual societies based on indigenous religious practices are a major source of institutional stability and social order.[87] In a number of rural districts, locally chosen popular kingships have been revived, and they function as key sources of social stability. Meanwhile, in urban areas such as Bissau and in the larger provincial towns such as Bafata, Bissora, and Catio, the Catholic Church is a major actor. The Bishop of Bissau has been highly supportive of democratic reform.

Although not formally organized, women also contribute to civil society. Guinea-Bissauan women often publicly encourage politicians to pursue the peaceful resolution of conflicts. Because they contribute to society's peaceful interethnic traditions of accommodation and negotiation, women constitute an important source of pressure on Guinea-Bissau's civil society.[88] The fact that the new head of the Supreme Court, Maria do Céu Silva Monteiro, is female may provide a boost to women's activism in Guinea-Bissauan society.

NGOs play a minor but growing role in politics. NGOs began to proliferate in the 1990s to carry out specific economic development projects (such as dam building and providing technical support to rice farmers) in the wake of the government's move toward privatization to reflect structural adjustment priorities. One particularly politically active NGO is the Legal Aid Center, which aggressively promotes human rights, individual liberties, free speech, free and open media, and other basic political and social freedoms. Although the Legal Aid Center has been periodically harassed by the government, it has persisted and has brought international attention to government repression.[89] Despite a diverse and vigorous panoply of forms of civil society in both rural and urban areas, the monopoly of political power remains strongly in the hands of elected autocrats and army generals.[90]

The Role of External Actors

As noted, Guinea-Bissau's main challenges are domestic. However, its neighbors, along with regional actors and international organizations, all play an important role in Guinea-Bissau's internal political and economic affairs. Additionally, in the 2000s, Guinea-Bissau has become financially dependent on external donors for essential public expenses. Because the central state lacks infrastructural capacity and national income depends on fluctuating revenues from agricultural crops, the government has been relying heavily on international aid, which represented about half of the gross national product (GNP) in 2004.[91] This section examines the contributions of external actors to Guinea-Bissau's peace and development prospects.

Immediate Neighbors

Guinea-Bissau is bordered by Senegal to the north and by the Republic of Guinea (also known as Guinea-Conakry) to the east and south. Neither of these countries can be considered a serious threat to Guinea-Bissau. Nonetheless, since the mid-1980s, tensions have arisen periodically between Senegal and Guinea-Bissau, in part reflecting disputes over access to a shared seabed potentially containing deposits of oil.

Additionally, since the 1990s, the Senegalese region of Casamance on the southern border of Guinea-Bissau (of which it was a part until 1886) has been embroiled in a secessionist war. In the mid-1990s, the Senegalese government became concerned that Guinea-Bissau's armed forces might be providing weapons and other support to the Casamancian rebels.[92] President Vieira supported Senegal's effort to contain the rebels by investigating possible instances of illegal gunrunning within the Guinea-Bissauan army. In doing so, Vieira accused a number of purportedly innocent soldiers and antagonized a number of military personnel.[93] Vieira's direct intervention in military affairs represents one factor behind the army's 1998–1999 revolt. In return for Vieira's efforts to curtail illicit army support to the Casamancians, Senegal sent 3,000–4,000 troops to Bissau and several provincial towns to help Vieira defend his regime against the rebel uprising. However, rebel army fighters killed hundreds of Senegalese soldiers and the remainder fled back across the border. This rebel success enabled the army to oust Vieira from the presidency.[94] Subsequent regimes have successfully restored peaceful relations with Senegal, and military support from Guinea-Bissau to the Casamancian rebels appears to have been brought to a halt.[95]

Subsequently, President Abdoulaye Wade of Senegal has played a particularly noteworthy role in encouraging domestic reconciliation within Guinea-Bissau. For example, President Wade invited the three leading Guinea-Bissauan presidential candidates to Dakar in mid-2005 just as former President Yala was threatening to destabilize Bissau due to his discontent with the results of the first electoral round. After meeting with President Wade, Yala announced his acceptance of the results.[96]

Regional Actors

The regional institution with which Guinea-Bissau has the most significant relations is the Economic Community of West African States (ECOWAS). In 1998 and 1999, ECOWAS, through its military wing, the Economic Community of West African States Monitoring Group (ECOMOG), briefly and ineffectually tried to intervene in the Guinea-Bissauan civil war.[97] The central problem was that ECOMOG sided with Vieira, which lessened its legitimacy in the eyes of the rebel army.[98] Another problem was inadequate cooperation by ECOWAS with the Comunidades dos Países de Língua Portuguesa (CPLP; Community of Portuguese-speaking Countries). Eventually, the CPLP was more successful in crafting a peace pact because it was viewed as politically neutral.[99]

During Yala's rule (2000–2003), ECOWAS repeatedly sent officials, including its respected Council of Elders, to Guinea-Bissau in an effort to curtail Yala's abuses, but its efforts were to no avail.[100] Thereafter, ECOWAS learned from its mistakes and, from 2003 to 2005, used multiple diplomatic means to engage Guinea-Bissau. ECOWAS leaders (including President Olusegun Obasanjo of Nigeria and President Wade of Senegal) displayed diplomatic skill, political neutrality, and willingness to cooperate with other international actors such as the UN Peacebuilding Support Office in Guinea-Bissau (UNOGBIS) and the CPLP.[101] For example, in September 2003, an ECOWAS delegation produced a commitment to civilianize the new Guinea-Bissauan government within forty-eight hours of General Seabra's coup. After the coup d'état of October 2004, ECOWAS provided US$500,000 for the payment of army salary arrears, and both ECOWAS and the CPLP sent delegations to Bissau to encourage a return to the process of democratization.[102] After the 2005 elections, political pressure from ECOWAS helped calm the political waters set roiling by the initial refusal of PAIGC leaders to cooperate with reelected President Vieira.[103] ECOWAS now has permanent offices in Guinea-Bissau and has continued to promote political stability and democratization, both in collaboration with UNOGBIS and independently, with varying degrees of success.[104]

International Mediation Efforts

Since 1999, the UN Security Council has sent representatives to Guinea-Bissau in order to encourage the peaceful resolution of internal disputes, advance democracy, improve the efficiency of governmental institutions, and promote political stability. Organized into UNOGBIS, these representatives have worked closely with government officials and civil society leaders as well as other international actors in Guinea-Bissau. These include Portugal and France, international financial institutions such as the World Bank and the IMF, the European Union (EU), the CPLP, the African Union (AU), ECOWAS, and various UN agencies and specialized agencies, such as the UNDP and UNICEF (UN Children's Fund).[105] An important goal of UNOGBIS has been to help coordinate and more effectively target democratization programs.[106] UNOGBIS also works to encourage "national reconciliation, the rule of law, respect for human rights, constitutional normality," the voluntary collection of arms from civilians, and peace with Guinea-Bissau's neighbors.[107]

During Yala's presidency from 2000 to 2003, UNOGBIS held regular discussions with a broad spectrum of government officials and civil society representatives on a wide range of issues related to good governance. However, it was not until after the 2003 coup that UNOGBIS included armed forces officers in these discussions—a mistake that was internally acknowledged and rectified.[108] Since the military's concerns were and are intimately linked to political stability, they merit special attention. For example, UNOGBIS has strongly supported both a small-arms collection program and the effort to demobilize and reintegrate excess army personnel that was begun in 2000 under President Yala. Although little progress has been made with respect to small-arms collection, as of 2005 11,445 soldiers had applied for demobilization and reintegration funding, and 7,186 had received it.[109] Army pay is another policy issue with immediate political implications. For example, in October 2004, in order to facilitate the government's allocation of army back pay, the UN and ECOWAS accelerated the provision of funds to the Bank of Guinea-Bissau.[110] Immediate full payment of the soldiers' salaries probably helped to avoid yet another round of intramilitary fighting.

Perhaps the single most important contribution UNOGBIS has made to peacebuilding was its effort to marshal and coordinate international support for Guinea-Bissau's elections in 2004 and 2005. The Union Economique et Monétaire Ouest Africaine (UEMOA; Economic and Monetary Union of West Africa) provided US$2.7 million to help fund parliamentary elections in 2003,[111] and the EU provided 100 electoral observers as well as US$11 million for presidential elections in 2005.[112] The collaboration between UNOGBIS and the UNDP was especially effective in providing technical electoral support and helped to produce relatively efficient balloting processes and fairly contested elections.[113]

Apart from UNOGBIS, in 2002, the UN Economic and Social Council (ECOSOC) established the Ad Hoc Advisory Group on Guinea-Bissau with the aim of fostering partnerships between the national government and international stakeholders. The group has organized meetings between Guinea-Bissauan authorities and potential donors to encourage domestic peace, political stability, and the rule of law as well as to channel development aid and emergency economic funding.[114] Although some of the activities overlapped with those of UNOGBIS, the latter has carved out a distinctive role in capacity building, such as providing technical support for elections and training for bureaucrats.[115] Additionally, while acknowledging the "extreme sensitivity" of the topic,[116] both UNOGBIS and the Ad Hoc Advisory Group have supported efforts toward "reform of the security sector"[117] and a "professionalization of the army," including both a review of "career structures" and "a reformulation of the role of the armed forces."[118] However, these latter efforts have achieved at best modest success in the wake of repeated coup d'état efforts through the first decade of the 2000s.

International Financial Institutions (IFIs)

From 1984 to 1998, the World Bank and the IMF provided loans to Guinea-Bissau while pressing for privatization and economic structural adjustments. As previously noted, the privatization reforms did generate income growth from cashew production, but they were inadequate to offset the national deficit and the growing foreign debt. After the economically devastating war in 1998 and 1999, the amount of aid provided by the World Bank and the IMF increased significantly, despite the latter's suspension of funding during the 2000–2003 Yala regime.

Since 2000, government revenue has been inadequate to cover such basic public expenses as salaries for teachers, clerks, and armed forces. In 2003, the World Bank provided a US$2.5 million loan to pay teachers' salaries, which were nearly one year overdue.[119] Furthermore, the World Bank and the IMF provided 100 percent of Guinea-Bissau's debt relief in 2002, 2003, and 2004.[120] Although Guinea-Bissau is one of thirty-eight countries eligible for debt relief by the G8, it did not qualify for immediate relief in June 2005 due to its incomplete control over fiscal management.[121]

In January 2004, the World Bank provided US$13 million in emergency aid to Guinea-Bissau to keep afloat the central bank, the Banco Internacional da Guiné-Bissau, and to pay for property damage incurred during the civil war.[122] The year after, the World Bank approved disbursements totaling US$309 million, divided among nine projects: support for basic education; national health development; private sector rehabilitation; energy and mining; industry; transportation; law, justice, and public administration; water and sanitation; and support for the global mitigation of HIV/AIDS.[123] Ten percent of Guinea-Bissau's population is infected with HIV/AIDS. In 2004, the World Bank allocated US$7 million for the distribution of antiretroviral drugs.[124]

International Donors

Throughout the 1980s and 1990s, there was little coherence in donors' strategies for financing development programs in Guinea-Bissau. Only after the country had fallen into deep financial crisis due to the 1998–1999 war did a shared sense of postconflict emergency inspire international agencies and bilateral donors to improve the coordination of their aid programs through fora and meetings—including those organized by UNOGBIS and the Ad Hoc Advisory Group.[125] International aid programs appropriately target the most needy sectors: food supply, health care, and economic development. Although these programs have not generated any noteworthy economic growth, they have helped to keep the country from economic and institutional collapse.

The UNDP proceeded to set up an Emergency Economic Management Fund (EEMF) that made it possible to resume salary payments to approximately 11,000 civil servants from twenty-four government ministries and other state organs. At the end of 2003, the EEMF covered the US$18.3 million budget deficit, paying the salaries of teachers, health workers, and employees of the state-owned water and electric company. The money was also used for technical assistance to improve financial management within the government and to reform the civil service.[126] In addition to covering salaries, the EEMF funded some basic expenses of government ministries and key social services. For example, it gave US$1 million to the Ministry of Education to print textbooks.[127] The principal contributors to the EEMF were the World Bank and the IMF, the African Development Bank, and the UNDP, as well as bilateral donors such as the Netherlands (providing US$2 million), Sweden (nearly US$1 million), France (US$620,000), Portugal (US$500,000), and Brazil (US$50,000).[128] In 2005, the EU provided an additional US$5.9 million toward payments of civil service salaries.[129]

International aid is not only paying some public salaries and financing governance reform but also supporting special programs such as demining, vaccination, and food relief. Canada, Germany, the Netherlands, the EU, the UK, and the United States together provided the funds to demine 81,930 square miles, removing more than 26,000 unexploded ordnance left over from the 1998–1999 civil war.[130] UNICEF provided US$23 million to cover a range of social programs, including those focused on child vaccination, primary education (not least among girls), and nutritional health.[131] The vaccination programs appear to have been very effective in limiting the spread of tropical diseases, despite a 2005 cholera epidemic that provoked interventions by the World Health Organization (WHO), UNICEF, and the World Food Programme. The WHO and UNICEF also managed a nationwide polio immunization campaign in November 2005.[132]

As already mentioned, given the decline in rice production and distribution in Guinea-Bissau, foreign aid has been necessary to forestall serious food shortages in the 2000s. For example, the WFP provided food aid to about 100,000 Guinea-Bissauans in 2003.[133] While there has been suspicion that some WFP rice wound up in the hands of government officials, corruption appears to have declined (at least at the highest levels of the government) in the wake of the fiscal reforms of 2004 and 2005.

Finally, with the cooperation of the Food and Agriculture Organization (FAO) and UNICEF, the UNDP has sponsored and managed rural income-generating programs and infrastructure rehabilitation.[134] In 2006 it initiated a US$5 million development program in the Gabu region with the aim of strengthening the administrative capacity of local development committees.[135] This program appears promising especially because the decisionmaking process is intended to be decentralized across local communities.

Examining the Role of External Actors

As we have demonstrated, international actors have been intensely involved in Guinea-Bissau's domestic affairs. Through the activities of UNOGBIS and ECOSOC's Ad Hoc Advisory Group, considerable attention has been given to peacebuilding activities, including the promotion of political tolerance and democracy. Despite repeated setbacks, political progress has included the organization of free and fair parliamentary elections in 2004 and presidential elections in 2005. To be sure, domestic actors were primarily responsible for this progress, but it should be acknowledged that UNOGBIS and the Ad Hoc Advisory Group assured adequate international aid to carry out the elections, persistently urged a return to democracy after the coups of 2003 and 2004, and worked behind the scenes to help the government avoid serious violence following the 2005 presidential election.[136] Mediation by UNOGBIS during military rule in 2004 helped to bring together members of civil society, political parties, and government officials to discuss key policy issues.[137] Additionally, UNOGBIS and the Ad Hoc Advisory Group facilitated the disbursements of multimillion-dollar aid packages from international institutions and bilateral donors to strengthen governmental agencies.

Given Guinea-Bissau's alternation between democratic and military rule from 1994 to 2009, an outside observer could reasonably conclude that the performance of UNOGBIS and the Ad Hoc Advisory Group is mixed. However, evaluating the impact of external actors is a complex task. It would be unfair to criticize them for failing to prevent coups. External actors cannot quickly reverse internal political dynamics rooted in historic divisions, although they can exacerbate such divisions if their intervention strengthens certain negative forces in the country. It does not appear that UNOGBIS or the Advisory Group have done the latter, as they have sought to facilitate intergroup accommodation. In regard to fiscal contributions on the part of a broader range of external actors (the World Bank, IMF, EU, and AU, as well as Portugal, France, and Sweden), some interventions appear to be effectively targeted and highly popular, including food, health, and educational programs; cash support for the central bank; postwar reconstruction; national debt coverage; and payment of civil servants' salaries.

The massive financial involvement of these donors raises an important question. Given their role in supporting primary state functions—namely providing needed social services that the government is unable to provide and enabling certain government agencies to function—to what extent are international donors substituting for the government? Have they collectively become a protostate? External intervention is clearly useful in carrying out functions that the government cannot perform; on the other hand, the international community increasingly risks being perceived as a de facto neocolonial—and therefore illegitimate—power in the eyes of Guinea-Bissauans. In truth, thus far it appears—however paradoxically—that state fragility (as reflected in the lack of domestic institutional capacity) severely limits the impact of constructive international interventions. Furthermore, despite the expanding role of international actors, national leaders remain in control of the country's basic policy directions; thus, to describe the government as a neocolonial protostate at this point would be to project an overblown image.

Meanwhile, the emergence of a transnational threat such as narcotrafficking highlights the relative vulnerability of Guinea-Bissau and suggests strong links among political instability, economic vulnerability, and state fragility. In this regard, the lack of domestically generated state revenues has contributed to an institutional context in which the fragile state is unable to curtail the growth of illegal transnational activities.

Serial Policy Failures

As described above, Guinea-Bissau's political order has been characterized by the periodic centralization of presidential power and repression followed by rising levels of political conflict, economic backsliding, rescue efforts by the international community, and then coups d'état. These coups have, in turn, been followed by a recentralization of presidential power, developmental crises, more coups—and the cycle has continued. Meanwhile, the emergence of narcotrafficking and transnational crime has further complicated the country's chronic political problems.

Guinea-Bissau's predicament reflects the difficulty of reversing mutually reinforcing and deep-rooted security and development challenges. However, it is difficult to single out specific policy decisions to blame for the country's backsliding. For example, it would be deceptive to suggest that democratization in the early 1990s contributed to the civil war of 1998 or that elections had a direct impact on economic growth or the national standard of living. Similarly, no particular economic policy can be associated with the country's chronic political crises. Even though economic factors have contributed to the army's grievances, repeated coups d'état have reflected internal factionalism rooted in political dynamics rather than specific policy choices.

Over time, three different development strategies have been pursued—albeit with little success. The first, socialism (1974–1984), was domestically generated and led to economic stagnation. The second, privatization and structural adjustment (1984–1998), was largely supported by international agencies. Privatization caused generalized economic deterioration and severe social dislocation, with benefits accruing to only a very small proportion of farmers and traders. The overreliance on cashew crops led to food scarcity, out-migrations, and cash outflows. Third, since the war of 1998 and 1999, the macroeconomic policy framework can best be described as oriented toward economic survivalism, with the political elite increasingly relying on the international community to provide basic services and emergency funding in ever-larger and more extensive policy domains. Meanwhile, reforms associated with structural adjustment such as bureaucratic downsizing and fiscal and budgetary accountability have accentuated insecurity in the military and contributed, at least indirectly, to the intensification of political factionalism. Thus, all three approaches have failed to foster noteworthy progress toward either development or security.

Meanwhile, on the political front, there is no evidence that instances of democratization, such as the multiparty elections of 1994, 1999, 2004, and 2005, defused internal conflict in ways conducive to sustaining democratic processes. On the contrary, each period of democratic opportunity was accompanied or followed by political or social instability. Overall, elections have had a mixed impact on security. On the one hand, they have provided an inclusive participatory means for restoring political order. On the other hand, they have enabled leaders to hide an increase in governmental repression behind the shield of democratic legitimacy. To date, most elected presidents in Guinea-Bissau have not shown significant restraint from ruling as virtual dictators. In turn, neither Parliament nor the Supreme Court has been able to serve as an effective check on their power.

Thus, on the whole, broad policy strategies, whether ideologically or practically motivated (by, say, proponents of socialism, privatization, or poverty reduction), have failed to generate noteworthy change. Instead, the most effective policies have involved pragmatic measures (such as payment of salary arrears) or micro development aid to meet basic needs. Through such policies, the international community has aided the government's effort to prevent massive social decay and perhaps nation-state collapse.

In light of Guinea-Bissau's record to date, the most likely development scenario over the next three to five years is a continuation of bare-bones survivalism, accompanied by economic inefficiency. The most likely security pattern involves periods of election-based democratic reform followed by coup attempts from different sections of the military. As we have discussed, the failure to assure the armed forces of regular income, the perception on their part that sitting presidents have interfered in army officer appointments, and political maneuvering among intra-army factions have all contributed to coup efforts. The particular combination of incentives for staging a coup shifts from moment to moment and is extremely difficult to predict. Since transnational threats like narcotrafficking are of relatively recent origin and have already attracted strong international attention, their long-term impact on Guinea-Bissau's security is difficult to estimate. However, the country's fragile institutional framework is clearly at further risk, especially considering the danger that the narcotics trade poses for bureaucratic corruption and deeper administrative dysfunction.

Policy Implications

In this chapter, I have sought to demonstrate the growing severity of Guinea-Bissau's security and development challenges and to draw attention to the primacy of domestic political factors in the perpetuation of these problems. Guinea-Bissau is at an advantage insofar as its social and political divisions are relatively horizontal. The central political problem is factionalism among similarly resourced groups. As a result, conflict resolution should be more realizable than it is in countries marked by more vertical, class-based divisions or deep ethnic inequalities. Strategies to mitigate intra-elite cleavages are essential for peacebuilding as well as development.

However, in this chapter I have also underlined the potentially positive role that external actors can play in supporting Guinea-Bissau with regard to governance and development. In that light, I make the following recommendations, which direct international actors to four key areas: (1) political and diplomatic efforts; (2) macrolevel policy and budget support; (3) the strengthening of state capacities, especially in order to combat drug trafficking and organized crime; and (4) microlevel development assistance.

Political and Diplomatic Efforts

In Guinea-Bissau, informal negotiation efforts by the UN, the EU, and Portuguese and West African officials have helped to calm existing political tensions at key moments. At the same time, the constructive role played by Armed Forces Chief of Staff Na Wai in Guinea-Bissau's 2005 transition to electoral democracy needs to be recognized. Although he remained largely aloof from the political process, when political tensions rose and violence seemed imminent Na Wai made it clear to political leaders that he would not tolerate deviance from the electoral path. He also helped to keep Guinea-Bissau stable by holding a series of meetings inside military barracks throughout the country to sensitize army personnel to the importance of reconciliation and respect for the parliamentary and electoral processes.[138] Clearly, then, there are domestic-leadership forces in the government and the armed forces that aim to build constructive peace-oriented coalitions, and the international community would be well advised to support local actors like Na Wai in their efforts to consolidate Guinea-Bissau's democratic process.

Macrolevel Policy and Budget Support

International aid has had an increasingly positive impact since 2003, reflecting the growing coordination of external interventions by major players such as UNOGBIS, ECOSOC's Ad Hoc Advisory Group, the EU, ECOWAS, the World Bank, the IMF, France, and Portugal. Yet, as previously noted, ambitious policies involving fundamental reforms in an environment of political instability have little chance of success. This fact suggests that external economic and social interventions need to be specifically targeted to address particular policy problems. These include support for raising the producer price of rice; debt relief; funding for civil service back pay on an emergency basis; assistance with vaccinations; funding for national elections; oversight reforms that strengthen fiscal accountability; and fiscal support for the refurbishment of military barracks and the voluntary demobilization of soldiers.

The macroeconomic policy adjustment that would have the greatest positive impact on development in the near future is a rise in the producer price of domestic rice through subsidies. The energetic response of farmers to the high price fetched by cashew nuts relative to rice in the 1990s points to potential in this area. Raising the producer price of rice, which is a cash crop as well as the country's staple food, would likely encourage rice planting on a level that could return the country to food self-sufficiency. In this respect, every euro (or dollar) spent on boosting the producer price of rice is likely to yield a better result than any other single macroeconomic policy program in terms of both income generation and raising the living standard. This would especially be the case if price support for rice were sustained over a five- to ten-year period.

International financial assistance in paying teachers, civil servants, and soldiers has also proved helpful and should remain an important policy instrument. It should be emphasized that funding for salaries has a pragmatic political as well as economic aim: in addition to securing needed cash for urban workers, it helps to hinder the likelihood of intense social conflict in the event of failure to pay wages—especially in the case of the military. In this sense, international financial support to the government for salary disbursements can be considered an important aspect of conflict prevention. Yet it also risks creating a cycle of dependency that would be difficult to reverse.

Strengthening State Capacities Against Organized Crime

One important but highly sensitive area for donor support relates to state building in Guinea-Bissau, with a special focus on strengthening the state's security sector against the growing threat from transnational organized crime, including narcotrafficking. Once again, external actors in this area ought to avoid attempting wholesale reform. In its November 2006 security sector reform plan, the government recognized the need to address the chronic problems confronting the country's security forces. However, the Guinea-Bissauan armed forces are intensely proud of not only their internal command system but also their historical accomplishments, including the nationalist war of independence, the ouster of Vieira in 1999, and the ouster of Senegalese troops in the 1998–1999 war. The Guinea-Bissauan army is comprised of peasant soldiers who hail from a broad range of village communities; for this reason, it is perceived as a people's army, not merely one of the state. External efforts to promote either a restructuring of the security sector or a reorganization of the system of military ranks and appointments are bound to provoke resentment and could be viewed as politically provocative. Moreover, there is a delicate balance of factional alliances within the army that could be upset by undue restructuring efforts. The contemporary history of coups throughout Africa makes it clear that attempts to intervene in the internal affairs of the armed forces are important factors in setting off coup attempts. Then again, the ongoing process of demobilizing and reintegrating excess army personnel is locally popular and merits continued external support.

The development priority of the international community should be to help the government achieve internal stability by supporting select macrolevel political and economic policies as well as basic food- and health-related needs.

Microlevel Development

Given Guinea-Bissau's poor record in implementing far-reaching economic reforms, development assistance at the microlevel is essential. Project-level support ranges from improving crop yields and protecting natural ecozones to providing direct support for digging wells, installing stalls in trading posts, and repairing fishing boats. Such projects represent a first step toward economic growth because they create employment and prevent social dislocations. However, in the context of bureaucratic fragility and inadequate administrative capacity, microlevel projects need effective community involvement. In the 1990s, NGOs in the rural areas tended to undertake projects that were driven by urban elites who understood neither rural society nor the specific and differing economic needs of individual regions, sectors, and communities.[139] As a result, project designs were often out of sync with local production processes (as with those that emphasized wet-rice production to people who actually specialized in dry-rice growing), and project resources did not reach their intended beneficiaries.[140] Experience confirms that microlevel development needs the active involvement of community leaders and project clients. Elders, both male and female, tend to be respected and influential in local communities, although in some areas heads of younger ages also wield important influence. Since age-based and gender-based identities result in separate economic functions, it is important to emphasize that not only male elders but also women and younger men who head age-group units ought to be included in decisions on grassroots development projects.[141]

As this chapter has sought to demonstrate, in the shorter term (three to five years), the international community can potentially contribute to an increase in security in Guinea-Bissau through diplomatic initiatives to promote political reconciliation; strengthen the capacities of the state to avoid state collapse, especially as a result of transnational organized crime; support existing peacebuilding initiatives by local and regional actors; and provide policy assistance in carefully selected issue areas. At the same time, aid to support higher crop prices for farmers and financial assistance for microlevel development projects led and managed by community leaders would represent important development initiatives.

Meanwhile, despite Guinea-Bissau's pressing domestic and external challenges, the external community should be wary of overstepping its bounds by seeking to act as a surrogate state or by strengthening the state primarily as an instrument to combat organized crime. External actors need to remember that Guinea-Bissau's long-term prospects for self-sustaining peace and development depend upon its ability to resolve its chronic political instability through internal peacebuilding processes—in which external actors have only limited influence.

Notes

1. Mustafah Dhada, *Warriors at Work: How Guinea Was Really Set Free* (Boulder, CO: University Press of Colorado, 1993); Patrick Chabal, *Amílcar Cabral: Revolutionary Leadership and People's War* (New York: Cambridge University Press, 1983).

2. Joshua B. Forrest, *Guinea-Bissau: Power, Conflict, and Renewal in a West African Nation* (Boulder, CO: Westview, 1992), 46–62.

3. It is still unclear whether actual coups took place or Vieira used the accusation of coup plotting to imprison or execute distrusted governmental and military officials. See Joshua B. Forrest, "Guinea-Bissau Since Independence: A Decade of Domestic Power Struggles," *Journal of Modern African Studies* 25, no. 1 (March 1987): 95–116.

4. Mustafah Dhada, "Guinea-Bissau: Towards a Pluralism of Sorts," *Africa Contemporary Record* 25 (2001): B86–B97.

5. Joshua B. Forrest, "Guinea-Bissau," in *A History of Post-Colonial Lusophone Africa,* ed. Patrick Chabal (London: Hurst, 2002), 236–263.

6. Joshua B. Forrest, *Lineages of State Fragility: Rural Civil Society in Guinea-Bissau* (Athens, OH: Ohio University Press, 2003), 229–231.

7. Alexander K. D. Frempong, "The Internal and Regional Dynamics of the Cycle of War and Peace in Guinea-Bissau," paper presented at the CODESRIA International Colloquium, "Lusophonie" in Africa: History, Democracy and Integration, Luanda, Angola, April 28–30, 2005, 11–14.

8. Joshua B. Forrest, "Democratization in a Divided Political Culture: Guinea-Bissau," in *The Fate of Africa's Democratic Experiments: Elites and Institutions,* eds. Leonardo Alfonso Villalón and Peter Vondoepp (Bloomington: Indiana University Press, 2005), 246–266.

9. Forrest, "Democratization in a Divided Political Culture: Guinea-Bissau."

10. Andrea E. Ostheimer, "The Structural Crisis in Guinea-Bissau's Political System," *African Security Review* 10, no. 4 (2001), http://www.iss.co.za/pubs/ASR/10No4/Ostheimer.html; UN Secretary-General, *Report of the Secretary-General on Developments in Guinea-Bissau and on the Activities of the United Nations Peacebuilding Support Office in That Country*, UN Doc. S/2002/312, March 26, 2002.

11. Frempong, "The Internal and Regional Dynamics," 14.

12. BBC News, "Q & A: Guinea-Bissau Coup," September 14, 2003, http://news.bbc.co.uk/2/hi/africa/3108310.stm.

13. "Campanha Eleitoral na Guine-Bissau Sem Incidentes," *Publico* [Lisbon newspaper], March 9, 2004.

14. Frempong, "The Internal and Regional Dynamics," 17; UN Secretary-General, *Report of the Secretary-General on Developments in Guinea-Bissau and on the Activities of the United Nations Peacebuilding Support Office in That Country*, UN Doc. S/2004/969, December 15, 2004, 12.

15. Frempong, "The Internal and Regional Dynamics," 18.

16. "Guinea-Bissau: Looking for an End to Upheaval," *The Africa Report* no. 1 (May 2005): 155.

17. Emma Birikorang, "Democracy for Guinea-Bissau? An Analysis of the 2005 Presidential Elections," Kofi Annan International Peacekeeping Training Centre (KAIPTC) Paper no. 8 (Accra: KAIPTC, August 2005), 9.

18. Birikorang, "Democracy for Guinea-Bissau?" 10.

19. "Guinea-Bissau President Shot Dead," BBC News, March 3, 2009; "Renegade Soldiers Kill Guinea-Bissau President," Yahoo News, March 2, 2009; "Edge of the Abyss," Economist Intelligence Unit Wire Service, March 4, 2009.

20. UNDP, "Human Development Index," in *Human Development Report 2005: International Cooperation at a Crossroads—Aid, Trade and Security in an Unequal World* (New York: UNDP, 2005).

21. Forrest, *Guinea-Bissau: Power, Conflict, and Renewal.*

22. Forrest, *Guinea-Bissau: Power, Conflict, and Renewal,* 76–110.

23. Forrest, "Guinea-Bissau," pp. 242–243.

24. World Bank, "Project Appraisal Document on a Proposed Credit in the Amount of 3DR 21.0 Million (US$26.0 Million Equivalent) to the Republic of Guinea-Bissau for a Private Sector Rehabilitation and Development Project," Doc. no. 23508-GUB, (Washington, DC: World Bank, February 28, 2002).

25. Forrest, "Guinea-Bissau," 257.

26. "Guinea-Bissau: Looking for an End to Upheaval," *The Africa Report.*

27. UN Economic and Social Council (ECOSOC), *Report of the Ad Hoc Advisory Group on Guinea-Bissau,* UN Doc. E/2004/10, February 6, 2004, 5.

28. ECOSOC, *Report of the Ad Hoc Advisory Group on Guinea-Bissau,* UN Doc. E/2004/10, and ECOSOC, *Report of the Ad Hoc Advisory Group on Guinea-Bissau,* UN Doc. E/2005/8, December 23, 2004, 5.

29. Frempong, "The Internal and Regional Dynamics," 19.

30. Gerald Gaillard, "Etude sur l'exode rural dans la region de Tombali Sud en Guinee Bissau," Report for the University of Lille, May 1995, Lille, France.

31. IRIN News, "Guinea-Bissau: Government Imports Rice to Counter Steep Price Rises," July 12, 2004, http://www.irinnews.org/report.aspx?reportid=50610.

32. Gerald Gaillard, "L'usage des terres en Guinea-Bissau," Report for the University of Lille, October 2004, Lille, France, 439–458; Gaillard, "Etude sur l'exode rural."

33. Forrest, *Lineages of State Fragility*, 162–167 and 224–225.

34. Forrest, "Guinea-Bissau."

35. Gaillard, "Etude sur l'exode rural."

36. CIA, "World Factbook: Guinea-Bissau," October 5, 2006, http://www.cia.gov/cia/publications/factbook/geos/pu.html.

37. See Peacebuilding Commission Country-Specific Configuration on Guinea-Bissau, "Background Paper on Drug Trafficking in Guinea-Bissau," paper prepared for Thematic Discussion on Drug Trafficking in Guinea-Bissau and Strengthening of the Justice Sector, May 28, 2008, http://www.un.org/peace/peacebuilding/Country-Specific%20Configurations/Guinea-Bissau/28.05.2008%20Background%20Paper%20Drug%20Trafficking.pdf. See also ECOSOC, *Report of the Ad Hoc Advisory Group on Guinea-Bissau,* UN Doc. E/2007/57, May 7, 2007, and UN Secretary-General, *Report of the Secretary-General on Developments in Guinea-Bissau and on the Activities of the United Nations Peacebuilding Support Office in That Country*, UN Doc. 2/2007/576, September 28, 2007.

38. See Peacebuilding Support Office, "Mapping of Resources and Gaps for Peacebuilding in Guinea-Bissau," April 7, 2008, http://www.un.org/spanish/peace/peacebuilding/AnnexGB07April2008.pdf.

39. See International Crisis Group (ICG), "Guinea-Bissau: In Need of a State," Africa Report series no. 142 (Brussels: ICG, July 2008).

40. See UN Security Council, "Letter Dated 11 December 2007 from the President of the Security Council to the Chairperson of the Peacebuilding Commission," December 14, 2007, UN Doc. A/62/736–S/2007/744, http://daccessdds.un.org/doc/UNDOC/GEN/N08/269/33/PDF/N0826933.pdf ?OpenElement.

41. Economist Intelligence Unit Wire Service, "Edge of the Abyss."

42. Forrest, *Guinea-Bissau: Power, Conflict, and Renewal*, 85–87.

43. CIA, "World Factbook: Guinea-Bissau."

44. "Country Profile: Guinea-Bissau," *The Africa Report,* November 2008.

45. Forrest, *Guinea-Bissau: Power, Conflict, and Renewal*, 84–95.

46. Forrest, *Lineages of State Fragility*, 181–204.

47. CIA, "World Factbook: Guinea-Bissau."

48. Forrest, *Guinea-Bissau*, 55–62.

49. Philip J. Havik, "Mundasson i Kambansa: espaco social e movementos politicos na Guine-Bissau," *Revista Internacional de Estudos Africanos,* nos. 18–22 (1999): 115–167.

50. Gaillard, "La guerre en son contexte: histoire d'une erreur politique," *Soronda: Revista de Estudos Guineenses* (December 2001): 221–283.

51. Frempong, "The Internal and Regional Dynamics," 25.

52. It is not yet clear who was behind the March 2009 assassination of President Vieira.

53. Dhada, *Warriors at Work.*

54. Forrest, *Guinea-Bissau: Power, Conflict, and Renewal,* 87–91.

55. Havik, "Mundasson i Kambansa."

56. IRIN News, "Guinea-Bissau: Government Imports Rice."

57. Gaillard, "Etude sur l'exode rural."

58. UN Secretary-General, *Report of the Secretary-General on Developments in Guinea-Bissau and on the Activities of the United Nations Peace-building Support Office in That Country*, UN Doc. S/2002/312.

59. Ostheimer, "The Structural Crisis in Guinea-Bissau."

60. Marina Padrão Temudo, "Western Beliefs and Local Myths: A Case Study on the Interface between Farmers, NGOs, and the State in Guinea-Bissau Rural Development Interventions," in *Between a Rock and a Hard Place: African NGOs, Donors, and the State,* eds. Jim Igoe and Tim Kelsall (Durham, NC: Carolina Academic Press, 2005), 253–277.

61. Government of Guinea-Bissau, "Interim National Poverty Reduction Strategy Paper," working paper (Bissau: Ministry of Social Solidarity, Reinsertion of Combatants and Fight Against Poverty, September 2000).

62. Government of Guinea-Bissau, "Interim National Poverty Reduction Strategy Paper," 10.

63. ECOSOC, *Report of the Ad Hoc Advisory Group on Guinea-Bissau,* UN Doc. E/2004/10, 5.

64. The results were: PAIGC, forty-five seats with 31.5 percent of votes; PRS (Social Renovation Party), thirty-five seats with 24.8 percent of votes; PUSD (United Social Democratic Party), seventeen seats with 16.1 percent of votes; UE (Electoral Union), two seats with 4.1 percent of votes; and APU (United People's Alliance), one seat with 1.3 percent of votes. See "Campanha Eleitoral na Guine-Bissau Sem Incidentes."

65. The International Peace and Prosperity Project (IPPP), "Guinea-Bissau: 'Failed State' Looking to Recover: Update and Prospective," working paper (Ottawa: IPPP, January 2006), 3; IRIN News, "Guinea-Bissau: New Government Named But National Unity Still a Long Way Off," November 10, 2005, http://www.irinnews.org/report.asp?ReportID=50040&SelectRegion=West_Africa&SelectCountry=GUINEA-BISSAU.

66. Ostheimer, "The Structural Crisis in Guinea-Bissau."

67. UN Secretary-General, *Report of the Secretary-General on Developments in Guinea-Bissau and on the Activities of the United Nations Peacebuilding Support Office in That Country,* UN Doc. S/2005/752, December 2, 2005, 2–3.

68. IRIN News, "Guinea-Bissau: New Government Named."

69. IRIN News, "Guinea-Bissau: Woman Chosen as New Head of Supreme Court," January 27, 2004, http://www.irinnews.org/report.asp?ReportID=39155&SelectRegion=West_Africa&SelectCountry=GUINEA-BISSAU.

70. IRIN News, "Guinea-Bissau: Prime Minister Says Doesn't Recognise New President but Won't Resign," August 23, 2005, http://www.irinnews.org/report.asp?ReportID=48716&SelectRegion=West_Africa&SelectCountry=GUINEA-BISSAU.

71. Birikorang, "Democracy for Guinea-Bissau?" 4–5.

72. Birikorang, "Democracy for Guinea-Bissau?" 4–5.

73. IRIN News, "Guinea-Bissau: High Court Deems New Premier Legal, Sparks Protest from Leading Party," January 30, 2006, http://www.irinnews.org/report.asp?ReportID=51427&SelectRegion=West_Africa&SelectCountry=GUINEA-BISSAU.

74. Forrest, *Lineages of State Fragility*, 228–229.

75. One noteworthy silver lining is the Ministry of Public Health, which has the country's best reputation for nationwide distribution of services, in part because of generous external support for vaccination programs and the distribution of medications.

76. IRIN News, "Guinea-Bissau: Government Imports Rice."

77. UN Secretary-General, *Report of the Secretary-General on Developments in Guinea-Bissau and on the Activities of the United Nations Peacebuilding Support Office in Guinea-Bissau,* UN Doc. S/2001/1211, December 14, 2001, 2.

78. ECOSOC, *Report of the Ad Hoc Advisory Group on Guinea-Bissau,* UN Doc. E/2004/10, 8.

79. IMF, "IMF Executive Board Concludes 2004 Article IV Consultation with Guinea-Bissau," Public Information Notice (PIN) no. 04/138, December 10, 2004; ECOSOC, *Ad Hoc Advisory Group on Guinea-Bissau,* UN Doc. E/2004/10, 2.

80. UN Secretary-General, *Report of the Secretary-General on Developments in Guinea-Bissau and on the Activities of the United Nations Peacebuilding Support Office in That Country,* UN Doc. S/2005/575, September 12, 2005, 3, and ECOSOC, *Ad Hoc Advisory Group on Guinea-Bissau,* UN Doc. E/2004/10, February 6, 2004, 3.

81. IRIN News, "Guinea-Bissau: World Bank Provides $13m to Shore Up Broke Government," January 7, 2004, http://www.irinnews.org/report.asp?ReportID=38788&SelectRegion=West_Africa&SelectCountry=GUINEA-BISSAU.

82. UN Secretary-General, *Report of the Secretary-General on Developments in Guinea-Bissau and on the Activities of the United Nations Peacebuilding Support Office in Guinea-Bissau,* UN Doc. S/2005/752, 4.

83. ECOSOC, *Report of the Ad Hoc Advisory Group on Guinea-Bissau,* UN Doc. E/2005/8, December 23, 2004, 5.

84. IPPP, "Guinea-Bissau Update: Report from a Recent Trip of the International Peace and Prosperity Project," (Ottawa: IPPP, July 4, 2005), 6.

85. Ostheimer, "The Structural Crisis in Guinea-Bissau."

86. Gerald Gaillard, "Islam et Politique Dans la Guinee-Bissau Contemporaine," Report for the Center of Political Islam of Bordeaux, University of Bordeaux, Bordeaux, France, February 2000.

87. Forrest, *Lineages of State Fragility*, 211–221.

88. Havik, "Mundasson i Kambansa."

89. IRIN News, "Guinea-Bissau: Prime Minister Says Doesn't Recognise New President."

90. Forrest, *Lineages of State Fragility*, 213–232.

91. UN Secretary-General, *Report of the Secretary-General on Developments in Guinea-Bissau and on the Activities of the United Nations Peacebuilding Support Office in Guinea-Bissau*, UN Doc. S/2005/752, 4.

92. Gaillard, "La guerre en son contexte."

93. Mustafah Dhada, "Guinea-Bissau: Politics, Intrigues, and Vieira's Last Stand," *Africa Contemporary Record* 26 (2002): B89–B97.

94. Forrest, "Guinea-Bissau," 258.

95. Frempong, "The Internal and Regional Dynamics," 15.

96. Birikorang, "Democracy for Guinea-Bissau?" 10.

97. Simon Massey, "Multi-faceted Mediation in the Guinea-Bissau Civil War," *Scientia Militaria: South African Journal of Military Studies* 32, no. 1 (2004): 76–95; Frempong, "The Internal and Regional Dynamics," 16.

98. Massey, "Multi-faceted Mediation," 89.

99. Massey, "Multi-faceted Mediation," 94–95.

100. Birikorang, "Democracy for Guinea-Bissau?" 9.

101. Frempong, "The Internal and Regional Dynamics," 16.

102. Frempong, "The Internal and Regional Dynamics," 17.

103. Frempong, "The Internal and Regional Dynamics," 11.

104. ECOSOC, *Report of the Ad Hoc Advisory Group on Guinea-Bissau,* UN Doc. E/2005/8, 4.

105. UN Secretary-General, *Report of the Secretary-General on Developments in Guinea-Bissau and on the Activities of the United Nations Peacebuilding Support Office in Guinea-Bissau,* UN Doc. S/2005/575, 2–3.

106. African Studies Center, "IRIN interview: Samuel Nana-Sinkam [19991127]," November 24, 1998, http://www.africa.upenn.edu/Hornet/irin-112799.html; UN, "United Nations and Guinea-Bissau," Peace and Security Section, Department of Public Information (New York: UN, October 2000); UN Secretary-General, *Report of the Secretary-General on Developments in Guinea-Bissau and on the Activities of the United Nations Peacebuilding Support Office in That Country,* UN Doc. S/2001/1211; UN Secretary-General, *Report of the Secretary-General on Developments in Guinea-Bissau and on the Activities of the United Nations Peacebuilding Support Office in That Country,* UN Doc. S/2004/456, June 4, 2004; UN Secretary-General, *Report of the Secretary-General on Developments in Guinea-Bissau and on the Activities of the United Nations Peacebuilding Support Office in Guinea-Bissau,* UN Doc. S/2005/575.

107. IRIN, "Guinea-Bissau: UNOGBIS Mandate Extended," November 20, 2003, http://www.irinnews.org/report.asp?ReportID=38000&SelectRegion=West_Africa&SelectCountry=GUINEA-BISSAU.

108. Author's information from UN official (anonymous by request), New York City, December 2004.

109. Birikorang, "Democracy for Guinea-Bissau?" 12.

110. IRIN News, "Guinea-Bissau: UN Funds Payment of Arrears to Army Mutineers," October 25, 2004, http://www.irinnews.org/report.asp?ReportID=43827&SelectRegion=West_Africa&SelectCountry=GUINEA-BISSAU; ECOSOC, *Report of the Ad Hoc Advisory Group on Guinea-Bissau,* UN Doc. E/2005/8, 8.

111. World Bank, "Guinea-Bissau Country Brief," April 2005, http://web.worldbank.org/WBSITE/EXTERNAL/COUNTRIES/AFRICAEXT/GUINEABISEXTN/0,menuPK:356680~pagePK:141132~piPK:141107~theSitePK:356669,00.html.

112. Birikorang, "Democracy for Guinea-Bissau?" 4.

113. UN Secretary-General, *Report of the Secretary-General on Developments in Guinea-Bissau and on the Activities of the United Nations Peacebuilding Support Office in Guinea-Bissau,* UN Doc. S/2005/575, 5.

114. ECOSOC, *Report of the Ad Hoc Advisory Group on Guinea-Bissau,* UN Doc. E/2004/10, 3.

115. Analysis based on UNOGBIS reports and ECOSOC, *Report of the Ad Hoc Advisory Group on Guinea-Bissau,* 2002–2005.

116. ECOSOC, *Report of the Ad Hoc Advisory Group on Guinea-Bissau,* UN Doc. E/2004/10, 8.

117. UN Security Council, *Report of the Security Council on Developments in Guinea-Bissau and on the Activities of the United Nations Peacebuilding Support Office in Guinea-Bissau,* UN Doc. S/2005/752, 4,

and UN Secretary-General, *Report of the Secretary-General on Developments in Guinea-Bissau and on the Activities of the United Nations Peacebuilding Support Office in Guinea-Bissau,* UN Doc. S/2005/575, 4.

118. ECOSOC, *Report of the Ad Hoc Advisory Group on Guinea-Bissau,* UN Doc. E/2005/8, 3, 7.

119. IRIN News, "Guinea-Bissau: Schools Reopen, World Bank Pays Teachers," October 29, 2003, http://www.irinnews.org/report.asp?ReportID=37542&SelectRegion=West_Africa&SelectCountry=GUINEA-BISSAU.

120. World Bank, "Guinea-Bissau Country Brief."

121. BBC News, "Cautious Welcome for G8 Debt Deal," June 12, 2005http://news.bbc.co.uk/1/hi/business/4084574.stm.

122. IRIN News, "Guinea-Bissau: World Bank Provides $13m to Shore Up Broke Government."

123. World Bank, "Guinea-Bissau: Country Brief."

124. IRIN News, "Guinea-Bissau: Government Launches First Big Push Against AIDS," July 27, 2004, http://www.irinnews.org/report.asp?ReportID=42380&SelectRegion=West_Africa&SelectCountry=GUINEA-BISSAU.

125. IRIN News, "Guinea-Bissau: World Bank Provides $13m to Shore Up Broke Government."

126. IRIN News, "Guinea-Bissau: UN Supervises $18.3 Million Emergency Fund for Government," December 24, 2003, http://www.irinnews.org/report.asp?ReportID=38587&SelectRegion=West_Africa&SelectCountry=GUINEA-BISSAU.

127. ECOSOC, *Report of the Ad Hoc Advisory Group on Guinea-Bissau,* UN Doc. E/2005/8, 6.

128. ECOSOC, *Report of the Ad Hoc Advisory Group on Guinea-Bissau,* UN Doc. E/2005/8, 5, and UN Secretary-General, *Report of the Secretary-General on Developments in Guinea-Bissau and on the Activities of the United Nations Peacebuilding Support Office in That Country,* UN Doc. S/2005/380, June 10, 2005, 4.

129. Frempong, "The Internal and Regional Dynamics," 19.

130. UN Secretary-General, *Report of the Secretary-General on Developments in Guinea-Bissau and on the Activities of the United Nations Peacebuilding Support Office in Guinea-Bissau,* UN Doc. S/2005/752, 5.

131. World Bank, "Guinea-Bissau Country Brief."

132. UN Secretary-General, *Report of the Secretary-General on Developments in Guinea-Bissau and on the Activities of the United Nations Peacebuilding Support Office in Guinea-Bissau,* UN Doc. S/2005/752, 4.

133. World Bank, "Guinea-Bissau Country Brief."

134. UN Secretary-General, *Report of the Secretary-General on Developments in Guinea-Bissau and on the Activities of the United Nations Peacebuilding Support Office in that country,* UN Doc. S/2001/1211, 5.

135. United Nations Development Program Report, "PNUD e governo da Guiné-Bissau assinam hoje documento official do projecto," Report by the Programme des Nations Unies pour le Dévéloppment en Guiné-Bissau, February 16, 2006.

136. AllAfrica Global Media, "Post-Transition Guinea-Bissau," September 15, 2005, Accessed at http://allafrica.com; page no longer accessible.

137. ECOSOC, *Report of the Ad Hoc Advisory Group on Guinea-Bissau,* UN Doc. E/2005/8, 3.

138. Birikorang, "Democracy for Guinea-Bissau?" 12.

139. Temudo, "Western Beliefs and Local Myths."

140. Temudo, "Western Beliefs and Local Myths," 259–263, 266–267.

141. Regarding the importance of female elders in economic marketing, see Philip J. Havik, "Female Entrepreneurship in a Changing Environment: Gender, Kinship, and Trade in the Guinea-Bissau Region," in *Negotiation and Social Space,* eds. Carl Risseuw and Kamala Ganesh (London: Sage, 1998), 205–225. For detailed agronomic examples of the roles of male elders, female elders, and heads of younger age groups, see Ursula Funk, "Land Tenure, Agriculture, and Gender in Guinea-Bissau," in *Agriculture, Women, and Land,* ed. Jean Davidson (Boulder, CO: Westview, 1987), 33–58; and Rosemary E. Galli and Jocelyn Jones, *Politics, Economics, and Society* (London: Pinter, 1987), 147–160.

8

Namibia: A Success Story?

Gretchen Bauer and Christiaan Keulder

In March 1990, Namibia became one of the last African countries to obtain its political independence. First colonized by Germany in the mid-1880s, Namibia became a de facto colony of South Africa after World War I when the League of Nations made it a de jure trust territory. Though South Africa was unsuccessful in its efforts to incorporate Namibia as a fifth province, it was successful in imposing its policies of segregation and apartheid on its neighbor. After World War II, Namibians formed their first nationalist movements. Within decades, the leading movement, the South West Africa People's Organization (SWAPO), had commenced an armed struggle against South Africa's occupation of Namibia and established exile bases in independent countries in the region. At the same time, given Namibia's status as a de jure mandate of the UN, appeals for independence were also directed internationally. Ultimately, the efforts of a contact group of Western nations combined with Angolan efforts to secure an end to war, resulting in UN-sponsored independence for Namibia. During a year-long transition to independence in 1989, UN-supervised universal franchise elections were held to select a constituent assembly to draft a constitution. In March 1990, power was handed over to a new government headed by the long-standing SWAPO leader, Sam Nujoma, who became president.

Coinciding with the end of the Cold War and the collapse of the Soviet Union, Namibia's transition to independence was remarkable in many respects. First, it formed part of a much larger geopolitical transition in southern Africa. South Africa, with the help of the United States, had managed to tie the Namibian peace process to the presence of Cuban troops in warring Angola. This complicated and frustrated the process, as Namibian independence became dependent on cooperation among a number of foreign countries, namely the Soviet Union, the United States, Cuba, Angola, and South Africa. Namibian actors thus played only a minor part in setting the conditions for independence; rather than being the result of a settlement among local elites, it was the product of negotiations among foreign powers, some of whom had no immediate stake in the outcome in Namibia.[1] Second, despite the lack of significant local input, Namibia's transition was remarkably speedy and peaceful once the core agreements were in place. This was due in part to the collapse of the Soviet Union and the ensuing changes in the global political climate and in part to the UN's supervision of the transition. Third, with mounting political unrest and economic decline at home, South Africa could no longer sustain its presence in Namibia and the war in Angola had become too costly both financially and militarily. In short, the timing of Namibia's independence—as the Cold War ended and a third wave of democracy extended to Africa—cannot be underestimated.

This chapter examines security and development in Namibia in its first fifteen years of independence (1990–2005). By and large, Namibia's story is one of a modicum of development success despite stark inequalities of wealth and income among a diverse population, continued heavy reliance on primary commodities, shortages of key natural resources such as arable land and water, ongoing struggles against poverty and disease, and the demands of democratic transition and consolidation. Moreover, in the decade and a half since independence, relative domestic peace and security have been maintained—despite Namibia's involvement in two regional wars (in Angola and Democratic Republic of Congo or DRC, respectively); an attempted secession by an armed rebel movement with ethnic ties to neighboring Zambia; ongoing border disputes with both Botswana and South Africa; and an influx of refugees from Angola. Against this complex background, Namibia's postindependence trajectory warrants analysis undertaken with a view to identifying to what extent national, regional, and international policies have contributed to the country's relative security and development successes.

Postindependence Challenges and Trends

With national independence in 1990, the new SWAPO government faced a host of challenges. Namibia's economy and society were marked by sharp dualism. This was evident in the stark contrast between the productiveness of the nation's mining and fishing industries as well as its commercial agricultural ventures on the one hand and that of subsistence agriculture on the other. At the same time, even the productive primary sector was under stress. The country's minerals and fishing stocks had been depleted under South African rule, and commercial agriculture faced recurrent drought. Moreover, local resources, under foreign control, were exported with very few benefits to the Namibian people. An exploitative migrant labor system ensured that foreign-owned enterprises had a constant supply of cheap local labor. As for the two societies—one was wealthy, educated, healthy, and European; the other was poor, illiterate, malnourished, and African. To categorize them thus is not, however, to gloss over the large racial and ethnic divides in the very small Namibian population—divides that had only been exacerbated by South African colonial policies entailing separate administrations and so-called ethnic homelands.

In addition, upon the achievement of independence, tens of thousands of returning Namibian exiles—some of whom had been away for two decades or more—had to be reintegrated into Namibian society. Once at war, soldiers in the People's Liberation Army of Namibia (PLAN) and the South West Africa Territorial Force (SWATF) had to be united to form a single national army, the Namibian Defense Force (NDF). Meanwhile, northern Namibia, which was home to nearly half of the nation's population and had for decades been a war zone under martial law with a dusk-to-dawn curfew, needed to be reconstructed and developed. Finally, a fragile democratic transition had to be consolidated. The majority of Namibians had lived their entire lives bereft of the most basic civil and political rights, despite two South African–inspired attempts at transitional governments. A progressive constitution adopted upon independence and hailed as one of the most democratic in the world laid the foundation for a significant transformation of the Namibian polity. However, an authoritarian political culture brought back from exile camps, together with the legacy of decades of apartheid colonial rule inside the country, threatened the nascent democracy.

Socioeconomic Development

With a fairly clear mandate from the Namibian people (who gave it 57 percent of the vote in the late 1989 transitional election), the ruling SWAPO party adopted a generous policy of national reconciliation and a mixed approach to its postindependence economy and development. From the beginning, the government's economic policies have been aimed at sustainable growth, a tangible increase in per capita income, a diversified economy, expanded employment opportunities, and improved education and health services. Economic development goals have been set out in two five-year national development plans: NDP1 and NDP2. The objectives of NDP1 are the same as those identified at the time of independence, to which NDP2 adds gender equality and equity, the reduction of regional development inequalities, and good governance.[2] Further, NDP2 aims to reduce poverty and create jobs through the promotion of small and medium enterprises and an increase in manufacturing to garner 20 percent of all formal sector employment. More is also to be spent on decentralizing some central government functions to the country's thirteen regions.[3] NDP1 and NDP2 set average annual gross domestic product (GDP) growth-rate goals of 5 percent and 4 percent, respectively. An average annual real GDP growth rate of 4.7 percent from 1994 to 1997 was sufficient to produce a 1.6 percent average annual real increase in GDP per capita. Agriculture; diamond and other types of mining; manufacturing (including onshore fish processing); tourism; and financial services recorded their strongest growth during this period. From 1998 to 2002, the average real GDP growth rate decelerated to 3.2 percent, with growth per capita at only 0.7 percent, owing to a contraction in output from agricultural and fish processing, lower mining sector growth resulting from a contraction in nondiamond minerals output, and slower growth in tourism and financial services. Projections for 2004–2006 forecast a 4.1 percent annual GDP growth rate owing to a recovery in diamond and fishing output, with annual average growth of 10 percent in other manufacturing activities as a result of increased production of refined zinc by the Skorpion mine and melted copper at the Tsumeb plant (see Table 8.1).[4]

In 2004 the Namibian government published its millennium development goals.[5] These are to eradicate extreme poverty and hunger; achieve universal primary education; promote gender equality and empower women; reduce child mortality; improve maternal health; combat HIV/AIDS, malaria, and other diseases; ensure environmental sustainability; and develop a global partnership for development. So far, Namibia has made good progress toward three of these goals: achieving universal primary education, promoting gender equality, and ensuring environmental sustainability. According to a 2005 UN report, however, Namibia faced a triple threat to its national development that year: an epidemic of HIV/AIDS, persistent and potentially worsening food insecurity problems, and the ineffective delivery of critical social services.[6]

Table 8.1 Selected Economic Indicators for Namibia, 1993–1999

	1993	1994	1995	1996	1997	1998	1999
GDP in N$ millions	9,302	11,549	12,707	15,012	16,795	18,887	21,124
GDP per capita in N$	6,205	7,470	7,972	9,137	9,902	10,792	11,703
GDP growth rate (real)		7.3	4.1	3.2	4.5	3.5	3.8
Increase in GDP per capita	–4.7	4.1	1.0	0.1	1.2	0.3	0.7
Exports as % of GDP	51.9	48.5	49.5	50.6	47.4	45.8	46.8
Imports as % of GDP	56.7	51.3	55.7	58.6	57.4	57.7	58.4
Government expenditure as % GDP	31.6	28.3	30.0	30.1	29.9	29.3	29.3
Budget deficit as % GDP	3.6	1.8	3.9	6.5	2.9	3.9	4.6
Yearly inflation rate (CPI)	8.6	10.8	8.9	9.1	8.8	6.2	8.6
Aid per capita US$	93	83	95	106	98	109	118
Aid as % GDP	4.5	3.6	4.5	5.0	4.6	5.5	6.6

Source: UN Development Programme (UNDP), *Namibia Human Development Report,* Windhoek: UNDP, 2000, 158.

The government has eschewed major intervention in the economy, instead promoting growth by (1) facilitating foreign direct investment in priority sectors such as nontraditional manufacturing and tourism; (2) partnering with the private sector; and (3) creating an attractive legislative and fiscal environment, for instance by establishing multiple export processing zones. As in South Africa, in Namibia black economic empowerment has been a growing feature of new partnerships with foreign private investors.[7] Abundant natural resources, good infrastructure, and improved access to regional and overseas markets provide a basis for developing a more diversified economy, although inadequate labor skills and high transport costs pose significant hindrances.[8]

A long-term policy document called "Namibia Vision 2030" calls for transforming the country into an industrialized economy.[9] Indeed, Namibia's high average per capita income (US$2,250 in 2003) disqualifies it for least developed country (LDC) status at either the UN or the World Bank, although the country does have an as-if LDC status.[10] Such status is certainly warranted in that the high average per capita income in Namibia conceals a highly uneven distribution of income. In 2005 the UN declared Namibia the most unequal country in the world, far ahead of South Africa, Zimbabwe, and Zambia. Indeed, Namibia was the only country *in* the world with a higher income inequality than the overall figure *for* the world.[11] Namibia's extreme inequalities of income and wealth are attributable in large measure to the decades of South Africa–imposed apartheid rule.

Indeed, decades of apartheid rule reinforced divisions within Namibia's multiethnic and multiracial population of nearly 2 million. About 6 percent of the population is white and another 6 percent of the population are mixed-race "coloreds," to use the local parlance. The remainder of the population is divided among several African-ethnic groups. The largest of these is the Ovambo, comprising about half of the Namibian population and residing largely in the north. Other groups include the Herero and Kavango—each comprising about 10 percent of the population—and the smaller Nama, Damara, Caprivi, and San groups.[12] Since independence, however, the government of Namibia has not included racial categories in its official population surveys, so the disparities in income and wealth are hard to capture. Instead, region has become a proxy for race/ethnicity, as particular groups tend to concentrate in particular areas. Namibia's thirteen administrative regions, then, do more than provide a subnational level of government; they also reveal the many disparities in the Namibian economy and society. For example, the bulk of historically disadvantaged Namibians (HDNs) live in the northern regions of Caprivi, Kavango, Ohangwena, Omusati, Oshana, and Oshikoto. Other regions such as Khomas and Erongo are home to far more advantaged populations, including the majority of white Namibians who enjoy first-world living standards.

The UNDP *Human Development Report* for Namibia in 2000 provides data for the country disaggregated by region, urban versus rural location, gender, and language group. In so doing, the report illustrates the country's inequalities in wealth and development and indicates the challenges still facing Namibia as it seeks to undo the legacies of colonialism and apartheid. The Human Development Indices for Namibia (see Table 8.2) show a national average life expectancy of only 43 years in 2000, with a regional low of 32.6 years in Caprivi and a regional high of only 47.2 years for Erongo. The low life-expectancy figure reflects the fact that Namibia is one of the most severely HIV-infected countries in the world.

In contrast, Namibia's 1999 national adult literacy rate of 81.4 percent compares favorably with other parts of the developing world. Adult literacy rates are generally high in Erongo, Karas, and Khomas and in the northern regions of Omusati, Oshikoto, and Oshana (where they range from 82 to 85 percent).[13] This reflects a postindependence increase in school enrollment across all regions—one made possible in part by an extensive rural school-building program. After independence, a national education system was established to replace the previous race-based system. Every year since, the government has

Table 8.2 Human Development Index (HDI) for Namibia, 2000

Region	Life Expectancy	Adult Literacy	School Enrollment	Income N$[a]	Adjusted Income[b]	HDI 2000	HDI 1999	HDI 1998
Caprivi	32.6	75.4	95.3	1,598	3,773	0.517	0.541	0.538
Erongo	47.2	88.5	89.7	5,423	4,339	0.713	0.754	0.810
Hardap	41.6	80.7	85.8	5,945	4.446	0.667	0.706	0.822
Karas	42.0	88.6	89.5	6,655	4,505	0.700	0.734	0.787
Khomas	46.1	94.0	83.7	11,359	4,777	0.769	0.821	0.853
Kunene	45.5	64.3	94.9	2,203	3,939	0.588	0.616	0.608
Ohangwena	43.0	76.0	93.7	1,070	3,569	0.544	0.582	0.546
Kavango	40.3	73.1	96.7	1,763	3,762	0.554	0.584	0.569
Omaheke	44.1	64.0	79.0	3,944	4,236	0.605	0.644	0.706
Omusati	42.6	82.5	99.3	1,452	3,725	0.585	0.624	0.614
Oshana	43.5	85.4	99.5	1,922	3,869	0.618	0.659	0.648
Oshikoto	40.3	81.9	94.1	1,680	4,322	0.654	0.686	0.604
Otjozondjupa	41.1	72.0	79.4	3,659	4,198	0.601	0.636	0.735
Namibia	43.0	81.0	94.5	3,608	4,190	0.648	0.683	0.770
Urban	46.4	91.7	96.2	7,651	4,575	0.749	0.787	0.808
Rural	41.7	73.7	93.7	1,875	3,856	0.574	0.608	0.601
Female	45.6	79.6	95.3	2,188	3,935	0.622	0.660	0.653
Male	40.6	82.6	93.5	4,454	4,299	0.653	0.685	0.767

(continues)

Table 8.2 continued

Language Group	Life Expectancy	Adult Literacy	School Enrollment	Income N$[a]	Adjusted Income[b]	HDI 2000	HDI 1999	HDI 1998
Caprivi	32.6	75.4	95.3	1,598	3,773	0.517	0.541	0.538
Afrikaans	67.2	96.1	87.4	13,995	4,884	0.885	0.887	0.865
Caprivi	56.6	79.9	89.0	1,692	3,803	0.613	0.640	0.579
English	66.9	98.6	89.9	1,708	5,108	0.895	0.926	0.873
German	75.0	99.4	92.2	30,459	5,283	0.960	1.000	0.930
Nama	58.6	71.1	74.7	2,404	3,983	0.611	0.642	0.618
Oshiwambo	61.3	82.8	88.9	1,707	3,807	0.641	0.673	0.613
Otjiherero	64.1	72.3	75.7	3,077	4,162	0.667	0.702	0.711
Rukavango	55.9	72.8	83.0	1,652	3,791	0.585	0.613	0.550
San	48.1	16.0	18.3	1,315	3,674	0.326	0.359	0.279
Tswana	61.7	81.0	85.7	5,326	4,390	0.721	0.751	0.782

Source: UN Development Programme (UNDP), *Namibia Human Development Report,* Windhoek: UNDP, 2000, 156.

Notes: a. These income figures are average adjusted per capita income figures taken from the *1993/1994 Namibia Household Income and Expenditure Survey.* The per capita income figures are adjusted to reflect the age composition of members of the household, the assumption being that younger members of a household consume less. The figures are still relevant for purposes of comparison across regions.

b. The HDI adjusts real income above a certain threshold, the underlying assumption being that people need a certain income to attain a decent standard of living and that income beyond a certain level has a diminishing marginal utility. The global HDI defines an income threshold for an acceptable standard of living as the world average income. The Namibian income threshold has been defined as the Namibian national average income.

allocated a sizable portion of the national budget to education, from the primary through the tertiary level. In the 2004–2005 budget, the allocation was 23.3 percent of total expenditure, down from a high of 28 percent in 1997–1998.[14]

The Human Poverty Indices for Namibia (see Table 8.3) also show the disparities among regions and groups. For example, in most of the country—Erongo and Khomas are the exceptions—nearly 40 percent of the population (89 percent in the case of Omaheke) has no access to health facilities. Similarly, although almost everyone in Erongo, Karas, and Khomas has safe drinking water, in many other regions of the country significant portions of the population have no access to safe water. The government's priorities since independence have been to expand access to health clinics in both rural areas and underserved urban areas and to expand primary care services, in contrast to the preindependence authorities who favored the wealthier urban areas. In the 2004–2005 national budget, 13.5 percent of total expenditure was allocated to health, including social security and welfare.[15] As noted, HIV/AIDS remains the country's foremost health challenge, as it has spread rapidly since the first cases were identified in 1986 (see Table 8.4).

Government and Politics

Namibia is a unitary state with three tiers of government: national, regional, and local. At the national level, legislative authority rests with a bicameral parliament that provides both popular and territorial representation. The lower house, the National Assembly, consists of seventy-two elected and six appointed members. Members are elected at five-year intervals through a closed-list proportional representation (PR) electoral system; the six appointments are the prerogative of the president. The upper house, the National Council, consists of twenty-six members elected from thirteen regional councils. Each of the regional councils elects two members from its own ranks to serve in the National Council, thereby ensuring equal representation for each of the country's administrative territories.

Regional councils are effectively rural local authorities; they came about as a result of a trade-off between political parties during the preindependence constitutional negotiations. As established by law in 1992, regional councils are the principal governing bodies for the regions and their primary function is regional planning. Beyond that, they have no legislative capacity or powers of taxation. Their major sources of income are levies from intraregional local authori-

Table 8.3 Human Poverty Index (HPI) for Namibia, 2000

Region	Nonsurvival to Age 40	Illiteracy	Low Child Weight	Lack of Safe Water	Lack of Health Facilities	More Than 80% of Income Spent on Food	HPI-N[a] 2000	HPI-G[a] 2000	HPI-N[a] 1999	HPI-N[a] 1998
Caprivi	53.7	24.6	8.4	25.2	42.0	7.0	36.0	39.6	32.7	25.0
Erongo	25.7	11.5	4.6	0.3	27.0	7.1	17.1	18.7	15.3	11.2
Hardap	36.2	19.3	13.9	3.3	43.0	4.7	25.0	27.5	22.8	19.1
Karas	35.5	11.4	16.7	0.2	43.0	4.1	23.8	26.2	21.4	16.0
Khomas	27.6	6.0	18.5	0.2	17.0	1.1	17.9	19.7	15.8	9.6
Kunene	28.7	35.7	4.2	10.2	47.0	11.3	27.0	29.6	26.3	24.8
Ohangwena	33.5	24.0	13.8	45.1	64.0	9.9	31.2	34.2	32.6	31.8
Kavango	38.5	26.9	17.8	34.6	38.0	19.6	30.3	32.6	29.7	27.2
Omaheke	31.2	36.0	4.9	4.2	89.0	25.1	31.7	33.4	31.0	30.5
Omusati	34.0	17.5	9.0	50.5	38.0	9.0	27.1	29.7	28.1	26.6
Oshana	32.4	14.6	15.5	18.5	54.0	5.5	25.0	27.5	24.3	22.0
Oshikoto	38.6	18.1	16.2	21.0	68.0	9.0	29.9	32.9	29.0	24.9
Otjozondjupa	37.0	28.0	5.6	1.4	52.0	10.8	27.3	29.9	25.3	21.0
Namibia	33.5	19.0	12.0	17.1	45.0	8.7	24.7	27.1	23.4	20.5
Urban	27.3	8.3		0.1	7.0	2.6	17.4	19.1	15.2	16.7
Rural	36.1	26.3		29.1	65.0	11.8	29.0	31.8	36.4	24.7
Female	36.9	20.4		21.8	45.0	9.6	26.0	28.5	28.7	25.4
Male	30.1	17.4		14.2	45.0	8.1	21.7	23.8	24.2	22.6

(continues)

Table 8.3 continued

Language Group	Nonsurvival to Age 40	Illiteracy	Low Child Weight	Lack of Safe Water	Lack of Health Facilities	More Than 80% of Income Spent on Food	HPI-N[a] 2000	HPI-G[a] 2000	HPI-N[a] 1999	HPI-N[a] 1998
Afrikaans	11.9	3.9		0.3	25.0	0.9	8.4	9.2	9.3	10.3
Caprivi	27.0	20.1		11.5	45.0	5.2	20.5	22.6	23.1	37.6
English	12.4	1.4		0.0	10.0	0.0	7.9	8.7	7.0	7.1
German	3.8	0.6		0.0	29.0	0.0	6.2	6.8	9.2	9.2
Nama/Damara	24.1	28.9		1.9	51.0	8.6	22.3	24.4	23.7	28.6
Oshiwambo	20.1	17.2		29.4	50.0	7.8	20.0	22.0	29.4	38.8
Otjiherero	16.2	27.7		5.6	55.0	16.5	21.2	22.4	24.6	31.2
Rukavango	28.1	27.2		38.3	35.0	19.5	25.2	26.7	31.4	39.9
San	40.2	84.0		10.4	36.0	28.7	56.0	61.3	58.1	59.9
Tswana	19.5	19.0		2.1	38.0	0.0	16.1	17.7	17.2	19.0

Source: UN Development Programme, *Namibia Human Development Report,* Windhoek: UNDP, 2000, 157.
Notes: All figures are expressed as percentages.
a. HPI-N stands for Human Poverty Index: Namibian Formula; HPI-G stands for Human Poverty Index: Global Formula.

Table 8.4 Demographic Impact of HIV/AIDS in Namibia, 1991–2006

Indicator	1991	1995	2001	2006
Annual number of deaths from AIDS	360	1,440	13,880	23,220
Crude death rate	11.4	11.2	16	18.8
Total population (millions)	1.1	1.6	1.9	2.1
Population growth rate (%)	3.6	3.1	2.1	1.5
Life expectancy at birth	60	58.3	43.8	40.2
Infant mortality rate	71.6	71.5	70.1	62.9
Mortality rate of those under five years (/1000)	104	98	106.2	100.9
Number of orphans due to AIDS (< fifteen years)	50	1,630	31,290	118,050

Source: UN Development Programme (UNDP), *Namibia Human Development Report*, Windhoek: UNDP, 2000, 12.

ties and grants from the central government. This effectively means that rural Namibia is administered by weak and underresourced structures, a fact that has had a significant impact on development there. Richer regions are better off, and the gap between them and the poor regions has only widened since these structures were put in place. Local authorities are responsible for the administration of Namibia's proclaimed urban areas, which are subdivided into four types according to their size and governed by legislative councils with between seven and fifteen members. These councils have powers of taxation and derive their income from service fees and property levies. They have the authority to pass and enforce bylaws and provide a number of important functions, including traffic control, emergency services, refuse removal, health control, sewerage, and the provision of water and electricity.

The Namibian judicial system consists of a supreme court, a high court, and regional and magistrates' courts. Although not part of the formal legal system, traditional or customary courts were retained with limited powers after independence. Between these two court systems, most Namibians have access to some form of legal recourse, albeit often with much delay and frustration. Though guaranteed by the constitution, judicial independence is often countered by calls from within the ranks of the ruling party for more SWAPO sympathizers to be appointed to the bench. Still, a number of rulings show that the judiciary remains independent, most notably the one calling for a recount of the 2004 parliamentary election.

Fifteen years into independence, Namibia is clearly a dominant party state, although opposition parties do freely exist and free and fair elections have been held regularly since 1989 (of which more to come). In March 2005, Namibia experienced its first presidential succession since independence as President Sam Nujoma's handpicked successor and longtime comrade-in-exile Hifikepunye Pohamba was elected president. Though the independence constitution had limited presidential terms to two five-year administrations, the ruling party, which had enjoyed two-thirds majorities in both houses of Parliament since 1994, amended the constitution in 1998 to make an exception for President Nujoma, allowing him a third term of office. In retrospect, this may have been a prudent move, as presidential successions often constitute crisis points in nascent democracies. In any event, the handover of power was accomplished smoothly and peacefully.

The Changing Nature of Security

Up to mid-2009, there had been no specific internal or external security threats against Namibia from hostile neighbors, exiled rebel groups, or internal dissident organizations. Since independence in 1990, there has been no major armed conflict such as civil war, political violence in the form of assassinations or bombings, or armed insurgency (with one possible exception); nor has there been intercommunity violence. The main security challenges since independence have been (1) insecurities along the northern border caused by the war in Angola and its spillover into Namibia and (2) unrest, marked by a brief armed uprising, in Caprivi. In addition, Namibian armed forces were involved for a brief period in the war in neighboring DRC.

At the time of independence, Namibia had no officially constituted army, as combatants on both sides of the liberation conflict had been demobilized during the transition.[16] This meant that the recruitment of soldiers into the new NDF occurred gradually and individually rather than via a wholesale merger of the two aforementioned, previously hostile units, PLAN and SWATF. The new government did not pursue military tribunals or prosecutions against its former enemies, seeking instead a balance between both sides in the new NDF. These measures were an extension of the policy of national reconciliation declared by President Nujoma shortly after independence.

Once the NDF was established, new recruits received training from Kenyan and British soldiers, who focused on attaining professionalism in the new army and integrating the formerly warring soldiers. Such training also brought about a change in the military ethos, one that no longer reflected the Soviet model that had been dominant among PLAN forces but instead resembled that of the Commonwealth countries. The consequences of this were significant for nation building; as Andre du Pisani puts it, "Standardized military training and a common military doctrine fed into the project of national reconciliation and of nation building. These provided the new state with values and practices around which the members of the NDF could draw together. In this respect, the NDF, from its inception, worked to support the politics of national reconciliation and directly assisted with both state formation and the consolidation of state power. The ethic became one of 'service to the nation.'"[17] At the senior level of the military, the new government appointed leaders who were loyal and had significant military and political experience; in so doing, it ensured that there was continuity between the military and the state executive. Moreover, although the government recognized that without an effective and professional army the new state would lack crucial capacity and face decreased statehood, it was adamant that there be civilian control over the military.[18]

NDF troops numbered about 9,000 in 2005, with a planned recruitment of an additional 1,000 ex-combatants.[19] Another 6,000 troops had joined the Special Field Force (SFF) as of 2003, the paramilitary police unit recruited primarily from among former PLAN combatants in the mid-1990s. The NDF and SFF share responsibility for Namibia's internal security. Compared to other countries in the region (for instance, South Africa, Zimbabwe, and Angola), Namibia has limited military capabilities as measured by weapons holding and armed personnel. The aggregate number of heavy weapons increased from five in 1997 to ninety in 2000 and the number of armed forces personnel increased from 6,000 in 1996 to 12,000 in 1999, though it decreased to 9,000 in the early 2000s.[20]

Though Namibia was not itself threatened, its military was active outside Namibia's borders for about four years, from 1998 to 2002. In August 1998, President Nujoma ordered the deployment of Namibian troops in DRC. Namibian involvement in the DRC war was justified on the grounds of regional solidarity and the need to secure Namibian peace, stability, and democracy. Indeed, many observers stress the salience of close political ties between SWAPO and the ruling parties in Angola and Zimbabwe—ties forged during the nations' respective armed struggles against internal rebels or colonial occupiers—for Namibia's decision to join the two countries in the war in DRC. But by 2002, all NDF soldiers had been withdrawn.

In December 1999, Namibia became involved in the long-standing war in Angola when the government gave permission to the Armed Forces of Angola (FAA) to launch attacks from northern

Namibia into southern Angola against UNITA (Union for the Total Independence of Angola) troops. This decision by the Namibian government prompted retaliatory action by UNITA against Namibia, which in turn prompted NDF involvement in the conflict. By early May 2000, the NDF had set up military bases inside Angola in an attempt to prevent UNITA rebels from carrying out retaliatory attacks on Namibian soil. Expansion of the Angolan war into Namibia had swift and significant consequences, including civilian casualties. As fear caused by the fighting spread and trips to Namibia were canceled, losses to the tourism industry mounted. The extension of Angola's civil war into Namibia also resulted in widespread charges of human rights abuses carried out by both NDF and SFF members in the Kavango and Caprivi regions, where the fighting was concentrated. Those abuses decreased significantly once cross-border fighting from Angola came to an end following the Angolan cease-fire in April 2002.

Finally, during the same period, Namibia's military and security forces became involved in an internal conflict. In August 1999, separatists calling themselves the Caprivi Liberation Army demanded independence for the Caprivi region and launched armed attacks on the police station, army base, and Namibian Broadcasting Corporation office in Katima Mulilo, Caprivi's largest town. The Namibian government responded by declaring a state of emergency in the region and detaining hundreds of suspected rebel collaborators. The rebellion was led by one-time opposition leader and Caprivi native Mishake Muyongo. The harsh military response to the alleged secession attempt prompted thousands of ordinary Caprivians to flee to Botswana. By 2002, tensions in the region had largely subsided, though NDF and SFF members continued to kill alleged secessionists, while several others accused of high treason for involvement in the plot died in police custody.[21]

The failed rebellion in Caprivi showed that despite its small size and relative lack of arms, Namibia's military had sufficient capacity to suppress any group-based challenge and defend the nation.[22] Indeed, no existing domestic group can match or seriously challenge the armed capabilities of the Namibian state, and the loyalty of the armed forces to the president and his government means that challenges from within the military are unlikely.[23] Moreover, though some security units have at times seemed to be acting at the arbitrary behest of the president, it would be inaccurate to describe any of them as a personal or private army.[24]

Over time, with its military involvement in DRC and Angola and its participation in peacekeeping in Liberia, the security establishment has gained influence over national policymaking. This is well reflected in government expenditure: the Ministry of Defense's national budget allocation increased from 5.5 percent in 1990–1991 to almost 10 percent in 1999–2000 (mainly to cover improved pay, training programs, and the aforementioned external interventions), though it went down to 8.6 percent in 2004–2005.[25] The latter period also saw a doubling of the budget allocation of the National Intelligence Security Agency (located in the Office of the President) as well as a substantial increase in the allocation to the SFF. Another result of this military involvement in regional conflicts has been the emergence of a small refugee population in Namibia. From 2000 to 2003, 20,000 to 30,000 refugees and asylum seekers entered Namibia annually, primarily from Angola, with about 1,500 coming from DRC, Rwanda, and Burundi in 2003 alone.[26] Of these, very few have returned home; rather, tens of thousands of refugees now reside in Namibian refugee camps administered by the Office of the UN High Commissioner on Refugees (UNHCR). During the period following the armed uprising in Caprivi, many Caprivians fled Namibia for Botswana, fearing the retaliatory response by Namibian security forces. Those Namibians have by and large since returned. Aside from these two instances, there has been no significant population displacement in or out of Namibia in the years since independence.

Assessing Risk Factors and Domestic Responses

A number of factors pose potential risks to Namibia's long-term security, growth, and development. These factors and some of the state responses to them are discussed in this section.

The Structure of the Economy

As noted, the Namibian economy is small—roughly 40 times smaller than that of its immediate neighbor South Africa. It is also highly skewed. Indeed, with a Gini coefficient of 70.7, it is the most highly skewed economy in the world. Moreover, it is dependent on exports from three primary sectors—mining, fishing, and agriculture—and is thereby at high risk. The mining sector is dominated by diamonds (though the country also produces zinc, uranium, and a number of base metals such as gold, copper, silver, and lead). In 2002, Namibia produced close to 1.7 million carats of diamonds, with a total value of N$4.45 billion (equivalent to US$704,746,500).[27] Overall, Namibia is the world's sixth largest producer of diamonds by value.[28] Diamond mining is dominated by NAMDEP—a joint venture by the government of Namibia and De Beers, one of the world biggest diamond mining companies—which produces about 80 percent of Namibia's diamonds. In 2002 and 2003, tax revenue from diamond companies amounted to about N$1.16 billion (US$183,709,200) or approximately 26 percent of all revenue from taxes on income and profits. Overall, the diamond industry makes up about one-tenth of the total Namibian economy. About 3,500 Namibians are employed in the industry, making it one of the economy's largest employers.

The Namibian government remains in firm control of diamond mining; no other group has private access to rough diamonds. The Minerals (Prospecting and Mining) Act of 1992 vests ownership of all minerals in the Namibian government. It also regulates mining rights and stipulates the rights and obligations of license holders, as well as royalties payable on unprocessed minerals. The Diamond Act of 1999 imposes strict controls over the possession, purchase, and sale of rough diamonds and provides for a framework to guard against what are known as blood diamonds or conflict diamonds. Revenue from the diamond industry remains firmly under government control and ultimately finds its way back to the Namibian population through the annual budget. In addition, all mining companies are obliged to train and employ Namibian staff and are urged to give preference to Namibian products and services.

Fishing and fish processing contribute between 6 and 9 percent of Namibia's annual GDP.[29] Since almost all Namibian fish is exported, this sector is an important earner of export revenues (N$2.8 billion in 2000 or US$443,436,000), and it is a major source of employment. Since 1994, employment at sea has fluctuated between 6,000 and 8,000; after aggressive measures to Namibianize the industry, approximately 65 percent of all crew is now Namibian.[30] Before independence, Namibians had little control over the country's rich pelagic and other marine resources. Since then, a number of measures have been adopted to protect fish resources and give Namibians a greater stake in the industry. First, the government limits the volume of fish that can be legally caught each year through a total allowable catch quota on the six main fish species. Second, the government provides incentives to encourage onshore fish processing in order to add more value and create more employment locally. The reforms have been relatively successful in Namibianizing the industry. As of the mid-2000s, however, the fishing sector is under duress; pelagic fishing adds very little value, and the sector is plagued by labor unrest.

Namibia's agricultural sector is constrained by its highly dualistic nature—a commercial subsector dominated by white farmers and a communal subsector consisting of black subsistence farmers. Moreover, agricultural production is shaped by the availability of arable land and water, both of which are scarce. Indeed, land and water scarcity constitutes another risk factor for Namibia. Only about 8 percent of Namibia's total land area is suitable for crop production; about 90 percent of the country's land mass is classified as dry land area, suitable only for livestock production, which requires vast tracts to be commercially viable.[31] Dry lands are also very vulnerable to degradation, which, together with bad soil quality and limited water resources, causes great human vulnerability and food insecurity. In 2002, some 12 percent of the Namibian population was estimated to be vulnerable (that is, food insecure).[32]

Despite the harsh conditions, agriculture remains an important source of employment and contributor to the Namibian economy. It has accounted for approximately 4 percent of GDP annually since 1995. In 2000, some 113,000 people (excluding unpaid family workers) were employed in the agricultural sector, the majority in subsistence farming.[33] The number of commercial farmers stood at 3,700 in 1991 and remained nearly constant until 1997, when it dropped sharply. Since 1997, some commercial farmers have ceased operations altogether; some have sold their farms, while others have moved into tourism, transforming their farms into guest or hunting lodges.

Land Distribution and Reform

Despite the hardships of farming in Namibia, the government regards the agriculture sector as crucial to the alleviation of poverty. It also forms an integral part of the government's policies on land reform and resettlement. Yet it is plagued by political uncertainty. After 1995, the year in which the Agricultural (Commercial) Land Reform Act was passed, a number of white commercial farmers began registering their farms as closed corporations in an attempt to avoid expropriation. Moreover, many white commercial farmers do not reinvest in their farming operations, reflecting concern about the future.

The unequal distribution of farmland is regarded by many as a potential threat to postindependence political stability. Politically, the land issue is extremely pliable. It embodies racial and class inequalities, historical injustices between colonizers and the colonized, and elements of ethnic identity politics. Economically speaking, "land reform is widely regarded as the precondition for meaningful rural development and poverty alleviation across the party spectrum."[34] Although Namibia has not experienced farm invasions, in some areas on-farm confrontations between farmers and farm workers or their unions have occurred. When required to intervene, law enforcement agencies have acted professionally and effectively so as to avoid violence.[35]

The Namibian government has adopted two main strategies for redressing the unequal distribution of farmland. First, it has put in place an affirmative action loan scheme (AALS) through the Agricultural Bank of Namibia to assist historically disadvantaged farmers in purchasing commercial farmland by means of government-subsidized loans. From 1992 to 2003, full-time black farmers obtained 1.8 million hectares of land, while part-time farmers obtained approximately 1.3 million hectares of land.[36] Insofar as AALS has contributed to the transfer of farmland to black farmers, it has been successful. It has not been very successful, however, in contributing to increased agricultural output. Real growth in value added to commercial farming has remained at around 1 percent per year since 1994.[37] Thus, AALS farmers have added little if any value to the economy. Given this, it is possible that the AALS will experience more serious problems in the future, when the subsidy period comes to an end.[38] This could cause repayment problems for many farmers, which could in turn be costly to the government, namely in the event that subsidies are extended.[39] Although the additional fiscal burden could be justified by local political actors as an investment in political stability, the donor community may not be keen to share this burden.

Second, the government adopted a national resettlement policy (NRP) in 1992. According to the NRP, farmers wishing to sell commercial farms must offer them first to the government to be used for resettlement. If the government does not want them, the farmers are free to sell their farms on the open market. Those Namibians wishing to be resettled must show that they are landless (though they are allowed to have income and/or livestock). Once approved, applicants are awarded a section of a resettlement farm and are granted a ninety-nine-year right-to-use contract with the government. By the end of 2003, 829,486 hectares of land had been purchased for resettlement at a cost of N$121 million (US$19,162,770).[40] This is about three-and-a-half times less land than was redistributed through the AALS.

Under both instruments, about 11 percent of farmland has been redistributed since 1990.[41] At this rate, it would take about forty years for half the available farmland to be redistributed. Besides being slow, land reform is also costly, with resettlement being more expensive than subsidized loans. To redistribute about half of all available farmland would cost the Namibian government approximately N$3,033 million (US$480,336,210) or a single year's development budget.[42] It is thus not surprising that many have criticized the government for the slow pace of land reform, as well as for the introduction in 2005 of a land tax to provide more resources for land redistribution. In the final instance, it is difficult to assess popular demand for land and land reform in Namibia. No political party has embraced the land question as its main election platform or mobilizing issue. Even within SWAPO, views differ: at a political rally in Walvis Bay in mid-2005, President Hifikepunye Pohamba called for greater reconciliation, whereas the trade unions called for land invasions. To date, most ordinary Namibians do not regard land reform as an immediate policy priority for government. Rather, they suggest that creating jobs, expanding education, and fighting HIV/AIDS should be the three main policy concerns of government.[43]

Water Shortages

In addition to the scarcity and maldistribution of its arable land, Namibia faces the possibility of significant water shortage. Bordered on the east and west by two of the world's largest and oldest deserts, Namibia's most frequent natural disaster is drought. It is estimated that Namibia experienced drought every four years between 1975 and 2000.[44] Indeed, Namibia is subject to both absolute water scarcity and high water stress.[45] Both are the result of low and variable rainfall (it received an annual precipitation of about 500 millimeters or fewer between 1961 and 1990). Moreover, the fact that Namibia shares the water of its three perennial rivers with neighboring states means that fluvial usage will always be contentious. To manage these resources and their ecosystems, the Southern African Development Community (SADC) has developed a number of regional protocols that are working effectively. At the time of this writing, there are no conflicts between member states over these rivers.

Ethnic Diversity

Namibia's multiethnic society potentially constitutes another risk factor. Given that Namibia's indigenous peoples were subject to colonial policies of racial inequality and ethnic differentiation for almost a century, it is not surprising that ethnicity is often considered the dominant force in postcolonial politics. But Namibia is not as heterogeneous as is often assumed. Table 8.5 shows the effective number of

Table 8.5 Effective Number of Ethnic Groups by Region

Region	Number of Groups
Caprivi	1.82
Erongo	3.83
Hardap	2.33
Karas	2.95
Kavango	1.22
Khomas	3.92
Kunene	2.98
Ohangwena	1.02
Omaheke	3.32
Omusati	1.02
Oshana	1.04
Oshikoto	1.27
Otjozondjupa	3.88

Source: Christiaan Keulder, "Conflict Vulnerability and Sources of Resilience Assessment for Namibia," report prepared for USAID Namibia, Windhoek: IPPR, 2003.

ethnic groups by region.[46] Nearly half (six) of Namibia's thirteen regions have fewer than two effective ethnic groups and are thus nearly homogeneous. At least five of these are also politically homogeneous and together account for close to 60 percent of the ruling party's overall national support.

Namibia's case illustrates that ethnic conflict is by no means a natural consequence of ethnic diversity, despite the predictions encapsulated by primordial theories of ethnic conflict. Barring the 1999 uprising in Caprivi, the country has been free from ethnic conflict. There is no oppression of ethnic minorities, and since the Caprivi insurgency there have been no active ethnic brokers challenging Namibian statehood or nationhood.[47] This is not to say that there are no ethnic sentiments; on the contrary, given the emphasis on ethnic identity during the prolonged colonial occupation, it is not surprising that many Namibians still attach great salience to it. In 2002, only 14 percent of respondents surveyed regarded their ethnic identities as more important than the national one; in 2004, this number increased to 23 percent. Although these two data points should not be considered a trend, they do suggest that there is substantial ethnic awareness and that the issue will have to be managed carefully over time.[48]

Still, the majority regard themselves first and foremost as Namibians. Indeed, opinion polls show that Namibians generally view their communities as relatively conflict free.[49] Nearly half view their communities as either devoid of conflict or rent by it only on rare occasions. Overall, intragroup conflicts are perceived to be more common than intergroup conflicts, with different patterns observed for urban and rural areas. Urban citizens perceive intergroup conflicts to be more prominent than do rural residents, who consider intragroup conflicts to be more prevalent. Furthermore, intragroup conflicts are seen to be most frequent in regions that are ethnically homogeneous.[50] These findings suggest that groups that are more frequently exposed to ethnic diversity (such as urban residents) are more likely to have an ethnic view of conflict, whereas those who are not exposed to such diversity (such as rural dwellers and those living in homogeneous areas) are more likely to focus on other (specifically intragroup) factors. Urban dwellers are exposed much more often than rural dwellers to competition for scarce resources such as housing, social services, and wage-based employment and markets; in their highly competitive environment, winners and losers are clearly visible.

That said, when asked about potential sources of future conflict, only a small minority (13 percent) of Namibians mention ethnicity or identity.[51] Some of the more frequently mentioned sources of conflict include social problems such as alcohol abuse, drugs, and crime as well as domestic problems such as abuse and unwanted pregnancies. These types of problems are unlikely to lead to violent group-based conflict, especially in comparison with some of the political and economic problems listed. These include corruption, interparty competition, wealth-based inequalities, unemployment, and low wages. Meanwhile, although urban dwellers are more likely to justify it than are rural dwellers, the fact that the latter outnumber the former means that few Namibians believe that violence constitutes just political action.[52] Survey data also shows that there is some correlation between support for the government and the rejection of violence as justified political action.[53] Both trends are positive for the future of Namibia, as most citizens still align themselves closely with the state.

Demographic Factors

Namibia's demographic profile, which skews very young, and its associated health and education trends pose another risk factor for the young nation.[54] Some 13 percent of the population is younger than five years, 39 percent is younger than fourteen years, and 7 percent is older than sixty years. The 2005 population growth rate was 2.6 percent, down from 3.1 percent in 1991. HIV/AIDS was first diagnosed in Namibia in 1986, and it has had a significant impact on the Namibian population ever since. First, life expectancy for women has declined from sixty-three years in 1991 to fifty years in 2001. For men, it has decreased from fifty-nine years in 1991 to forty-eight years in 2001. This means that the gains in the health of the population made in the latter part of the twentieth century have been eradicated. Second, female fertility rates have fallen from 6.1 children per woman in 1991 to 4.1 in 2001. Third, throughout the country, the number of households with deaths annually has increased steadily since 1991. Fourth, HIV/AIDS has been an important factor in orphanhood. Almost 15 percent of children under the age of fifteen years have been orphaned by their mothers, fathers, or both. Fifth, in regions with the highest rates of HIV, the largest number of deaths occurs among the age groups most at risk from HIV—namely those between twenty and forty-five years, who also constitute the most economically active segment of the population.

The official literacy rate in Namibia in 2001 was 81 percent, a slight improvement over the 1991 figure of 76 percent. School attendance increased significantly in the same period: in 1991, 26 percent of the population older than fifteen years had never attended school; in 2001 it was only 15 percent. As of 2005, 34 percent of school-age Namibians older than fifteen years are still full-time students. By the standards of the developing world, Namibia's literacy and school enrollment rates are encouraging. However, the standard of education remains a problem, as a large segment of the population leaves school before completing the secondary level. While this is largely a legacy of the South African–imposed, so-called Bantu education, it remains a serious problem that affects the quality of the labor market and, subsequently, the rate of unemployment.

Significant population movements have occurred in Namibia since independence. According to the Economist Intelligence Unit, "[The] Khomas region, most of whose inhabitants live in Windhoek and its immediate area[,] which was only the third most populous region in 1991, is now the most highly populated, with 250,000 inhabitants. Much of this growth is the result of migration from the countryside—around 600 arrive in the capital every month" (see Table 8.6).[55] At the same time, the fastest growth rate since 1991 has been recorded in the Erongo region—including Swakopmund and Walvis Bay, two rapidly growing coastal towns—and Kavango to the north, into whose capital, Rundu, a large number of Angolans have immigrated.

Demographic factors are hardly ever a direct source of violent conflict, yet they can cause strain on existing economic and environmental resources, which leads to conditions of scarcity that in turn

Table 8.6 Total Population by Region, 2001 Census

Region	Total Population	Percentage
Caprivi	79,852	4.4
Erongo	107,629	5.9
Hardap	67,998	3.7
Karas	69,677	3.8
Kavango	201,093	11.0
Khomas	250,305	13.7
Kunene	68,224	3.7
Ohangwena	227,728	12.5
Omaheke	67,496	3.7
Omusati	228,364	12.5
Oshana	191,977	10.5
Oshikoto	160,690	8.8
Otjozondjupa	135,723	7.4
Total	1,826,854	100

Source: National Planning Commission of Namibia, "Namibia 2001 Population and Housing Results," March 2003, http://www.npc.gov.na/census/index.htm.

lead to increased competition and, sometimes, violent conflict. This scenario is especially typical of densely populated areas where two or more groups are competing for the same resources. In the era of South African rule, ethnic groups in Namibia were kept apart, even in urban areas, via the homeland system; as a result, they did not directly compete for scarce resources such as land and water. Though the system was abolished long ago, its legacy persists in rural Namibia today. The communal farming areas are, for the most part, ethnically homogeneous, meaning that there is no intergroup competition. Moreover, a low population density of 2.2 people per square kilometer means that contact between groups is low; the great distances between groups make it relatively difficult to mobilize large numbers of people around specific issues. The most rugged, isolated areas of the country, best suited for undetected military activity, are also the least densely populated.

The Political System

In the postindependence period, a dominant-party political system has emerged in Namibia, a fact that constitutes another potential risk factor in the view of some. Despite fifteen years of independence, the most important political cleavage in Namibia remains that of the liberation struggle. It defines and shapes electoral politics much more than ethnicity, race, class, or ideology. Apart from two very small parties to the left and right, the major political parties are all clustered around the center. The ruling party, SWAPO, meanwhile, continues to mobilize support on the basis that it was the successful liberation movement while denouncing opposition parties as stooges of the South African colonial administrations.

Voting patterns show a strong rejection of opposition parties in those parts of the country heavily militarized during the liberation struggle. These north-central regions, containing more than half of the country's population, have no floating or independent voters and are the only regions in the country with fewer than two effective parties (see Table 8.7).[56]

Further, strong partisanship in these regions negates the effects of the proportional representation (PR) electoral system. Since these regions have (1) dominant-party systems and (2) numerical superiority, the country as a whole has a de facto dominant-party system. In the context of these unified voting patterns, Namibia's PR electoral system has failed to bring about a true multiparty system, defined as having at least three parties of roughly equal size.[57] In fact, the number of parties has contracted with every election since 1989. Though the PR system has produced a larger number of opposition parties, none have grown to a substantial size. Indeed, the system provides no incentives for small parties to merge into bigger ones; on the contrary, it provides incentives for fragmentation. This fact is in part

Table 8.7 Effective Number of Parties by Region

Region	Number of Parties
Caprivi	2.19
Erongo	2.4
Hardap	2.86
Karas	2.36
Kavango	1.65
Khomas	2.27
Kunene	3.43
Ohangwena	1.05
Omaheke	2.61
Omusati	1.07
Oshana	1.10
Oshikoto	1.21
Otjozondjupa	2.87

Source: Christiaan Keulder, "Conflict Vulnerability and Sources of Resilience Assessment for Namibia," report prepared for USAID Namibia, Windhoek: IPPR, 2003.

responsible for an interesting paradox in Namibian politics: although voter volatility is high, it does not make the party system more unstable, nor does it lead to larger numbers of effective parties. Namibia thus has a dominant-party system with substantial volatility.

Each of Namibia's national elections has been declared free and fair by both domestic and international observers, and most Namibians believe that elections thus far have indeed been free and fair.[58] Political parties contesting elections generally adhere to a code of conduct, and elections are generally free of violence and conflict. Namibia's exemplary election-management record was stained in 2004, when two opposition parties successfully contested the results of that year's National Assembly elections in the High Court. With a full bench, the court declared the results null and void and ordered the Election Commission to conduct a full recount. Although the recount did not alter the overall distribution of votes, it did reveal many administrative errors and shortcomings.[59] In mid-2005, the two parties contemplated a new case to seek a rerun of the 2004 elections based on the evidence uncovered during the recount, which threatened to create Namibia's first major constitutional crisis.

Despite the emergence of the dominant-party political system, political parties remain free to register voters, operate unencumbered, and campaign for votes. Entry requirements for new political parties are low; citizens who meet the legal requirements for candidacy are allowed to register as candidates for their parties and registered voters are allowed free and secret ballots. Over the years the Electoral Commission has gone to great lengths to ensure that all Namibians have adequate opportunity to register and vote. Citizens without formal identification cards or passports are allowed to register by means of sworn statements, and mobile voting stations have been employed extensively to ensure that voters in remote areas can cast ballots. Special provisions have been made to accommodate voters outside of their resident constituencies.

It is not impossible for dominant-party systems to be democratic. Although they are qualified as "uncommon democracies," they do not necessarily produce inferior democracy.[60] That said, it is the case that under dominant parties, the chances for abuse of power are greater and voters are likely to have fewer meaningful choices at the ballot box. These two factors could cause any number of serious governance-related problems. Still, dominant-party systems also provide the much-needed political stability that is often critical to new democracies. These are polities with little or no experience with democracy and with few democrats at the elite or mass levels. Chances are good that when threatened at the polls, incumbent leaders will abolish the democratic project so as to retain their positions.

Leadership

In Namibia, the threat to democracy is real. Namibians at both the elite and mass levels have experienced more than 100 years of authoritarianism under colonialism (and even in exile). By contrast, they have experienced only fifteen years of democracy. Opinion polls show that support for democracy in Namibia is still incomplete and that there is considerable support for nondemocratic alternatives.[61] With control of more than two-thirds of the national legislature, the ruling party is in a position to unilaterally change the constitution and claim popular support for such changes. At the same time, SWAPO's dominance at the polls means that it need not be threatened by democracy. It can tolerate a free press, an active civil society, and opposition parties at almost no political cost.

Sam Nujoma, Namibia's president for the first fifteen years of independence and the leader of SWAPO since its formation in the early 1950s, remains enormously popular. As president, he demonstrated a leadership style that was both heavy-handed and reconciliatory. As party president, he managed the ruling party with an iron fist and did not tolerate opposition. Nujoma made sure that his longtime ally Hifikepunye Pohamba became Namibia's second president. Many have argued that since (1) Nujoma has not retired from his position as the SWAPO party leader and (2) he has successfully installed his own choice as president, he will continue to remain the power behind the throne.

A committed pan-Africanist and Namibian nationalist, Nujoma has at times railed against the role of so-called Western imperialist powers in Africa, a stance that has not endeared him to international donors. He has publicly lambasted gays and lesbians, white Namibians, commercial farmers, and the domestic media for promoting foreign interests or being unpatriotic. He has maintained close ties with Zimbabwe's president, Robert Mugabe, throughout that country's political and economic turmoil and has even defended Mugabe at public forums. Nujoma's close friendships with Laurent Kabila and MPLA (Movement for the Popular Liberation of Angola) cadres in Angola are thought to explain, at least in part, his decision to commit Namibian troops to the war in DRC and to allow

FAA troops to mount attacks on UNITA forces from northern Namibia.

At the same time, Nujoma has advocated a policy of national reconciliation from the earliest days of independence; among other things, he included white Namibians in every one of his cabinets. Nujoma is also lauded as a champion of women's and children's rights in the quest for gender equality. Women's Affairs was first a department in the Office of the President before being transformed into a full-scale ministry. Nujoma also played an important role in passing the 1996 Married Persons Equality Bill, which has proven to be a landmark in the struggle for gender equality. As president he also routinely included a large number of women among his picks for National Assembly candidate slates.[62]

Early in his tenure, Nujoma's successor, President Pohamba, seems to have set his policy focus on curtailing corruption. This will win him favor with most Namibians—but especially with the still predominantly white business sector. In a surprising move aimed at reconciliation in early 2005, President Pohamba received leaders from the two opposition political parties to discuss the 2004 National Assembly and their successful efforts to have the results of that year's presidential elections officially recounted. President Nujoma, by contrast, never held official talks with the opposition.

The Bloated State Apparatus

A final risk factor for the postindependence Namibian government has been the severely bloated state apparatus inherited at independence. The colonial state, with its various homeland bureaucracies, had to be dismantled and replaced with a single, unified administrative system that served all citizens, not just the privileged few. This meant that the new state was built on the old one, rather than from scratch. Moreover, Article 140 of the Namibian constitution states that all laws valid prior to independence would remain valid until such time as they were lawfully revoked. Article 141 states that all personnel employed by the colonial administration at the time of independence would remain in the employ of the new administration until they retired, resigned, or were transferred or removed, in accordance with the law. This meant that the bloated colonial state became an even more bloated postcolonial state as a significant number of new recruits were added to the existing administration. According to Henning Melber, the number of civil servants in the country grew by nearly 50 percent from 1990 to 1995.[63]

Between the bloated-state legacy of colonialism and its own commitment to a mixed economy, the government is able to enjoy a substantial share of the economy. Government expenditure on GDP averaged around 30 percent (measured at market prices) from 1990 to 2003.[64] The government owns some of the most crucial services in the economy, including water, electricity, and rail and air transport, and is a major player in other sectors. A recent concern has been the ineffectiveness of state-owned enterprises. The national airline, Air Namibia, is clearly unprofitable and is costing Namibian taxpayers millions of dollars in subsidies. In 2003 and 2004 alone, Air Namibia received N$400 million (US$63,348,000) in state subsidies, some twenty times more than the N$20 million (US$3,167,400) it received in 2000 and 2001.[65] The Namibia Broadcasting Corporation and the rail transport company Transnamib have also received substantial transfers from central government in recent years. In 2003, transfers to parastatals amounted to approximately 3.8 percent of GDP at market prices.

At an average of roughly one-fifth of the total, education is the single largest expenditure item in the Namibian budget. The second largest item is general public services, covering legislative and executive organs, financial and fiscal affairs, general personnel services, and government buildings. Health care constitutes approximately 10 percent of the total budget. In small economies such as Namibia's, it is crucial that the government strike the right balance between maintaining efficient public services and promoting development. Yet Namibia appears unable to do so due to its excessive expenditure on general public services. Add to this such luxury items as a new statehouse (at an estimated cost close to N$90 million or US$14,253,300) and jets for the head of state as well as ventures like a state-funded movie on the ex-president's life and perpetually insolvent parastatals, and it seems that much-needed resources for development are being wasted elsewhere.

As far back as 1996, the government adopted a decentralization policy that has, however, done little to ameliorate bloat. The aim of this policy was rather to relegate more functions and resources to regional councils and local authorities, thereby bringing government closer to the people. Initially, many line ministries were unwilling to shed functions, personnel, and resources in favor of regional councils and local authorities, so implementation of the policy was slow. By the mid-2000s, the policy had all but ceased to exist in light of the serious management and governance problems many local authorities are experiencing. There is a real danger that such weak and vulnerable institutions will not be able to cope with the additional demands imposed by devolved functions and that they will therefore ultimately go under.

Mitigating Factors

A number of factors serve to mitigate somewhat the impact of the risk factors we have identified.

The Constitution

At the core of the Namibian constitution is an entrenched bill of rights that guarantees citizens the usual political and civil rights found in any liberal democracy, and these have been fairly well respected since independence. Namibia is also a signatory of international human rights instruments such as the UN's Universal Declaration of Human Rights and the International Covenant of Civil and Political Rights.[66] Not surprisingly, Namibia is considered a free country by international monitors such as Freedom House. Indeed, Freedom House has ranked Namibia a free country every year since its independence, with average scores of two on the political rights index and three on the civil liberties index (where one is most free and ten is least free).[67]

The Namibian constitution also protects the right to peaceful protest, and protest action has indeed been a regular feature of Namibian politics since independence. Various groups have chosen to express their discontent in this manner: trade unions have decried employer practices; ex-combatants have demanded jobs and benefits from the government; residents have requested services from their local authorities; members have challenged their political parties; and nongovernmental organizations (NGOs) have engaged the government. More important, protesters have generally been allowed to demonstrate peacefully in practice as well as on paper, even though some events have attracted the attention of security forces. For example, ex-combatants were allowed to camp in the parliamentary gardens for days as they waited for the president to return from a trip abroad and receive their complaints. Marches by women's groups and activists have become a regular feature of International Women's Day celebrations. Overall, the government's response to public protests contrasts markedly with that of the colonial administrations, which used blatant force to quell any hint of political protest or unrest.

Traditional Leadership

Another institution that helps to mitigate the potential for conflict in Namibia is traditional leadership. As in most African countries, much of rural Namibia is still under the control of traditional leaders. These leaders and their councils allocate land, preside over customary courts, and manage community affairs, and, in so doing, serve as important vehicles for conflict mediation and management at the local level. Indeed, they are often the only mechanism through which communities can be reached and mobilized, and without their cooperation development projects are more likely to fail.

Though viewed as archaic by some, the institution of traditional leadership is still highly regarded by many Namibians. It is often their only link to the state, the only agency through which to articulate interests and needs. Surveys show that many Namibians still turn to traditional leaders to resolve local conflicts. In fact, traditional leaders provide the second most popular type of conflict mediation after that of the security forces (that is, the army and police); they are more popular than modern courts, the government, NGOs, and churches.[68]

Ironically, there is very little that is traditional about so-called traditional leadership today. Many aspects of the institution and the customs that underpin it are being changed to make it more compatible with the demands of representative democracy and with government policy objectives. Many communities today elect their traditional leaders, especially village headmen. In some instances, local customary law has been codified, making it less arbitrary and dynamic. Some aspects of customary law were changed to conform to the constitution and its provisions for equality and the protection of human rights. One area of reform, for instance, involved widows and their right to inherit common property from deceased husbands. Another reform abolished corporal punishment from customary courts because it is prohibited by the constitution. Although the number of women in traditional offices is still small, it is no longer unheard of for women to be appointed or elected to traditional leadership positions.[69]

The constitution provides for the Council of Traditional Leaders to serve as an advisory body to the Namibian parliament and president. This body meets a few times a year to discuss matters such as communal land issues and leadership disputes. Although it has no real policy-making powers, it does tie the institution of traditional leadership to the state, thereby helping to promote peace and stability in rural areas. Through the council, leaders of all major ethnic groups have access to the state, and rural communities have an additional mechanism by which to raise their concerns and express their interests.[70]

Civil Society and the Media

Suppressed under colonialism and apartheid, civil society and the media have sought to mitigate government excesses since independence. For example, outside the white community, groups with public interests were not allowed to be formally organized; the result was that informal personal networks became the dominant and most effective instrument for mobilization. The main exceptions were trade unions and other community-based organizations, which emerged primarily from a few urban townships during the 1980s.[71] This meant that at the time of independence, Namibia's civil society was small and exclusive. Moreover, after a boom period of rapid expansion, it has again waned considerably, despite the fact that it is now easy and relatively inexpensive to formally register nonprofit organizations. A lack of resources, overdependence on donor support, and skills shortages—though not the lack of free political space—restrict the growth of civil society in Namibia today. By and large, rural interests are still unorganized; excepting churches, civil society organizations have failed to penetrate and capture these interests. For this reason, in August 2005, delegates from the eighty-five-member Namibia Non-Governmental Organizations Forum (NANGOF) met with the prime minister to urge the adoption of a policy document fostering relations between the government and civil society.[72]

Colonialism has also had a huge impact on the media in Namibia. First of all, the colonialist authorities prevented black ownership of the media and stifled the growth of community-based media. Radio remains the most far-reaching medium and, other than a few commercial stations, is firmly in government hands. The same applies to television, which is thoroughly dominated by the Namibian Broadcasting Corporation. In addition, access to computers and the Internet remains fairly limited. Still, Namibia has four large independent newspapers, all of which have been allowed to report freely and critically. Although the government has banned all government advertising in one of the four, it has not adopted any measures to curb media freedom. No journalists have been detained, nor have any newspapers been closed down. Indeed, two or three independent dailies act as significant government watchdogs.

Finally, Namibia is regarded as one of the least corrupt countries in Africa. In 2001, Transparency International ranked Namibia thirtieth overall on its Corruption Perceptions Index (CPI) with a score of 5.4 (where ten is highly clean and zero is highly corrupt). It was the second cleanest African country after Botswana.[73] In 2002, Namibia's ranking improved to twenty-eighth with a score of 5.7, the highest since independence.[74] Thereafter it declined, and in 2004 Namibia was ranked fifty-fourth with a score of 4.1.[75] A 2005 study of print media reports on actual cases of corruption showed that the media is free to report on corruption and that it has done so extensively. Since 1990, the main newspapers have carried 1,247 articles on 467 cases of corruption. Nearly half the cases (44 percent) occurred in a government ministry or department, 11 percent within another government agency, and 16 percent within a parastatal. This means that nearly 70 percent of corruption cases involved agencies of the state. The study also showed that Namibia has had a significant case of corruption once every two years, although the overall number of corruption cases reported in the print media has been declining since 1992. At the same time, the intensity with which the print media covers key cases has increased.[76]

In the mid-2000s, Parliament passed an anticorruption law that provides for an anticorruption agency to be established. This agency was set up and funds for its operations were provided for in the 2005–2006 annual budget. In addition to the Anti-Corruption Agency, two other government institutions deal with corruption. The Office of the Auditor General audits the government's accounts and the Office of the Ombudsman investigates civil service transgressions.

Regional and International Factors and Policies

Namibia participates in several southern African bodies and receives both bilateral and multilateral development assistance. It is a member of two important regional organizations: the aforementioned SADC and the Southern African Customs Union (SACU). As a member of SADC, Namibia is a signatory to several treaties, protocols, and agreements that govern its relations with its neighbors in areas as diverse as water, trade, illicit drugs, tourism, education, mining, health, conservation, firearms, corruption, election standards, and social rights.[77] A concrete manifestation of regional cooperation has been the establishment of transnational game parks. These parks were formed by merging adjacent existing national game parks and removing all customs requirements for tourists traveling within the larger, transnational entity. The SADC Parliamentary Forum (SADC-PF) monitors elections in the region and has developed a set of regional standards. It has also developed standards for gender equality; for example, in 1997, SADC heads of state pledged that 30 percent of decisionmaking positions would be held by women by 2005—a target that Namibia met at the local level and nearly met at the national level.[78] Although these norms and standards are not yet enforceable, they do provide a cross-regional set of yardsticks by which an individual country's performance can be measured.

The SACU links Botswana, Lesotho, Namibia, Swaziland (known collectively as the BLNS states), and South Africa. Historically, SACU gathered excise duties on local production and customs duties on member states' imports from outside the union area. These were then paid to all member states using an agreed revenue-sharing formula. After a decade of negotiations to reform SACU, a new agreement that addressed many long-standing problems came into effect in July 2004. Namibia is also a member of the African Union (AU).[79]

Given the international community's close involvement in the Namibian independence struggle and peace process, it is not surprising that the country attracted significant donor assistance once independence was achieved. Indeed, at the time of independence, Namibia had the highest foreign aid per capita of any African country.[80] Together, Germany and the Scandinavian countries account for more than half the aid given to Namibia since independence. These countries have strong historical links to Namibia. In the case of Germany, the link dates back to 1884; indeed, as a former colonizer, Germany is under renewed pressure to rectify the wrongs of the past. In 2004, the German government officially apologized for the war against the Herero and Nama people that led to the deaths of thousands of men, women, and children in the early twentieth century, though it stopped short of admitting to genocide. In May 2005, the German government announced that it would significantly increase its aid to Namibia and that the Herero and Nama peoples would receive a substantial proportion of the increase—an attempt to compensate them for their suffering. The Germans anticipate focusing their development assistance much more on land reform in the future.

The Scandinavian countries' aid to Namibia is a continuation of their extensive support to the liberation movement prior to independence, as well as, in the case of Finland, even longer-standing missionary ties. Sweden alone has accounted for one-fifth of bilateral aid to Namibia since independence, although that assistance has now fallen dramatically. By 2008, Swedish bilateral aid was replaced by commercial, contract-financed technical cooperation; collaboration between municipalities in Sweden and Namibia; and NGO cooperation between the two countries.[81]

Figure 8.1 shows the breakdown of aid to some of the key target sectors for the period 1991 to 2003. Education was the prime target sector, followed by economic infrastructure. The latter includes various subsectors such as transport and storage, communications, energy, and banking. Overall, the main targets for assistance reflect the priority sectors in the Namibian economy (mining, agriculture, and fishing) as well as the main challenges to development and a better quality of life (education, water, health, and environmental protection).

Still, development assistance to Namibia overall is falling, as is the number of bilateral donors. Figure 8.2 shows that the volume of aid has declined steadily over time, hitting its lowest level in 2001 and then recovering somewhat by 2003. Total grants to Namibia fell from a high of US$180 million in 1991 to just under US$130 million in 2003 (which was, however, up from US$100 million in 2001). Moreover, several bilateral donors have been withdrawing from the

Figure 8.1 Aid by Sector, 1991–2003

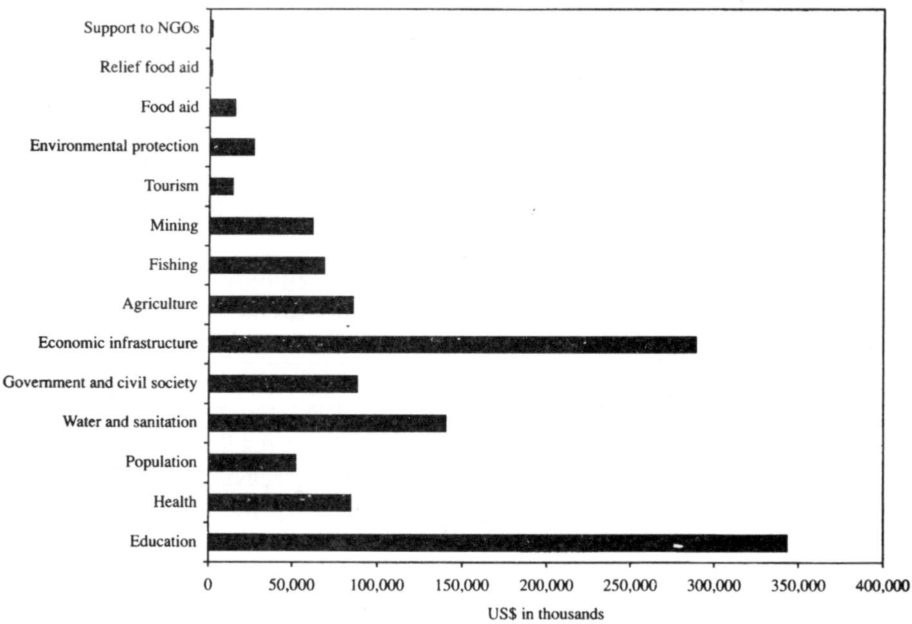

Source: Organization for Economic Cooperation and Development, various years.

Figure 8.2 Volume of Aid (total grants)

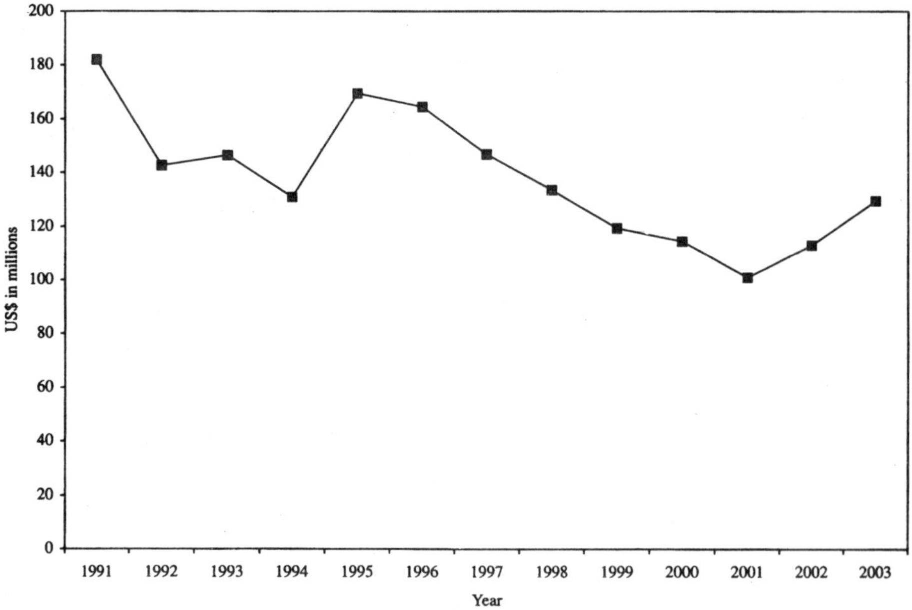

Source: Organization for Economic Cooperation and Development, various years.

country. In 2003, Portugal and the UK's Department for International Development (DFID) ended their Namibian programs. In 2006, another of Namibia's important donors, the Netherlands, phased out its assistance and will eventually terminate its presence in the country altogether. Finland has also been winding down its long-standing support to Namibia.

The United States, too, considered decreasing its aid to Namibia, channeled through the US Agency for International Development (USAID), in the early 2000s. However, compelling arguments from the Windhoek USAID office based on the probability of continued successes in the new democracy convinced Washington to change course and not draw down its assistance. After reaching a low of US$9.5 million in 2000, US bilateral aid increased steadily to US$29.2 million in 2003.[82] At the time of this writing, US development aid to Namibia focused on basic education, community-based natural resource management, and democracy and governance.[83]

The European Commission (EC) is the largest multilateral donor to Namibia. EC aid to Namibia fell to a historic low of US$24.6 million in 2003, then increased in 2004 mainly in support to education; the government, civil society, and NGOs; the private sector of business, trade, and tourism; and agriculture, forestry, and fisheries.[84] Overall, multilateral assistance to Namibia fell steadily from US$60.4 million in 1999 to US$34.4 million in 2003 (although the low of US$31.2 million came in 2001).[85]

The Importance of Democracy to Security and Development

Fifteen years after a successful transition to democracy, Namibia remains, against substantive odds, one of Africa's most stable democracies. Its small but highly skewed economy, its history of ethnic and racial animosity and discrimination, its dependence on a few natural resources for economic growth and experience with significant shortages of others—all pose potential risks to political stability and democratic consolidation. Yet only Botswana and Mauritius have experienced longer periods of uninterrupted democratic rule in southern Africa.

Namibia provides evidence that democracy can take root in a society with little or no democratic experience. Compared to most other countries in the region, popular demand for more democracy is relatively low in Namibia, yet the supply is high, suggesting that the consolidation of the democratic regime remains incomplete.[86] There are a number of factors that explain why the country remains politically stable despite its incomplete consolidation of democracy. First, the protracted nature of the Namibian transition to independence meant that all actors involved in the process had to agree on substantive issues such as core constitutional principles before the final handover of political power. For the most part, all the political actors remain committed to these principles and to the constitution as a whole. Despite some shortcomings raised earlier in this chapter, the democratic regime functions well enough to largely ensure political stability. The rule of law is respected and the judiciary plays an important part in mitigating political conflict, as evidenced by the aforementioned ruling that the 2004 parliamentary election results be recounted.

Second, Namibia's dominant-party system also accounts for much of the country's political stability. Given the widespread lack of experience with democracy, the liberation movement–turned–ruling party's immediate electoral dominance meant that it had sufficient time to get used to the opportunities and constraints imposed on it by the democratic system. Its dominance afforded it time to find its way as the new government and to pursue its policies without fear of electoral defeat. The fact that the liberation movement achieved and maintained its electoral dominance by means of free and fair elections meant that there was no need to revert to subversive strategies to maintain power, as has been the case in nearby Zimbabwe. Even after fifteen years of democracy, the ruling party is under no pressure to abort or subvert the democratic system; in fact, the potential costs of not having democracy are higher than the costs of maintaining it. The electoral dominance of the ruling party also ensures that the Namibian state has sufficiently high levels of public trust and legitimacy to pursue its socioeconomic development agenda. As a result, there have been no political or violent challenges from any significant social grouping within the Namibian polity.

Third, Namibia is a functioning state with sufficient extractive, coercive, and symbolic capacity to incorporate all significant social groupings and suppress potential violent challenges to the government and the nation if and when they arise. It successfully dealt with the 1999 secession attempt in Caprivi, and no other group has posed a similar challenge since. Despite criticisms and shortcomings, all Namibians have benefited from government development policies—today there are more schools, clinics, water distribution points, and electricity connections than ever before. The standard of living of previously advantaged white Namibians has not deteriorated significantly, while that of previously disadvantaged black Namibians has improved (albeit at a very slow rate). Also, compared to some other governments in southern Africa, the Namibian government has not committed serious political or policy blunders that have caused widespread political discontent.

It was relatively easy for the Namibian government to implement a development policy framework after independence for at least two reasons. First, during the liberation struggle, SWAPO maintained links with both the capitalist West and the socialist East, which meant that at the time of independence it did not have to revise its ideological position to win favor with the international community. Moreover, with the collapse of the socialist East, no debilitating ideological alliance with one side or the other was necessary, as it had been for many countries in the days of the Cold War. Second, the preference for developmentalism was and is shared by all major political actors and parties in the country. Hence, there are no major challenges either to the policies of the government or to its emphasis on developmentalism by means of a mixed economy. Namibia's liberation struggle was ultimately a nationalist struggle for self-determination, not an ideological struggle for a society shaped by socialism or capitalism. Thus, by the time independence arrived, there were no major unresolved ideological struggles between local political actors or global political contenders to fuel violent conflict as there were in both Angola and Mozambique.

Fourth, Namibia's lack of political violence and conflict can be partly attributed to the interaction of geographic and demographic factors. Although these factors cannot be attributed to deliberate policy decisions or seen as the outcome of any single strategy, their contribution is important. Included in this list of incidental factors are extremely low population densities that inhibit social organization and networking, vast areas of inhospitable land that cannot sustain human activity of any kind, and the location of the country's natural resources. Diamonds, for example, are found either deep in the Namibian desert or at sea, a fact that adds considerably to mining costs and thus makes gaining illegal access to them (much less transforming them into blood or conflict diamonds, as happens in Angola) nearly impossible. These factors make it extremely difficult for any social group to organize, network, or finance antistate conflict on a significant scale.

Finally, from 1995 to 2005, southern Africa has become a much less hostile neighborhood for democratic countries such as Namibia. The liberation struggle in South Africa ended with black-majority rule and a democratic polity. Malawi and Zambia moved from single-party regimes to multiparty democracies. The protracted wars in Mozambique and Angola were brought to an end, and although the latter remains a continuing challenge, the former has since conducted three national multiparty elections. A fragile peace accord in DRC has meant that Namibia could withdraw its troops from that conflict situation. The fact that neighboring countries such as Angola and Zambia provided assistance to the ruling party during the liberation struggle has meant not only that Namibia has always had positive relations with its neighbors but that very little of their conflicts have spilled over into Namibian territory. The continuing turmoil in Zimbabwe is too far away from Namibia to affect it in any immediate way. Unlike neighboring Botswana and South Africa, Namibia has not received any significant number of Zimbabwean refugees.

Having laid the foundations on which democracy could prosper, Namibia continues to face serious challenges in addressing human development and human security. Poverty, together with vast inequalities in income and living standards, remains a potential source of future instability. The speed of development thus far remains slow, and as the positive effects of political gains wear off, much more tangible results will be required. For starters, this means that the development goals set by the government must be met if not exceeded. For that to happen, more and faster economic growth must be achieved—a task that is all the more difficult given the reductions in foreign aid and the problems being experienced by prominent economic sectors such as fishing. Many more new jobs are required, and corruption must be curtailed (signs from the Pohamba administration are encouraging on this front). As generational changes occur among voters and the political benefits of the immediate postindependence period continue to wear off, the ruling party must determine how best to maintain its electoral dominance. Although there is little evidence to suggest that it will lose its dominant position any time soon, SWAPO will have to find new ways to appeal to an ever-changing voter corps—sooner rather than later.

Notes

1. For accounts of the transition see Lionel Cliffe, Ray Bush, Jenny Lindsay, and Brian Mokopakgosi, *The Transition to Independence in Namibia* (Boulder, CO: Lynne Rienner Publishers, 1993); Joshua B. Forrest, *Namibia's Post-Apartheid Regional Institutions: The Founding Year* (Rochester, NY: University of Rochester Press, 1998); and Gerhard Erasmus, "The Constitution: Its Impact on Namibian Statehood and Politics," in *State, Society, and Democracy: A Reader in Namibian Politics,* ed. Christiaan Keulder (Windhoek: Gamsberg Macmillan, 2000).

2. UN, *United Nations Development Assistance Framework 2001–2005: Co-ordination and Co-operation of the United Nations System in Namibia*, 41, http://www.undg.org/archive_docs/770-Nambia_UNDAF_-_2001-2005.pdf.

3. Economist Intelligence Unit (EIU), *Namibia Country Profile 2004* (London: EIU, 2004), 44.

4. EIU, *Namibia Country Profile 2004*, 49.

5. Government of the Republic of Namibia—National Planning Commission, "Namibia: 2004 Millennium Development Goals," Windhoek, 2000, http://www.sarpn.org.za/documents/d0001012/index.php.

6. Lindsay Detlinger, "Namibia Remains the Most Unequal Country in the World," *The Namibian*, September 15, 2005, http://www.namibian.com.na/index.php?id=28&tx_ttnews[tt_news]=20617&no_cache=1.

7. EIU, *Namibia Country Profile 2004*, 45.

8. EIU, *Namibia Country Profile 2004*, 44.

9. Government of Namibia, "Namibia Vision 2030: Policy Framework for Long-Term National Development" (Windhoek, 2004); EIU, *Namibia Country Profile 2004*, 44.

10. UN, *United Nations Development Assistance Framework 2001–2005: Co-ordination and Co-operation of the United Nations System in Namibia*, 9.

11. Detlinger, "Namibia Remains the Most Unequal Country in the World."

12. EIU, *Namibia Country Profile 2005* (London: EIU, 2005).

13. UNDP, *Namibia: Human Development Report 2000*, Windhoek: UNDP, 2000, 27.

14. EIU, *Namibia Country Profile 2004*, 35.

15. EIU, *Namibia Country Profile 2004*, 36.

16. Some 57,000 former combatants were demobilized. These included 32,000 PLAN fighters, 25,000 SWATF fighters, 2,000 San soldiers, and 3,000 from Koevoet. See Andre Du Pisani, "The Role of the Military in the Formation and Consolidation of the Namibian State," in *Demilitarisation and Peace-Building in Southern Africa, Volume III: The Role of the Military in State Formation and Nation-Building*, eds. Peter Batchelor, Kingma Kees, and Guy Lamb (Burlington, VT: Ashgate, 2004), 69.

17. Andre Du Pisani, "The Role of the Military in the Formation and Consolidation of the Namibian State," 70.

18. Andre Du Pisani, "The Role of the Military in the Formation and Consolidation of the Namibian State," 68.

19. EIU, *Namibia Country Profile 2005*, 17.

20. Christiaan Keulder, "Conflict Vulnerability and Sources of Resilience Assessment for Namibia," unpublished report prepared for USAID Namibia, 2003, 56.

21. Gretchen Bauer, "Namibia: Ushering in the Second Decade of Independence," *Africa Contemporary Record 28: 2000–2002* (New York: Holmes and Meier, 2006).

22. Keulder, "Conflict Vulnerability and Sources of Resilience Assessment for Namibia," 56.

23. Keulder, "Conflict Vulnerability and Sources of Resilience Assessment for Namibia," 57.

24. On one occasion, after a heated speech in which the former president had lashed out against homosexuality, members of the SFF openly harassed gay citizens in Katutura, claiming that they were following the president's wishes.

25. EIU, *Namibia Country Profile 2004*, 33.

26. UN High Commission for Refugees (UNHCR), *Statistical Yearbook 2003: Trends in Displacement, Protection and Solutions* (New York: UNHCR, 2003).

27. In this chapter, conversions from Namibian dollars to US dollars have been calculated at a 2004 average rate.

28 Only Botswana, Russia, Angola, South Africa, and Canada are bigger producers by value. For a detailed analysis of the diamond industry in Namibia, see Martin Boer and Robin Sherbourne, "Getting the Most Out of Our Diamonds: Namibia, De Beers, and the Arrival of Lev Leviev," IPPR [Institute of Public Policy Research] Briefing Paper no. 20 (Windhoek: IPPR, 2003).

29. Robin Sherbourne, "Namibia's Great White Hope," IPPR Briefing Paper no. 7 (Windhoek: IPPR, 2001).

30. Sherbourne, "Namibia's Great White Hope."

31. Dry land areas are land areas that fall within three of the world's six aridity zones: arid, semiarid, and dry subhumid. Dry land areas have an aridity index (defined as the ratio of average precipitation to average evapotranspiration) of between .05 and .65. See World Resources Institute, "Earth Trends: Environmental Information," http://earthtrends.wri.org.

32. Keulder, "Conflict Vulnerability and Sources of Resilience Assessment for Namibia."

33. Martin Angula and Robin Sherbourne, "Agricultural Employment in Namibia: Not the Engine of Wage Employment Growth," IPPR Briefing Paper no. 16 (Windhoek: IPPR, 2003).

34. Werner Wolfgang, "The Land Question in Namibia," in *Contemporary Namibia: The First Landmarks of a Post-Apartheid Society,* eds. Ingolf Diener and Oliver Graefe (Windhoek: Gamsberg Macmillan, 2001), 259.

35. Although not directly related to the land issue, a number of attacks on farmers have increased tensions. In the mid-2000s, a number of white farmers were murdered in attacks that appear to be inspired either by robbery or revenge. In one such incident, a recently dismissed farm worker killed a farmer, his wife, and eight other staff members, including a number of children.

36. Robin Sherbourne, "A Rich Man's Hobby," IPPR Opinion paper no. 11 (Windhoek: IPPR, 2003), 6.

37. Sherbourne, "A Rich Man's Hobby," 6.

38. According to the AALS, full-time farmers are expected to pay full interest rates (11.75 percent) ten years into the loan. During the first three years, no interest is paid; for years four to six, interest is charged at 2 percent; at 4 percent for years seven and eight; and at 8 percent for year nine. Part-time farmers are expected to pay interest from year one but at a reduced rate, depending on the size of the loan.

39. AALS farmers are not allowed to sell their farms during the first ten years, the period during which they receive interest subsidies.

40. Robin Sherbourne, "Rethinking Land Reform in Namibia: Any Room for Economics?" IPPR Opinion paper no. 13 (Windhoek: IPPR, 2004), 4.

41. Robin Sherbourne, "Rethinking Land Reform in Namibia: Any Room for Economics?" 4.

42. Robin Sherbourne, "Rethinking Land Reform in Namibia: Any Room for Economics?" 4.

43. Christiaan Keulder and Tania Wiese, "Democracy Without Democrats? Results from the 2003 Afrobarometer Survey in Namibia," Afrobarometer Working Paper no. 47 (Cape Town: Institute for Democracy in South Africa [IDASA], 2005).

44. Keulder, "Conflict Vulnerability and Sources of Resilience Assessment for Namibia."

45. Brian Jones, *Selected Natural Resource Management and Limited Rural Development Assessment* (Windhoek: USAID Namibia, 2003), 14.

46. The effective number of ethnic groups creates an index that takes into account the relative size of each group by weighting each group by its size. The following formula is used: *EGeff* = 1/™*egi*2 ; where *egi* is the size of the Ith ethnic group.

47. Ted Robert Gurr and Monty Marshall, *Peace and Conflict 2003: A Global Survey of Armed Conflict, Self-Determination Movements, and Democracy* (College Park, MD: University of Maryland, 2003).

48. Keulder and Wiese, "Democracy Without Democrats?"

49. Christiaan Keulder, "Conflict Vulnerability and Sources of Resilience Assessment for Namibia."

50. Christiaan Keulder, "Conflict Vulnerability and Sources of Resilience Assessment for Namibia," 37.

51. Christiaan Keulder, "Conflict Vulnerability and Sources of Resilience Assessment for Namibia," 40.

52. Christiaan Keulder, "Conflict Vulnerability and Sources of Resilience Assessment for Namibia," 41.

53. Christiaan Keulder, "Conflict Vulnerability and Sources of Resilience Assessment for Namibia," 42.

54. The data for this section comes entirely from the Government of the Republic of Namibia, *2003 National Census Report* (Windhoek: National Planning Commission, 2003).

55. EIU, *Namibia Country Profile 2004*, 33–34.

56. Calculated using the Laakso-Taagepera Index (1979) index of effective parties, where *Peff* = 1/™ *pi 2* and *pi* is the vote share of the Ith party. Markku Laakso and Rein Taagepera, "'Effective' Number of Parties: A Measure with Application to West Europe," *Comparative Political Studies* 12, no. 1 (1979): 3–27.

57. Namibia uses a PR system for national and local legislative elections and a first-past-the-post system for regional elections. The PR system used is of the closed-list variety and incorporates a Hare quota. For National Assembly elections, the country is treated as a single constituency and there is no legal threshold for representation. The large district magnitude together with the lack of legal thresholds makes it very easy for small parties to gain representation. This makes Parliament more inclusive but contributes to a fragmentation of party politics.

58. Christiaan Keulder, *Voting Behaviour in Namibia III: Presidential and National Assembly Elections 1999* (Windhoek: Friedrich Ebert Stiftung, 2000); Christiaan Keulder, *Voting Behaviour in Namibia I: Local Authority Elections 1998* (Windhoek: Friedrich Ebert Stiftung, 1999); Christiaan Keulder, *Voting Behaviour in Namibia II: Regional Council Elections 1998* (Windhoek: Friedrich Ebert Stiftung, 1999).

59. In one instance, some 900 valid ballot papers were discarded during the recount because their markings became illegible due to rainwater seeping into the ballot box while in storage.

60. T. J. Pempel, *Uncommon Democracies: The One-Party Dominant Regimes* (Ithaca, NY: Cornell University Press, 1990).

61. Keulder and Wiese, "Democracy Without Democrats?"

62. Gretchen Bauer, "'The Hand That Stirs the Pot Can Also Run the Country': Electing More Women to Parliament in Namibia," *Journal of Modern African Studies* 42, no. 4 (2004): 479–509.

63. Henning Melber, "Public Administration: Constraints and Challenges," in *Contemporary Namibia: the First Landmarks of a Post-apartheid Society*, eds. Ingolf Diener and Olivier Graefe (Windhoek: Gamsberg Macmillan, 2001), 93–109.

64. Institute for Public Policy Research (IPPR), available at http://www.ippr.org.na.

65. Ibid.

66. Gerhard Erasmus, "The Constitution: Its Impact on Namibian Statehood and Politics," in *State, Society, and Democracy: A Reader in Namibian Politics*, ed. Christiaan Keulder (Windhoek: Gamsberg Macmillan, 2000).

67. For more statistical information on civil liberties in Namibia from Freedom House, see www.freedomhouse.org.

68. Christiaan Keulder, "Conflict Vulnerability and Sources of Resilience Assessment for Namibia," 41.

69. Christiaan Keulder, "Traditional Leaders," in *State, Society and Democracy: a reader in Namibian politics*, ed. Christiaan Keulder, (Windhoek: Gamsberg Macmillan, 2000), 150–171.

70. Christiaan Keulder, "Traditional Leaders," 150–171.

71. Gretchen Bauer, *Labor and Democracy in Namibia, 1971–1996* (Athens, OH: Ohio University Press, 1998).

72. "Civil Society Meets with the PM," *The Namibian*, August 5, 2005, http://www.namibian.com.na/index.php?id=28&tx_ttnews[tt_news]=12383&no_cache=1 .

73. Transparency International. *Global Corruption Report 2001*, 234, http://www.transparency.org/publications/gcr/gcr_2001.

74. Transparency International. *Global Corruption Report 2003*, 264, http://www.transparency.org/publications/gcr/gcr_2003.

75. Transparency International. *Global Corruption Report 2005*, 236, http://www.transparency.org/publications/gcr/gcr_2005.

76. Christiaan Keulder, *The Print Media and Reports on Corruption 1990–2004* (Windhoek: Namibia Institute for Democracy, 2005).

77. For more on SADC, see http://www.sadc.int.

78. Bauer, "'The Hand That Stirs the Pot Can Also Run the Country.'"

79. EIU, *Namibia Country Profile 2005*, 57.

80. Lindsay Detlinger, "Namibia Could Have Done Much Better," *The Namibian*, December 7, 2005, http://www.namibian.com.na/index.php?id=28&tx_ttnews[tt_news]=13349&no_cache=1.

81. Sweden International Development Cooperation Agency (SIDA), personal correspondence.

82. EIU, *Namibia Country Profile 2005*, 80.

83. "US Aid to Namibia to Focus on Education, Conservancies," *The Namibian,* August 18, 2005, http://www.namibian.com.na/index.php?id=28&tx_ttnews[tt_news]=12527&no_cache=1.

84. EC, personal correspondence, on file with Christiaan Keulder.

85. EIU, *Namibia Country Profile 2005,* 80.

86. Keulder and Wiese, "Democracy Without Democrats?"

9

The Security-Development Crisis in Guyana

Perry Mars

In this chapter, I examine the causes and consequences of political and ethnic conflict in Guyana and assess the utility and impact of various national and international interventions, especially those involving development assistance, aimed at addressing such conflict. The focus is on security and development trends since 1985, following the sudden death of Forbes Burnham, who had been Guyana's president since 1964. More specifically, I explore how fluctuations in economic trends correlate with variations in the levels of political and ethnic conflict in the country. Additionally, I look closely at particular localized regions that are experiencing both economic vicissitudes and civil conflicts, particularly Buxton, the Bauxite Belt, and the Sugar Belt, to examine the impact of government policy interventions on security and developmental outcomes in these areas and, ultimately, in the country as a whole. Finally, I also attempt to estimate the risk of ethnic rebellion and insurgency facing Guyana and the extent to which the particular combinations and sequences of domestic and international policy interventions—particularly those involving poverty reduction—can help transform the prospect of a serious escalation of violence into the assurance of a more peaceful developmental process in the country.

Background and History

Guyana is the only English-speaking country on the mainland of South America. It is situated north of Portuguese-speaking Brazil, west of Dutch-speaking Suriname, and east of Spanish-speaking Venezuela (it borders the Atlantic Ocean to the northeast). The country is highly urbanized—about 40 percent of the total population lives in either the capital city of Georgetown or one of the two other main hubs, New Amsterdam and Coriverton.[1] Its relatively small population of about 750,000 people is heavily concentrated on a small strip of northern coastland that constitutes less than 10 percent of Guyana's land space. The rest of the country is remote hinterland or forested (jungle) terrain where scattered populations of Amerindians, itinerant miners, and loggers live. The historical demand of what is known as king sugar—that sugar plantations be located near the seaports on the coastland—has led to the neglect of hinterland development, even though this area is rich in natural resources such as gold, diamonds, and precious hardwoods.

The country is racially and ethnically diverse, comprising at least six different ethnic groups, the most sizeable of which are the East Indians or Indo-Guyanese, with about 49.4 percent of the population, and the Afro-Guyanese, with about 35.6 percent. People of mixed ethnic/racial ancestry and the Amerindians each make up approximately 7 percent of the population, while the Chinese, Europeans (both white and Portuguese), and others total the remaining 1 percent.[2] Ethnic diversity is reflected in both the economic and political spheres of life in Guyanese society.[3]

An ethnic-based division of labor, which stems from deliberate colonial policies, exists in the sense that the primary sectors of the economy—agriculture, industry, and service—are distinguishable by high concentrations of differing ethnic populations in each sector. For example, agricultural production of sugar and rice on the rural coastland tends to be dominated by East Indians, while mining (concentrated in the interior) and the public service (concentrated in the urban areas) tend to be the preserves of the Afro-Guyanese. The native Amerindians work largely in logging and peasant farming in the forested hinterland, while mixed and other lighter-skinned populations (including the Chinese and Portuguese) predominate in mainly urban commercial business settings. This ethnic segmentation, rather than serving as a buffer against interethnic conflict by providing safe havens for every group, in fact demonstrates the stark inequalities among groups and has precipitated many of the political and ethnic conflicts Guyana has witnessed over the years.

Guyana's political system has evolved from one of colonial domination, which seriously restricted democratic participation, to a full electoral democracy based on the British parliamentary system. Various European powers colonized Guyana—first the Dutch, then the French, and finally the British, who granted independence in

1966. It was only as recently as 1951 that Guyana obtained a modern constitution from the British, namely the Waddington Constitution, granting the colony universal electoral suffrage. In 1953, the first democratic elections were held. The then-nationalist movement led by Dr. Cheddi Jagan and his People's Progressive Party (PPP) swept the polls, only to be met with a vicious response from the British authorities, who defined the PPP as communist and therefore intolerable within the British Empire. The PPP government was swiftly dismissed from office. The party itself soon succumbed to a calculated British effort to split the movement, first by jailing Jagan along with those they regarded as his extremist cohorts and then by using his supposedly more moderate archrival, Forbes Burnham, to challenge Jagan for the party leadership in 1955.[4] In 1958, Burnham broke away to form his own party, the People's National Congress (PNC).

Although the basis for the 1955 PPP split was initially ideological, the fact that Jagan was East Indian and Burnham was Afro-Guyanese soon led to polarized ethnic voting patterns, particularly as of the 1961 elections. By the time of the critical preindependence elections of 1964, East Indians had almost exclusively identified with the PPP while the Afro-Guyanese had similarly adhered to the PNC. The other lighter-skinned and mixed ethnicities, including Amerindians, identified with a procolonial party, the United Force (UF).

The most intense levels of political violence in Guyana took place between 1962 and 1964 following the PPP's return to power in 1957. The violence was instigated by a combination of domestic, political, and ethnic hostilities in the wake of domestic contestations of political power and external Cold War–related interventions—mainly on the part of the United States and the UK, which were seeking to prevent the supposedly Marxist PPP from gaining power on the eve of independence.[5]

It was a period in which political violence and ethnic polarization coincided and reinforced each other in the form of retaliatory killings between East Indian and Afro-Guyanese populations. British involvement in imposing the proportional representation (PR) electoral system in 1964 generated heated, indeed violent opposition from PPP supporters, who claimed to have been cheated of victory at the 1964 polls. Between 1962 and 1964, over one hundred persons were killed and untold numbers uprooted from their homes, particularly in ethnically mixed neighborhoods—a turn of events that led to the creation of polarized ethnic enclaves throughout the Guyana coastlands.[6]

The introduction of the PR system in 1964 was intended to open up political space for more inclusive ethnic group participation in electoral politics. However, the opposite has occurred due to ethnic polarization around the two major political parties, the PPP and PNC, each of which has mobilized popular support on the basis of negative ethnic appeals and the instigation of fear of the other. Although PR has in fact brought multiple ethnic groups into Parliament, the result is not significantly different from that of earlier elections based on the first-past-the-post constituency system. More importantly, parliamentary multiethnicity has had very little effect on political policy and decisionmaking, since Parliament is merely a relatively ineffectual debating chamber whereas real, binding decisions remain in the hands of the cabinet and president, which is to say the executive branch of government.[7]

The fact also that the executive branch is invariably dominated by the typically ethnicity-based majority party makes for the indefinite exclusion of opposition parties and minority ethnic groups from meaningful participation and the rewards of the political system. The exclusive dominance of the winning party, which usually garners less or little more than 50 percent of the popular vote, suggests the operation of a zero-sum democracy whose existence is usually attributed to the electoral democratic framework that Guyana inherited from the British via their Westminster system of government. Many of the political and ethnic conflicts in Guyana, particularly since the advent of PR in 1964, stem from the skewed ethnic representation arising from its winner-take-all form of political decisionmaking.[8]

The years following independence saw the rise to power of the very repressive and authoritarian PNC regime that had succeeded the PPP at the polls in 1964. The slogan of Burnham's PNC regime "Peace Not Conflict" cleverly played on the party's initials. Yet the postindependence period bore witness to some of the most intensely violent events. The 1969 Amerindian secessionist uprising in the interior Rupununi region, for instance, was swiftly put down by the newly formed Guyana Defense Force (GDF) at the cost of many casualties on both sides. The 1973 protest march against electoral rigging led to similar army intervention and the killing of two opposition PPP supporters. The 1977 sugar workers' strike, led by the PPP-affiliated Guyana Agricultural and General Workers' Union (GAWU), lasted 135 days but was severely repressed and ultimately defeated by a combination of the regime's military and paramilitary forces. The 1989 general strike against the PNC-sponsored International Monetary Fund (IMF) economic austerity program was followed by the government's dismissal of the striking workers.

Despite sporadic violence, the PNC administration—including

both the Burnham (1964–1985) and the Hoyte (1985–1992) regimes —lasted some twenty-eight years. Those twenty-eight years of autocratic rule within ostensibly democratic parameters were characterized by political repression and autarchic economic regimens that resulted in large-scale capital flight, brain (and brawn) drain, and chronic public unrest due to mass discontent with an increasingly isolated political establishment. Public protest against continual electoral rigging by the PNC led, after Burnham's sudden death in 1985, to the intervention of several international humanitarian and political organizations, including the Carter Center. The PNC government, which by then meant the Hoyte administration, grudgingly consented to a return to free and fair elections and to the restoration of representative democracy. Also within this period, the Hoyte administration introduced the IMF-inspired Economic Recovery Program (ERP) to liberalize the Guyanese economy.

The Changing Nature of Conflict

The various political conflicts in Guyana can be characterized as follows: electoral/political strife in the 1950s; racial/political violence with foreign instigation during the 1960s; violent political repression during the 1970s; a brief, uneasy period of peaceful overtures between the government and the opposition during the 1980s; a return to electoral violence and ethnic conflict in the 1990s; and a degeneration into politicized gangsterism, particularly since 2000, when excessive police and military forces and death squads began targeting various ethnic-based militant groups. The conflicts in the post-Burnham period can be more specifically divided into three phases, as suggested in Table 9.1.

The first phase (1985–1991) began with the succession to power of the new Hoyte administration and ended on the eve of a free and fair election in 1992, which was won by the People's Progressive Party/Civic (PPP/C) party. This first phase is identified as a crisis phase, characterized by the popular unrest surrounding global economic impacts as well as by massive labor protests and general strikes against the IMF and the ERP, which had imposed economic austerity on the country. The culminating events of this phase were the 1989 general strike and public protests staged against electoral rigging and for free and fair elections; these unfortunately resulted in repressive governmental interventions, including the dismissal of public service and university workers.[9]

Table 9.1 Characteristics of Post–Cold War Conflicts in Guyana

Phase	Conflict Level	Major Policy Interventions	Description of Events	Results
Phase I 1985–1991	Crisis	IMF/ERP: economic austerity	1989 general strike; civil society street protests for "free and fair elections"	State dismissal of public workers; CCC intervention; end of strike
Phase II 1992–1998	Limited violent conflict	Carter Center; CARICOM: international mediation	Postelection violence (1992); postelection violence (1997); protests; ethnic targeting; arson; PNC boycott of Parliament and calls for civil disobedience	Police interventions/ violence; CARICOM and Commonwealth mediations leading to Herdmanston Accord and St. Lucia Statement; call for dialogue
Phase III 1999–2005	Armed confrontations, gangsterism	Coercive/ Military Emphasis	Politicized criminal violence; Buxton "guerrilla" campaign; ethnic targeting; death squad killings; kidnappings; police deaths; storming of Presidential Secretariat	Extensive police/ military/death squad operations; civil society, GHRA interventions; breakdown of dialogue

Sources: Compiled from The Caribbean Community (CARICOM) Mission to Guyana, "Herdmanston Accord, Measures for Resolving Current Problems," signed in Guyana, January 17, 1998; *Stabroek News,* various issues; *Guyana Chronicle,* various issues; and *New Nation,* various issues.

The second phase (1992–1998) represented a shift from crisis to what could be called limited violent conflict, when the political protests primarily against the results of the 1992 and 1997 elections sometimes erupted into a combination of street riots, violent ethnic targeting, and coercive state and police interventions to quell the disturbances. Now sporadic, now massive interethnic violence between supporters of the PPP and the PNC, particularly following the 1997 elections, threatened to escalate even further in intensity. The major opposition party, the PNC, boycotted Parliament during this period—which, however, ended with the humanitarian interventions of both the Carter Center and CARICOM (the Caribbean Community and Common Market), culminating in the signature of two peace agreements in 1998 between the PPP/C regime and the PNC opposition. Afterward, the PNC returned to Parliament.[10]

The Carter Center had intervened at the invitation of the Hoyte regime in the wake of the political protests. As a former president of the United States, Jimmy Carter had himself succeeded in brokering an agreement with the government for the international monitoring of the 1992 elections and had further recommended the establishment of continuous dialogue between governing and opposition parties in the interests of political stability. By 1997, however, talks between the two parties had broken down. The country returned to a more elevated phase of political violence, following claims by the PNC and other opposition parties that the 1997 elections were rigged in favor of the PPP/C regime. It was at this stage that CARICOM was invited by the two parties to help broker yet another peace agreement between them. CARICOM's efforts resulted in the 1998 Herdmanston Accords, which called for an international audit of the election results and a return to dialogue by the two parties.[11] However, the government's failure to implement these agreements led to further intervention by CARICOM as well as to the signing of the St. Lucia Statement later that year, which recommended a halt to the violence and established a facilitator for the resuscitation of the dialogue process between the two contending parties.[12]

The third phase of political conflict in Guyana (1999–2005) entailed a sharp shift from limited violence to a more elevated form of conflict that could be thought of as organized armed confrontation directly involving military and paramilitary forces. This third phase included armed attacks on the police, the politicization of narco- and other criminal forms of gangsterism, further ethnic targeting and violence, joint police and army operations against suspected village guerrillas, and the extensive use of paramilitary death squads in support of police operations. More specifically, this third phase saw turmoil within the labor movement and an escalation of bellicose rhetoric between the two major parties. The opposition leader, Desmond Hoyte, called for massive civil disobedience, which the PPP/C president Bharat Jagdeo likened to terrorism.[13] It was within this escalatory context that a storming of the Presidential Secretariat by opposition supporters took place, resulting in the deaths of two protestors at the hands of the police and the arrest on charges of treason of two protest leaders in July 2002.[14]

However, it was the events in Buxton that came to symbolize the organized armed (or at least more militarized) nature of political and civil conflict during this third phase. Buxton, a predominantly Afro-Guyanese village about twelve miles outside of Georgetown, provided, with its high levels of unemployment among youth, a convenient milieu for escaped prisoners, drug traffickers, and other deadly criminals. Police killings of several armed youths in Buxton led to the retaliatory killings of several policemen by gangs, giving rise to President Jagdeo's call to the armed forces to "clean out Buxton" in May 2003.[15] Two of the main political characteristics of these Buxton-based events were (1) the overt politicization of gang activities (the gangsters defined themselves as freedom fighters and gained tacit support from the political opposition),[16] and (2) the targeted killing of East Indians in apparent vengeance attacks against the PPP/C government, which received heavy East Indian support.[17]

After 2005, the levels of conflict continued to escalate as burgeoning criminal gangs engaged in virtual guerrilla warfare in the jungles; although operating principally against the security forces in tit-for-tat armed exchanges, they also targeted particular communities on both sides of the ethnic divide. Early in 2008, bloody massacres took place in three communities: the East Indian village of Lusignan on the east coast; the ethnically mixed mining town of Bartica in the northern interior region; and along the upper reaches of the Berbice River, mainly among Afro-Guyanese diamond miners at Lindo Creek.[18]

One indicator of escalating levels of political violence is the number of casualties over time. In Guyana, an accurate assessment of the number of casualties of political violence is difficult to come by, since no credible statistics exist. The peculiar conflation of political activism with criminal activities during the third phase further adds to the difficulty. However, there are some figures on police killings over the years that provide some intimation of the intensity of crime-related violence and political tension in the country. For instance, reports of civilian deaths from police violence increased from an annual average of fifteen during the first phase (ending in 1991) to seventeen during the second phase[19] to, eventually, twenty during the more elevated third phase.[20] From 2000 to 2003, the most critical years of the third phase, the number of killings by police—excluding the unknown numbers of civilians murdered by death squads—dramatically increased to twenty-three. Also over this three-year period, scores of police officers were killed by armed criminal and politicized gangs.[21] Notably, it was during this post-2000 period of heightened politicized violence that the rise of the notorious death squads became most evident as well, contributing to the intensity of violence overall during this period. The death squad has often been referred to as the phantom squad because of its shadowy character. It is said to have arisen in response to the deteriorating security situation in the country, one characterized by both the precipitous rise in violent crime following the prison breakout of some notorious criminals in

2002 and the deportation of drug and other criminal offenders from the United States back to Guyana in 2003.[22]

Opposition charges that the death squad was nurtured by the Guyanese government—specifically by then Minister of Home Affairs Ronald Gajraj—and financed by wealthy businessmen[23] were not borne out by the government-imposed Commission of Inquiry in 2004, particularly after key witnesses either died in execution-style killings by unknown assailants[24] or otherwise failed to show up at the proceedings. Many killings of youths in the country are attributed to operatives of the phantom squad.[25] Conflicts in Guyana tend to be located in economically depressed regions or areas, which also have heavy concentrations of Afro-Guyanese populations that are largely supportive of opposition political parties—areas such as the city of Georgetown, mainly black villages on the coastland like Buxton, and mining towns such as Linden.

In general, ethnic and racial divisiveness, disparities, and polarization in Guyana are usually seen in the context of the distribution of critical resources, from land and businesses to political posts and representation. In these respects, East Indians are perceived to be better placed in Guyanese society than their Afro-Guyanese counterparts. Such perceptions often give rise, particularly among opposition political parties and their mainly Afro-Guyanese supporters, to allegations of discrimination in government policies, while countercharges from the governing PPP/C and its mainly East Indian supporters claim that criminal violence from the Afro-Guyanese section of the population is overwhelmingly directed against East Indians in the country. As such, both PPP/C and PNC election rhetoric and mobilization efforts tend to inflame antagonisms and hostilities between the two major ethnic groups that respectively support them.

Development Trends

Macroeconomic Trends

Guyana's economy is traditionally based mainly on three export commodities: sugar, rice, and bauxite. World Bank figures for 2005 suggest that the service sector, primarily public, contributes 44 percent of Guyana's gross domestic product (GDP), followed by agriculture (mainly sugar and rice) with 31 percent and industry (mainly mining and small-scale manufacturing) with 24 percent of the GDP.[26]

The levels of economic development in Guyana have fluctuated depending on international as well as domestic factors and policies. In 1989, for example, upon the IMF's request, the Hoyte administration introduced the aforementioned ERP, which was intended to liberalize the economy through a strong emphasis on privatization.[27] However, the ERP instead led to a 5 percent fall in GDP and an inflation rate that had risen to 100 percent by 1991.[28] This was followed by a respite in the economy beginning in 1991, which the PPP/C extended when it took control in 1992. As a result of modernization and structural reforms in the economy, the new PPP/C government realized single-digit inflation rates, a 7.4 percent growth in real output, and increases in per capita income from US$380 to US$750 in 1996.[29] There was also significant growth in the rice and sugar industries during this period, particularly between 1990 and 1998.[30]

Since 1996, however, economic growth has consistently slowed due to exogenous factors, including a decline in commodity prices, unfavorable weather conditions, and endogenous factors that include what the Guyanese government conceded was "a difficult political and industrial environment"—presumably an allusion to the period of industrial unrest and political instability that both preceded and followed the controversial 1997 elections.[31] Between 1999 and 2005, the economic growth rate in Guyana averaged about 0.6 percent. In 2005, for instance, the rate plummeted to a depth of negative 3 percent, although it recovered in 2006 with a growth rate of 4.7 percent.[32] In addition, according to World Bank figures, the rate of private investment decreased significantly—from 13.4 percent of GDP in 1998 to 6.6 percent in 2003.[33] At the same time, the Guyanese budget deficit widened from 4.9 percent of GDP in 2000 to as much as 13.2 percent of GDP by 2003.[34] Meanwhile, the external debt gradually increased, reaching approximately US$1.2 billion in June 2005.[35]

In general, then, the Guyanese economy has tended toward consistent decline since the mid-1990s. Another significant indicator of the downturn is the currency rate, which has declined markedly every year since the country introduced a floating exchange rate in 1988. Thus, while the exchange rate was 27.1 Guyana dollars (G$) to one US dollar (US$) in 1989, it was 125 to one in 1992 when the government changed hands; in 1998 it was 150 to one, and in 2000 it fell even further to 184.7 to one.[36] In 2005, the rate stood at about 200 to one.

On a world scale, Guyana ranks somewhere between the lower and middle ranges of economic development. The 2005 Human Development Index (HDI) indicates that Guyana ranks 107th out of 177 countries, while Haiti, the lowest in the hemisphere, ranks 153rd and Barbados, one of the highest in the world, comes in at thirty.[37] In 2006, Guyana further declined with respect to HDI value (ranking 110th), while Haiti made some gains with a ranking of 148.[38] In terms of GDP, only Haiti is ranked lower than Guyana in the hemisphere, as it is for containing the highest percentage of people living below the poverty line.[39]

Socioeconomic/Demographic Trends

In addition to its poor macroeconomic performance, Guyana suffers from stark levels of economic inequality. For example, the share of income or consumption by the poorest 10 percent of the population is estimated to be at 1.3 percent, while the share controlled by the richest 10 percent is as high as 33.8 percent.[40] Such economic inequalities can also be detected across regional levels within the country. The distribution of extreme poverty rates in the country (per 1999 figures) is as follows: 19 percent for the country as a whole, 70.8 percent for interior (hinterland) communities, 18.1 percent for rural coastal areas, and 8.2 percent for the city of Georgetown.[41]

Although government statistics put the unemployment rate at about 10 percent, it is more probable that the real rate hovers between 15 and 50 percent, depending on the region, locality, or stratum in question.[42] Unemployment levels are highest among youth and in rural peasant farming areas and hinterland communities. Meanwhile, more than 40 percent of the working-age population (fifteen years and older) is described as being "outside [the] labor force or economically inactive."[43]

Guyana's general population increased from 723,673 in 1991 to 751,223 in 2002, with significant ethnic and regional variation. While, for example, the Afro-Guyanese and East Indian populations declined by 2 percent and 5 percent respectively, the Amerindian and mixed populations increased by 3.5 percent and 3.2 percent respectively. In fact, the Amerindian population jumped from 46,722 in 1991 to 68,819 in 2002, representing a 47.3 percent increase.[44]

In terms of regional distribution (among the ten official geographic/administrative regions in Guyana), the most populated area is Region 4 (which includes the city of Georgetown and villages like Buxton on the east coast of Demerara), with 41.3 percent of the population; its nearest rival, Region 6, follows with 17 percent. However, the largest population decline—by 18,600 persons or about 3.2 percent of its 1991 share of the population—has also occurred in Region 6 (East Berbice).[45] Also significant is a population decline in the city of Georgetown, although there was some growth in the suburbs and outlying regions; a major newspaper in Guyana stated that "growth in Region 4 is concentrated outside of the city and along the East Coast and East Bank Demerara areas."[46]

With regard to poverty rates for Guyana, a government review of the 2006 Poverty Reduction Strategy Paper (PRSP) suggests that 33 percent of the population lives below the poverty line, while those in extreme poverty constitute 18 percent.[47] These figures represent a slight improvement over earlier estimates such as the UN Common Country Assessment for 2005, which put the figures at 36.3 percent and 27.7 percent respectively.[48] Steep inequalities are demarcated along both class and ethnic lines. Eighty-eight percent of Amerindians and 43 percent of Afro-Guyanese occupy the lowest rungs of the economic ladder, compared with the 33 percent of East Indian Guyanese who fell below the poverty line in 2000.[49]

The economic downturn after 1996 appears to have been greater within those economic enclaves dominated by the Afro-Guyanese working classes, such as the mining and public service sectors. Bauxite mining, for instance, has suffered from declining production, resulting in the return of workers to their native coastlands. Production of calcined bauxite, for example, has fallen steadily every year since the 1980s—from 529,000 metric tons in 1984 to 106,000 metric tons in 2000.[50] Also significant for Afro-Guyanese unemployment on the coastlands is the drastic decline of public sector jobs. Between 1987 and 2000, for instance, employment in central government declined from 27,411 to 8,885; in the remaining areas of the public sector, it dropped from 47,167 to 23,510. The total public sector decline was from 74,578 to 32,395, which represents a drop of about 56 percent.[51] Significant unemployment and labor unrest within these sectors facilitated the emergence of large numbers of idle youth, further thwarting efforts toward political stability.

By contrast, production in the more East Indian–dominated sugar and rice industries has tended to steadily increase over the years, largely because of government subsidies or protected markets. Between 1990 and 2000, production in the rice industry increased steadily from 93.4 thousand metric tons to 291.9 thousand metric tons, with an export value rising from G$513.2 million (US$2.5 million) to G$7.4 billion (US$37 million) between these years. In the case of sugar, production rose from 129.7 thousand metric tons in 1990 to 273.3 thousand metric tons in 2000, with an export value increasing from G$3.2 billion (US$16 million) to G$22.1 billion (US$110 million) over these years.[52]

Development and Conflict

As I have now demonstrated, there is a close relationship between escalating levels of civil and political conflict and declining levels of economic performance and development in Guyana as a whole. The main exception seems to be the atypical economic growth spurt that occurred between 1991 and 1996, when the level of political conflict was increasing from that of the crisis phase of unstable peace witnessed from 1985 to 1991 to that of the second phase, characterized by limited violent conflict (1992–1998). This second phase was in fact a period not only of economic growth but also renewed democratization, acquiescence to external mediation, and greater openness to international economic processes. It was also the period of dialogue between the two major parties. But the third phase (1999–2005) represented a return to the marked coincidence of economic decline and increased political and ethnic violence.

The evidence thus far presented suggests, however, that the incidence of poverty per se, which is particularly characteristic of both rural and hinterland Guyana, is less significant as a predictor of civil unrest and violence alone than it is in combination with the positioning of economic inequalities along class, community, and ethnic lines. More specifically, disparities in poverty levels among demographically significant communities and a sense of powerlessness among disadvantaged groups are critical factors in the generation of political and civil unrest. For example, the dislocation of peasant farmers in the rural coastland and the high levels of unemployment and political disempowerment among youth in economically depressed urban enclaves have caused concentrations of major civil, largely Afro-Guyanese, unrest.

The relationship between poverty and violent political conflict constitutes a vicious cycle. Chronic poverty within depressed communities (such as the rural peasantry) and among dispossessed groups (such as the unemployed youth of impoverished urban enclaves) tends to coincide with a higher incidence of political and social unrest, leading to criminality and ethnic violence. The rise of violent crime (including some associated with drug trafficking) occurs predominantly in these areas characterized by economic dispossession mainly because it is often linked to the opportunity to increase material benefits and rewards. This spiral of poverty and violent conflict is observed to deepen within such disadvantaged communities and spread throughout the society as a whole. In turn, social unrest and political violence contribute to further economic decline and the consequent deepening of poverty levels. In the case of Guyana, persistent political instability tends not only to destroy existing economic structures but also to chase away local capital and skilled personnel, as well as potential foreign investments.[53]

Therefore, a more appropriate economic measure than overall GDP of potential violent conflict is the level of economic development of the most depressed and potentially violent communities; statistics on the development of particular industries such as bauxite, sugar, and the service sector tend to be more helpful in understanding the causal connections between economic forces and combined levels of civil unrest and political violence. That said, economic indicators, although important, cannot adequately explain how conflict levels have escalated and mutated in Guyana. What is also necessary here is an understanding of the political dimensions of conflict. In this respect, the politicization of issues such as economic deprivation and discrimination, the fairness of elections and political representation, and approaches to conflict interventions are critical factors to consider.

Another important question: to what extent are recent demographic trends significant as an explanation of variations in the levels of social and political conflict around the country? The 2002 Guyanese census indicates that declining populations might be experiencing increased migration and therefore what some might see as a safety-valve effect, lessening the overall intensity of conflict. However, the fact that the overwhelming majority of the population decline is in Region 6, which is relatively low in conflict proneness, makes this outcome rather unlikely. By the same token, the possibility that the population increase in the outskirts and suburbs of Georgetown contributes to youth unemployment in conflict-prone areas like Buxton and Agricola is tenable only up to a point and only in a very limited way, since the shifts in total population register only in the hundreds rather than in the thousands.

The main significance of the population shifts appears simply to be their potential to escalate political and electoral conflicts as a result of their influence on the fierce debate between the People's Progressive Party/Civic (PPP/C) government and the People's National Congress/Reform (PNC/R) and other opposition parties over verification of the voter list. This polarized debate enraged the country during the 2006 election campaign as the principal electoral institution, the Guyana Elections Commission (GECOM), became sandwiched in the middle. Whereas the PNC/R and opposition parties seemed anxious to remove migrant populations from the existing electoral list, which was based on the 2001 election, the PPP/C government not only praised the list as adequate and insisted that those listed had the right to vote in 2006 but also stridently condemned the opposition parties for objecting to its use.[54]

However, the 2006 elections were relatively, not to mention quite uncharacteristically, peaceful despite the strongly contentious campaign rhetoric of the two major parties. Even more surprising was the fact that for the first time since Guyana's independence in 1966, the main opposition party unconditionally accepted the election results. The opposition PNC acknowledged the legitimacy and results of the 2006 elections, which returned the PPP to government with 53 percent of the votes. What had changed, it seemed, was the quality of the leadership of the major opposition party; PNC head Robert Corbin was by this time pressing the issue of power sharing with the PPP government.[55] In turn, President Jagdeo had made strong promises to employ more inclusive governance and more directly involve opposition parties.[56] However, this nuanced approach by the PNC leader led to a fracas as his leadership was challenged within the party.[57] Meanwhile, by the end of 2008, the PPP government had failed to act on its preelection promises toward governmental inclusiveness.

Risk Factors and Capacities for Peace

The telltale signs of Guyana's moderate to relatively high level of conflict risk are multiple. They include the existence of deep ethnic and political polarization;[58] the economic discontent affecting major ethnic sections of society and the generalized poverty from which rebel recruitment and mobilization spring;[59] security forces that are weak, undermanned, underfunded, and outgunned compared to criminal gangs; the politicization of narco- and other criminal forms of gangsterism; arms trafficking and stockpiling by politicized groups; and intransigence on the part of both the government and the opposition. Other factors contributing to the country's precarious situation include its Cold War–era history of ideological struggles involving foreign intervention and divisive policies,[60] the heavy emphasis on coercive and repressive strategies for conflict management at the state level,[61] and a political system that fosters a zero-sum contest for political power among competing groups.[62]

Table 9.1 demonstrates the consistent elevation of conflict levels in Guyana from crisis (1985–1991) to limited violent conflict (1992–1998) to organized (or militarized) armed confrontation (1999–2005). Given the political, economic, and social conditions of conflict risk in Guyana, it is not inconceivable that unless careful, strategic preventive measures such as Michael Lund's "preventive diplomacy"[63] are adopted, conflict levels could escalate further to what Stanley Samarasinghe and others identify as insurgency,[64] involving increased attempts to usurp power, organized armed threats to the government, or even the emergence of a state within the state. Further adding to the high risk of escalating conflict is what appears to be the serious weakness of existing political and social institutions and structures that help maintain political and ethnic stability. The 1953 and 1962–1964 conflicts left a legacy of highly politicized ethnic divisiveness reinforced by an electoral system that allowed for Westminster-style zero-sum contention for power among rival political groups. The introduction of the PR electoral system in 1964, which was intended to pressure parties to engage in coalition politics and thereby cut across or neutralize racial political representation in Parliament, did not succeed as expected. Instead, it helped to institutionalize ethnic voting patterns in Guyana.[65] The PR electoral system that is still in force today also polarizes ethnic representation in Parliament, with more than 60 percent of East Indians representing the PPP and a similar percentage of African-Guyanese representing the PNC.

The main problem with the Westminster electoral system as practiced in Guyana is that it fosters a politics of frustration and indefinite exclusion for opposition parties or out-groups.[66] Political opposition groups in Guyana have continually expressed the hopeless feeling of permanent exclusion from authoritative decisionmaking; this was the case for the PPP opposition during the autocratic Burnham years just as it is for the PNC opposition today under the PPP/C regime. This system also feeds the tendency toward intransigence on the part of ruling parties as well as the perception among opposition and civil society groups of discrimination in political decisions and policies. This generalized perception is even acknowledged in the government's aforementioned PRSP, which admits the presence of "racial and political discrimination" at local levels—including within the Regional Democratic Council (RDC) and Neighborhood Democratic Council (NDC), which function as subdivisions in each of Guyana's ten administrative regions.[67] Within this context, the probability of violent political conflict remains high.

To accurately assess the risk of conflict escalation one must also take into account a given country's history of violent conflict. In the case of Guyana, the events of both 1953 and the 1962–1964 period involved high levels of largely foreign-instigated political violence and ethnic polarization. In both 1953 and 1964, British colonial and US-sponsored interventions aimed at defeating Jagan's supposedly

Marxist politics included (1) politically, ideologically, and ethnically divisive tactics; (2) the provision of financial resources for the labor movement and opposition political parties; and (3) propaganda intended to instigate violent political upheavals in the country.[68] Undoubtedly, one of the main reasons the current conflict situation has not escalated to the level of extreme ethnic rebelliousness characteristic of the 1960s is that in the post–Cold War period divisive ideological interventions and destabilizations in Guyana are no longer a priority for powerful foreign states.

Today, external destabilizing interferences are more closely related to criminal activities such as international drug trafficking. Guyana is fast becoming a favorite location for drug transshipment with all its implications for illegal arms trafficking, violent gangsterism, and potential political destabilization. In 2005, the International Narcotics Control Strategy Report (a report prepared annually for the US Congress) cited the massive seizure of drugs from Guyana at international ports such as London, New York, and Toronto as evidence that narcotrafficking is on a steep increase in Guyana, due in part to the porous borders the nation shares with Venezuela and, indirectly, Colombia and in part due to high-level state corruption.[69] The report further suggested that "every commodity that Guyana exports has been used to ship cocaine out of the country," alluding to the high-profile seizures of cocaine hidden in coconuts, timber, frozen fish, rice, and molasses by agents in the US and UK in 2004.[70]

Directly associated with drug trafficking is money laundering. The report further suggested that money laundering is a large part of the informal economy—which is in turn thought to encompass between 40 and 60 percent of all the nation's economic activity—and concluded, "There are suspicions that high levels of drug trafficking and money laundering are propping up the Guyanese economy." In addition, the report referred to widespread allegations of corruption reaching government levels that "continue to go uninvestigated."[71] This corruption also extends to arms trafficking. In 2002, Desmond Hoyte, then leader of the main opposition party, complained that the PPP government was engaging in a cover-up of the illegal gun trade and failing to prosecute dealers who'd been caught red-handed with the most powerful weapons in the business.

As we have emphasized, given the overlapping political, social, and institutional challenges facing Guyana, the risk of escalating political and ethnic conflict is estimated to be high.[72] Thus it is particularly important to understand Guyana's security and development prospects in light of the nature and appropriateness of the responses by the government, nongovernmental organizations (NGOs), and other stakeholders to the said risk.

Domestic Responses

Guyana has transitioned from taking a typically statist developmental approach during the Burnham era (1964–1985) to adopting the free market strategy dictated by the IMF according to its structural-adjustment conditionalities and reflected in the Hoyte-era ERP to, finally, the combination of free market and poverty reduction measures the PPP/C regime introduced in 2000. These latter indicated a move away from a centrally directed or public-centered economy to one based essentially on privatization strategies and what are conceived to be the requirements of economic globalization. For this reason, the private sector is intended to displace state-controlled policies in the Guyana economy.

Economic Strategies

Guyana's economic strategies are based principally on the government programs relating to poverty reduction outlined in its 2002 PRSP and on the Carter Center's recommended program, which is in turn outlined in the National Development Strategy (NDS), a civil society document adopted by the PPP/C government in 2005. Since 2002, Guyana's government has developed strategies for economic development that focus on poverty reduction and economic growth. As presented in the PRSP, the government's goals for economic and political stability can be summarized as follows: (1) creating jobs by increasing economic growth, putting an emphasis on foreign private investments; (2) strengthening public institutions for better governance, putting an emphasis on equal treatment of all stakeholders in the system; (3) decentralizing public services and legislating against discrimination in areas like land distribution; (4) investing in both human and physical capital, including health, education, water and sanitation, and general environmental protection; and (5) improving safety nets and continuously addressing regional pockets of poverty.[73]

How the proposed funds are to be allocated indicates more specific priorities within the government's overall development strategy. Briefly, these priorities are economic growth, the modernization of the sugar and rice sectors, and a shift from bauxite to other minerals on the one hand and, on the other hand, good governance and political stability, police reform (including community policing), and a stronger judiciary.[74] Even more specific projects are identified at regional or local levels: for the bauxite region, the goals are the privatization of the industry and the encouragement of small businesses and entrepreneurial development in the area; for the Amerindian communities, the establishment of a Ministry of Amerindian Affairs and the creation of the Amerindian Development Fund are priorities; and for local communities and village councils, the main concern is the promotion of greater autonomy to deal with such public funding programs as the Social Impact Amelioration Program (SIMAP).

Guyana's investment strategy emphasizes the private sector, the development of a skilled labor force, a movement away from primary production into the service and manufacturing industries, and equitable distribution of economic activity.[75] This perspective is derived from the comprehensive NDS of 2005, which became the inspiration for the Guyanese government's overall poverty reduction strategies. The NDS outlines the need for increased economic growth if Guyana is to significantly develop by 2010. It further identifies the urgency of addressing the problem of racial and ethnic conflict as a precondition for economic development in the long run. Finally, it suggests a multipronged, geographically equitable economic strategy that encompasses export promotion, private capital investment, infrastructure development, inclusive governance, and the remigration of skilled Guyanese from abroad—all aimed at the elimination of poverty.[76]

Policy Results

The policies for addressing poverty and conflict in Guyana have resulted in some generally positive outcomes. In general, Guyana has significantly and steadily increased its scores on HDI trends from 1985 to 2003 as follows: 0.677 (1985), 0.683 (1990), 0.685 (1995), 0.714 (2000), and 0.720 (2003).[77] Also, the government claims that between 2002 and 2006 the Guyana Office of Investment (GO-Invest) was able to attract seventy foreign investment projects and seventy-four domestic investors for a total of US$424 million; between 2003 and 2004 specifically, both export and import volumes increased by 14.8 percent and 13.4 percent, respectively.[78]

Efforts to strengthen public institutions have borne some fruit, especially in the case of the much-needed, government-created Ethnic Relations Commission (ERC), which is very active in investigating allegations of racial and ethnic discrimination, mainly those that occur at the workplace. The ERC was established by a parliamentary act in 2000 and given a mandate "to promote ethnic harmony" via investigative, facilitative, educative, and research functions.[79] By 2004, the ERC had investigated eighteen complaints from both groups and individuals, although only two of these had been concluded or resolved up to 2006. Meanwhile, the ERC complains of having serious resource limitations.[80] Similarly, other critical public institutions such as the judiciary and security forces remain relatively weak because of limited resources.[81] For this reason, crime, particularly for gun violence, is alarmingly high.

Since its first meeting in 2003, the ERC has been very active in investigating and settling matters related to ethnic and racial discrimination. However, the ERC's potential tends to be limited by several other factors beyond lack of adequate resources, including training and expertise, as well as an overload of complaints with which part-time commissioners must cope.[82] A major problem for the ERC is the largely negative image it has among significant sections of the Guyanese people. According to the commission's CEO, such suspicion is based on "a lack of knowledge of the ERC and its commissioners."[83] Decisionmaking needs to be decentralized so as to give louder voice to local communities on such issues as the distribution of economic resources and local ethnic representation—issues that are now relegated to what appears to be an increasingly overburdened ERC. Investment in human capital has yet to produce strong results, as illustrated by the poor and apparently declining quality of public education[84] as well as by the brain drain embodied by numerous educated and skilled laborers (including teachers and nurses) seeking overseas job opportunities.[85]

The policy objectives of the Guyana PRSP fall short of satisfactorily addressing the more serious causes of political and ethnic tension, particularly communal divisiveness and noninclusive government. The drafting of the PRSP itself was a missed opportunity for the government to involve the opposition parties and private sector representatives. The result is a PRSP document that is not sufficiently conflict sensitive. Meanwhile, Guyana's efforts toward poverty reduction and the main goals of the PRSP are still unrealized. Economic growth rates have remained stagnant since 1999, while adequate amounts of private foreign investment have so far failed to materialize.[86]

A major problem with the Guyanese government's declared economic policy objectives is the lack of analysis of the relationship between economic objectives and security conditions—as reflected in the levels of ethnic and political stability in the country. Though the

NDS (unlike the PRSP) is most emphatic about the need to address governance and ethnic-instability problems, it has failed to demonstrate precisely how this need is linked to its economic analyses and projections. No causal analysis of trends related to political conflict and violence is suggested as a basis for understanding how different approaches to economic development may help in the resolution or mitigation of conflict, or, conversely, how conflict management may affect economic trends. The NDS also reflects ambiguities about democratic governance; on the one hand, it demands increased democratic participation, while on the other hand it denigrates labor strikes and political protests (including marches and demonstrations) as both indicative of "bad governance" and inimical to the prospects of economic development.[87] Both the PRSP and the NDS, therefore, lack sufficient conflict sensitivity.

Policy Limitations

It is hard to evaluate the impact of government policies on local communities where it matters most—in terms of poverty reduction. This difficulty was acknowledged by the presidential secretary, Roger Luncheon, in a June 2005 address to the regional and local stakeholders at the second annual progress report on the PRSP program, wherein he pointed to the urgent need for data collection to more properly address the practical eradication of poverty on the ground. Local representatives reacted, complaining about the lack of progress in program implementation, the inability to secure necessary financial resources, their exclusion from the decisionmaking process, and government corruption. In particular, the representative from Region 4 complained of the overcentralization of decisionmaking in the Office of the President to the exclusion of Parliament. In addition, he asserted that the government had approved the allocation of only 18 percent of what had originally been stipulated for his region's budget.[88]

Within the government's policy framework, one usually overlooked group that can have a positive impact on both poverty reduction and conflict mediation is the Guyanese diaspora. It contributes to the Guyanese economy via a high volume of remittances. In the 2003–2004 period, gross diaspora remittances to Guyana from the United States alone totaled approximately US$230 million, reflecting a significant increase from US$54 million in 1997.[89] These remittances are said to represent 83 percent of official development assistance (ODA), 134 percent of foreign direct investment (FDI), and 13 percent of overall GDP.[90] In addition, they constitute about 80 percent of the personal income of their recipients and about 50 percent of per capita GDP.[91] However, these remittances generally support living expenses rather than business investments. Apart from its capacity for domestic economic investment, the diaspora also has the ability to mediate the conflict situation in Guyana—though mediation is generally neglected as a tool for addressing the nation's security problems.

As much as 89 percent of the most educated segment of the Guyanese population lives overseas.[92] Meanwhile, Guyanese political parties often receive significant sums of money from expatriates for campaigns and mobilization efforts.[93] In light of these statistics, it is no wonder the Guyanese diaspora can be seen as either a source of both conflict stimulation and conflict mitigation at home. However, if properly organized to overcome their own ethnically divisive limitations, members of the diaspora—being as they are sources of expertise, remittances, and party contributions—could muster the leverage necessary to influence the direction of party policies in their homeland.[94]

The Security Sector

Guyana's military and security forces have struggled over the years due to relatively weak manpower and an inadequate budget. The strength of the security forces usually remains at about 1,400 for the GDF and 3,000 for the police.[95] Government military expenditure relative to the GDP declined from 1.7 percent in 1994 to 0.8 percent in 2003; indeed, the military often complains about low salary.[96] Historically, the Guyana security forces tended to be disproportionately Afro-Guyanese—the International Commission of Justice (ICJ) report in 1965 put the figures at 73.5 percent African, 19.9 percent East Indian, and 6.6 percent other.[97] The disproportionate ratio of Afro-Guyanese to East Indians in the security forces has gone largely unchanged, although some efforts have been made to recruit more East Indians and Amerindians.

Despite their resource handicap, the military and security forces have played an independent, professional role since the nation's return to democracy in 1992 in defending the new PPP regime against opposition-inspired protests and violent activism. Constitutionally, civilian officials control the military and police forces; however, the rule of law has been under threat due to their ruthless approach toward suspected and wanted criminals. Beyond official police efforts, overwhelming deadly force has been used against criminals in the form of an ominous secret paramilitary force, the phantom squad or death squad, which targets suspects alleged to be associated with violent criminal activities.

In response to increasing political pressure from opposition parties, civil society, and international sources, the Guyanese government created the Commission of Inquiry in 2004 to investigate allegations that the death squad was supported and possibly organized by government officials, primarily then minister of home affairs Ronald Gajraj.[98] The Commission's findings cleared the minister but still led to public and international outcry for his resignation, which eventually occurred in May 2005. The following month, the Guyanese government, with assistance from the Organization of American States (OAS), launched its five-year Drug Strategy Master Plan, which emphasized law enforcement.[99] A report on a proposed review of this plan in 2008 alluded to several advances toward its implementation, including "identification of funding from local sources, signing and ratifying international agreements/conventions," and "computerizing the Immigration and Criminal Investigation Departments."[100]

Since 2002, the Guyana government has made fighting crime a top priority, passing several laws aimed at combating terrorism, particularly the Prevention of Crimes (Amendment) Act of 2002. However, according to Amnesty International, the term *terrorism* in this act was too broadly defined; furthermore, it has facilitated the use of "arbitrary arrest, detention, ill-treatment and torture."[101] The impunity adopted by the Guyanese police toward the arbitrary killing of citizens led to a massive outcry from domestic sources such as the Guyana Human Rights Association (GHRA), the Guyana Bar Association, the Guyana Trade Union Congress (GTUC), and the University of Guyana Students Association (UGSA), as well as opposition political parties, Amnesty International, US officials from the State Department, and the Carter Center, among others. Consequently, two police officers were tried for the killing of a University of Guyana student in 2003—although they were eventually acquitted by the courts.[102]

What is most striking in this context, however, is the failure of the government and security forces in Guyana to significantly impact the levels of political instability and violent criminality in the country. Certainly, efforts have been made to increase the budget for the police and military forces. Yet the police continue to complain that they do not have sufficient firepower to compete with heavily armed criminal elements. Meanwhile, the crime rate, particularly for violent crime, is reported to be increasing. Since 2002, the Guyanese police have made several seizures of illegal weapons caches, but few detainees have been incarcerated or prosecuted.[103] Between 2003 and 2004, the crime rate, according to the Minister of Home Affairs Gail Teixeira, had increased by 2 percent, including a rise in rape and other acts of violence against women.[104] In November 2004, the police warned about an increase in illegal gun acquisitions.[105] A 2005 editorial in government newspaper *The Guyana Chronicle* sounded the alarm regarding "terror in the streets," alluding to a renewed spate of gun violence targeting people using public transportation.[106] Meanwhile, according to a government report in May 2005, violence and killings continued unabated in Buxton.[107]

Institutions of Governance and Conflict Resolution

The Guyanese Parliament is also a troubled institution. First, it is heavily polarized along ethnic lines. In addition, opposition parties have claimed for years that it is nothing more than "a useless talk shop," to use the PNC's term—a mere rubber stamp on ruling-party (PPP/C) decisions.[108] Lengthy boycotts of the institution by the main opposition parties (that is, the PPP in the Burnham years and the PNC under the present PPP/C government) have made matters worse. A report by Commonwealth Senior Staff Parliamentary Advisor Michael Davies, who was invited by the Guyanese government in 2005 to investigate the functioning of Parliament, concluded that the current PPP/C-controlled body was unresponsive to opposition proposals, rife with malfunctioning committees, and too controlling of the parliamentary process, such that opposition parties and the private sector felt shut out from the parliamentary process altogether.[109]

The lack of sufficient outreach or inclusiveness Guyana's government demonstrates might well be a function of the Guyanese electoral system, which (as we have noted) rests on a winner-take-all foundation. The tendency toward autocratic rule was a feature of the last PNC government (1964–1992, but particularly under Burnham), just as it is of the PPP/C government today. One example of such lack of inclusiveness is the PPP/C government's reluctance to ensure the participation of significant civil society groups and opposition parties in the process of drafting the government's PRSP in 2002. Opposition parties claimed that "the consultations were not truly open to all groups, were dominated by government leaders, and did not include many poor areas."[110] The NDS paper, which was produced in 2003 as the result of a very popular civil society initiative led by the Carter Center and other international NGOs, was slighted by the PPP/C government until 2005.[111]

The role played by NGOs in particular has been constructive, however limited. A Social Partners group, for instance, comprising the Private Sector Commission (PSC), the GTUC, and some religious organizations, offered to mediate during the stalled dialogue between the ruling PPP/C and the opposition PNC/R parties, although without much success.

The leader of the PNC, Desmond Hoyte, initiated the call for dialogue in 2001, which was very enthusiastically embraced by President Jagdeo and the ruling PPP/C party. The initial conditions for the dialogue included the creation of several sectoral committees to investigate and address issues relating to critical matters such as border and national security, bauxite resuscitation, land distribution and house-lot allocation, depressed communities, radio monopoly, and local government reform.[112] PNC/R's complaints about a lack of progress in the implementation of these conditions were later echoed by the PSC and the Social Partners group. In the following year, therefore, the PNC/R unilaterally suspended the dialogue over the nonimplementation issue.

The negative public perception of the ERC is reflected more significantly in the unwillingness of two of the nation's most ethnically conscious organizations, the African Committee for Development and Action (ACDA) and the Guyana Indian Heritage Foundation (GIHF), to participate in ERC programs.[113] Six other Afro-Guyanese organizations—the Pan-African Movement, the African Welfare Convention, the Guyana Rastafarian Council, the Nubian Research Center, the All-African Guyanese Council, and the Ile Ifa group—sent a petition to the ERC, signed May 10, 2006, against participation in the institution's proposed annual cultural festival. Among the ten specific complaints against the ERC contained in the petition were (1) its failure to "articulate a national approach to ethnic inclusion," (2) its engagement with private businesses whose hiring practices were significantly ethnically skewed, (3) its apparent tendency toward favoritism, (4) its failure to articulate a public position on the interparty controversy over house-to-house verification of the voter list, and (5) its prior dismissal of earlier complaints emanating from these groups.[114]

So far, little effort has been made by the Guyanese government to synchronize or even explain the relationship between its socioeconomic policies and its political-security policies. Yet the former have a significant effect on the level of political instability in the country. In some ways the economic strategies themselves harbor seeds of political and ethnic discontent. For example, the shift away from bauxite has led to large-scale retrenchment in the mining town of Linden, leading to much unrest among the largely Afro-Guyanese residents as well as on the coastland, where most of the bauxite miners come from. Furthermore, little consideration has been given to strategies for making privatization policies compatible with efforts to redistribute economic resources and functions to depressed geographic communities on the coastlands, where political unrest and violence tend to concentrate and thus discourage private capital investment.

In addition, the focus on private sector development has led to a decline in the public sector; the reduction of appropriate incentives has contributed not only to the migration of but also to corruption and incapacity among public servants. Indeed, low pay in the police and security forces compels many to participate in the competing drug trade and thereby create conflicting loyalties among members of the force, who are thus unable to deal effectively with crime, corruption, and other threats to the country's social and political stability. Meanwhile, there is as yet no legislation against discrimination in land distribution, although the problem in terms of both land and housing seems to be mounting, as can be gauged from the range of complaints to the ERC.[115]

International Outlook

Guyana's international orientation has shifted from one of nonalignment and protectionism during the Cold War era and Burnham's reign to one of commitment to IMF-directed free trade and open market policies during the Hoyte administration to one that under the PPP/C government of the early postmillennium emphasizes not only a free market but private foreign investment. Since 1992, Guyana has finally been considered part of "the international community of multiparty democracies."[116]

Economic Relations

In shifting toward a more open free trade policy, Guyana has brought its approach to international economic relations more closely in line with IMF-favored policies as well as with US and G7/8 economic interests in the region.[117] However, the 2005 decision by the European Union (EU) to reduce its historically preferential prices for Guyanese sugar exports by 39 percent has threatened the survival of Guyana's main export and income source.[118] Over 70 percent of Guyana's sugar exports go to Europe, and the revenue derived from this preferential trade has generally accounted for over 50 percent of

Guyana's agricultural production and about 20 percent of its GDP. In addition, sugar accounts for the livelihood of 26,000 workers who concomitantly "provide a living for 150,000 people out of a total population of 750,000."[119] This sizeable reduction of the EU preferential prices for Guyana's sugar will probably result in a significant reduction in living standards for a large proportion of Guyana's poorer rural population.[120] In 2008, for example, civil and labor unrest in the sugar sector has increased due to the greater economic hardship felt by sugar workers throughout the country.[121]

Guyana's international trade contributes significantly to its overall economic development strategy, which is based on export-led growth. The aims of this strategy are to advance Guyana's regional and bilateral trading interests and identify and pursue new markets and opportunities for resource mobilization through technical cooperation with other countries. The Guyanese government also sees the Caribbean Single Market and Economy (CSME) that was established in 2006 as "the vehicle for advancing national economic and social interests of Member States," including Guyana.[122] However, since its establishment, the CSME has run into serious difficulties, as member states have resisted opening their doors to one another, particularly with respect to the free movement of Caribbean populations and exchanges of skills.[123]

Guyana's main export market has shifted from the United States in 2001 and 2002 to the UK in 2003 and Canada in 2004, while its main CARICOM export market has shifted from Jamaica (2001–2003) to Trinidad and Tobago (2004). The value of Guyana's exports has increased from US$490 million in 2001 to US$589 million in 2004. The 2004 earnings from merchandise exports alone represent an increase of 9.2 percent over the 2003 figures (US$512 million). While the overall contribution of exports to the GDP in Guyana climbed from 81.4 percent in 2001 to 90.2 percent in 2004, it is noteworthy that the value of imports in relation to GDP also climbed, from 96.9 percent in 2001 to 99 percent in 2004. Meanwhile, the balance of trade fell from 93.6 percent in 2001 to 57.9 percent in 2004, and the trade deficit fell by 1.5 percent between 2003 and 2004.[124] Since 2004, trade balances have fluctuated but still ended on the downside in mid-2007, with a deficit of US$8.6 million following a mid-2006 surplus of US$17 million.[125]

Foreign investors have also made a modest contribution to Guyana's overall economic development. GO-Invest was set up by the post-1992 Guyanese government to facilitate and coordinate foreign and domestic investment projects. The UN Conference on Trade and Development (UNCTAD), in its 2002 World Investments Report, ranked Guyana nineteenth among 140 countries in terms of FDI in relation to economy size for the period 1998–2000.[126] By 2005, GO-Invest had managed to attract 139 investment projects—eighty-nine of which were fully operating and ninety-one of which were new that year—and had created 4,145 jobs. Of these, the number of new direct jobs was 1,686. Most of these new industries involve agroprocessing (thirty-four), followed by ecotourism (twenty-six) and wood products (twenty-one). Most (56 percent) are located in the most populous Region 4. The overall contribution to the Guyanese GDP of investments inspired by GO-Invest was G$69.2 billion (equivalent to about US$346 million) in 2005, representing a sizeable increase from the G$11.2 billion (about US$56 million) invested in 2002.[127]

Development Assistance

Since 1985, Guyana has maintained a solidly amicable relationship with the international community. The strength of this relationship is indicated in the significant increases in international aid to Guyana since 1992, especially as compared to the Cold War years under the Burnham regime, when foreign aid seriously plummeted. For example, the high point of foreign aid for the then-PNC government was in 1981, when Guyana received a total sum of about US$71 million.[128] Since 1992, with the advent of the new PPP/C regime, Guyana's total ODA from international quarters has greatly increased—although it has varied widely in the process, reaching a peak of US$325 million in 1996 but plummeting to US$94 million in the 1998–2000 period.[129] Still, by 1997 Guyana was receiving by far the most ODA per capita (US$124); the average for South America at the time was US$13, whereas the world average was only US$10.[130] By 2003, ODA to Guyana had declined to US$86.6 million and constituted only 11.7 percent of GDP, as compared to 42.6 percent of GDP in 1990.[131] However, the following year (2004) recorded a steep increase in ODA, namely to the amount of US$145 million.

The top ten largest international aid donors for Guyana for 2002–2003 were the Inter-American Development Bank (IDB), the UK, the International Development Association (IDA) of the World Bank, the United States, the Caribbean Development Bank (CDB), the IMF, Germany, Canada, Japan, and the EU. However, the international donor agencies with the most conflict-sensitive agendas for Guyana—those specifically addressing issues of security and conflict resolution—are the US Agency for International Development

(USAID), the Canadian International Development Agency (CIDA), and the UN aid agencies, particularly the UN Development Programme (UNDP). The main policy objectives of these donors, as can be observed by comparing their main policy agendas, may be summarized as follows: (1) supporting export-led economic growth, with privatization and foreign investment as the main pillars; (2) strengthening democratic institutions to encourage greater participation and inclusiveness as well as local government reform; (3) aiding police and judicial reforms; (4) strengthening NGOs and civil society; (5) supporting human development efforts, including the advancement of education and health care, public sector and technical training, flood and disaster relief, and development for indigenous Amerindians; and (6) assistance for HIV/AIDS reduction and control. Beyond these largely consensual policy objectives, individual donors also target more specific problem sectors of the economy; the IMF focuses on debt relief, for instance, while the EU maintains interest in infrastructure and agricultural development.[132]

The UN takes its policy agenda further, encouraging the development of the government's managerial capacity by providing policy advice, data collection, and monitoring capabilities; it also encourages the institutional strengthening of key entities and rights-based approaches to development. For this reason, the UN Country Team (UNCT) for Guyana, in its Development Assistance Framework, advocates for "custom-made initiatives" or pilot projects to reach the most deprived segments of the population and to counteract the hazards of globalization. The UNCT argues further that the main cause of poverty is discrimination and inequality, and therefore it places much emphasis on good governance to overcome these problems. Within this context, the UNCT recommends a comprehensive development framework that emphasizes affirmative-action policies and "mass campaigns toward peace, tolerance, and appreciation of diversity." The UN is further interested in aiding the drug control strategy of the government, as projected in the Drug Strategy Master Plan introduced in 2005.[133]

Implementation Challenges

The foregoing UN interests in Guyana are based on the assumption that the nation remains constrained by severe weakness in governance, insufficient participation, corrupt administrative practices, insufficient accountability, and serious inequities in access to economic resources and social services. What is needed, however, to enhance the UNCT Development Assistance Framework for Guyana is greater focus on the linkages between the foregoing developmental issues and the perceived security crises in the country.[134]

In the UNCT framework, there is inadequate conceptualization of the relationship between security and economic growth or development and thus of the mechanisms that might ensure that specific aspects of the Guyana proposals for economic growth and poverty reduction can successfully increase security and political stability and mitigate ethnic conflict. Appropriate standards for assessing the progress of the various measures proposed for economic growth and conflict reduction are hardly addressed. The UNCT seems to prioritize the strengthening of the health and education sectors, which at best are only indirectly connected to the processes of economic growth and conflict resolution. The security forces and judicial system, as well as the economic agencies that work for youth employment (particularly by developing strategies to attract job-creating industries to the more economically depressed areas in the country) tend to be slighted in the framework. While the UNCT quite appropriately suggests improving data collection processes, it is not specific regarding the type of institutional framework needed to do so (for instance, the Statistics Bureau, the University of Guyana, or a new framework altogether). Finally, while the UNCT places principal importance on rights-based changes, it should recognize that the quest for rights alone, in the absence of resource redistribution initiatives, is not sufficient to ensure the economic inclusion of hitherto excluded or conflict-prone groups.

In developing countries like Guyana, international donor policies supportive of export-led growth and private foreign investments are indeed relevant to poverty reduction and economic growth strategies. However, as the example of the UNCT framework suggests, these policies offer few directives either for the alleviation of economic discontent born of skewed resource distribution or for any significant reduction of economic inequality based on ethnicity or class.[135]

The actual implementation of these projects tends to be rather limited and difficult to manage, primarily due to a lack not only of adequate data but also of government accountability and policy transparency.[136] Examples of the failure of international aid to fully accomplish its proposed objectives in Guyana are increasing crime rates, particularly related to drug trafficking; increasing turmoil over the issues, such as the voters list controversy, that surrounded the national elections in August 2006; the indefinite postponement of local government elections; and the large-scale migration of the country's most qualified teachers overseas where better opportunities await. The massive out-migration of the most skilled Guyanese and the related matter of their potential contribution to both economic development and conflict resolution back home are seriously neglected issues within the international assistance framework.

Mediation and Peacebuilding Prospects

The international environment impacts Guyana's prospects for peace and security in various ways. The post–September 11 shift of US policy under the George W. Bush administration to preemptive and militarized interventions has created an environment within which the Guyanese government could easily abandon conciliatory policies and step up its military and coercive tactics against disruptive or potentially violent political protests. It is within this context that President Jagdeo's comparison of street protests to "terrorist activities," which tended to justify the use of harsh police tactics against opposition political activists, can best be comprehended.[137] In 2002, the government passed several laws aimed at dealing with terrorism, at least one of which Amnesty International contends "undermines the principles of legal certainty and the presumption of innocence" and further constitutes a "threat to freedom of expression and association."[138] It is also within this context that opposition charges of police brutality and excessive use of force can be understood. The governing and opposition parties' diametrically opposed perspectives on military intervention in domestic security matters can only exacerbate political tensions and have undoubted multiplier effects on the country as a whole.

Among international aid agencies, the UNDP is perhaps most sensitive to the resolution of domestic political and ethnic conflicts in Guyana. The UNDP office in Guyana has initiated a joint endeavor with the Ministry of Local Government and Regional Development called the Building Social Cohesion Project (BSCP), which aims to "strengthen the capacity" of the RDCs to reduce "social tensions" and give "disadvantaged youths a greater voice in the development activities in their areas," as well as to conduct conflict transformation workshops for RDC counselors and youth leaders.[139] The BSCP has also financed police training workshops with the joint participation of the Guyana Human Rights Association.[140]

By far the most effective aspect of the UNDP's BSCP program in Guyana is the series of joint programs and workshops it conducts with the ERC. In 2006, the UNDP, in conjunction with the ERC, launched a series of multi-stakeholder forums, inviting the participation of community leaders throughout the country.[141] Its objective was to facilitate dialogue among the various ethnic groups with a view toward common understanding and resolution of grievances. However, despite the importance of the objective, the turnout was relatively low, indeed moderate at best—particularly in the regions with the most intense and contentious political demands. Whereas the predominantly African-dominated Region 4, for example, had a turnout of only 22 percent, turnout in the overwhelmingly East Indian–dominated Region 6 was only modestly better at 33 percent.

The revelations in these deliberations were interesting. Issues of an economic nature, such as demands for infrastructure improvements and job creation (particularly for youth), took precedence over political and social issues such as governance, ethnic harmony, and drug addiction. And although the matter was raised, there was hardly any sustained discussion on what participants perceived to be the nature of the interconnection between security and development issues. Discussions on political unity, for instance, tended to be devoid of any references to the need for good or inclusive governance. In Region 4, the area with the most violent conflict (particularly in Buxton, Friendship, and Sophia), the issues of ethnic differences, resource allocation, and opportunities for youth were most prominently raised, whereas governance and democracy were very low priority. The primary concerns of the Amerindian communities, who demonstrated a 52 percent turnout rate at the stakeholders' forum in Region 1, included job creation, ethnic marginalization, and corrupt land allocation practices.

These jointly sponsored discussions involving stakeholders at the local and regional levels seem, in short, to have been largely amicable and focused largely on socioeconomic rather than more divisive political or ideological issues. The rather pragmatic orientation of local communities underscores the fact that the causal factors of conflict and insecurity in Guyana reside principally at the elite level, particularly within the leadership of the PPP/C and the PNC/R. With a history of contention and violent discord between them, these two parties demonstrate a high preference for ethnic mobilization as a strategy—whether electoral or extraparliamentary—toward the attainment or retention of political power.

International support for reconciliation and mediation also comes from nongovernmental and regional bodies like the aforementioned Carter Center, the Commonwealth Secretariat, and CARICOM.[142] However, their efforts, though generous and initially effective—in that they usually inspire a momentary lull in violence—tend to be short lived. Violence returns very soon after the initial objective (such as bringing the contenders to the table) is met, followed by usually abrupt withdrawals of the international bodies from the scene. The short-lived nature of such interventions is evident in the case of the 1992 postelection violence, which followed very soon after the mediation efforts by Jimmy Carter. Another classic example of postelection violence even in the presence of international mediators is the violent Public Service Union (PSU) strike in 1999, which occurred shortly before the eventual signing of the 1998 CARICOM Herdmanston and St. Lucia Accords. This particular event resulted in the injury of seventeen protesters after police opened fire.[143] At best, these conciliatory policies can be said to result in temporary and limited, rather than sustained and comprehensive, success. To be fair, however, their relative success or productivity must be judged against Guyanese history, which lacks any precedent for political conflict mediation or negotiation, as well as against the apparent reluctance of the political leadership to agree on the necessity of third-party interventions.[144]

Conclusion

The Guyanese experience suggests that although economic factors generally loom large in ethnopolitical conflict, there is not necessarily a direct correlation between specific dimensions of economic growth and particular levels of political conflict in the country. The more significant factor seems to be the performance of those economic sectors that coincide with significantly large segments of particular ethnic populations. Between 1985 and 2005, the mining (mainly bauxite) and public (particularly central-government) sectors, which absorb mainly Afro-Guyanese employees, tended to face consistent declines in production and employment levels relative to the East Indian–dominated rice and sugar industries, which have demonstrated increasing growth. The indirect impact of increased poverty and unemployment created by downward trends in the Afro-dominated economic sectors has been to generate labor and youth unrest. These factors, combined with a national history of political discontent, have in turn led to sometimes intensive social conflict and recurrent political and criminal violence within disadvantaged communities. Such tends to be the case in Buxton and in the impoverished urban enclaves of Georgetown and of Linden, the principal bauxite-mining town in the interior of Guyana.

The pertinent recommendation here, therefore, is that Guyana should undertake more comprehensive economic reconstruction with the goal of implementing economic distribution policies that enhance security and reduce conflict, particularly within the more economically depressed regions of the country. Such policies should facilitate poverty reduction, job creation, and multiethnic, collaborative entrepreneurial initiatives, such as cooperative enterprises and neighborhood construction projects. In this regard, ongoing development projects in the interior mining towns planned by government-supported entrepreneurial training programs like the aforementioned LEAP in Linden, should be extended to depressed villages on the coast as well.

Notwithstanding successive governments' use of overwhelming force to suppress civil unrest and political violence, conflicts in Guyana have steadily escalated and mutated over the years from generalized crises to sporadic and limited violence to highly organized armed (or militarized) confrontations. The more conciliatory policies—which involved both international mediation and domestic consultations with civil society groups and which also coincided with the more economically prosperous second phase of conflict (1992–1998)—were either not sustained or were applied only in an ad hoc fashion. The recommendation here, therefore, is that the authorities rely less exclusively on coercive strategies to place a greater emphasis on community policing, consistent training in peaceful and noncoercive crowd and crime control, and inquests into the killing of citizens by police. The government should also seek international assistance to develop intelligence gathering and informational capabilities to more effectively combat transnational crime and narcotrafficking, which require resources and expertise beyond the immediate reaches of the local security forces.[145]

In addition, it is necessary for the Guyanese government to continually take the initiative to conduct peace talks and implement peace agreements (such as the Herdmanston Accords) with opposition parties and minority interest groups promptly and transparently, with the objective of counteracting the recurrent and systematic violence that consumes significant sections of the Guyanese population. Indeed, the onus is on the government to ensure the success of conciliatory initiatives directed toward opposition and minority forces, particularly the dialogue process.

The reasons for the continual breakdown of the dialogue process—as illustrated particularly by the breaking of the agreements brokered by the Carter Center and CARICOM—are rooted in historical contingencies, such as the lack of a tradition of accepting outside mediation and conciliation efforts. Central to the problems here is the relative intransigence of the powers that be—their inability to be conciliatory in victory shaped by the zero-sum character of Guyana's electoral process. What is therefore recommended here is a serious reexamination of the electoral system, with a view toward making the necessary structural changes to ensure both a higher stake for and the greater involvement of minority parties in the parliamentary and governmental decisionmaking processes. The objective here is the realization of a more inclusive government—or, at the very least, parliamentary reform that pays more attention to minority views both within committees and in the deliberating body as a whole.

There is also the need for more sustained efforts on the part of not only the government and the opposition parties in Guyana but all stakeholders in the Guyanese peace process, particularly international donors, toward facilitating the emergence and development of third-party mediating forces, domestically and regionally. Building the capacity of such NGOs in Guyana as the PSC and the unified trade union movement (combining GTUC and FITUG), and supporting the maintenance of a permanent desk at CARICOM for conflict interventions in the region, would be part of these combined efforts toward more lasting political stability. Within this context, both the Guyanese government and international donor agencies should seek the direct involvement of the multiethnic Guyanese diaspora, taking advantage of their negotiating and investing expertise. A serious study of the potential influence of this multiethnic diaspora is needed to determine the extent to which its members can mediate the conflict situation between the two major parties through their capabilities and behind-the-scenes access. Beyond its use as a source of private remittances, the diaspora should be addressed as a source of public investments that could be directed to the neglected communities and interior regions.

Additionally, to provide intellectual and scientific support for the foregoing projects, Guyana needs to build new and independent institutions for generating knowledge and understanding about political and criminal violence and conflict resolution. In this regard, both governmental and international donors should support the establishment and institutionalization of research facilities on conflict and ethnic issues with data collection, policy analysis, and publications capabilities. Such a development is already on the agenda of the ERC but could also be implemented by other relevant institutions such as the University of Guyana.

International aid to build institutional or state capacity is relevant and important to peacebuilding efforts. Some aid agencies such as USAID and the UK's Department for International Development (DFID) have committed to supporting the capacity building of Guyana's security forces, judicial system, educational programs, and civil society organizations. However, what needs greater emphasis on the part of international donors is funding directed specifically toward the facilitation of interethnic working relationships at the communal level—for example, pilot projects that reward interethnic collaborative efforts, such as the creation of cross-communal recreational facilities and multiethnic neighborhoods.

However, in light of the probability of high-level corruption, international aid to Guyana should be closely monitored through the establishment of transparency and accountability standards that ensure that the aid reaches its intended targets at the local levels. These standards should tie future aid to demonstrated success in the peaceful resolution of violent conflict and/or in the establishment of better relations among different ethnic interests and between the two main political parties.

There should also be persistent efforts to broker and sustain domestic peace initiatives such as those made by the UNDP via its Building Social Cohesion Program, which supports capacity building for multipartisan national institutions (such as the ERC and regional and local democratic councils) that have the constitutional mandate to lead efforts aimed at dialogue and reconciliation in Guyana. Beyond this, what is needed is a joint international-domestic arrangement, like the UNDP-ERC multi-stakeholder meetings at the regional and local levels, geared toward the development of strategies that directly engage the leaders of the PPP/C and the PNC/R in face-to-face workshops to examine and transcend their own negative and mutually self-defeating perceptions of each other. Economic development and political stability are possible in Guyana only if each of the two major parties recognizes that the cooperation and contribution of the other are indispensable to the realization of these necessary objectives.

Notes

1. Government of Guyana, "Poverty Reduction Strategy Paper (PRSP)" (Georgetown: Poverty Reduction Strategy Secretariat, 2002), 8; UN, "Common Country Assessment for the Cooperative Republic of Guyana," (Georgetown: UN, 1999), 8.

2. Government of Guyana, "Report on Household Income and Expenditure Survey 1992–1993," (Georgetown: Bureau of Statistics, September 1993), 154.

3. In Guyana, race and ethnicity overlap in such a way that they are almost interchangeable. However, the former, with its historical, hierarchical (white-dominant/black-subordinate) characteristics, has given way to the latter, with its pluralistic (multicultural) considerations, as the principal defining concept of group identity in the country. Hence, the same identity groups that include racial characteristics (East Indian, African, Chinese, Amerindian, and European) are today invariably and officially being referred to as ethnic groups, as reflected, for instance, in the appellations of the constitutionally derived Ethnic Relations Committee and in terminology of the Guyana Census. See Government of Guyana, "Population and Housing Census 2002: Summary Results," (Georgetown: Bureau of Statistics, October 17, 2005). This chapter therefore follows the official line of using ethnicity to identify Guyanese groups.

4. See Government of Great Britain, *Report of the British Guiana Constitutional Commission 1954* (London: Her Majesty's Stationery Office [HMSO], 1954); Government of Great Britain, *Report of a Commission of Inquiry into Disturbances in British Guiana in February 1962* (London: HMSO, 1962); Cheddi Jagan, *The West on Trial* (Berlin: Seven Seas, 1972); and Leo Despres, *Cultural Pluralism and Nationalist Politics in British Guiana* (Chicago, IL: Rand McNally, 1967).

5. Some of the PPP policies, such as the Labor Relations Bill (1962) to democratize trade unions and the Kaldor Budget (1963)—named after the Cambridge University professor Nicolas Kaldor, who designed the bill to tax capital gains—were seized upon by trade union leadership and opposition parties. These groups, which were actively supported and financed by the CIA, the American Federation of Labor and Congress of Industrial Organizations (AFL-CIO), and other US and international sources, used the policies as pretexts for unleashing violence. For more information, see Jagan, *The West on Trial* and Philip Reno, *The Ordeal of British Guyana* (New York: Monthly Review, 1964).

6. See Government of Guyana, "Report of the National Rehabilitation Committee" (Georgetown, September 1965), 5–9.

7. See "Parliament Sector Committees Hampered by Unresponsive Government, Other Factors: Report," *Stabroek News,* March 4, 2005, 1.

8. See "The Necessity for Power Sharing in Guyana," *Stabroek News,* January 12, 2008, 2.

9. See Bert Wilkinson, "Guyana Strikes Collapse," *Caribbean Contact,* June 1989, 5.

10. The Caribbean Community and Common Market (CARICOM), "Caribbean Community Mission to Guyana: Measures for Resolving Current Problems" (Georgetown: CARICOM Secretariat, January 1998); CARICOM, "Guyana: The St. Lucia Statement" (Georgetown: CARICOM Secretariat, July 1998).

11. CARICOM, "Caribbean Community Mission to Guyana."

12. CARICOM, "Guyana: The St. Lucia Statement."

13. Amnesty International, "Guyana, Human Rights, and Crime Control: Not Mutually Exclusive," AI Index no. AMR 35/003/2003, January 13, 2003, http://www.amnesty.org/en/library/info/AMR35/003/2003/en.

14. Mark Ramotar, "'Well Orchestrated Ploy' Behind Current Tension: President Jagdeo," *Guyana Chronicle,* July 19, 2002, http://www.

guyanachronicle.com/ARCHIVES/archive%2019-07-02.html#Anchor—31861.

15. See PNC/R Press Release, mimeo, July 8, 2003.

16. See "Escapee Douglas Shot Dead," *Guyana Chronicle,* August 27, 2002, 1, http://www.guyanachronicle.com/ARCHIVES/archive%2027-08-02.html#Anchor—21670.

17. Guyana Human Rights Association (GHRA), "Guyana Concerns Are Only for Victims," press release, June 10, 2003, http://www.waveguyana.org/PRESS%20RELEASE%20FROM%20THE%20GUYANA%20HUMAN%20RIGHTS%20ASSOCIATION.htm.

18. See Guyana Police Public Relations Office, "Guyana Police Release on Lusignan Massacre and Eve Leary Attack," press release, Georgetown, January 26, 2008; Gaulbert Sutherland and Alva Solomon, "Bartica Slayings: Hard Times for Those Scarred by Bartica Massacre," *Stabroek News,* February 16, 2009, 1; Olieatoyin Allen, "Lindo Creek Massacre: DNA tests to be done," *Stabroek News,* July 14, 2008.

19. See Joan Mars, *Deadly Force, Colonialism, and the Rule of Law: Police Violence in Guyana* (Westport, CT: Greenwood, 2002), 138; US Department of State, *Guyana: Country Reports on Human Rights Practices* (Washington, DC: Bureau of Democracy, Human Rights and Labor, 1999), 2.

20. The data for this statistical average were culled together by examining the country reports for Guyana over a four-year period (1999–2003). See US Department of State, "Guyana: Country Reports on Human Rights Practices" (Washington, DC, 1999–2004). For 2003 alone, unlawful killings by the Guyana police amounted to thirty-nine. See US Department of State, "Guyana: Country Report on Human Rights Practices 2003" (Washington, DC: Bureau of Democracy, Human Rights and Labor, 2004).

21. US Department of State, "Guyana: Country Report on Human Rights Practices 2003." These tit-for-tat killings between criminal gangs frequently occurred in Buxton, and the combined police-military forces continued operations in the area up to January 2008. Army personnel incurred at least two deaths that year in these operations. See *Stabroek News*, January 24, 2008.

22. Patrick Denny, "520 Deportees in 2003—60 for Drugs and Serious Offences," *Stabroek News,* January 5, 2004, http://www.stabroeknews.com/index.pl/article?id=1955886.

23. "Gajraj: Killing Squad Offer Mere Allegation—Corbin Storms Out of Police Commission Swearing In," *Stabroek News,* January 10, 2004, http://www.stabroeknews.com/index.pl/article?id=2197797; "Opposition Declares Gajraj Probe a Farce," *Stabroek News,* May 16, 2004, http://www.stabroeknews.com/index.pl/article?id=8129001.

24. Caribbean Net News, "Guyana Death Squad Witness Shot Dead," June 25, 2004, http://www.caribbeannetnews.com/2004/06/25/witness.htm.

25. Rickford Burke, "Guyana Government Responsible for Bacchus' Assassination," Caribbean Net News, June 25, 2004, http://www.caribbeannetnews.com/2004/06/25/assassination.htm.

26. World Bank, "Guyana Country Data Profile," 2007, http://web.worldbank.org/WBSITE/EXTERNAL/COUNTRIES/LACEXT/GUYANAEXTN/0,,menuPK:328300~pagePK:141132~piPK:141109~theSitePK:328274,00.html.

27. Commonwealth Advisory Group, "Guyana: Economic Recovery and Beyond" (London, August 21, 1989).

28. Government of Guyana, "Poverty Reduction Strategy Paper (PRSP)," (Georgetown: Poverty Reduction Strategy Secretariat, 2007), 7.

29. Government of Guyana, "Poverty Reduction Strategy Paper," 2007, 7.

30. Government of Guyana, "Poverty Reduction Strategy Paper," 2000, 56.

31. Government of Guyana, "Poverty Reduction Strategy Paper," 2000, 56.

32. The figures collected from the Ministry of Finance, Guyana, are as follows: 1999 (3.0), 2000 (-1.4), 2001 (1.9), 2002 (1.1), 2003 (-0.6), 2004 (1.6), and 2005 (-3.0). Data from personal interviews with budget adviser of the Ministry of Finance, Government of Guyana, June 19, 2006, and December 2007. See also Ministry of Finance, "Budget 2007 Building a Modern and Prosperous Guyana," (Georgetown, February 2, 2007), 54.

33. World Bank, "Guyana: Country Brief," 2004, 2, http://web.worldbank.org/WBSITE/EXTERNAL/COUNTRIES/LACEXT/GUYANAEXTN/0,,menuPK:328284~pagePK:141132~piPK:141107~theSitePK:328274,00.html.

34. US Agency for International Development (USAID), "USAID Guyana: Country Strategic Plan (CSP), 2004–2008" (Washington, DC: USAID, September 2003), 8.

35. See Central Intelligence Agency (CIA), "World Factbook: Guyana," 2005, http://www.cia.gov/library/publications/the-world-factbook/geos/gy.html.

36. Government of Guyana, "Poverty Reduction Strategy Paper," 2000.

37. UNDP, *Human Development Report 2005* (New York: Oxford University Press, 2005).

38. See UNDP, Human Development Report, "Guyana: The Human Development Index—Going Beyond Income," Statistical Update, 2008.

39. UK Department for International Development (DFID), "Regional Assistance Plan for the Caribbean," (London: DFID, June 2004), http://www.dfid.gov.uk/Pubs/files/rapcaribbean.pdf.

40. UN Conference on Trade and Development (UNCTAD), "World Investment Report Country Fact Sheet: Guyana," 2004, http://www.unctad.org/sections/dite_dir/docs/wir04_fs_gy_en.pdf.

41. UN, "Common Country Assessment of Development Challenges in Guyana," (Georgetown: UN, 2005), 48.

42. Government of Guyana, "Report on Household Income and Expenditure Survey 1992–1993," (Georgetown, 1993), 64–65.

43. Government of Guyana, "Report on Household Income and Expenditure Survey 1992–1993," 139.

44. Government of Guyana, "Population and Housing Census 2002," 25–26, 46.

45. Government of Guyana, "Population and Housing Census 2002," 17.

46. "Census Unveiled—Population Increases to 749,190: Berbice Sees 18,600 Decline," *Stabroek News,* May 14, 2004, 1.

47. See Government of Guyana, "The Guyana Poverty Reduction Strategy Paper," 2002, 5.

48. UN, "Common Country Assessment 2005," 48.

49. UN, "Common Country Assessment 2000," (Georgetown: UN, 2000), 19.

50. Government of Guyana, "Statistical Bulletin," (Georgetown: Bureau of Statistics, September 2001), 28.

51. Government of Guyana, "Statistical Bulletin," 64.

52. Government of Guyana, "Statistical Bulletin," 24–25.

53. World Bank, "Guyana: Country Brief," 2.

54. Gordon French, "Political Impasse Threatens Elections in Guyana," Caribbean Net News, May 22, 2006, http://www.caribbeannetnews.com/cgi-script/csArticles/articles/000016/001692.htm.

55. International Foundation for Elections Systems (IFES), "Guyanese Opposition Urges Power Sharing," September 8, 2006, http://www.ifes.org/features.html?title=Guyanese%20Opposition%20Urges%20Power%20Sharing.

56. See BBC Caribbean, "Jagdeo Pledges Role for Opposition," September 4, 2006, http://www.bbc.co.uk/caribbean/news/story/2006/09/060904_guyana0409.shtml.

57. See RadioJamaica.com, "Robert Corbin Faces Strong Challenge from Vincent Alexander for PNC/R Top Post," July 20, 2007, 1.

58. Much more empirical work has to be done to correctly ascertain Guyana's precise risk of conflict. One quantitative measure, Carleton University's Country Indicators for Foreign Policy (CIFP) project, coded Guyana's risk potential for "ethnic rebellion" at a global rank score of 4.0 on a 9-point scale (CIFP), Carleton University, Ottawa, 2004 (cifp@carleton.ca). However, a proper scoring of the level of political/ethnic conflict for Guyana has to take into consideration more critical factors such as the country's history of intense political and ethnic violence since 1953, coupled with its relatively poor record of economic, political, and social performance; these latter measures, most theorists agree, are among the most important conditions for estimating conflict risks in a particular country. See Ted Robert Gurr, *Minorities at Risk: A Global View of Ethnopolitical Conflicts* (Washington DC: United States Institute of Peace, 1993); Stanley Samarasinghe, Brian Donaldson, and Colleen McGinn, "Conflict Vulnerability Analysis: Issues, Tools, and Responses," working paper (Washington, DC: USAID, April 2001); and John Davies, "Conflict Early Warning and Early Response for Sub-Saharan Africa," CERTI (Linking Complex Emergency Response and Transition Initiative) paper (College Park: Center for International Development and Conflict Management [CIDCM] at the University of Maryland, September 2000).

59. Institute of Development Studies (IDS), "Proceedings of IDS Colloquium on Poverty in Guyana: Finding Solutions, March 18–19, 1993," *Transition* 20–21 (1993): 5–243.

60. See Jagan, *The West on Trial,* and Hilbourne Watson, "Guyana, Jamaica, and the Cold War Project: The Transformation of Caribbean Labor," in *Caribbean Labor and Politics: Legacies of Cheddi Jagan and Michael Manley,* eds. Perry Mars and Alma H. Young (Detroit, MI: Wayne State University Press, 2004).

61. Perry Mars, "State Intervention and Ethnic Conflict Resolution: Guyana and the Caribbean Experience," *Comparative Politics* 27, no. 2 (January 1995): 167–186; J. Mars, *Deadly Force.*

62. Perry Mars, "Ethnic Politics, Mediation, and Conflict Resolution: The Guyana Experience," *Journal of Peace Research* 38, no. 3 (May 2001): 353--372.

63. Michael Lund, *Preventing Violent Conflicts: A Strategy for Preventive Diplomacy* (Washington DC: United States Institute of Peace, 2001).

64. Samarasinghe et al., "Conflict Vulnerability Analysis."

65. The PR system eliminates the pressure on the two ethnic-based parties to find multiracial slates to contest elections. In the earlier first-past-the-post (FPTP) system, parties needed to find individuals from different ethnic groups to contest the many different ethnic-based constituencies. The more multiracial the party slates at elections, the more multiracial would be the representation of each party within the Guyanese parliament. The PPP would be forced to put up black candidates in black-based constituencies, whereas the PNC would have to find more East Indian candidates for East Indian-dominated constituencies. In this system, electoral boundaries were important, particularly where many constituencies cut across ethnic lines.

66. The introduction of PR in 1964 had the effect of ensuring the PPP was defeated at the polls without resolving the winner-take-all Westminster syndrome. In fact, PR has the tendency of reinforcing ethnic voting patterns, particularly insofar as PPP and PNC electoral slates are dominated by candidates of a single preferred ethnic group. At the same time, PR allows for proportionality only within Parliament, whereas the winner-take-all factor operates at the level of the cabinet, which is exclusively formed by the majority party (now the PPP/C) and which usually fully controls government decisions to the total exclusion of all opposition or rival parties and ethnic groups.

67. Government of Guyana, "Poverty Reduction Strategy Paper," 2000, 19.

68. Jagan, *The West on Trial;* Reno, *The Ordeal of British Guiana*; Government of Great Britain, *Report of the British Guiana Constitutional Commission 1954.*

69. US Department of State, "International Narcotics Control Strategy Report: The Caribbean," *Bureau of International Narcotics and Law Enforcement,* vol. 1, Washington, DC, March 2005, 26, http://www.state.gov/p/inl/rls/nrcrpt/2005/vol/html/42365.htm.

70. US Department of State, "International Narcotics Control Strategy Report: The Caribbean," 26.

71. "Drug Fight Here Weak: US Report Joint Guyana-US Operation Compromised by Corruption," *Stabroek News,* March 5, 2005, 1, http://www.stabroeknews.com/index.pl/article?id=12957909.

72. The use of the Tulane University Conflict Vulnerability Analysis (CERTI Project) framework—Instrument C—supports this hypothesis. This framework assesses the level of intensity of conflict between groups based on a five-point scale, with one referring to the low presence and five referring to the high presence of identifiable factors pertaining to "social fragmentation," "economic and political inequality," and "politicization of differences/repression of groups" (see Samarasinghe et al., "Conflict Vulnerability Analysis," 23–24). Completing the coding and process for these three indicators reveals the following scores for Guyana: social fragmentation = 3.5; economic and political inequality = 3.7; politicization of

differences/repression of groups = 3.7, making for a total average score of at least 3.6 out of 5.

73. Government of Guyana, "Poverty Reduction Strategy Paper," 2002.

74. Ibid., pp. 31, 32, 35.

75. Tourism and Hospitality Association of Guyana (THAG), "Guyana Open for Business: Many Changes and Opportunities," in *Explore Guyana: The Official Tourist Guide of Guyana 2006* (Georgetown: THAG, 2006), 22.

76. Government of Guyana, "National Development Strategy (2001–2010): A Policy Framework—Eradicating Poverty and Unifying Guyana," Civil Society Document (Georgetown, 2000).

77. Government of Guyana, "National Development Strategy (2001–2010)."

78. GO-Invest, "Summary of Investment Projects in 2004," http://www.goinvest.gov.gy/SUMMARY%20OF%20INVESTMENT%20PROJECTS%20IN%202004.doc; for more positive summaries of investments in Guyana for this period, see also Government Information Agency (GINA), "GO-Invest Oversees Significant Investments Last Year: Increases in Investments Expected in 2003," press release (Georgetown: GINA May 28, 2003).

79. Ethnic Relations Commission, "Promoting Harmony and Good Relations," Georgetown, 2005, 1, http://www.ethnicrelations.org.gy/about.html.

80. Government of Guyana, *ERC Annual Report 2004* (Georgetown: Ethnic Relations Commission, 2004).

81. GINA, "Guyana Police Force Response to Drug Trafficking in Guyana," press release (Georgetown: GINA, March 13, 2004).

82. Government of Guyana, *ERC Annual Report 2004,* 18.

83. Personal interview with Christine King, chief executive officer of the ERC, Georgetown, June 2006.

84. Government of Guyana, "National Development Strategy (2001–2010)," 197.

85. William J. Carrington and Enrica Detragiache, "How Extensive Is the Brain Drain?" *Finance and Development* 36, no. 2 (June 1999): 46–49; untitled speech by Ambassador Odeen Ishmael presented at the University of Guyana Guild of Graduates Dinner, Toronto, September 18, 1999, http://www.guyana.org/Speeches/ishmael_torontouniversity.html.

86. See World Bank, "Guyana: Country Brief," 2.

87. Government of Guyana, "National Development Strategy (2001–2010)," 8, 9.

88. See "Poverty Report: Low Growth Key Problem—Negative Rates Seen This Year, 2006," *Stabroek News,* June 27, 2005, 3. http://www.stabroeknews.com/index.pl/article?id=22905529.

89. Manuel Orozco, "Distant But Close: Guyanese Transnational Communities and Their Remittances from the United States," draft of a report commissioned by US Agency for International Development, January 2004, 31.

90. Manuel Orozco, "Remitting Back Home to Guyana: Issues and Options," *Inter-American Dialogue*, November 7, 2002, 24, http://www.guyana.org/govt/GuyanaPresentation.pdf.

91. Orozco, "Distant but Close," 14.

92. Carrington and Detragiache, "How Extensive Is the Brain Drain?"

93. Sheila V. Holder, "Political Party and Campaign Financing in Guyana," in *From Rhetoric to Best Practices: The Challenge of Political Financing in the Americas,* eds. Steven Griner and Daniel Zarotta: OAS Unit for the Promotion of Democracy–International IDEA, Washington, DC, 2004).

94. See Perry Mars, "The Guyana Diaspora and Homeland Conflict Resolution," in *The New African Diaspora,* ed. Isodore Okpewho (Bloomington: Indiana University Press, 2009).

95. See Library of Congress, "Guyana: Mission, Organization, and Capability," Country Studies, Washington, DC: Library of Congress Federal Research Division, January 1992. The Guyana Police Force's 2000 report put the existing strength of the Guyana police force at 3,146. See Commissioner of Police, *Guyana Police Force Annual Report 2000* (Georgetown: Police Headquarters, 2000).

96. CIA, "World Factbook: Guyana."

97. International Commission of Jurists (ICJ), *Report of the Commission of Inquiry into the Security Forces of Guiana* (Geneva: ICJ, 1965).

98. Amnesty International, "Guyana: Urgent Action Needed on Witness Protection," AI Index no.AMR 35/004/2004, June 25, 2004, http://www.amnestyusa.org/document.php?id=80256DD400782B8480256EBE005EF0B2&lang=e; "Opposition Declares Gajraj Prove a Farce," *Stabroek News,* 1.

99. GINA, "National Drug Strategy Master Plan to be Launched Later this Month—Content Programmatic, says Dr. Luncheon," press release (Georgetown: GINA, June 8, 2005), http://www.gina.gov.gy/archive/daily/b050608.html; "Law and Order Commission to Energise National Crime Plan—$30M Subvention for Community Policing," *Stabroek News,* June 22, 2005, http://www.stabroeknews.com/index.pl/article?id=22551483.

100. "US Drug Report Notes Gov't Official Benefits from Proceeds of Drug Trafficking—Minister Rohee: Drug Master Plan for Review in March," GINA, March 4, 2008, 3, http://www.gina.gov.gy/archive/daily/b08304.html.

101. Amnesty International, "Guyana, Human Rights and Crime Control."

102. US Department of State, "Guyana: Country Reports on Human Rights Practices" (Washington, DC: Bureau of Democracy, Human Rights and Labor, 2003), 2, and US Department of State, "Guyana: Country Reports on Human Rights Practices" (Washington, DC: Bureau of Democracy, Human Rights and Labor, 2005), 2.

103. Haynes, "Easy Guns, Deadly Violence—Police Grapple with 'Greatest Threat.'" In early 2006, the GDF discovered missing from its armory a large quantity of high-powered weapons. Its vigorous pursuit of suspects has netted several ex-GDF personnel and has suggested a connection between the theft and prominent businessmen, some of whom are said to have links with the previously discussed death squad. So far none have been tried for any offense linked to the missing weapons, even though one of the weapons has been found.

104. See "Efforts Being Made to Tackle Gun Running but It's a Huge Task—Texeira," *Stabroek News,* September 3, 2005, 1.

105. Andre Haynes, "Easy Guns, Deadly Violence—Police Grapple with 'Greatest Threat,'" *Stabroek News,* November 30, 2004, http://www.stabroeknews.com/index.pl/article?id=8669730.

106. "Terror on the Streets," *Guyana Chronicle,* June 27, 2005.

107. GINA, "Police Undaunted by Criminal Elements in Buxton," press release (Georgetown: GINA, May 20, 2005), http://www.gina.gov.gy/archive/daily/b050520.html.

108. See Aubrey C. Norton, "From the General Secretary's Desk: Parliamentary Changes—A Victory for the People," *New Nation,* July 18, 1998, 2.

109. "National Assembly Not Playing Proper Role in Governance: Report—Independence Needed from Executive," *Stabroek News,* March 3, 2005, http://www.stabroeknews.com/index.pl/article?id=12738206; "Parliament Sector Committees Hampered by Unresponsive Govt, Other Factors: Report," *Stabroek News,* March 4, 2005, p.1; Daniel Da Costa, "Commonwealth Adviser Report on Parliament One-sided—Jagdeo," *Stabroek News,* March 9, 2005, http://www.stabroeknews.com/index.pl/article?id=13305730.

110. IMF, "Guyana: Poverty Reduction Strategy Paper, Joint Staff Assessment," (Washington, DC: IMF, August 30, 2002), 3.

111. IMF, "Guyana: Poverty Reduction Strategy Paper, Joint Staff Assessment."

112. "Jagdeo/Hoyte Caucus: Leaders Agree to Menu of Measures," *Stabroek News,* April 25, 2001, 18.

113. "Jagdeo/Hoyte Caucus: Leaders Agree to Menu of Measures."

114. Pan African Movement (PAM), et al., "Why We Cannot Participate in ERC's 'Cultural-Fest'!" circular letter (mimeo), May 10, 2006.

115. See Government of Guyana, *ERC Annual Report 2004.*

116. UN, "United Nations Development Assistance Framework: Guyana (2001–2003)," (Georgetown: United Nations Country Team, 2001), 7.

117. See Kathy McAffee, *Storm Signals: Structural Adjustment and Development Alternatives in the Caribbean* (Cambridge, MA: South End, 1991).

118. "Biting the Bullet," *Kaieteur News,* July 7, 2005, 4.

119. Ellen Huan-Niemi, "The Future of Trade Preferences for Sugar," European Network of Agricultural and Rural Policy Research Institutes (ENARPRI) Policy Brief no.1, University of Connecticut, September 2003, 1.

120. Sara Evans, "Callousness Redefined: How EU and US Economic Policies Spell a Bitter End for the Caribbean Sugar Industry," Council on Hemispheric Affairs, Washington, DC, June 24, 2005, 1; Caribbean Regional Negotiating Machinery (CRNM), "Caribbean Concerned over Sugar Reform Proposals: Steep Price Cuts to Have Devastating Effects on Region's Fragile Economies," News Release no. 08/2005, June 23, 2005.

121. See "Wages Talks Break Down Again . . . Sugar Grinds to Halt," *Stabroek News,* August 27, 2008, 1.

122. President Bharat Jagdeo, "Feature Address to the National One Day Summit on the CARICOM Single Market and Economy," Georgetown, December 1, 2003, 19.

123. See "Jagdeo Slams Barbados on Guyanese Treatment," *Stabroek News,* May 23, 2009, 1; "Paranoia Grips Guyanese Community in Barbados," *Kaieteur News,* May 28, 2009, 1.

124. Government of Guyana, "Review of Guyana's Foreign Trade,"

2003–2004, (Georgetown: Ministry of Foreign Trade and International Cooperation [MOFTIC], 2004).

125. Bank of Guyana, "Half Year Report," (Georgetown: Bank of Guyana, 2007), 14.

126. GO-Invest, "Sectoral Analysis of Projects Facilitated by GO-Invest in 2002 and the 1st Quarter of 2003," May 2003, http://www.goinvest.gov.gy/Documents/2002Q12003SectorAnalysisofProjectsfacilitatedbyGOINVEST.doc.

127. GO-Invest, "Reports: Summary of Investments Projects for 2005," http://www.goinvest.gov.gy/reports.html.

128. Library of Congress, "Guyana: Mission, Organization, and Capability."

129. Central Intelligence Agency, "World Factbook: Guyana," 1996, http://www.cia.gov/library/publication/the-world-factbook/geos/gy.html.

130. Earth Trends, *Country Report: Economic Indicators—Guyana*, World Resources Institute, 2003, 1, http://earthtrends.wri.org/pdf_library/country_profiles/eco_cou_328.pdf.

131. UNDP, "Country Report," in *Human Development Report 2005* (New York: Oxford University Press, 2005), 281.

132. This summary is derived from a comparison of the policy objectives of several of the major international aid donors to Guyana. See Inter-American Development Bank (IDB), "IDB Reaffirms Its Commitments at Summit of Americas: Ten-Point Action Plan for Latin America and the Caribbean," IDB press release, April 18, 1998, http://www.iadb.org/exr/PRENSA/1998/summite.htm; IDB, "IDB Approves Debt Relief for Guyana Under Enhanced HIPC," IDB press release, December 4, 2002, http://wwww.iadb.org/exr/PRENSA/2002/cp28202e.htm; IMF, "IMF Completes Second Review of Guyana's Performance Under the PRGF Arrangement, Approves Disbursement of US$8.8 Million," IMF Press Release no. 04/160, Washington, DC, July 28, 2004; World Bank, "Guyana: Country Brief," 2004; USAID, "Guyana: USAID Program Profile," May 1, 2006, http://www.usaid.gov/locations/latin_america_caribbean/country/program_profiles/guyanaprofile.html; USAID, "USAID Guyana: Country Strategic Plan, 2004–2008"; "Guyana Building Community Capacity Project," Canadian International Development Agency (CIDA), May 15, 2005, http://www.acdi-cida.gc.ca/CIDAWEB/acdicida.nsf/En/EMA-218121250-NU8; DFID, *Regional Assistance for the Caribbean;* European Commission, "Development: EU Relations with Guyana," September 7, 2006, http://ec.europa.eu/comm/development/body/country/country_home_en.cfm?cid=gy&status=new; Chris Spies, "Report on the Post Conference Opportunities Workshop held January 9, 2004, and the Meeting on January 12, 2004," UNDP Building Social Cohesion Program, http://www.sdnp.org.gy/csoc/reports/Report_on_9_January.rtf.

133. UN, "United Nations Development Assistance Framework: Guyana (2001–2003)," 6, 16, 19.

134. UN, "United Nations Development Assistance Framework: Guyana (2001–2003)," 6, 16, 19.

135. See Caroline Thomas, *Global Governance, Development, and Human Security* (London: Pluto, 2000); McAffee, *Storm Signals*; and John

Rapley, *Globalization and Inequality: Neoliberalism's Downward Spiral* (Boulder, CO: Lynne Rienner Publishers, 2004).

136. See John Gaffar, *Guyana: From State Control to Free Market* (New York: Nova, 2003), 293.

137. "PPP Criticizes PNC/R Protest," *Guyana Chronicle,* April 10, 2002, 3.

138. Amnesty International, "Guyana, Human Rights, and Crime Control."

139. "Project Launched to Strengthen Capacity of RDCs to Reduce Social Tensions," *Stabroek News*, July 6, 2005, 12, http://www.stabroeknews.com/index.pl/article?id=23591067.

140. UNDP, *Promoting Social Cohesion in Guyana: A Strategy for the Prevention and Mitigation of Electoral Violence* (Georgetown: UNDP, 2006).

141. UNDP, "Report of Multi-Stakeholder Forums Held in Region 1"; "Report of Multi-Stake holder Forums Held in Region 4"; "Report of Multi-Stakeholder Forums Held in Region 6" (Georgetown: UNDP, 2006)

142. Carter Center, "Activities by Country: Guyana," September 2006, http://www.cartercenter.org/countries/guyana.html; CARICOM, *Caribbean Community Mission to Guyana*; CARICOM, *Guyana: The St. Lucia Statement.*

143. See "Public Service Strike Turns Violent: Seventeen Injured in Wharf Confrontation—Police Fire Tear-gas, Pellets," *Stabroek News,* May 19, 1999, 1.

144. See Perry Mars, "State Intervention and Ethnic Conflict Resolution: Guyana and the Caribbean Experience," 167–186.

145. At the request of the government of Guyana, the British (through DFID) responded in 2007 with the offer of a grant worth 3 million pounds sterling for improvements and capacity building in Guyana's security sector (called the Security Sector Reform Project). However, as of June 2009, the implementation of this project is still in limbo and mired in much controversy between the Guyanese government and the British authorities in the country, primarily over the issue of "country ownership" of the project. See "Top Guyana Official Withdraws from Security Sector Reform Negotiations," *Caribbean NetNews,* May 28, 2009, http://www.caribbeannetnews.com/article.php?news_id=16738.

10

At the Crossroads of Hegemonic Powers: The Kyrgyz Republic

Anara Tabyshalieva

Kyrgyzstan's peaceful separation from the Soviet Union in 1991 was a remarkable feat. It was not preceded by a national liberation struggle, nor did it lead to serious political turmoil. Indeed, the country's abrupt break with its long history first of colonization under Russia and then of extended union within the Soviet Union was nonviolent and orderly. However, in the fifteen years that followed the secession, Kyrgyzstan experienced a painful transition process, culminating in the March 2005 upheavals and the resultant change in leadership.

The March 2005 Tulip Revolution was a broad-based popular response to an increasingly corrupt and repressive presidency. Although President Askar Akayev's administration (1990–2005) was not as authoritarian as the regimes in neighboring countries, state institutions were too weak to curb intense elite competition, corruption, and the involvement of criminal groups in politics. Despite complaints of high-level corruption by local civil society groups and the business community, donor organizations and international financial institutions continued providing loans and grants to the unpopular government. The authoritarian and corrupt presidency undermined economic progress, and increasing alienation between political elites and the public led to mass protests in 2002 and 2005. The Tulip Revolution was a missed opportunity for the country to embark on democratic reforms, end corruption, and promote economic and social development. Instead of delivering on his electoral promises of reform, the incoming president, Kurmanbek Bakiyev, has continued the policies of his predecessor in consolidating presidential power and distributing economic and political power among his patronage network.[1] In this chapter, I review Kyrgyzstan's postindependence transition. During this eighteen-year period, the country has made significant progress in enhancing its security and development, building a modern state, and integrating into the international community. I identify the trends and relationships in security and development outcomes in Kyrgyzstan and analyze the possible causal connections between security and development. I then examine the domestic and international factors contributing to the country's current socioeconomic and security status. Noting that Kyrgyzstan's security and development problems are interlinked, I conclude with a series of policy recommendations.

Security: Challenges and Implications

Inherited colonial legacies and geography contribute greatly to Kyrgyzstan's security and development situation. Small and landlocked Kyrgyzstan borders Kazakhstan, China, Uzbekistan, and Tajikistan. High mountains divide the state into northern and southern regions, leading to the development of regional identities. Mountainous terrain dominates most of Kyrgyzstan, leaving only 9 to 10 percent of its total territory suitable for permanent residence and agriculture.[2]

With the collapse of the Soviet Union, Kyrgyzstan emerged on the international scene as an independent state in 1991. The peaceful transition to independence created the illusion of an unproblematic future. After all, Kyrgyzstan's path to independence was not forged by a national liberation movement fighting colonial rule; it seemed instead a gift of history following the demise of the multiethnic USSR. Since independence, however, Kyrgyzstan has faced many transitional challenges. More than 150 years of colonial history and Russian domination significantly impacted the fledgling state's political experience, governance, and conflict-management capacity. With only limited experience of self-governance, the country was ill prepared to deal with the destabilizing effects of economic and political liberalization. This problem was aggravated by economic and liberalization policies that inflamed underlying social tensions and elite rivalries.

Since the transition, Kyrgyzstan has faced three tiers of conflict. At the community level, ethnic and subethnic conflicts have arisen over the distribution of irrigated land and water, political power, and economic assets. Intracommunal conflict has also been fueled by intolerance of an increasing number of Christian converts from Muslim backgrounds. Nationally, the Tulip Revolution erupted due to unjust distribution of wealth and power, poor governance, and widespread unemployment. At the international level, Kyrgyzstan has had to deal with problems related to the autocracy in Uzbekistan and the spillover of political rebels and refugees from neighboring Tajikistan and Uzbekistan. Moreover, Kyrgyzstan is not only in a relatively unstable neighborhood, but it is also an arena of significant geostrategic import to three hegemons: Russia, China, and the United States.

Ethnopolitical Dynamics

Kyrgyzstan developed as part of the Russian colonial empire in the mid-nineteenth century, eventually becoming an autonomous province and then a full-fledged union republic of the Soviet Union. Subjected to 150 years of Russian domination, Kyrgyzstan continues to contend with its colonial legacy. The land reform issues facing Kyrgyzstan, for instance, can be traced to early Russian colonial practices and policies. The confiscation by the Russian administration of Kyrgyz tribal pastures, fertile lands along rivers, and traditional transportation routes led to a rebellion in 1916. The Czarist administration responded to these riots through a campaign of brutal repression that amounted to an ethnic massacre of the inhabitants of the area. As a result of the massacres, thousands of Kyrgyz families fled to China, leading to a decrease of over 40 percent of the Kyrgyz population in the northern provinces. About 200,000 Kyrgyz died in a wintertime exodus across glacial gorges. Although the February 1917 revolution in Russia stopped the persecution of the Kyrgyz, the subsequent Great October Socialist Revolution did not change Czarist policies for land distribution. Thus land disputes between the natives and Russian farmers continued. Furthermore, Stalin's programs of forced sedentarization and collectivization dramatically altered the livelihoods of Kyrgyz seminomadic and settled peoples and led to the loss of a significant part of their livestock. These colonial policies have left enduring legacies that have affected land reform initiatives in Kyrgyzstan by, for example, complicating attempts by the Kyrgyz Parliament to discuss land privatization in the 1990s.

There is also significant tension in the largest cities over the distribution of land. The source of these is another Soviet policy, the resident permit *(propiska)* system, which lasted until the late 1980s. The system limited the internal migration of rural Kyrgyz to cities so as to maintain jobs for Russian and Ukrainian workers and professionals, who were encouraged to reside in Kyrgyz cities. With the relaxation of the permit system after independence, there has been an increase in rural-urban migration, leading to population pressures in urban areas and sparking conflict over land around the largest cities, Bishkek and Osh.[3]

Migration policies under Soviet rule also explain many of the territorial ethnicity patterns seen in contemporary Kyrgyzstan. In the mid-nineteenth century, the percentage of Kyrgyz within the total population was sharply reduced following a massive migration of Russians and Ukrainians into the area. While Russians and Ukrainians were encouraged to move into the satellite republics, movement of the local population was restricted. Even in the national capital, the Kyrgyz constituted a minority.

Under the Soviet state, Kyrgyzstan's multiethnic character was subsumed under the rhetoric of proletarian internationalism, the "brotherhood of all nations," Soviet citizenship, and the pursuit of a "new society." Yet the USSR enforced an ethnic hierarchy through privileges that actually reinforced divisions among ethnic groups. Russians were often given privileged positions at the expense of the natives of the non-Russian republics. In the capital, Bishkek, the natives comprised a minority and the use of the Kyrgyz language was severely restricted. The centrally controlled administrative and military apparatuses enforced stability by immediately suppressing any ethnic, religious, or social discontent. During Soviet domination of the region, ethnic identities and rivalries were submerged under Moscow's dictate declaring all peoples in the USSR as part of the Soviet new society. However, as the Kremlin's power began to weaken in the late 1980s and the economy slowed down, ethnic tensions over the distribution of natural resources began to flare in local communities. For example, in 1990 interethnic conflicts broke out in southern Kyrgyzstan (namely the cities of Osh and Uzgen) over the distribution of irrigated land.[4] Almost immediately, separatist political slogans accompanied these clashes. At the time, the local Communist Party leadership was unprepared to effectively handle such turmoil. After independence, newly elected President Akayev capitalized on the fierce interelite competition to consolidate his presidential power. Market-oriented privatization reforms only facilitated his ability to redistribute assets through his patronage network.[5]

Since the economic crisis in the late 1980s, the disintegration of the Soviet Union in 1991, and the declaration of the Kyrgyz language as the national language during independence, there has been a mass out-migration of Russians, Ukrainians, and other Russian-speaking people. Russians comprised 9 percent of the 2007 population, down 21 percent from their numbers in 1992.[6] Over the 150-year history of colonial domination, the Russian language has had a privileged status as the language of the administrative system, trade, higher education, and science. Russian is still dominant in public life since it is the common language among the country's diverse ethnolinguistic groups; according to national statistics, 33 percent of Kyrgyz and Uzbeks, 81 percent of Kazakhs, and 98 percent of Ukrainians speak fluent Russian. However, since independence, the Kyrgyz language has begun to play a larger role in all spheres of the public life.[7] About half of the country's population is bilingual, speaking both Russian and Kyrgyz. English is spoken by only 1 percent of the population—mostly young people in the capital.[8]

Kyrgyz, Russians, and Uzbeks comprise the largest ethnic groups in Kyrgyzstan. But there are also dozens of smaller ethnic groups: Ukrainians, Germans, Uyghurs, Koreans, Dungans, Tartars, Tajiks, and peoples from the Caucasus and Crimea. The Kyrgyz, who were historically divided into tribes and subtribes, made up 70 percent of the total population as of 2008. According to the Ministry of Internal Affairs, there are around 600,000 ethnic Kyrgyz living in neighboring countries—including 360,000 in Uzbekistan and 160,000 in Xinjiang, China. Currently, the largest ethnic minorities—Uzbeks (14.5 percent) and Russians (9 percent)—live predominantly in lowlands and enjoy access to key market centers. These ethnic minorities have sizable kin groups residing in adjacent Uzbekistan and Russia.[9] Tension over language in multiethnic communities is exacerbated by the differing policies of the three states sharing the Ferghana Valley: Uzbekistan, Kyrgyzstan, and Tajikistan. The sizable Uzbek community living at the Kyrgyz-Uzbek border is interested in improving bilateral relations. By contrast, Uzbekistan's own education and language policies reflect an attempt to distance the state from Soviet-Russian legacy. For example, Uzbekistan has converted to the Latin alphabet, whereas Kyrgyzstan and Tajikistan continue to use a Cyrillic script. This means that students at Uzbek-language schools in Kyrgyzstan, mostly in the Osh and Jalalabat provinces, face problems in continuing their education across the border.[10]

Religious Tensions

The religious and cultural traditions of Muslims have shaped the dominant belief systems in Kyrgyzstan. Almost 90 percent of the country's people—Kyrgyz, Uzbeks, Turks, Uyghurs, Tartars, Dungans, and others—are Sunni Muslim of the Hanafi school. There are, however, some historical differences between the religious practices of different

Muslim groups. The Islam of the formerly nomadic Kyrgyz includes many elements of pre-Islamic faith; that of the sedentary populations of the lowlands—the Uzbeks, Tartars, Dungans, and Uyghurs—incorporates fewer. Domestic membership in the Russian Orthodox Church, the second largest religious denomination, has decreased since the 1990s due to the steady out-migration of Russians and the increased presence of various Protestant churches.

The rise of religious conflict is a relatively new and significant development, bringing another layer of complexity to ethnic and subethnic conflicts. As a Soviet republic, Kyrgyzstan was subject for seventy years to the policy of state atheism. However, after independence, Kyrgyzstan's program of political liberalization included the recognition of religious freedom. This has in turn rendered Kyrgyzstan fertile ground for proselytism and the emergence of nontraditional religious groups. One example is the illegal Islamic party Hizb ut Tahrir (Party of Liberation). Externally sponsored and ideologically based, Hizb ut Tahrir demands the establishment of an Islamic caliphate. Similar to other movements of radical political Islam, Hizb ut Tahrir condemns secular government and Western influence and calls for the boycott of elections.[11] However, the movement has a very limited base of support, with only an estimated three thousand members along the southern border of Kyrgyzstan.[12]

Since independence and the end of state atheism, the intense proselytizing efforts of foreign Protestant missionaries have led to intracommunal conflict. Prior to Russian colonization, Islam was the only religion of native people. Thus, the presence of Protestant missionaries from the United States, South Korea, and Europe has led to increasing tension between newly converted Christians from Muslim families and the Muslim community. As a result of intolerance, grassroots, intraethnic clashes occur sporadically between the relatives of recently deceased Kyrgyz Protestants and Kyrgyz Muslims, since most rural communities only have Muslim graveyards.[13]

These transition-based sources of conflict should not be underestimated in the Kyrgyz case. Kyrgyzstan has had to create a viable, independent state while managing a radical political and economic transition in a particularly unstable region. Religious conflicts resulting from newfound political and personal freedom are important indicators of some of the deleterious effects of liberalization policies in Kyrgyzstan.

The Bitter Lessons of the 2005 Tulip Revolution

The postindependence challenges were so unexpected that the local leadership was largely unprepared to respond adequately to the security problems and abrupt changes that subsequently followed. Nevertheless, in the early 1990s, the Democratic Movement of Kyrgyzstan, led by intellectuals and civil servants, mobilized the people to vote for the first president of the country, Askar Akayev, born in the north of the country. Early in his presidency, Akayev, a gifted physicist, promised liberal economic and political reforms. Yet over the term of his presidency, Akayev increasingly concentrated his political power through three broad strategies. He systematically consolidated the power of the presidency, mobilized government resources to maintain patronage networks that would keep him in power, and marginalized his opponents.[14]

Akayev incrementally increased his control over the legislative and judicial branches and downplayed the roles of the prime minister and Parliament. As the power of the presidency expanded, it began to overlap with the administrative powers of the prime minister. In effect, the prime minister began losing the independence and power required to govern the provinces.[15] In fourteen years, Akayev effectively removed seven prime ministers, targeting many of them as scapegoats for economic and social problems. Furthermore, he pushed through parliamentary amendments to the 1993 constitution in 1996, 1998, 2001, and 2003 that in effect increased presidential power and minimized that of Parliament. In addition to passing amendments, Akayev used his influence over the judiciary to maintain his hold on power for a third term. Since a third term was unconstitutional, it became possible only after the court ruled that Akayev's first term fell under the Soviet-era constitution.

It should be noted that after independence, both the legislature and the judiciary attempted to be active and independent from the executive. However, most judicial reforms were never enacted and over time the judiciary became corrupt, serving the interests of the ruling patronage networks to the detriment of common citizens.[16] In dealing with the political opposition, Akayev pursued various strategies—from government appointments to targeted tax inspections and imprisonment. For example, he persecuted members of the popular party Ar Namys (Dignity) and jailed its leader, Feliks Kulov, while limiting the influence of other popular opposition leaders by offering them positions abroad as ambassadors.[17] The domestic and foreign policies of Akayev's administration led to mass social protests and political instability. In March 2002, voters from rural Aksy in the remote southern province of Jalalabat, mobilized to protest the arbitrary arrest of opposition politician and lawmaker Azimbek Beknazarov. Beknazarov accused President Akayev of signing a border agreement that ceded lands to China without consulting

Parliament. Although the protesters organized a peaceful demonstration, the brutal response of the law-enforcement forces resulted in the deaths of five protestors and injuries among dozens more.[18]

It was the 2005 parliamentary elections that triggered the March 2005 revolution. The capture of parliamentary seats by many of Akayev's allies and relatives—including his twenty-nine-year-old son and thirty-two-year-old daughter—was seen as a clear indication that Akayev was using government resources to collect votes and rig the elections.[19] On March 24, 2005, about ten thousand protestors from all regions of Kyrgyzstan gathered on the central square for a peaceful demonstration. Like that of the 2003 Georgian and 2004 Ukrainian protests, the goal of the antigovernment protest leaders was to start a multiday strike that would compel Akayev to negotiate with opposition forces. Yet, unlike the revolutions in Georgia and Ukraine, the Kyrgyz opposition was not well organized and did not rally around one particular charismatic leader. When progovernment forces attacked, protesters spontaneously responded by storming the presidential administration. Much to the protesters' surprise, Akayev had already fled the country.

The March revolution was a nationwide response to Akayev's increasing authoritarianism, the corruption in the administration, the sluggish development of the economy, and continued poverty. The opposition forces were organized under a short-lived bloc, the Coordination Council of the People's Unity. The opposition held together in part because of the alliance of several political rivals—Bakiyev, Atambayev, Beknazarov, and many others. The opposition leaders, many of whom were from southern provinces, promised decentralization and a reduction in the power of the presidency. In fact, it was Bakiyev's promise to fight corruption, resume economic reforms, and launch decentralization measures that won him the July 2005 presidential election. Bakiyev's anti-Akayev stance allowed him to collect "roughly 90 percent of the vote."[20]

Yet after the elections, disagreement over the distribution of political power led to the fragmentation of the opposition, renewed instability, and business as usual. Despite his reformist preelection agenda, President Bakiyev quickly reneged on such campaign promises as power-sharing. He took direct control of profitable state agencies and security forces and appointed his brother as head of the State Security Service. Instead of decentralization reform he diminished the role of prime minister. With a firm grip on the reins of power, the president unseated three prime ministers between 2005 and 2007. Like his predecessor, Bakiyev selected an ethnic Russian as fourth prime minister, since a non-Kyrgyz would not be perceived as a political rival. Furthermore, the period following the revolution was marked by a redistribution of resources that was in turn associated with several political killings and protest movements in the capital and provinces.[21] There was instability in the capital, too, as thousands of squatters tried to unlawfully expropriate land and property.[22] The revolution also led to the reactivation of criminal groups—some of whom claimed that they were working to defend the revolution, when in fact they were only redistributing property. The dissatisfaction pickets were primarily due to the redistribution of economic assets and the rise of new political groups in the country; the March revolution had shifted political power from northern clans, who dominated the upper echelons of power during much of the Communist period (1961–1985) as well as from 1990 to 2004, to southern elites.

Despite the revolution's success in overthrowing an unpopular president from the north, Kyrgyzstan's institutions have been unable to contain the fierce competition among elites. The continued struggle over the redistribution of power and economic resources has fragmented the political leadership into competing factions, which have mobilized broad social discontent to further fuel competition between groups in an attempt to gain the political and economic advantage.

Insecurity is critically linked to Kyrgyzstan's development problems, which will be discussed in the next section. Unemployment, rural-urban migration, and ill-conceived land-reform policies have all led to increased social tensions that sometimes escalate into conflict. Postindependence economic decline and the unequal geographical distribution of employment opportunities have in part been responsible for high urbanization rates, as young people migrate from villages to large cities in search of better jobs and access to new markets. Bishkek and Osh have become magnets for unemployed and underemployed youth from affected areas.[23] Unable to find housing, some migrants have resorted to seizing land plots and constructing squatters' camps on the outskirts of large cities. Redistribution of land plots by Bakiyev's adminitration following the March 2005 upheavals have only exacerbated tensions in densely populated urban areas.[24]

Many reasons are given for the initial success of the relatively peaceful Tulip Revolution, including mass social mobilization, unified opposition leadership, and weak security forces. Yet there is significant concern that the one-day unrest inadvertently set a precedent whereby the coup becomes the operative mechanism for regime change in the face of ongoing problems. Since the revolution, Kyrgyzstan has continued to struggle with an increasingly authoritarian presidency, fierce intraelite competition, and weak state institutions. The judiciary remains an ineffective check against presidential power; the underpaid civil service is prone to corruption; and the police have been unable to effectively respond to transnational crime. In short, the political situation remains highly unstable and precarious.[25]

As a result of the authoritarian policies of the postrevolutionary leadership and wide use of administrative resources, the parliamentary elections failed to meet a number of commitments to the Organization for Security and Cooperation in Europe (OSCE).[26] Hurriedly formed in October prior to the elections, Ak-Jol (Best Way), a propresidential party, received majority seats in the rubber-stamp Kyrgyz Parliament in December 2007—whereas popular opposition parties such as Ata-Meken ("Fatherland") did not get any seats at all. Before the presidential elections in 2009, Bakiyev, the southern president elected after the revolution, concentrated even more power in his hands than did his ousted predecessor. He crushed the opposition groups and signed a law in 2009 that allows the defense forces to be used against domestic dissent.[27]

Crime and the Drug Trade

According to an Asian Development Bank (ADB) report, Kyrgyzstan benefits from a relatively low crime rate. With over 8,700 police officers (one for every 600 people), it enjoys one of the highest rates of protection in the world.[28] Despite the numbers, however, police and security forces are not well trained and are often underequipped and underpaid. The low wages of police officers have caused many to seek kickbacks from people involved in illegal activities, primarily sex workers, drug users and dealers, and smugglers. There is also rampant corruption in the penitentiary system, as revealed by the media coverage of the suppression of a series of prison riots from 2005 onward.[29]

Economic liberalization has also been accompanied by an increase in drug trade and the organization of criminal groups. According to an International Crisis Group report, security forces are unable to stop the growth of organized crime.[30] The overthrow of the previous administration "left not only a political vacuum but also a criminal vacuum. Businessmen had long complained that members of the [former] presidential family in effect ran rackets requiring payment of protection money."[31] Since the March 2005 revolution, criminal networks have gained more influence both in the state and in society because of the weakness of the new government, the inability of security forces to respond, and the extent of corruption in the system.[32] For instance, Bayaman Erkinbaev (who was assassinated after the March revolution), was elected three times to the Parliament—despite his reputation as a narcobaron.[33]

Kyrgyzstan is also a strategic transportation corridor between South Asia and Russia.[34] Narcotics dealers competing for access to transit routes contribute to insecurity in the affected region. According to UNODC statistics, heroin seizures in Kyrgyzstan increased from 105 kilograms in 2003 to 431 kilograms in 2007, while opium seizures increased from 46 to 271 kilograms in the same period.[35]

Despite cooperation by the law-enforcement agencies of Tajikistan, Kyrgyzstan, and Uzbekistan, drug trading remains a profitable endeavor, even tempting underpaid public servants. Although Kyrgyzstan formed its own national forces and border patrol upon independence, these forces have been unable to respond effectively to the security challenges posed by the drug trade and transnational insurgency groups in the region.[36] During the 1999 and 2000 incursions by the Islamic Movement of Uzbekistan (IMU) into the country, the ill-equipped army was unable to muster an effective tactical operation on the mountainous terrain.[37]

Cross-border Movements and Foreign-funded Insurgency

Kyrgyzstan has to contend with the diverse security challenges of an unstable region. Internal political instability in Uzbekistan has been a particular source of insecurity in Kyrgyzstan. On May 13, 2005, bloodshed in the Uzbekistani city of Andijon—located sixty kilometers from the largest Kyrgyz city, Osh—led to instability in the Ferghana Valley.[38] Hundreds of Uzbek citizens, including women, children, and injured civilians, escaped the bloodshed by crossing into Kyrgyzstan. From this group, 439 Uzbek asylum seekers found shelter in Kyrgyzstan.[39] Despite diplomatic and economic pressure from the Uzbek government on Kyrgyzstan to extradite refugees, almost all were sent to Romania with the aid of the UN High Commissioner for Refugees (UNHCR) and the OSCE. In response, the Uzbek prosecutor-general blamed UNHCR for defending terrorists[40] and officials in Tashkent, the Uzbek capital, threatened to cut off gas to Kyrgyzstan.[41] Uzbekistan's president, Islam Karimov, accused Kyrgyz leadership of sheltering rebels and inspiring Uzbek citizens to initiate their own March revolution.[42]

There are also significant security challenges posed by the rise of political Islam in the region. The aforementioned IMU, which seeks to replace the ruling elite in Uzbekistan with an Islamic caliphate, has transformed itself into a transnational insurgency group operating in four countries: Uzbekistan, Tajikistan, Kyrgyzstan, and Afghanistan. The movement originated in the Uzbek region of the Ferghana Valley. Expelled from Uzbekistan in the early 1990s, the IMU was later supported by the United Tajik Opposition (UTO), Al-Qaida, and the Taliban. The membership base of the group is relatively young, even though most of its backing seems to come from more established groups like Al-Qaida and the Taliban. Allegedly, renaming itself the Islamic Movement of Turkestan (central Asia), the former IMU has broadened its goals to operate not only Uzbekistan but in the central Asian region.[43] There are reports that Kyrgyz students are illegally attending jihadist madrassas in Pakistan, which are known to be fertile recruiting grounds for such groups.

The transnational activities of the IMU have had serious security implications for Kyrgyzstan. For example, in 1999 and 2000, several hundred IMU militants were led by the warlord Juma Namangani through the gorges of Tajikistan into Kyrgyzstan. While in Kyrgyzstan, the rebels held twenty-five people hostage and demanded safe passage into Uzbekistan. The incident revealed two important vulnerabilities: (1) the inability of the local army to effectively respond to attacks by insurgent groups and (2) the susceptibility of local, unemployed men to recruitment by these groups. On this second point, it is important to note that the local population did not support this group ideologically; instead, some Kyrgyz joined the IMU probably just to receive payment for their services. The incursion into Kyrgyz territory revealed the weakness of the border patrol. Set up in 2002, the Kyrgyz Border Service remains underfunded and unable to respond immediately to attacks by armed religious extremists. After the disintegration of the Soviet Union, borders became a new source of unofficial income for border guards and custom officers. Although the government attempts to regulate cross-border movement of arms flow and illegal trade, corruption is rampant throughout the system. Since the IMU incursions into Kyrgyzstan, Russia, the United States, and China have provided aid to strengthen the border troops.

Three large ethnic enclaves of Tajikistan and Uzbekistan in the Kyrgyz Republic created under Soviet rule have also contributed to rising ethnic and interstate tensions. The Vorukh enclave, which is a part of Tajikistan, has numerous economic and social problems that Tajik authorities have not been able to resolve. The other two enclaves, Shakhimardan and Sokh, are inside Kyrgyzstan, though they are administered from Uzbekistan. The Sokh enclave, populated mostly by ethnic Tajiks, maintains a particularly difficult border to cross. Kyrgyz citizens have to pass through unfriendly custom and border controls when they travel across the south of their own country. Furthermore, attempting in 2000 to limit illegal cross-border movement, Uzbek authorities put land mines around their enclaves on the Kyrgyzstan border, leading to increased tension between the two neighbors. Under pressure by Kyrgyzstan, Uzbekistan began the demining process in 2004–2005.[44]

Development Trends: Rising Tides Do Not Lift All Boats

Although Kyrgyzstan was able to absorb the shock of a major transformation from a command to a market economy in the 1990s and early 2000s, its fundamentals remain greatly affected by its geography and natural resource base. The country does not have as much mineral wealth as its resource-rich neighbors; nonetheless, its mountains contain deposits of gold, rare earth metals, iron, bauxite, copper, tin, molybdenum, mercury, and antimony. Kyrgyzstan's greatest natural assets are vast reserves of water trapped in glaciers and bodies of water. The water is an important source of hydroelectric energy in the country. Kyrgyzstan's mountain ranges have also been compared to the Swiss Alps; with appropriate development policies, they could eventually be a tourist draw.

Yet the mountainous territory also presents an important set of liabilities. It is a dangerous habitat, afflicted by a variety of natural disasters. Avalanches and annual landslides disrupt the lives and livelihoods of populations to the south. The country is subject to earthquakes and one of the most seismically unstable areas in Central Asia.[45] The rugged landscape also impedes government agencies in responding to emergencies or detecting and controlling narcotrafficking and guerrilla movements from neighboring states. And just as it provides ideal cover for drug trafficking, the terrain also limits legitimate interregional trade. Landlocked Kyrgyzstan lacks easy access to international trade routes and markets. Meanwhile, its Soviet-era transportation network has meant a continued economic orientation towards Russia.

Shifting Economic and Social Policies

Upon independence, the main challenges faced by policymakers were the institutional weakness of the state, the erosion of social safety nets, and the predominance of Soviet-based administrative systems. Under the USSR, Kyrgyzstan was an industrial-agricultural republic whose economy was tightly linked to those of the Russian Federation and other Soviet republics. The industrial sector was mostly developed in the north of the country, whereas the southern lowlands remained predominantly agricultural. Since independence, Kyrgyzstan has been undergoing a process of deindustrialization; today industrial production is far below preindependence levels. This industrial disintegration closely parallels the dissolution of Kyrgyzstan's links with former Soviet republics. Meanwhile, deindustrialization processes have caused the stagnation of Kyrgyzstan's large enterprises and industrial economy. Industry contributes to approximately 15 percent of the gross domestic product (GDP).[46] Since the late 1990s, exports as a percentage of GDP have been on the rise, mostly as a result of the development of the Kumtor gold mine.[47]

Increasingly, the present-day Kyrgyz Republic is becoming an agrarian country, with agriculture currently comprising 35 percent of the GDP. Agricultural producers were able to overcome the initial shocks of the decollectivization of farms. Yet, further land reform and privatization measures may lead to conflicts over the distribution of irrigated land.[48]

The euphoria following independence was challenged by the economic and social crises of the early 1990s, which led to the decline of Kyrgyzstan's real GDP by 50 percent. In 2008, the Kyrgyz Republic remains heavily indebted, with about US$2.3 billion in external debt.[49] Meanwhile, it depends heavily on its agricultural sectors and the export of gold to drive the economy. Indeed, it is overreliant on its gold exports to Switzerland, Germany, and the United Arab Emirates, which constituted about 40 percent of total export earnings and 7 percent of GDP in 2004.[50] This leaves Kyrgyzstan vulnerable to the fluctuation of gold prices. Although it also exports minerals, fuel, textiles, and electricity, the country has not yet been successful in sufficiently diversifying its export base.

Over the first dozen years of the postindependence era, between 1993 and 2003, GDP per capita has fallen from US$450 to US$330. The local economy was hit hard by the 1998 Russian financial crisis and recovered only slowly over the next five years (Figure 10.1).

Upon independence, Kyrgyzstan embarked on an ambitious program of market liberalization and structural reform. In 1993, the government established control of its monetary policy by introducing a national currency to replace the Russian ruble. Over time, monetary

Figure 10.1 GDP per Capita in the Kyrgyz Republic, 1993–2003 (US$)

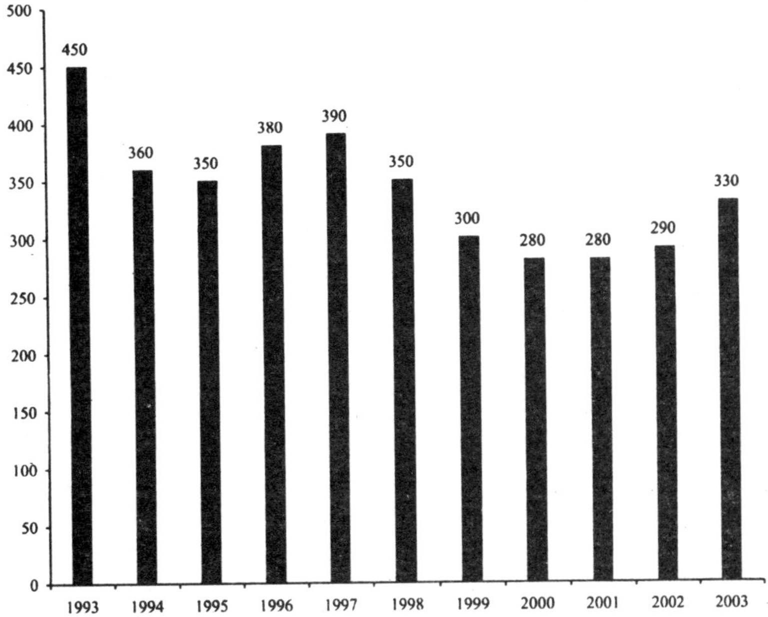

Source: UNDP, National Human Development Report, "The Influence of Civil Society on the Human Development Process in Kyrgyzstan" (Bishkek, 2005), Annex, http://hdr.undp.org/en/reports/nationalreports/europethecis/kyrgyzstan/KYRGYZSTAN_2005_en.pdf.

policies effectively reduced inflation from 855 percent in 1992 to 4.1 percent in 2004.

An extensive privatization program encouraged the emergence of a private-sector middle class. However, the country continues to struggle with attracting foreign direct investment (FDI) partly because of an unfavorable business environment and rampant corruption. Presumably, the shadow economy now accounts for over 40 percent of economic activity.[51] Although real GDP growth has reduced poverty, living standards remain low. According to a 1999 World Bank survey, between 49 and 69.7 percent of the population then lived below the poverty line.[52] In addition, poverty has clear regional dimensions. It is higher in rural areas. The ethnic Kyrgyz population scattered in the remote provinces of Naryn and Talas are poorer than people in other regions. And despite the fact that the densely populated southern provinces of Jalalabat and Osh suffer frequent natural disasters, national expenditure for the prevention and management thereof is only 0.6 percent of GDP.[53] There are fears that in the case of an emergency, any unfair distribution of humanitarian aid and corruption on the part of government officials would lead to ethnic conflict. Increased transparency, community participation, and progressive environmental policies are critical to preventing intercommunal violence over natural resources.

After independence, the government steadily decreased budget expenditures on social and health services, potentially endangering impressive achievements in literacy, life expectancy, and health care. Health care expenditure as a percentage of government expenditure fell from 3 percent in 1993 to 2.3 percent in 2003. Similarly, social security spending fell from 0.6 percent in 1993 to 0.2 percent in 2003. Meanwhile, whereas expenditures for social services decreased, military spending increased from 0.7 percent to 1.5 percent within the same period (Figure 10.2).

Recovering after the disintegration of the Soviet Union, the government has gradually begun to increase its allocation of public funds for social services. Though public expenditures on social services as a percentage of GDP fell from 18 percent in 1995 to 8.4 percent in

Figure 10.2 Expenditures of the Government Budget (as a percentage of GDP)

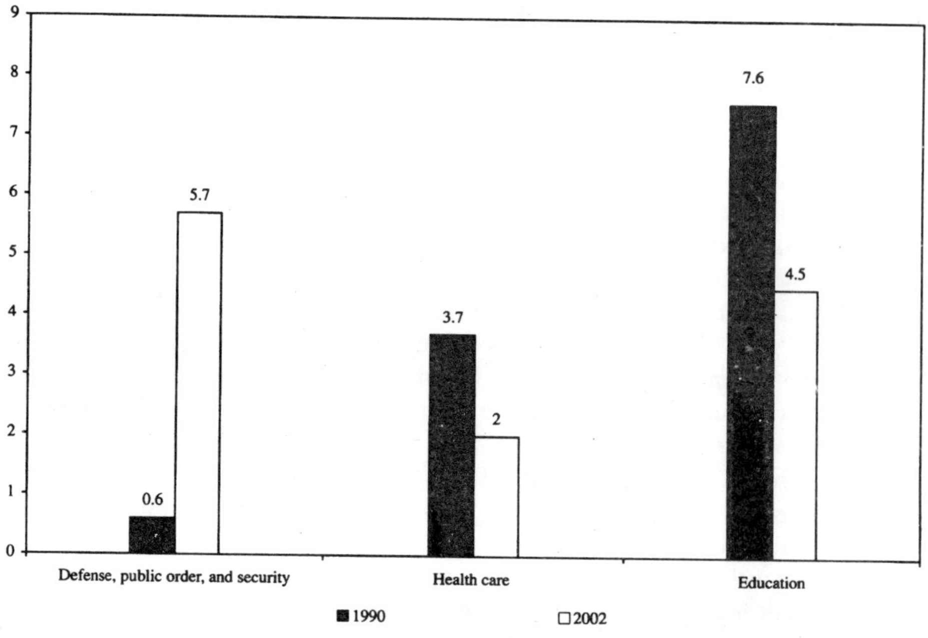

Source: "The UN System in the Kyrgyz Republic," *Common Country Assessment* (Bishkek, 2003), 2003, p. 48.

2000, they increased in 2003 to 11.6 percent.[54] Successively, the country adopted the National Sustainable Human Development Strategy in 1997, the Comprehensive Development Framework (CDF) for 2003–2010, and the National Poverty Reduction Strategy (NPRS) in 2003. The Millennium Development Goals (MDGs) mobilize domestic and international players to address poverty.[55]

Sixty-two percent of the population is of working age—from fifteen to sixty-four years old.[56] Official statistics report that only 3 percent of the workforce is unemployed. However, according to the International Labor Organization (ILO) and the International Monetary Fund (IMF), unemployment rates range from 8 to 20 percent.[57] The lack of reliable statistics is partly a function of the distrust citizens of post-Soviet republics have for the state.[58] Half of those unemployed are women. The high level of gender equality in employment achieved under Soviet policies is dropping. In 2003, the salaries of male employees exceeded the salaries of female employees by 1.6 times.[59] Gender disparities have increased in many other spheres of life, including politics, education, and social protection. Local patriarchal traditions and modern consumerist images of the West contribute to gender discrimination.[60]

Unemployment has also contributed to the growth of a criminal economy: the transnational drug trade. Official sources reveal that more than 95 percent of the people arrested for drug-related crimes in 2002 were unemployed.[61] Furthermore, the number of people involved in human trafficking, drug smuggling, and opium poppy cultivation is on the rise. Police corruption disproportionately affects at-risk groups like sex workers and drug users, who have to bribe police officers in part because of a series of draconian laws against their activities.[62]

Another strategy for coping with the high level of unemployment is migration. Internal and external migration has greatly affected the socioeconomic and ethnic map of Kyrgyzstan. Regardless of ethnicity, poverty has driven people abroad in search of employment. About 500,000–700,000 people, which is to say a quarter of Kyrgyzstan's able-bodied citizens, have migrated to Russia and Kazakhstan. According to the IMF, in mid-2004 the average monthly wage in Kazakhstan and Russia was over US$200, whereas in Kyrgyzstan it was only US$47.[63] Kyrgyz migrant laborers mostly work in shuttle trade and the construction sector in Siberia and the Far East. Many economic migrants encounter difficulties in registering for permission to work in Russia. Over US$150 million in remittances was sent to Kyrgyzstan from Russia in 2004 alone.[64]

Income disparities have also encouraged rural-urban migration. Since independence, the restrictive residency permit system has been relaxed and young migrants from rural areas are now able to move to urban areas and establish squatter camps. This trend has led to increasing tension over land in urban areas.[65] Although official statistics, based on the old Soviet method of residency registration, underestimate the scale of rural-urban migration, it is clear that the trend has important implications for both security and development in Kyrgyzstan.

The health of the environment has been significantly degraded by human activities, thus aggravating the possibility of natural disasters. Forests cover 6 percent of the country but are being depleted as people use wood for heating.[66] Deforestation, overgrazing, and road and canal construction all contribute to flash floods, mudslides, and avalanches, which in turn damage communication infrastructure. Between 1990 and 2002, there were 357 flood-related emergencies.[67] In addition, Soviet planners left damaging uranium tailings along riverbanks. For example, the dangerous materials left in Mailuu Suu could leak into the Syr Darya River, resulting in a cross-border ecological disaster.

Kyrgyzstan inherited relatively high levels of social well-being and infrastructure from the Soviet Union. The country still enjoys high levels of universal literacy. And despite cuts in public expenditure in health care and education, life expectancy at birth has not changed much since 1990; in 2002, it remained at 64.4 years for men and 72.1 for women.[68] In fact, the collapse of the socialist safety net has severely affected populations in the high mountains and lowlands. With few public funds to maintain it, the transportation and communication infrastructure has greatly deteriorated since independence.[69]

Meanwhile, however, there has been a rapid spread of tuberculosis and HIV through the population. Between 1990 and 2003, the number of tuberculosis cases per 100,000 people tripled. Between 2000 and 2003, there was a ninefold increase in notification rates of HIV. According to a World Bank study, by 2015, Kyrgyzstan will need US$4.4 billion to pay for the antiretroviral treatment alone.[70] The flourishing drug trade in the country also undermines HIV prevention efforts.[71] The number of drug addicts in Kyrgyzstan is estimated at about 2 percent of the total population of the country or approximately 80,000 to 100,000 people. Among them, 68 percent are intravenous drug users—of whom 93.4 percent are males (2003).[72]

Corruption

Among the many obstacles to establishing good governance in Kyrgyzstan is the deep-rooted tradition of patronage. These patronage networks mean that relatives and allies often receive appointments to government positions or economically profitable sectors. For instance, under former President Akayev, ruling patronage networks controlled some of the most important segments of Kyrgyzstan's economy: energy, gold, communication, customs, fuel, and alcohol. In addition, any appointments to government agencies receiving external aid, loans, and tax revenues were highly sought after. The tiny ruling elite also funneled state resources through their patronage networks to remain in power.

Especially given the patronage tradition, postindependence liberalization policies seem to have created the ideal environment for pervasive corruption. The increased competition between political elites has encouraged the use of informal payments. Over the fifteen years since independence, bribery and favoritism have become rampant in executive and judicial agencies. For many individuals, bribing state officials is cheaper than dealing with state overregulation and taxation, licensing, registration, and complicated and lengthy documentation.[73] Civil servants are particularly vulnerable to corruption, being often underpaid and unprotected from arbitrary and politically motivated removals from office.

Measuring the extent of corruption in Kyrgyzstan is difficult because bribes have evolved to become part of local tradition. For example, some public administrators receive cash from businessmen customarily as gifts and as demonstrations of respect. Furthermore, a new practice has been established that requires businessmen and state officials to donate to charitable funds in support of festivals, marathons, and other events. Since these transactions are cash contributions to local funds, they are easy neither to trace nor monitor. Postrevolutionary investigations have revealed that local state budget organizations were required to transfer funds to Akayev's wife, the former first lady.[74]

Indeed, the ruling family's corruption adversely affected the nascent business and middle classes, who began to oppose Akayev's authoritarian tendencies. The business community was especially discontent over the activities of Akayev's son and son-in-law, who monopolized key assets and the most profitable enterprises in the country. FBI investigations have revealed that they embezzled hundreds of millions of dollars from Pentagon fuel contracts.[75]

Ironically, anticorruption campaigns were one strategy that Akayev used to deal with the opposition. Under pressure from the international community to fight corruption, Akayev launched campaigns targeting his opponents and disloyal businessmen. Journalists and activists from nongovernmental organizations (NGOs) who openly discussed corruption in the president's family and among his allies were immediately silenced.[76]

Building Civil Society

Political liberalization and external aid have helped Kyrgyzstan build elements of a vibrant civil society. Since 1991, over 8,000 civil society groups and nongovernmental organizations (NGOs) have entered the national arena. NGOs partner with state agencies in reforming education, promoting human rights, and protecting the environment. However, there is growing concern that many of the NGOs that are externally funded will only be viable as long as external support exists.

In Kyrgyzstan, urban residents have relatively good access to various media outlets. The majority of the population (60 percent) watches television, one-fifth listens to radio, and only a quarter read newspapers. People watch mostly Russian television programs—largely because of their higher technical quality and their coverage of international news.

In contrast to radio and television shows, the Kyrgyz public has more options in print media. However both local newspapers and television stations face significant financial burdens, leading to the disappearance of many outlets.[77] Among its neighbors, Kyrgyzstan has the highest share of Internet users per capita, with 54 users per 1,000 people in 2005 (compared to 34 for Uzbekistan, 27 for Kazakhstan, 8 for Turkmenistan, and 1 for Tajikistan). Although Internet use is expensive, it is not fully regulated by the government and has become quite popular.

Kyrgyzstan's Dilemma: Authoritarian Neighbors vs. the International Donor Community

With its domestic security complicated by the difficulty of maintaining good relations with its unstable neighbors, Kyrgyzstan also has to contend with the competing interests of three hegemons: Russia, China, and the United States. US and Russian airbases coexisted uneasily around the capital, Bishkek—a fact that has brought pressure from China as well as Russia, who want the United States to diminish its military presence in the region. As a landlocked and resource-poor country, Kyrgyzstan is heavily dependent on donor countries, its neighbors, and Russia. Because of the conflicting desires of all these actors, Kyrgyzstan is pulled in multiple policy directions. For example, Western donors encourage political and economic reforms in the country, whereas neighbors express concern over the destabilizing consequences of such liberalization processes. The instability created by liberalization, combined with economic stagnation, poverty, unemployment, and government corruption, undoubtedly contributed to the events that triggered the 2005 Tulip revolution.

Kyrgyzstan is a member of several organizations whose aim is to broaden economic and security cooperation among states in the region. However, its overlapping membership in both international and regional organizations has led to conflicting obligations. The international community and Western donors have been encouraging political liberalization and a market economy in Kyrgyzstan, whereas its neighbors and regional superpowers Russia and China resist these trends. According to the US-based Freedom House, the situation in Kyrgyzstan looks better than in Russia, China, Kazakhstan, and other neighbors, as illustrated in Figure 10.3.

The Russia-centered Commonwealth of Independent States (CIS) was established in December 1991. It was intended to fill the institutional vacuum left by the rapid disintegration of the Soviet Union and to restore the domination of Russia in the former Soviet republics. Although its numerous decisions and statements remain largely ineffective, the CIS has served to prevent the expression of hostility among the former Soviet republics. Under its own initiative, Russia founded the 1992 Collective Security Treaty (CST) with Armenia, Belarus, Kazakhstan, Kyrgyzstan, and Tajikistan. In April 2003, the CST became the Collective Security Treaty Organization (CSTO). The CSTO seeks to address the emerging security threats within the region, including terrorism and drug trafficking. Within this framework, Russia established an airbase in Kyrgyzstan to expand its influence in central Asia.

In 1994, the leaders of Kazakhstan, Kyrgyzstan, and Uzbekistan established the Central Asian Regional Union (CARU) with the goal of enhancing regional stability and security by creating a common market. In 1998, after limited results from cooperation, CARU first became the Central Asian Economic Community (CAEC) and then the Central Asian Cooperation Organization (CACO). Yet the name

Figure 10.3 Internet Users in Central Asia per 1,000 People (MDG), 2002

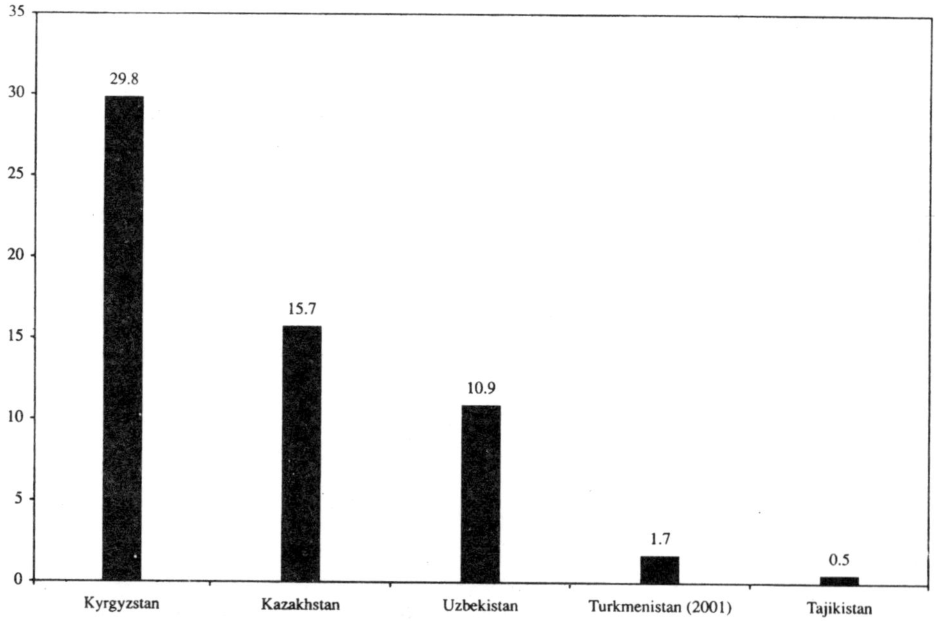

Source: UNDP, *Human Development Report 2004* (New York, 2004), 181–182.

changes did not improve regional relations or mask the regional ambitions of the two largest states, Uzbekistan and Kazakhstan. In October 2005, CACO merged with the Eurasian Economic Community (EurAsEC), which includes Russia, Belarus, Kazakhstan, Kyrgyzstan, Tajikistan, and Uzbekistan. Created in 2000, EurAsEC aims to establish a common custom tariff among its members, following the earlier but unsuccessful Custom Union between Russia, Belarus, Kazakhstan, and Kyrgyzstan in 1995.[78]

Meanwhile, the China-led Shanghai Cooperation Organization (SCO), established in 1996, includes Russia, Kazakhstan, Kyrgyzstan, Tajikistan, and Uzbekistan. The SCO was developed to counterbalance the influence of the United States and NATO in central Asia. The presence of the US military in the central Asian republics greatly concerns Beijing.[79] There have been efforts at military cooperation in the region, although they have met with limited success. In 1996, Kazakhstan, Kyrgyzstan, and Uzbekistan established a regional battalion of peacekeepers, Tsentrazbat. Funded by NATO's Partnership for Peace program (PfP), Tsentrazbat focuses on developing joint political action rather than military coordination.[80]

Despite those efforts, regional economic and political cooperation has been an elusive goal. Cooperation has been ineffective in part because national governments have developed differing sectoral policies, whether on anti-drug trafficking, water management, or migration, under the mandate of the regional organizations.[81] These differing policies are partly a function of different national interests and partly the reflection of a difference in the national pace of economic reforms and political liberalization. The competition among the central Asian republics for donor aid and foreign investment also impedes regional cooperation. Asymmetries in power prohibit partnership on an equal basis and often engender distrust among regional partners. Yet, as Robert Keohane points out, cooperation is not the "absence of conflict—which is always at least a potentially important element of international relations—but a process that involves the use of discord to stimulate mutual adjustment."[82] For all these reasons, the bilateral agreements we will now discuss have thus far been more effective than regional organizations.

Post-Soviet Neighbors: Kazakhstan, Uzbekistan, and Tajikistan

In arid central Asia, conflict over water in the Aral Sea Basin is a threat to regional stability. Kyrgyzstan inherited from the Soviet era the largest central Asian water reservoir, which was built to accumulate an adequate amount of water for seasonal regulation in Uzbekistan and Kazakhstan. These two countries rely on water from the upstream neighbors in the spring and summer for irrigation, whereas Kyrgyzstan needs water for electric power production during the winter. There has been no long-term agreement for the management of water resources. Although interstate tensions have occasionally arisen, they are unlikely to escalate into armed conflict. So far, each year the neighbors have been able to reach agreements that accommodate differing water and energy needs.[83]

Similar rates of economic and political liberalization and similar linguistic and cultural roots allow Kyrgyzstan and Kazakhstan to maintain mutually beneficial economic relations. Kazakhstan's companies are increasingly involved in Kyrgyzstan's economy, with hundreds of joint ventures operating in the country. Kyrgyzstan benefits from economic growth in Kazakhstan through tourism and cross-border trade.

As noted previously, the tense internal situation in Uzbekistan has complicated Uzbek-Kyrgyz relations. There are also specific natural resource conflicts that strain the ties between Uzbekistan and Kyrgyzstan. Uzbekistan relies on Kyrgyzstan's control of water supplies, while Kyrgyzstan depends on supplies of natural gas from Uzbekistan. Thus, Kyrgyzstan is vulnerable to any unilateral decision to cut off its natural gas supply. Aggravating this situation are long-term disagreements about the shared use of the Naryn/Syr Darya river system and the ownership of oil deposits in border regions.

Despite a poor human rights record, Uzbekistan acts as regional cop for its smaller neighbors, capitalizing on the terrorist threat in Central Asia. Uzbekistan's president, Islam Karimov, has publicly blamed the leadership of Tajikistan and Kyrgyzstan for their lack of order, excessive tolerance of opposition groups, and harboring of terrorists. Tashkent introduced a visa regime for Kyrgyz nationals and, in both 1999 and 2000, placed land mines along both the nations' common borders and those of Uzbek enclaves within Kyrgyzstan.[84] As a response to this serious breach of its territorial integrity, Kyrgyzstan, with aid from Japan and the Asian Development Bank (ADB), has built new roads that bypass Uzbekistan. Meanwhile, Kyrgyz human rights activists have complained that the Uzbek National Security Service has kidnapped several Kyrgyz citizens in Kyrgyz territory since 1999, imprisoning them for between twelve and sixteen years in Uzbekistan.[85] In 2007, a vocal critic of the Uzbek leadership, journalist Alisher Saipov, was assassinated in Osh.[86]

For landlocked Tajikistan, Kyrgyzstan is a major corridor to the outside world. In 2001, Uzbekistan introduced a visa regime for Tajikistan and closed down all Uzbek-Tajik transportation and communication links. On a daily basis, hundreds of Tajik migrants pass through Kyrgyzstan's borders to go to Russia and Kazakhstan. Yet Vorukh, the Tajik enclave in Kyrgyzstan, is potentially unstable. Minor conflicts over irrigated land and water occur along the Tajik-Kyrgyz border.

At the Crossroads of Three Hegemons

In recent years, Kyrgyzstan has become an arena for competition among three great powers: Russia, the United States, and China. By providing political and military support to nations in the region, each power seeks to limit the influence of the others. Since September 11, Kyrgyzstan has become central to the so-called war on terror led by the United States.

The US military presence around the Kyrgyz capital concerns both Beijing and Moscow. The Manas Air Base in Kyrgyzstan, with about a thousand US troops, was used for combat support, transport, refueling, tanker and cargo shipments, and ground operations in Afghanistan; it has also hosted coalition forces.[87] According to former Foreign Minister Askar Aitmatov, the Kyrgyz government rejected the request of the United States and NATO to station Airborne Warning and Control System (AWACS) reconnaissance aircraft at the air base.[88] This decision most likely reflects Kyrgyzstan's sensitivity to its relations with Russia and China. In 2009, under pressure from Russia, the Kyrgyz leadership decided to close the Manas Air Base in exchange for a Russian loan of US$2 billion.[89]

There are concerns among civil society groups in Kyrgyzstan about the country's relations with the United States. According to a study by A. Cooley, "There is a general attitude that the United States is in Kyrgyzstan to preserve its security interests and does not particularly care about promoting democracy and human rights."[90] A Kyrgyz NGO leader has noted that since the establishment of the base, US embassy officials are less responsive to democracy-related concerns.[91] Environmental problems related to aircraft refuelers dumping fuel at the base have also been raised by local civil society groups.[92] For political and economic reasons, Kyrgyzstan maintains good relations with Russia, on which it remains highly dependent. Following an agreement in September 2003, Russia established an air base in Kant, twenty miles from the Manas Air Base. Constructed under the auspices of the CSTO, the Russian base was established on the pretext of combating international terrorist groups in Kyrgyzstan. Russia linked the building of the base to Kyrgyzstan's outstanding debt, agreeing to direct part of the sum owed toward the reconstruction of the Kant air base. Economically, Russian companies have also proposed making several significant investments. Two major hydroelectric power stations have been proposed for the Naryn River: Kambarata-1 and Kambarata-2. Furthermore, Russian companies are cooperating with Kyrgyzstan to set up aluminum production facilities in Kyrgyzstan.

Despite its strategic interests in the regime, Russia has generally refrained from interfering openly in Kyrgyzstan's internal affairs, especially during the March 2005 revolution. This is probably due in part to its failed efforts to influence domestic developments in Ukraine and Georgia. However, on the day of the March revolution, the Akayev family was allowed to flee from the Russian air base to a safe haven in Russia. With the Russian war against Georgia in 2008, the Kremlin's heavy hand is more visible in the transformation of the Kyrgyz geopolitical landscape.

As a rising global hegemon, China has attempted to influence security issues in Central Asia through the SCO. Since the latter's independence, China has also attempted to establish friendly bilateral relations with Kyrgyzstan. There are, however, two major issues challenging the relationship. First, the Chinese leadership sees the political activism of Uyghur leaders as a potential threat to stability in Xinjiang. There are more than 50,000 ethnic Uyghurs in Kyrgyzstan, some of whom fled from Xinjiang in the 1960s. China attempts to monitor Uyghur national activity in Kyrgyzstan. Beijing has labeled separatist organization Ittipak a Uyghur Unity Association. According to Ittipak's leader, Uyghurs have come to Kyrgyzstan seeking asylum for different reasons.[93] Second, there are continued tensions surrounding the demarcation of the Kyrgyz-Chinese border. In 1996 and 1999, agreements were signed by Akayev and Chairman Jiang Zemin that ceded 125,000 hectares of land to China. These agreements were seen as illegitimate by the opposition, which accused Akayev of not following appropriate ratification procedures.[94]

Foreign Aid

Since independence, dozens of foreign donors and multilateral organizations have been operating in the country. The most active international financial institutions include the IMF, the World Bank, and the ADB.

Coordination between the World Bank and the ADB has greatly increased in the last few years. Kyrgyzstan was included as a pilot country at the Rome High Level Forum on Harmonization of Donor Assistance in 2004. This meeting convened the ten most active donors in the country[95] and fourteen multilateral organizations to discuss donor cooperation.[96] It represented a major attempt at donor coordination and the alignment of donor programs with national priorities.

Kyrgyzstan received several times more official development aid (ODA) per capita than any of its central Asian neighbors. For instance, between 1992 and 2002 the country was given seven times more aid per capita than Uzbekistan and three times more than Kazakhstan (Figure 10.4).[97] In 2005, ODA was US$268 million, approximately 114 percent of GNI.[98]

As of June 2004, Kyrgyzstan had received twenty-two loans totaling US$536 million from the ADB.[99] Transportation and communications sectors have received the largest share (27 percent of the total loans distributed by the ADB to Kyrgyzstan), followed by the

Figure 10.4 Official Development Assistance to Central Asian Countries, 1992–2002 (per capita US$)

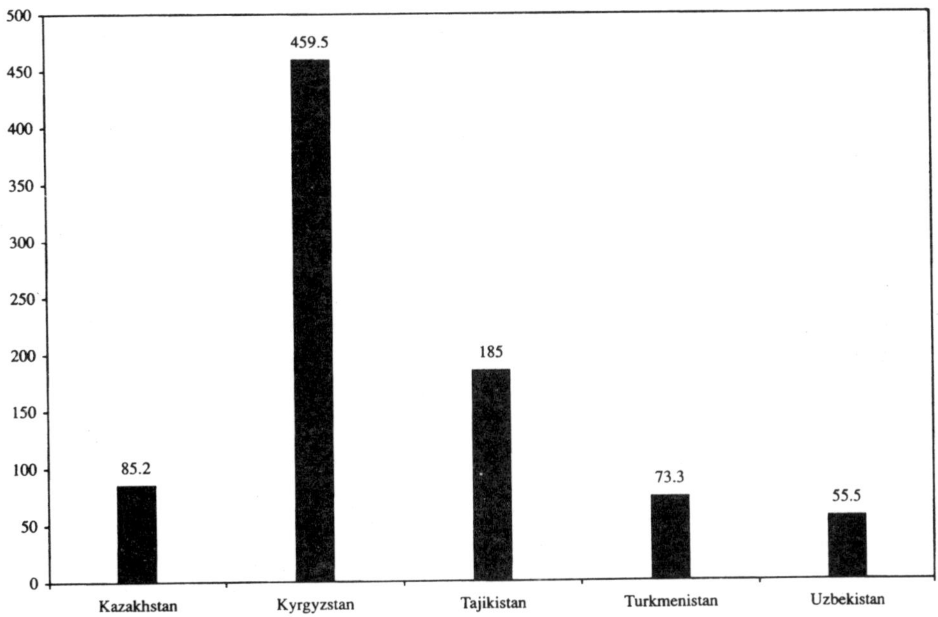

Source: World Development Indicators 2004.

financial sector (22 percent) and social infrastructure (16 percent).[100] The US Agency for International Development (USAID) is one of the largest donors to Kyrgyzstan. Since 1992, the United States, through USAID/Central Asian Republics (USAID/CAR), has approved more than US$170 million in assistance to Kyrgyzstan. USAID's grants are designed to improve governance, livelihoods, and quality of life.[101]

Japan provides aid for communication, governance, health, and agriculture through the Japanese International Cooperation Agency (JICA). Since 1999, JICA has dispatched hundreds of Kyrgyz specialists to Japan for technical training in the fields of economy, finance, administrative policy, and development policy. JICA has also carried out development study projects in the areas of TV and radio broadcasting, industrial development, and mining development, and has assisted the health care sector through a grant.[102]

Another key donor, the government of Germany, provides assistance to programs in agricultural reform, education, and environmental protection.[103] Since 1997, the UK Department for International Development (DFID) has collaborated with the Kyrgyz government in three key areas: rural livelihoods, health, and governance and statistics. According to the DFID website in 2008, expenditure on the bilateral program is about £7 million per year (US$10 million).[104] Meanwhile, Switzerland has provided humanitarian, technical, and financial assistance. The Swiss government also supports development in the energy and agricultural sectors, aids increased regional cooperation and conflict prevention, and contributes to the development of national statistics. In terms of trade, the Swiss government has partnered with Kyrgyzstan to implement the aforementioned CDF, which promotes the export of Kyrgyzstan's goods and services, until 2010. Most projects are implemented by multilateral partners and international organizations as well as by Swiss NGOs and companies.[105] In addition to bilateral aid from European governments, Kyrgyzstan also receives modest aid from the European Union (EU). The EU provides assistance through TACIS (Technical Aid to the Commonwealth of Independent States) and its food security programs.[106]

Several agencies, including USAID, the Swiss Development Corporation (SDC), and the UNDP have also developed a conflict prevention strategy for Kyrgyzstan as part of their conflict-sensitive development assistance. The SDC has been involved at the community level, supporting local NGOs in their work on conflict prevention and mediation. In keeping with its growing interest in conflict prevention, DFID has also undertaken conflict assessment in Kyrgyzstan.[107] USAID has funded reports analyzing the causes of conflict in Kyrgyzstan and has provided recommendations about tracking conflict risks at national and subnational levels. USAID's conflict prevention activities are also focused on the south. Southern Kyrgyzstan experiences many tensions due to trade restrictions stemming from the closing of international borders, land shortages, unemployment, and governance problems in the Ferghana Valley.[108]

Several international organizations have united with local partners to promote high standards of governance and human security. International and regional organizations provide significant support in building key government and civil society institutions. The OSCE has greatly increased its presence in Kyrgyzstan to become involved in election monitoring, among other things. In 2004, the OSCE established an academy in Bishkek that provides education to young specialists in conflict prevention and resolution as well as postconflict rehabilitation. UN organizations provide programs in development and governance. However, UN assistance failed to prevent the rigging of the parliamentary elections in February 2005 that triggered the March Revolution. At the critical moment when the opposition forces confronted Akayev, Western-funded civil society groups played only a marginal role. With the exception of several opposition newspapers that received technical support from Freedom House, there is no evidence that opposition forces have received foreign funds.[109]

For that matter, even in areas of high donor activity, the impact of development assistance has been diminished by corruption, political instability, and the dispersal of funds across many different development projects. In 2004, donors at a consultative meeting expressed concern over corruption and the succession crisis in the country. In the first dozen years of independence, inconsistent and incoherent policies by national actors and international donors alike have contributed to Kyrgyzstan's external debt and aid dependency.[110]

Increasingly, donor countries and international organizations are pursuing joint strategies through initiatives like the Poverty Reduction Strategy Paper (PRSP), the UN Development Assistance Framework (UNDAF) and Common Country Assessment (CCA), and the aforementioned MDG. Regional cooperation initiatives like the Central Asia Regional Economic Cooperation (CAREC) and the Aral Sea organizations are linking actors across sectors and organizations with the Kyrgyz government to improve coordination.[111] Despite these collaborative efforts, however, most Central Asian regional projects have been unsuccessful, due partly to resistance from large states such as Uzbekistan and Kazakhstan and partly to the lack of long-term donor support. Nevertheless, efforts at continued coordination persist. For example, a website has been established to support donor coordination, providing an overview of priority sectors for development and helping donors avoid overlaps in assistance.

Conclusion

Since independence, Kyrgyzstan has made significant progress in development and security. The government's program of political and economic liberalization assisted the country in overcoming many colonial legacies, provided greater political freedom, and strengthened civil society. In spite of its promise, the path to liberalization was not without problems. The open political environment allowed the country's new president to consolidate his power by slowly transferring state assets to his patronage network. To this day, Kyrgyzstan must contend with the legacy of corruption, criminality, and authoritarianism.

Despite the successful ousting of Akayev in the March 2005 revolution, the economic and political situation in the country remains fragile. In the postmillennium, the policies of donors and international financial institutions have become more coherent, and attempts at coordination have been relatively successful. However, the lack of coordination that remains, combined with the institutional weakness of the government through which aid is funneled, has contributed in large part to top-level corruption. External aid has encouraged the corrupt segments of the ruling elite to strengthen the presidency, concentrate political and economic power in the hands of the few, and silence civil society groups and political opponents, thus provoking mass upheavals.

Two scenarios are possible for Kyrgyzstan's future. In the more pessimistic scenario, authoritarianism and corruption continue. If this turns out to be the case, then it is most likely that the influence of the drug trade and criminal groups will continue to dominate parts of the country and eventually the top echelons of government. If the government does not deal assertively with organized crime, it is possible that criminal elements may mobilize the poor to elect their own president. In addition, instability in neighboring autocratic countries such as Uzbekistan and Tajikistan could continue, thereby creating an inflow of refugees into the south of the country that would be highly destabilizing.

In the optimistic scenario, the government is able to mobilize the required political will and resources to reform governance, including the security sector, and to provide legitimate employment opportunities to stem the tide of criminality. It is highly probable that Kyrgyzstan will remain heavily dependent on its neighbors and the three hegemons. Although each of the three great powers is attempting to limit the influence of the other two, they all have an important stake in ensuring security in the region. If Kyrgyzstan is able to partner effectively with all three, the country might be able to control the flow of transnational crime.

With its transition now firmly in place, national policies can be greatly improved. The following recommendations, based on an analysis of security and development patterns, reflect lessons learned to date.

1. Political and security reforms need to be consolidated. Civil society organizations and the business community need to become effective countervailing forces against increasing presidential authoritarianism and nepotism. State institutions such as the judiciary, Parliament, and the police need to be strengthened in order to deal

with the crime problem. Professional security forces (police, military, and intelligence forces) need to be modernized through the expanding and continuing programs of the OSCE and others. Anticorruption efforts should be consistent and coherent so as to minimize the influence of criminal groups on politics and the economy.

2. To decrease the appeal of extremist groups, socioeconomic policies need to address the diverse sources of insecurity affecting vulnerable populations that have been identified in this chapter. Government transparency, civic participation in political and social life, and proactive environmental policy are critical steps on the path to addressing insecurity. Indigenous mechanisms for conflict management need to be studied and built upon to manage intercommunal conflicts over natural resources and bridge ethnic and religious divides.

3. Given its limited power and resources, Kyrgyzstan needs to participate more effectively in international organizations in order to increase its security. It also needs to manage its external relations carefully to avoid becoming too closely associated with authoritarian hegemons that have a direct interest in its affairs.

4. On the development front, international financial institutions and donor countries should continue to support democratic reforms and socioeconomic development in Kyrgyzstan. It is important for the international community to focus more on institution building, indigenous and domestic mechanisms of governance, and donor and government accountability in development programs.

5. Implementation of the relevant development frameworks and action programs are vital to creating effective partnerships among the Kyrgyz government, civil society groups, and international agencies. Donors should focus on income-generating activities and infrastructure both in the southern provinces and in the new, poor neighborhoods adjacent to large cities.

6. Kyrgyzstan needs to diversify its export economy to reduce its overreliance on gold. It also has to establish a favorable business environment for private investment. This means enhancing the professionalism of the civil service so as to strengthen local anticorruption mechanisms. Donors, the national government, and civil society must look at the interrelationship between aid and corruption. Donors need to monitor their anticorruption conditionalities. Aid needs to be linked to anticorruption programs, decentralization, accountability, and participation.

7. Consultative mechanisms for monitoring and evaluating external aid, debt, and the national budget need to be locally established.

With the support of the donor community and the private business sector, civil society groups need to strengthen their capacity to monitor and evaluate the government's development and security agenda, aid dependence and effectiveness, and the implementation of governmental commitments to public reforms, especially anticorruption efforts.

As this chapter has sought to demonstrate, the country's security and development problems are interlinked, although they both require targeted responses. National as well as international agencies are already beginning to develop more coherent and integrated policies to address security and development problems simultaneously. This trend has to be deepened and broadened to ensure that Kyrgyzstan can meet the multifaceted challenges of its transitional period as an independent state.

Notes

1. AKIpress, "Kyrgyz MP: Previous Authority Jailed People; the New Authority Shoots Them," September 22, 2005, available with subscription at http://www.akipress.com.
2. UNDP, *Kyrgyzstan National Human Development Report 1998: Role and Influence of the State* (Bishkek: UNDP, 1998), 50.
3. Anara Tabyshalieva, "Kyrgyzstan's Tenuous Hold on Democracy," *Far Eastern Economic Review* 168, no. 4 (April 2005): 26–29.
4. Anara Tabyshalieva, "The Challenge of Regional Cooperation in Central Asia: Preventing Ethnic Conflict in the Ferghana Valley," Peaceworks Paper Series no. 28 (Washington, DC: United States Institute of Peace, June 1999), 20.
5. International Crisis Group (ICG), "Kyrgyzstan at Ten: Trouble in the 'Island of Democracy,'" ICG Asia Report series no. 22 (Brussels: ICG, August 28, 2001).
6. UNDP, *Kyrgyzstan National Human Development Report 2001: Democratic Governance: Alternative Approaches to Kyrgyzstan's Future Development,* (Bishkek: UNDP, 2001), 60; The Kyrgyz Republic, "International Religious Freedom Report 2008," Bureau of Democracy, Human Rights, and Labor, US Department of State, http://2001-2009.state.gov/g/drl/rls/irf/2008/108502.htm.
7. Still, only about 50 percent of Kazakhs and 25 percent of Uzbeks speak Kyrgyz fluently, even though these three languages have a great linguistic similarity, and only 3 percent of Russians speak Kyrgyz fluently. See UN, "Kyrgyzstan Common Country Assessment," (Bishkek: UN, 2001).
8. UN, "Kyrgyzstan Common Country Assessment," 2001.
9. See more about ethnic relations in Anara Tabyshalieva, "The Kyrgyz Republic on the Verge of Change?" *Helsinki Monitor* 14, no. 3 (2003): 227–228.

10. UN, "Common Country Assessment 2003: The UN System in the Kyrgyz Republic," (Bishkek: UN, 2003), 33.

11. Anara Tabyshalieva, "Hizb-ut Tahrir's Increasing Activity in Central Asia," *CACI Analyst,* January 14, 2004, http://www.cacianalyst.org/?q=node/1759.

12. ICG, "Radical Islam in Central Asia: Responding to Hizb Ut-Tahrir," ICG Asia Report series no. 58 (ICG: Brussels, June 30, 2003).

13. Anara Tabyshalieva, "Political Islam in Kyrgyzstan," in *OSCE Yearbook, 2002,* ed. Ursel Schlichting (Baden-Baden: Institute for Peace and Security Policy at the University of Hamburg, 2003), 83–92; see also Anara Tabyshalieva and Georgi Derluguan, "The 'Religious Factor' in Central Asia and the Caucasus," *Perspectives on Central Asia* 2, no. 3 (June 1997), http://www.eisenhowerinstitute.org/themes/past_themes/centasia/pubs/june_1997.dot.

14. The president approves appointments to the central government, including the head of the Office of the General Prosecutor and the head of the Chamber of Accounts. He appoints heads of commissions, first deputies of ministers, and governors at the provincial level, as well as all judges at the local level of government.

15. UN, "Common Country Assessment 2003," 14.

16. ICG, "Kyrgyzstan: After the Revolution," ICG Asia Report series no. 97 (Brussels: ICG, May 4, 2005).

17. Such leaders include ex-Speaker of Parliament Medetkan Sherimkulov, ex-Minister Roza Otunbaeva, and former Rector of Osh State University Bakyt Beshimov. Anara Tabyshalieva, "Kyrgyz Turmoil over a Border Agreement," *CACI Analyst,* May 22, 2002, http://www.cacianalyst.org/?q=node/253; Eurasianet, "Victims of Kyrgyz Clashes Buried," March 21, 2002, http://www.eurasianet.org/resource/kyrgyzstan/hypermail/200203/0061.shtml.

18. Anara Tabyshalieva, "Kyrgyz Turmoil over a Border Agreement," CACI Analyst, May 22, 2002, http://www.cacianalyst.org/?q=node/253; Eurasianet, "Victims of Kyrgyz Clashes Buried," March 21, 2002, http://www.eurasianet.org/resource/kyrgyzstan/hypermail/200203/0061.shtml.

19. Tabyshalieva, "Kyrgyzstan's Tenuous Hold on Democracy."

20. Eurasianet, "Kyrgyz President-Elect Outlines Next Steps," July 12, 2005, http://www.eurasianet.org/resource/kyrgyzstan/hypermail/200507/0006.shtml.

21. For instance, Usen Kudaibergenov, an organizer of civil defense brigades, and three members of the Parliament—Jyrgalbek Surabaldiev, Baiaman Erkinbaev, and Tynchbek Akmatbayev—were killed within the first year of the new administration.

22. Eurasianet, "Police, Squatters Clash in Kyrgyz Capital," May 18, 2005, http://www.eurasianet.org/resource/kyrgyzstan/hypermail/200505/0028.shtml.

23. ICG, "Youth in Central Asia: Losing the New Generation," ICG Asia Report series no. 66 (ICG: Brussels, October 31, 2003).

24. ICG, "Kyrgyzstan: A Faltering State," ICG Asia Report series no. 109 (ICG: Brussels, December 16, 2005).

25. Anara Tabyshalieva, "Political Violence on the Rise in Kyrgyzstan," *CACI Analyst,* January 25, 2006, http://www.cacianalyst.org/?q=node/3691.

26. OSCE, "Statement of Preliminary Findings and Conclusions," http://www.osce.org/documents/odihr/2007/12/28916_en.pdf.

27. Erica Marat, "Bakiyev Strengthens Control over Armed Forces Ahead of Opposition Revolts," *Eurasia Daily Monitor* 6, no. 15, January 23, 2009, http://www.jamestown.org/programs/edm/single/?tx_ttnews[tt_news]=34406&tx_ttnews[backPid]=27&cHash=e67bf3351d.

28. Gulnaz Baiturova, Sheradil Baktygulov, Michael Heppell, Robert Hood, et al., "Governance Assessment Study for Sound Development, Management, and Poverty Reduction in the Kyrgyz Republic," paper prepared for the Asian Development Bank (ADB), May 2004, http://www.adb.org/Documents/Papers/Governance_KGZ/KGZ_Governance_Assessment.pdf.

29. See further ICG, "Kyrgyzstan: A Faltering State"; ICG, "Kyrgyzstan's Prison System Nightmare," *Asia Report* no. 118, August 16, 2006.

30. ICG, "Kyrgyzstan: After the Revolution," 14.

31. ICG, "Kyrgyzstan: After the Revolution," 14.

32. ICG, "Kyrgyzstan: A Faltering State," 16–17.

33. Tabyshalieva, "Political Violence on the Rise in Kyrgyzstan."

34. See more in UN Office on Drugs and Crime (UNODC), "The Opium Economy in Afghanistan: An International Problem," (Vienna: UNODC, 2003); UNODC, *World Drug Report 2005* (Vienna: UNODC, 2005), 56.

35. UNODC Regional Office for Central Asia, "Drug Seizures," UNODC ROCA Online Databases, http://www.dbroca.uz/?act=seizures.

36. International Institute for Strategic Studies (IISS), *The Military Balance, 2003/04* (London: IISS, 2004).

37. UN, "Kyrgyzstan Common Country Assessment," 2001, 95–96.

38. Human Rights Watch, "Burying the Truth: Uzbekistan Rewrites the Story of the Andijan Massacre," Report Series vol. 17, no. 6 (September 2005), http://www.hrw.org/reports/2005/uzbekistan0905/5.htm.

39. Radio Free Europe/Radio Liberty (RFE/RL), "Factbox: Andijon Timeline," September 20, 2005, http://www.rferl.org/content/article/1061536.html.

40. Eurasianet, "Uzbekistan Accuses UN of Aiding 'Terrorists'," August 25, 2005, http://www.eurasianet.org/resource/kyrgyzstan/hypermail/200508/0040.shtml.

41. According to Eurasianet, "Kubanychbek Jusupov, deputy head of the Kyrgyz gas company Kyrgyzgaz, told the BBC on 27 August that Uzbekistan has unilaterally withdrawn from a July agreement on gas shipments to Kyrgyzstan." See Eurasianet, "Kyrgyz Official Says Uzbekistan Nixes Gas Agreement," August 29, 2005, http://www.eurasianet.org/resource/kyrgyzstan/hypermail/200508/0044.shtml.

42. UzReport, "Uzbek President Blames Islamic group for Events in Andijan," May 14, 2005, http://news.uzreport.com/main.cgi?lan=e.

43. See Ahmed Rashid, *Jihad: The Rise of Militant Islam in Central Asia* (New Haven, CT: Yale University Press, 2002).

44. Relief Web, "Kyrgyzstan-Tajikistan: Landmine Threat Along Uzbek Border Removed," October 31, 2005, http://www.reliefweb.int/rw/RWB.NSF/db900SID/NKUA-6HPR5E?OpenDocument.

45. IRIN News, "Kyrgyzstan: Avalanche Kills Four in South," January

30, 2006, http://www.irinnews.org/report.asp?ReportID=51437&Select Region=Asia.

46. Economist Intelligence Unit (EIU), *Kyrgyz Republic: Country Profile 2004* (London: EIU, 2004).

47. EIU, *Kyrgyz Republic: Country Profile 2004.*

48. ICG, "Kyrgyzstan: A Faltering State." This report details the conflict that has ensued due to land reform measures.

49. EIU, "Kyrgyz Republic: Country Report," November 1, 2008.

50. EIU, *Kyrgyz Republic: Country Profile 2004.*

51. Eurasianet, "Kyrgyz Deputy Prime Minister Advocates Legalizing Shadow Economy," January 28, 2003, http://www.eurasianet.org/resource/kyrgyzstan/hypermail/200301/0065.shtml.

52. World Bank, *World Development Report 2005: A Better Investment Climate for Everyone* (Washington, DC: World Bank, 2005).

53. World Bank, *World Development Report 2005,* 258.

54. EIU, *Kyrgyz Republic: Country Profile 2004.*

55. See UNDP, "Millennium Development Goals National Progress Report 2008," http://www.undp.kg.

56. Among them are 1,607,396 males and 1,669,612 females. See Central Intelligence Agency (CIA), "World Factbook 2006: Kyrgyzstan," July 20, 2006, http://www.cia.gov/cia/publications/factbook/geos/kg.html.

57. UN, "Common Country Assessment 2003," 11.

58. In former Soviet republics, self-employed people often identify themselves as unemployed. There is still a Soviet habit of only recognizing the employment of those who work in the state sector.

59. UN, "Common Country Assessment 2003," 12.

60. Anara Tabyshalieva, "Revival of Traditions in Post-Soviet Central Asia," in *Making the Transition Work for Women in Europe and Central Asia,* World Bank Discussion Paper no. 411 (Washington, DC: World Bank, 2000).

61. UN, "Common Country Assessment 2003."

62. See more in UNDP, *AIDS in Kyrgyzstan: Five Years of Resistance* (Bishkek: UNDP, 2003).

63. International Monetary Fund (IMF), "Kyrgyz Republic: Sixth Review Under the Three-Year Arrangement Under the Poverty Reduction and Growth Facility and Request for New Three-Year PRGF Arrangement," Country Report Series no. 05/119 (Washington, DC: IMF, March 2005), 5.

64. IRIN News, "Kyrgyzstan: Focus on Labour Migration," May 19, 2005, http://www.irinnews.org/report.asp?ReportID=47187&SelectRegion=Asia.

65. UN, "Kyrgyzstan Common Country Assessment," 2001.

66. UN, "Kyrgyzstan Common Country Assessment," 2001, 121–122.

67. UN, "Common Country Assessment 2003," 33.

68. UNICEF, "The TransMONEE Database 2004," http://www.unicef-icdc.org/resources/transmonee.html.

69. See more in UNDP, *Central Asia Human Development Report 2005* (Bratislava: UNDP, 2005), 49–81.

70. Joana Godinho et al., "Reversing the Tide: Priorities for HIV/ AIDS Prevention in Central Asia," paper prepared for World Bank, November 2004, http://siteresources.worldbank.org/ECAEXT/Resources/258598-1102016393263/ReversingtheTide.pdf, 22–23.

71. UNDP, *AIDS in Kyrgyzstan: Five Years of Resistance.*

72. UN, "Common Country Assessment 2003," 15.

73. ADB, "Governance Assessment Study for Sound Development, Management, and Poverty Reduction in the Kyrgyz Republic," 44–50.

74. RFE/RL, "Former Kyrgyz First Lady Subject to Probe," April 27, 2005, http://www.rferl.org/newsline/2005/04/2-TCA/tca-270405.asp.

75. See more in David S. Cloud, "Pentagon's Fuel Deal Is Lesson in Risks of Graft-Prone Regions," *New York Times,* November 15, 2005, 1-A.

76. ADB, "Governance Assessment Study for Sound Development, Management, and Poverty Reduction in the Kyrgyz Republic."

77. Tajikistan joined this union in 1999.

78. See more in UNDP, *Central Asia Human Development Report 2005,* 185–203.

79. For more on NATO's Partnership for Peace, see http://www.nato.int/issues/pfp/index.html.

80. See more in UNDP, *Central Asia Human Development Report 2005.*

81. Robert O. Keohane, "Hegemony in the World Political Economy," in Robert J. Art and Robert Jervis, eds., *International Politics: Enduring Concepts and Contemporary Issues* (New York: Pearson Longman, 2005), 309.

82. Marat Iskakov and Anara Tabyshalieva, "Cold Winters Upstream, Dry Summers Downstream in Central Asia," *CACI Analyst*, January 30, 2002, http://www.cacianalyst.org/?q=node/152.

83. Bruce Pannier, "Uzbekistan: Government Announces Effort to Clear Borders of Land Mines," RFE/RL, August 19, 2004, http://www.rferl.org/featuresarticle/2004/08/c1aea32e-58e4-46e6-956e-8914562f48ef.html.

84. ICG, *Central Asia: Uzbekistan at Ten—Repression and Instability*, ICG Asia Report series no. 21 (Brussels: ICG, August 21, 2001), 20–21.

85. See Gulnoza Saidazimova, "Kyrgyzstan: Friends Cry Foul as Authorities Link Slain Journalist to Islamists," RFE/RL, October 31, 2007, http://www.rferl.org/featuresarticle/2007/10/1d4d356f-8e3e-4e1c-a9d7-9f959ec5329d.html.

86. Wojciech Bartuzi, "US Appears Set to Expand Cooperation with Kyrgyzstan in 2003," Eurasianet, December 5, 2002, http://www.eurasianet.org/departments/insight/articles/eav120502.shtml.

87. RFE/RL, "Kyrgyz Ex-Foreign Minister Says US Asked to Put Spy Planes in Kyrgyzstan," November 15, 2005, http://www.hri.org/news/balkans/rferl/2005/05-11-15.rferl.html#24.

88. David Trilling and Deirdre Tynan, "Kyrgyzstan: President Bakiyev Wants to Close US Military Base Outside Bishkek," Eurasianet, February 3, 2009, http://www.eurasianet.org/departments/insightb/articles/eav020309b.shtml.

89. Alexander Cooley, "Depoliticizing Manas: The Domestic Consequences of the US Military Presence in Kyrgyzstan," Program on New Approaches to Russian Security (PONARS) Policy Memo no. 362 (Washington, DC: Center for Strategic and International Studies, February 2005), 7.

90. Cooley, "Depoliticizing Manas," 4.

91. MosNews, "US Aircraft Dump 80 Tons of Fuel over Kyrgyz Capital," September 27, 2005, http://www.mosnews.com/news/2005/09/27/kerosenebishkek.shtml.

92. IRIN News, "Kyrgyzstan: Interview with the Chair of National Uyghur Society," February 17, 2005, http://www.irinnews.org/report.asp?ReportID=45626&SelectRegion=Asia.

93. Eurasianet, "A Daily Review of News from Kyrgyzstan," January 10, 2001, http://www.eurasianet.org/resource/kyrgyzstan/hypermail/200201/0028.shtml.

94. Namely Germany, France, Iran, Japan, Sweden, Turkey, Russia, Switzerland, the UK, and the United States.

95. Namely the Aga Khan Development Network, ADB, European Bank for Reconstruction and Development (EBRD), European Commission, International Finance Corporation (IFC), IMF, International Office for Migration (IOM), Islamic Development Bank (IDB), Organization for Security and Co-operation in Europe (OSCE), UNICEF, UNDP, UNODC, World Bank, and World Health Organization (WHO).

96. Aid per capita includes both official development assistance (ODA) and official aid and is calculated by dividing total aid by the mid-year population estimate.

97. World Bank, *World Development Indicators 2007*, http://siteresources.worldbank.org/DATASTATISTICS/Resources/table6_11.pdf.

98. Seven of the loans were program loans aimed at providing support to policy reforms to facilitate the transition to a market economy; the remaining fifteen were project loans.

99. At present, twelve loans with a net approved loan amount of US$288 million are ongoing. ADB's annual lending levels averaged about US$66 million during 1994–2001. See Donors.kg, "Asian Development Bank (ADB)," http://www.donors.kg/en/donors/adb.

100. For more information on USAID grants, see Donors.kg, "US Agency for International Development (USAID)," http://www.donors.kg/en/donors/usaid.

101. For information on JICA donor activities in Kyrgyzstan, see "Japan International Cooperation Agency (JICA)," Donors.kg, http://www.donors.kg/en/donors/jica.

102. See "Deutsche Gesellschaft für Technische Zusammenarbeit GmbH (GTZ)," Donors.kg, http://www.donors.kg/en/donors/gtz.

103. For more information on DFID's donor activities in Kyrgyzstan, see "Department for International Development (DFID)," Donors.kg, http://www.donors.kg/en/donors/DFID.

104. For more information on Swiss donor activities, see "Welcome," Swiss Cooperation, http://www.swisscoop.kg/index.php?userhash=26082579&.

105. For more information on the TACIS program, see http://europa.eu.int/comm/external_relations/ceeca/tacis.

106. Tony Vaux and Jonathan Goodhand, *Conflict Assessments: Disturbing Connections—Aid and Conflict in Kyrgyzstan* (London: University of London, 2001).

107. USAID/CAR, "Conflict Prevention," http://www.usaid.gov/locations/europe_eurasia/car/caip_pci.html.

108. Craig S. Smith, "US Helped to Prepare the Way for Kyrgyzstan's Uprising," *New York Times*, March 30, 2005, 4-A.

109. ICG, "Political Transition in Kyrgyzstan: Problems and Prospects," 19.

110. Eurasianet, "Donors Note Shortcomings in Kyrgyzstan Programs," November 29, 2004, http://www.eurasianet.org/resource/kyrgyzstan/hypermail/200411/0024.shtml.

111. CAREC, The Central Asia Regional Economic Cooperation Program, is an ADB-supported initiative that was created in 1997 to encourage economic cooperation among countries in the central Asian region, focusing on infrastructure, transport, energy, and trade. CAREC includes Azerbaijan, China, Kazakhstan, Kyrgyzstan, Mongolia, Tajikistan, and Uzbekistan. In 2003, CAREC expanded to include the EBRD, IMF, Islamic Development Bank, UNDP, and World Bank. See http://www.adb.org/CAREC/default.asp.

11

Conflict and Postconflict in Tajikistan

Shirin Akiner

Tajikistan, situated in the southwest of central Asia in the high mountains bordering Afghanistan and China, was one of the fifteen constituent republics of the Soviet Union. Its remote, landlocked location and relatively limited resource base hindered economic development. Consequently, it was one of the poorest of the Soviet republics, heavily dependent on the central government for subsidies and development aid. When the Soviet Union was formally dissolved at the end of 1991, Tajikistan was almost immediately engulfed by civil unrest. Within months this had escalated into internecine warfare. The outlook at this time seemed very bleak.

For a while it seemed as though Tajikistan would cease to exist as an independent, unified state. Yet in a relatively short time, the balance shifted in favor of cohesion. Peace negotiations (known as the Inter-Tajik Peace Talks) were started in 1994; in June 1997, they ended with the signing of a comprehensive peace treaty between the warring factions. This remains in force today. There are many unresolved problems, but a degree of national and societal recovery has been achieved that in the immediate aftermath of the war would have been regarded as impossible.

The aim of this chapter is to map security and development trends in Tajikistan over two decades (from the mid-1980s to the mid-2000s) and to indicate how national and international policies have influenced those changes.[1] The chapter is organized into six parts. The first part examines Tajikistan's historical and geographical inheritances; this contextual background is essential for understanding subsequent events. The second and third parts, respectively, chart emerging social tensions in the immediate preconflict period and the escalation of local confrontations into civil war. The progress of postconflict recovery and reconstruction is examined in the fourth part, while the fifth part identifies new security challenges. The chapter concludes with a tentative assessment of the situation in Tajikistan and prospects for the future.

Tajikistan's Inheritance

Tajikistan became an independent state upon the disintegration of the Soviet Union. Inevitably, the social, political, and economic legacies of the Soviet era exerted a significant influence on the development of the newly independent state. The country is also shaped by its physical geography. Such features as high mountain ranges, the scarcity of arable land, and the uneven distribution of natural resources (especially water) have largely determined agricultural practices, industrial development, transportation systems, and infrastructure development in both the Soviet and post-Soviet periods. They also account, in part, for the centrifugal nature of regional political and socioeconomic tendencies.

Physical Geography

Tajikistan encompasses a territory of some 143,100 square kilometers. Over 90 percent of this land is covered by mountains, glaciers, and windswept plateaus. Some twenty-eight ranges divide the country into a patchwork of isolated, or at best semi-isolated, areas of habitation. There are relatively few passes across the mountains, and many are closed by snow for several months of the year. Only 7 percent of the territory of Tajikistan is settled by humans; only 5 percent of the land is arable.[2] Four geographic zones can be distinguished. Historically, each of these had—and to some extent still preserve—distinctive patterns of trade with and transport to and from adjacent regions. The largest zone, the province of Gorno-Badakhshan, occupies the eastern part of the country and almost half its total territory. The second zone lies in the center of Tajikistan and is dominated by massive mountain ranges that represent a formidable north-south barrier. The third zone, the Khatlon province, is in the southwest. Traditionally, this area constituted the divide between the mountain dwellers and the plains dwellers. The fourth zone, the Soghd province, encompasses the lowlands to the north of the central mountain ranges.[3] In terms of valuable resources, this is the richest part of the country, with substantial reserves of hydrocarbons and other minerals as well as good arable land.

Tajik History

Tajik historiographers trace the origins of national statehood back to the Samanid Empire, which, at its height in the tenth century, stretched from the Syr Darya to the Hindu Kush, from the Pamirs to northern Iran. The territory of present-day Tajikistan occupies only a small and peripheral area of this state. However, the modern Tajiks are Persian speakers and share a common ethnic and cultural heritage with the Samanids. Thus, they see themselves as heirs to an ancient dynasty. This identification is all the more powerful since their neighbors (the Uzbeks, Kazakhs, Kyrgyz, Turkmen, and Uighurs) are of Turkic stock.

Traditionally, there was a divide between the plains (northern Tajikistan) and the mountains (most of the rest of the country); this was reflected in very different cultural, economic, and political patterns of development. Within these two broad divisions, virtually every city, valley, and oasis was home to a separate microcommunity, each with its own dialect and material culture. By religion, the overwhelming majority of Tajiks were Sunni Muslims, followers of the Hanafi school (as are most other central Asians, except for Iranian nationals, who are Shia). However, the southwestern part of Gorno-Badakhshan was home to small groups of eastern Iranian peoples, collectively known as the Pamiris, whose languages were not mutually comprehensible with Tajik.[4] By religion, they were almost all Ismaili Muslims (spiritual followers of the Aga Khan). Consequently, despite the consensus of belief in a common history, the Tajik nation that came into being in the twentieth century was in reality composed of a mosaic of disparate groups.

Soviet power was established in central Asia soon after the Bolshevik revolution. In 1924, the National Delimitation of Central Asia was carried out, as a result of which five territorial-administrative entities were created. One of these was the Tajik Autonomous Soviet Socialist Republic (ASSR). In 1929, the province of Khujand (corresponding approximately to the modern-day Soghd province) was transferred from Uzbek jurisdiction to Tajik jurisdiction, and the status of Tajikistan was upgraded to that of a constituent republic of the Soviet Union (the Tajik SSR).[5] The borders that were fixed at that time remain in force today.

Soviet Development Policies

Under Soviet rule, wide-ranging social, cultural, and economic changes were introduced. These included the emancipation of women (defined as gender equality before the law, in education, and in employment), free and compulsory education, and comprehensive health care. Later, higher educational facilities were developed, as well as advanced research institutes.[6] By the 1960s, literacy rates were close to 100 percent. Modern state institutions were established and Tajik civil servants (male and female) were incorporated into the administration at all levels of responsibility. There was also a rapid expansion of print and broadcast media; these were important tools for bonding the nation and did much to foster a sense of communal identity. In the economic sphere, a program of electrification was introduced and new industrial complexes were established. Most of these were located in northern Tajikistan (the Soghd province), where there were substantial reserves of minerals.[7] Agriculture was transformed by the introduction of collectivization.[8] Other developments during this period included the creation of modern communication and transport networks. In the early 1920s, many parts of Tajikistan were accessible only on foot or horseback. In the 1930s the state initiated the large-scale construction of railway lines and roads. Regular air links were established between the Tajik capital of Dushanbe and Tashkent, the capital of Uzbekistan, as well as within the republic, namely between Dushanbe and the main towns.

Demography

Massive population movements also took place in the first half of the twentieth century, uprooting and atomizing communities. The first great upheaval took place in the early 1920s, when over a quarter of the Tajik population fled to Afghanistan.[9] Shortly thereafter, the Soviet authorities introduced a policy of enforced migration, shifting communities from areas that were considered to have little economic potential, mainly in the mountains, to more productive land on the plains in the center and south of Tajikistan. Several of the leading figures in the subsequent civil war were from these uprooted communities.[10]

There were two other migration flows that significantly altered the demographic balance. One was of Slavs, mainly Russians, who came to Tajikistan as administrators and aid and development workers.[11] The other influx was of deportees, mainly Germans from the Volga region, exiled for alleged treason during World War II. They were mainly settled in the southwest.[12] In the 1980s, the population flow was reversed, as many of the more recent immigrants, particularly Slavs, began to leave in search of better economic prospects elsewhere. Some of the forced migrants also began to return to their original homes in other parts of Tajikistan.

On the eve of the breakup of the Soviet Union, Tajikistan had a population of just over 5 million. It was a multiethnic republic; Tajiks constituted some 62 percent of the total population, while other sizable groups were Uzbeks (23.5 percent) and Russians (7.6 percent). Some 95 percent of the population was concentrated in the western half of the country, whereas the eastern part—the autonomous province of Gorno-Badakhshan—was very sparsely peopled. Approximately one-third of the total population lived in urban areas. The population was young (45 percent was under fifteen years of age) and there was a high rate of demographic growth.[13]

The Prelude to the Civil War, Circa 1985–1991

In the early decades of Soviet rule, the central government made major investments in the social sphere in Tajikistan. There was also capital investment in priority sectors of the economy. These included large-scale infrastructural projects, high-technology industries (mostly related to the military defense sector), and cotton production. There was a constant demand for labor. Some of this demand, particularly in heavy industry and some of the technical professions, was met by immigrants (voluntary as well as deported), but there were ample employment opportunities for Tajiks. The high demand for labor absorbed the ever-increasing workforce created by the demographic explosion. Life was stable and there was a fairly high degree of social mobility. Though regional identities and loyalties remained strong, they were contained within and mediated by larger national and pan-Soviet structures.

By the 1970s, the Soviet economy as a whole was moving into recession. This had an adverse impact on Tajikistan, which depended highly on budgetary transfers from the central government. Over the next decade, there was a proliferation of economic and social problems. Moreover, competing ideologies emerged at this time. New political leaders gave definition and voice to popular grievances, mobilizing latent discontent into open disaffection. The combination of these factors created a stressed and vulnerable societal environment, characterized by decreasing levels of security and material hardship for much of the population.[14] In the late 1980s, this found expression in a spate of local riots in various parts of Tajikistan. These relatively small-scale clashes, often between different ethnic communities, were largely triggered by competition over access to scarce resources—water, land, housing, and jobs.[15]

Youth Unemployment and Antisocial Behavior

The first serious problem to emerge was the rise in unemployment, particularly in rural areas of Tajikistan, where the majority of Tajiks were located. Jobless youths drifted to the cities in search of work but found it difficult to integrate into urban life. They remained on the margins of society and were easily drawn into antisocial behavior. Soldiers returning from service in Afghanistan became a ready source of narcotics; small arms, too, began to circulate illegally. Sports groups specializing in martial arts acquired great popularity at this time; many of these had a criminal character. Thus, a youth subculture developed that was characterized by alienation, frustration, and pent-up aggression.[16]

Corruption

Corruption, bribery, theft of public goods, and other abuses of office were familiar features of Soviet society (and possibly of pre-Soviet society). Such practices often had a regional-factional component, which meant that powerful regional-factional groups frequently captured public institutions, filling the key posts with their own people, who in turn advanced the interests of their patrons. When the economy was flourishing, such practices were accommodated without apparent strain.[17] In the 1980s, however, the economic decline meant that resources and goods were scarcer, which ensured in turn the greater power of those who were in charge of distribution. Inevitably, they favored their own ethnic-social networks, thereby aggravating latent regional tensions.[18]

The Islamic Resurgence and Division

A third stress factor in the prelude to the civil war was the resurgence of Islam.[19] Religious practitioners here, as elsewhere in the Soviet Union, had suffered decades of repression and persecution. As a result, although the overwhelming majority of Tajiks continued to regard themselves as Muslims, Islam had become more a marker of cultural identity than a faith that was actively practiced. By the 1980s, though, an Islamic revival was underway. This was a complex phenomenon, marked by internal schisms and rivalries. There were two competing factions. One was led by Akbar Turajonzade, an energetic young cleric who had received a sound orthodox Islamic education.[20] Working within the framework of the existing laws, he promoted Muslim regeneration, achieving some notable successes.[21] The other faction, led by Said Abdulla Nuri, was inspired by the teachings of Muslim scholars who had remained outside the Soviet system.[22] At first the main focus of such groups was ritual observance and the study of religious texts, but in the 1970s a radical trend toward the goal of establishing an Islamic state began to emerge. The radical Muslim leaders of this trend were dubbed Wahhabis.[23]

Initially, Turajonzade's faction was more influential. It not only enjoyed a degree of support, or at least toleration, from the government at the time, but it also appealed to the majority of the urban Tajik intelligentsia, who were in favor of retaining the separation of religion and state. Yet by the beginning of the 1990s, the balance of power was changing. The radical faction was better organized and more proactive in attracting new adherents, particularly from among the marginalized urban youth. Crucially, it had branches all over Tajikistan. In 1990, faction leaders created the Islamic Rebirth Party (IRP) of Tajikistan; it was formally registered as a political party in October 1991.[24]

New Political Activists

The fourth factor that impacted societal dynamics in the late 1980s was the emergence of new, sociopolitical strains of activism.[25] In a more stable, cohesive society, these new movements might have been a first step toward a multiparty system. However, instead of consolidating political platforms and building up organizational structures, they relied on populist demagoguery. Lack of political acumen and a perhaps limited understanding of national trends led them into an illusory alliance with the IRP (more of which to come). When tensions escalated into conflict, they were soon marginalized. Meanwhile, the Communist Party (CP) was still by far the strongest political organization. As societal tensions mounted, many people held fast to their image of the CP as the guarantor of stability and national unity. In particular, those who were disturbed by the growing strength of the IRP believed that only the CP could safeguard the secular nature of the state.

Civil War, 1992–1997

The conflict began almost imperceptibly. There was no specific event, declaration, or ultimatum that marked the onset of civil war. Rather, it was an acceleration of the cycle of action and reaction, destruction and revenge, that transformed a series of localized incidents into a prolonged campaign. Nevertheless, even at the height of hostilities, only some parts of the country were affected. Most of the fighting took place in the south (the Bokhtar region).[26] Elsewhere, the situation was relatively stable. The government in Dushanbe continued to function and during this period even acceded to a number of international organizations, including international financial institutions (IFIs). These bodies, particularly the International Monetary Fund (IMF), provided support for economic restructuring and reform, albeit of a limited nature (as we will see later on).

The Evolution of the Conflict

In retrospect, the first distinct portent of the troubles to come was the rioting in Dushanbe in February 1990. The rioting was triggered by the (unfounded) rumor that large numbers of Armenians—refugees from the internecine ethnic conflict in Azerbaijan—were to be rehoused in Dushanbe, supposedly taking priority over those who had been on the city's housing list for a long time. It took three days for the authorities to regain control, by which time some twenty-five people had been killed and over 700 injured.[27]

In August 1991, Dushanbe was again engulfed by mass public protests, this time lasting for several weeks. Thousands of demonstrators took to the streets to call for the resignation of the Tajik leadership and the organization of free presidential elections. It was against this turbulent background that in November the first free, nationwide presidential election was indeed held. It was a remarkably open contest, with the nine contenders representing a wide spectrum of political stances. Rahmon Nabiev, a former first secretary of the CP, was the winner, gaining 57 percent of the vote (a modest lead by subsequent electoral standards). According to official estimates, his chief opponent, Davlat Khudonazarov, the candidate of an odd alliance of Islamists and so-called democrats, received some 35 percent.[28] His supporters accused the authorities of fraud and insisted that he had won a far larger share of the vote. But there was a genuine feeling at the time that Nabiev did enjoy the confidence of a large section of the population and that whatever irregularities there might have been had not significantly distorted the ballot results.

At the end of December 1991, the Soviet Union was suddenly dissolved. The government of the now fully independent Tajikistan found itself bereft of the support and protection of the central government. It had neither a national army nor reliable internal security forces, thus no means of enforcing law and order.[29] Within weeks, the security situation began to spiral out of control. The incident that triggered the crucial confrontation between government and opposition forces came in March 1992 in the form of a televised address delivered by the Speaker of Parliament, who used the occasion to criticize the head of the Ministry of the Interior. This was not merely a procedural matter. It encapsulated underlying regional tensions, since the Speaker was regarded as a representative of the dominant northern elite, while the head of the Ministry of the Interior was a Pamiri from the east of the country. Pamiris regarded the nationwide transmission of this confrontation as a deliberate ethnic affront. In response, they gathered spontaneously in the center of Dushanbe, calling for the speaker's dismissal.

The Pamiris formed the core of the protest group, but they were joined by people from other parts of the country. The prevailing mood was one of hostility toward the government and support for the Islamists and other opposition factions. There was also a strong anti-Russian vein. A rival demonstration of progovernment, anti-Islamist factions soon formed nearby. This consisted mainly, though by no means exclusively, of Kulobis from the southwest. The standoff continued for weeks, with each side continually provoking the other. At the end of April, a third crowd assembled in another part of Dushanbe.

In early May, fighting broke out between pro- and antigovernment groups. Calm was only restored by the intervention of troops from the local garrison of the Russian Army's 201st Motor Rifle Division (MRD). President Nabiev, now little more than a figurehead, agreed to the formation of a coalition—the Government of National Reconciliation (GNR). However, in September, Nabiev was forced to step down; in November the GNR resigned. A new government strongly opposed to the GNR coalition was formed under the leadership of Imomali Rahmonov, a southerner from Kulob (he formally changed his surname to Rahmon in March 2007, but for the sake of consistency Rahmonov is used throughout this chapter).

The focus of the conflict shifted to the south, where armed clashes of increasing ferocity took place between supporters of the government and opposition supporters. With this progression came a degree of formalization. Political and military structures were created, physical headquarters established, and alliances both internal and external forged. On the macro level, this provided a certain clarity, as the warring factions constituted two identifiable blocs—on the one hand the government, on the other the umbrella alliance of the United Tajik Opposition (UTO).

Yet the reality was more complex. Not only were there other strands of political opinion (most notably the Party of People's Unity, founded by former Prime Minister Abdumalik Abdullojonov), but there were also splits and rivalries within the two main blocs. Moreover, field commanders often acted autonomously, pursuing their own ambitions rather than any common group strategy. As for the population at large, ideological, regional, communal, and generational fractures cut across one another, further fragmenting society. There were no neatly defined, easily identifiable blocs of combatants, only blurred and fluid allegiances.

Foreign Actors

Several foreign actors, both state and nonstate, were involved militarily and/or politically in the Tajik conflict. The chief state actors were Russia, Uzbekistan, Afghanistan, and Iran. It is unlikely that either of the warring factions could have survived had it not been shored up by these external sponsors, yet the support was never sufficient to allow either side to gain decisive superiority.[30] It is not easy to evaluate the impact of this foreign involvement. First, there was often considerable divergence—or at least lack of coordination—between official policies and initiatives taken by those on the ground. Second, publicly made commitments were not always implemented as promised. Third, the capabilities, not to mention the broader policy aims, of would-be sponsors differed greatly. Russia certainly had the military resources to intervene decisively in the Tajik conflict but was constrained by other priorities, not least the war in Chechnya. Uzbekistan, the dominant regional power, was a very new state and its policies, domestic as well as foreign, were in flux. Afghanistan was being torn apart by civil strife, and its involvement in Tajik affairs was entirely factional (primarily on the part of the Taliban and the Northern Alliance). Iran was not only simply too far away but also concerned with internal problems, particularly a weak economy, and with its delicately balanced international position to become very deeply embroiled. Thus, none of these players was able to contemplate a serious commitment in Tajikistan.

The Consequences of the Civil War

For a time it seemed as though the country would be dismembered by secessionist factions in the north and east. The very concept of a unified Tajik nation was called into question as regional allegiances assumed predominance. In late 1992 and early 1993, there was a mass exodus of opposition leaders, antigovernment fighters, and civilians to bases in northern Afghanistan; in 1994, this coalition of antigovernment forces constituted the aforementioned UTO. The hot phase of the conflict lasted from mid-1992 to late 1996. The most intense clashes occurred in the first eighteen months of the war. Thereafter, the fighting was more localized and sporadic. Both sides suffered from internal divisions, mutinies, and defections; neither was strong enough to win a decisive victory. During the conflict, nearly one-sixth of the population (over 778,000 people) fled Tajikistan. Some 700,000 people were displaced within the country itself. By the time hostilities ceased, the country's economy had been devastated and thousands of refugees had been left homeless and destitute. The death toll was conservatively estimated at 50,000 (the overwhelming majority of fatalities occurred in the period of 1992–1993), with many more individuals missing, lost without a trace. Some 55,000 children were orphaned and thousands of women were widowed. In financial terms, the cost of damage to the country (including damage to agriculture, transportation, communication, health care, education, and so on) ran into the billions of dollars.[31]

The Dushanbe Government: Institutional and Economic Reform

Despite the ferocity of the war in some areas, other parts of the country remained relatively stable. In the area that was under government control, there were some attempts at institutional and economic reform. A new constitution was adopted in November 1994 that established the division of executive, legislative, and judicial powers. Shortly thereafter, a presidential election was held. Inevitably, voting procedures could not be properly implemented in several districts on account of the continuing hostilities. Moreover, an estimated 800,000 refugees had left the country by this time; some attempt was made to set up polling stations in places such as Moscow and parts of northern Afghanistan, but with little success.[32] There were only two candidates: Imomali Rahmonov, the incumbent acting head of state, and Abdumalik Abdullojonov, then Tajik ambassador to Moscow. The contest was closer than might have been expected, with Rahmonov receiving 60 percent of the vote, Abdullojonov 35 percent. There were undoubtedly many shortcomings in the whole undertaking, but arguably it did represent a step toward normalization of the country's political life. Parliamentary elections were held in 1995, and as expected, yielded a body of deputies that was strongly propresident.

Some progress was also made in the economic sphere. On the eve of independence, Tajikistan had adopted pioneering reforms. These included the Law on Deregulation and Privatization of Property, which was passed in February 1991; enterprise restructuring began later that year. In 1992, Tajikistan became one of the first ex-Soviet states to create commercial banks. These reforms were all but nullified by the civil war; all sectors of the economy were devastated. Output shrank disastrously and hyperinflation set in, reaching over 2,000 percent in 1993.[33] The country remained dependent on trade within the Commonwealth of Independent States (CIS), exporting traditional commodities such as cotton and aluminum in return for manufactured goods and foodstuffs.[34]

The situation gradually began to improve after Imomali Rahmonov took office in late 1992. There are two interlocking sets of factors that help to explain this positive trend. On the domestic level, Rahmonov was able to consolidate his position and exert authority over the state apparatus. As a result, he succeeded in creating a crucial minimum degree of certainty and stability. As we have noted, this enabled the institutions of state management inherited from the Soviet era to continue to function (albeit imperfectly) in a large part of the country.

At the international level, the major powers were jockeying for influence. This trend might have led to a proxy war, with interested parties covertly supporting their favored candidates. This did not in fact happen to any great extent, most likely because the potential players had other priorities and preoccupations at the time, as we have seen. However, a certain element of competition was to be observed in the provision of aid. In the West, there was a widespread perception that Iran or, more probably, Russia would try to use the Tajik conflict as a way of strengthening its grip on central Asia.[35] To counter this perceived threat, efforts were made to draw Tajikistan into the Western orbit through involvement in international organizations. It was thus that IFIs became engaged in Tajikistan, despite the fact that the fighting between government and opposition forces was at its height and the future of the country was very much in the balance.

Tajikistan joined the World Bank Group and the IMF during the 1993–1994 period. The IMF undertook a number of missions to Tajikistan from 1993–1995 and provided some technical assistance.[36] In May 1996 the IMF approved a US$22 million standby arrangement.[37] A new privatization program was launched that year with World Bank assistance.[38] Other international financial organizations also provided support. One of the first to become involved was the European Bank for Reconstruction and Development (EBRD), which

Tajikistan had joined in 1992. Until 1996 the EBRD had focused primarily on technical cooperation, notably the implementation of a vital project—carried out in conjunction with the Dutch government, which provided a grant of US$4 million—to repair the runway at Dushanbe airport; the project was completed in October 1996. Subsequently, EBRD strategic priorities included the strengthening of the financial sector and support for private enterprise—for example, the provision of a credit line worth US$8.6 million to small and medium enterprises, and a loan of 1.5 million (approximately US$2.1 million at current exchange rates) to a private-sector food packaging company.[39]

The Peace Process

The peace process was initiated in early 1994, under the aegis of the UN and observer nations, among them Iran and Russia.[40] It took three years and eight rounds of negotiations to reach a settlement, yet by 1993, well before the process began, there had been signs of stabilization and national recovery. From 1992 onward, foreign donors—the governments of Iran, Russia, Turkey, and the United States, among others—had begun to provide significant humanitarian assistance.[41] International agencies—UN and nongovernmental—were also able to establish a presence in the country and to provide various forms of support.[42] As a result of these interventions, as well as of the increasingly secure environment the government had managed to create in a large part of the country, thousands of refugees and internally displaced persons (IDPs) began to return to their places of origin. By early 1995, approximately 65 percent of the estimated 60,000 people who had fled to Afghanistan and more than 96 percent of some 700,000 IDPs had returned; out of almost 38,000 wholly or partially destroyed houses, some 16,600 were rebuilt.[43] Thus, by the mid-1990s, the conflict situation, though still fragile, was no longer as critical as it had been in the first half of the decade.[44]

The landmark Protocol on Military Issues, which set out the conditions and modalities for the disarmament and reintegration of opposition forces into government units, was signed during the seventh round of talks, held in Moscow between February 26 and March 8, 1997.[45] The eighth and final round of peace talks was convened a month later in Tehran. In the interim, the leaders of the opposing factions met to resolve outstanding issues such as the establishment of a joint Central Election Commission, the reform of national and local government on the basis of a 30 percent UTO quota, and the lifting of all restrictions on opposition parties immediately following the incorporation of UTO units into the government armed forces. The General Agreement on the Establishment of Peace and National Accord in Tajikistan was signed on June 27, 1997 and registered with the secretariat of the UN.[46] In July, the Pact on Mutual Forgiveness was signed and endorsed by the newly formed Commission for National Reconciliation (CNR).[47] In September 1997, five years after leaving for Afghanistan, the leader of the UTO returned to Dushanbe.

In 1999, two years after the signing of the peace treaty, a grand jubilee was held to mark the 1,100th anniversary of the founding of the Samanid state. The underlying political narrative was the celebration of the rebirth of the nation and the start of a new era of unity. From a purely economic point of view the event was an extravagance that the country could ill afford, but the psychological effect was very positive, generating as it did a surge of optimism and renewed belief in the national idea. At the same time, there was some improvement in interethnic relations; the xenophobia that had surfaced in the early stages of the conflict began to subside. Granted, it is possible that this was because the exodus of so many non-Tajiks had rendered Tajikistan a more ethnically homogeneous state than it was at the time of independence.[48]

Factors Leading to a Successful Peace Process: Provisional Conclusions

Compared to other armed conflicts (both within the CIS and elsewhere), the speed with which a peace agreement was reached was extraordinary. There were several contributing factors; some were preindependence legacies. First, Tajikistan (unlike neighboring Afghanistan, for example) has no socially sanctioned culture of violence—there is no tradition of blood feuds, honor killings, the everyday bearing of weapons, or other structural forms of aggression. Historically, the Tajiks have tended to follow occupations that flourish in a peaceful environment, such as trade, agriculture, and scholarship. Second, despite the many microdivisions in Tajik society, there are no deep-seated group antagonisms. Consequently, although there was a certain degree of regionalization and ethnicization of the conflict, it was not dominant; the lack of historical, ethnicity-based hatreds undoubtedly rendered compromise easier than it might otherwise have been. Third, the Tajiks are ethnically Iranian and acutely feel their isolation in the midst of what is predominantly a Turkic environment. So whatever regional differences they may have, they nevertheless share a deep sense of common ethnic and cultural identity.[49]

There were also several contemporary factors that aided the peace process. These included able and decisive leadership on both sides. Imomali Rahmonov and Said Abdullo Nuri, representing the government and the opposition respectively, had sufficient natural authority to be able to make difficult (and sometimes unpopular) decisions and still retain the confidence of most of their followers.[50] The ongoing process of government in parts of the country (especially the capital and the economically developed north) throughout the civil war also maintained a certain degree of continuity in post-Soviet institution building. There was also at least the skeleton of a functioning civil service, which meant that even during the conflict, some progress, however modest, could be made toward economic reform. Additionally, the violence was relatively localized; as we have noted, only parts of the country—mainly to the center and the south—were directly affected. Moreover, even in the areas most afflicted, the hot phase of the conflict did not last for much more than a year.

Consequently, the conflict did not take place amid the total breakdown of society. A state presence existed throughout, albeit with limited territorial control. Externally, on the regional level, there was cooperation rather than hegemonic rivalry among the main players (Iran, Russia, and to a lesser extent Uzbekistan); as we will see, such regional unity was underpinned by sustained international support for the peace talks. The combination of these factors created an environment that enabled a successful outcome to the peace process.

Postconflict Recovery and Reconstruction

The peace agreement continued to hold, and gradually the security environment improved. By 2000, there had been substantial progress on several fronts, including those of institution building and the renewal of political processes, demobilization and disarmament, repatriation, media reform, and a decrease in political violence. This positive trend continued, with varying degrees of enthusiasm and efficiency, throughout the 2000s. As of the time of this writing in 2009, there are still major domestic challenges, notably with regard to human development, but by comparison with the immediate postwar period there has been an extraordinary degree of recovery. In international relations the trend is also encouraging. Tajikistan has expanded its cooperation with international agencies and strengthened its relationship with foreign states, especially those within the region.

National Policies: Institutional (Re)building

In 1999 the single-chamber legislative body that was inherited from the Soviet era was transformed into a bicameral system comprising a standing lower house of elected deputies, an upper house of deputies elected by the regional assemblies, and eight additional presidential nominees. Local government was also reformed to create a multilayered system of jurisdiction, hierarchically ranked from the provincial level down to the village level with representative and executive bodies at each tier. In theory, the different levels were meant to function autonomously, with direct control over local matters (fiscal, social, and so on). In practice, however, there were many problems, mostly caused by a severe shortage of financial and human resources.

Presidential elections occur at regular intervals (originally specified as every five years, they were extended to seven years in September 1999, when a number of other constitutional changes were also approved by referendum). Any citizen, regardless of gender, religion, or ethnic origin, is eligible to run for the presidency. The first postwar presidential election was held in November 1999. The registration process and media coverage revealed heavy bias in favor of the incumbent, Imomali Rahmonov. At first it seemed as though he would stand unchallenged, but shortly before the election, in response to international expressions of concern, a rival IRP candidate was allowed to register. In the event, Rahmonov received 97 percent of the vote. The next presidential election was held on schedule in November 2006. Apart from the sitting president, there were four other contenders. As anticipated, President Rahmonov was reelected, though by a somewhat reduced majority; this time he received 76.4 percent of the vote.

During the civil war, opposition parties had been outlawed, but in 1999 the ban was lifted and independent parties began to reappear. However, they faced considerable difficulties in establishing a viable electoral base. Most were small, underfunded, and dominated by a single individual. They were unable to satisfy the strict criteria for official registration (a prerequisite for participation in elections).[51] Yet six parties did qualify for registration and in February 2000 fielded their candidates to the newly created lower house. The outcome of the elections was marred by numerous irregularities such as proxy voting, lack of proper voter identification, lack of transparency during the vote count, and interference by government officials.[52] Not surprisingly, the People's Democratic Party of Tajikistan headed by President Rahmonov took the lion's share of the vote. In February 2005, another bout of parliamentary elections was held. Again, foreign observers and opposition parties alleged fraud.[53] Nevertheless, there was general agreement that the elections were conducted in a calm and orderly fashion and were a distinct improvement over the previous ballot.

Economic Restructuring

During the civil war, Tajikistan suffered devastating economic disruption. This was due not only to the conflict but also to the consequences of the collapse of the Soviet economic system and its web of interdependence.[54] Supplies of essential goods and materials were suddenly halted, while traditional markets disappeared virtually overnight. Agriculture and industry were the most severely affected sectors; during the civil war, many enterprises operated at a third of their normal capacity. From 1990 to 1994, output declined by an average of 20 percent per year; the cumulative decline during this period was 69 percent. The contraction continued, though somewhat more slowly, from 1995 to 1999.[55] However, following the formal conclusion of hostilities, the government was able to embark upon a policy of economic reform. Strict monetary and fiscal policies were introduced. Inflation was brought under control and for the first time since independence, there was real economic growth. Small private enterprises began to appear, especially in the trade and service sectors. In agriculture, too, there were signs of recovery.[56]

Post-2000, there was significant progress in structural reform. Important developments included land reform and farm privatization, the privatization of strategic state-owned enterprises, the restructuring of the energy sector, and the reform of the banking system. The implementation of these programs was by no means perfect, but progress was made, however haltingly. Economic growth from 1997 to 2001 averaged 7.5 percent. This trend was sustained over the following years; in 2004, gross domestic product (GDP) grew by 10.6 percent in real terms. Average monthly wages increased significantly and unemployment fell (according to official statistics, the number of unemployed people decreased by 6,000, while the number of employed people grew by 12,000).[57] Agriculture (cotton, grain, fruits and vegetables, animal husbandry) and industry (aluminum, mining, chemicals, power generation, and manufacturing) each accounted for approximately a quarter of GDP, while services accounted for 52 percent. In 2007, a healthy 7.5 percentage rate was recorded; for 2008, just over 7 percent was projected.[58] By the end of that year, however, turmoil in global markets resulted in a worldwide slump in commodity prices. The revenue from Tajikistan's main exports—cotton and aluminum—fell sharply. At the time of this writing in 2009, neither the extent of the global economic crisis nor its duration could be predicted, but it was already clear that it would severely impede Tajikistan's economic development for years to come.

In the postconflict period, key policy priorities were the modernization and development of the cotton, aluminum, and mining sectors. Realizing that foreign investment was crucial, the government took steps to improve the business environment, introducing tax privileges and other incentives for foreign investors. However, Tajikistan was, and still is, seen as a relatively high-risk country by investors. There were many factors that contributed to this perception, from residual fears about Tajikistan's political stability to uncertainty about the prospects for regional cooperation, particularly as they might affect cross-border transport and communication networks. There were also concerns about the weakness of the regulatory framework and the high incidence of corruption at all levels of society.[59] Nonetheless, the number of joint ventures with foreign partners steadily increased, an indication of growing confidence in Tajikistan's potential.[60] In 2009, owing to the global recession, there was a retrenchment in foreign investment. This caused delays in and the cancellation of some projects.

Human Development: Poverty, Health, and Education Indicators

Since independence, Tajikistan has seen a significant decline in human development indicators. After the collapse of the Soviet Union, it experienced a crisis in the provision of essential social services, particularly education and health care—sectors that had largely been funded by the central Soviet government.[61] This problem was exacerbated by the civil war, which not only caused massive devastation but also hampered social and economic reform and restructuring.[62] One of the legacies of the conflict was chronic unemployment, which in turn created widespread poverty.[63] There has been some improvement since the turn of the millennium, with poverty falling from 82 percent in 1999 to 64 percent in 2003; according to some estimates, by 2005 it had fallen to 45 percent.[64] Nevertheless, in 2004, the average monthly wage for government employees was still only the equivalent of US$25, with teachers and health workers making even less; in agriculture, the average monthly wage was lower still—whereas in the nongovernmental, nonagricultural sectors, the average was around US$52.[65] Moreover, the distribution of poverty was uneven, marked by regional and seasonal variations.[66] Poverty was particularly acute in cotton-producing areas, where reform was slow and farmers had high levels of debt.

Poverty was also experienced through limited access to social services. In the Soviet era, education and health care were free and universally available; there was also a range of welfare benefits available, for instance, to children, mothers, invalids, and the elderly. These have now been so drastically reduced as to be almost nonexistent, particularly in rural areas. Such problems have only been exacerbated by a high birth rate; despite the losses of the war, in the period 1989–2007, the population increased from 5 million to an estimated 7 million.[67] In recent years there has been some reduction in the birth rate, but the population is still predominantly young, with a median age of 21.3 years as of July 2007.[68]

Another problem area is education. Official sources still record adult literacy levels at almost 100 percent for men and women alike.[69] In theory, nine years of education is compulsory. However, since the end of the Soviet period the education system has been in chronic decline, particularly in rural areas. School premises are often in a state of semi-ruin and lack adequate teaching staffs, schoolbooks, and basic equipment. Although education is nominally free, parents are increasingly expected to pay teachers' wages and cover the costs of books and maintenance. Corruption is rife; indeed, bribes are usually required to ensure satisfactory examination results. It is very difficult to collect exact data, but a study by the UN Children's Fund (UNICEF) in 2001 estimated a dropout rate of 14 percent; a year later, the UN Development Programme (UNDP) estimated that the average enrollment for people at all levels of education (ages six to twenty-three) was down to 62.1 percent. Dropout rates tended to be higher among girls than among boys. Government spending on education, at 2.4 percent of the budget, is insufficient to reverse the decline in education. Efforts are being made to address this problem; important initiatives include the Education Modernization Project launched in 2003 by the Tajik Ministry of Education.[70]

The provision of primary health care has also suffered since independence. The government is implementing programs aimed at increasing the quality and availability of the health service, with particular emphasis on reducing infant mortality. Other health issues include the prevalence of diseases such as malaria and tuberculosis. Inadequate access to safe drinking water and poor sanitation also create serious health hazards. There are no reliable statistics on the incidence of HIV/AIDS; for instance, according to the United Nations Office on Drugs and Crime (UNODC) in 2006, the officially stated figure was 506; however, unofficial estimates put the figure at 4,900.[71] Given the increase in intravenous drug users, there is the potential for HIV to become a bigger problem in the future.

The Informal Economy

When assessing poverty levels in Tajikistan, the large informal economy must be taken into account. Some transactions take the form of monetary bribes, but many are based on a mutual, unofficial exchange of services and favors. Such benefits cannot be captured by conventional accounting, just as the support that is provided by extended family networks cannot be calculated. The support of kin networks frequently overrides the urban-rural divide, as relatives in the countryside will send gifts of local produce to family members in the town and receive other forms of assistance in return. As a result of this informal support system, life for most of the population is not as harsh as the bare statistics might suggest—an impression that is certainly borne out by firsthand observation. Those who suffer the most hardship are the elderly and nonindigenous populations (such as Russians and other Soviet-era immigrants), as they do not have family networks or other informal connections to turn to for help.[72]

Labor Migration and Remittances

Another factor that impacts poverty levels is labor migration and the remittances it yields from abroad. Precise figures for migrants are not available, since many Tajiks who leave the country in search of work do so illegally and hence are unregistered. In 2008, it was estimated that between 600,000 and 1 million Tajiks were abroad at any one time.[73] This was a significant proportion of the labor force. Most were males; some sought short-term seasonal employment, others left for several years at a time. The main destination was Russia, which absorbed over 90 percent of the migrants. It is difficult to estimate the amount of money that these migrants sent home, since many used informal methods of transfer. In 2004, according to IMF estimates, remittances made to Tajikistan through the banking system alone amounted to US$433 million; the total inflow, including informal transfers, was estimated at US$1 billion (some 50 percent of GDP).[74] There was a social cost of the prolonged absence of so many able-bodied, active members of families and communities. However, their financial support was indispensable, and thus it was seen as a necessary evil. In 2009, the flow of Tajik labor migrants was suddenly reversed as the global financial recession led to a sharp downturn in the Russian economy and, as a result, many construction projects were canceled or delayed. Consequently, large numbers of Tajik labor migrants were made redundant and forced to return home. This placed a massive strain on Tajikistan's fragile economy. At the time of writing (mid-2009), the Tajik government was struggling to find ways of minimizing the social and economic effects of this new challenge.

Civil Society Development and Media Freedom

During the civil war, journalists were frequently subjected to physical abuse; several were assassinated. After peace was restored, there was a significant improvement in the security environment, enabling journalists to operate with some degree of safety once again. However, despite moves to establish a legal basis for independent print and broadcasting companies, the state continued to exercise a virtual monopoly over the media. Journalists were commonly harassed and intimidated. Laws protecting state secrets and presidential honor were frequently invoked as pretexts for closing down independent outlets. The result has been a high degree of self-censorship with respect to political content.[75]

Censorship, direct or indirect, is not the only problem for journalists. Production, especially paper, costs are exorbitant. This is a huge burden that is not confined to the private sector; state-owned newspapers, too, experience financial difficulties. Overall, there is a dearth of information available to the general population. Access to the Internet is restricted to a tiny urban segment of society. Foreign broadcasts obtained from Russian television channels, the BBC World Service, Voice of America, Radio Liberty, and the Iran-funded Voice of Free Tajikistan, provide valuable news coverage, but not all are accessible to the population at large. However, international organizations such as the Organization for Security and Cooperation in Europe (OSCE), the US Agency for International Development (USAID), and others are providing training and start-up capital for independent media bodies, and the response, particularly in the north, has been encouraging.

Nongovernmental Organizations

The presence of Western-style nongovernmental organizations (NGOs) is a relatively new phenomenon. A law on so-called public associations was adopted in 1991, covering political parties as well as NGOs. In 1998, separate laws were adopted on the two types of formations. Among other provisions, NGOs involved in charitable work with children, young people, disabled people, and others were granted tax exemptions and, in some cases, reduced registration fees.[76] By 1999, over 400 such bodies had been registered, most of which were concerned with youth and gender issues.[77] However, the majority were underresourced and poorly managed. Many failed to show any signs of activity after registration.

By 2000, about 200 NGOs were still functioning. They were involved in a variety of sectors, including health, education, social protection, human rights, and environmental protection, but as much as a third of the total were concerned with the promotion of gender parity.[78] Moreover, many NGOs were founded and directed by women. Several were supported by international organizations, in particular the UNDP's Women in Development program. The emphasis on gender issues was prompted by the reduced role of women in the public sphere as compared to the Soviet period, when women had equal opportunities in education and work. In 1998, the Tajik government took steps to reverse this trend by launching the comprehensive National Plan for the Advancement of Women 1998–2005, which included sections on health care, education and training, poverty and economics, women's rights, and violence against women; some sixty NGOs helped in the formulation of this program.[79] A number of other measures have also been introduced that aim to promote women's rights and raise awareness of gender issues, particularly through research; consequently, the Centre for Gender Studies was established within Tajik State University in 2000.[80] Such initiatives have brought about some improvement in the lives of women in urban areas but have had limited impact in rural areas, where the great majority of the population lives. Nevertheless, the fact that there is recognition that these problems exist and require attention is in itself encouraging.

Traditional forms of community organization—notably the *mahalla,* an informal neighborhood-based institution—still provide the main source of moral and practical support for the majority of the population. Attempts in recent years by the government and by international aid organizations to use the *mahalla* as a conduit for the implementation of projects has distorted its function, giving it semi-bureaucratic status. In some areas *mahalla* officials now receive regular salaries.

The most successful attempts to develop civil society have been initiated by the Aga Khan Development Network (AKDN). The AKDN has been present in Tajikistan since the early 1990s, when it provided much-needed humanitarian relief to Gorno-Badakhshan. Its activities have since expanded into an integrated program of economic, social, educational, and cultural development. It collaborates with the Tajik government and a wide range of national and international partners. The main (though not exclusive) geographic focus of the activities of the AKDN is Gorno-Badakhshan and the neighboring region. One of the organization's priorities has been the strengthening of institutional structures at the village level so as to enhance community participation in decisionmaking. The aim is to promote social cohesion, cooperative behavior, and sustainable self-sufficiency. In general, these projects are well-managed and show promising results. However, the conditions in Gorno-Badakhshan are very favorable, not least because the majority of the local people are Ismailis and predisposed to support the objectives of the AKDN. Elsewhere in Tajikistan the environment may not be so receptive; hence, it may not be possible to replicate this model of development throughout the country.[81]

International Policies and Foreign Aid

A donors' conference was held in Vienna in November 1997 under the aegis of the UN. Further donor meetings were held in subsequent years, resulting in substantial pledges of aid; these included a meeting in Tokyo in 2001, at which a total of US$430 million was committed, and the fourth Consultative Group meeting in 2003, where donors pledged US$900 million to be disbursed over the period 2004–2006. Tajikistan has also received substantial assistance from international organizations, institutional donors, national governments, and national governmental agencies.[82] Additionally, a number of foreign NGOs are active in Tajikistan, engaged primarily in such fields as medical aid and social protection.[83]

IFIs have endorsed Tajikistan's efforts at economic restructuring and reform, despite some weaknesses in policy implementation. In January 2000 the IMF signaled its approval by granting a new US$18 million credit. The World Bank was likewise sufficiently reassured by the progress of reform to launch a further Country Assistance Strategy, focusing on such areas as poverty reduction, postconflict rehabilitation, and institution building and public administration. Other IFIs and multilateral donors—notably the Asian Development Bank (ADB) and the Islamic Development Bank (IDB), both of which Tajikistan joined in 1998, the European Union (EU), the UNDP, and the AKDN—also have country strategies and assistance programs for Tajikistan that focus on similar issues. The ADB prioritizes projects in the agricultural sector, infrastructure (especially energy and transport), and the social sector, while IDB investments are directed mainly toward public utilities, transport and communication, and social sector reform. The EU, in addition to programs focusing on such areas as poverty alleviation and community development, also supports regional cooperation, particularly with respect to border management and counternarcotics operations.[84]

This external assistance has helped Tajikistan to embark upon the immense and difficult tasks of recovery and reconstruction. However, there have been problems in managing aid effectively. These include the poor monitoring and implementation of projects, resulting in wasted effort and money, as well as differing expectations of what can realistically be achieved. Corruption, too, has been a serious problem, not only among Tajiks but also on the part of foreign partners who sometimes behave with less probity than would be expected of them in their home countries.[85]

Another serious issue has been the cost of international assistance. At the time of independence, Tajikistan was free of external debt. Over the following years, however, it became the recipient of a large flow of loans. Concomitantly, Tajikistan has rapidly accumulated a massive debt burden; by 2000, it had reached 128 percent of GDP.[86] The government first attempted to address the problem in 1995, to little effect. It was only in the early 2000s that a combination of measures, including debt-rescheduling negotiations with its main creditors and tighter policies on contracting new debt, helped to stem the growth of the debt burden. At the end of 2004, the two largest multilateral creditors were the World Bank and the IMF; the largest bilateral creditor was Uzbekistan (debt to Russia was reallocated as part of a comprehensive package of accords concluded in 2004, of which more to come). The situation was further improved in December 2005 when, under the Multilateral Debt Relief Initiative, the IMF approved 100 percent debt relief on all outstanding debt incurred by Tajikistan before January 1, 2005.[87] This decision reflected the IMF's positive assessment of Tajikistan's "overall satisfactory recent macroeconomic performance" and progress in other areas such as poverty reduction and improved public expenditure management.[88]

Membership in International and Regional Organizations

Tajikistan was formally accepted as a member of the UN on March 2, 1992. The newly independent state subsequently joined the main UN funds, programs, and special agencies, as well as non-UN international governmental organizations. In total, Tajikistan's membership within these bodies reflects a desire to balance competing international power blocs, avoid being drawn into any exclusive political grouping, and retain a nonaligned stance as much as possible. Thus, Tajikistan is a member of such diverse international structures as the CIS, the OSCE, the Collective Security Treaty Organization (CSTO), the Organization for Islamic Conference (OIC), the North Atlantic Cooperation Council (NACC), and the NATO Partnership for Peace program (PfP). It has also joined the main IFIs, including the ADB, the IDB, and the EBRD.

Tajikistan's remote, landlocked location makes regional cooperation a vital element in promoting security and development. During the 1990s, the civil war hindered Tajikistan's full participation in regional structures. Since then, the deepening of the peace process has enabled the country to play an increasingly active part in the Eurasian Economic Community (EurAsEC), whose other members are Belarus, Kazakhstan, Kyrgyzstan, Russia, and Uzbekistan;[89] the Economic Cooperation Organization (ECO), whose membership comprises all five central Asian states, as well as Azerbaijan, Afghanistan, Iran, Turkey, and Pakistan; and the Shanghai Cooperation Organization (SCO), whose other members are China, Kazakhstan, Kyrgyzstan, Russia, and Uzbekistan.[90] The summit meeting of the EurAsEC heads of state was held in Dushanbe in October 2007. Following the agreed rotational principle, Tajikistan assumed chairmanship of the organization in 2008.

The primary emphasis in these bodies is on cooperation in economic development, including the expansion of trade and transport infrastructure. However, since the early 2000s, increasing attention has been paid to the need to combat security threats, especially drug trafficking, terrorism, and separatist movements. Two separate but overlapping regional security organizations have been created: under the aegis of the SCO is the Regional Anti-Terrorist Structure Organization (RATS), inaugurated in June 2004 during the aforementioned summit meeting and based in Tashkent; and under the aegis of the CIS is the antiterrorist Rapid Reaction Force, formally inaugurated in August 2001 and based in Bishkek.[91] Participation in these organizations has not yielded spectacular benefits for Tajikistan, but it certainly has helped to further bilateral links with member states, notably Russia, China, and Iran.

Bilateral Foreign Relations

Tajikistan has long borders with Afghanistan (1,206 kilometers), Uzbekistan (1,161 kilometers), and Kyrgyzstan (870 kilometers) and a shorter border with China (414 kilometers). At the time of the collapse of the Soviet Union, several stretches of Tajikistan's external border had not been fully demarcated. By the end of 2005, that process had largely been completed through peaceful negotiation by the contiguous state.[92] The current priority for the Tajik government is to improve regional trade and transport links while maintaining effective border controls. This task presents major challenges—not only are there the physical problems of distance, difficult terrain, and extreme climatic conditions, but there are also transnational security threats such as drug trafficking and terrorism. Tajikistan is still at an early stage in formulating its national security strategy. Uzbekistan, however, already has a well-defined concept of national security to which border protection is key. This can present problems for operating a mutually acceptable border regime that permits the legitimate movement of goods and people but provides adequate protection against transborder criminal activities. The dilemma was starkly demonstrated in 1999 when Uzbekistan, in response to an insurgency of some 500 armed guerrillas allegedly based in Tajikistan and Afghanistan, unilaterally planted mines in an unmarked zone along the border to deter further attacks.[93]

Nevertheless, despite such problems, from 2000 onward formal trade operations have increased markedly, as has informal shuttle trade between Tajikistan and its neighbors. By 2006, road connections with neighboring states had been substantially improved. The first stage of the Tajikistan-China highway was completed at the end of 2005. Projects to connect Tajikistan with Kyrgyzstan and Afghanistan were at various stages of completion in 2009.

Tajikistan's most important but also most difficult bilateral relationship is with Uzbekistan. Sensitive issues include border and transit regimes; illegal labor migrants (mostly from Tajikistan to Uzbekistan); cross-border trade; allegations of interference in each other's domestic affairs; the treatment of ethnic diasporas (namely Tajiks in Uzbekistan and Uzbeks in Tajikistan); and energy supplies. During the late 1990s, relations between the two countries were often strained, but since 2003 there have been some signs of greater cooperation. Uzbekistan also began to destroy the mines it had laid in the border zone (from 1999 to 2005, more than seventy Tajiks were killed and eighty injured by mines in this area).[94] Other matters have remained a cause of friction. In 2005, cross-border trade was seriously hindered by bureaucratic delays, high fees, and corruption on the Uzbek side.[95] Another major cause of tension was the price demanded by Uzbekistan for gas supplies. This reached a crisis point in January 2009 when the Uzbek authorities introduced a massive price hike, demanding US$300 per 1,000 cubic meters (almost double the previous rate). Tajikistan, already suffering from a severe economic downturn, was unable to meet this new price. The result was a catastrophic energy shortage during one of the worst winters in living memory. The situation was aggravated by Turkmenistan's suspension of electricity supplies to Tajikistan. In 2007, Turkmenistan had agreed to supply 1.2 billion kilowatt hours of electricity per year to Tajikistan via the Uzbek power grid. However, when Tajikistan failed to reach an agreement with Uzbekistan over the transit fee, Turkmenistan reneged. At the time of this writing (mid-2009), the matter had still not been resolved.

The other crucial relationship for Tajikistan is with Russia, which was strengthened in 2004 by the conclusion of a comprehensive set of bilateral accords. These included agreement on the establishment of a permanent, 5,000-strong Russian military base on Tajik territory and the lease of the Nurek space-tracking station for forty-nine years for a nominal rent of US$0.39 per year.[96] Other agreements included a timetable for the withdrawal of Russian troops from the Afghan border and the transfer of responsibility for border security to the Tajik authorities (which was completed in 2005). Agreement was also forged on measures to regularize the status of the thousands of Tajik migrants who are employed, often illegally, in Russia. In return, most of Tajikistan's US$300 million debt to Russia was either written off or converted into investment in the Tajik economy. The extent of Russian public and private sector investment in Tajikistan from 2005 to 2010 is expected to total around US$2 billion.[97]

Since the end of the civil war, other regional relationships have also progressed. Iran is an important economic partner, whose activities include providing funds for strategic projects such as the construction of the Anzob tunnel, which links northern and central

Tajikistan, and the Sangtuda hydropower station. Multisectoral ties with first China and then India, Pakistan, and Afghanistan are being developed, whereby Tajikistan may integrate into a broader network of partnerships stretching eastward and southward. However, President Rahmonov is careful to avoid an exclusively regional orientation. Tajikistan maintains good relations with the United States and Europe—in October 2004, a cooperation agreement was signed with the EU.[98] Following the commencement of Western-led military operations against the Taliban and Al-Qaeda in Afghanistan in autumn 2001, Tajikistan provided some logistical support. A small French military contingent, mostly providing transit and refueling faculties, was granted leave to establish a temporary base at Dushanbe International Airport.[99] In 2009, the Tajik government agreed to allow US forces to use Tajikistan as a transit route for non-military cargoes destined for Afghanistan.

Postconflict Security Challenges

Despite significant progress toward consolidating the peace process, Tajikistan faces new security challenges. These can be divided into two broad categories, global and local, which constantly intersect and interact. This duality heightens the threat even as it limits the government's ability to take action to resolve the situation. Drug trafficking and other forms of organized crime clearly present serious security threats for Tajikistan, but they are global phenomena, driven by complex dynamics that extend far beyond the region—not least by the demands of rich Western societies.[100] Therefore, although measures can and must be taken to combat the local impact of these problems, they cannot eradicate it. At best they can contain and mitigate some of the consequences. Similarly, it would be disingenuous to view the emergence of radical, potentially (if not already) militant Islamist movements in Tajikistan as an isolated development. It is clearly part of a worldwide trend, even though at this stage it is difficult to assess what the precise linkages between different groups are. Again, the Tajik authorities can adopt policies that will limit the spread of extremist movements, but they cannot fully resolve the problem. Of course, when exogenous threats such as these coincide with local grievances and resentments, they can constitute the catalyst for conflict. In Tajikistan, this convergence of internal and external challenges increases the likelihood that political projects may be pursued through not democratic processes but political violence. Moreover, the centrifugal forces of regionalism could be revitalized by continued societal grievances based on perceived inequalities in access to power and resources.

Drug Trafficking

According to the UNODC's *Afghanistan Opium Survey 2007*, Afghanistan accounted for 93 percent of the world's production of opium, the basic ingredient in heroin. In 2008 and 2009, there was no appreciable improvement in the situation. Tajikistan has long been the principal conduit for drug traffic from Afghanistan. There are two main routes through Gorno-Badakhshan in the east and Kulob in the southwest. In both regions, unemployment is high and drug trafficking is often the only available source of income. The price that illegal narcotics can command in Tajikistan is a tiny fraction of what they fetch further afield; nevertheless, by local standards, the profits are colossal and far outweigh the risks involved.[101]

In 2003, seizures of over five tons of drugs were made, an increase of 26 percent from 2002. The massive flow of illegal narcotics—once mainly raw opium, now increasingly pure heroin—from Afghanistan into the central Asian states continues to grow. In 2006, total drug seizures by law enforcement bodies in Tajikistan amounted to 4,759.8 kilograms and included 2,097.5 kilograms of heroin, 1,386.8 kilograms of opium, and 1,305.5 kilograms of marijuana.[102] It is generally accepted that such hauls account for 10 percent of the total cross-border flow at most.[103]

The fight against drug trafficking is complicated by widespread corruption and criminal complicity at all levels of counternarcotics operations. This fact was highlighted by the case of Ghaffur Mirzoev, who was appointed to head the Tajik Drug Control Agency in early 2004 despite the fact that he was widely believed to be one of the region's chief drug barons. Ultimately the appointment was revealed to be a skillful means of entrapping him; in the months that followed it, the security services gathered a massive dossier of incriminating material against him. He was arrested in August 2004; it is perhaps not insignificant that he was allegedly plotting a coup d'état. He was tried in camera in 2006; a life sentence was handed down.

After the disintegration of the Soviet Union, the 2000-kilometer Afghan-Tajik border was patrolled by Russian troops. In autumn 2005, as part of a comprehensive set of Russian-Tajik accords, control of the border was handed over to the Tajik authorities. International assistance was offered to Tajikistan to help train its border guards, and a Russian operational border unit was created to collaborate with the Tajiks in countering drug trafficking and international terrorism.[104] Nevertheless, fears remain that border protection will deteriorate.

Concerns about drug trafficking tend to highlight the threat it poses to Western societies. However, the damage to a country as vulnerable as Tajikistan is even more serious. Drug trafficking fosters every type of criminal activity, including money laundering, protection racketeering, and human trafficking. It is also leading to a rise in drug addiction within Tajikistan, particularly among the young. No reliable statistics are available, but according to local accounts Kulob has been especially hard hit. An estimated 80 percent of male adolescents and a smaller but growing number of females there were reportedly addicted to drugs in 2000.[105]

Militant Islamism

Before the civil war, Soviet rule in Tajikistan was actively contested by an alternative political project. This was not the vague democratic vision of the secular opposition parties but the firm idea of an Islamic state as propagated by the IRP. By the late 1980s, this movement had a nationwide network of adherents who were mentally and physically prepared to fight to achieve their goal. When the Soviet Union collapsed, they intensified their efforts and, arguably, came close to accomplishing their aim. Today, the IRP has lost much of the moral authority that it once enjoyed, due in large measure to the perception that the Islamists achieved very little in the areas that were under their control during the civil war. At that time they did not in fact demonstrate greater morality or concern for social justice. Women, in particular, saw a sharp diminution of their civil rights, accompanied by the imposition of strict Islamic codes of dress and behavior; those who did not conform were liable to be assaulted and, by some accounts, raped.[106] Whereas in 1990 the IRP, in contrast to the incumbent regime, seemed to offer a real hope of change for the better, in the postconflict era the party compares unfavorably to the present government.

Yet the mission of creating an Islamic state has not been abandoned. It is now being pursued by a new generation of clandestine organizations, such as Hezb-i Tahrir (Party of Liberation), the Islamic Movement of Uzbekistan (IMU), and Bayat (Allegiance).[107] In some ways these organizations resemble the IRP as it existed in the late 1980s, but there is an important difference: the IRP was a homegrown movement, with deep roots in society, and was therefore able to draw on a degree of local sympathy if not active support. These newer movements are less anchored in local communities, drawing instead on a transnational support base and propounding global aims. To date their appeal appears to be more limited. Although the challenge they offer to the incumbent government is similar to that which the IRP mounted in the 1990s, in practical terms it is weaker. Consequently, the emerging radical groups are (at least for the foreseeable future) less likely to be able to pursue their goal with the same vigor as the IRP. Nevertheless, the present government is taking no chances. In March 2009 it introduced a tough new law, the Law on Religion and Religious Associations, which significantly increased state control over all religious activities. Among other provisions, it banned prayer both at work and in military units and legitimized state censorship of religious material.

Regionalism

Regionalism in Tajikistan is understood both as solidarity among people from the same region and as a manifestation of the interests of that region. Regionalism is often identified as a cause (and sometimes even the main cause) of conflict. By extension, it becomes possible to depict the civil war in terms of a struggle between geographically defined blocs (corresponding to the zones we have described). But it would be misleading to do so. There were and still are strong regional loyalties; nevertheless, at the beginning of the conflict it was not uncommon for members of a single community or even a single family to support different factions.[108] As the conflict progressed, those who constituted the ideological minority in areas of conflict either fled or were killed. As a result, by the end of the war, geographic boundaries did indeed coincide fairly closely with the spread of political allegiances, thereby emphasizing regional divisions.[109]

One of the most obvious consequences of the civil war was the rise to power of southerners from Kulob, the home region of President Rahmonov, whereas the senior posts in the government during most of the Soviet period had been dominated by northerners. This has created resentment, particularly in the northern Soghd province, where people often complain of discrimination and lack of economic opportunity. This discontent is understandable. During the Soviet period, Soghd was the most prosperous province in Tajikistan; in the 1990s, however, it experienced a dramatic deterioration in its economy.[110] Although the Soghd province was not directly involved in the conflict, it suffered from the disruption of trade and transport links. Moreover, many of the large state-owned enterprises that had previously been major employers and producers of wealth proved to be uncompetitive when the country began to embrace market reforms; consequently, they were forced either to close or to operate well below capacity, resulting in devastating job losses. Subsequently, joint ventures were established with foreign partners and some Soviet-era factories were successfully refurbished; the owners were then able to find new, more profitable markets. Agriculture, too, began to recover, and some progress was made in developing new, untraditional exports. Its rich resources and relatively good transport systems helped to make the province an attractive destination for investment. In 2002, more than half the foreign investment in Tajikistan (both direct and indirect) went to the Soghd province.[111] Yet for many people the standard of living was still far below the Soviet period—thus the sense of resentment.[112] It was only exacerbated by the fact that some of the largest and most profitable enterprises were taken over by Kulobis from the south.

However, the government is less dominated by Kulobis than might be expected. Not only are some of the most senior posts held by non-Kulobis, but there is also bitter infighting among the Kulobis themselves; since the end of the civil war, the president's most serious rivals have largely emerged from within his own inner circle of family and allies. A similar situation was to be observed during the Soviet period, when the main political rivalries were to be found among the northerners, rather than between northerners and people from other parts of the country. Thus, despite the perception of regional solidarity, it is intraregional rather than interregional competition that characterizes Tajik society. One advantage of this scenario is that a single actor is rarely strong enough to act alone; instead, it is necessary to seek allies in other regions and even outside the country. This in turn ensures that whoever is in power will need to construct a broad network of support and maintain a balance of interests.

Natural Disasters and Environmental Challenges

In addition to its many economic and social difficulties, Tajikistan also faces serious environmental problems. It regularly suffers natural disasters that result in severe human and material losses. Every year heavy rains, flash floods, mudslides, and avalanches cause major agricultural damage and destroy property and infrastructure (roads, bridges, drainage systems, irrigation canals, and so on). Hundreds of lives are lost and thousands are left homeless. In 1997, for example, some 12,650 people were affected by floods; nearly 300 people were killed and almost 1,000 required resettlement.[113] Droughts such as that of 1999–2001 threaten the food supply. Other natural hazards include earthquakes as well as glacial melting and other problems attributed to global climate change.[114]

This recurring cycle of calamities causes periodic dislocation of the population and places yet more strain on the meager resources of the state. The worst affected parts of the country are usually the southern and central zones—the very regions that were the most affected by the civil war. Potential catastrophes include the overflow of Lake Sarez, which would unleash a tidal wave of destruction.[115] In 2004, equipment for monitoring the situation was installed as part of a risk-mitigation project to provide early warning for the surrounding population.

These natural calamities complicate Tajikistan's attempts to establish a sustainable basis for development. The international community has provided some disaster relief, but it is generally too little, too late. Consequently, the brunt of these disasters is shouldered by the local population.[116] This in turn creates conditions in which anger and resentment against the government, even in reference to quite separate issues, can readily be inflamed. Thus, natural disasters have the potential to become political issues. The challenge for the authorities, therefore, is not only to address the physical damage these events cause but also to ensure that they do not cause further damage in the form of political protests.

Conclusion

As we have noted, the Tajik conflict began in 1992 and was formally brought to an end by the signing of a peace treaty in 1997. Yet as early as 1993, the process of recovery and reconstruction was already beginning. Several factors contributed to this positive trend; of particular importance were three structural elements. One was competent leadership of the government. Imomali Rahmonov became head of state in November 1992. Relatively young at forty and inexperienced, he seemed unlikely to prove more than an ephemeral figure. In fact, he not only succeeded in consolidating his position, he showed a capacity to take advice and implement policy in a consistent manner. The second structural element was a functioning state apparatus and a critical mass of trained professionals. The third element was the timely provision of assistance by international financial institutions. In 1993, when the first IMF mission was undertaken, circumstances could scarcely have seemed propitious. Yet whatever the motivation (as we have suggested, it might have been political rather than economic), this early intervention laid the foundation for long-term engagement.

Other interventions were also important. Emergency humanitarian relief was provided by multilateral and bilateral donors during the worst period of the conflict. Later, as the situation stabilized, assistance was widened to include social, economic, and infrastructural projects. Again, the existence of state institutions and experienced personnel facilitated the implementation of these programs. The UN and the Organization for Security and Cooperation in Europe (formerly known as the Conference for Security and Co-operation in Europe), together with Russia, Iran, and other states, played an important role in the peace process. Jointly, they initiated and supported the series of peace talks that eventually led to the signing of the peace treaty.

The UN and CSCE/OSCE were also mandated to promote the development of democratic institutions.[117] In this area progress was very slow. Neither the UN mission in Tajikistan nor the OSCE sent observers to the presidential election in November 1994 on the grounds that it did not conform to democratic principles. In hindsight, it appears perhaps unrealistic to expect a country that had only recently emerged from some seventy years of Soviet rule and was still in the grip of a civil war to conduct free and fair elections.[118] For the Tajik government, the election was undoubtedly seen not as an exercise in democracy but as a means of legitimizing the incumbent regime.[119] Even so, it was not an empty political gesture; in most parts of the country the situation was showing signs of stabilization. Refugees and IDPs were returning to their homes and the assassinations and kidnappings that had been commonplace in the early days of the conflict were becoming less frequent. This improvement was largely owed to the government's growing ability to enforce law and order on the streets.

After the signing of the peace treaty, the economy began to improve; from 2000 onward, the growth rate was impressive. Corruption remained a major problem but violent crime decreased.[120] Streets and other public spaces again became lively and busy. There was also a revival of cultural activities such as concerts and art exhibitions, which had been prominent features of Tajik society in the preconflict era. Another sign of normalization was Tajikistan's increasing confidence in the conduct of its foreign affairs. It continued to have close ties with Russia but balanced them with a wide range of multilateral and bilateral ties with Asian and Western states. As we have noted, in 2001 Tajikistan even agreed to host a support base for Western-led coalition operations in Afghanistan and, in 2009, to permit its territory to be used as a transit route for nonmilitary supplies to Afghanistan.

The postconflict recovery of Tajikistan was accompanied by a growing concentration of power in the hands of the president. Some independent parties were granted registration, but partly owing to internal divisions, as well as harassment by officials, they were unable to establish a strong political presence.[121] The independent media also came under pressure; opposition newspapers were frequently suspended on minor technicalities, and journalists who criticized the government were liable to be charged with tax evasion and other such irregularities. Critics of the regime highlighted the lack of democratic reform and labeled Tajikistan an authoritarian state.[122]

However, as we have outlined, in many respects the peacebuilding process has been a success.[123] This inevitably brings into question "the assumption that solutions to the conflict can best be found through Western-style democratic and constitutional reforms."[124] It is too soon to attempt to provide a definitive answer, but analysis of events over the course of the twelve-odd years since the signing of the peace treaty reveals a pattern of sustained progress in development and security. It is unlikely that this could have been achieved, given the difficult and volatile conditions of Tajikistan, under a different style of leadership.

While the trauma of the civil war is receding, there are other challenges to stability. How well the Tajik government will be able to cope with these problems remains an open question. As noted, one of the main issues is the rise of militant Islamism. It could be regarded as a development problem, requiring socioeconomic solutions, yet that is perhaps too facile a linkage—one not supported by demographic evidence. The data that exist on members of militant Islamic groups indicates, in Tajikistan as in other countries, that there is little correlation between individual socioeconomic status and ideological response. The Tajik government regards religious extremism as a security threat and has adopted a predominantly punitive strategy. Some believe that a more productive way forward would be through dialogue and compromise.[125] Their view is based on the Tajik experience of postconflict peacebuilding. Yet today, the rise of Al-Qaida and other transnational militant networks appears to have created a different dynamic. Approaches that have worked in the past will probably no longer be effective. Meanwhile, drug trafficking is another major challenge that confronts the Tajik government. Again, some argue that the best way to combat it is by improving socioeconomic conditions. This view surely ignores the global scale of the issue. The Tajik authorities work closely with international agencies to fight drug trafficking, but whether their work will be sufficient to contain the local impact of the problem remains to be seen.

As these few examples show, Tajikistan is still faced with many uncertainties. To date, it has proved able to cope with immediate postconflict challenges, but it is nevertheless still vulnerable to a variety of internal stresses. It is also vulnerable to external upheavals, as shown by the impact of the 2009 global recession. Nevertheless, Tajikistan will most likely continue to preserve a balance between security and development. Whether it will be helped or hindered in its balancing act by the slow pace of democratic reform remains a matter of debate. Without doubt, in time, Tajikistan will find solutions that accord with its own unique cultural and historical traditions. It is unlikely that they could easily be replicated elsewhere. Leo Tolstoy, in the opening lines of his novel *Anna Karenina*, famously commented that "all happy families resemble one another, but each unhappy family is unhappy in its own way." The same sentiment could be applied to vulnerable states.

Notes

1. This chapter draws on material presented in more depth in Shirin Akiner, *Tajikistan: Disintegration or Reconciliation?* (London: Royal Institute of International Affairs, 2002). It gives bibliographic references to the main works consulted in this study.

2. Saodat Olimova, Sobir Kurbonov, Grigory Petrov, Zebo Kahhorova, Firuz Kataev, and Muzaffar Olimov, Regional Cooperation for Development of Human Capacity and Human Security in the Region of Central Asia: Country Report on Tajikistan (Dushanbe: SHARQ Scientific and Research Centre, 2005), 6; International Monetary Fund (IMF), "Republic of Tajikistan: Selected Issues and Statistical Appendix," IMF Country Report no. 05/131 (Washington, DC: IMF, April 2005), 68.

3. Also spelled Sughd. This province has undergone several name changes; it was known as Khujand uyezd from 1918–1926, then as Leninobod oblast' in 1939. It was again renamed as Soghd veloyat in 2000.

4. Today the Pamiri peoples in Tajikistan number about 150,000; there are also Pamiri communities in the adjacent regions of Afghanistan, China, and Pakistan. See Akiner, *Tajikistan*, 9; Kamoludin Abdullaev and Shahram Akbarzadeh, *Historical Dictionary of Tajikistan* (London: Scarecrow, 2002), 161.

5. Despite this redrawing of the border, half a million Tajiks—and much of the land that Tajiks regard as part of their traditional territory—were left under Uzbek jurisdiction. The most sensitive areas were the historic cities of Bukhara and Samarkand. For the Tajiks, this is an ongoing source of grievance. See Rahim Masov, *Istoriya topornogo razdeleniya* (Dushanbe: Irfon, 1991).

6. The Tajik State University was founded in 1948, the Tajik Academy of Sciences in 1951. Scholarship in the specialized institutes was of a high caliber. The Tajik Institute of Medicine, for example, was one of the foremost centers of medical research in the entire Soviet Union. See further Abdullaev and Akbarzadeh, *Historical Dictionary of Tajikistan*, 3.

7. See B. G. Gafurov, ed., *Istoriya Tadzhikskogo naroda* 3, no. 1 (1964), especially 203–246, 306–325.

8. Collective farms varied in size and range of activities. Some were very large, the equivalent of an entire administrative district; they had their own budgets and provided their members with such facilities as schools, healthcare centers, youth clubs, and leisure amenities. See also Pavel Luknitsky, *Soviet Tajikistan* (Moscow: Foreign Languages, 1954), 87–101.

9. Kamol Abdullaev, *Exiles of Bolshevism: Central Asian Emigration 1918–1932* (unpublished book manuscript, 1999).

10. Abdullo Said Nuri and Muhammad Sharif Himmatzosda, for instance. See Akiner, *Tajikistan*, 23–24.

11. By 1979, there were some 395,000 Russians in Tajikistan (over 10 percent of the population), mostly located in Dushanbe and the industrial centers in the north and south. See the Soviet census survey for 1979, Central Statistical Administration, *Vestnik Statistiki* (Moscow, 1979–1983). See also V. I. Bushkov and D. V. Mikul'skii, *Anatomiya grazhdanskoi voiny v Tadzhikistane* (Moscow: Institut Etnologii i Antropologii RAN, 1997), 26–46.

12. By the 1980s, in parts of this area, up to 90 percent of the inhabitants were new settlers. See Bushkov and Mikul'skii, *Anatomiya grazhdanskoi voiny v Tadzhikistane*, 26–46.

13. Demographic data from the 1989 Soviet census. The average crude birth rate was estimated at 41.8 per 1,000, infant mortality (occurring within the first year) 46.7 per 1,000. Average life expectancy was 69.7 years. See Central Statistical Administration, *Vestnik Statistiki* (Moscow, 1991).

14. See M. Khrustalev, *Grazhdanskaya voina v Tadzhikistane: istoki i perspektivy* (Moscow: Issledovanie TsMI MGIMO, 1997).

15. The first such clash to be widely reported took place in 1989, in the northeast, between Tajiks and Kyrgyz. Similar conflicts occurred elsewhere that year, including clashes between Tajiks and Uzbeks in the west of the country. There were similar ethnic conflicts in the Ferghana Valley (Uzbekistan) between Uzbeks and Meskhetian Turks (wartime deportees) in 1989 as well as between Uzbeks and Kyrgyz in Uzgen (Kyrgyzstan) in 1990. See Bushkov and Mikul'skii, *Anatomiya grazhdanskoi voiny v Tadzhikistane,* 46–55.

16. Khrustalev, *Grazhdanskaya voina v Tadzhikistane,* 29.

17. Akiner, *Tajikistan,* 25–27.

18. The Ministry of the Interior, for example, was dominated by Pamiris. Among the many scandals linked to this body was the mass misappropriation and sale of official vehicles, as a result of which the militia were

stranded, unable to pursue criminals. Fraudulent deals connected to the construction of much-needed housing in the capital were also laid at the door of this network. In popular perception, all Pamiris were tainted by these abuses. See Akiner, *Tajikistan,* 26–27; Stephane Dudoignon, "Political Parties and Forces in Tajikistan, 1989–1993," in *Tajikistan: Trials of Independence,* eds. Mohammad-Reza Djalili, Frédéric Grare, and Shirin Akiner (London: Curzon, 1998), 52–85, 57 in particular.

19. See Muriel Atkin, "The Subtlest Battle: Islam in Soviet Tajikistan," *International Journal of Middle East Studies* 23, no. 3 (August 1991): 471–473; Akiner, *Tajikistan*, 28–33; Shirin Akiner, "Islam, the State, and Ethnicity in Central Asia in Historical Perspective," *Religion, State, and Society: The Keston Journal* 24, nos. 2–3 (June–September 1996): 91–132.

20. He was educated in religious institutions in Bukhara and Tashkent and later at Amman University in Jordan. See Sergei Gretsky, "Profile: Qadi Akbar Turajonzoda," *Central Asia Monitor* 3, no. 1 (1994): 16–24.

21. For example, he opened an Islamic Institute in Dushanbe in 1990; he also published numerous booklets on Islam and opened over a hundred community or so-called Friday mosques. See Gretsky, "Profile."

22. One of the most influential of such teachers was Muhammad Hindustani Rustamov, known as Haji Domla. Born in Kokand in 1892, he studied in Bukhara, Afghanistan, and India; he eventually returned to Tajikistan and died in Dushanbe in 1989. Several of his disciples became influential religious leaders. See Bakhtiyar Babadjanov and Muzaffar Kamilov, "Muhammadjan Hindustani (1892–1989) and the beginning of the 'Great Schism' among the Muslims of Uzbekistan," in *Islam in Politics in Russia and Central Asia,* eds. Stephane Dudoignon and Komatsu Hisao (New York: Kegan Paul, 2001), 195–219.

23. The term was widely used in the Soviet press; it implied that these Muslims were fanatics as well as traitors working for a foreign power (presumably Saudi Arabia). There is no known evidence to justify the latter insinuation and little to support the former. See Akiner, "The Politicisation of Islam in Post-Soviet Central Asia," *Religion, State, and Society: The Keston Journal* 31, no. 2 (2003): 97–122, p. 98 in particular.

24. An all-Union Islamic party had been created a few months previously in Astrakhan. Later that year the Tajiks decided to set up a branch party; this later became autonomous. Hereafter the abbreviation IRP will only be used to refer to the Islamic Rebirth Party of Tajikistan.

25. Three relatively large sociopolitical movements were formed at this time: the Rastokhez (Rebirth) National Front; the Democratic Party of Tajikistan; and La'l-i Badakhshan (The Ruby of Badakhshan). See further Akiner, *Tajikistan,* 33–34; Stephane Dudoignon, "Political Parties," in *Tajikistan: Trials of Independence,* edited by Mohammad-Reza Djalili, Frédéric Grare, and Shirin Akiner (London: Curzon, 1998), 52–85.

26. UNDP, *Tajikistan Human Development Report 1995* (Dushanbe: UNDP, 1995), 50.

27. Official sources give the death toll as twenty-two—see Bushkov and Mikul'skii, *Anatomiya grazhdanskoi voiny v Tadzhikistane,* 51—but eyewitness accounts suggest that it was slightly higher (personal communication to author, November 2005).

28. This alliance was all the more surprising in view of Khudonazarov's

opinion of Islam, which he compared unfavorably to Christianity (see Gretsky, "Profile").

29. The other newly independent central Asian states declared jurisdiction over the military personnel, equipment, and bases that were located on their territory at the time of the collapse of the Soviet Union. They were able to implement this decision because a critical mass of the men and their commanding officers belonged to the titular ethnic group of the state. In Tajikistan this was not the case—the great majority of the troops were Slavs, veterans of the Afghan campaign. Moreover, the ongoing crises in the country meant that the government was unable to exercise the authority needed for such a move. During the 1990s, however, the Tajik government established a national army and other defense and security forces. The aim was to develop a small professional army. Currently, there is still compulsory military conscription of two years for males aged eighteen years. Military expenditure accounts for just under 4 percent of the budget. See Central Intelligence Agency (CIA), "World Factbook: Tajikistan," November 2, 2006, http://www.cia.gov/cia/publications/factbook/geos/ti.html.

30. Akiner, *Tajikistan,* 44–50; see also Lena Jonson, "The Tajik Civil War: A Challenge to Russian Policy," Discussion Paper no. 74 (London: Royal Institute of International Affairs, 1998); Sergei Gretsky, *Russia's Policy Toward Central Asia* (Moscow: Carnegie Endowment for International Peace, 1997); and Mohammad-Reza Djalili and Frédéric Grare, "Regional Ambitions and Interests in Tajikistan: the Role of Afghanistan, Pakistan, and Iran," in *Tajikistan: Trials of Independence,* eds. Mohammad-Reza Djalili, Frédéric Grare, and Shirin Akiner (London: Curzon, 1998), 119–131.

31. There are no agreed statistics on war damage (including deaths, displaced persons, destruction of property, economic dislocation, and so on). The estimates given here are based on UNDP, *Tajikistan Human Development Report 1995,* 47–59; UNDP, *Tajikistan Human Development Report 1998,* 35; and Open Society Institute (OSI), "Tajikistan: Refugee Reintegration and Conflict Prevention," Forced Migration Projects of the Open Society Institute (New York: OSI, 1998), 6–8.

32. The Conference (later renamed Organization) on Security and Cooperation in Europe (CSCE/OSCE) did not send election monitors on the grounds "that constitutional restrictions on the participation of opposition parties were in contradiction with democratic principle." See Oliver Brenninkmeijer, "International Concern for Tajikistan: UN and OSCE Efforts to Promote Peace-building and Democratisation," in *Tajikistan: The Trials of Independence*, eds. Mohammad-Reza Djalili, Frédéric Grare, and Shirin Akiner (London: Curzon, 1998) 180–215, 202 in particular. Russia and the United States did accept the results as legitimate. See Khrustalev, *Grazhdanskaya voina v Tadzhikistane: istoki i perspektivy*, 56.

33. Inflation was still at around this level in 1995. See UNDP, *Tajikistan Human Development Report 1995,* 64.

34. See UNDP, *Tajikistan Human Development Report 1995,* 13–18, for an overview of the economic situation at this time.

35. See Jonson, "The Tajik Civil War," for a representative Western assessment of Russian intentions in Tajikistan at this time.

36. A senior US diplomat confirmed to the author (in a discussion in

Dushanbe, June, 2002) that the US government had indeed actively lobbied the IMF to provide assistance to Tajikistan during this period.

37. European Bank for Reconstruction and Development (EBRD), "Tajikistan: 1998 Country Profile," May 9, 1998, 8–9, http://ebrdrenewables.com/sites/renew/countries/Tajikistan/profile.aspx.

38. EBRD, "Tajikistan: 1998 Country Profile," 22.

39. For details of these and other EBRD projects, see EBRD, "Tajikistan: 1998 Country Profile," 23–25; and EBRD, "Strategy for Tajikistan," document prepared for the EBRD, November 2005, 8–15.

40. In May 1993, UN Special Envoy Ismat Kittani went to Dushanbe to hold talks with all parties. In early 1994, following preliminary contacts between Iranian officials and Russian Deputy Foreign Minister Anatoly Adamishin, the latter held meetings with Tajik opposition leaders in Moscow and Tehran. This paved the way for the first round of Inter-Tajik Peace Talks.

41. Russian government aid to Tajikistan in the period 1992–1994 included humanitarian assistance estimated at 2 billion rubles as well as support for the peace negotiations and help with the return of refugees and internally displaced persons (IDPs). Iran donated emergency aid worth US$16.5 million—for medicine, food, clothes, blankets, tents, and so forth—as well as credits and a wide range of grants for training and education. Turkey provided humanitarian assistance equivalent to US$500,000. In 1994, the United States began giving large sums of aid; this included a donation of US$50 million and a similar amount in credits, as well as large deliveries of food and other supplies worth some US$2 million. Various forms of technical assistance were provided, including training and educational programs. NGOs such as Save the Children and Aga Khan Development Network (AKDN) also received grants form the US government to implement special programs (UNDP, *Tajikistan Human Development Report 1995,* 52–53).

42. The International Committee of the Red Cross (ICRC) carried out its first mission to Tajikistan in 1992 and opened an office in Dushanbe the following year, as well as a temporary base in Khorog in the mountainous Badakhshan province to the east. In 1993, the UN High Commissioner for Refugees (UNHCR) and the UN Children's Fund (UNICEF) commenced operations; the latter was particularly concerned with the distribution of medicine and high-nutrient foods. The Belgian and Dutch branches of Medicins sans Frontiers (Doctors Without Borders), the World Health Organization (WHO), and other humanitarian organizations also had projects in Tajikistan during this period. Amnesty International produced its first report on Tajikistan in the spring of 1993. See Amnesty International, "Hidden Terror: Political Killings, 'Disappearances' and Torture Since December 1992," AI Index no. EUR 60/04/93, April 30, 1993, http://www.amnestyusa.org/document.php?id=7102D71EAD97FC85802569A6006030AE&lang=e. See also UNDP, *Tajikistan Human Development Report 1995*, 52–53. See Jean-Marc Bornet, "The International Committee of the Red Cross and the Conflict in Tajikistan," in *Tajikistan: The Trials of Independence*, eds. Mohammad-Reza Djalili, Frédéric Grare, and Shirin Akiner (London: Curzon, 1998), 219–228, for a detailed account of Red Cross activities, including its cooperation with the Tajik Red Crescent.

43. UNDP, *Tajikistan Human Development Report 1995,* 50–51.

44. UNDP, *Tajikistan Human Development Report 1998,* especially 63–78.

45. For the text of the main documents of the peace process, see *News About Peace (Documents),* compiled by Abdunabi Sattorzoda et al., the Tajikistan Commission on National Reconciliation (CNR), and the United Nations Mission of Observers in Tajikistan (UNMOT) (Dushanbe: Oli Somon Printing House, 1998).

46. The General Agreement on the Establishment of Peace and National Accord in Tajikistan was signed in Moscow in the presence of Russian President Boris Yeltsin, Iranian Foreign Minister Kamal Kharrazi, and senior officials from the UN and observer states. For an account of the peace process, see Kamol Abdullaev and Catherine Barnes, eds., "Politics of Compromise: The Tajikistan Peace Process," Accord Iss. 10 (London: Conciliation Resources, 2001).

47. *News About Peace,* 65–67.

48. According to the 2000 census, the ethnic composition of the population in that year was Tajik, 79.9 percent; Uzbek, 15.3 percent; Russian, 1.1 percent; Kyrgyz, 1.1 percent; other, 2.6 percent. See CIA, "World Factbook: Tajikistan," December 13, 2007, http://www.cia.gov/library/publications/the-world-factbook/geos/ti.html.

49. Akiner, *Tajikistan,* 7–8. For a discussion of modern Tajik identity, see Guissou Jahangiri, "The Premises for the Construction of a Tajik National Identity, 1920–1930," in *Tajikistan: Trials of Independence*, eds. Mohammad-Reza Djalili, Frédéric Grare, and Shirin Akiner (London: Curzon, 1998) 14–41. Several of the new political activists of the late 1980s, particularly those connected with parties such as Rastokez and the Democratic Party of Tajikistan, made the revival of Tajik (Iranian) culture a central plank of their programs (Akiner, *Tajikistan,* 33).

50. For a review of the careers of Rahmonov and Nuri, see Akiner, *Tajikistan,* 51–53.

51. To register, parties were required to have at least 1,000 members drawn from all parts of Tajikistan, to provide a written manifesto, and to pay a substantial registration fee.

52. OSCE, "Final Report: Elections to the Parliament 27 February 2000—Republic of Tajikistan," report prepared for the OSCE Office for Democratic Institutions and Human Rights, Warsaw, May 17, 2000.

53. OSCE, "Final Report: Elections to the Parliament 27 February and 13 March 2005—Republic of Tajikistan," report prepared for the OSCE Office for Democratic Institutions and Human Rights, Warsaw, May 31, 2005.

54. In 1988, trade accounted for 41.6 percent of Tajikistan's GDP, of which 86.3 percent was interrepublican; by 1991, the percentage of interrepublican trade had risen to 96 percent. Michael Kaser and Santosh Mehrotra, "The Central Asian Economies After Independence," paper prepared for the Post-Soviet Business Forum, Royal Institute of International Affairs, London, 1992, 63–64.

55. IMF, "Republic of Tajikistan," 8–13.

56. For surveys of the economic situation after independence, see UNDP, *Tajikistan Human Development Report 1995*, 13–23; UNDP, *Tajikistan Human Development Report 1998,* 63–83; UNDP, *Tajikistan Human Development Report 1999,* (Dushanbe: UNDP, 1999), 17–20; also IMF, "Republic of Tajikistan," 71–76.

57. Asian Development Bank (ADB), "Tajikistan: Country Strategy and Program Update 2006–2008," Manila, July 2005.

58. See, for example, ADB, "Tajikistan," particularly the section titled "Economic Assessment and Outlook." See also "Asian Development Outlook 2007," Asian Development Bank, http://www.adb.org/Documents/Books/ADO/2007/taj.pdf. Other international financial institutions (IFIs) give similarly upbeat prognoses.

59. In 2005, Tajikistan was ranked 150th out of 159 in Transparency International's annual Corruption Perceptions Index. See Jeremy Bransten, "World: UN Convention Against Corruption Takes Force," Radio Free Europe/Radio Liberty (RFE/RL), December 14, 2005, http://www.rferl.org/featuresarticle/2005/12/C844447E-7C38-4D54-A2CD-2D7FDD4F207F.html. For a review of the commercial environment in Tajikistan, see EBRD, "Strategy for Tajikistan," 49–56.

60. In 2003, 151 joint ventures were operating in Tajikistan. The main sectors were the extraction of ores and precious stones, construction, commerce, and the processing of agricultural products. See Saodat Olimova et al., *Regional Cooperation for Development of Human Capacity and Human Security in the Region of Central Asia,* 35.

61. In 1991, the central government subsidy to Tajikistan was greater than Tajik revenue from taxation. See Kaser and Mehrotra, "The Central Asian Economies After Independence," 49.

62. Shortly after independence, Tajikistan was ranked 88th out of 174 countries in the UNDP Human Development Index; in 2003 it was ranked 113th out of 175. See UNDP, *Tajikistan Human Development Report 1999*, 13; UNDP, *Tajikistan Human Development Report 2000*, 17; UNDP, *Human Development Report 2003: Millennium Development Goals—A Compact Among Nations to End Human Poverty* (New York: Oxford University Press, 2003), 239.

63. At the end of the 1990s, according to official estimates, some 33 percent of the population was very poor and almost 20 percent was destitute (that is, with a per diem income of below US$1.075 at PPP). Poverty existed in terms of not only income but also access to resources. See UNDP, *Tajikistan Human Development Report 2000*, 61; also Payam Foroughi, "Socio-Economic Survey of Households, Farms, and Bazaars in Tajikistan" (Dushanbe: USAID, 1999, unpublished).

64. See the entry for Tajikistan in EBRD, *Transition Report 2005: Business in Transition*, London, November 2005, 188. This optimistic assessment was doubted by some. However, at the formal presentation of the report in Dushanbe on January 19, 2006, a senior EBRD representative defended this finding, pointing out that much depended on the sources consulted. He added that the people's perception of the situation showed a significant and positive change. See EBRD MEMO on the Presentation of the EBRD, "Transition Report 2005: Business in Transition," prepared by the EBRD Office of the Chief Economist, London, May 2005.

65. IMF, "Republic of Tajikistan," 22–23.

66. UNDP, *Tajikistan Human Development Report 2000,* 86–90.

67. There are no reliable population statistics; most estimates range from 6.7 million to 7 million. The higher figure seems the most likely, given the habitual underreporting of births in rural areas and of babies born to unregistered multiple wives, as well as the relatively high registration fee. (See UNDP, *Tajikistan Human Development Report 1999*, 15–17; UNDP, *Tajikistan Human Development Report 2000*, 53; Margarita Khegai,

"Sovremennye formy brachnykh otnoshenii v Tadzhikistana i prava cheloveka," in *Nekotorye aspekty gendernykh issledovanii v Tadzhikstane: Sbornykh materialov nauchnyjkh seminarov* (Dushanbe: Centre for Gender Research, Tajik Branch of the Open Society Institute, 2002), 55–67.

68. See CIA, "World Factbook: Tajikistan"; see also Olimova et al., Regional Cooperation for Development of Human Capacity and Human Security in the Region of Central Asia, 6.

69. CIA, "World Factbook: Tajikistan," based on statistics given in Tajikistan's national 2000 census, estimates that 99.5 percent of the population aged fifteen years and up (99.7 percent of males and 99.2 percent of females) could read and write. UNICEF and other international agencies give similar statistics. Official sources claim that there are an average of 16.7 students per teacher—20.2 in urban areas and 15.6 in rural areas. See Olimova et al., *Regional Cooperation for Development of Human Capacity and Human Security in the Region of Central Asia*, 12–13.

70. This was supported by a loan of US$20 million from the World Bank. See IRIN News, "Tajikistan: World Bank Approves US $20 Million for Education," May 21, 2003, http://www.irinnews.org/report.asp?ReportID=34244&SelectRegion=Central_Asia&SelectCountry=TAJIKISTAN.

71. See UN Office on Drugs and Crime (UNODC), "Country Factsheet Tajikistan 2006," 2007, http://www.unodc.org/uzbekistan/en/fact_taj.html; see also Olimova et al., *Regional Cooperation for Development of Human Capacity and Human Security in the Region of Central Asia*, 62.

72. Personal discussions with members of Russian and other non-Tajik communities during research trips to Tajikistan from 2000 to 2003.

73. Since a large proportion of the migrants are illegal, no precise data is available. For a review of the situation see Olimova et al., *Regional Cooperation for Development of Human Capacity and Human Security in the Region of Central Asia*, 31–35.

74. IMF, "Republic of Tajikistan," 51–55; World Bank, "Tajikistan Trade Diagnostic Study," World Bank Report no. 32603-TJ (Washington, DC: Poverty Reduction and Economic Management Unit, Europe and Central Asia Region, December 13, 2005), 58–64.

75. The treatment of Mukhtor Boqizoda, editor-in-chief of the independent weekly *Neru-i Sukhan*, illustrates the harassment that journalists face. The newspaper was shut down by the Tajik authorities in January 2005 for alleged tax evasion. Publication was resumed on July 4, 2005, but halted again nine days later. In August the editor was accused of stealing electricity and sentenced to two years of corrective labor as well as the payment of a hefty fine. See Rustam Nazarov, "Tajikistan's Open-and-Shut Newspaper," Reporting Central Asia no. 396 (London: Institute for War and Peace Reporting, July 18, 2005), http://www.iwpr.net/?p=rca&s=f&o=255938&apc_state=henirca2005; Bruce Pannier, "Tajikistan: Crisis of Independent Media Sparks International Criticism," RFE/RL, September 9, 2005, http://www.rferl.org/featuresarticle/2005/09/7aa1d61f-272a-428c-8847-02018b928a24.html. Other independent journalists have experienced similar problems. See Michael Hall, "Tajikistan at the Crossroads of Democracy and Authoritarianism," in *Prospects for Democracy in Central Asia*, ed. Birgit N. Schlyter, (New York: I. B. Tauris, 2006), 25–40.

76. UNDP, *Tajikistan Human Development Report 1999*, 33.

77. UNDP, *Tajikistan Human Development Report 1999,* 34.
78. UNDP, *Tajikistan Human Development Report 2000,* 31.
79. UNDP, *Tajikistan Human Development Report 2000,* 31, 49.
80. UNDP, *Tajikistan Human Development Report 2000,* 48–54.
81. See further Shirin Akiner, "Prospects for Civil Society in Tajikistan," in *Civil Society in the Muslim World: Contemporary Perspectives,* ed. Amyn B. Sajoo (London: Tauris, 2002), 149–193.
82. For a comprehensive list of agency profiles, see the website of the UN Coordination Unit in Tajikistan, http://www.untj.org.
83. Over thirty foreign aid organizations are working in Tajikistan, including the Agency for Technical Cooperation and Development (ACTED), the AKDN, Caritas, Merlin, Mercy Corps, Oxfam, and the main UN agencies (UNICEF, UNDP, and so on). For the most comprehensive list available, including regional distribution, project descriptions, and sectoral breakdown, see the website of the UN Coordination Unit in Tajikistan, http://www.untj.org.
84. For detailed information on the country strategies and program updates of these IFIs and multilateral donors, see EBRD, "Strategy for Tajikistan," 37–40.
85. Personal interviews with senior UN officials, conducted in central Asia in 2004.
86. IMF, "Republic of Tajikistan," 56.
87. IMF, "IMF to Extend 100 Percent Debt Relief to Tajikistan Under the Multilateral Debt Relief Initiative," Press Release no. 05/303, December 23, 2005, http://www.imf.org/external/np/sec/pr/2005/pr05303.htm.
88. IMF, "IMF to Extend 100 Percent Debt Relief to Tajikistan Under the Multilateral Debt Relief Initiative."
89. Tajikistan was a member of the Central Asian Cooperation Organization (CACO), along with Kazakhstan, Kyrgyzstan, Russia, and Uzbekistan. The CACO went through a number of transformations in the ten years after it was founded in 1994. In October 2005, CACO leaders gathered in St. Petersburg for a summit meeting and, in a surprise move, signed a declaration merging this organization with the Eurasian Economic Community (EurAsEC). Uzbekistan, which was not originally a member of this body, acceded to EurAsEC in January 2006; it withdrew in November 2008.
90. For a history of these organizations, see Shirin Akiner, "Regional Cooperation in Central Asia," in *Economic Developments and Reforms in Cooperation Partner Countries: The Interrelationship Between Regional Economic Cooperation, Security, and Stability,* eds. Patrick Hardouin, Reiner Weichhardt, and Peter Sutcliffe (Brussels: NATO Economics Directorate, 2001), 187–208.
91. The capacity of the rapid reaction force was greatly boosted by the opening of a Russian airbase in Kyrgyzstan at Kant, about 25 kilometers from Bishkek, the capital, in October 2003.
92. The presidents of China and Tajikistan signed the final agreement on border demarcation in May 2002. See Government of the People's Republic of China, "China's Territorial and Boundary Affairs," Ministry of Foreign Affairs, June 30, 2003, http://www.fmprc.gov.cn/eng/wjb/zzjg/tyfls/tyfl/2626/t22820.htm. At the time of this writing, some outstanding issues with Uzbekistan and Kyrgyzstan remain to be resolved.
93. It is not clear who they were, but it is generally accepted that the

guerrillas were probably members of the banned Islamic Movement of Uzbekistan. See Akiner, "The Politicisation of Islam in Post-Soviet Central Asia," 108; Vitaly V. Naumkin, "Militant Islam in Central Asia: The Case of the Islamic Movement of Uzbekistan," Berkeley Program in Soviet and Post-Soviet Studies Working Paper Series (Berkeley, CA: University of California, Berkeley, July 1, 2003). See especially 38–48.

94. See Shirin Azizmamadova, "Uzbeks Clear Mines from Tajik Border," Reporting Central Asia no. 417 (London: Institute for War and Peace Reporting, October 30, 2005), http://www.iwpr.net/?p=rca&s=f&o=257316&apc_state=henirca2005.

95. World Bank, "Tajikistan Trade Diagnostic Study," 26, 38–40.

96. RIA Novosti, "Nurek Agreements to Keep Russian Space Troops Assured for Half-Century: Defense Minister," October 16, 2004, accessed at http://en.rian.ru/rian/index.cfm?prd_id=160&msg_id=4976209&startrow=1&date=2004-10-16&do_alert=0 (page now discontinued).

97. BBC News, "Inside Central Asia," April 16, 2005, http://news.bbc.co.uk/2/hi/in_depth/asia_pacific/2005/central_asia/default.stm.

98. A Partnership and Cooperation Agreement was signed between the EU and Tajikistan in October 2004. From 1992 to 2002, Tajikistan was by far the largest beneficiary of the European Union (EU), receiving more than 350 million euros, mostly in grant form; see further EU, "Ceremony for Signature of the EU-Tajikistan Partnership and Cooperation Agreement," Press Release no. 13294/04, October 11, 2004, http://ue.eu.int/ueDocs/cms_Data/docs/pressData/en/er/82200.pdf; see also The European Commission' Delegation to Kazakhstan, Kyrgyzstan, and Tajikistan, http://delkaz.ec.europa.eu/joomla/.

99. Part of this force was withdrawn from Tajikistan in November 2005. However, it was strengthened again in the spring of 2006 in support of NATO operations in Afghanistan. See RFE/RL, "Central Asia Report: May 19, 2006," http://www.rferl.org/reports/centralasia/2006/05/15-190506.asp; see also Jeremy Bransten, "World: UN Convention Against Corruption Takes Force," RFE/RL, December 14, 2005, http://www.rferl.org/featuresarticle/2005/12/C844447E-7C38-4D54-A2CD-2D7FDD4F207F.html.

100. In 2000, it was estimated that one kilogram of opium in Afghanistan cost US$30; in Western Europe, one kilogram of heroin (made from 10 kilogram of opium) cost US$150,000; overall, the retail trade in opium cultivated in Afghanistan in that year was worth US$100 billion. See Nancy Lubin, Alex Kaits, and Igor Barstein, "Narcotics Interdiction in Afghanistan and Central Asia: Challenges for International Assistance," report prepared for the Open Society Institute, New York, 2002, 5. By 2007, the average farm-gate price (weighted by production) of fresh opium at harvest time was US$86 per kilogram; of dry opium, the price was US$122 per kilogram. See UNODC, *Afghanistan Opium Survey 2007,* (Kabul: UNODC, 2007), 1.

101. See Lubin et al, "Narcotics Interdiction in Afghanistan and Central Asia."

102. Data as of January 1, 2007. See UNODC, *Compendium: Drug Related Statistics 1996–2007* (Vienna: UNODC Regional Office for Central Asia, 2007). See also annual reports of *Information Bulletin on Drug Related Situation: The Central Asian Region*, prepared by the National Information Analytical Center on Drug Control under the Cabinet of Ministers of the

Republic of Uzbekistan, supported by the OSCE, Tashkent (http: www.ncdc.uz), which collates information from all the central Asian states on drug control issues.

103. International Crisis Group (ICG), "Tajikistan: An Uncertain Peace," Asia Report series no. 30 (Brussels: ICG, December 24, 2001) 19.

104. BBC News, "Inside Central Asia," October 23, 2005, http://news.bbc.co.uk/2/hi/in_depth/asia_pacific/2005/central_asia/.

105. Author's personal communication with teachers from Kulob University, April 2000.

106. Personal communications to the author on research trips to Tajikistan in 1997, 1998. See N. Khalimova, "Ustnaya istoria i istoria zhenschshin," in *Nekotorye aspekty gendernykh issledovanii v Tadzhikstane: Sbornykh materialov nauchnyjkh seminarov* (Dushanbe: Centre for Gender Research, Tajik Branch of the Open Society Institute, 2002), 88–94, for a rare account in print of a female perspective on this period.

107. Hezb-i Tahrir (transliterated in various forms, usually translated as Liberation Party) is a transnational Islamist organization, which was created in 1953 in Jerusalem. It is now banned in many countries as a dangerously subversive organization. The movement seems to have established a presence in Uzbekistan in the early 1990s; from there it spread throughout the region. It is proscribed in all the Central Asian states. In Tajikistan, many of its members have been arrested and imprisoned. It probably has a following of around 8,000 people. For a description of the aims and tactics of the movement and its social structure, see K. Mukhabbatov, "Religiozno-oppozitsionnyje gruppy v Tadzhikistane: Khizb-ut-Tahrir," in *Religioznyj ekstremizm v Tsentral'noj Azii, Materialy konferentsii, Dushanbe, 25 aprelya 2002 g* (Dushanbe: OSCE, 2002), 72–86. For a somewhat different view of this and similar movements, see Kamol Abdullaev, "State, Islam, and Opposition in Central Asia," in *Stumbling but Struggling: Political Opposition in Former Post-Soviet Countries,* ed. Romana Careja (Moscow: Strategy Publishing House, 2004), 145–152. The Islamic Movement of Uzbekistan (sometimes called the Islamic Movement of Turkestan) is also active in Tajikistan—see Abdullaev, "State, Islam, and Opposition in Central Asia." Bayat is a much smaller organization and to date appears to operate only in Tajikistan. It was first mentioned in the Tajik press in early 2004. Its members, too, have been arrested and given long prison sentences. The avowed aim of all these movements is to create an Islamic state.

108. In 1991, for example, three Pamiris, all born in the town of Khorugh, represented very different political stances: Davlat Khudonazarov (b. 1944) stood as a candidate for the presidency of a united Tajikistan, supported by, among others, the IRP; Atobek Amirbekov (b. 1950) headed the party La'l-i Badakhshan, which advocated autonomy for Badakhshan; and Shody Shabdollov (b. 1943) led the Communist Party. A similar range of political allegiances was to be found in other regional groupings (Akiner, *Tajikistan,* 40–42).

109. Saodat Olimova, "Regionalism and Its Perception by Major Political and Social Powers of Tajikistan," in *Tajikistan at a Crossroad: The Politics of Decentralisation,* ed. Luigi De Martino (Geneva: CIMERA Situation Report 4, January 2004), 85–118.

110. In 1991, more than two-thirds of Tajikistan's industrial enterprises

were located here; the province contributed 37.5 percent to the republic's GDP. By 1996, this had fallen to 16.3 percent. Thereafter it gradually recovered, and in 2002 its share in the national GDP was 36.4 percent. See Alijon Boymatov, "Economic Relations Between Centre and Periphery: The Case of Sughd Province," in *Tajikistan at a Crossroad: The Politics of Decentralisation* ed. Luigi De Martino (Geneva: CIMERA Situation Report 4, January 2004), 47–85 (see especially p. 48).

111. Boymatov, "Economic Relations Between Centre and Periphery," 63–65.

112. In 2002, annual GDP per capita in Soghd stood at US$216; this was higher than the national average (US$182) but still less than 40 percent of the level in 1991. Boymatov, "Economic Relations Between Centre and Periphery," 48.

113. Gulchehra Mansurova, "Ecological Migration in Tajikistan: In the Name of People's Life," [*sic*] *Tajikistan Economic Review* 23, no. 61 (December 1998).

114. In September 2001, a senior representative of the UN World Food Programme (WFP) warned that over 1 million people in Tajikistan were at risk of starvation; there was a deficit of 341,000 metric tons of grain for the coming winter. The drought, which began in 2000, was the worst in seventy-five years (UNDP, *Tajikistan: Human Development Report 2000*, 78). In the event, however, these fears were not realized: there were food shortages, but not of a critical, life-threatening nature. For regular updates on humanitarian emergencies caused by natural disasters in Tajikistan, see regional reports by UN Office for Coordination of Humanitarian Affairs (OCHA), particularly IRIN News reports (available at www.irinnews.org)—for example, "Tajikistan: Climate Change Threatens Livelihoods of Mountain Villagers," June 2007, http://www.alertnet.org/thenews/newsdesk/IRIN/12ba718922687l9599a1659079095fc8.htm; see also the Situation Reports of the Disaster Relief Emergency Fund (DREF) of the International Federation of Red Cross and Red Crescent Societies, for example, "Tajikistan: Earthquake and Floods," July 2007, http://www.ifrc.org/docs/appeals/rpts07/EarthquakeRashtIB.pdf.

115. Located in central Gorno-Badakhshan, the lake formed when the river Murghab was blocked as a result of the 1911 earthquake. It now holds 10,000 cubic kilometers of water; see IRIN News, "Lake Sarez Disaster Preparedness Proceeding Well," May 23, 2007, http://www.irinnews.org/report.aspx?ReportID=72328.

116. Olimova et al., Regional Cooperation for Development of Human Capacity and Human Security in the Region of Central Asia, 39–41.

117. Brenninkmeijer, "International Concern for Tajikistan," 193.

118. Brenninkmeijer, "International Concern for Tajikistan," 206.

119. Brenninkmeijer, "International Concern for Tajikistan," 193.

120. UNDP, *Tajikistan Human Development Report 2000*, 91.

121. As of May 2006, these were the Democratic Party, the Islamic Revival Party, the Social Democratic Party, the Socialist Party, and the Communist Party.

122. See, for example, Hall, "Tajikistan at the Crossroads of Democracy and Authoritarianism," 25–39.

123. Abdullaev, "State, Islam, and Opposition in Central Asia," 154.

124. Brenninkmeijer, "International Concern for Tajikistan," 206.

125. See Jean-Nicolas Bitter et al., *Postroenie doveriya mezhdu islamistami i sekulyaristami—tadzhiksii eksperiment* (Dushanbe: Devashtich, 2004).

12

Conclusion

Neclâ Tschirgi, Michael S. Lund, and Francesco Mancini

The contributors to this volume set out to examine the utility—as well as the limits—of the call to integrate security and development policies as part of the evolving international agenda to assist developing countries at risk of conflict. Because security and development studies proceeded on separate tracks during much of the Cold War, it is only since the 1990s that a robust body of knowledge has begun to develop on their linkages and interdependence. This study was designed to contribute to the evolving body of knowledge, policy, and practice by examining the actual interplay between security and development.

We approached security and development empirically, from a thematic as well as a country-specific perspective. While Chapters 1 through 4 examine the interconnections among poverty, environmental, and demographic pressures, insecurity, and underdevelopment, the subsequent seven case studies investigate a broader range of factors that account for the commonalities and differences in their subjects' security and development attainments. The overriding objective of this approach was to go beyond the equally unhelpful assertions that (1) development and security are always interdependent and that (2) each country case is unique.

Collectively, the eleven chapters provide useful insights on the complex and variable interplay among a host of factors in contributing to insecurity and underdevelopment. Three main conclusions help to frame the discussion that follows. First, although their authors do not claim to identify direct causal linkages, the thematic chapters underscore the heightened security and development risks of certain socioeconomic and environmental trends. The effects of these trends accumulate over time and require long-term investments and sustained policy interventions to be reversed. Second, the country case studies demonstrate that security and development are related in multiple configurations and are mediated through local political processes and institutions, thus leading to different outcomes in different countries. At that level, political uncertainty and instability emerge as pivotal causes rather than mere consequences of development failures and insecurity. Third, the case studies confirm that external trends and policies at both the regional and global levels have far-reaching influence on the development and security achievements of individual countries—significantly constraining or expanding their options. These findings bring into question some of the orthodoxies underlying international policy responses to violent conflict and insecurity in many developing countries, and thus they call for more differentiated and locally grounded approaches. The following sections elaborate on the main conclusions from the volume and extract their broader policy implications.

Poverty, Environment, and Demography: Critical Connectors

Although the thematic chapters do not claim direct causal relations between poverty-based, environmental, and demographic pressures on the one hand and conflict on the other, they do point to a number of important potential connections that constitute identifiable risk factors. Recognizing the strong statistical correlation between poverty and civil war, Sakiko Fukuda-Parr presents the main structural explanations of violent conflict. These include low incomes and stagnant growth, horizontal inequalities and social exclusion, environmental pressures and competition over resources, dependence on primary commodities, demographic structures, the youth bulge, and neighborhood effects. But even as she shows how conflict impedes development, she notes that current treatments of the so-called conflict-poverty trap are neither universally accepted nor conclusive. In fact, the multidimensional nature of conflict and development militates against simple mechanistic explanations. Thus, Fukuda-Parr makes a strong plea for a synthesis of various approaches to gain a fuller understanding of the cumulative consequences of development failures and of the extent to which current development policies may increase conflict risks and perpetuate stagnation. In her words, "The development cooperation agenda is not designed to deal effectively with the dynamics of poverty and conflict; its logic even leads to policies that are perverse, often achieving the opposite of what is needed in terms of priorities for aid allocation among countries, criteria for evaluating aid effectiveness, and approaches for engaging with fragile states about aid."

In Chapter 3, Richard Matthew argues against the assumption that environmental change is directly linked to insecurity and low development, noting that environmental factors come into play in indirect ways. Environmental degradation can invite or exacerbate violent conflict, contribute to vulnerability and inequity, and bolster infectious disease. Moreover, policy responses involve complex feedback loops that can lead to unanticipated outcomes. But conflicts often have long histories going beyond environmental stress. Research on resource scarcities and the resource curse has provided a growing understanding of how environmental factors contribute to conflict in different contexts. However, Matthew points out that explanations involving both the scarcity-conflict link and the resource curse tend to downplay—if not explicitly deny—the capacity of communities at all levels to adapt to many forms of stress, including environmental stress. Human history, he adds, records few Easter Islands—that is, states that disappear due to environmental stress and violence—and many Rwandas, or states that eventually overcome environmental stress and violence (albeit at very high costs).

One of the most fruitful insights Matthew unearths from the extensive literature on environmental stress is the interplay between vulnerability and resilience. As he explains, there is "a growing recognition that social vulnerability is latent in human systems prior to the onset of an environmental stress: disaster occurs when stress exceeds the coping capacity of the human system." Thus, an important conclusion concerns the relationship between stresses and coping capacity. Initially, concepts such as the population explosion and the youth bulge have served as entry points for understanding demographic and environmental conflict issues. Operating within general population trends, demographic (including gender) inequities have also emerged as critical factors.

Framing these issues in terms of inequality involves recognizing their different consequences for regions or social groups that are more vulnerable to stresses. For example, climate change is more likely to place burdens on poor and fragile communities, since they lack the resilience to adapt and the capacity to mitigate effects. As a result, equity-based responses to global environmental change must go beyond technical solutions. Conservation efforts designed to protect living systems for sustainable development, for example, have at times generated conflict and insecurity, especially for the poor. Similarly, strategies to address climate change that are not accompanied by broad support for poverty alleviation and appropriate adaptation technologies are likely to contribute to human insecurity and conflict.

In Chapter 4, Richard Cincotta identifies several conditions and trends of a demographic nature that affect security and development: a youthful age structure; the declining availability of natural resources; the rapid growth of and deteriorating human conditions in urban slums; high rates of death in the working-age population (largely from HIV/AIDS); demographic aging and population decline; differential population growth rates among ethnic populations; cross-border and domestic migration; and an unusually high marriage-age sex ratio that demonstrates the demographic dominance of males. Among these, there is strong evidence to indicate that countries with very youthful age structures have an elevated risk of experiencing conflict. In each decade since 1970, 80 to 85 percent of all civil conflicts involving the state emerged in countries experiencing a youthful age structure.

Cincotta notes that "both controlled and comparative studies suggest that the conflict-risk levels associated with a large youth bulge are of roughly similar magnitude to risks associated with low levels of economic development or with high levels of infant mortality—around 2.3 times that of background risks." But although it is a clear risk factor, youthful age structure is neither a necessary nor sufficient condition for the initiation of political violence. Nor do declines in the youth bulge affect ongoing civil war. Current research indicates that civil violence tends to persist long after a country's age structure has matured. However, there are indications that increasing maturity, along with economic development, does make recruitment for fighters more difficult and affects the conflict environment. The impact of other demographic factors on conflict is also at best indirect. For example, although countries with a high rate of urban population growth were about twice as likely as other states to experience an outbreak of civil conflict in the 1990s, this statistic was inseparable from the risks associated with low per capita income. Nonetheless, Cincotta argues that these demographic factors are not unimportant: "They can and often do produce stresses that seriously impede social and economic development, widen rifts between regional and ethnic groups, confine communities and families to poverty, and erode the legitimacy of governments."

In short, poverty, environment, and demography are critical determinants of security as well as development insofar as their interplay creates or exacerbates societal vulnerabilities. Policy interventions are needed on multiple levels to reduce particular vulnerabilities as well as strengthen societal resilience and institutional capacities. For example, steady investments in gender, education, and youth employment can build social and institutional resilience as well as retard or reverse potentially dangerous demographic trends. Although these measures take a long time to show results, they set into motion new dynamics that can help alleviate stresses such as rural-urban migration, extreme urbanization, and environmental degradation. Similarly, equity-based approaches to poverty and environmental degradation not only contribute to development but also potentially enhance security by reducing vulnerabilities at the individual or societal levels.

If vulnerability and resilience together provide a key to understanding how broad factors such as environmental and demographic changes affect development and security, what determines the extent to which particular societies are able to cope with such changes effectively? The seven country studies present a range of experiences to help us examine this question.

Divergent Trajectories in Security and Development

Before we turn to the sources of the seven countries' varying attainments, it is instructive to compare the attainments themselves and the dynamics between security and development in each case. A comparison of their profiles reveals that the countries differ greatly, that their security problems have changed in important ways over time, and that their differing courses have been highly contingent on actions taken at the domestic and international levels. As is consistent with findings from the statistical research covered in Chapter 2, we see that there is a clear correlation over the long term between security and development in all seven countries. The two more developed countries (Namibia and Guyana) have attained greater peace while the least secure (Somalia and Guinea-Bissau) have seen the least development. However, in the short and medium terms, the case studies trace distinct trajectories in the relationship between security and development as intermediated by other factors.

Among the seven countries, the most successful in attaining relative security and development is Namibia. As Bauer and Keulder note, having obtained its independence in 1990 after a long armed struggle, Namibia by and large enjoys "a modicum of development success despite stark inequalities of wealth and income among a diverse population, continued heavy reliance on primary commodities, shortages of key natural resources such as arable land and water, ongoing struggles against poverty and disease, and the demands of democratic transition and consolidation." Meanwhile, relative peace and security have been maintained in spite of the country's participation in two regional wars, an attempted secession by an armed rebel movement, border disputes with Botswana and South Africa, and an influx of refugees from Angola. Various factors have contributed to Namibia's ability to address pressing domestic problems without conflict: the post–Cold War geopolitical transitions in southern Africa, the international community's close involvement in Namibia's independence struggle and peace process, generous donor assistance postindependence, and increased regional cooperation following South Africa's democratic transition. As a result, Namibia was able to overcome a violent history to become "a functioning state with sufficient extractive, coercive, and symbolic capacity to incorporate all significant social groupings and suppress potential violent challenges to the government and the nation." Thus, of the seven countries, Namibia has come closest to escaping the conflict-poverty trap and provides insights to guide policy.

Somalia's trajectory as a state sharply contrasts with that of Namibia. Since the 1990s, following thirty years of independence, its economy and security have deteriorated to the point of civil war and state collapse. In the process, Somalia has witnessed, in Kenneth Menkhaus's words, the "continuing devolution of warfare to lower and lower levels of clan lineages." This fragmentation of power has created successive challenges to peacebuilding and statebuilding. And insecurity in Somalia has only been exacerbated by growing exposure to both terrorist activity and the counterterrorist strategies of the US and regional allies. Nevertheless, Menkhaus shows that even in the grip of the conflict-poverty trap and the absence of a central government, "evolving local interests in basic public order and the revival of commerce" reflect Somalia's potential "to slow, if not reverse, the vicious circle of insecurity and underdevelopment." Indeed, lacking a state, the country has been ruled by shifting coalitions of clans, clerics, and businessmen. They operate their own courts, security forces, and locally administered infrastructure and services. Meanwhile, an urban-based, private commercial economy under the control of particular clans and warlords has emerged in the economic centers. It has generated export diversification and small-scale manufacturing; facilitated the building of roads, ports, and other infrastructure, including communication networks; and led to the establishment of health and social services, supplemented where feasible by humanitarian aid from international agencies and nongovernmental organizations (NGOs). The situation in Somalia remains extremely fluid and precarious following successive failures by a range of groups (with external support) to establish and expand political control.

The other five countries arrange themselves along a spectrum between these two extremes. Guinea-Bissau provides a classic example of the security consequences of failing to address the connections among chronic development problems, political tensions, and diminishing state capacities. Guinea-Bissau's problems have been long in the making. Following its independence in 1974, the country made little progress toward development as it struggled with multiple coups and a short civil war in 1998 and 1999. Already an extremely poor country, Guinea-Bissau was never able to recover from the devastation wrought by the war. However, as Joshua Forrest notes, it was less the war than recurrent factional fighting among leaders that hampered Guinea-Bissau's efforts to address chronic socioeconomic problems; led to migration flows, urban food shortages, and infrastructural inefficiencies; and generated the growing budget deficits and excessive debt that have shaped the country's current predicament. After thirty years as an independent state, it is still one of the world's poorest nations and now faces a threat from narcotraffickers, whose proceeds are estimated to exceed the country's total gross domestic product (GDP). As a result, it is not the risk of another civil war that confronts Guinea-Bissau today but chronic poverty and the capture of its weak state by criminal networks.

Although it has also experienced civil war, Yemen currently faces different problems. Following its unification in 1990 and a short civil war in 1994, Yemen has had to tread a difficult course between, in Bonnefoy and Detalle's words, "regional and international security pressures on the one hand and domestic priorities on the other." Like Guinea-Bissau, Yemen is a low-income, low-human-development country that faces mounting domestic problems, including widespread poverty; rapid population growth; a heavily armed population; social, economic, and religious cleavages; and endemic urban and rural violence—all as it is trying to democratize. Since September 11, 2001, its government has come under intense pressure to play an active role in the US-led global war on terror, a scenario that constitutes the so-called security paradox. The authors argue that by responding to external pressures, the government risks undermining the country's social and political equilibrium and fragile democratization process, thereby increasing its own insecurity. Yet the country is heavily dependent on external assistance to solve its domestic problems. Thus, it is caught in a difficult predicament as it tries to manage competing and even conflicting pressures.

As neighbors and former Soviet republics, Kyrgyzstan and Tajikistan share many features. Interestingly, however, they have followed divergent trajectories since independence and experienced different security challenges. Shortly after the Soviet Union was dissolved in 1991, Tajikistan fell into unrest, followed by a six-year civil war. As Shirin Akiner explains, the roots of the conflict go back to the decline of the Soviet economy, but the Tajik civil war erupted in the power vacuum created by the collapse of the Soviet Union. It extracted a heavy human and financial toll and exacerbated the country's economic problems, although the comprehensive peace treaty has held since 1997. Although it is still considered a high-risk country, Tajikistan's return from the brink has been notable. With strong external assistance and economic reforms, Tajikistan was able to reverse its negative economic growth, registering a growth rate of 10.6 percent in 2004. Today, the country faces many uncertainties and new challenges for security and development, including drug trafficking, militant Islam, and cronyism.

Although Kyrgyzstan, too, faced the near collapse of its economy, it did not experience widespread violent conflict following its separation from the Soviet Union in 1991. However, notes Anara Tabyshalieva, the country is increasingly facing latent conflict on several fronts. At the community level, ethnic and subethnic conflicts have been rising over the distribution of irrigated land and water, political power, and economic assets. At the national level, the nonviolent March 2005 revolution erupted due to the uneven distribution of wealth and power, widespread unemployment, and poor governance. Since then, the country has faced growing internal and external problems compounded by the uncertainties of its political transition. At the regional level, Kyrgystan is affected by problems relating to neighboring Uzbekistan as well as to spillover of political rebels and refugees from other neighboring states. In addition to its location in an unstable region, Kyrgyzstan is also increasingly influenced by rivalries between Russia, China, and the United States.

Finally, Guyana lies just above the cutoff point for low-income countries. It enjoys medium human development and actually scores the highest of the seven countries on the human development index. However, it has been afflicted by recurrent political conflict and violence. Perry Mars maintains that signs of instability and insecurity have been increasing, among them

> the existence of deep ethnic and political polarization; the economic discontent affecting major ethnic sections of society and the generalized poverty from which rebel recruitment and mobilization spring; security forces that are weak, undermanned, underfunded, and outgunned compared to criminal gangs; the politicization of narco- and other criminal forms of gangsterism; arms trafficking and stockpiling by politicized groups; and intransigence on the parts of both the government and the opposition.

Guyana's rising security problems seem directly traceable to a political system that essentially sponsors a zero-sum contest for political power among competing groups while perpetuating economic inequalities based on ethnic cleavages.

Explaining Security and Development Trajectories

The case study chapters detail the unique mix of factors that has influenced the level of and interplay between security and development in each country. They display the rich fabric of local and national dynamics (such as substate politics and local conflict management capacities) that influence country-specific outcomes, identifying the particular circumstances that enable certain factors to serve as escalators or de-escalators of violence. However, the divergent and changing security trajectories of the seven countries also raise an important question for policymakers. What factors may be of greatest importance in accounting for differences in states' ability to deal with security risks and develop? The answer to this question may help policymakers shape appropriate responses to promote both security and development. From among the range of factors identified in Chapter 1, the seven case studies point to three sets of factors that may determine the extent to which certain countries are more vulnerable than others and explain why some have proved more effective in addressing and overcoming security risks and development challenges. The first set of factors relates to the long-term socioeconomic and environmental dimensions of development covered in the thematic chapters. The second set involves the context-specific political dynamics and institutional features of the seven countries examined here. And the third set of factors concerns the regional and international dynamics over which a given country has only limited influence. We will now elaborate upon these findings and address their policy implications in the final section of this chapter.

Socioeconomic and Environmental Factors

A comparative review of the physical environments, demographic stresses, ethnic compositions, and levels of poverty and inequality in the seven countries provides a mixed picture of their importance relative to other factors.

Physical environment and natural resources. According to the case studies presented here, there is no uniform pattern to discern in the role the physical environment (defined as a combination of location, terrain, and climate) plays in vulnerability to conflict. The countries examined are all geographically small or medium-sized. Tajikistan and Kyrgyzstan are landlocked countries, while the others lie on the seacoast. They all have temperate climates conducive to agriculture and inhospitable physical terrains. Moreover, they are all periodically subject to some type of natural disaster, such as droughts and windstorms, floods, earthquakes, landslides, and insect plagues. Yet their physical similarities do not ensure similar security and development experiences. For example, both more peaceful and developed countries like Namibia and Guyana and highly insecure and impoverished ones like Somalia and Guinea-Bissau have access to the sea as well as areas inhospitable to development.

Natural-resource endowments help somewhat to explain the different levels of security and development in the seven countries. Given their heavy reliance on agriculture and subsistence economies, competition over scarce local resources such as land and water has fueled localized conflicts within each country. Land tenure issues, often linked to political rights and representation, are a constant source of tension. However, there is limited evidence of interstate or intrastate conflict over natural resources, and nowhere has such conflict affected their differences. Of the seven countries, unstable Somalia is the most resource poor, but it is followed by more peaceful Kyrgyzstan, while the rest all have potentially valuable but underexploited mineral, forest, oil, and/or water resources. Excluding Namibia, Guyana, and Yemen, underground resource reserves are either untapped or only partially tapped. Some offshore oil resources, like those in Guinea-Bissau, have been contested, but to a degree that falls short of armed conflict. Several of the countries rely on certain exportable mineral assets (such as oil and gas in Yemen, oil in Namibia, gold in Kyrgyzstan, and bauxite in Guyana) for large portions of their GDP. Such assets shape the basic structures of their economies and societies and make them vulnerable to fluctuating global prices and resulting social tensions, as in Guyana and Kyrgyzstan. Uniquely, in Namibia, government control of rich diamond resources has been a source of stability. In the central Asian states, interdependence as a function of natural resource monopolies has generally served to foster peaceful equilibrium, as seen in the exchanges of water and power between small Kyrgyzstan and Tajikistan on the one hand and larger Uzbekistan and Kazakhstan on the other.

Demographic stresses. As discussed in Chapter 4, population pressures are widely considered to hurt development and increase the risk of conflict. Yet in these seven countries, neither population density nor youth bulge shows a consistent relationship to low development or insecurity. Ranging in population size from three-quarters of a million (Guyana) to 21 million (Yemen), the seven countries have relatively low population densities and differ significantly in terms of their average growth rates, from 0.02 percent (Guyana) to 3.7 percent (Yemen). Guinea-Bissau and Tajikistan have low population growth rates. Namibia is a clear exception, since its population growth declined rapidly from 1991 (3.1 percent) to 2001 (2.6 percent) due to the impact of HIV/AIDS. But, both the poorer and more violent countries (Somalia and Yemen) and the relatively better off and more secure countries (Guyana and Kyrgyzstan) have high population growth.

Also believed to have some impact on security and development goals is a large number of unemployed young people, especially men. The populations of all seven countries have high percentages of people under the age of fifteen. However, this impact seems to be significantly mitigated by out-migration, particularly in Yemen, Tajikistan, Guyana, Guinea-Bissau, and Somalia. In fact, in all seven countries, diaspora remittances constitute a significant contribution to national income, providing both a safety valve and cushion that reduces the impact of unemployment and low household incomes.

At the same time, the effects of large movements of populations in the form of urban migration, refugee flows, and internal displacement have created social strains in all cases—and most prominently in conflict-torn countries such as Guinea-Bissau, Tajikistan, Yemen, and Somalia. Yemen's economy was adversely affected by the return of Yemeni workers from neighboring Arab states after the 1991 Gulf War and by the internal displacement caused by its short civil war. In

Kyrgyzstan, squatter communities of rural migrants grew up around Bishkek after the end of Soviet-era residence restrictions. These likely contributed to the events that deposed President Akayev in March 2005 as well as to the periodic protests since then. In the south of Kyrgyzstan, a large number of people who fled from the war in Tajikistan still have not been settled. Those who fled into Kyrgyzstan in 2005 after the Andijan crisis in Uzbekistan were a source of tension between the two governments. The potential effect on Tajik politics of the workers returning from Russia has yet to be seen. In contrast once again, Namibia has not experienced political tensions despite its high rate of rural-to-urban migration. In sum, the case studies confirm that population pressures are a potentially important but not definitive risk factor.

Ethnic composition. It is hypothesized that the relative size and depth of group cleavages within a population impact security. In the seven countries, however, the extent to which populations are ethnically homogeneous does not correspond consistently to levels of security or development. Instead, several patterns emerge. Ethnically homogeneous Somalia and Yemen have had civil wars and recurrent intragroup violence along clan and tribal lines. On the other hand, since independence, heterogeneous Namibia has been peaceful, thus illustrating, according to Bauer and Keulder, "that ethnic conflict is by no means a natural consequence of ethnic diversity." Even so, ethnically heterogeneous Guinea-Bissau has experienced a civil war. Meanwhile, Kyrgyzstan, Tajikistan, and Guyana represent ethnic-dominant countries, where large ethnic groups coexist among several minorities. Whereas Kyrgyzstan has been relatively peaceful, Tajikistan has experienced a brutal civil war. However, Shirin Akiner notes that war was characterized by "blurred and fluid allegiances" rather than ethnic or regional divides. Guyana is a classic case of ethnic dominance, with almost 75 percent of its population composed of two large groups of Indians and blacks (the first of which is somewhat larger than the second) in addition to several considerably smaller settler groups and indigenous peoples. Yet, as Perry Mars explains, Guyana has not experienced a major war, even though ethnic factors consistently fuel political tensions. In comparative perspective, the variations in ethnic composition do not appear to constitute a consistent determinant of particular security or development differences independent of other factors such as economic disparity or political mobilization, which remain to be discussed.

Poverty and inequality. Poverty is a consistent reality across the countries, including Namibia and Guyana. However, because it has been widespread and persistent over time, it is not the fact but the character of poverty that emerges as the potential risk factor. Conforming to the analysis provided by Fukuda-Parr and the theory of horizontal inequalities, all the case studies confirm that disparities across regions, ethnic or identity groups, and the rural-urban divide matter more than the mere prevalence of poverty. This is most sharply demonstrated by the case of Guyana, where, according to the 2006 Poverty Reduction Strategy Paper (PRSP), 33 percent of the population lives below the poverty line, with 18 percent living in extreme poverty. Steep inequalities are demarcated along both class and ethnic lines. Eighty-eight percent of the Afro-Guyanese population and 43 percent of Amerindians occupy the lowest rungs of the economic ladder, compared with 33 percent of East Indian Guyanese. This disparity is reflected in the high incidence of political and civil unrest among the economically depressed Afro-Guyanese communities. Nevertheless, notes Perry Mars, this unrest has not evolved into civil war, apparently due to certain mitigating factors we will review.

Surprisingly, another case of severe inequality is Namibia. Bauer and Keulder show that Namibia's extremely high level of income inequality is compounded by huge geographic disparities. While the government does not use racial categories in its official population census, taking region as a proxy for race/ethnicity reveals that the bulk of historically disadvantaged Namibians live in the northern regions of the country, including Caprivi, which has a low regional life expectancy of 32.6 years. It is also the region that experienced a brief armed uprising in 1999.

On the other hand, in Yemen, where poverty is primarily rural, some of the poorest areas have been spared violence due to their sheer isolation from national political and security crises. Rather, it is the fast economic growth in urban areas that has contributed to a sense of increasing inequality and caused rising social and economic tension. Bonnefoy and Detalle note that this trend was reflected in the riots occurring in July 2005 over a reduction in fuel subsidies, which left some fifty people dead and hundreds wounded. Meanwhile, the Yemenis' reliance on the informal sector, community loans, and self-help mechanisms helps to explain why risk factors such as accelerating urbanization and rising urban poverty have not led to large-scale crime and insecurity. Thus, the Yemeni case also shows that low income does not automatically translate into impoverishment. In this case, the poor had historically developed coping mechanisms and resilience with little support from the state. However, the breakdown of traditional coping mechanisms—usually due to violent conflict, environmental and economic crisis, and/or instability—emerges as an important factor in the equation of poverty with insecurity. Thus, the war of 1998–1999 in Guinea-Bissau led to massive food insecurity along with displacement and external migration. Meanwhile, Kyrgyzstan and Tajikistan provide interesting examples insofar as they had historically enjoyed far-reaching social protections under the Soviet system. The economic collapse, social erosion, and rise in corruption both countries have seen since independence partly explain their rising insecurity, although only the latter fell into a major war.

Political and Institutional Factors

As this discussion demonstrates, socioeconomic and environmental factors have generated serious pressures and vulnerabilities in all seven countries. However, these factors fall short of explaining the major insecurity that exists in some instances and not in others. The case studies point to another set of factors relating to a country's political arrangements and institutions that appear to be more pivotal. As noted in Chapter 1, the nature of the state is considered a powerful explanatory variable in the academic literature on conflict and development. Similarly, the dynamics of state formation consistently emerge as critical in the case studies. The role of democratization remains limited, largely due to the fragility of the process as it is unfolding among the seven countries.

All seven countries are relatively new states. The oldest is Somalia, which became independent in 1960, while the youngest are Namibia, Kyrgyzstan, and Tajikistan which are post–Cold War states. More than longevity, however, the nature of each state's initial formation, combined with its subsequent ability to engage with substate political actors, appears to correlate closely with the level of stability and security it has attained. Because factors having to do with political transition loom large in all cases, their similarities and differences deserve closer attention. Namibia is at one end of the spectrum; one of the newest states, it is also the most stable. Somalia is at the other end, having become stateless after more than three decades of independence. From a comparative perspective, the seven countries display three distinct patterns with regard to the nature of their transition to self-rule: (1) gradual, managed transition from colonial rule to democratization; (2) abrupt and unexpected independence; (3) prolonged, incomplete state formation. In each case, the transitional phase shaped the ability of the postindependence state to consolidate enough political authority to enact effective economic and social development policies.

The countries that were institutionally better prepared for self-rule were more likely to channel political struggles for power along nonviolent paths, allowing them to begin earlier the task of addressing domestic problems. Namibia and Guyana experienced managed transitions to independence and democracy that are reflected in their relative security—although Namibia also benefited from changing Cold War dynamics and hands-on involvement by international actors. Unique among the seven cases is the fact that, long before power was handed over to Namibians, there was agreement on the core features of the political system. Despite regular elections since 1989, Namibia has functioned as a single-party state ruled by the nationalist movement SWAPO under President Sam Nujoma. In 1998, when the constitutional term of office of President Nujoma was due to expire, the ruling party amended the constitution to allow him a third term of office—a practice that in other contexts is often criticized. But Bauer and Keulder explain that "this may have been a prudent move, as presidential successions often constitute crisis points in nascent democracies." When power was eventually transferred to Nujoma's handpicked successor in March 2005, the handover was peaceful. With strong political control, the government was able to pursue a national development framework to address potentially volatile problems such as widespread poverty, inequitable land distribution, and grave income inequalities without confronting violent conflict.

Like Namibia, Guyana had a gradual transition to self-rule. However, Perry Mars demonstrates how the centralized Westminster model of parliamentary government was overlaid on an ethnically divided society, thereby planting the seeds of the country's polarized political system. Cold War politics divided the Guyanese leadership even further. As a result, ethnically based groupings became institutionalized into competing political parties. Since then, Guyana has operated as an alternating one-party state vis-à-vis an electoral winner-take-all system that heightens the country's ethnic political polarization. The state's institutions (including the military and security forces) have proved resilient enough to avert widespread conflict and to enable socioeconomic policies to address pressing problems. However, the country's polarized politics have consistently hindered efforts to contain localized and economically based ethnic violence and rising criminality.

Tajikistan and Kyrgyzstan followed an unusual path to statehood.

When the Soviet Union collapsed in 1991, both central Asian countries had a tradition of delegated government and Soviet-trained civil servants to run the new states. But when power struggles emerged within the political leadership in each country, only Tajikistan quickly fell into civil war. Without a strong central leadership and a national army, the independent Tajik republic could not manage latent regional tensions and socioeconomic collapse, and thus ensued a struggle for political power by regional and religion-based factions. An externally supported political process led to a comprehensive peace treaty in 1997. Despite regular elections, power has remained concentrated in the hands of President Rahmonov, and the institutionalization of democratic processes has been extremely slow. Nevertheless, the peace accord has held for ten years and the peacebuilding process has led to sustained economic progress.

Kyrgyzstan, on the other hand, avoided civil war. Yet even as he proudly enacted liberal economic and political reforms, President Akayev increasingly consolidated the powers of the presidency, mobilized government resources to maintain patronage networks, and alienated opponents. In fourteen years, Akayev removed seven prime ministers and pushed through several constitutional amendments to increase presidential powers at the expense of the parliament. The reaction to the Akayev regime gathered force over time, with mass social protests and political instability; but it was the 2005 parliamentary elections that triggered the March 2005 revolution leading Akayev to flee the country suddenly. Corruption, patronage, and increasing authoritarian rule have proved difficult to reverse under the new president, Kurmanbek Bakiyev.

Of the seven countries, Guinea-Bissau, Yemen, and Somalia were the least prepared for independence and continue to struggle to create effective political authority at the center. Upon independence from Portugal, Guinea-Bissau was united under the PAIGC party, a political outgrowth of the liberation movement. However, because the rules of the political game were not institutionalized, rivalries soon broke out within the ruling elite, composed of the army and the PAIGC. These factional struggles have continued ever since and help to explain the fragility of the postindependence state.

Yemen also had difficulty creating effective central institutions due to its divided history. North Yemen was ruled by the Zaydi Imamate until a Nasserist military takeover in 1962, whereas South Yemen was a British colony until 1967. Fueled by regional and international Cold War politics, the ensuing civil war between republicans and royalists continued until 1970 and led to the emergence of two republics. When they were finally unified in 1990, they had already experienced two wars (in 1972 and 1979), continuous cross-border guerrilla activities, and various plots and assassinations. Thus, although Yemen has made some progress toward unifying power at the center, its process of state formation has been greatly complicated by separate ideologies, institutions, and leadership as well as continuing factionalism. Moreover, as Bonnefoy and Detalle demonstrate, Yemen's political transition has consistently been undermined by external factors that have hampered the central government's efforts at political accommodation with subnational actors.

Somalia resembles Yemen in that it has had to deal with the consequences of being divided—in this case, between two colonial powers—and unresolved issues of political rule. British Somaliland (now northern Somalia) differed in character from Italian colonial rule in the center-south of the country. The British exercised indirect rule, which allowed traditional structures to survive, whereas Italians largely displaced or corrupted traditional authorities. When Somalia achieved independence in 1960, its newly established multiparty system proved dysfunctional. Under the autocrat Siad Barre, it quickly degenerated into a police state and was not able to create a cohesive political system. Nonetheless, Somalia's repressive regime was propped up by Cold War patrons and foreign aid. When the Cold War ended and foreign aid was frozen on human rights grounds, the regime could not survive on its own. Kenneth Menkhaus argues that establishing a central government in Somalia has proven particularly difficult because it has always been a mediated state. During the colonial and postcolonial periods, governments ceded authority over the judiciary and public sector to clan elders. Since collapse of the central state, it has proved particularly difficult to recreate an effective mediated national state.

In comparative perspective, the extent to which a country was prepared for self-rule under colonial administration and the effectiveness of the subsequent process of consolidating central political authority emerge as powerful explanations for its ability to address structural socioeconomic problems and security threats.[1] Thus, a major amendment to the current security-development discourse is the explicit inclusion of politics as a pivotal third element that vitally determines whether lasting security and development are made possible.

External Factors

Although domestic political cohesion, largely influenced by preindependence legacies, has proved paramount across the case studies, regional as well as international pressures have also played an influential role in defining domestic security and development outcomes. Situated in different regions of the world and confronted with specific geopolitical realities, the seven countries have each been affected differently by key external factors. Nonetheless, regional neighborhoods, transnational threats, and international policies stand out as consistently important.

All seven countries have faced threats to their physical security from extensive and exposed borders, ethnic affiliations across their boundaries, and periodic cross-border disputes with neighboring countries. But their degree of vulnerability has varied. In the cases of both Yemen and Somalia, neighboring countries contributed to internal strife. Yemen has seen the movement of forces and arms from Saudi Arabia in support of various clans, while the Ethiopian military has been engaged periodically in Somalia's clan rivalries. The role of the Ethiopian military in supporting the transitional government in Somalia in 2007 is an exception to the post–Cold War decline in direct engagement with neighboring countries. Although Guinea-Bissau was spared major spillover from conflicts in neighboring Senegal and Guinea, the conflict in the Senegalese southern region of Casamance fed into Guinea-Bissau's civil war in 1998 and 1999.

In other cases, regional neighbors have played a less harmful or even more positive role. In Namibia, the end of the apartheid regime in South Africa lifted a potential source of conflict and created opportunities for closer economic ties. At the same time, Namibia participated in two regional wars in Angola and the Democratic Republic of Congo. In Guyana, border disputes have recurred with Venezuela but not led to war. In Tajikistan and Kyrgyzstan, several regional factors were instrumental in discouraging major armed conflicts: their economic interdependence, use of Russian as a regional lingua franca, and membership in new regional security organizations—not to mention Russia's strong interest in avoiding the fallout from any ensuing regional conflict. Tajikistan was not affected by spillover from the civil war in neighboring Afghanistan thanks to the presence of Russian peacekeeping troops along the river that forms the boundary between the two countries.

Transnational threats are another aspect of troubled regional neighborhoods, bringing an added global dimension. All seven countries with the limited exception of Namibia face rising security threats that are global in nature and increasingly transported across borders by nonstate actors. Among these, three merit special attention: transnational organized crime, especially narcotrafficking;

cross-border movement of militants and terrorists; and radical Islamic movements. Yemen, Somalia, Kyrgyzstan, Tajikistan, Guyana, and Guinea-Bissau all struggle with one or more of these threats originating outside their borders. Tajikistan, for example, was unable to keep extremists from forming into the Islamic Movement of Uzbekistan and launching insurgencies into southern Kyrgyzstan. However, Namibia seems to be relatively shielded from these threats. What is noteworthy about transnational security threats is their potential for reinforcing domestic sources of conflict while simultaneously affecting the geostrategic interests of external actors. Thus, as is acutely reflected in the country case studies, the domestic handling of such threats is often complicated by the need to respond to externally driven pressures and policies.

As noted in individual chapters, the Cold War—or more precisely, the spillover effects thereof—had profound impacts on all seven countries. The end of the Cold War has also unleashed contradictory consequences. The civil wars in Yemen, Somalia, and Tajikistan were the consequence of changing international balances of power that affected domestic policies. Equally important, however, has been the nature of international engagement in the seven countries. The stance of international actors and the extent of their engagement has varied greatly, ranging from prolonged neglect (as in Guinea-Bissau) to peacemaking (as in Namibia and Tajikistan) to forceful intervention (as in Somalia). While this volume does not lend itself to a systematic weighing of the different kinds and degrees of engagement, it does reveal the fact that international involvement tends to be ad hoc and crisis oriented. The most poignant case is Somalia. In Chapter 6, Kenneth Menkhaus notes that international involvement in Somalia went through four distinct phases, each having a "dramatically different—and often unintended—impact on Somalia's security and development." The 1993–1994 UNOSOM was, at the time, the largest and most ambitious peace enforcement mission in UN history. Curiously, although it is generally considered a failure, its economic impact was enormous and largely positive—helping to create a business class engaged in legitimate or quasi-legitimate commerce. However, where there was concerted international strategy, as in Namibia and Tajikistan, the role of the UN and other international and regional actors was instrumental to the peace process and offers useful lessons about the potential value of robust international peacemaking and peacebuilding. In Guinea-Bissau, Guyana, Kyrgyzstan, and Yemen, international involvement has been shallower and more selective.

Traditionally, the role of international actors involves types of engagement that were driven by larger geopolitical concerns, which impacted country-level political dynamics. The policies of the Cold War blocs to influence security and development in each of the seven countries are described in the case studies. More recently, the global war on terror after September 11 has generated external pressures that are widely felt. As noted in Chapter 1, the state-based international system is in a state of flux, with new cleavages and tensions that have far-reaching ramifications. While the impact of the fallout from the changed international security environment after September 11 is not yet fully understood, several case study authors argue that the global war on terror has already negatively affected domestic security. The four countries with Muslim populations—Kyrgyzstan, Tajikistan, Yemen, and Somalia—are particularly at risk due to domestic militant movements with external links. As a result, they find themselves under strong external pressure to play a more active role in combating these movements as part of a larger security agenda. This is most acutely seen in the case of Yemen, although both Kyrgyzstan and Tajikistan also face similar pressures. In the meantime, without a central state, Somalia has become particularly open to infiltration by radical and terrorist groups. What becomes amply clear from the seven country case studies is that international geopolitical considerations and global security concerns still need to be factored into current approaches to conflict prevention in developing countries as diverse as Guinea-Bissau and Kyrgyzstan.

Extracting Broader Policy Lessons

In this study we have set out to examine the call to integrate security and development policies as a strategy for conflict prevention, particularly in countries with experiences of civil wars or of latent or sporadic violence. So far, the security-development nexus has proved a truism that inspires policymakers to make concerted efforts to overcome the established boundaries between sectorally defined institutions and policies by developing more coordinated, holistic strategies at the national and international levels. However, we have sought to go beyond this popular mantra to investigate the critical connections between security and development that are found both in research and on the ground as well as in the societal and other circumstances that produce those connections. In line with the general caution against overgeneralizing, the authors of individual chapters offer their own targeted recommendations that address issue- and country-specific challenges. The broader policy lessons that follow draw on the overall patterns that have been presented in this chapter and identify key elements for country-focused strategies. They capitalize on the studies main finding that durable and compatible security and development are achieved through cohesive and legitimate political processes that are context specific.

Structural Prevention: Rethinking Development

In its 1997 report, *Preventing Deadly Conflict,* the Carnegie Commission made a compelling case for adopting a strategy of primary prevention that addresses the structural causes and manifestations of incipient conflict.[2] The chapters in this volume demonstrate that knowledge about the security-development linkages has deepened considerably since then.

The fact that many of the broad structural risk factors have only an indirect causal relationship to conflict and stagnant development is certainly not a warrant for ignoring them in international policies or for dealing only with their manifestations. Not only are reducing poverty and other development goals important in their own terms, but they also contribute to reducing the risk of conflict and societal breakdown. To address them effectively, however, a deliberate policy of structural conflict prevention is required. This means that the dual goals variously captured by the terms *structural stability, secure development,* and *preventive peacebuilding* have to become a more explicit goal in development aid. As Fukuda-Parr convincingly argues, the main policy challenge in ensuring security is not simply accelerating development or addressing development failures. Instead, the challenge is to realign instruments of development cooperation such as funding mechanisms and debt relief with projects to alleviate the security risks that are inevitably unleashed by the development process, especially in poor societies and fragile states with weak coping mechanisms for managing rapid change.

The thematic chapters offer concrete policies that can reverse or retard the negative consequences of mounting economic, demographic, and environmental pressures through better targeted and specially tailored programs. Unfortunately, these approaches are difficult to incorporate into standard aid policies and practices. Nothing is more revealing of the continued disconnect between the security and development agendas than the publication of the UN's *2008 Least Developed Countries Report*, which approaches the development challenges of LDCs without reference to conflict and security issues.[3]

Viewing sectoral development strategies through a conflict lens requires a fundamental paradigmatic shift within the development community. As Sakiko Fukuda-Parr notes in Chapter 2, with the MDGs and so-called aid effectiveness as the main drivers of current development policies, mainstreaming conflict-sensitive programs into development planning and implementation remains an elusive goal. Thus, a strategy for effective structural conflict prevention is needed to explicitly infuse development policies with a heightened commitment to identifying and addressing security risks and thus achieve more sustainable development results.

Preventive Diplomacy at the Country Level

Beyond structural prevention, however, there is an acute need for proactive international engagement with internal processes of political accommodation, national dialogue, and conflict management at all levels of society as a prerequisite for synthesis of security and development. Given the constraints of national sovereignty, such initiatives in sustained, hands-on intrastate diplomacy are currently limited and small-scale, tending to focus primarily at the local level. Yet, countries like Namibia and Tajikistan have greatly benefited from robust international efforts to resolve major domestic political and policy problems. Examples exist of other conflict transformation initiatives in Guyana and Guinea-Bissau, and other countries with lower visibility that have produced discernible results. These experiences suggest that international actors can play an important role in mediating intrastate conflicts.

However, the international community currently does not provide adequate resources for ongoing preventive diplomacy in intrastate conflicts beyond a small number of countries. In particular, the UN's standard instruments of preventive diplomacy, good offices, mediation, and peacemaking were designed for conflicts between states and are not immediately adaptable for addressing internal conflicts. As a result, international efforts to support preventive diplomacy in countries like Yemen, Guinea-Bissau, Guyana, and Somalia have remained quite limited. Instead, there has been a proliferation of programs such as constitution building and political party assistance, which tend to be more technocratic than political in design and thus fall short of addressing the underlying political problems and tensions in a conflict-prone society. Hence, there is urgent need for more support for conflict management and preventive diplomacy at the country level. The creation of new UN institutions like the Mediation

Support Unit of the Department of Political Affairs as well as the Peacebuilding Commission are encouraging signs of the search for new tools and instruments to assist countries with domestic political problems. As of March 2008, the United Nations also has an international team of mediation experts on standby to assist in political negotiations, which represents a significant innovation.[4]

Building Capacities and Resilience

The ultimate purpose of preventive diplomacy, as suggested by the 2007 *Principles for Good International Engagement in Fragile States and Situations* of the Organization for Economic Cooperation and Development–Development Assistance Committee (OECD-DAC), is to make effective statebuilding "the central objective of international partnerships in fragile situations and countries emerging from conflict."[5] This volume has confirmed the importance of building societal and institutional mechanisms to strengthen coping capacities and resiliency in conflict-affected and fragile states. Yet the definitions of state fragility and statebuilding are far from clear.

Most fragile states are actually states in the early stages of formation. The diverse historical experiences of the seven states reviewed in this study confirm the need for country-specific approaches that are firmly grounded in the specificities of state formation in each country. The differences between chronically unstable countries like Guinea-Bissau, new states like Kyrgyzstan, weak states like Yemen, stateless societies like Somalia, and postconflict states like Namibia and Tajikistan are significant. It is counterproductive to classify uniformly a diverse group of states as fragile and to seek to buttress them through externally initiated and mandate-driven program designs such as security sector reform without an acute consciousness of how such programs can profoundly alter the domestic political dynamics of a fragile polity. Despite considerable academic literature that cautions against a technocratic approach to statebuilding, current policies still favor building the formal institutions of the state at the expense of nurturing the compact between state leaders and their societies that has historically been central to state formation.[6] The country studies in this volume and other recent literature usefully remind us that statebuilding is not necessarily peacebuilding.[7]

Moreover, the recent policy focus on statebuilding is heavily motivated by international security concerns and thus risks shortcutting the long, tortuous, and messy political processes accompanying the creation of modern states. Just as Cold War policies were partly responsible for the creation of artificially propped-up states, the post-9/11 statebuilding agenda may lead to the support of regimes that do not enjoy domestic legitimacy or, conversely, the neglect of governments are considered unstable by external actors. In both cases, statebuilding policy can be conflict inducing.

Assessment, Planning, and Monitoring through a Local Lens

Coming in the wake of the Cold War, the conflict prevention agenda initially focused primarily on the security and development concerns of individual countries at risk of conflict. However, September 11 ushered in an international dimension by bringing the hard security interests of major powers into an already complex equation. Whose security is at stake? What types of security strategies are being developed?[8] What impact will they have on conflict and security at the country level? Can the post-9/11 international peace and security agenda address the root causes of conflict and underdevelopment in specific countries? It is still too early to answer these questions definitely. There is a real danger that the concerns of the poorest and least stable developing countries will be sidelined by narrowly conceived security agendas of powerful states, as was the case during the Cold War. Several case studies in this volume document the negative fallout from such one-dimensional post-9/11 international security policies, which have generated domestic insecurity in various countries. Thus, it cannot be assumed that international security policies will necessarily support lasting security in countries that are currently facing domestic security challenges. The appropriate strategies need to be formulated through a structural conflict-prevention lens that pays due attention to those compacts between leaders and citizens that will be perceived locally as legitimate and durable.

The question that naturally follows is what kinds of concrete processes for conflict-sensitive assessment and policy planning at the country level are most likely to produce the holistic strategies that may be tailored to specific contexts, locally owned, and thus accepted as legitimate. In a nutshell, such processes involve a semistructured procedure that brings together influential governmental and nongovernmental local actors with donors to perform an assessment using one of the available conflict and fragility assessment tools.[9] It also allows for the review of existing domestic and international policies and development programs to gauge their appropriateness and formulates multisectoral strategies to be implemented and periodically evaluated in terms of realistic security and development benchmarks. In trying to forge social compacts between governments and their citizens, various country agencies and some NGOs have undertaken projects of this nature. However, more international leverage is often needed to encourage meaningful participation on the part of key local powerbrokers.

Peacebuilding as Structural Prevention

Finally, it should be noted that the UN's current policies and institutional arrangements for primary conflict prevention and postconflict peacebuilding are out of sync. Five out of the seven countries included in this volume have had violent internal conflicts, yet only Somalia remains in conflict. Although they continue to face multiple security risks and pressing development problems, the other four have not had a relapse. Roughly a decade after the end of their respective conflicts, they are not high-risk countries that qualify for postconflict support from the UN's Peacebuilding Commission. Nonetheless, as Guinea-Bissau's recent inclusion on the agenda of the Peacebuilding Commission and its latest bout of violence amply demonstrate, the underlying problems addressed by postconflict peacebuilding and conflict prevention are often similar. Having created the UN's new peacebuilding architecture, the UN and national governments are reluctant to see postconflict peacebuilding and conflict prevention as part of the same agenda because of member-state sensitivities about national sovereignty. Thus, the UN continues to deal with these as separate policy areas. By now, it is widely recognized that the challenges facing countries emerging from conflict are particularly acute and require special attention, and that postconflict peacebuilding cannot be seen as a short-term undertaking to follow a peace agreement with elections. By the same token, it needs to be accepted that conflict prevention is not simply a matter of heading off imminent crises in fragile, conflict-prone environments. Postconflict peacebuilding and primary conflict prevention are two sides of the same coin, and both need to attend to the underlying and immediate causes that generate conflict and perpetuate economic stagnation.

All in all, the current international environment provides an unusual opportunity to align development and security policies domestically and internationally. Never before in modern history have the conditions of millions of people in the poorest countries of the world occupied so high a place on the agendas of the UN, international institutions, governments, and NGOs. There is an unusual degree of agreement that what happens in the far corners of the developing world may have major implications for the rest of the world, including the most prosperous and industrialized nations. If promoted and applied in effective and locally legitimated ways with an emphasis on engendering political cohesion, a more integrated perspective on security and development could save lives and improve living standards for many more people as well as address wider international security concerns. It is hoped that this volume will not only contribute to reducing the gap between rhetoric and reality vis-à-vis the security-development nexus but also to the continuing search for differentiated, multifaceted, and grounded approaches to structural prevention in both primary prevention and postconflict settings.

Notes

1. For a similar argument, see Stefan Lindemann, "Do Inclusive Elite Bargains Matter? A Research Framework for Understanding the Causes of Civil War in Sub-Saharan Africa," LSE Development Studies Institute, discussion paper, February 2008.

2. Carnegie Commission on Preventing Deadly Conflict, *Preventing Deadly Conflict: Final Report* (New York: Carnegie Corporation of New York, 1997).

3. UN, *Least Developed Countries Report 2008: Growth, Poverty and the Terms of Development Partnership*. UN Doc. UNCTAD/LDC/2008, January 7, 2008.

4. See United Nations Department of Political Affairs, "UN Peacemaker," http://www.un.org/peacemaker.

5. For a synthesis of initial findings from the OECD-DAC's Fragile States Group on the nature of statebuilding in situations of state fragility, see "State Building in Situations of Fragility: Initial Findings," August 2008, http://www.oecd.org/dataoecd/62/9/41212290.pdf.

6. The difficulties inherent in externally supported statebuilding operations are usefully covered in *The Dilemmas of Statebuilding: Confronting the Contradictions of Postwar Peace Operations,* eds. Roland Paris and Timothy D. Sisk (London: Routledge, 2009).

7. For a recent contribution to this debate, see *Building States to Build Peace,* eds. Charles T. Call and Vanessa Wyeth (Boulder, CO: Lynne Rienner, 2008). Concomitant OECD-DAC documents also recognize the distinction between statebuilding and peacebuilding.

8. Stephen Baranyi, ed. *The Paradoxes of Peacebuilding Post-9/11* (Vancouver: University of British Columbia Press, 2008).

9. For a list of assessment tools, see "Survey of Donor Approaches to Governance Assessment," report prepared for the OECD Development Assistance Committee, February 2008.

Bibliography

Adger, Neil. "Commentary: The Right to Keep Cold." *Environment and Planning A* 36 (2004): 1711–1715.

Agyeman, J., R. D. Bullard, and B. Evans, eds. *Just Sustainabilities: Development in an Unequal World.* Cambridge, MA: MIT Press, 2003.

Ahmed, Ismail. "Remittances and Their Economic Impact in Post-War Somaliland." *Disasters* 24, no. 4 (2000): 380–389.

Akbarzadeh, Shahram. *Historical Dictionary of Tajikistan.* London: Scarecrow, 2002.

Akiner, Shirin. "Islam, the State, and Ethnicity in Central Asia in Historical Perspective." *Religion, State, and Society: The Keston Journal* 24, nos. 2–3 (June–September 1996): 91–132.

———. "The Politicisation of Islam in Post-Soviet Central Asia." *Religion, State, and Society: The Keston Journal* 31, no. 2 (2003): 97–122.

———. "Prospects for Civil Society in Tajikistan." In Amyn B. Sajoo, ed., *Civil Society in the Muslim World: Contemporary Perspectives.* London: Tauris, 2002, 149–193.

———. "Regional Cooperation in Central Asia." In Patrick Hardouin, Reiner Weichhardt, and Peter Sutcliffe, eds., *Economic Developments and Reforms in Cooperation Partner Countries: The Interrelationship Between Regional Economic Cooperation, Security, and Stability.* Brussels: NATO Economics Directorate, 2001, 187–208.

Al-Enazy, Askar Halwan. "The International Boundary Treaty (Treaty of Jeddah) Concluded Between the Kingdom of Saudi Arabia and the Yemeni Republic on June 12, 2000." *The American Journal of International Law* 96, no. 1 (2002): 161–173.

Al-Suwaidi, Jamal S., ed. *The Yemeni War of 1994: Causes and Consequences.* London: Saqi, 1995.

Anderson, Mary B. *Do No Harm: How Aid Can Support Peace—or War.* Boulder, CO: Lynne Rienner Publishers, 1999.

Archer, John. "Gender Roles as Developmental Pathways." *British Journal of Social Psychology* 23 (1984): 245–256.

Asian Development Bank. *Emerging Asia: Changes and Challenges.* Manila: ADB, 1997.

Atkin, Muriel. "The Subtlest Battle: Islam in Soviet Tajikistan." *International Journal of Middle East Studies* 23, no. 3 (Aug. 1991): 471–473.

Babadjanov, Bakhtiyar, and Muzaffar Kamilov. "Muhammadjan Hindustani (1892–1989) and the Beginning of the 'Great Schism' Among the Muslims of Uzbekistan." In Stephane Dudoignon, and Komatsu Hisao, eds., *Islam in Politics in Russia and Central Asia.* New York: Kegan Paul, 2001, 195–219.

Balmford, Andrew, Joslin L. Moore, Thomas Brooks, Neil Burgess, Louis A. Hansen, Paul Williams, and Carsten Rahbek. "Conservation Conflicts Across Africa." *Science* 291, no. 5513 (2001): 2616–2619.

Banuri, Tariq. "Human Security." In Naqvi Nauman, ed., *Rethinking Security, Rethinking Development: An Anthology of Papers from the Third Annual South Asian NGO Summit.* Islamabad: Sustainable Development Policy Institute, 1996, 163–164.

Barber, Charles. "Global Environmental Security and International Cooperation: Conceptual, Organizational, and Legal Frameworks." Paper prepared for World Resources Institute, Washington, DC, 1989.

Barnett, Jon. "In Defense of the Nation-State: Securing the Environment." *Sustainable Development* 6, no. 1 (1998): 8–17.

———. "Reclaiming Security." *Peace Review* 9, no. 3 (1997): 405–410.

———. *The Meaning of Environmental Security: Ecological Politics and Policy in the New Security Era.* London: Zed Books, 2001.

Bauer, Gretchen. "'The Hand That Stirs the Pot Can Also Run the Country': Electing More Women to Parliament in Namibia." *Journal of Modern African Studies* 42, no. 4 (2004): 479–509.

———. *Labor and Democracy in Namibia, 1971–1996.* Athens, OH: Ohio University Press, 1998.

———. "Namibia: Ushering in the Second Decade of Independence." *Africa Contemporary Record* 28 (2001–2002).

Bauer, John G. "How Japan and the Newly Industrialized Economies of Asia Are Responding to Labor Scarcity." Asia-Pacific Research Report 3. Honolulu: East-West Center, 1995, 5–12.

Besteman, Catherine, and Lee V. Cassanelli, eds. *The Struggle for Land in Southern Somalia: The War Behind the War.* Boulder, CO: Westview Press, 1995.

Bhagat, Ram B. "Religious Identity, Demography, and Social Tension in India." Paper presented at the conference Population Association of America Meeting, Atlanta, May 9, 2002.

Birikorang, Emma. "Democracy for Guinea-Bissau? An Analysis of the 2005 Presidential Elections." Kofi Annan International Peacekeeping Training Centre Paper no. 8. Accra, August 2005.

Bloom, David E., David Canning, and Jaypee Sevilla. "The Demographic Dividend: A New Perspective on the Economic Consequences of Population Change." RAND Monograph Report Series. Santa Monica, CA: RAND, 2002.

Boer, Martin, and Robin Sherbourne. "Getting the Most Out of Our Diamonds: Namibia, De Beers, and the Arrival of Lev Leviev." IPPR Briefing Paper no. 20. Windhoek: Institute of Public Policy Research, 2003.

Bongaarts, John. "Fertility Transitions in Developing Countries: Progress or Stagnation?" Poverty, Gender, and Youth Working Paper Series no. 7. New York: Population Council, 2008.

———. "Population Policy Options in the Developing World." *Science* 263, no. 5148 (1994): 771–776.

Bongaarts, John, and Susan Cotts Watkins. "Social Interactions and Contemporary Fertility Transitions." *Population and Development Review* 22, no. 4 (1996): 639–682.

Bornet, Jean-Marc. "The International Committee of the Red Cross and the Conflict in Tajikistan." In Mohammad-Reza Djalili, Frédéric Grare, and Shirin Akiner, eds., *Tajikistan: The Trials of Independence*. London: Curzon, 1998, 219–228.

Boymatov, Alijon. "Economic Relations Between Centre and Periphery: The Case of Sughd Province." In Luigi De Martino, ed., *Tajikistan at a Crossroad: The Politics of Decentralisation*. Geneva: CIMERA Situation Report 4, January 2004, 47–85.

Bradbury, Mark, Adan Yusuf Abokar, and Haroon Ahmed Yusuf. "Somaliland: Choosing Politics over Violence." *Review of African Political Economy* 30, no. 97 (September 2003): 455–478.

Brenninkmeijer, Oliver. "International Concern for Tajikistan: UN and OSCE Efforts to Promote Peace-building and Democratisation." In Mohammad-Reza Djalili, Frédéric Grare, and Shirin Akiner, eds., *Tajikistan: The Trials of Independence*. London: Curzon, 1998, 180–215.

Brock, Lothar. "Peace Through Parks: The Environment on the Peace Research Agenda." *Journal of Peace Research* 28, no. 4 (1991): 407–423.

———. "Security Through Defending the Environment: An Illusion?" In Elise Boulding, ed., *New Agendas for Peace Research: Conflict and Security Reexamined*. Boulder, CO: Lynne Rienner Publishers, 1992, 79–102.

Brower, Jennifer, and Peter Chalk. *The Global Threat of New and Reemerging Infectious Disease: Reconciling US National Security and Public Health Policy*. Arlington, VA: RAND, 2003.

Brown, Donald. "The Importance of Expressly Examining Global Warming Policy Issues Through an Ethical Prism." *Global Environmental Change* 13, no. 4 (2003): 229–234.

Brown, Lester. *Redefining National Security*, no. 14. Washington, DC: Worldwatch Institute, 1977.

Bryden, Matt. "No Quick Fixes: Coming to Terms with Terrorism, Islam, and Statelessness in Somalia." *Journal of Conflict Studies* 23, no. 2 (Fall 2003): 24–56.

Bulatao, Rudolfo A. "The Value of Family Planning Programs in Developing Countries." RAND Monograph Report Series. Santa Monica, CA: RAND, 1998.

Burnside, Craig, and David Dollar. "Aid, Policies, and Growth." *American Economic Review* 90, no. 4 (2000): 847–868.

Carapico, Sheila. *Civil Society in Yemen: The Political Activism in Modern Arabia*. Cambridge, UK: Cambridge University Press, 1998.

Carrington, William J., and Enrica Detragiache. "How Extensive Is the Brain Drain?" *Finance and Development* 36, no. 2 (June 1999): 46–49.

Chabal, Patrick. *Amílcar Cabral: Revolutionary Leadership and People's War.* New York: Cambridge University Press, 1983.

Chengappa, Raj, and Ramesh Menon. "The New Battlefields." *India Today*, January 31, 1993, 28.

Chomsky, Noam. *Hegemony or Survival: America's Quest for Global Dominance.* New York: Metropolitan, 2003.

Choucri, Nazli. *Population Dynamics and International Violence: Propositions, Insights, and Evidence.* Cambridge, MA: MIT Press, 1973.

Cincotta, Richard P. "From Ultrasound to Insurgency." *Environmental Change and Security Project Report* 11 (2005).

———. "How Democracies Grow Up." *Foreign Policy*, March–April 2008, 92–93.

Cincotta, Richard P., Robert Engelman, and Daniele Anastasion. *The Security Demographic: Population and Civil Conflict After the Cold War.* Washington, DC: Population Action International, 2003.

Cincotta, Richard P., and Elizabeth Leahy. "A Metric Characterizing Population Age Structure and Its Relation to Armed Conflict." Paper presented at the annual meeting of the International Studies Association, San Diego, CA, March 22, 2006.

Cliffe, Lionel, Ray Bush, Jenny Lindsay, and Brian Mokopakgosi. *The Transition to Independence in Namibia.* Boulder, CO: Lynne Rienner Publishers, 1993.

Collier, Paul. *The Bottom Billion: Why the Poorest Countries are Failing and What Can Be Done About It.* Oxford: Oxford University Press, 2007.

———. "Economic Causes of Civil Conflict and Their Implications for Policy." In Chester A. Crocker, Fen Osler Hampson, and Pamela Aall, eds., *Turbulent Peace: The Challenges of Managing International Conflict.* Washington, DC: United States Institute of Peace, 2001, 143–161.

———. "On the Economic Consequences of Civil War." *Oxford Economic Papers* 51 (1999): 168–183.

Collier, Paul, and David Dollar. "Development Effectiveness: What Have We Learnt?" *The Economic Journal* 114 (2004): F244–F261.

Collier, Paul, and Anke Hoeffler. "Aid, Policy, and Peace." Working Paper no. 28125. Washington, DC: World Bank, 2002.

Cortright, David, and G. A. Lopez. *The Sanctions Decade: Assessing UN Strategies in the 1990s.* Boulder, CO: Lynne Rienner Publishers, 2000.

Crocker, David A., and Toby Linden, eds. *Ethics of Consumption: The Good Life, Justice, and Global Stewardship.* Lanham, MD: Rowman and Littlefield, 1998.

Crosby, Alfred. *America's Forgotten Pandemic: The Influenza of 1918.* Cambridge, UK: Cambridge University Press, 1990.

Cross, Harry, Karen Hardee, and John Ross. "Completing the Demographic Transition in Developing Countries." POLICY Occasional Paper 8. Washington, DC: The Futures Group, 2002, 5–12.

Dalby, Simon. "Ecopolitical Discourse: 'Environmental Security' and Political Geography." *Progress in Human Geography* 16, no. 4 (1992): 503–522.

———. "The Environment as Geopolitical Threat: Reading Robert Kaplan's 'Coming Anarchy.'" *Ecumene* 3, no. 4 (1996): 472–496.

———. "Threats from the South? Geopolitics, Equity, and Environmental Security." In Daniel Deudney and Richard A. Matthew, eds., *Contested Grounds: Security and Conflict in the New Environment Politics*. Albany, NY: SUNY Press, 1999, 155–185.

Daly, Martin, and Margot Wilson. *Homicide*. New York: Aldine de Gruyter, 1988.

Department for International Development (DFID). *Regional Assistance Plan for the Caribbean*. London: DFID, June 2004, http://www.dfid.gov.uk/Pubs/files/rapcaribbean.pdf.

———. "Why We Need to Work More Effectively in Fragile States." London: DFID, January 2005.

Despres, Leo. *Cultural Pluralism and Nationalist Politics in British Guiana*. Chicago: Rand McNally, 1967.

Detalle, Renaud. "Ajuster sans douleur? La méthode yéménite." *Maghreb-Machrek* no.155 (1997): 20–36.

———. "Les islamistes yéménites et l'Etat: vers l'émancipation?" In Basma Kodmani-Darwish and May Chartouni-Dubarry, eds., *Les Etats arabes face à la contestation islamiste*. Paris: Ifri-Armand Colin, 1997, 271–298.

———, ed. *Tensions in Arabia: The Saudi-Yemeni Fault Line*. Baden Baden: Nomos Verlagsgesellschaft, 2000.

Deudney, Daniel. "Bringing Nature Back In: Geopolitical Theory from the Greeks to the Global Era." In Daniel Deudney and Richard A. Matthew, eds., *Contested Grounds: Security and Conflict in the New Environment Politics*. Albany, NY: SUNY Press, 1999, 25–57.

Dhada, Mustafah. "Guinea-Bissau: Politics, Intrigues, and Vieira's Last Stand." *Africa Contemporary Record* 26 (2002): B89–B97.

———. "Guinea-Bissau: Towards a Pluralism of Sorts." *Africa Contemporary Record* 25 (2001): B86–B97.

———. *Warriors at Work: How Guinea Was Really Set Free*. Boulder, CO: University Press of Colorado, 1993.

Diamond, Jared. *Guns, Germs, and Steel: The Fates of Human Societies*. New York: W. W. Norton, 1997.

Djalili, Mohammad-Reza, and Frédéric Grare. "Regional Ambitions and Interests in Tajikistan: the Role of Afghanistan, Pakistan, and Iran." In Mohammad-Reza Djalili, Frédéric Grare, and Shirin Akiner, eds., *Tajikistan: Trials of Independence*. London: Curzon, 1998, 119–131.

Dresch, Paul. *A History of Modern Yemen*. Cambridge, UK: Cambridge University Press, 2000.

———. *Tribes, Governments, and History in Yemen*. Oxford: Clarendon, 1993.

Dresch, Paul, and Bernard Haykel. "Stereotypes and Political Styles: Islamists and Tribesfolk in Yemen." *International Journal of Middle East Studies* 27, no. 4 (1995): 405–431.

du Bouchet, Ludmila. "La politique étrangère américaine au Yémen." *Chroniques Yéménites*, no. 11 (2004): 101–121, http://cy.revues.org/document154.html.

du Pisani, Andre. "The Role of the Military in the Formation and

Consolidation of the Namibian State." In Peter Batchelor, Kingma Kees, and Guy Lamb, eds., *Demilitarisation and Peace-Building in Southern Africa, Volume III: The Role of the Military in State Formation and Nation-Building*. Burlington, VT: Ashgate, 2004, 62–84.

Dudoignon, Stephane. "Political Parties and Forces in Tajikistan, 1989–1993." In Mohammad-Reza Djalili, Frédéric Grare, and Shirin Akiner, eds., *Tajikistan: Trials of Independence*. London: Curzon, 1998, 52–85.

Easterlin, Richard A. *Birth and Fortune: The Impact of Numbers on Personal Welfare*. Chicago: University of Chicago Press, 1987.

Ehrlich, Paul. *The Population Bomb*. New York: Ballantine, 1968.

Erasmus, Gerhard. "The Constitution: Its Impact on Namibian Statehood and Politics." In Christiaan Keulder, ed., *State, Society, and Democracy: A Reader in Namibian Politics*. Windhoek: Gamsberg Macmillan, 2000, 97–107.

Fagan, Brian. *Floods, Famines, and Emperors: El Niño and the Fate of Nations*. New York: Basic Books, 1999.

Fearon, James. "Primary Commodity Exports and Civil War." *Journal of Conflict Resolution* 49, no. 4 (2005): 483–507.

Fearon, James, and David Laitin. "Ethnicity, Insurgency, and Civil War." *American Political Science Review* 97, no. 1 (February 2003): 75–90.

Forrest, Joshua B. "Guinea-Bissau." In Patrick Chabal, ed., *A History of Post-Colonial Lusophone Africa*. London: Hurst, 2002, 236–263.

———. "Guinea-Bissau: Democratization in a Divided Political Culture." In Leonardo Alfonso Villalón and Peter VonDoepp, eds., *The Fate of Africa's Democratic Experiments: Elites and Institutions*. Bloomington: Indiana University Press, 2005, 246–266.

———. *Guinea-Bissau: Power, Conflict, and Renewal in a West African Nation*. Boulder, CO: Westview Press, 1992.

———. "Guinea-Bissau Since Independence: A Decade of Domestic Power Struggles." *Journal of Modern African Studies* 25, no. 1 (March 1987): 95–116.

———. *Lineages of State Fragility: Rural Civil Society in Guinea-Bissau*. Athens, OH: Ohio University Press, 2003.

———. *Namibia's Post-Apartheid Regional Institutions: The Founding Year*. Rochester, NY: University of Rochester Press, 1998.

Frempong, Alexander K.D. "The Internal and Regional Dynamics of the Cycle of War and Peace in Guinea-Bissau." Paper presented at the CODESRIA International Colloquium, "Lusophonie" in Africa: History, Democracy and Integration, Luanda, Angola, April 28–30, 2005, 11–14.

Fuller, Gary. "The Demographic Backdrop to Ethnic Conflict: A Geographic Overview." Paper presented at the conference The Challenge of Ethnic Conflict to National and International Order in the 1990s: Geographic Perspectives, Washington, DC, September 30, 1993.

Fuller, Gary, and Forrest R. Pitts. "Youth Cohorts and Political Unrest in South Korea." *Political Geography Quarterly* 9, no. 1 (1990): 9–22.

Funk, Ursula. "Land Tenure, Agriculture, and Gender in Guinea-Bissau." In Jean Davidson, ed., *Agriculture, Women, and Land*. Boulder, CO: Westview Press, 1987, 33–58.

Funke, Odelia. "Environmental Dimensions of National Security: The End of the Cold War." In Jyrki Kakonen, ed., *Green Security or Militarized Environment.* Brookfield, VT: Dartmouth, 1994, 55–82.

Galli, Rosemary E., and Jocelyn Jones. *Politics, Economics, and Society.* London: Pinter, 1987, 147–160.

Garrett, Laurie. *The Coming Plague: Newly Emerging Diseases in a World Out of Balance.* New York: Farrar, Straus, and Giroux, 1994.

Gibbons, Elizabeth D. *Sanctions in Haiti: Human Rights and Democracy Under Assault.* Washington, DC: Praeger, 1999.

Gizewski, Peter, and Thomas Homer-Dixon. "Urban Growth and Violence: Will the Future Resemble the Past?" *Project on Environment, Population and Security.* Washington, DC: American Association for the Advancement of Sciences, 1995.

Gleditsch, Nils Petter. "Armed Conflict and the Environment: A Critique of the Literature." *Journal of Peace Research* 35, no. 3 (1998): 381–400.

Gleick, Peter H. "The Implications of Global Climate Changes for International Security." *Climate Change* 15 (1989): 303–325.

Godinho, Joana, Adrian Renton, Viatcheslav Vinogradov, Thomas Novotny, and Mary-Jane Rivers. "Reversing the Tide: Priorities for HIV/AIDS Prevention in Central Asia." Paper prepared for World Bank, November 2004, http://siteresources.worldbank.org/ECAEXT/Resources/258598-1102016393263/ReversingtheTide.pdf.

Goldstone, Jack A. "Demography, Environment, and Security: An Overview." In Myron Weiner and Sharon Staunton Russell, eds., *Demography and National Security.* New York: Berghahn, 2001, 38–61.

———. *Revolution and Rebellion in the Early Modern World.* Berkeley, CA: University of California Press, 1991.

Goodhand, Jonathan. "Enduring Disorder and Persistent Poverty: A Review of the Linkages Between War and Chronic Poverty." *World Development* 31, no. 3 (2003): 629–646.

Gore, Al. *Earth in the Balance: Forging a New Common Purpose.* Boston, MA: Houghton Mifflin, 1992.

Grant, Jonathan, Stijn Hoorens, Suja Sivadasan, Mirjam van het Loo, Julie DaVanzo, Lauren Hale, Shawna Gibson, and William Butz. "Low Fertility and Population Aging: Causes, Consequences, and Policy Options." Paper prepared for the European Commission, RAND Europe, Cambridge, UK, 2004.

Gretsky, Sergei. "Profile: Qadi Akbar Turajonzoda." *Central Asia Monitor* 3, no. 1 (1994): 16–24.

———. *Russia's Policy Toward Central Asia.* Moscow: Carnegie Endowment for International Peace, 1997.

Griffin, Michele. "The Helmet and the Hoe: Linkages Between United Nations Development Assistance and Conflict Management." *Global Governance* 9, no. 2 (2003): 295–361.

Gurr, Ted Robert. *Minorities at Risk: A Global View of Ethnopolitical Conflicts.* Washington DC: United States Institute of Peace, 1993.

Gurr, Ted Robert, and Monty Marshall. *Peace and Conflict 2003: A Global Survey of Armed Conflict, Self-Determination Movements, and Democracy.* College Park, MD: University of Maryland, 2003.

Hall, Michael. "Tajikistan at the Crossroads of Democracy and

Authoritarianism." In Birgit N. Schlyter, ed., *Prospects for Democracy in Central Asia*. New York: I. B. Tauris, 2006, 25–40.

Halle, Mark, Richard Matthew, and Jason Switzer, eds. *Conserving the Peace: Resources, Livelihoods, and Security*. Geneva: International Institute for Sustainable Development, 2002.

Halliday, Fred. "The Third Inter-Yemeni War and Its Consequences." *Asian Affairs* 26, no. 2 (June 1995): 131–140.

Hauge, Wenche, and Tanya Ellingsen. "The Causal Pathway to Conflict: Beyond Environmental Security." *Journal of Peace Research* 35 (1998): 299–317.

Havik, Philip J. "Female Entrepreneurship in a Changing Environment: Gender, Kinship, and Trade in the Guinea-Bissau Region." In Carl Risseuw and Kamala Ganesh, eds., *Negotiation and Social Space*. London: Sage, 1998, 205–225.

———. "Mundasson i Kambansa: espaco social e movementos politicos na Guine-Bissau." *Revista Internacional de Estudos Africanos,* nos. 18–22 (1999): 115–167.

Haykel, Bernard. *Revival and Reform in Islam: The Legacy of Muhammad al-Shawkânî*. Cambridge, UK: Cambridge University Press, 2003.

Holder, Sheila V. "Political Party and Campaign Financing in Guyana." In Steven Griner and Daniel Zarotta, eds., *From Rhetoric to Best Practices: The Challenge of Political Financing in the Americas*. OAS Unit for the Promotion of Democracy–International IDEA, Stockholm, 2004.

Homer-Dixon, Thomas. *Environment, Scarcity, and Violence*. Princeton, NJ: Princeton University Press, 1999.

———. "Environmental Scarcities and Violent Conflict: Evidence from Cases." *International Security* 19, no. 1 (1994): 5–40.

———. "The Ingenuity Gap." *Population and Development Review* 21, no. 3, (1995): 587–612.

———. "On the Threshold: Environmental Changes as Causes of Acute Conflict." *International Security* 16, no. 2 (1991): 76–116.

Howe, Neil, and Richard Jackson. "Battle of the (Youth) Bulge." *The National Interest* 96, no. 4 (2008): 33–41.

Hudson, Valerie, and Andrea Den Boer. *Bare Branches: The Security Implications of Asia's Surplus Male Population*. Cambridge, MA: MIT Press, 2004.

Human Rights Watch. "We Have No Orders to Save You: State Participation and Complicity in Communal Violence in Gujarat." *Human Rights Watch* 4, no. 3C (2002).

Human Security Centre. *Human Security Report 2005: War and Peace in the 21st Century*. New York: Oxford University Press, 2005.

———. "Mapping and Explaining Civil War: What to Do About Contested Datasets and Findings?" Workshop report, Oslo, August 18–19, 2003. Vancouver: University of British Columbia, 2003.

Humphreys, Macartan. "Economics and Violent Conflict." Review paper. Cambridge, MA: Harvard University Press, 2003, http://www.prevent-conflict.org/portal/economics/Essay.pdf.

Humphreys, Macartan, and Ashutosh Varshney. "Violent Conflict and the Millennium Development Goals: Diagnosis and Recommendations."

Working Papers Series Center on Globalization and Sustainable Development. New York: The Earth Institute at Columbia University, 2004.

Huntington, Samuel P. *The Third Wave: Democratization in the Late Twentieth Century.* Norman, OK: University of Oklahoma, 1991, 115–116.

Institute of Development Studies (IDS). "Proceedings of IDS Colloquium on Poverty in Guyana: Finding Solutions, March 18–19, 1993." *Transition* 20–21 (1993): 5–243.

International Crisis Group (ICG). "Somaliland: Democratisation and its Discontents." *ICG Africa Report* no. 66. Brussels, July 28, 2003.

———. "Tajikistan: An Uncertain Peace." *Asia Report* no. 30. Brussels, December 24, 2001.

———. "Yemen: Coping with Terrorism and Violence in a Fragile State." *Middle East Report* no. 8. Brussels, January 2003.

Jagan, Cheddi. *The West on Trial.* Berlin: Seven Seas, 1972.

Jahangiri, Guissou. "The Premises for the Construction of a Tajik National Identity, 1920–1930." In Mohammad-Reza Djalili, Frédéric Grare, and Shirin Akiner, eds., *Tajikistan: Trials of Independence.* London: Curzon, 1998, 14–41.

Jones, Brian. *Selected Natural Resource Management and Limited Rural Development Assessment.* Windhoek: USAID Namibia, 2003.

Jonson, Lena. "The Tajik Civil War: A Challenge to Russian Policy." Discussion Paper no. 74. London: Royal Institute of International Affairs, 1998.

Kahl, Colin H. "Population Growth, Environmental Degradation, and State-sponsored Violence: The Case of Kenya, 1991–1993." *International Security* 23, no. 2 (1998): 80–119.

Kaplan, Robert. "The Coming Anarchy." *The Atlantic,* February 1994, 61.

Kaser, Michael, and Santosh Mehrotra. "The Central Asian Economies After Independence." Paper prepared for the Post-Soviet Business Forum, Royal Institute of International Affairs, 1992.

Kemfert, Claudia, and Richard Tol. "Equity, International Trade, and Climate Policy." *International Environmental Agreements: Politics, Law and Economics* 2 (2002): 23–48.

Keohane, Robert O. "Hegemony in the World Political Economy." In Robert J. Art and Robert Jervis, eds., *International Politics: Enduring Concepts and Contemporary Issues.* New York: Pearson Longman, 2005.

Keulder, Christiaan. "Conflict Vulnerability and Sources of Resilience Assessment for Namibia." Report prepared for USAID Namibia, 2003.

———. *The Print Media and Reports on Corruption 1990–2004.* Windhoek: Namibia Institute for Democracy, 2005.

———. "Traditional Leaders." In Christiaan Keulder, ed., *State, Society and Democracy: A Reader in Namibian Politics.* Windhoek: Gamsberg Macmillan, 2000, 150–171.

Khan, Qayser, and Susan Chance. "Yemen and the Millennium Development Goals." World Bank Discussion Paper, Middle East and North Africa Working Paper Series no. 31. Washington, DC: World Bank, March 2003, http://www-wds.worldbank.org/external/default/WDSContent

Server/WDSP/IB/2003/10/20/000090341_20031020140717/Rendered/PDF/270220PAPER0MNA031.pdf.

Khegai, Margarita. "Sovremennye formy brachnykh otnoshenii v Tadzhikistana i prava cheloveka." In *Nekotorye aspekty gendernykh issledovanii v Tadzhikstane: Sbornykh materialov nauchnyjkh seminarov.* Dushanbe: Centre for Gender Research, Tajik Branch of the Open Society Institute, 2002, 55–67.

Lauprecht, Christian. "Demographic Change and Ethnic Relations: Mauritius and Fiji in Comparative Perspective." Paper presented at Public Policy and ICAR Seminar Series, Arlington, VA, March 13, 2005.

Le Billon, Philippe. "The Political Ecology of War: Natural Resources and Armed Conflicts." *Political Geography* 20 (2001): 561–584.

Le Sage, Andre. "Stateless Justice in Somalia: Formal and Informal Rule of Law Initiatives." Policy paper. Nairobi: UNDP, Rule of Law and Security Programme, January 2005.

Le Sage, Andre, with Ken Menkhaus. "The Rise of Islamic Charities in Somalia: An Assessment of Impact and Agenda." Paper presented at the International Studies Association Conference, Montreal, March 2004.

Leahy, Elizabeth, Robert Engelman, Carolyn G. Vogel, Sarah Haddock, and Tod Preston. *The Shape of Things to Come: Why Age Structure Matters to a Safer, More Equitable World.* Washington, DC: Population Action International, 2007.

Lederberg, Joshua, ed., *Biological Weapons: Limiting the Threat.* Cambridge, MA: MIT Press, 1993.

Lee, Ronald, and Andrew Mason. "What Is the Demographic Dividend?" *Finance and Development* 43, no. 3 (2006): 16–17.

Leichenko, Robin, and Karen O'Brien. *Double Exposure: Global Environmental Change in an Era of Globalization.* New York: Oxford University Press, 2005.

Little, Peter. *Somalia: Economy Without State.* Bloomington: Indiana University Press, 2003.

Lonergan, Steve. "Global Environmental Change and Human Security Science Plan." International Human Dimensions Programme on Global Environmental Change Report 11, Bonn, 1999.

Lubin, Nancy, Alex Kaits, and Igor Barstein. "Narcotics Interdiction in Afghanistan and Central Asia: Challenges for International Assistance." Report prepared for the Open Society Institute, 2002.

Lund, Michael. *Preventing Violent Conflicts: A Strategy for Preventive Diplomacy.* Washington DC: United States Institute of Peace, 2001.

Lyons, Terrence, and Ahmed I. Samatar. *Somalia: State Collapse, Multilateral Intervention, and Strategies for Political Reconstruction.* Washington, DC: Brookings Occasional Papers, 1995.

Malone, David M., and Heiko Nitzschke. "Economic Agendas in Civil Wars." Discussion Paper no. 2005/07. New York: UNU WIDER, April 2005.

Malthus, Thomas. *An Essay on the Principle of Population.* 1798, http://www.econlib.org/library/Malthus/malPop.html.

Mansurova, Gulchehra. "Ecological Migration in Tajikistan: In the Name of People's Life." [*sic*] *Tajikistan Economic Review* 23, no. 61 (December 1998).

Maren, Michael. *The Road to Hell: The Ravaging Effects of Foreign Aid and International Charity.* New York: Free Press, 1997.

Mars, Joan. *Deadly Force, Colonialism, and the Rule of Law: Police Violence in Guyana.* Westport, CT: Greenwood, 2002.

Mars, Perry. "Ethnic Politics, Mediation and Conflict Resolution: The Guyana Experience." *Journal of Peace Research* 38, no. 3 (May 2001): 353–372.

———. "State Intervention and Ethnic Conflict Resolution: Guyana and the Caribbean Experience." *Comparative Politics* 27, no. 2 (January 1995): 167–186.

———. "The Guyana Diaspora and Homeland Conflict Resolution." In Isodore Okpewho, ed., *The New African Diaspora.* Bloomington: Indiana University Press, 2009.

Mason, Karen O., Noriko O. Tsuya, and Minja Kim Choe. *The Changing Family in Comparative Perspective: Asia and the United States.* Honolulu: East-West Center, 1998.

Massey, Simon. "Multi-faceted Mediation in the Guinea-Bissau Civil War." *Scientia Militaria: South African Journal of Military Studies* 32, no. 1 (2004): 76–95.

Matthew, Richard A. "Environment and Conflict in Northern Pakistan." *Environmental Change and Security Project Report* 7 (2001): 21–35.

———. "Environmental Stress and Human Security in Northern Pakistan." *Environmental Change and Security Project Report* 7, 2001.

———. "In Defense of Environment and Security Research." *Environmental Change and Security Project Report* 8 (2002): 109–124.

———. "The Environment as a National Security Issue." *Journal of Policy History* 12, no. 1 (2000): 101–122.

Matthew, Richard A., Ted Gaulin, and Bryan McDonald. "The Elusive Quest: Linking Environmental Change and Conflict." *Canadian Journal of Political Science* 36, no. 4 (2003): 111–137.

Matthew, Richard A., and Bryan McDonald. "Cities Under Siege: Urban Planning and the Threat of Infectious Disease." *Journal of the American Planning Association* 72, no. 1 (2006): 109–117.

Matthews, Jessica. "Power Shift." *Foreign Affairs* 76, no. 1 (1997): 50–66.

———. "Redefining Security." *Foreign Affairs* 68, no. 2 (1989): 162–177.

McAffee, Kathy. *Storm Signals: Structural Adjustment and Development Alternatives in the Caribbean.* Cambridge, MA: South End, 1991.

McNeil, William H. *Plagues and Peoples.* New York: Anchor, 1998.

McNeill, John. *Something New Under the Sun: An Environmental History of the Twentieth Century World.* New York: W. W. Norton, 2002.

Meadows, Donella, Dennis Meadows, Jorgen Randers, William W. Behrens. *Limits to Growth.* New York: Universe, 1972.

Melber, Henning. "Public Administration: Constraints and Challenges." In Ingolf Diener and Oliver Graefe, eds., *Contemporary Namibia: The First Landmarks of a Post-Apartheid Society.* Windhoek: Gambsberg Macmillan, 2001.

Menkhaus, Ken. "International Peacebuilding and the Dynamics of Local and National Peacebuilding in Somalia." In Walter Clarke and Jeffrey Herbst, eds., *Learning from Somalia: The Lessons of Armed Humanitarian Intervention.* Boulder, CO: Westview Press, 1997, 42–63.

———. "Quasi-States, Nation-Building, and Terrorist Safe Havens." *Journal of Conflict Studies* 23, no. 2 (Fall 2003): 7–23.

———. *Somalia: State Collapse and the Threat of Terrorism.* Adelphi Paper no. 364. Oxford: Oxford University Press, 2004.

Menkhaus, Ken, with Lou Ortmayer. "Somalia: Misread Crises and Missed Opportunities." In Bruce Jentleson, ed., *Preventive Diplomacy in the Post–Cold War World: Opportunities Missed, Opportunities Seized, and Lessons to be Learned.* New York: Carnegie Commission on Preventing Deadly Conflict, 1999.

Mesquida, Christian G., and Neil I. Wiener. "Human Collective Aggression: A Behavioral Ecology Perspective." *Ethology and Sociobiology* 17, no. 4 (1996): 247–262.

———. "Male Age Composition and the Severity of Conflicts." *Politics in the Life Sciences* 18, no. 2 (1999): 181–189.

Milanovic, Branko. "Why Did the Poorest Countries Fail to Catch Up?" Carnegie Paper no. 62. Washington, DC: Carnegie Endowment for International Peace, November 2005.

Miller, Derek B. "Demand, Stockpiles, and Social Controls: Small Arms in Yemen." Small Arms Survey Occasional Paper, no. 9. Geneva, May 2003.

Mische, Patricia. "Ecological Security and the Need to Reconceptualize Sovereignty." *Alternatives* 14, no. 4 (1992): 389–427.

Moller, Herbert. "Youth as a Force in the Modern World." *Comparative Studies in Society and History* 10, no. 3 (1968): 237–260.

Moore, Mick. "Political Underdevelopment: What Causes 'Bad Governance.'" *Public Management Review* 1, no. 3 (2001): 385–418.

Mosely, Paul, John Hudson, and Arjan Verschool. "Aid, Poverty Reduction, and the New Conditionality." *The Economic Journal* 114 (2004): F217–F243.

Mubarak, Jamil. "The Hidden Hand Behind the Resilience of the Stateless Economy in Somalia." *World Development* 25, no. 12 (December 1997): 2027–2041.

Müller, Benito. "Equity in Climate Change: The Great Divide." Oxford Institute for Energy Studies, 2002.

Murdoch, James, and Todd Sandler. "Economic Growth, Civil Wars, and Spatial Spillovers." *Journal of Conflict Resolution,* 46, no. 1 (2002): 91–110.

Murshed, Syed Mansoob. "The Conflict-Growth Nexus and the Poverty of Nations." United Nations DESA, DESA Working Paper no. 43, UN Doc. ST/ESA/2007/DWP/43, June 2007, http://www.un.org/esa/desa/papers/2007/wp43_2007.pdf.

Myers, Norman. *Ultimate Security: The Environmental Basis of Political Stability.* New York: W. W. Norton, 1993.

Nafziger, Wayne, Frances Stewart, and Raimo Vayrynen, eds. *War, Hunger, and Displacement: The Origins of Humanitarian Emergencies,* vols. 1 and 2. New York: Oxford University Press, 2000.

Nandra, A. R., and Carl Haub, *The Future Population of India: A Long-range Demographic View.* Washington, DC: Population Reference Bureau, 2007.

National Intelligence Council. *Growing Global Migration and Its Implications for the United States.* Washington, DC: NIC, 2001.

Nauman, Naqvi, ed. *Rethinking Security, Rethinking Development: An Anthology of Papers from the Third Annual South Asian NGO Summit.* Islamabad: Sustainable Development Policy Institute, 1996.

Naumkin, Vitaly V. "Militant Islam in Central Asia: The Case of the Islamic Movement of Uzbekistan." Berkeley Program in Soviet and Post-Soviet Studies Working Paper Series. Berkeley, CA: University of California, Berkeley, July 1, 2003.

Newcomb, James. *Biology and Borders: SARS and the New Economics of Biosecurity.* Cambridge, MA: Bio-Era Research Associates, 2003.

O'Brien, Karen, and Robin Leichenko. "Winners and Losers in the Context of Global Change." *Annals of the Association of American Geographers* 93, no. 1 (2003): 99–113.

Ohlsson, Leif. "Livelihood Conflicts: Linking Poverty and Environment as Causes of Conflict." Policy Paper. Stockholm: SIDA Environmental Policy Unit, 2000.

Olimova, Saodat. "Regionalism and Its Perception by Major Political and Social Powers of Tajikistan." In Luigi De Martino, ed., *Tajikistan at a Crossroad: The Politics of Decentralisation.* Geneva: CIMERA Situation Report 4, January 2004, 85–118.

Ophuls, William. *Ecology and the Politics of Scarcity.* San Francisco: W. H. Freeman, 1976.

Orozco, Manuel. "Distant But Close: Guyanese Transnational Communities and Their Remittances from the United States." Paper prepared for USAID, January 2004.

———. "Remitting Back Home to Guyana: Issues and Options." *Inter-American Dialogue*, November 7, 2002, http://www.guyana.org/govt/GuyanaPresentation.pdf.

Osborn, Fairfield. *Our Plundered Planet.* New York: Grosset and Dunlap, 1948, 200–201.

Ostheimer, Andrea E. "The Structural Crisis in Guinea-Bissau's Political System." *African Security Review* 10, no. 4 (2001), http://www.iss.co.za/PUBS/ASR/10No4/Ostheimer.html.

Paris, Ronald. "Human Security: Paradigm Shift or Hot Air?" *International Security* 26, no. 2 (2001): 87–102.

Peluso, Nancy, and Michael Watts, eds. *Violent Environments.* Ithaca, NY: Cornell University Press, 2001.

Pempel, T. J. *Uncommon Democracies: The One-Party Dominant Regimes.* Ithaca, NY: Cornell University Press, 1990.

Rapley, John. *Globalization and Inequality: Neoliberalism's Downward Spiral.* Boulder, CO: Lynne Rienner Publishers, 2004.

Rashid, Ahmed. *Jihad: The Rise of Militant Islam in Central Asia.* New Haven, CT: Yale University Press, 2002.

Rawson, David. *The Somali State and Foreign Aid.* Washington, DC: US Department of State Foreign Service Institute, 1993.

Refugee Policy Group (RPG). *Lives Lost, Lives Saved: Excess Mortality and the Impact of Health Interventions in the Somalia Emergency.* Washington, DC: RPG, 2004.

Richards, P., ed. *No Peace, No War: An Anthropology of Contemporary Armed Conflicts.* Oxford: James Currey, 2005.

Ross, Michael L. "What Do We Know About Natural Resources and Civil Wars?" *Journal of Peace Research* 41, no. 3 (2004): 337–356.

Sahnoun, Mohamed. *Somalia: The Missed Opportunities.* Washington, DC: US Institute of Peace, 1994.

Samarasinghe, Stanley, Brian Donaldson, and Colleen McGinn. "Conflict Vulnerability Analysis: Issues, Tools, and Responses." Paper prepared for USAID, April 2001.

Samatar, Ahmed I., ed. *The Somali Challenge: From Catastrophe to Renewal.* Boulder, CO: Lynne Rienner Publishers, 1994.

Savage, Timothy M. "Europe and Islam: Crescent Waxing, Cultures Clashing." *Washington Quarterly* 27, no. 3 (2004): 25–50.

Schmitter, Philippe C. *Speculations About the Prospective Demise of Authoritarian Regimes and Its Possible Consequences.* Washington, DC: Woodrow Wilson Center, 1980.

Schrijver, Nico. "International Organization for Environmental Security." *Bulletin of Peace Proposals* 20, no. 2 (1989): 115–122.

Shain, Yossi. "Democrats and Secessionists: US Diasporas as Regime Destabilizers." In Myron Weiner, ed., *International Migration and Security.* Boulder, CO: Westview Press, 1993.

Smolinski, Mark S., Margaret A. Hamburg, and Joshua Lederberg. *Microbial Threats to Health: Emergence, Detection, and Response.* Washington, DC: National Academies, 2003.

Staveteig, Sarah. "The Young and the Restless: Population Age Structure and Civil War." Environmental Change and Security Project Report no. 11. Washington, DC: Woodrow Wilson Center for International Scholars, 2005.

Stevenson, Thomas. "Yemeni Workers Come Home: Reabsorbing One Million Migrants." *Middle East Report* 181 (March 1993): 15–20.

Stewart, Frances. "Conflict and the Millennium Development Goals." *Journal of Human Development* 4, no. 3 (2003): 325–351.

———. "Crisis Prevention: Tackling Horizontal Inequalities." *Oxford Development Studies,* 28, no. 3 (2000): 245–262.

Stewart, Frances, and Valpy Fitzgerald. "The Costs of War in Poor Countries: Conclusions and Policy Recommendations." In Frances Stewart and Valpy Fitzgerald, eds., *War and Underdevelopment, Volume I: Economic and Social Consequences of Conflict.* New York: Oxford University Press, 2001, 225–245.

Stewart, Frances, Cindy Huang, and Michael Wang. "Internal Wars: An Empirical Overview of the Economic and Social Consequences." In Frances Stewart and Valpy Fitzgerald, eds., *War and Underdevelopment, Volume I: Economic and Social Consequences of Conflict.* New York: Oxford University Press, 2001, 67–103.

Stillwaggon, Eileen. *AIDS and the Ecology of Poverty.* Oxford: Oxford University Press, 2006.

Suhrke, Astri, and Ingrid Samset. "What's in a Figure? Estimating Recurrence of Civil War." *International Peacekeeping* 14, no. 2 (April 2007): 195–203.

Tabyshalieva, Anara. "The Challenge of Regional Cooperation in Central Asia: Preventing Ethnic Conflict in the Ferghana Valley." Peaceworks Paper Series no. 28. Washington, DC: United States Institute of Peace, June 1999.

———. "Kyrgyzstan's Tenuous Hold on Democracy." *Far Eastern Economic Review* 168, no. 4 (April 2005): 26–29.

———. "Political Islam in Kyrgyzstan," In *OSCE Yearbook 2002*. Baden-Baden: Institute for Peace and Security Policy at the University of Hamburg, 2003, 83–92.

———. "Revival of Traditions in Post-Soviet Central Asia." In *Making the Transition Work for Women in Europe and Central Asia*, World Bank Discussion Paper, no. 411. Washington, DC, 2000.

———. "The Kyrgyz Republic on the Verge of Change?" *Helsinki Monitor* 14, no. 3 (2003): 227–228.

Tabyshalieva, Anara, and Georgi Derluguan. "The 'Religious Factor' in Central Asia and the Caucasus." *Perspectives on Central Asia* 2, no. 3 (June 1997).

Tehranian, Majid, ed. *Worlds Apart: Human Security and Global Governance*. London: I. B. Tauris, 1999.

Teitelbaum, Michael S., and Jay Winter. *A Question of Numbers: High Migration, Low Fertility, and the Politics of National Identity*. New York: Hill and Wang, 1998.

Temudo, Marina Padrão. "Western Beliefs and Local Myths: A Case Study on the Interface Between Farmers, NGOs, and the State in Guinea-Bissau Rural Development Interventions." In Jim Igoe and Tim Kelsall, eds., *Between a Rock and a Hard Place: African NGOs, Donors, and the State*. Durham, NC: Carolina Academic Press, 2005, 253–277.

Thomas, Caroline. *Global Governance, Development, and Human Security*. London: Pluto, 2000.

Thomas, Caroline, and Peter Wilkins, eds. *Globalization, Human Security, and the African Experience*. Boulder, CO: Lynne Rienner Publishers, 1999.

Tilly, Charles. "War Making and State Making as Organized Crime." In Peter Evans, Dietrich Rueschemeyer, and Theda Skocpol, eds., *Bringing the State Back In*. New York: Cambridge University Press, 1985, 169–191.

Tonn, Bruce. "An Equity-First, Risk-Based Framework for Managing Global Climate Change." *Global Environmental Change* 13, no. 4 (2003): 295–306.

Ullman, Richard. "Redefining Security." *International Security* 8, no. 1 (1983): 129–153.

UN. *A More Secure World: Our Shared Responsibility*. UN Doc. A/59/565, December 2, 2004.

———. *2005 World Summit Outcome*. UN Doc. A/RES/60/1, October 24, 2005.

———. *United Nations Millennium Declaration*. UN Doc. A/RES/55/2, September 18, 2000.

UN Development Programme (UNDP). "Human Development Index." In *Human Development Report 2005: International Cooperation at a Crossroads—Aid, Trade and Security in an Unequal World*. New York: UNDP, 2005.

———. *Human Development Report 1994*. Oxford: Oxford University Press, 1994.

———. *Human Development Report 2003: Millennium Development Goal—A Compact Among Nations to End Human Poverty*. New York: Oxford University Press, 2003.

———. *Human Development Report 2004: Cultural Liberty in Today's Diverse World*. New York: UNDP, 2004.

———. *Human Development Report 2005.* New York: Oxford University Press, 2005.

———. *Human Development Report 2007/2008: Fighting Climate Change—Human Solidarity in a Divided World.* New York: UNDP, 2007.

UN High Commission for Refugees (UNHCR). *Statistical Yearbook 2003: Trends in Displacement, Protection and Solutions,* 2003.

UN Office for West Africa (UNOWA). *Youth Unemployment and Regional Insecurity in West Africa.* New York: United Nations, 2005.

UN Office on Drugs and Crime (UNODC). "The Opium Economy in Afghanistan: An International Problem," paper prepared for UNODC, Vienna, 2003.

———. *World Drug Report 2005.* Vienna: UNODC, 2005.

UN Population Division, *World Population Prospects: The 2006 Revision.* New York: United Nations, 2007.

UN Secretary-General. *In Larger Freedom: Towards Development, Security and Human Rights for All.* UN Doc. A/59/2005, March 21, 2005.

———. *Report of the Secretary-General on Developments in Guinea-Bissau and on the Activities of the United Nations Peacebuilding Support Office in That Country.* UN Doc. 2/2007/576, September 28, 2007.

Urdal, Henrik. "A Clash of Generations? Youth Bulges and Political Violence." *International Studies Quarterly* 50, no. 3 (2006): 607–630.

Uvin, Peter. *Aiding Violence: The Development Enterprise in Rwanda.* West Hartford, CT: Kumarian Press, 1998.

———. "The Development/Peacebuilding Nexus: A Typology and History of Changing Paradigms." *Journal of Peacebuilding and Development* 1, no. 1 (2002): 5–22.

———. "The Influence of Aid in Situations of Violent Conflict." Paper prepared for the DAC Informal Task Force on Conflict, Peace, and Development Cooperation. Paris: OECD-DAC, 1999.

van Hear, Nicholas. "The Socio-economic Impact of the Involuntary Mass Return to Yemen in 1990." *Journal of Refugee Studies* 7, no. 1 (1994): 18–38.

Varisco, Daniel. "The Elixir of Life or the Devil's Cud: The Debate Over *Qat* (*Catha edulis*) in Yemeni Culture." In Ross Coomber and Nigel South, eds., *Drug Use and Cultural Context: Tradition, Change, and Intoxicants Beyond "The West."* London: Free Association Books, 2004, 101–118.

Vaux, Tony, and Jonathan Goodhand. *Conflict Assessments: Disturbing Connections: Aid and Conflict in Kyrgyzstan.* London: University of London, 2001.

Vlassenroot, Koen, and Tim Raeymaekers. "The Politics of Rebellion and Intervention in Ituri: The Emergence of a New Political Complex?" *African Affairs* 103 (July 2004): 385–412.

Ware, Helen. "Demography, Migration, and Conflict in the Pacific." *Journal of Peace Research* 42, no. 4 (2005): 435–434.

Weiner, Myron. *The Global Migration Crisis.* New York: Longman, 1995.

Weisfeld, Glen. "Aggression and Dominance in the Social World of Boys." In John Archer, ed., *Male Violence.* New York: Routledge, 1994, 42–69.

Westing, Arthur. "Comprehensive Human Security and Ecological Realities." *Environmental Conservation* 16, no. 4 (1989): 295–298.

Wolfgang, Werner. "The Land Question in Namibia." In Ingolf Diener and Oliver Graefe, eds., *Contemporary Namibia: The First Landmarks of a Post-Apartheid Society.* Windhoek: Gamsberg Macmillan, 2001.

World Bank. *Assessing Aid: What Works, What Doesn't and Why.* New York: Oxford University Press, 1998.

———. *The East Asian Miracle: Economic Growth and Public Policy.* Oxford: Oxford University Press, 1993, 40–43.

———. *MiniAtlas of Millennium Development Goals.* Washington, DC: World Bank, July 2005.

———. "Project Performance Assessment Report: Yemen Vocational Training Project." World Bank Report no. 32593. Washington, DC: World Bank June 14, 2005, http://www-wds.worldbank.org/external/default/WDSContentServer/IW3P/IB/2005/06/21/000160016_20050621174604/Rendered/INDEX/32593.txt.

World Commission on Environment and Development. *Our Common Future.* New York: Oxford University Press, 1987.

World Health Organization (WHO). *The World Heath Report 2004: Make Every Mother and Child Count.* Geneva: World Health Organization, 2004.

———. *The World Heath Report 2005: Changing History.* Geneva: World Health Organization, 2005, http://www.who.int/whr/2005/en/index.html.

WSP-International. *Rebuilding Somaliland: Issues and Possibilities.* Lawrenceville, NJ: Red Sea, 2005.

Würth, Anna. *Ash-sharî'a fî Bâb al-Yaman: Recht, Richter und Rechtpraxis an det familienrechtlichen Kammer des Gerichts Süd-Sanaa, Republik Jemen (1983–1995).* Berlin: Duncker and Humblot, 2000.

Xenos, Peter. "Demographic Forces Shaping Youth Populations in Asian Cities." In Lisa M. Hanley, Blair A. Ruble, and Joseph S. Tulchin, eds., *Youth, Poverty, and Conflict in Southeast Asian Cities.* Washington, DC: Woodrow Wilson International Center for Scholars, 2004.

Yates, T. L., J. N. Mills, C. A. Parmenter, T. G. Ksiazek, R. R. Parmenter, J. R. V. Castle, C. H. Calisher, S. T. Nichol, K. D. Abbott, J. C. Young, M. L. Morrison, B. J. Beaty, J. L. Dunnum, R. J. Baker, J. Salazar-Bravo, and C. J. Peters. "The Ecology and Evolutionary History of an Emergent Disease: Hantavirus Pulmonary Syndrome." *Bioscience* 52, no. 11 (2002): 989–998.

Zolberg, Aristide R., Astri Suhrke, and Sergio Aguayo. *Escape from Violence: Conflict and the Refugee Crisis in the Developing World.* New York: Oxford University Press, 1989.

Zureik, Elia. "Demography and Transfer: Israel's Road to Nowhere." *Third World Quarterly* 24, no. 4 (2003): 619–630.

The Contributors

Shirin Akiner has much firsthand experience of central Asia and has written and lectured widely on the region. She was awarded the Sir Percy Sykes Memorial Medal by the Royal Society for Asian Affairs in 2006, and in December 2008 she was granted an honorary fellowship at the Ancien Association of NATO Defense College in Rome. Currently a fellow of the Cambridge Central Asia Forum at the University of Cambridge, she has also held research and teaching posts at the University of London (1974–2008) and served as visiting professor at several universities including Oberlin University, Uppsala University, and the National University of Seoul.

Gretchen Bauer is a professor in the Department of Political Science and International Relations at the University of Delaware, where she teaches courses on African politics and women in politics. She is the author of *Labor and Democracy in Namibia, 1971–1996;* coauthor with Scott Taylor of *Politics in Southern Africa: State and Society in Transition;* and coeditor with Hannah Britton of *Women in African Parliaments.* In 2009, she was a visiting researcher in the Department of Sociology at the University of Botswana.

Laurent Bonnefoy is CNRS/ANR postdoctoral fellow at the Institut de Recherches et d'Etudes sur le Monde Arabe et Musulman (IREMAM–University of Provence, France). A specialist in religious movements in the Arabian Peninsula, he is currently conducting more fieldwork in Yemen and has written various articles in both French and English on Salafism and the contemporary political system in Southern Arabia.

Richard P. Cincotta is a consulting demographer to the Long Range Analysis Unit of the US National Intelligence Council (NIC). His research focuses on demographic transition, human migration, and their relationships to natural resource dynamics, human health, regime type, and the onset of civil conflict. His publications on these topics have appeared in *Foreign Policy*, *Nature*, and *Science*. He also contributed to the NIC's 2009 global analysis, *Global Trends 2025: A Transformed World.*

Renaud Detalle is human rights officer in the Middle East and North Africa Unit of the Office of the UN High Commissioner for Human Rights. An expert on Yemen, he has written extensively on the country.

Joshua B. Forrest is associate professor of history and political science at La Roche College in Pittsburgh and adjunct professor at the University of Pittsburgh's Graduate School for Public and International Affairs. He has twice received Fulbright-funded field research fellowships to Africa and has been a research fellow at Harvard University's Academy for International and Area Studies. His books include *Subnationalism in Africa: Ethnicity, Alliances, and Politics* (2004), and *Lineages of State Fragility: Rural Civil Society in Guinea-Bissau* (2003).

Sakiko Fukuda-Parr is a professor of international affairs at the New School. From 1995 to 2004 she was director of the UNDP's *Human Development Reports.* Her current work includes poverty and human rights, conflict prevention, the Millennium Development Goals (MDGs) and international development agendas, and global technology. Her many publications include *The Gene Revolution: GM Crops and Unequal Development*, as well as numerous articles in journals and reviews. She serves as editor of the *Journal of Human Development,* which she founded, and as a member on the Editorial Board of Feminist Economics.

Christiaan Keulder is a political scientist, who has worked for Namibia's Institute for Public Policy Research, as well as Media Tenor Namibia, a research institute forcused on media analysis. His writings on the country have been widely published.

Michael S. Lund is a conflict policy researcher at the Woodrow Wilson International Center; a senior specialist for conflict and peacebuilding at Management Systems International, Inc.; author of

Preventing Violent Conflicts (1996) as well as numerous studies in conflict assessment, conflict prevention, postconflict peacebuilding, and the interactions of development and conflict; and coeditor and contributor to four other books. He has done analyses of countries in sub-Saharan Africa, the Balkans, Caucasus, central Asia, east Asia, and Latin America for government agencies of the United States and other nations; the UN, EU and other multilateral organizations; and NGOs.

Francesco Mancini is the deputy director of studies at IPI and heads the IPI program *Coping with Crisis, Conflict, and Change.* Mancini is also an adjunct assistant professor at Columbia University's School of International and Public Affairs, a position he also held for two years at New York University. Prior to joining IPI, he served as an associate at the EastWest Institute in New York. From 1996 to 2001, Mancini was a senior management consultant at Groupe CRCI in Paris, where he focused on business strategy and change management.

Perry Mars is professor of Africana studies at Wayne State University in Detroit. His work has been published in various international scholarly journals, including *Latin American Perspectives, Comparative Politics, Journal of Peace Research, Social and Economic Studies,* and *Ethnic and Racial Studies.* His books include *Ideology and Change: The Transformation of the Caribbean Left* (1998) and *Caribbean Labor and Politics: Legacies of Cheddi Jagan and Michael Manley,* a volume he coedited with Alma Young (2004).

Richard A. Matthew is associate professor at the University of California at Irvine and founding director of the Center for Unconventional Security Affairs. He studies global threat networks and the environmental dimensions of conflict and postconflict reconstruction and has done extensive field work in conflict zones in South Asia and East Africa.

Kenneth Menkhaus is a professor of political science at Davidson College, where he has taught since 1991. He specializes in the Horn of Africa, focusing primarily on development, conflict analysis, peacebuilding, and political Islam.

Anara Tabyshalieva focuses on different aspects of peace in the history of Asia and Eurasia. She was a senior fellow at the United

States Institute of Peace and a Fulbright scholar at SAIS, Johns Hopkins University. In addition, she coedited UNESCO's volume on the history of civilizations of Central Asia. More recently, she has issued a report, commissioned by UNESCO, that examines human security in eight Asian countries.

Neclâ Tschirgi was vice president of the International Peace Academy from 2001 to 2005, where she led the Security-Development Nexus Research Program, upon which this volume is based. Subsequently, she served as a senior policy adviser to the Peacebuilding Support Office at the United Nations until March 2009. Her current research focuses on the changing landscape of international relations since the end of the Cold War, including the evolution of international responses to conflict prevention and peacebuilding.

Index

About the Book

Although policymakers and practitioners alike have enthusiastically embraced the idea that security and development are interdependent, the precise nature and implications of the dynamic interplay between the two phenomena have been far from clear. The authors of *Security and Development: Searching for Critical Connections* realistically assess the promise and shortcomings of integrated security-development policies as a strategy for conflict prevention. Addressing cross-cutting issues and also presenting detailed country case studies, they move beyond rhetoric and generalization to make an important contribution to the international conflict prevention agenda.

Neclâ Tschirgi is senior policy adviser in the United Nations Peacebuilding Support Office. **Michael S. Lund** is senior associate, conflict and peacebuilding at Management Systems International, Inc. **Francesco Mancini** is deputy director of studies at the International Peace Institute.